4^{00}

D1210289

The Union Cavalry in the Civil War, Volumes I–III
Winner of the Jules F. Landry Award for 1985

Union Cavalry Under Fire at Reed's Bridge, Battle of Chickamauga
Drawing by Alfred Waud, from *Harper's Weekly*

STEPHEN Z. STARR

The Union Cavalry in the Civil War

VOLUME III
The War in the West
1861–1865

Louisiana State University Press
Baton Rouge and London

Published with the assistance of a grant from
the National Endowment for the Humanities

Library of Congress Cataloging in Publication Data

(Revised for vol. III)
Starr, Stephen Z
  The Union cavalry in the Civil War.
  Includes bibliographies and indexes.
  CONTENTS: v. 1. From Fort Sumter to Gettysburg,
1861–1863.—v. 2. The War in the East, from Gettysburg
to Appomattox, 1863–1865.—v. 3. The War in the West, 1861–1865
    1. United States. Army. Cavalry—History—Civil
War, 1861–1865. 2. United States—History—Civil War,
1861–1865—Campaigns and battles. I. Title.
E492.5.S7   973.7'41   78-26751
ISBN 0–8071–0484–1 (v. 1)
         0–8071–0859–6 (v. 2)
         0–8071–1209–7 (v. 3)

To the memory of
the officers and men of the Union cavalry,
whose story this is

The story of the Seventh Kansas will never be written—can never be written. The story of a few battles—not a tenth part told; a sketch of many skirmishes—but briefly related, are mere suggestions of four years of energetic action, of hardship and suffering, and of gratification that strength had been given to endure it all. I have not told the story of marches under a midday sun that . . . seemed to shrivel up the brain as you gasp for breath in the dust beaten up by the horses' feet; of marches through mud and never-ceasing rain that soaked you, saturated you . . . of marches through winter storms of sleet and driving snow, without hope of shelter or rest; of struggles against almost irresistible drowsiness when sleep had been denied you for days and to sleep now would be death; of weeks of tossing in the fever ward of a field hospital where the oblivion of stupor came to you as a blessing . . . this part of the story has not been told. The thrill and excitement of battle were wanting in all this; it was only plain, monotonous duty, made endurable by the grim humor that jeered at suffering and made a joke at the prospect of death. . . . A cavalry regiment does not usually suffer a heavy loss in any one engagement; it is one here, two or three there—a constant attrition that is ever wearing away the substance; it is the aggregate that tells the story. The dead are scattered here and there, buried by the wayside where they fell. Few have been gathered into the national cemeteries, but they rest as well, and the same glory is with them, wherever they may sleep.

First Lieutenant and Regimental Adjutant Simeon M. Fox, 7th Kansas Volunteer Cavalry, "The Early History of the Seventh Kansas Cavalry"

Contents

Illustrations

Maps

Preface

A COMBINATION OF INTELLECTUAL CHALLENGE AND LOVE affair that began in 1963 has reached its consummation with the completion of this, the third and mercifully the last, volume of *The Union Cavalry in the Civil War*. Volumes I and II described the raising, organization, equipping, training, and teething troubles of the mainly volunteer Union cavalry, in both East and West, and went on to describe its development and operations in the East, the painfully slow growth of its competence at all levels, and its ultimately decisive contribution, under Philip Sheridan, to the winning of the war.

The present volume tells the far more diffuse story of the Union cavalry in the West, its development in its own fashion and at its own pace into an effective element of the Union armies, and its role in the numerous campaigns that were waged over the length and breadth of the vast region extending from the Ohio River to the Gulf and from the Alleghenies to the Kansas-Missouri border.

With few exceptions, the literature—certainly the popular literature—on the Union cavalry has been of the "Boots and Saddles" variety, permeated, as were the cavalry recruits in the early months of the war, with the supposed glamor of the cavalry service. The present study has had as its objective the portrayal of the life and campaigns of the Union cavalry as they were experienced and fought by its troopers and officers. These men had their share of moments of glamor, to be sure, moments of exaltation, of a sense of accomplishment, of the pleasures of companionship, but these were the intervals of sunshine in the midst of long spells of hardship, pain, defeat, hunger, boredom, and fear. The glamor of service in the Union cavalry did not blossom until, decades after the war, the sedate survivors relived the days of their youth and wrote their reminiscences and regimental histories.

No one studying the accounts of the Civil War as experienced by the officers and troopers of the Union cavalry—their wartime letters and diaries—can fail to be impressed, and at times moved, by their dedication and patriotism. They were guilty of every sin in the long catalog of military vices, but they also chose as volunteers to brave hardships beyond the comprehension of later generations, as well as the daily risk of mutilation and death, out of a sincerely held belief that they were, indeed, fighting to ensure "that this nation, under God, shall have a new birth of freedom; and that government of the people, by the people, and for the people, shall not perish from the earth." For that reason, this volume is dedicated to their memory.

Out of consideration for the long-suffering reader, to say nothing of a long-suffering university press, this account does not cover cavalry operations on the periphery of the Civil War—in Texas and the Southwest, against the Plains Indians in the Northwest, and by the bodies of pro-Union and pro-Confederate Indian cavalry in what is now Oklahoma. Interesting as these operations may be, they add little to the tale of the main lines of development of the Union cavalry in the fighting in the more settled lands farther east. For the same reason, considerably less than justice has been done to the contributions of the horse artillery to the operations of the cavalry brigades and divisions to which they were attached.

It is impossible to be immersed in a study like this for any length of time without being constantly aware of areas that one must regretfully leave untouched. For example, who produced the millions of horseshoes the cavalry needed? What was the source of the many thousands of saddles and sets of tack issued to the cavalry, and of the leather from which such items were produced? On a less mundane plane, much more could be said about certain facets of the life of the cavalry in the days and weeks when "nothing was happening," when, except for caring for their horses and performing the routine duties of camp, they had their time and energy and thoughts to themselves. What were their reactions to news of their families' lives back home or to political developments, local and national? How did they view life around them when they got south of the Mason and Dixon Line? What were their reactions to southerners, white and black, to slavery, to the southerners they had to fight? Much of this must remain untold and indeed unstudied, for there are always archives that one could not examine, letters and diaries of cavalrymen, both Blue and Gray, unread, documents not seen.

My grateful acknowledgments are due in the first instance to L. E. Phillabaum and Beverly Jarrett of the Louisiana State University Press, and their staff, for their long-suffering, good-humored patience with a sometimes refractory author. Second, I must thank my good friend, Thomas F. Thiele, who has read every word of all three volumes of this study and has given me his perceptive and helpful advice and suggestions. My gratitude is due also to Messrs. Roy Stonesifer, Jr., of Edinboro State College, Edinboro, Pennsylvania, and Thomas L. Connelly, University of South Carolina, who have read the present volume in manuscript and have done their best—not always with success—to save the author from the consequences of his sometimes idiosyncratic notions about the Union cavalry.

Information, photocopies of monographs, and photographs have been furnished the author by Mrs. Frances Forman of the Cincinnati Historical Society; Mr. L. L. Tucker, Director of the Massachusetts Historical Society; Mr. James L. McDonough of David Lipscomb College; Miss Betty J. Starns of Eli Lilly and Company; Arnold Gates of the New York Civil War Round Table; and Mr. Joseph W. Snell, Executive Director of the Kansas State Historical Society. The late Mr. David L. Bacon of North Haven, Connecticut, has kindly given me a copy of his compilation of the Civil War letters of his grandfather, Colonel (later Brigadier General) Thomas J. Jordan, 9th Pennsylvania Cavalry. And I must not fail to mention with gratitude the most enjoyable and instructive tour of the Westport battlefield to which I was treated by Messrs. L. F. Buresh and O. N. Fitts of the Kansas City Civil War Round Table.

Having dedicated my first book (an outgrowth of my interest in Civil War cavalry) to my dear wife, I cannot very well dedicate another book to her, but I do offer her this volume as a wholly inadequate token of my love, and of my gratitude for her patience, tolerance, and interest. It is a special pleasure for me to offer her the completed manuscript a few weeks short of our fiftieth wedding anniversary.

It would be churlish to end this Preface without quoting the old army expression "If you ain't cavalry, you ain't."

The Union Cavalry in the Civil War

I

Come in Your War Array

THE "CENTER OF POPULATION" OF THE UNITED STATES IN 1860 was a mythical point a few miles north of Portsmouth, an Ohio River town a hundred miles east of Cincinnati. Fifty years earlier, in 1810, the Center of Population was located at Charles Town, Virginia. In the intervening years, the population of the new republic had increased from 7,240,000 to 31,433,000, and in the same years the westward migration had shifted the Center of Population three hundred miles to the west. Six of the new states admitted to the Union between 1810 and 1860 were part of the "Old Northwest": Indiana, Illinois, Michigan, Iowa, Wisconsin, and Minnesota.[1] The 1860 census credited these six states with a population of 5,436,000. With the addition of Ohio, the earliest-admitted of the states formed out of the Northwest Territory, and of Kansas, admitted in January, 1861, after its long travail as the battleground between freedom and slavery, the population of these eight western states very nearly equaled that of the free states of the "Central Tier"—Pennsylvania, New Jersey, and New York—plus all of New England. With the population of the border states of Kentucky and Missouri—of dubious loyalty in 1861—included with that of the eight states of the Old Northwest, it was evident that the portion

1. Indiana had been admitted in 1816, Illinois in 1818, Michigan in 1837, Iowa in 1846, Wisconsin in 1848, and Minnesota in 1858.

of the North lying west of the Alleghenies was in the process of becoming the heartland of America.[2]

It has long been recognized that westward migrants generally followed the parallels of latitude. Thus, there was a sizable emigration from Virginia and North Carolina by way of Kentucky to southern Indiana, southern Illinois, and Missouri; for the most part, however, the explosive growth in this new western country—most conspicuously in Illinois, whose population increased elevenfold, from 157,000 to 1,772,000, in the thirty years from 1830 to 1860—was the result of emigration from the central and New England states and from the British Isles and Germany.

This area, known in 1861 as the Northwest, was what may not improperly be called a new nation in process of formation, a fluid society of newcomers, many of them recent immigrants from Europe. How would they react to the secession of the southern slave states, to the disruption of the Union? The answer came swiftly, in their response to the news of the attack on Fort Sumter and the president's proclamation three days later calling out the "militia of the several States of the Union to the aggregate number of 75,000" to suppress the insurrection against the national government. The Chicago *Tribune* spoke for the entire region when it declared, "The gates of Janus are open; the storm is upon us. Let the cry be, The Sword of the Lord and of Gideon!" Without waiting for the War Department's assignment of quotas to the several states, Governor William Dennison of Ohio wired the president: "What portion of the 75,000 militia . . . do you give Ohio? We will furnish the largest number you will receive." When Dennison learned that Governor Beriah Magoffin had refused to furnish militia from Kentucky "for the wicked purpose of subduing her sister Southern States," he telegraphed Washington, "If Kentucky will not fill her quota, Ohio will fill it for her." This was no idle boast, for within days of the announcement that Ohio's quota was thirteen thousand men, thirty thousand were enrolled. And Ohio's response was typical of the entire region. Everywhere companies and regiments

2. The population figures in this paragraph and the next are from Jos. C. G. Kennedy, *Preliminary Report on the Eighth Census, 1860*, 37th Cong., 2nd Sess., House of Representatives, Executive Documents No. 116 (Washington, D.C., 1862), *passim*. The population of Ohio in 1860 was 2,340,000, and of Kansas, 107,000. The population of the two border slave states, Kentucky and Missouri, was 1,156,000 and 1,182,000, respectively.

were being formed, and the governors of all the western states were besieged by commanding officers begging to have their units accepted.

The regiments of infantry and batteries of artillery formed in this period of patriotic ebullition were eagerly accepted by the War Department. Not so, however, the numerous mounted units that were being organized at the same time by men eager to offer their services to the government. Winfield Scott, the aged general-in-chief of the army, considered the five mounted regiments (increased to six in the summer of 1861) of the Regular establishment ample for the needs of the army in what he professed to believe would be a short war; that, further, the terrain on which he expected the war to be fought was unsuitable for the operations of large bodies of cavalry; and lastly, that the war would be over long before volunteer cavalrymen could be trained well enough to fulfill a useful role in it.[3] On the basis of these views the War Department declined to accept regiments of mounted troops offered by the governors of Indiana, Minnesota, Iowa, and Illinois.[4] This, however, did not deter gentlemen of an adventurous disposition from organizing cavalry companies and squadrons of cavalry in the expectation that Washington would eventually relent and accept their units. Many of these organizations were in fact accepted. Illinois had, serving in the West, Thielmann's Dragoons, and Carmichael's, O'Harnett's, Stewart's, Delano's, Jenks's, and Smith's companies of cavalry. Similar small units were mustered in Kansas, Kentucky, and Missouri, two of the Missouri units bearing the ornamental names "Benton Hussars" and "Fremont's Hussars," respectively.

Then, following the humiliating defeat of the Union army at Bull Run on July 21, came the realization that to put down the rebellion and restore the Union was a task beyond the capabilities of the minute Regular Army joined for ninety days by the 75,000 militia called forth by the president's proclamation of April 15. In response to the president's call for 500,000 men to serve for three years, the manhood of the North hastened to enlist. Regiments of infantry and batteries of artillery were being organized at every hand by local worthies representing every profession but (with insignificant exceptions) the military, im-

3. Stephen Z. Starr, *The Union Cavalry in the Civil War*, Volume I: *From Fort Sumter to Gettysburg* (Baton Rouge, 1979), 67ff.

4. Thomas F. Thiele, "The Evolution of Cavalry in the American Civil War, 1861–1863" (Ph.D. dissertation, University of Michigan, 1951), 32.

pelled by a fiery patriotism and a praiseworthy ambition to serve their country as officers in the volunteer army.[5]

The bars were now down to the formation of mounted regiments of volunteers, with the result that within a month after Bull Run, thirty-one such regiments had been organized and mustered in, followed by fifty-one more by the year-end. Many of the seventy-eight mounted regiments that were enlisted in Indiana, Ohio, Illinois, Michigan, Wisconsin, Iowa, and Kansas in the course of the war to serve for three years or longer were raised in the summer and fall of 1861; for example, nine of the seventeen regiments of Illinois cavalry and six of the thirteen Ohio regiments were mustered in before December 31, 1861.[6] It should be mentioned also that with the exception of the 2nd Ohio, the 3rd Indiana, the 8th Illinois, and the 1st, 5th, 6th, and 7th Michigan (these last forming the splendid Michigan Brigade, whose soldierly qualities were instrumental in making George A. Custer a major general), all these "western" regiments served in the West and Southwest thoroughout the war and are hence the dramatis personae of this segment of the history of the Union cavalry.[7]

It must be pointed out for the sake of factual accuracy that as a result of one of the vagaries of army administration, the 3rd Indiana became divided; six of its companies served in the East with the Army of the Potomac, while the others served in the West.[8] The 1st Ohio was

5. One of the exceptions was Captain Albert G. Brackett, 2nd United States, authorized by Secretary of War Simon Cameron on August 6, 1861, to proceed to Illinois "or any other of the Western States" to raise a regiment to be known as the "First Western Cavalry," of which he was to be the colonel. Brackett had the regiment raised and organized by September 30, and it was mustered in as the 9th Illinois. Edward A. Davenport, *History of the Ninth Regiment Illinois Cavalry Volunteers* (Chicago, 1888), 14–15.

6. Two of the Ohio cavalry regiments, the 4th and 5th, as well as the 3rd Iowa, were formed on the basis of authority granted by General John C. Fremont with the understanding that when raised, the regiments were "to be attached to his command in Missouri." Lucien Wulsin, *The Story of the Fourth Regiment Ohio Veteran Volunteer Cavalry* (Cincinnati, 1912), 9; Lurton D. Ingersoll, *Iowa and the Rebellion* (Philadelphia, 1866), 396.

7. As in the first two volumes of this study, the word *Cavalry* will be omitted, in the text as well as in the notes, from the names of mounted regiments unless needed to avoid confusion. Thus, we shall speak of the 1st Ohio, 7th Kansas, 4th United States, *etc.*, but of the 4th Kentucky Cavalry, to distinguish it from the 4th Kentucky Mounted Infantry.

8. William N. Pickerill, *History of the Third Indiana Cavalry* (Indianapolis, 1865), viii; *The War of the Rebellion: A Compilation of the Official Records of the Union and Confederate Armies* (128 vols.; Washington, D.C., 1880–1901), Series I, Vol. XXXIX,

the victim of a similarly permanent cleavage; two of its companies served throughout the war in the East and the rest of the regiment in the West.[9] The 2nd Ohio began its campaigning in Missouri, Kansas, and the Indian Territory (the present state of Oklahoma); then, having returned to Ohio for reorganization, it served in Kentucky and Tennessee and, after reenlisting as veterans in early 1864, finished the war in the East.[10]

The tale of the organization of these volunteer regiments in the early months of the war is recounted in the first volume of this study and, as well, the trials and tribulations of their first few weeks or months in the service, the characteristics of their officers and enlisted men, the halting steps whereby officers and men alike began to surmount their state of military ignorance and acquire the first smatterings of military skills and (more painfully and imperfectly) discipline. The first volume also tells of their emergence from a dismally low average level of horsemanship and of the painfully slow process whereby they became possessed of armament (frequently makeshift) and equipment. In all these respects the Union cavalrymen in the West and their brethren in the East were generally alike and shared a generally similar experience. It will become apparent, nevertheless, as this account proceeds, that there were significant differences between the Union cavalry in the East and in the West.[11] In what may be called the spiritual realm, there was a striking but wholly natural difference: a greater informality in the West at every level, in dress and behavior, in the relations between officers and enlisted men, and in a casual lack of reverence for the orthodoxy, sanctioned by West Point and Carlisle, of

---

Pt. 3, p. 758, hereinafter cited as *Official Records.* Unless otherwise indicated, all citations are to Series I.

9. William L. Curry, *Four Years in the Saddle: History of the First Regiment Ohio Volunteer Cavalry* (Columbus, Ohio, 1898), 21.

10. Whitelaw Reid, *Ohio in the War: Her Statesmen, Her Generals and Soldiers* (2 vols.; Cincinnati, 1868), II, 757–59. After the war was already over, the 2nd Ohio was shipped to Missouri and put in a few weeks of peacekeeping duty before returning to Ohio for muster-out.

11. In the first few months of the war, regiments and smaller units of cavalry were raised and disposed of in an atmosphere of utter confusion. General Don Carlos Buell wrote in November, 1861, that Governor Oliver P. Morton of Indiana raised "a company of cavalry . . . as a body guard to General Alexander McD. McCook" and that his own "brigade commanders have their cavalry and their batteries which they tell the division commander he has nothing to do with." *Official Records*, Vol. VII, 443.

traditional cavalry doctrine imported from Europe. In the material realm, especially with respect to armament, the western cavalry, unlike the infantry and artillery, suffered throughout from a disadvantage that seemed to have the force of a law of nature: the greater the distance from Washington, the poorer the weapons.

One of the unexamined imponderables of the operations of the Union cavalry west of the Alleghenies is the extent and precise nature of the effect that its frequently unsuitable and unreliable weapons, especially in the first two years of the war, had on the evolution of its tactics. It will therefore be useful, and indeed necessary, to consider, in greater detail than was appropriate earlier in this study, the provision of arms and equipment for the Union cavalry serving in the West.[12] A convenient point of departure is the military satrapy in St. Louis of one of the tragicomic figures of American military history, John Charles Fremont. He was sent west with the vaguest of directives—"I have given you carte blanche; you must use your own judgment and do the best you can" were the president's parting words to him as they said good-bye on the steps of the White House. His mission was to take military and political command of the "Western Department," an enormous area embracing Illinois, Kentucky, and all the states and territories beyond the Mississippi River as far west as the Rocky Mountains.[13]

The Federal troops in the department when Fremont assumed command on July 25 were still for the most part the militia called out by the president's proclamation of April 15. After ninety days in the service, all the initial enthusiasm was gone; they were largely a mutinous rabble, untrained, undisciplined, unequipped, unarmed, and unpaid. Receiving no help from the authorities in Washington—not even funds to pay the troops he already had—Fremont was faced within a short time after his arrival in St. Louis with the descent upon him of a tidal wave of regiments raised in the aftermath of Bull Run, all of which he was expected to equip, arm, organize, and conduct against the enemy. His difficulties were monumental. Typically, John McClernand, commanding a brigade of Illinois infantry stationed at Cairo, Illinois, a position critically important for the Union to hold, reported that the little more than half of his men who had arms of any kind had seven

---

12. See Vol. I, Chapter IV, of the present work, esp. pp. 124–29.
13. Allan Nevins, *The War for the Union: The Improvised War, 1861–1862* (New York, 1959), 309.

different patterns of muskets, three American-made and four imported, a high percentage of all of them being defective and dangerous to the men who would have to use them.[14] Not only arms for the troops, but everything needed to equip them for the field—ambulances, wagons, medical supplies, blankets, tents, the bits and pieces of personal gear required even in that relatively simple age, from shoes to canteens—was lacking.

As was to be the case throughout the war, the cavalry, simply because it needed more gear than did the footsoldiers and the gunners, was beset by shortages to a greater extent than either the infantry or the artillery. Senator James H. Lane, authorized in an aberration not uncommon in the chaotic first months of the war to raise a force to "protect Kansas," wrote Fremont on August 16: "We should be supplied with artillery and small arms, horse equipments, etc. Kansas is destitute. I have a thousand horses now arriving and eager men to mount them, but without arms and equipments. Our men are without uniforms, blankets, or shoes."[15] John Pope, then a mustering officer in Chicago, telegraphed Fremont: "We need speedily, to fit out one or two regiments of cavalry, sabers and revolvers. There are absolutely none in this part of the country."[16] General David Hunter, sent West to assist Fremont as second-in-command, reported from Missouri on October 5: "The command were exposed to a violent storm all night, without tents. The cavalry and artillery are without overcoats. . . . The cavalry have but two rounds of cartridges." He reported a week later that "Colonel Ellis' cavalry" (not otherwise identified) were "without ammunition, cartridge boxes, swords, pistols, and great-coats, and many of them are greatly in want of clothing."[17] Major William McLaughlin's battalion of Ohio cavalry, a part of the Sherman Brigade, was posted in Kentucky in January, 1862, without carbines. Colonel (later General and later still, President) James A. Garfield armed them with the rifles of "such of the Forty-Second Ohio Infantry [his own regiment] as were sick and on detached duty"; the cavalrymen had received "a full sup-

14. *Ibid.*, 320.
15. *Official Records*, Vol. III, 446. A week earlier, Fremont had wired Frank P. Blair, Jr., in Washington: "Major Hagner telegraphs . . . that all my cavalry equipments and harness, arranged for . . . in New York, have been ordered to Washington. I do not think this is quite right." *Ibid.*, 432.
16. *Ibid.*, 396. The telegram was sent on July 17, 1861.
17. *Ibid.*, 522, 531–32.

ply" of cartridges for their pistols, but not caps, without which the cartridges were useless.[18]

Some cavalry regiments, more fortunate than the rest, were issued arms in the autumn or winter of 1861. And what arms they were! The 3rd Ohio, exceptionally favored, received a full complement of good modern carbines, but they were of three different types, the Sharps, Burnside, and Remington.[19] Most regiments, however, had to make do with what the historian of the 4th Iowa called a "villainous equipment of arms," which in the case of his regiment were "heavy sabers, Starr's revolvers, holster-pistols (old pattern, smooth bore) and Austrian rifles. Of the pistols and rifles, there were enough for half the men."[20] The 4th Ohio departed on its first campaign in February, 1862, without carbines, armed only with sabers and unreliable revolvers; one company only of the regiment was armed with the Colt revolving rifle, obtained by means of "considerable diplomacy" from the Ordnance Depot in Louisville.[21] The 7th and 9th Pennsylvania, the two cavalry regiments from the Keystone State that served in the West throughout the war, started out with Belgian infantry rifles, "about as worthless as a military weapon could be."[22]

18. *Ibid.*, Vol. VII, 27. On December 28–31, General Lew Wallace was on a scout from Paducah with a detachment including 130 men of the 2nd Illinois, some of whom he had to arm with rifles borrowed from the 11th and 13th regiments of Indiana infantry. Some of the rifles, Wallace reported, were "carelessly lost" or thrown away by the cavalrymen. *Ibid.*, 67.

19. Thomas Crofts, *History of the Service of the Third Ohio Veteran Volunteer Cavalry* (Toledo, 1910), 19.

20. Ingersoll, *Iowa and the Rebellion*, 419. In his formal history of the regiment, the historian, speaking of the spring of 1863, wrote: "The clumsy Austrian (infantry) rifles, issued when the regiment was first equipped, were still in the hands of those men who had not had the hardihood or ingenuity to 'lose' them. Some had revolvers of the Starr and other bad kinds, many had the single-barreled holster pistols, with ramrods, of the pattern in use in the Mexican war. . . . Every man saw, and what was much worse, felt the insufficiency of the arms." William F. Scott, *The Story of a Cavalry Regiment: The Career of the Fourth Iowa Veteran Volunteers* (New York, 1893), 63.

21. Wulsin, *Story of the Fourth*, 28.

22. William B. Sipes, *The Seventh Pennsylvania Veteran Volunteer Cavalry* (Pottsville, Pa., n.d.), 9; John W. Rowell, *Yankee Cavalrymen: Through the Civil War with the Ninth Pennsylvania Cavalry* (Knoxville, 1971), 41. (A third Pennsylvania cavalry regiment, the 15th, that served in the West had so strange and in some ways sad a history that it cannot be counted with the 7th and the 9th.) At the end of January, 1862, the 7th Pennsylvania was rearmed, part with Burnside and part with the Smith carbines. As to the 9th, Colonel Edward C. Williams reported that when he ordered his men to fire by companies, "sometimes three guns would go off out of sixty or seventy."

The 7th Kansas, which was to earn a not entirely unwelcome notoriety as "Jennison's Jayhawkers," started the war with "many diverse patterns of weapons," including a strange hybrid muzzle-loader described as "pistol carbines." The commanding officer of the regiment, Lieutenant Colonel Daniel R. Anthony, complained in June, 1862, that the "Prussian rifles" with which part of the regiment was armed were "entirely unfit for service." Six months later, in December, Lieutenant Colonel Thomas P. Herrick, who had succeeded Anthony, excused the tardiness of a report he had been ordered to submit to the Cavalry Bureau on the number, kind, and caliber of the regiment's firearms with the explanation that he had been "obliged to alter the [report] form in order to suit the great diversity of arms in [the] regiment. Permit me to call your attention to . . . the unfortunate condition of arms in my command."[23] This complaint of the commanding officer of a regiment engaged in active operations points up the fallacy of the commonly accepted notion that northern industry, going into high gear as soon as the war broke out, supplied the Union armies (and via captures, a sizable percentage of the Confederate armies as well) with a super-abundance of all the weapons and gear they needed to overwhelm the agricultural South. However true as a general proposition this piece of conventional lore may be, it is certainly not true of arms for the Union cavalry, particularly those serving in the West, who, generally speaking, were not even moderately well armed until the latter part of 1863 and not properly armed—quite different from being moderately well armed—until well into 1864, and some units, never.

The men of the western states who hastened to enlist in cavalry regiments, or were persuaded to do so, were undistinguishable from their counterparts in the East or, for that matter, from their brethren, now become their adversaries, hailing from the seceded western states. Nor were their motivations different for enlisting in the cavalry rather than in the infantry or the artillery. There were "personality" differences between East and West, but only in the most superficial and general sense; much more important were the similarities. There was a greater predominance of country boys in the western regiments than in those from the East, but this did not necessarily imply a greater familiarity with horses or a greater initial ability to ride, control, and care

23. Stephen Z. Starr, *Jennison's Jayhawkers* (Baton Rouge, 1973), 82–83.

for the untrained animals that were issued to them. At all levels of the military hierarchy, there was the same ignorance in the West as there was in the East of all things military, aggravated in the West by a considerably smaller leavening of professionally trained officers. With the exception of a small number of units made up entirely or mainly of German immigrants who had had some military training in the Old Country, there was in the western regiments an even lesser regard for the superficial niceties of dress and conduct than there was in the East and, more important, an even more casual attitude toward discipline. Previously quoted was the remark of the historian of the 51st Indiana Mounted Infantry that would have been subscribed to wholeheartedly by the overwhelming majority of western cavalrymen: "We had enlisted to put down the Rebellion, and had not patience with the red-tape tomfoolery of the regular service."[24] It was of course taken for granted that every freeborn American in the ranks of a cavalry regiment knew by instinct the difference between necessary discipline and "red-tape tomfoolery," and regulated his conduct accordingly. There was a fair degree of discipline in battle—the instinct of self-preservation saw to that—but little in camp or on the march.

It would be "invidious," in the language of the day, to make comparisons in so sensitive an area, but a number of Kentucky, Tennessee, and Arkansas regiments in the Union army became notorious for the extraordinarily free and easy habits of their men. The 1st Kentucky in particular made itself a byword for indiscipline in every possible form. Colonel Garfield described the regiment as riddled by desertion ("A large number . . . refused to come into the mountains, and many that started deserted") and as a "demoralized, discouraged" body of men.[25] Time failed to work its usual magic with the Kentuckians, for in July, 1862, General James S. Negley reported them as "in truly a deplorable condition," and added that, having supplied them with clothing, sabers, and revolvers, he was trying to discipline them.[26] Three more months went by, and Colonel, later Major General, William B. Hazen,

24. William R. Hartpence, *History of the 51st Indiana Veteran Infantry* (Indianapolis, 1894), 36. This remark is quoted in Vol. I, p. 166 of the present work.

25. *Official Records*, Vol. VII, 32. In the same report Garfield describes the 14th Kentucky Infantry as "composed of excellent material, but . . . in a wretched state of discipline. . . . It can be considered but little better than a well-disposed, Union-loving mob." These words fit the 1st Kentucky to a T.

26. *Ibid.*, Vol. XVI, Pt. 2, p. 95.

commanding the pursuit after the battle of Perryville, reported that two companies of the regiment "at the first discharge of the enemy retreated in disorder . . . and were with difficulty found. . . . The entire regiment seemed greatly deficient in anything approaching military drill, and it was with difficulty that . . . [his] orders, given in the simplest military language, were understood."[27] The Kentuckians' most conspicuous vice was straggling; they were described by the historian of another mounted regiment as being "everywhere at the same time. They . . . seemed to have carte blanche to go when and where they pleased, and to return when ready."[28] The story of their contest of wills with General George Stoneman, related with considerable unction by the regimental historian as "a question of which should yield— the iron will of Stoneman, or the habits and rather free ways" of the Kentuckians, has as its focus the march of the regiment from Kentucky in May, 1864, to join in Sherman's Atlanta Campaign, and has been mentioned briefly in Volume I of this study. Before the march began, Stoneman issued strict orders forbidding straggling; a commissioned officer was to ride behind each company, and a rear guard behind each regiment, to keep the men in the ranks. But, the regimental historian relates, General Stoneman, "not yet . . . informed of all our boys' peculiarities . . . had neglected to make efficient provisions for front and flank guards to keep them in the column." Of the eight hundred officers and men who started the march, only seventy-three were present when the regiment arrived in Burnside, Kentucky, on the evening of the second day. But most (not all, however) of the absentees had caught up with the regiment when it reached its destination in Georgia nine days later.[29]

27. *Ibid.*, Pt. 1, p. 1137.

28. B. F. Thompson, *History of the 112th Regiment of Illinois Volunteer Infantry in the Great War of the Rebellion* (Toulon, Ill., 1885), 30. Thompson adds: "They knew but little about drill, and discipline was a stranger to them, but the men had the utmost confidence in their colonel [Frank Wolford] and he in them. Every man was a brigadier on his own hook, and the majority of them believed themselves superior to the average brigadier." *Ibid.*, 30. See also R. M. Kelly, Thomas Speed, and Alfred Pirtle, *The Union Regiments of Kentucky* (Louisville, 1897), 112.

29. Eastham Tarrant, *The Wild Riders of the First Kentucky Cavalry (Union)* (Louisville, 1894), 315–19; Vol. I, p. 171 of the present work; *Official Records*, Vol. XXXII, Pt. 3, p. 530. Shortly before the regiment's departure for Georgia, General Stephen G. Burbridge asked to have it ordered out of its home state: "The quiet of the State demands that they be removed as soon as possible." *Ibid.*, 293.

Another western cavalry regiment, which became by common consent one of the most dependable combat units in the western armies, was the 7th Kansas, credited to that state notwithstanding that of its ten companies one, Company K, was recruited in northeastern Ohio by John Brown, Jr., eldest son of the martyr, and three others, Companies D, E, and F, and about thirty men of a fourth, Company B, came from Illinois. Companies D and E are deserving of special notice on two counts: first, because they were so eager to get into the fight that, having learned after being recruited in August, 1861, that Illinois had already filled the quota assigned to it under the post–Bull Run call for 500,000 men, they traveled to Leavenworth in the hope that there would be room for them in the Kansas quota and that they would be accepted there; and second, although they had enlisted to serve as infantry, they voted in good democratic fashion, upon their arrival in Kansas, to accept Colonel Charles R. Jennison's invitation to join his cavalry regiment, then in the process of formation.

The tone of the 7th Kansas was set by the colonel himself and by the Kansans in the regiment, particularly those in Companies G and H, many of them veterans or survivors of the long agony of "Bleeding Kansas," men who, under the command of Jennison himself and of other leaders of gangs of free-state guerrillas, had fought a bitter eye-for-an-eye-tooth-for-a-tooth border war with the proslavery Border Ruffians from Missouri, concentrating their martial endeavors on shootings, hangings, arson, and robbery, and especially the last, in the Missouri counties adjacent to Kansas, all in the name of retaliation. "Jayhawking" became a specialty of the regiment, practiced as enthusiastically by the men from Illinois and even by the Missourians as by their authentically Kansan comrades.[30] Operating in the border counties of Missouri south of Kansas City from November, 1861, on, the Jayhawkers robbed, burned, and killed with such gusto that the War Department was obliged to remove them from Missouri, first to Kansas and then to Tennessee.[31] There they continued their evil ways, claiming nearly always that "burthened with a false reputation for robbery,

30. Company I of the regiment had in its ranks a sizable contingent of men from St. Joseph, Missouri. Starr, *Jennison's Jayhawkers*, 77.
31. On April 17, 1862, shortly before their removal to Tennessee, the officers of the regiment published a series of resolutions declaring that "the charges made against 'Jennison's Regiment' of pillage, arson and brutality *are inventions of envious, designing and unprincipled liars*, than whom there are not in the service, or out of it, more con-

rapine and all crimes" that had accompanied them to Tennessee, they were being blamed for all the depredations committed by every other Union cavalry regiment in the area. Eventually, Grant took the drastic step of ordering their wages stopped to pay for sugar and tobacco they had taken or destroyed in Trenton, Tennessee.[32]

The 1st Kentucky and the 7th Kansas have been singled out, it is hoped not unfairly, to demonstrate the two most common and closely intertwined vices of the Union cavalry: straggling and marauding. Given the tremendous difficulty of hauling on the primitive roads of the day, for dozens and sometimes hundreds of miles from railhead or the nearest navigable stream, the huge quantities of supplies needed to keep an army of any size and its animals fed, it was inevitable that from time to time the men should have had to fall back on foraging to stay alive themselves and to keep their animals alive. Moreover, the dreary monotony of army rations, even when rations were available, made the henroosts, orchards, pigpens, smokehouses, larders, and vegetable patches of every farmhouse within reach irresistibly tempting. Taken so far, foraging may be considered a not entirely illegitimate concomitant of warfare. But only too often, and despite an endless stream of prohibitions, exhortations, and threats, "legitimate" foraging led to the plundering of defenseless civilians, friendly and enemy alike. In January, 1864, General Samuel D. Sturgis reported from Sevierville, in Unionist east Tennessee, that "it is a pity that circumstances should compel us to entirely exhaust the country of these loyal people. . . . The necessity of pressing supplies leads so immediately to plundering that soldiers find no difficulty in taking the step from one to the other. . . . It is distressing to witness the sufferings of these people at the hands of . . . friends."[33] General David S. Stanley, promoted in the fall of 1862 to chief of cavalry of the Army of the Cumberland, wrote: "This disposition to plunder was pretty general. It was natural to use and destroy property belonging to those whose dearest hope was to kill us, and unless the general commanding an army took a decided stand against plundering, the practice soon ran through an

temptible and utterly abandoned objects of pity and scorn." For Kansas rhetoric, this was relatively restrained. Starr, *Jennison's Jayhawkers*, 139.

32. Simeon M. Fox, "The Story of the Seventh Kansas," *Transactions of the Kansas State Historical Society, 1903–1904*, VIII (Topeka, 1904), 31; Starr, *Jennison's Jayhawkers*, 186–89.

33. *Official Records*, Vol. XXX, Pt. 1, p. 114.

army and was ruinous to all property except land, and in turn reflected upon the invading force, for invariably a plundering force lost effectiveness and discipline in time of hard marching and battle."[34]

Viewing the situation from a less exalted rank, Sergeant Lyman B. Pierce, 2nd Iowa, wrote in his regimental history that "foraging was made the means of many great wrongs inflicted on the citizens . . . many stopped not when their necessities were supplied, but . . . carried on a wholesale robbery business. Money, watches, jewelry and valuables of any kind were stolen by them, calling themselves foragers."[35] Much, and perhaps most, foraging was carried on without supervision, by troopers acting alone, in pairs, or in small groups, and the anonymity bestowed by the uniform lessened the chances of detection and punishment of plunderers. Officers found it convenient to close their eyes to what was going on and in some cases even took the lead in expeditions that ended in marauding, whatever their ostensible military purpose may have been.[36] Even after the war had officially ended, General Emory Upton thought it necessary to order a thorough search of his Fourth Division, made up of the 3rd, 4th, and 5th Iowa, the 1st and 7th Ohio, and the 10th Missouri, of James H. Wilson's cavalry corps, "in order to seize all plunder that may have been collected by the men" on the march from Selma, Alabama, to Macon, Georgia. Wilson ordered his other two division commanders, Edward M. McCook of the First Division and Robert H. G. Minty of the Third, to follow Upton's example; the two divisions between them contained two Illinois, four Indiana, one Iowa, four Kentucky, one Pennsylvania, and two Ohio regiments.[37]

The makeup of these three cavalry divisions is given in detail to demonstrate the point that marauding was not the specialty of a few particularly vicious units like the 7th Kansas or of units (again like the

34. David S. Stanley, *Personal Memoirs of Major-General David S. Stanley, U.S.A.* (Cambridge, Mass., 1917), 118.

35. Lyman B. Pierce, *History of the Second Iowa Cavalry* (Burlington, Ia., 1865), 114; Vol. I, p. 170 of the present work.

36. Starr, *Jennison's Jayhawkers*, 113, 117. The historian of the 51st Indiana Mounted Infantry informs us that "strict orders were issued forbidding foraging. . . . In time the veterans learned to circumvent all such orders, and to modify the cruel penalty by a system of division with the officers . . . who allowed the boys to construe orders to suit their needs." Hartpence, *History of the 51st Indiana*, 31.

37. *Official Records*, Vol. XLIX, Pt. 2, p. 486. (The composition of the three divisions appears in *Ibid.*, Pt. 1, pp. 402–403.)

7th Kansas) that could plead as an excuse for their marauding that they were repaying in kind what had been done to their families and friends. Moreover, a reading of the surviving letters, diaries, and reminiscences of the officers and men of the 7th Kansas, and of cavalrymen generally, makes it evident that they were not congenital criminals and ruffians to whom marauding came naturally, but overwhelmingly, young men and boys who had been brought up in decent, God-fearing homes. Marauding was only one of the symptoms of the removal of normal restraints by the war; there were others.

Those whose baggage Generals Upton, McCook, and Minty were to have searched, had plundered with knowledge of General Wilson's Special Field Orders No. 5, of January 14, 1865, which directed his division and brigade commanders to establish "strong guards . . . about the camps, in order to prevent the men from leaving camp for improper purposes. Marauding and pillaging must be stopped, and for this purpose, all officers of the command are authorized to shoot at once those caught in the act of stealing or destroying wantonly the property of unoffending citizens."

Three months later, this order obviously forgotten or ignored (there is no indication in the records that any marauder was shot pursuant to it), Wilson tried again, issuing on April 11 Special Field Orders No. 20.

The attention of division commanders is called to orders heretofore published in regard to pillaging. The evil has increased to such an extent as to call for the most prompt and decided measures, and all officers and men are enjoined to aid in suppressing a practice dishonorable and unbecoming a Christian soldiery. Hereafter no enlisted man, servant, or employee belonging to the cavalry corps will be allowed to enter a house under any pretense whatever, except under the direction of a commissioned officer. . . . Any violation of this order may be punished by death. . . . This order is to be read to every regiment . . . every day until it is thoroughly understood.

Only two weeks after the publication of this order, patrols had to be sent out of Macon "in every direction . . . to arrest all men engaged in marauding."[38]

Marauding, or in a more general sense "depredations," which included the wanton destruction of property, was in most respects the most serious disciplinary problem with which commanding officers had to deal, but it was far from being the only one. Cavalrymen of the

38. *Ibid.*, Vol. XLV, Pt. 2, p. 589, Vol. XLIX, Pt. 2, pp. 319, 452.

western armies, like those in the East, were guilty at one time or another of every imaginable form of indiscipline. Personal hygiene and camp sanitation were systematically neglected; troopers were dirty and ragged, their camps in "filthy condition," dead horses and the offal resulting from the butchering of beef cattle in and near camp left unburied, kitchens "filthy," firearms discharged in camp or on the march, cartridges swept into the nearest campfire, horses habitually neglected or abused, civilian clothing substituted for parts of the uniform, guard and picket duty negligently performed, drunkenness widespread, orders disobeyed—the list is endless. The western armies generally (apparently to a greater degree than those in the East), and the cavalry in particular, seemed to be manned largely by members of a resolutely individualistic generation unaccustomed to discipline and commanded by officers who for the most part, at least at the company officer level, were as disdainful of discipline as their men, were not convinced of its necessity, and, what is perhaps worst of all, were unaccustomed to the exercise of authority.[39]

As mentioned earlier, the conventional wisdom in 1861 was that under "the most favorable circumstances," a minimum of one year was required to produce a properly trained cavalryman.[40] There were a few exceptions, which will be mentioned shortly, but for the most part, from the beginning of the war to the end, the training cavalry regiments received ranged from none to inadequate. It should be noted also that recruits added to cavalry regiments from time to time received no preliminary training whatever; their only "training" was what they picked up from their veteran fellow troopers after they joined their regiments.

The 7th Pennsylvania, recruited in September, 1861, was considered "ready for service" by mid-December.[41] The 1st Kentucky lacked "military training and discipline," as its historian confessed, but, he

39. The Regimental and Company Order and Letter Books of cavalry regiments in the National Archives (Record Group 94) are filled with messages, circulars, orders, and exhortations dealing with these disciplinary problems. See in particular the Order and Letter Books of the 2nd Iowa, 2nd Michigan, 3rd Ohio, and 7th Pennsylvania. See also, by the present author, "Hawkeyes on Horseback: The Second Iowa Volunteer Cavalry," *Civil War History*, XXIII (1977), 212–27; "The Second Michigan Volunteer Cavalry: Another View," *Michigan History*, LX (1976), 161–82; "The Third Ohio Volunteer Cavalry: A View from the Inside," *Ohio History*, LXXXV (1976), 306–18.

40. Moses Harris, "The Union Cavalry," MOLLUS, Commandery of Wisconsin, *War Papers*, I (Milwaukee, 1891), 350.

41. Sipes, *The Seventh Pennsylvania*, 6.

hastened to explain, "stern military necessity never allowed them the opportunity" to acquire either.[42] In early January, 1862, by which time it was on active duty, the McLaughlin Battalion of the Sherman Brigade of Ohio was reported to have had "very little drill and cannot be relied on for much service, except scout and messenger duty."[43] One of the best and most thoughtful of the historians of western cavalry regiments recorded that

the practice of separating cavalry regiments into parts, and sending the different parts upon different services, so that a whole regiment was seldom within reach of its commander for many days together, prevailed widely during the first years of the war; and it was a practice most injurious and demoralizing. Among the serious evils that followed it was the almost inevitable failure or inability of the several detachments to keep up any important amount of drill or instruction. It was in the practical school of the necessities and emergencies of each day, therefore, that the volunteers were made soldiers.[44]

The 4th Michigan, described by a member of another cavalry regiment as "the most distinguished of all the noted regiments from the peninsula State," was mustered in on August 29, 1862, left the state on September 26, and was in action against John Hunt Morgan's horsemen in Kentucky on October 10.[45] Obviously, the regiment could not have had anything worthy of the name of training, even by the unexacting standards of 1862. Moreover, as a general rule, the lack of time or opportunity for drill and training lasted well beyond "the first years of the war." The 1st Alabama (Union) was reported in April, 1863, to be "poorly drilled."[46] On October 26, 1864, a detachment of the 10th Indiana was sent on a scout from Decatur, Alabama, the regiment having

42. Tarrant, *Wild Riders of the First Kentucky*, 30.
43. *Official Records*, Vol. VII, 27.
44. Scott, *Story of a Cavalry Regiment*, 374.
45. Joseph G. Vale, *Minty and the Cavalry: A History of Cavalry Campaigns in the Western Armies* (Harrisburg, Pa., 1886), 98–100.
46. *Official Records*, Vol. XXIII, Pt. 1, p. 247. This regiment was formed in southwest Missouri by Colonel M. LaRue Harrison from refugees from western Arkansas. These men "could not stay at home and . . . had been living in the mountains and out of the way places since early in the war[;] when they came into the Federal lines [they] were ragged . . . with long hair and unkempt beards, they had the appearance of wild men or cave men, and could hardly recognize themselves in their improved appearance when they had discarded their old clothing, had their hair cut and beards trimmed up and put on the new blue uniform of the Union army." Wiley Britton, *The Union Indian Brigade in the Civil War* (Kansas City, 1922), 108, 190. In February, 1865, "portions" of the regiment, then in Arkansas, were reported to be "committing the most outrageous excesses, robbing and burning houses indiscriminately." *Official Records*, Vol. XLVIII, Pt. 1, p. 1008.

been "mounted and equipped as cavalry only the day before."[47] In a special category of preventable futility were the short-term cavalry companies, squadrons, battalions, and even regiments, raised by the government for periods of enlistment of thirty, sixty, ninety, and a hundred days, three and six months, and one year, to cope with some actual or fancied emergency. Such short periods of enlistment were obviously insufficient to allow for any worthwhile training; they allowed hardly enough time for the officers to learn the names of their men or for the men to feel reasonably at ease with or on their horses.[48]

Some few regiments did receive a fair amount of training. The 1st Iowa, for instance, had five hours of drill every day, frequent sham battles, and saber practice; they even had the opportunity to train their horses to jump over ditches and fallen logs.[49] This was in September, 1861; in the same month, the 5th Iowa also had ample drill, including practice in charges against infantry and artillery, "training of horses to run up on the muskets and mouths of the cannons, while firing and also being drawn up in line when the foot would charge on them with muskets & fixed bayonets."[50] The 4th Ohio, recruited in the Cincinnati area in the late summer of 1861, received its horses before the ranks of the regiment were full, and had four hours daily of mounted drill for four months before it began active service in Kentucky in January, 1862.[51] These, however, were exceptional cases; more typical was the 2nd Illinois, which had a total of only four weeks of drill, two on foot and two on horseback, before commencing active service near Paducah.[52]

The unifying theme of the first volume of this study is that a principal factor in the advancement of the Federal cavalry in the East from

47. *Official Records*, Vol. XXXIX, Pt. 1, p. 700.

48. In July, 1862, to try to cope with J. H. Morgan's "First Kentucky Raid," General Jeremiah T. Boyle raised, with the approval of the War Department, the 8th, 9th, and 10th Kentucky, all to serve for one year. *Ibid.*, Vol. XVI, Pt. 1, pp. 743, 744, 746, 749, 752; see also Kelly, Speed, and Pirtle, *The Union Regiments of Kentucky*, 192, 202.

49. Max Hendricks Guyer (ed.), "The Journal and Letters of Corporal William O. Gulick," *Iowa Journal of History and Politics*, XXVIII (1930), 217, 222, 245.

50. Charles Alley, "Excerpts from the Civil War Diary of Lieut. Charles Alley," *Iowa Journal of History*, XLIX (1951), 246.

51. Wulsin, *Story of the Fourth*, 56.

52. Samuel F. Fletcher, *The History of Company A, Second Illinois Cavalry* (Chi-

COME IN YOUR WAR ARRAY

futility to competence was its liberation from attachment in driblets to brigades, divisions, and corps of infantry, its organization into brigades, divisions, and eventually corps of its own, under its own officers exercising operational command as well as administrative authority, and its being granted the freedom, ultimately, to operate as an autonomous fighting force. This was the pattern of organization that the Confederate cavalry in the East had enjoyed almost from the beginning of the war and, under the great "Jeb" Stuart, exploited as a major source of its "bulge" over the Union cavalry until midway through the war. And, as will be seen, this was also the organizational pattern that was being evolved in a halting, undirected, pragmatic way by (or more accurately, for) the Union cavalry in the western armies as early as June, 1862, six months before it was proposed for the Army of the Potomac by General Alfred Pleasonton and eight months before General Joseph Hooker ordered that the cavalry of that army be "consolidated into one corps." [53]

There was, of course, no formal organism in the Union army whose responsibility it was to analyze new technical, organizational, or tactical developments, to try to determine why they worked if indeed they did. Nor was there any formal mechanism for the transmittal from one theater of war to another of useful technical information—organizational or tactical—and even less for seeing to it that a pattern or procedure that had been evolved and seemed for whatever reason to work in one theater, was adopted or given a try elsewhere. Neither Secretary Stanton nor Henry W. Halleck, general-in-chief from July, 1862, on, did so, notwithstanding that the latter, at any rate, had the daily burden of trying to deal with the stream of dispatches in which area and army commanders set forth the problems, difficulties, and dissatisfactions their mounted troops were causing them. Eventually, a properly organized, autonomous cavalry emerged in the West as well as in the East, and while cavalrymen in the West were never as effectively armed as were their brethren in the East, or as they should have been—as late as March, 1865, General Wilson had to persuade the

cago, 1912), 13. The regiment performed its saber drill with homemade wooden swords, as did the 4th Illinois. P. O. Avery, *History of the Fourth Illinois Cavalry Regiment* (Humboldt, Neb., 1903), 47.

53. *Official Records*, Vol. XXI, 815, Vol. XXV, Pt. 2, p. 51; Vol. I, pp. 326–27, 339 of the present work.

men of his Fifth Division to give up their Spencer carbines ("the only good arm this division has") so that he could arm properly General John T. Croxton's brigade of the First Division for the Selma Campaign—they did benefit greatly from a divisional and corps scheme of organization.[54]

For roughly the first year of the war, the Union cavalry in the West, like that in the East, was at loose ends; lacking a clear-cut mission, it was used almost entirely for patrolling, scouting, carrying dispatches, and escort duty. At the siege of Corinth, Mississippi, in May, 1862, four regiments of cavalry had to perform "the very unusual service to mounted men of building roads and bridges, earthworks for batteries, rifle pits, and lying in the trenches as infantry."[55] Not surprisingly, the cavalry's state of disorganization was in keeping with the trifling or "noncavalry" work it was called upon to do. In April, 1862, in the Armies of the Mississippi, the Ohio, and the Tennessee, the cavalry was attached to divisions of infantry, and to make this dispersion even worse, it was further fragmented, attached in units of a battalion or two, or a company or two, to infantry brigades or divisions. Nearly all these regiments of cavalry, after being pitchforked into service with little if any preliminary training, were prevented by being broken up into battalion or company-sized packets serving separate from one another, from any possibility of working their way into a state of military usefulness.[56] Cavalry colonels found it impossible to train and discipline their men or to teach by practice their line officers the elements of the proper functions of cavalry, or, indeed, to learn it themselves. It is not surprising, therefore, that after the battle of Shiloh, the cavalry

54. *Official Records*, Vol. XLIX, Pt. 1, p. 808, Pt. 2, p. 19. The suggestion that the Spencers of the Fifth Division be given to Croxton's brigade came from Colonel Datus E. Coon, commanding the Second Brigade of the Fifth Division. The Spencers were given up by the 2nd Iowa, and the 3rd, 6th, 7th, and 9th Illinois, all of whom had received them as a reward for reenlisting as veterans. For eight months before getting the Spencers, the 3rd and 7th Illinois had been "armed" with guns that had been condemned and turned in to the Ordnance people in Memphis. *Ibid.*, Pt. 2, p. 39.

55. *Ibid.*, Vol. X, Pt. 1, p. 726.

56. *Ibid.*, 100, Pt. 2, pp. 87, 147. The historian of the 1st Ohio reports that "on the day of the battle of Perryville [October 8, 1862] the regiment was again united, after having been cut up in detachments for more than two months." Curry, *Four Years in the Saddle*, 76. On July 12, 1862, Buell's chief of staff spoke of orders posting portions of the 7th Pennsylvania in Nashville, Murfreesboro, Tullahoma, and Cowan, Tennessee, respectively, and added, not surprisingly, "I am unable thus far to find out where all the companies of this regiment are." *Official Records*, Vol. XVI, Pt. 2, p. 130.

was "in great disrepute among . . . [the] entire army. At Shiloh the infantry said they had acted badly, and all assumed that all cavalry would
do the same."[57] Grant, one of those guilty of dividing up his cavalry into
less-than-regimental units that he subordinated to his infantry, complained of "the usual cavalry stupidity" without realizing that to a certain extent he was himself responsible for it. General Sherman, commanding a division in Grant's army and with a part of the 4th Illinois
(whom he reported as "a mere squad, and it is worse than [a] toothache to call upon them for hard work") attached to his command,
wrote Grant that he mistrusted their reports.[58] General David S. Stanley,
upon becoming chief of cavalry of the Army of the Cumberland (formerly Buell's Army of the Ohio) in November, 1862, wrote that the
cavalry he took over "had been badly neglected. It was weak, undisciplined, and scattered around, a regiment to a division of infantry."[59] General Wilson, writing many years later and probably not
averse to exaggerating the contrast between the low estate of the
mounted arm in the West prior to his assignment as Sherman's chief of
cavalry and its subsequent accomplishments at Nashville and Selma
under his command, commented that the "mounted service was looked
upon as both futile and discreditable" and "had come to be a scoff and
a byword to the other branches of service."[60]

General Halleck, in overall command in May, 1862, of the snail-like
Union advance to Corinth following the battle of Shiloh, had under
him Grant's Army of the Tennessee, Don Carlos Buell's Army of the
Ohio, and John Pope's Army of the Mississippi, in the first two of which
the cavalry had been parceled out among the divisions of infantry
in the manner we have described. On April 28, Halleck appointed
General A. J. Smith chief of cavalry of his entire force.[61] There is no
indication in the records that General Smith's duties were anything
more than administrative. A regimental historian, however, reports

57. Pierce, *History of the Second Iowa*, 18.
58. *Official Records*, Vol. X, Pt. 2, p. 87, Vol. XVII, Pt. 2, pp. 36, 79, 85. The cavalry
accused by Grant of stupidity was the 6th Illinois, commanded by Colonel Benjamin H.
Grierson. The "stupidity" was that, ordered to escort from Memphis a supply train to
Sherman, the regiment took the wrong road, leaving the train unprotected. It was
promptly captured by W. H. Jackson's Confederate cavalry.
59. Stanley, *Personal Memoirs*, 120; *Official Records*, Vol. XX, Pt. 2, p. 94.
60. James H. Wilson, *Under the Old Flag* (2 vols.; New York, 1912), II, 27–28.
61. *Official Records*, Vol. X, Pt. 2, p. 139.

that "this was the first movement of the cavalry in this department as a separate and independent organization, and after a careful inspection by the chief, several expeditions were planned and executed by the cavalry entirely independent of the infantry. . . . The cavalry regiments were still attached to and camped with the different infantry divisions, but were concentrated when any independent movement of the cavalry was contemplated."[62] If there was such a concentration of the cavalry following General Smith's appointment or any expeditions "by the cavalry entirely independent of the infantry," no record of either appears in the sources where one would expect to find it. The Corinth campaign was nearing its end when John Pope announced the expansion of the cavalry division he had established at the start of the New Madrid Campaign in February from two regiments to four, the 2nd Iowa and the 7th Illinois being added to the 2nd and 3rd Michigan; Gordon Granger, promoted to brigadier general, was to continue in command.[63] The organization of the division and the promotion of Gordon Granger to single-star rank had a momentous result: it started up the ladder of success an obscure infantry captain named Philip Henry Sheridan, then doing quartermaster's work at Halleck's headquarters. Governor Austin Blair of Michigan was persuaded to appoint Sheridan to the command of the 2nd Michigan that Granger's promotion had made vacant.

Pope's example, if it was noticed at all, was certainly not imitated by his two colleagues in army command, Buell and Grant. Their cavalry remained scattered among the infantry, and the operations of those mounted troops remained under the direction of the infantry officers to whose commands they happened to be attached.[64]

62. Curry, *Four Years in the Saddle*, 55. The same regimental historian tells us that the colonel of his regiment, Minor Milliken (killed at Stones River, December 31, 1862), "had always been very strongly in favor of organizing the cavalry into brigades and divisions, as he always claimed that they could be of much more service massed than by cutting them up into detachments and having them attached to divisions of infantry by regiments or battalions." *Ibid.*, 81–82.

63. General Orders No. 57, June 1, 1862, *Official Records*, Vol. X, Pt. 2, p. 241. It should be noted, however, that the "Organization of the Army of the Mississippi" on May 30, 1862, as it appears in *Ibid.*, 147, already shows the "Cavalry Division" commanded by Gordon Granger, and Granger's report of operations from April 23 to June 10 seems to imply that the division was already in being on the former date. *Ibid.*, Pt. 1, p. 726.

64. *Ibid.*, 149–54. General Braxton Bragg, who succeeded Beauregard in command of the Confederate Army of Tennessee, ordered on November 4, 1862, the grouping of his cavalry into two brigades, each of which he attached to a three-division corps of infantry. *Ibid.*, Vol. XX, Pt. 2, p. 388.

It may be taken for granted that Pope ordered his cavalry concentrated into a division with General Halleck's knowledge and consent. One may therefore wonder why Halleck, having agreed to the adoption of this form of organization by one of his three army commanders as a sensible move, or at least as a move worth trying, did not take the logical next step of urging or even ordering his other two army commanders to follow Pope's example. Buell's organization, at all events, defied all reason. In early June, 1862, he represented to the War Department that "with lines of great depth . . . swarming with the enemy's cavalry" to protect, he needed eight more regiments of cavalry in Tennessee and Kentucky.[65] He had at this time 3,714 mounted troops "present for duty." Three of his regiments, plus three companies of a fourth, were united to form a cavalry brigade; but four more of his regiments, the "Fry Kentucky Scouts," and the "Anderson Troop of Pennsylvania Cavalry" remained unattached; and two more regiments, plus one company of a third, were attached to a division and a brigade, respectively, of infantry. It is difficult to tell if this boxing of the organizational compass gave Buell the best or the worst of all possible worlds.[66]

After reporting, a month later, the existence in his army of a cavalry brigade of 574 officers and men under Colonel Edward M. McCook, of "unattached" cavalry numbering 2,543, and of another 1,864 horsemen attached to five different divisions of infantry, Buell tried another tack. On August 27, he set up a "Light Brigade," consisting of two regiments of Michigan infantry and two regiments, two battalions of a third, and a "group" of unknown size, of cavalry; it may be significant, or a mere accident of seniority, that the brigade was to be commanded by an infantry colonel.[67] A week later, Buell and his staff had another inspiration: they grouped their cavalry into two brigades, commanded by Colonels McCook of the 2nd Indiana and Lewis Zahm of the 3rd Ohio, respectively, with Colonel John Kennett, 4th Ohio, being given command of the whole.[68] Intentionally or otherwise, the two-brigade

65. The dispatch in which Buell made this request is not in the *Official Records*. In a dispatch of August 18, 1862, in which the quoted phrase occurs, he speaks of having made the request for eight more cavalry regiments "three months ago." *Ibid.*, Vol. XVI, Pt. 2, p. 361.

66. *Ibid.*, 5–9. This was Buell's table of organization as of June 10, 1862.

67. *Ibid.*, 120–21, 430, 438. The cavalry component of the Light Brigade was the 1st Kentucky, 2nd Indiana, and two battalions of the 4th (later corrected to the 5th) Kentucky. The "group" of unknown size was "Stokes' Tennessee Cavalry." Colonel J. F. Miller was appointed to command the brigade.

68. The "force" consisted of the 1st, 3rd, 4th, and 5th Kentucky, the 2nd Indiana,

unit was not called a division. Another month went by, and another turn of the organizational wheel took place. Colonel Kennett's command of 3,132 officers and men remained in being and was now called a division, but in addition to it, each of Buell's divisions of infantry was given a cavalry component of four, five, or six companies.[69]

William Rosecrans, who had been virtually exiled to the West, took John Pope's place on June 15 in command of the Army of the Mississippi and began forthwith a career that lasted as long as his time of command in Tennessee, of badgering and hounding everyone in authority from the president on down for more cavalry and more horses, more weapons, and more equipment for the cavalry he already had. In mid-November he asked Secretary Stanton and General Halleck, who was now in Washington, for four thousand revolving rifles to be used to arm infantry, who, "using saddles answering a double purpose for pack and riding saddles," would thereby and without further ado become "a very swift-moving body of light artillery [sic] . . . to be used against large moving columns of the enemy, to surprise and cut them to pieces."[70] Was Rosecrans indicating a conviction (it would not be the last time) that all that was needed to produce four thousand cavalrymen was to mount four thousand infantrymen on horses, or was his use of the word *artillery* intentional and an anticipation of what the Union cavalry was to develop into under other leadership: horses for mobility and overwhelming firepower for dismounted action? Rosecrans was aware, he said, "of the importance of keeping . . . [his] cavalry massed to the front," and he showed it by expanding Granger's division to four regiments and then turning it into a "legion" (which, however, militated against the development of an effective *cavalry*) with the addition of three regiments of infantry and three batteries of artillery.[71]

---

the 3rd and 4th Ohio, and one battalion of the 7th Pennsylvania. McCook's brigade had four of the regiments and the battalion of Pennsylvanians; Zahm had the other three regiments. *Ibid.*, 484.

69. *Ibid.*, Vol. XVII, Pt. 2, pp. 562–63 (October 1, 1862).

70. *Ibid.*, Vol. XX, Pt. 2, pp. 57, 58, 59. The "revolving rifles" Rosecrans asked for were the five-shot Colts. Secretary Stanton replied within twenty-four hours that "sixteen hundred revolving rifles, all that are now manufactured in the United States, have been purchased and are now being shipped to go at passenger-train speed to Louisville, and there be subject to your order." *Ibid.*, 64; see also p. 60. A month later, Rosecrans had the inspiration of mounting on "saddles or bare backs" infantry on "pack and other horses" to try to overtake J. H. Morgan, then on his "Christmas Raid." *Ibid.*, 236.

71. *Ibid.*, Vol. XVII, Pt. 2, p. 148 (July 5, 1862).

Grant, like Buell, seemed to find it difficult to decide on the form of his cavalry organization. He began by dutifully following Pope's lead and on June 11 ordered the establishment of a cavalry division to be commanded by Colonel T. Lyle Dickey, 4th Illinois, to be divided into three brigades and composed of all his mounted troops with the exception of the 1st Ohio. Nine days later this order was revoked, and the cavalry was ordered to "report to the commanding officers of the several divisions [of infantry] to which it was attached before the publication of . . . [the June 11] order." Another four days elapsed, and Colonel Dickey was then announced as "chief of cavalry force"—which may or may not have been an intentional deviation from the normal title of "chief of cavalry"—under Grant. Four months later, on November 26, Dickey himself announced, pursuant to an order of Grant's (footnoted "Not found" in the *Official Records*), his assumption of the command of Grant's cavalry division; its three small brigades were to be commanded respectively by Colonels A. L. Lee of the 7th Kansas, Edward Hatch of the 2nd Iowa, and Benjamin H. Grierson of the 6th Illinois. Each of the brigades was ordered attached to one of the three "wings" (under Generals Charles S. Hamilton, James B. McPherson, and W. T. Sherman) into which Grant's army was then divided. It is obvious, therefore, that Dickey's "division" was such for administrative purposes only and that Dickey's post, correspondingly, was that of a high-level staff officer limited to administrative functions.[72]

We have glanced briefly at western cavalry regiments, their genesis, personnel, their initial armament and equipment, their training such as it was, and their disciplinary problems, major and minor. We have also seen how the commanding officers of the major armies in the West sought to integrate their cavalry with the other arms in their commands. With the exception of John Pope's formation of brigades and a division of cavalry, these were mere shifts and expedients, the fumblings of officers groping for ways of making use of a strange and unfamiliar weapon. Not too many years later, first the tank and then the fighter plane were to present the United States Army high com-

72. *Ibid.*, 4, 20, 30, 363. It should be noted that the troops in the Department of Kansas were organized in August, 1862, into three brigades, each of which was a "legion" and included, in addition to cavalry regiments, batteries of artillery, regiments of infantry, and (an unusual touch) a regiment of "Indian Home Guards." *Ibid.*, Vol. XIII, 595.

mand with similar intellectual challenges, of defining the mission of a new weapon and of integrating it with the arms they had learned to handle with confidence if not always with success. It may be argued on behalf of the Hallecks, Grants, Buells, and Rosecrans of the western armies that they could not have anticipated the success their untrained, undisciplined, ill-armed, poorly officered horsemen would eventually attain when, having learned their trade, better armed and better led, they were grouped into brigades, divisions, and a corps. But John Pope, surely not one of the major intellects of the Regular Army, saw the light; so, to an even greater extent, did the Confederates in the East, with a success that was obvious as early as the spring of 1862; and so did at least one volunteer colonel in the West, which certainly suggests that there may have been others of the same mind.[73] In the meantime, any cavalryman in the western armies, with or without shoulder straps, shunted about organizationally from pillar to post and employed on what the least intelligent trooper could recognize as trifling duties, as military errand boys and escorts, might have been excused for wondering if there was a worthwhile role for him in the army.

We must now turn to the campaigns of the armies of which the western cavalry regiments were a part, in the course of which they evolved a body of cavalry doctrine that would have horrified any self-respecting officer of a European regiment of hussars, chasseurs, lancers, or cuirassiers but that in time was to produce spectacular victories for the Union.

73. See footnote 62, p. 22 above.

II

Let Slip the Dogs of War

WEST OF THE ALLEGHENIES AND SOUTH OF THE BORDER
states of Kentucky and Missouri lay five of the Confederate states: Alabama, Arkansas, Louisiana, Mississippi, and Tennessee, which occupied in many respects the same political, economic, and even spiritual position in relation to the seaboard states of the South as did the states of the Northwest in relation to the seaboard states of the Union. Settled (with the exception of Louisiana) by the southern phase of the same westward migration that populated Indiana, Illinois, and the other states of the Northwest, these "Cotton States" had in 1860 just a little less than half (2,389,000) of the total white population of 5,449,000 of the eleven states of the Confederacy.[1] Equally important was the geographic fact that four of these states were bounded by the lower Mississippi and hence could control access to the sea of the entire Mississippi basin, including the watersheds of its principal tributaries. The Mississippi River as a pathway to Europe for the farm produce of the Northwest, and as a pathway for its imports of European manufactures, was in the years before the war on the verge of being replaced by the development of the east-west trunk railroad system and the beginnings of track-width standardization. But in a historical phenomenon

1. Kennedy, *Preliminary Report on the Eighth Census, passim.* Kentucky and Missouri, which were both in and out of the Confederacy, had a total white population of 1,983,000 in 1860.

not at all uncommon, the Mississippi River retained a symbolic significance as a vital channel of commerce when its actual importance was
already on the wane. Indeed, one of the more visionary notions underlying the South's decision to secede was that its control of the Mississippi would force the northwestern states to leave the Union and join
the Confederacy. In any event, a key element in General Scott's "Anaconda Plan" and in the strategic thinking of the Washington administration was the goal of wresting control of the Mississippi from the
South, and this remained the principal strategic objective of the western armies of the Union until the capture of Vicksburg and Port Hudson in the summer of 1863. The liberation of east Tennessee was usually a secondary objective, but at times, for reasons that were perhaps
more sentimental than military, it seemed to be on a par with the opening of the Mississippi.

The Confederacy on its side pursued a somewhat rigid, mainly defensive strategy. Its occasional forays north, like General Lee's invasion
of Pennsylvania in 1863 or the Bragg–Kirby Smith invasion of Kentucky in 1862, were in the nature of counterpunches, rather than
moves in an offensive strategy. President Davis' attention—and in the
area of Confederate strategy, policies and decisions were expressions
of his views—was focused on the hundred miles between his capital
and that of the Union. The Washington government was not guilty of
quite the same degree of myopia, but it was still appropriate, as late as
February, 1864, for W. T. Sherman to write his friend Grant in Washington: "For God's sake and your country's sake, come out of Washington. . . . come out West; take to yourself the whole Mississippi Valley;
let us make it dead-sure, and . . . the Atlantic slope and Pacific shores
will follow its destiny as sure as the limbs of a tree live or die with the
main trunk. . . . Here lies the seat of the coming empire; and from the
West when our task is done, we will make short work of Charleston
and Richmond and the impoverished coast of the Atlantic."[2]

Any attempt to describe the operations and development of the
Union cavalry in the West faces a major difficulty in trying to present a
coherent account of events, campaigns, personalities, and trends. A primarily chronological approach would confuse the reader by skipping

2. Quoted in Lloyd Lewis, *Sherman: Fighting Prophet* (New York, 1932), 343.

from Kentucky and eastern and central Tennessee to northern Mississippi and western Tennessee and back again, with an occasional excursion beyond the Mississippi to the Missouri-Kansas-Arkansas area, to describe operations conducted more or less simultaneously but as like as not, without any intentional or even accidental strategic relation to one another. If on the other hand the approach is primarily geographic, the unifying key of the flow and relation of events in time is obscured or lost, and the reader is compelled to recall, if he can, in one geographical context what he has been told previously in another. For, obviously, even in the absence, certainly before the spring of 1864, of any central strategic coordination of the numerous Union armies, plans and events in one portion of the trans-Allegheny area did influence, more or less, operations in other portions. Similarly, the course of military operations and the feasibility of military plans for operations west of the Alleghenies were affected by what was happening, or what was intended to be done, east of the mountain chain. Equally with the North, the South, in allocating manpower and resources to its western armies, had to consider what was happening, or was likely to happen, along the Rappahannock or on the Peninsula or in the Shenandoah Valley. Hence, at some sacrifice of logic and at the risk of losing to some degree the benefits of chronology, which Winston Churchill rightly called "the key to easy narrative," this study of one aspect of the war in the West will endeavor to weave into a coherent web the two guiding threads of chronology and geography, in the hope of escaping the difficulties that would result from an exclusive reliance on either.

Basic to an understanding of the course of the war in the West is the need to grasp the fundamental strategies adopted by the two sides, partly as a reasoned choice and partly unconsciously, as steps taken intuitively in response to an urgent need, strategies to which later generations of military historians can impute their own penchant for an orderly design. To make good its objective in fighting the war, to wit, the restoration of the Union, the North had to conquer the South, defeat its armies in the field, occupy its territory, and through the medium of a military victory force its people to resume their allegiance to the Union. To accomplish this purpose, the North had to carry the war to the enemy, to fight an offensive war. The South, on the other hand, whatever its long-term difficulties might turn out to be, had a far simpler immediate problem than that faced by the North. To make good its secession and maintain its status as a separate nation, it had no need to conquer the North; it could reach its goal by means of a defensive strategy, similar to that which underlay the successful resistance of the thirteen colonies to the efforts of Great Britain to force them back to their allegiance.[3] The main drawbacks of a defensive strategy for the South were first, the surrender of the initiative to the North, and second, the difficulty of protecting, given its numerical inferiority, an 800-mile land frontier stretching from the Potomac at Washington to the confluence of the Ohio and the Mississippi, or a frontier of 1,150 miles if the distance from Cairo to the western border of Missouri is added. A defensive strategy forced upon the South the further burden of anticipating and defending against northern attacks on its sea frontier, all the way from Chesapeake Bay south around the Florida peninsula and west as far as Brownsville, Texas. An impossible task, given the severely limited resources of the Confederacy.

The decision of Virginia to secede established the Potomac as the line east of the mountains that the Confederacy had to defend. There was no such clear-cut boundary between the old Union and the new in the West. The secession of Arkansas in May and of Tennessee in June did not fix their northern boundaries as the dividing line between North and South, for the allegiance of their neighbors to the north, Missouri and Kentucky, remained in doubt. Had it not been that in the revolutionary atmosphere of 1861, not legalities but a resolute use of force determined the course of events, Missouri would have joined the Confederacy in fact, as it did in law. Because of the divided allegiance of its people, Missouri remained a no-man's-land to the end of the war, repeatedly fought over by the armies of both sides, the scene of all the horrors of a true civil war.

Kentucky, with a prosouthern majority but a large and determined minority of Unionists, took the strange and, given its geographic position, obviously untenable course of trying to remain neutral, its legislature resolving in May, 1861, "that this state and the citizens thereof should take no part in the civil war now waged, except as mediators

3. See, however, Russell F. Weigley, *The American Way of War: A History of United States Military Strategy and Policy* (New York, 1973), 96–97.

and friends to the belligerent parties and that Kentucky should, during the contest, occupy the position of strict neutrality."[4] It became quickly apparent that Kentucky and her people were faced with a situation that brought no blessings to peacemakers. For the moment, and until one side or the other decided to ignore openly Kentucky's declaration of neutrality, the belligerents' armed forces were kept away from each other's throats by the width of the state. As is common in such situations, however, both sides, while ostensibly observing Kentucky's neutrality, found ways of playing fast and loose with it, and it was just a question of time before one side or the other chose to do so openly. It was inevitable that Kentucky should eventually become aligned with the North or the South and inevitable also that because of its location, it should become a battleground as each belligerent tried to reach its enemy through its territory. In the event, the North was the first to end the charade of its observance of Kentucky's neutrality. General Robert Anderson, hero of Fort Sumter, set up his headquarters in Louisville, and William Nelson, a native of Kentucky who exchanged a lieutenancy in the navy for a major general's commission in the army, set up his in Maysville, Kentucky. Only fast action by Leonidas Polk, a West Point classmate and friend of President Davis's, who had given up his post as Episcopal bishop of Louisiana to become a major general in the Confederate army, forestalled by one day the occupation of Columbus, Kentucky, in the southwestern corner of the state, by Union General Ulysses S. Grant and his troops from Cairo; General Polk got there first, on September 4.

Thus the two border states of Missouri and Kentucky, with their stars in the flag of the Confederacy as well as in the Old Flag, became what Kentucky had been many years before, "a dark and bloody ground," and so they remained for four years, furnishing men, resources, and graves to both sides. In both these states, the Civil War was in truth a fratricidal war.

In command of 20,000 (eventually increased to 43,000) ill-equipped, poorly armed or unarmed Confederate troops guarding the line extending from the mountains of eastern Kentucky and Tennessee to the Kansas-Missouri border was General Albert Sidney Johnston, a native

4. Quoted in Stanley F. Horn, *The Army of Tennessee* (Indianapolis, 1941), 41.

of Kentucky, graduate of West Point, Class of 1826, and from 1855 on, colonel of the 2nd United States Cavalry, in which his lieutenant colonel was Robert E. Lee. Johnston's exiguous defenses, concentrated at three major posts—Columbus, Bowling Green, and Cumberland Gap, all in southern Kentucky—faced Federal armies commanded by Grant at Cairo, W. T. Sherman (until, judged not quite sane for suggesting that 200,000 men would be needed to clear Kentucky and carry the war to the enemy to the south, he was replaced by Don Carlos Buell) in west-central Kentucky, and General George H. Thomas in eastern Kentucky.[5] The first serious clash in the area—a mere skirmish, by later standards—took place on November 7, 1861, at Belmont, a mere name on the map, on the right bank of the Mississippi ten miles below Cairo and across the river from General Polk's base at Columbus. Grant staged the operation as a shipborne infantry raid. Only two companies of Grant's cavalry were involved, for, with a total of 17,000 troops in his command, he had only five companies of mounted troops, divided among three locations, plus apparently unorganized cavalry numbering 300. Of the three companies of cavalry he had at Cairo, only one was fully armed.[6] In reporting his lack of mounted troops, Grant sounded a note that was to run like a leitmotif through the preliminaries of nearly every operation of any magnitude throughout the West from the beginning of the war to the end. With the exception of Wilson as he organized his forces for the Selma Campaign, no commanding officer on the Union side ever thought he had as much cavalry as he needed. A few days after Grant complained of his lack of cavalry, General C. F. Smith sent him from Paducah six companies of the 2nd Illinois. These six companies, as well as the other four companies of the same regiment that he retained at Paducah, were "badly armed with old carbines" and lacked sabers and pistols; Smith's requisition for sabers and pistols, sent in "many weeks since," had failed to produce arms.[7]

5. Sherman had succeeded General Anderson on October 8, 1861, in command of what was designated the Department of the Cumberland. *Official Records*, Vol. IV, 297.

6. *Ibid.*, Vol. III, 497–98. Grant informed department headquarters in St. Louis on November 21 that his "cavalry force are none of them properly armed—the best being deficient in sword belts and having the old pattern carbines. Eight companies are entirely without arms of any description." *Ibid.*, Vol. VII, 442.

7. *Ibid.*, Vol. IV, 339. Three weeks later General Smith added the detail that each of the four "imperfectly armed" companies was short twenty sabers; none of the men had pistols, "and only some of them have carbines." *Ibid.*, Vol. VII, 464.

A week earlier, General Sherman had told General Thomas L. Crittenden, at Henderson, Kentucky, "Of course have lances made if you prefer and have not arms enough for your mounted men; the price is nothing."[8] At the opposite end of the state, General Nelson, having improvised a cavalry force made up in part of 142 men "mounted from the wagon teams" and in part of 36 "gentlemen, volunteers," to join his infantry for an attack on the Confederate troops at Ivy Mountain, near Piketon, Kentucky, claimed that he could have "taken or slain the whole of them" if he had had real cavalry.[9] General Albin Schoepf, in command of an infantry brigade at Somerset, Kentucky, reported on December 8 a scuffle between the 35th Ohio Infantry and the 1st Kentucky of his command, and "the enemy's cavalry," which he did not identify. The 1st Kentucky, he wrote,

as usual, behaved badly. They are a nuisance, and the sooner they are disbanded the better. They are scouring the country on their own account, lounging about the villages and drinking establishments, a nuisance and disturbance to the quiet citizens. . . . Captain [T. S.] Everett . . . reports a series of irregularities by stragglers of this regiment as having passed under his notice in the several villages through which he passed.

Is there no such thing as obtaining a regiment of *reliable* cavalry? Such a regiment is indispensable with this brigade at this time. The absence of such troops has kept me in the saddle until I am nearly worn down with fatigue.[10]

A day earlier, Schoepf had ended a dispatch with the disconsolate admission that "having no reliable cavalryman to carry . . . dispatches," he had to have "recourse to the mail, as it is more certain."[11]

At the western end of the long frontier between the old nation and the new, James H. Lane, a member of the Senate from the newly admitted state of Kansas, attracted President Lincoln's favorable notice in the feverish days following the attack on Fort Sumter by organizing all the Kansans in Washington into a "Frontier Guard" to protect the president's person. He returned from a hasty journey to Kansas with tales of an imminent invasion of the state with fire and sword by the

8. *Ibid.*, Vol. IV, 324. Sherman wrote in the same dispatch that he had no clothing for the volunteers appearing for muster-in, nor any arms other than "European muskets of uncouth pattern which the volunteers will not touch."

9. *Ibid.*, 225–26.

10. *Ibid.*, Vol. VII, 8–9. Major Francis W. Helveti, 1st Kentucky, described by the regimental historian as a "first class drillmaster," was captured by the enemy in this action. Tarrant, *Wild Riders of the First Kentucky*, 30.

11. *Official Records*, Vol. VII, 481.

secessionists in Missouri and was thereupon given the responsibility of protecting the state; made a brigadier general, he was empowered to raise two regiments of Kansas infantry for that purpose. By August, Lane had raised three regiments, not two. With these troops, whose needs in the way of uniforms, shoes, blankets, and firearms have been mentioned, he could, he thought, do more than merely protect Kansas; he proposed to free the Mississippi by a march on New Orleans, "administering on the way as many kicks as possible to the 'sore shin' of the Confederacy, namely slavery."[12] What little chance this harebrained scheme had of being turned into reality was erased by the invasion of Missouri in August by the forces—not much better endowed with arms and equipment, to say nothing of training and discipline, than Lane's—of Generals Sterling Price and Ben McCulloch. After defeating (and killing) General Nathaniel Lyon at Wilson's Creek, Price and McCulloch separated. McCulloch returned with his forces to Arkansas, while Price marched on toward Lexington, on the Missouri River. Lane was ordered to move his command south to Fort Scott, to be on the flank of Price's army as it moved northward to Lexington.

On August 25, Lane reported that he had about 1,200 men, half of them cavalry, at Fort Scott and that his horsemen would defend the Kansas border and disperse "such parties as they can reach"; he added in his inimitable manner, that if reinforced, he "could play hell with Missouri in a few days."[13] Lane did not identify or describe what he called his "cavalry." A few dozen of them were Charles R. Jennison's "Southern Kansas Jay-Hawkers," veterans of Bleeding Kansas days who, even before they joined forces with Lane, had taken advantage of the outbreak of the Civil War to conduct in the name of patriotism profitable forays into Missouri. The rest, ostensibly organized as the 5th and 6th Kansas, insofar as they were organized at all, were simply Kansans who chose to join Lane on horseback instead of on foot. The condition of the entire command, horse and foot, was thus described a few months later by Major C. C. Halpine, assistant adjutant general of the Department of Kansas:

12. For the genesis of the Lane Brigade, see Starr, *Jennison's Jayhawkers*, 43–46. Having served creditably in the Mexican War as colonel of the 3rd Indiana Infantry, Lane had a more legitimate claim to being appointed a brigadier general than did all but a tiny minority of officers commissioned from civil life.

13. *Official Records*, Vol. III, 455.

The regimental and company commanders knew nothing of their duties and apparently had never made returns or reports of any kind. The regiments appeared in worse condition than they could possibly have been during the first week of their enlistment, their camps being little better than vast pig-pens, officers and men sleeping and messing together; furloughs in immense numbers being granted, or, when not granted, taken; drill having been abandoned almost wholly, and the men constituting a mere ragged, half-armed, diseased and mutinous rabble, taking votes, as to whether any troublesome or distasteful order should be obeyed or defied.[14]

These were the troops with which Lane proposed to make the march from Kansas to New Orleans.

What Lane meant by playing hell in Missouri was demonstrated on September 24 at the town of Osceola, which his men burned to ashes after looting it of everything worth hauling away, Lane's own share of the loot being a fine carriage, a piano, and a quantity of silk dresses, which he sent off to his home in Lawrence, Kansas.[15] Captain W. E. Prince of the Regular Army, who had the thankless task of dealing with Lane, begged him to "adopt early and active measures to crush out this marauding which is being enacted in Captain Jennison's name, as also yours, by a band of men representing themselves as belonging to your command. . . . Please have a formal examination into the plundering of private and public buildings which has recently taken place . . . at Fort Scott."[16] Such gentle admonitions were useless; on December 19, by which time Jennison had organized the 7th Kansas and become its colonel, General Halleck reported to Washington that "the conduct of the forces under Lane and Jennison has done more for the enemy in . . . [Missouri] than could have been accomplished by 20,000 of his own army. I receive almost daily complaints of outrages committed by these men in the name of the United States, and the evidence is so conclusive as to leave no doubt of their correctness."[17] A month later, Halleck sent to Washington a copy of an

14. *Ibid.*, Vol. VIII, 615. Major Halpine also found among the many other irregularities in which these two regiments were involved that "horses in great quantity and at extravagant prices had been purchased . . . these horses being then turned over to men and officers who were then drawing 40 cents extra per day for them as private property." *Ibid.*, 615–16.

15. Starr, *Jennison's Jayhawkers*, 49.

16. *Official Records*, Vol. III, 482. It is to be noted that Fort Scott was in Kansas and not in what Kansas regarded as "enemy territory," *i.e.*, Missouri.

17. *Ibid.*, Vol. VIII, 499.

eyewitness report by a clerk of the Department of the Interior of the robberies, arson, and a murder ("they shot to death Mr. Richards, a good Union man, without cause or provocation") committed by Jennison's regiment in the area of Rose Hill, Missouri, and informed the adjutant general of the Army that he had ordered John Pope, then in command in northwest Missouri, to drive them out of the state. "They are," Halleck wrote, "no better than a band of robbers. . . . They disgrace the name and uniform of American soldiers and are driving good Union men into the ranks of the secession army." [18]

Lane and Jennison were not alone in tolerating or even encouraging "depredations" against the unfortunate Missourians. The behavior of Price's forces on their march north and subsequent retreat was equally reprehensible. And Major (later General) John M. Schofield reported from Montgomery City, west of St. Louis, that "the only cavalry force at my disposal is a battalion of Germans, utterly worthless for . . . [scouting]. If I trust them out of my sight for a moment they will plunder and rob friends and foes alike. I have arrested two of the officers and have five of the men in irons. I have asked General Halleck to recall this battalion and send me civilized human beings in their stead. If this be done . . . I shall hope to carry on my operations with success, and without making more enemies than friends to the Union." [19]

John Pope's first field command in the war was in Missouri, and he too had to deal with the McCulloch-Price invasion of the state. He did so in more responsible fashion than Senator Lane's. He took off in mid-December with a force of 4,000, horse and foot, to prevent the flow of recruits and supplies from northern Missouri to Price, then on the Osage River. One of Pope's two brigades, commanded by Colonel (later General) Jefferson C. Davis, found an enemy force near Sedalia encamped beyond the Blackwater River, "deep, miry, and impassable, except by a long, narrow bridge, which the enemy occupied in force." Davis ordered his cavalry to carry the bridge by assault. Two companies of the 4th United States, followed by five companies of the 1st Iowa, drove the Confederates off the bridge and, aided by the infantry, caused the entire force to surrender "at discretion." Davis' captures in-

---

18. *Ibid.*, 507–508. Other reports of and references to the misbehavior of the 7th Kansas in Missouri in late 1861 and January, 1862, are to be found in *Ibid.*, 45, 46, 55, 449, 546, and in Starr, *Jennison's Jayhawkers*, 96–118.

19. *Official Records*, Vol. VIII, 482.

cluded 1,300 officers and men, 500 horses and mules, 73 wagons heavily loaded with gunpowder and other supplies, and 1,000 stand of arms.[20]

With all the misconduct of Kansas troops and "Germans" in Missouri, the long toll of atrocities committed by the Missouri state militia against their prosouthern fellow citizens, and the horrors perpetrated by prosouthern guerrillas against both the armed forces of the Union and Unionist Missourians, there was an occasional lighter moment in the Civil War in that state.[21] One of the lesser causes of Fremont's downfall was that he surrounded himself with officers of foreign extraction: Germans and Hungarians for the most part, who had come to the United States after the defeat of the revolutionary movements of 1848. Ignored by Fremont's detractors was the fact that these refugees, who volunteered for service in the Union army, were a majority of the handful of men with military experience whose services were available to Fremont. It was their misfortune, as well as his, that many of them were unable to adapt their ways and manners to suit the tastes of midwestern Americans.

One of these émigré officers was Major Charles Zagonyi, veteran of the Hungarian War of Independence of 1848–1849 and commander of Fremont's bodyguard of about 150 cavalrymen. In early October, following Price's capture of Lexington, Fremont took the field against him. On October 25, Fremont's advance, led by Major Zagonyi and his troopers, reached Springfield, Missouri, held by a Confederate garrison of "about 2,000 or 2,200" (by the major's count) cavalry and infantry. The Confederates had learned of Zagonyi's approach and were drawn up under arms to receive him. To get at them, Zagonyi "had to pass 250 yards down a lane and take down a rail fence at the end of it" and then form up for the charge that, notwithstanding the grotesque disparity of numbers, he resolved to make. The charge, Zagonyi reported,

20. *Ibid.*, 39–40; see also Charles C. Lothrop, *A History of the First Regiment Iowa Cavalry Veteran Volunteers* (Lyons, Iowa, 1890), 43–44.

21. For an example of the mistreatment of fellow Missourians by the Unionist Missouri state militia, see *Official Records*, Vol. VIII, 357, 663. For the conduct of the 6th Kansas in August, 1862, on a march from Kansas City to Independence, see *Ibid.*, Vol. XIII, 255. "Jayhawking," *i.e.*, strong-arm robbery of livestock, farming implements, and household goods by Kansas civilians crossing over into Missouri, which the civil authorities of Kansas were unable or unwilling to suppress, became so widespread an evil that the army thought it necessary on February 8, 1862, to impose martial law in Kansas. *Ibid.*, 547.

was a smashing success, and the enemy, horse and foot, "retired" or fled. Zagonyi rallied his men "and charged through the streets in all directions about twenty times, clearing the town and neighborhood." [22] The major reported the loss of 15 of his men killed, 27 wounded, and 10 missing. Unquestionably, therefore, there was a fight of some severity, but what did actually happen at Springfield on October 25? Captain Patrick Naughton, who was there with his company of "Irish Dragoons," complained bitterly that Zagonyi failed to give *his* men due credit for their participation in the charge. Colonel William Preston Johnston wrote sixteen years after the event and on the basis of information given him "by those conversant with the facts"—that is, on the basis of secondhand information—that Zagonyi's report was "a picturesque fol-de-rol" and "merely the cloak for a disaster." Zagonyi, Johnston wrote, "was ambuscaded by militia, not more numerous than his own command, and severely handled, with the loss of only two or three of his opponents." [23]

A generally reliable regimental historian has an account of Zagonyi's charge that, at second hand, as was Colonel Johnston's, agrees in the main with the major's report. This account tells us that Captain (later General) David S. Stanley, 1st United States,

in command of all the cavalry in the Army of the Missouri, led two hundred and fifty men, including forty of Fremont's Body Guard, commanded by Lieutenant [sic] Zagonyi, in the great charge upon the rebel rearguard at Springfield. . . . This, being the first occasion in the war, in which a volunteer cavalry force participated in a saber charge, attracted great attention . . . and the charge of the "Fremont Guard" was so . . . advertised as to create the impression that no other troops were present. The fact is, however, that Captain Stanley led the fight, and the regulars [of the 4th United States] were equal participants with the volunteers. . . . In this engagement the entire rearguard of Price's army, over two thousand strong, was cut to pieces and destroyed. [24]

The truth of what actually happened in Springfield on this October day is lost beyond recovery; it may be taken for granted in any event that if the Fremont bodyguard did in fact charge the enemy, they did so un-

22. *Ibid.*, Vol. III, 249–51.

23. *Ibid.*, Vol. VIII, 252–53; see also Albert G. Brackett, *History of the United States Cavalry* (New York, 1865), 221–23, and Colonel William Preston Johnston, "Zagonyi's Charge with Fremont's Body-Guard—A Picturesque Fol-de-Rol," *Southern Historical Society Papers*, III (1877), 195–96. (The author of this paper was the son and biographer of General Albert Sidney Johnston.)

24. Vale, *Minty and the Cavalry*, 10–11.

aided by the inspirational effect of the thunderous war cry, reported by the major, of "Fremont and the Union."

There was to be more significant action two months later, in January, 1862, at the right-hand anchor of General Johnston's long defense line. General Thomas, who had taken William Nelson's place in command of the Union forces in that area, began planning as early as September, 1861—long before he had the necessary men, arms, or supplies—an advance into east Tennessee by way of Cumberland Gap. A successful invasion would relieve from Confederate occupation an area overwhelmingly Unionist in sentiment and would make possible the cutting of the East Tennessee & Virginia Railroad, a link in the Confederacy's vitally important connection between the seaboard and the Mississippi Valley.[25] Facing Thomas was General Felix K. Zollicoffer, ex-newspaperman and politician, who had advanced into Kentucky, crossed the Cumberland River, and encamped his troops with the river behind him, in violation of a basic rule of military prudence. Thomas, whose forces were a part of General Buell's Department of the Ohio, was ordered to move out from Lebanon, Kentucky, join forces with General Schoepf at Somerset, and attack Zollicoffer. Because of "the almost impassable condition of the roads" (an ever-recurring phrase in the reports of commanding officers), Thomas needed seventeen days to make the approximately eighty-mile march from Lebanon to Logan's Cross Roads, ten miles from the Confederate camp, where a West Pointer, George B. Crittenden, had superseded Zollicoffer in command.[26] Crittenden decided to attack Thomas before he had his forces fully assembled. In the ensuing battle of Logan's Cross Roads (or Mill Springs), fought on the dark and foggy morning of January 19 by roughly four thousand men on each side, Crittenden was defeated and driven from the field.[27] The cavalry component of Thomas' small army

25. The invasion of east Tennessee to relieve the Unionist population of the area and to "seize and hold a point of the railroad connecting Virginia and Tennessee" was one of the major operations proposed by the president in his "Memorandum for a Plan of Campaign" of early October, 1861. Quoted in Bruce Catton, *Grant Moves South* (Boston, 1960), 110.

26. *Official Records*, Vol. VII, 79; R. V. Johnson and C. C. Buel (eds.), *Battles and Leaders of the Civil War* (4 vols.; New York, 1887–88), I, 386, hereinafter cited as *Battles and Leaders*.

27. *Battles and Leaders*, I, 387–92; *Official Records*, Vol. VII, 79–100, 105–10. Zollicoffer was killed in the battle.

was four companies of the 1st Kentucky. On picket, as they should have been, on the morning of the battle, the Kentuckians reported the advance of Crittenden's troops. Then, led by their colonel, Frank Wolford, "conspicuous in the midst of danger," whose "martial appearance" was enhanced by his costume, consisting of an "old red hat [and a] home-spun brown jeans coat," and whose "face had been undefiled by water or razor for some time," they dismounted and fought as infantry throughout the action.[28] Crittenden's attacking force of two brigades of infantry was joined by a battalion and an independent company of Tennessee cavalry; another battalion of cavalry remained in reserve. Crittenden reported that only twenty-five of the men of one of these battalions (he did not say which one) did *not* run away.[29]

A few days before Thomas' fight at Logan's Cross Roads, Grant made what amounted to a large-scale armed reconnaissance or "demonstration in force" from his base at Cairo toward Camp Beauregard at Murray, Tennessee, and Fort Donelson, a short distance south of the Kentucky-Tennessee border. Halleck's orders directed Grant "by all means to avoid a serious engagement."[30] This reconnaissance, made on roads deep in mud, produced in a short time what could be seen in retrospect as one of the most momentous strategic moves of the war: Grant's campaign in February to capture Fort Henry, on the east bank of the Tennessee, and its twin, Fort Donelson, on the west bank of the Cumberland, twelve miles by road over the ridge separating the two rivers. Halleck's instructions to Grant for the February operation directed that "having invested Fort Henry," he was to send forward a cavalry force to break up the Memphis & Ohio Railroad, fifteen miles south of the fort.[31] As it turned out, Grant did not have to "invest" Fort Henry; its guns silenced by the fire of Flag Officer Andrew H. Foote's four gunboats, the fort was evacuated by its garrison and occupied by Grant's troops without a fight.[32] Grant's cavalry, made up of the independent companies of Illinois cavalry of Warren Stewart, James J. Dollins, M. James O'Harnett, and Eagleton Carmichael, the 4th Illinois,

28. Tarrant, *Wild Riders of the First Kentucky*, 57–65. The regiment lost four killed and nineteen wounded in the battle.
29. *Official Records*, Vol. VII, 110.
30. *Ibid.*, 533–34.
31. *Ibid.*, 121–22.
32. *Battles and Leaders*, I, 362–66. Foote was an officer in the U.S. Navy. Grant's infantry at Fort Henry was John A. McClernand's division of Illinois regiments.

and two companies of the 2nd Illinois, pursued the Fort Henry garrison for several miles on their retreat to Fort Donelson, attacked their rear guard, and captured some prisoners and six pieces of artillery.[33]

Nothing in the records indicates that Grant did anything, or had any intention of doing anything, to comply with Halleck's orders to send his cavalry to cut the Memphis & Ohio. Instead, he led his infantry, which now included a second division, to the capture of Fort Donelson.[34] He was to have the help once more of Foote and his gunboats, which had descended the Tennessee and steamed up the Cumberland to bombard the fort with their heavy guns.

On the evening of February 12, Grant deployed his infantry in a semicircle on the steep-sided hills, ridges, and ravines around the fort and the nearby town of Dover. Donelson turned out to be a much tougher proposition than Fort Henry; it was much more advantageously sited and far more powerfully armed, and its garrison, hastily reinforced to eighteen thousand, was much larger. A four-day siege in due form, with hard fighting and heavy casualties on both sides, was needed to capture the place. On February 16, General Simon Bolivar Buckner, who had succeeded former Secretary of War John G. Floyd and General Gideon Pillow in command, surrendered the fort and its garrison.[35] The phrase "unconditional surrender," which Grant used in his reply to Buckner's request for terms, and his own name, became instantly famous. A few regiments of Virginia infantry escaped from Dover before the surrender; the cavalry of Lieutenant Colonel Nathan Bedford Forrest and a sizable number of infantrymen who chose to take their chances under his leadership also escaped before daylight, by fording the icy backwater (or "slough") of Lick Creek, a hundred yards wide and in places three feet deep.[36]

The small cavalry force at Grant's disposal in these operations—a single regiment plus eight separate companies—had little to do as cavalry. They performed a traditional role by scouting in advance of the

33. *Official Records*, Vol. VII, 126, 129, 167.
34. Grant was joined at Fort Donelson by a third (General Lew Wallace's) division of infantry.
35. For the siege, see *Official Records*, Vol. VII, 159–253; *Battles and Leaders*, I, 403–28; Horn, *Army of Tennessee*, 88–97. Grant's casualties totaled 2,886.
36. John A. Wyeth, *That Devil Forrest: Life of General Nathan Bedford Forrest* (New York, 1959), 50–53; Robert Selph Henry, *"First with the Most" Forrest* (New York, 1944), 57–60; *Battles and Leaders*, I, 426.

infantry on the march from Fort Henry to Fort Donelson. In the siege itself, troopers of the 4th Illinois—Colonel T. Lyle Dickey's regiment, armed with Sharps' rifles—fought as sharpshooters with the 11th Illinois Infantry and "did good execution by picking off the enemy as they exposed themselves above the breastworks."[37] In the fighting on the fifteenth that decided outcome of the siege, Dickey's cavalrymen, on the right of the line of investment, prepared to go into action dismounted in an attack by the First Brigade of Wallace's division, but the foot soldiers gained their objectives on their own and were able to dispense with the assistance of the cavalry.[38]

The eastern end of General Johnston's defense line was gone, destroyed by Thomas' victory at Logan's Cross Roads. Grant's capture of the two forts not only unhinged the center of Johnston's line and opened the way for a Union invasion of middle Tennessee and the occupation of Nashville, but it also placed in jeopardy the Confederate strongholds on the Mississippi, at Columbus, on Island No. 10, at New Madrid, and eventually at Memphis, which constituted the western anchor of Johnston's line. Even before the loss of Fort Donelson, the capture of Fort Henry by Grant was sufficiently menacing to cause Johnston to order the evacuation of Bowling Green, Kentucky, the linchpin of the center of his line. On February 25, Nashville too was lost, occupied by Buell's troops. Johnston began to concentrate troops assembled from every point of the compass—Braxton Bragg's from Pensacola and Mobile, Daniel Ruggles' from New Orleans, P. G. T. Beauregard's from Columbus—to add to William J. Hardee's command from Bowling Green, at Corinth, Mississippi, an important railroad junction (the crossing point of the north-south Mobile & Ohio and the east-west Memphis & Charleston) just south of the Mississippi-Tennessee border and about twenty miles southwest of a spot on the map named Pittsburg Landing, on the Tennessee River.

General-in-Chief George B. McClellan in Washington, Halleck, and Buell were debating what the next moves in the campaign in Tennessee should be.[39] Halleck at the same time was busy chastising Grant for largely imaginary transgressions and delinquencies. The

37. *Official Records*, Vol. VII, 199.
38. *Ibid.*, 245.
39. The Tennessee River was the eastern boundary of Halleck's department; Buell and his Department of the Ohio therefore did not come under Halleck's command.

pause in operations that now ensued, much to the distress of military historians of later generations, would probably have occurred anyway, for at that season of the year movement by road for wheeled transport and artillery was virtually impossible, and even movement by boat on the Cumberland and Tennessee was made exceedingly difficult and hazardous by the spring floods.[40] Eventually, however, the problem of command in the area was worked out by moving the eastern boundary of Halleck's department eastward, so as to give him control of Buell and his army. Halleck's difficulties with Grant were quietly glossed over, and lastly, an officer whose role in the Civil War in the West became in time no less important than Grant's, namely William Tecumseh Sherman, came up the Tennessee at the head of a newly organized division to join Grant.[41]

The first military operation following the capture of Fort Donelson was entrusted to Sherman. He was to proceed by boat up the Tennessee (seventeen transports were needed to carry his division up the river) to some point below Eastport, in the northeastern corner of Mississippi, march thence to the Memphis & Charleston, which at that point ran a short distance south of the river, and break up the railroad at whatever point between Corinth and Tuscumbia, Alabama, he was able to reach.[42] The landings Sherman hoped to use were found to be occupied by Confederate artillery and infantry, so he dropped downriver a few miles and at 11 P.M. on March 14 disembarked his cavalry, consisting of six companies of the 5th Ohio, to start off on a twenty-mile march that would take them to the railroad at Burnsville, where they were to tear up the track and burn the depot buildings and the railroad company's repair shops.[43] As soon as the horsemen cleared

40. When in the second week in March Sherman made the abortive attempt, described in the following paragraph, to cut the Memphis & Charleston, the Tennessee rose fifteen feet in one twenty-four-hour period. Horn, *Army of Tennessee*, 117.

41. William T. Sherman, *The Memoirs of General William T. Sherman* (2 vols. in one; Bloomington, 1957), I, 225–26.

42. Sherman, *Memoirs*, I, 227; *Official Records*, Vol. X, Pt. 2, pp. 31, 34.

43. The 5th Ohio had been organized in 1861 pursuant to a call by General Fremont. The regiment had the benefit of more than four months of drill before it was ordered at the end of February, 1862, to join Sherman at Paducah. When the regiment left Ohio, its 1,142 men (twelve companies) had a total of 900 sabers, 419 Joslyn revolvers, and 120 "second hand" Sharps' carbines. Having been unable to get ammunition for their revolvers, on the way to Tennessee "details of men were made from each . . . [company] to mold bullets and make cartridges from the materials which had been drawn at Paducah and Fort Henry." Reid, *Ohio in the War*, II, 777–78.

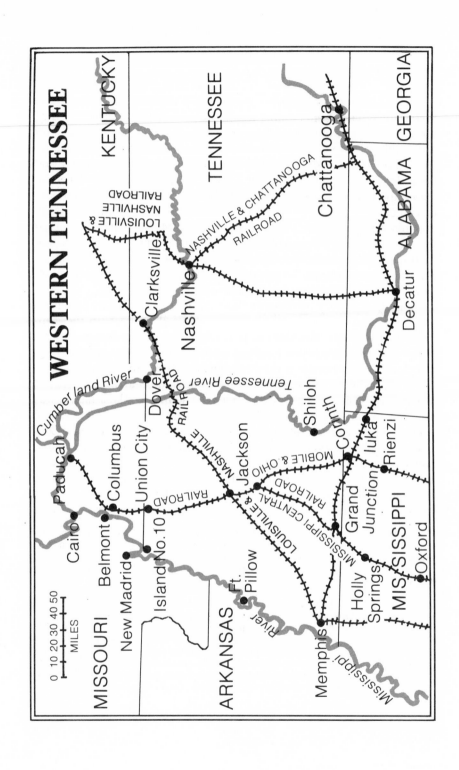

the landing, the infantry also disembarked and, in pitch darkness and in rain coming down "in torrents," marched off to follow the cavalry and give them whatever support they might need. At daybreak, after a six-mile march, the infantry met the cavalry, coming back. By swimming their horses, the cavalrymen had managed to cross several normally insignificant tributaries of the Tennessee, each of which, however, had become so swollen by the downpour that "mere brooks covered the whole bottom." But they lost several men carried away and drowned.[44] This was the 5th Ohio's introduction to active campaigning. Eventually, the Ohioans reached a stream they were unable to cross, and turned back. It was manifestly impossible to carry out the project, and even the return to the boats was beset with difficulties and dangers. Sherman reported that the artillery horses had to be unhitched and the guns dragged underwater by the men to get them back to the boats.[45]

Sherman and his bedraggled, water-soaked command returned to Pittsburg Landing, on the west bank of the stream, which had caught Sherman's eye on his way upstream, because he could see that a road from it led uphill to a large, level plateau high enough above the river to be well out of reach of the spring floods. Before setting up camp on this plateau on March 16 near a meetinghouse called Shiloh Church, Sherman tried once more to reach the railroad, sending this time a battalion of the 4th Illinois with the 5th Ohio, under the command of Lieutenant Colonel Thomas T. Heath of the Ohio regiment, in the direction of Corinth. Five miles out, Heath ran into the 2nd Alabama; there was an exchange of gunfire, and the Ohioans had the pleasurable experience of making their first mounted charge and taking a few prisoners, after which, in obedience to their orders, they returned to camp.[46]

In the next two weeks, as the rains ceased, the spring flowers appeared, and the dogwood, redbud, and peach trees burst into bloom, one division after another of Federal infantry came up the river and

44. Sherman, *Memoirs*, I, 227–28; Reid, *Ohio in the War*, II, 778.
45. Sherman, *Memoirs*, I, 228.
46. On March 13, four companies of the 5th Ohio made a dash to the Mobile & Ohio trestle bridge over Beach Creek near Bethel (about fifteen miles west of Shiloh), destroyed the bridge, tore up the track for some distance, and twisted the rails. *Official Records*, Vol. X, Pt. 1, p. 10. Presumably the purpose of the raid was to deny use of the railroad to Confederate troops coming south to Corinth from Columbus, Kentucky.

disembarked at Pittsburg Landing. Eventually, five divisions were encamped more or less haphazardly on the high ground above the river.[47]
Grant, restored at least outwardly to General Halleck's good graces,
was back in command, and established his headquarters at the settlement of Savannah, nine miles downstream from his troops. From
there, on April 2, he issued orders that, in keeping with normal procedure at this stage of the war, parceled out his cavalry among his six
divisions of infantry. In addition to eight odd companies of cavalry
(four independent companies of Illinois cavalry, two companies of
Regulars, and two companies of the 2nd Illinois) Grant now also had
three complete regiments, the 5th Ohio and the 4th and 11th Illinois;
these he divided by battalions among the infantry, two battalions of
each regiment going to each of three divisions of infantry, and one battalion of each regiment plus one or two of the "odd" companies going
to each of the other three divisions.[48] These orders of Grant's were to
have consequences, unlooked for by their author, four days later.

Notwithstanding Grant's and Sherman's indignant denials, the
Army of the Tennessee, as Grant's forces were now designated, was
taken completely by surprise at dawn on April 6 by the onslaught of
the army General Johnston had collected at Corinth. Having had the
initiative for weeks, it seemed not to occur to Grant, his staff, or his
subordinate commanders, that the Confederates might not be content
to make waiting to be attacked an invariable custom and might choose
to seize the initiative themselves. Sherman, who, being physically
present at Shiloh, must bear a major part of the blame, told Grant the
day before the battle that he did "not apprehend anything like an attack on . . . [his] position," and Grant assured Halleck the same day
that he had "scarcely the faintest idea" of a Confederate attack on his
forces at Shiloh.[49]

Generally overlooked by military historians is the one factor that
made it inevitable that if there was a Confederate attack on a major

47. A sixth division, that of Lew Wallace, was encamped at Crump's Landing, about
six miles downstream from Shiloh.
48. General Orders No. 33, April 2, 1862. *Official Records*, Vol. X, Pt. 2, pp. 87–88.
On March 9, Grant had reported 3,169 cavalry "present and for duty" in his command.
Ibid., 21.
49. Horn, *Army of Tennessee*, 126; Catton, *Grant Moves South*, 219; see also
Sherman to Grant, April 5, 1862: "I have no doubt that nothing will occur to-day more
than some picket firing." *Official Records*, Vol. X, Pt. 2, pp. 93–94.

scale at Shiloh, it would catch the Federals by surprise. Enough—more than enough—Federal cavalry was present at Shiloh to have been able to shake Sherman's complacency, his casual assumption that the Confederates would wait patiently at Corinth to be attacked, had that cavalry been used as it should have been, to patrol the roads leading up from Corinth, where the enemy was known to be, to Shiloh. Certainly both Sherman and Grant, graduates of the military academy, knew that patrolling in the direction of the enemy was a primary function of cavalry and should therefore have used their cavalry for that purpose. Why did they not do so? A part of the expanation is doubtless the perfectly human penchant to leave well enough alone; having assumed that there was no likelihood of a Confederate attack, neither Sherman nor Grant saw any need to patrol in the direction of Corinth. Why bother? But the more significant reason lies buried in a few casual words in a dispatch Sherman sent Grant on April 5: "We are in the act of exchanging cavalry, according to your order"—the order of April 2, quoted above, calling for the distribution (or redistribution) of the cavalry.[50] The cavalrymen who should have been out patrolling in the direction of Corinth and could thus have given Sherman a day's warning of Johnston's approach were too busy with the chores that needed doing to conform with Grant's redistribution order. They had no time for what they should have been doing in the near proximity of a large enemy force. Moreover, having just been shuffled about and finding themselves in strange surroundings and with strange associations, it is little wonder that in the battle the next day the cavalrymen "acted badly," in the opinion of the infantry, thousands of whom behaved equally "badly" or even worse.[51]

There was a further fact, mentioned by General Stephen A. Hurlbut, commander of the Fourth Division, in his report: "The ground was such that I was unable to use cavalry. Colonel [William H. H.] Taylor's Fifth Ohio Cavalry was drawn up in order of battle until near 1 o'clock [on April 6], in the hope that some opening might offer for the use of that arm, and none appearing, I ordered the command withdrawn from the reach of shot."[52]

50. *Official Records*, Vol. X, Pt. 2, p. 93.
51. See footnote 48, p. 46 above.
52. *Official Records*, Vol. X, Pt. 1, p. 206. General Hurlbut had under his command only two battalions of the 5th Ohio; the third battalion was attached to the Second Divi-

There was no pursuit worthy of the name when, on the afternoon of the second day of the battle, P. G. T. Beauregard, who succeeded to the command of the Confederate army when Johnston was killed, decided to call off the action and withdraw his greatly outnumbered forces. His own infantry, Grant thought, was too tired to pursue; hence the equally tired Confederate infantry made an undisturbed retreat. One regimental historian's account has it that "toward night the cavalry were all massed close to the front ready to charge the enemy as soon as they were routed at Snake creek, where it was believed the final struggle would be. The retreat of the rebels was well covered, and, there being but one single corduroy road for us to cross on, it was not deemed expedient for the cavalry to charge them so we were ordered back and accomplished nothing."[53] Another account has it that the two companies of the 2nd Illinois, the 7th Illinois (which the author has mistaken for the 4th Illinois), and the 5th Ohio "were placed under the command of Col. T. Lyle Dickey . . . who was ordered to pursue. These were fine regiments and we might have captured many prisoners had it not been for our commander. Dickey's cowardice, previously suspected, was soon demonstrated."[54]

Whatever the truth concerning Colonel Dickey's courage or lack thereof may have been, it is a fact that the only cavalrymen who came out of this battle with any credit were both Confederates. One was Nathan Bedford Forrest, whom his superiors did not recognize for the military genius he was until it was too late, and the other was a Ken-

---

sion. The cavalry's share of the total Union casualties at Shiloh of 1,754 killed, 8,408 wounded, and 2,885 captured or missing was 5 killed and 22 wounded. *Battles and Leaders*, I, 538; *Official Records*, Vol. X, Pt. 1, p. 100.

53. Avery, *History of the Fourth Illinois*, 62. On the first day of the battle, the 4th Illinois "was kept on the field all day shifting positions often but at no time far in the rear of our lines, and often in range of the enemy's artillery. Two or three times we were called upon to charge the enemy's lines, but before we got into action we were ordered back."

Ibid., 61–62.

54. Fletcher, *The History of Company A*, 53. Two of Grant's orders (one signed by John A. Rawlins, his chief of staff) dealt with pursuit by the cavalry. The first informed General McClernand that the 5th Ohio had been sent out "to ascertain if the enemy have retreated," and it concluded, "Should they [the enemy] be retreating, I want all the cavalry belonging to the entire command to follow them, supported by three or four brigades of infantry." The second order was a request to Buell: "Will you be good enough to order your cavalry to follow [the enemy] on the Corinth road and give two or three of your fresh brigades [orders] to follow in support." *Official Records*, Vol. X, Pt. 2, pp. 97–98. It will be noted that in both instances Grant wanted infantry supports for the cavalry.

tuckian with much more questionable credentials as a commander of cavalry, John Hunt Morgan. In the middle of the night after the first day's fighting, Forrest sent his scouts, wearing Union army overcoats, down to the landing and took to General Hardee the information they brought back, namely that Buell's fresh troops were being ferried over from the other side of the river to reinforce Grant and that thousands of stragglers were sheltering on the riverbank; he urged an immediate attack to take advantage of the disorder at the landing to drive the Union army into the river or, in the alternative, an immediate retreat to avoid defeat the next day by the fresh troops being brought across the river.[55] Neither course was adopted. Morgan, promoted to full colonel the day before the battle, led his men late in the afternoon of the first day in a mounted charge against the 6th Iowa Infantry, in which he lost four men killed; Basil Duke, his brother-in-law and second in command (and as some insisted, his brains), was among the wounded.[56] On the afternoon of the second day, Morgan joined Forrest's regiment in covering the retreat of the infantry toward Corinth.

Shiloh, with its nearly 24,000 casualties, a battle both sides could and did claim as a victory, was inconclusive in the sense that it neither put an end to a movement nor created the possibilities for one. The manifest surprise of the Union forces and their near loss of the battle on the first day shook Halleck's confidence in Grant's ability to command an army. Beauregard had seen fit to break off the action on the second day, and it now remained to be seen what use the Federals would make of the somewhat tainted success the Confederates thus handed to them. It also remained to be seen what use would be made by the Union armies to the east and to the west of Shiloh of the breach Grant had previously made in the Confederate defense line, a breach that Shiloh had precariously preserved.

55. Henry, *"First with the Most" Forrest*, 77–79; Horn, *Army of Tennessee*, 139.
56. Dee A. Brown, *The Bold Cavaliers: Morgan's 2nd Kentucky Cavalry Raiders* (Philadelphia, 1959), 50.

III

Fire Answers Fire

AT THE SAME TIME THAT GENERAL HALLECK WAS BUSILY supervising the progress of the portion of his forces commanded by Grant along what was then the eastern edge of his department and, urged on by the president, was trying to enlist the cooperation of the neighboring army of General Buell, he was also directing the operations of his other armies along the western edge and down the center of his huge area of command. There was something distinctly unappealing about Halleck's personality, a disagreeable quality that the lapse of 120 years has not succeeded in varnishing over; that and his strange reluctance to exercise to the full the functions of his position as general-in-chief, and thereby fulfill the hopes of a greatly overburdened president, have earned Halleck the disdain or active dislike of military historians. He has been denied credit for the truly remarkable job of organization he performed after he stepped into the military chaos and political witches' cauldron left behind by Fremont. Nor has he received his due for the vision and energy with which he planned, supervised, and to a degree directed a number of simultaneous military operations in his vast Department of the Missouri, in the conduct of which he was hampered by the inexperience of commanding officers and all the shortages that Fremont had been unable to cope with.

It will be worthwhile to note some of these shortages as they affected the cavalry in this the second year of the war. Halleck was told on February 1 that the Ordnance Bureau was about to send him 750 "short Enfield rifles with sword bayonets"—barely enough to arm two-thirds of a single regiment—with the explanation that "without the bayonets these will answer for cavalry until other arms can be supplied"; he was also promised 1,500 revolvers and 5,000 sabers.[1] Ten days later, General Buell, who with his cavalry was about to come under Halleck's command, was told by James W. Ripley, the commanding general of the Ordnance Bureau, that against his requisition for 5,000 carbines, "as many of the carbines as were on hand or could possibly be obtained" had been forwarded; but, Ripley explained: "Although we have out contracts for a large number of carbines, their deliveries are not sufficient to meet the many calls for this kind of arm. . . . Those purchased in Europe to meet immediate demands (by Mr. Schuyler) have turned out unserviceable."[2] Hence on March 21, Buell reported to Washington that of the eleven regiments plus fifteen odd companies of cavalry in his army, "but three of the . . . regiments are properly armed; some have sabers and rifles, some sabers and muskets, some sabers and a variety of pistols."[3] He did add, however, that his ordnance officer was "at length beginning to receive carbines, though of various descriptions."

What the lack of carbines could mean to a regiment of cavalrymen was pointed out in a report from Taberville, Missouri, by Colonel Fitz Henry Warren of the 1st Iowa. "The whole country," the colonel wrote, "is now in the brush, and we need carbines. . . . Carbines we must have. It is no better than murder to send men into these brush fights with Colt's army revolvers. Some of my command whom I took out had nothing but sabers."[4]

Another pair of reports, involving the 5th Ohio, whose presence at Shiloh has been mentioned, implies the important role the possession of adequate weapons had on the morale and ultimately the effectiveness of a regiment of cavalry. After the Ohioans had been moved to western Tennessee, General Hurlbut reported that they had an average of only eight carbines to a company and that, "as a charge is an impossible thing in the country over which the column passed, they were compelled to do skirmishing duty in thick timber and under-

1. *Official Records*, Vol. VII, 933.
2. *Ibid.*, 606.
3. *Ibid.*, Vol. X, Pt. 2, p. 613. Buell reported 11,496 aggregate total and 9,222 "for duty" cavalry under his command.
4. *Ibid.*, Vol. XIII, 201; see also *Ibid.*, Vol. VIII, 334–35, 337, involving detachments of the 1st and 3rd Iowa, respectively.

growth with the revolver alone."[5] A few months later Colonel Dickey, who commanded the hastily assembled cavalry force that pursued but failed to catch General Earl Van Dorn—another alumnus of Albert Sidney Johnston's 2nd United States—after he had raided and destroyed Grant's base at Holly Springs, Mississippi, reported that the 5th Ohio (and the 7th Illinois), which "had until very lately been illy armed, have proven themselves, with good arms in their hands, as effective in the face of the enemy as their most noted companions in the field."[6]

Cavalry regiments organized in the summer and fall of 1861 either came into the service with a full complement of horses or else were mounted by the government shortly after muster-in. The quality of the horses of this "first mount" was usually, but not always, the best the regiment would ever have; the horses issued to the 1st Ohio, for example, at its first camp in October, 1861, "proved to be very fine mounts . . . [the] handsomest and most serviceable horses we had during our service."[7] Other regiments fared less well; noted previously was the pained inquiry of Colonel Lewis Zahm of the 3rd Ohio whether he was obliged to accept horses furnished to his regiment that were manifestly unfit for service.[8] One of the strangest of the numerous strange procurement arrangements made by Fremont, or in his name, was with an enterprising citizen of Cincinnati named J. E. Reside, who, it was discovered, had been authorized to purchase horses for Fremont's cavalry at a maximum price of $130 and also to inspect the horses he bought, for a fee of 2½ percent of the purchase price.[9] It is

5. *Ibid.*, Vol. XVII, Pt. 1, p. 307. Not until after October 5, the date of General Hurlbut's report, did the 5th Ohio receive enough carbines to arm the entire regiment.

6. *Ibid.*, 495. Other shortages and deficiencies that plagued the cavalry in 1862 were defective cartridges for their carbines ("They shake to pieces in riding, and at the end of each day's march many of the men find instead of cartridges only a mixed mass of powder, ball and papers") and lack of horseshoes (General G. M. Dodge reported, "We have been without shoes for horses for a long time, and it renders one-half of the force unfit for service"). The 3rd and 4th Ohio and the 5th Kentucky lacked haversacks, canteens, and "horse equipments of all kinds." And fully as important were the unconscionable delays in paying the men; the 3rd Ohio, in October, 1862, had been unpaid for seven months. *Ibid.*, 143, and Pt. 2, p. 104, and Vol. XVI, Pt. 2, p. 568.

7. Curry, *Four Years in the Saddle*, 22; see also Lothrop, *A History of the First Regiment*, 34.

8. See Vol. I, p. 132 of the present work.

9. *Official Records*, Vol. VIII, 372; for other frauds in the purchase of horses see Russell F. Weigley, *Quartermaster General of the Union Army: A Biography of Mont-*

impossible to believe that an agreement so blatantly improvident and so obviously open to fraud had been entered into by army officers too naïve to know better. The agreement did, however, produce horses, whatever their quality may have been. But whether the horses supplied to a given regiment were good, bad, or indifferent, only a few weeks later a large percentage of them had perished of exposure, starvation, epidemics of disease, lack of proper care, or outright abuse, and from mid-1862 on, the War Department, the quartermaster general and his subordinates, the Cavalry Bureau (from the date of its establishment on July 28, 1863), and indeed everyone else in authority were besieged by commanding officers from every point of the compass clamoring or begging for horses for their dismounted cavalrymen. On June 30, 1862, when Buell had 4,981 cavalry present for duty, he ordered Colonel Thomas Swords, chief quartermaster in Louisville, to "commence at once buying cavalry horses to the number of 5,000." [10] From the early summer of 1862 on, the records are replete with inquiries, exhortations, complaints, and reports, all bearing on the senders' need for cavalry mounts and the recipients' efforts and difficulties trying to supply them. An obvious source of supply was the farms in the theater of operations, which, this early in the war, still had horses. Later, horses and mules were seized wherever found, but in these early months, cavalrymen in areas of divided allegiance were urged to observe "system and good order," to take no horses from those "known to be good Union men," and to be mindful of the rule that "animals must in no case be taken so as to leave an establishment without one horse." [11] None of these well-intentioned, compassionate rules survived for very long the harsh realities of war and the needs of the armies.

Near the western edge of Halleck's department, Confederate General Sterling Price was wintering in Springfield, Missouri, with the forces with which he had invaded the state in the late summer of 1861. Hav-

---

gomery C. Meigs (New York, 1959), 185–87, 194. The War Department specifications required horses bought for the cavalry "to be sound in all particulars, 15 to 16 hands high, not less than 4 or more than 9 years old, color to be bays, blacks or sorrels, good square trotters, bridle-wise." Thiele, "The Evolution of Cavalry," 184.

10. *Official Records*, Vol. XVI, Pt. 2, pp. 77, 120. Buell did not bother to explain why he needed 5,000 horses for 4,981 cavalrymen, many of whom presumably had mounts.

11. *Ibid.*, 296.

ing assumed command of the Department of the Missouri on November 9, Halleck felt it his first duty to drive Price out of the state. In late December, he assembled a force in Rolla, Missouri, of 12,000 officers and men—an army of four small divisions of infantry plus cavalry and artillery—under the command of General Samuel R. Curtis, for the campaign against Price.[12] It is worthy of note that Halleck was willing to risk exposing raw troops to the hazards of a winter campaign. In conformity with usage normal at the time, Curtis' cavalry was (with the exception of two "unassigned" units, the 3rd Iowa and W. D. Bowen's Battalion of Missouri Cavalry) divided among his four divisions of infantry. Two of the cavalry units, a legacy from the Fremont days, the "Fremont Hussars" and the "Benton Hussars," each commanded by a Hungarian refugee officer, were attached to the Second Division, which was also commanded by a veteran of the Hungarian War of Independence of 1848–1849—General Alexander Asboth.[13] The campaign got under way with an advance by the Federals on February 10, 1862. Considerably outnumbered, Price thought it best to retreat; nor did he halt until, after a toilsome march of about one hundred miles in midwinter weather, shedding stragglers and supplies all along the way, he reached Cove Creek, south of Fayetteville, Arkansas.[14] There he was joined by Earl Van Dorn, who assumed command of an army that consisted of the 6,800 troops Price had brought out of Missouri, General McCulloch's 8,400 men, and Albert S. Pike's 1,000-man Indian Brigade, made up mainly of "semi-civilized Cherokees, Choctaws, Chickasaws, Seminoles, and Creeks . . . totally . . . [lacking] discipline and training," their faces being "daubed with war paint." Van Dorn outnumbered Curtis three to two.[15]

12. *Ibid.*, Vol. VIII, 196.

13. The officers commanding the two "hussar" units (the latter of which evolved into the 5th Missouri) were Major Emeric Meszaros and Colonel Joseph Nemett, respectively. *Battles and Leaders*, I, 337.

14. Curtis had his cavalry snapping at Price's heels all the way south. There were small-scale skirmishes on February 14, 15, 17, 18, 20, and 23, which provided splendid training for the units involved. The only seriously untoward incident on the pursuit involving the cavalry occurred at a settlement named Mud Town, Arkansas, where 42 "of the officers and men of the Benton Hussars were poisoned . . . by eating rebel food or drinking rebel liquor." One of them Captain Louis Dulfer ("a gallant officer") actually died. *Official Records*, Vol. VIII, 59, 60, 61, 68, 69.

15. Albert Castel, *General Sterling Price and the Civil War in the West* (Baton Rouge, 1968), 70.

After following Price as far as Fayetteville, Curtis turned back and retreated to the settlement of Leetown, just south of a natural feature named Pea Ridge near the Arkansas-Missouri border. There, on March 6–8, the two armies fought the battle the North called Pea Ridge; the South named it the battle of Elkhorn Tavern.[16] It was a shapeless, fluid battle, quite unlike such orderly affairs as Gettysburg or Missionary Ridge. It provided the Union cavalry with opportunities to charge the enemy infantry, and thus to play a role in the battle itself, which came very seldom the cavalry's way. On the morning of the second day, March 7, near Leetown, Colonel Cyrus Bussey led a composite cavalry force, made up of portions of his own 3rd Iowa, the Benton Hussars, the 1st Missouri, and the Fremont Hussars, on a charge with revolvers against a large body of enemy infantry that he had stumbled on, and then exchanged charges and countercharges with the enemy's cavalry. The 3rd Iowa contingent lost 24 killed and 17 wounded in this encounter. It was found after the battle that 8 of the killed had been scalped by Pike's Indians, "and the bodies of others were horribly mutilated, being fired into with musket balls and pierced through the body and neck with long knives." The battle as a whole resulted in a severe defeat for the Confederates; what remained of Van Dorn's forces (McCulloch was killed and Price wounded) after his losses in the battle and the disappearance of "uncounted hundreds of stragglers and deserters" found sanctuary a week later in Van Buren, Arkansas, "weak, broken down, and exhausted."[17]

To make up for Curtis' losses in the battle, Halleck ordered Colonel S. H. Boyd at Rolla to send on to Curtis "all available forces . . . without delay." There had apparently been trouble with the 4th Iowa over their unwillingness to serve in Arkansas, for Halleck added, "If any of the Fourth Iowa Cavalry refuse to go forward immediately, arrest them for mutiny and place them in confinement."[18]

Missouri was the scene throughout the war of guerrilla warfare of the most vicious description; it was to be raided from the south time

16. The battle is described in *Battles and Leaders*, I, 314–34; Castel, *General Sterling Price*, 71–78; and Curtis' report in *Official Records*, Vol. VIII, 195–204. Of the total Union casualties of 1,384, the cavalry sustained 46 killed, 94 wounded, and 42 captured or missing. *Official Records*, Vol. VIII, 204–207.
17. *Official Records*, Vol. VIII, 232–35, 206, 208, 236; Castel, *General Sterling Price*, 74, 78.
18. *Official Records*, Vol. VIII, 632.

after time and subjected to a full-scale invasion by Price in the autumn of 1864. But Pea Ridge, or Elkhorn Tavern, freed it of Confederate occupation in 1862, and so it remained to the end of the war.

John Pope, seventeenth in rank of the graduates of the West Point Class of 1842, recipient of two brevets in the Mexican War, captain in the Corps of Topographical Engineers when the Civil War began, mustering officer at Camp Yates in Chicago (he was succeeded in that post by an ex-Regular named Ulysses S. Grant), promoted to brigadier general in the same batch of thirty-seven that also included W. T. Sherman and U. S. Grant, had command under Fremont of the District of North Missouri. He was now given command of the second major undertaking on Halleck's agenda: opening the Mississippi below Cairo. Blocking the river to navigation by the Union were a major Confederate fort at Columbus, Kentucky (the "Gibraltar of the West"), and, forty miles downstream as the crow flies, the twin strongholds of New Madrid, on the river's west bank, and Island No. 10, nine miles south but, due to the contortions in the course of the Mississippi caused by the New Madrid earthquakes of 1811–1812, nevertheless upstream from New Madrid. Columbus did not have to be taken; General Beauregard decided that Grant's captures of Forts Henry and Donelson had made the post untenable, and ordered its evacuation.[19] When a short time later the 7th Kansas, on its way to Tennessee, occupied a portion of the Columbus fortifications, it had to spend the first two days "performing a badly needed policing of its camp area, removing a large accumulation of 'brick—burnt logs—mud—old Hay—Tents clothing Beef Bones and other Bones—all half rotten and putrid.'"[20]

New Madrid and Island No. 10, however, had to be taken, and on February 14 John Pope was assigned to the job of doing it. So he set up an advanced base at Commerce, Missouri, connected with New Madrid, fifty miles to the south, by a corduroy road built on top of an embankment to raise it above the level of the "dismal and almost impassable" Great Mingo Swamp.[21] Within a week of his arrival at Commerce on February 21, Pope marched to New Madrid with approx-

19. The deserted post was first entered by a scouting party of the 2nd Illinois from Paducah. Much of the armament and many of the seventeen thousand men removed from Columbus went to strengthen the defenses of New Madrid and Island No. 10. Kenneth P. Williams, *Lincoln Finds a General* (5 vols.; New York, 1949–59), III, 297.
20. Starr, *Jennison's Jayhawkers*, 163.
21. *Official Records*, Vol. VIII, 80.

imately eighteen thousand troops, "most of them entirely raw," which he organized into five small divisions of infantry and, notably, a division of cavalry under Colonel Gordon Granger.[22] Granger's division was small by the standards of cavalry organizations of a later day; it contained only three regiments: the 2nd and 3rd Michigan and the 7th Illinois.[23] If any notice was taken by anyone in authority of Pope's unprecedented (and so far as can be determined, unauthorized) action in organizing a cavalry division, no evidence of it is to be found in the records. Among Pope's "Unassigned Troops" were the 2nd Iowa, two companies of the 2nd Illinois, and three companies of the 4th United States; nothing in the records indicates why these units were not included in Granger's division.[24]

Notwithstanding the difficulties of a march made in "drizzling snow and rain," and "after incredible labor and exposure, wading through swamps, and in many places dragging wagons and artillery by hand," Pope's men reached New Madrid on March 3. The siege artillery he needed arrived at sunset on March 12. It was set up in battery and began the bombardment of the fortifications at daylight on the thirteenth, and that night, taking advantage of a "furious thunderstorm," the garrison evacuated the fortifications, leaving behind thirty-three pieces of artillery, "several thousand stand of superior small-arms," and "immense quantities of property and supplies. . . . Nothing except the men escaped, and they only with what they wore."[25]

The conquest of Island No. 10 shows the Union armed forces at their ingenious, jack-of-all-trades best. It was a fascinatingly complex operation involving the running of ten Confederate batteries—five on the island and five on the mainland—aimed at the river, by the gunboats Carondelet (commanded by the "prompt, gallant, and cheerful"

22. Ibid., 94, 80. Granger, a New Yorker, had graduated thirty-fifth of forty-one in the West Point Class of 1845. After a year's service in the infantry, he transferred in 1846 to the Regiment of Mounted Riflemen. He received two brevets in the Mexican War and a brevet for Wilson's Creek before being appointed colonel of the 2nd Michigan on September 2, 1861. Sheridan, while serving under him, thought him a meddling busybody. George W. Cullum, Biographical Register of the Officers and Graduates of the U.S. Military Academy (2 vols.; New York, 1868), II, 133–35; Philip H. Sheridan, Personal Memoirs of P. H. Sheridan (2 vols.; New York, 1888), I, 170.

23. Official Records, Vol. VIII, 92; but Ibid., 95, and Battles and Leaders, I, 463, show Granger's division as containing only the two Michigan regiments.

24. Official Records, Vol. VIII, 93.

25. Ibid., 82–83.

Captain Henry Walke) and *Pittsburg,* the bombardment of the island
by thirteen-inch mortars mounted individually on mortar boats, and
the digging of a nine-mile canal that cut off the garrison of the island
from access to reinforcements and supplies and enabled Pope to attack
them from the rear.[26] These, however, were infantry, artillery, engineering, and inland navy operations almost entirely, and there was
little opportunity for the cavalry to assist.[27] Six companies of the 7th
Illinois, as a part of Pope's advance guard, had had a successful brush
with the enemy on March 1, returning with three pieces of artillery
and a number of prisoners. Colonel Washington L. Elliott's 2nd Iowa,
armed only with sabers and pistols, joined Pope's forces at New Madrid
after a march that on one occasion had the regiment wading through
water belly-deep to their horses for "near half a day." At Island No. 10,
before sunrise on April 8, Colonel Elliott discovered, and reported to
Pope, that the Confederates had evacuated the position.[28]

The trophies Pope had to show for the conquest of Island No. 10
were nearly 7,000 prisoners, 138 pieces of artillery, 7,000 stand of
small arms, and provisions by the boatload.[29] These operations, which
General Halleck rightly called a "splendid achievement," would entitle
Pope to a considerably higher place in the esteem of military historians
if, later in the year at Second Bull Run, he had not been the victim of
General Lee's and Stonewall Jackson's proudest achievement.

In the midst of his supervision of Grant's, Curtis', and Pope's operations, each of which involved him in a large volume of correspondence
by letter and telegraph, plus his correspondence with Washington,
plus the multitude of his administrative responsibilities, Halleck somehow found the time and the energy to initiate still another operation.
On March 1 he directed General Frederick Steele to advance from Pilot
Knob with a force of four to five thousand, "drive back or capture" Confederate forces at Pitman's Ferry, Missouri, "destroy the enemy's stores"
at the Arkansas towns of Pocahontas, Jacksonport, and Batesville, and,
if practicable, go on to Helena on the Mississippi and "occupy and for-
tify that place, so as to cut off [Confederate] steamboat communication

26. Pope's report of the capture of Island No. 10 is in *Ibid.,* 89–90; see also *Battles
and Leaders,* I, 439–47, and Williams, *Lincoln Finds a General,* III, 396–99.
27. Indeed, Pope expressed the opinion that the two Michigan regiments of cavalry,
"many of the companies armed with revolving rifles," could serve "admirably" as infantry. *Official Records,* Vol. VIII, 622.
28. *Ibid.,* 580; Pierce, *History of the Second Iowa,* 12–17.
29. *Official Records,* Vol. VIII, 89–90.

with Memphis." Steele was to have two regiments of cavalry in his command, the 5th and 13th Illinois. Halleck then learned that the Confederates had 5,000 men at Pitman's Ferry and Pocahontas, and he tried to persuade Pope to release the 2nd and 3rd Michigan to beef up Steele's forces. But Pope, following the nearly universal practice of commanding officers when asked to release some of their troops to another army, argued that his security in mounting his attack on New Madrid depended on his cavalry, and declined politely but firmly to release the two Michigan regiments. Eventually, in any event, on the receipt of information that the commands of Van Dorn and Price were marching east with the evident intention of crossing the Mississippi to join the Confederate forces at Corinth, Steele's operation was called off.[30]

Within days after the battle of Shiloh, reports in the newspapers, and doubtless via the army grapevine as well, of the surprise, the near defeat, and the enormous casualties of Grant's army had begun to reach department headquarters in St. Louis and the government in Washington. These reports and rumors reawakened Halleck's latent doubts about Grant's qualifications for command—and perhaps also his personal dislike and jealousy of his subordinate. Whatever Halleck's reasons, conscious or otherwise, may have been, he decided to take personal command of the combined armies of Grant and Buell (to which Pope's Army of the Mississippi was shortly to be added), a total of nearly 125,000 men, in a campaign against Beauregard's army in Corinth, which had been reinforced by the troops Van Dorn and Price had brought from across the Mississippi.

On April 11 Halleck set up his headquarters at Pittsburg Landing, and on May 4 he began a snail-like progress toward Corinth, twenty-three miles away, against enemy forces he outnumbered by considerably more than two to one. Slowed to some extent by rain and miry roads, but much more by Halleck's determination that there was to be no repetition of the Shiloh surprise, the Federals did not reach Beauregard's main defense line until May 28.[31] They were now in a

30. *Ibid.*, 578–79, 610, 672.
31. General Buell reported to Halleck that "the ground everywhere is intersected by creeks and marsh bottoms, over which corduroy roads have to be made, forming perfect defiles." Quoted in Williams, *Lincoln Finds a General*, III, 412. The same terrain had

position to come to grips with the enemy, but after a beautifully stage-managed exercise of military hocus-pocus, the last of Beauregard's 53,000 troops marched out of Corinth on the night of May 29, undetected and unhindered by the Federals, a few hours after Halleck's left wing began the bombardment of the already nearly unoccupied Confederate lines.

As Halleck's armies made their way south toward Corinth, Gordon Granger, commanding the cavalry division of Pope's army, now grown to four regiments divided into two brigades, was "laboriously employed in the advance."[32] Much of the time, the cavalry had the duty of "scour[ing] the country" ahead of the infantry and brought back information about the location and activities of the enemy, which Pope promptly sent on to Halleck.[33] At other times, however, as Granger reported, "the heavy rains would render the roads entirely impassable for wagons, and I was then obliged to pack out upon the saddle horses of my command the requisite supplies of rations and forage, thus doubling the labor of both men and animals." In addition to acting as a supply train for the infantry, Granger's cavalrymen were required also to perform "the very unusual service to mounted men of building roads and bridges, earthworks for batteries, rifle pits, and lying in the trenches as infantry"; these duties, Granger wrote, were performed "without a single murmur," as no doubt they were when he was within earshot.[34]

Shortly before the infantry reached Corinth, Granger sent Colonel Elliott and the Second Brigade on a wide circuit to the south of Corinth, to break up the Mobile & Ohio Railroad, Beauregard's lifeline of supplies from the south. Elliott's raid was eminently successful. He reached the railroad at Booneville, thirty miles south of Corinth, and after a "sharp skirmish" with enemy cavalry, he destroyed a lengthy train

---

not, however, prevented the Confederate army in April from covering the same distance in the opposite direction in two days.

32. It will be noted that within two weeks of reporting the existence of a two- or three-regiment division of cavalry, Pope had a four-regiment division, the addition being the 2nd Iowa, a regiment previously "unassigned." The division was divided into two brigades, the First (3rd Michigan, 7th Illinois) under Colonel John K. Mizner, and the Second (2nd Michigan, 2nd Iowa) under Colonel Washington L. Elliott. *Official Records*, Vol. X, Pt. 1, pp. 726–27.

33. *Ibid.*, Pt. 2, pp. 179, 181.

34. *Ibid.*, Pt. 1, p. 727.

"filled with arms, ammunition, baggage and equipments" (including General Leonidas Polk's personal baggage), the depot, and a sizable length of track.[35] On May 30, Granger himself led his First Brigade in pursuit of Beauregard's retreating forces. The tangible results of the pursuit were meager—two hundred of Beauregard's wounded and some supplies were captured—and when Granger got ten miles ahead of his own infantry, he "deemed it prudent" to halt. Nevertheless, the cavalry performed creditably throughout these operations, and William Rosecrans, who had command of three divisions of infantry in the pursuit, commended Granger in his report for "the signal ability in which he handled the cavalry."[36]

The 2nd Michigan, two battalions of which were armed with Colt's revolving rifles, had a new commanding officer when it rode out as part of Colonel Elliott's brigade to raid the Mobile & Ohio. The new colonel, named Sheridan—the outward marks of his rank, a well-worn pair of eagle shoulder straps, given him by General Granger, hurriedly sewed on his infantryman's jacket—arrived at his regiment's camp at Farmington, Mississippi, just as the men, in a hubbub of excitement, were preparing to leave on the raid.[37]

Slowly but surely, the cavalry attached to Halleck's forces—and it should be noted that these were cavalrymen whose regiments Pope had united and organized into brigades and a division—were making a name for themselves as a useful adjunct of an army. At least one of Pope's troopers had no doubts about the source of his fellow troopers' improved performance. Pope, he wrote, "showed the world that he could make this branch of the service very effective. Instead of mixing them with infantry in the same regiments and brigades, he organized cavalry brigades and divisions, placing them under cavalry officers, and when thus organized he assigned them to their appropriate duty."[38] On April 29, in the course of a reconnaissance by Elliott's brigade, his

35. *Ibid.*, 731, 862–65, and Pt. 2, pp. 226, 227, 235, 239, 245; Sheridan, *Personal Memoirs*, I, 144–50; Pierce, *History of the Second Iowa*, 23–24. Halleck called Elliott's exploit "splendid," and promised that "he shall be rewarded." *Official Records*, Vol. X, Pt. 2, p. 237.

36. *Official Records*, Vol. X, Pt. 1, p. 712.

37. Sheridan, *Personal Memoirs*, I, 14–48; Williams, *Lincoln Finds a General*, III, 414–15; for the 2nd Michigan, see Starr, "The Second Michigan Volunteer Cavalry," 161–82.

38. Pierce, *History of the Second Iowa*, 18.

2nd Iowa stumbled upon, and immediately charged, a "masked" battery, their casualties in the charge being "the first blood spilled by the Second Iowa on the altar of liberty."[39] A few days later the Iowans, now commanded by Lieutenant Colonel (eventually Major General) Edwin Hatch, made a successful raid on the Memphis & Charleston; the regiment destroyed a "trestle work" and "otherwise render[ed] useless" a stretch of the road. Moreover, Colonel Hatch performed an essential duty of cavalry, a duty neglected more often than not by cavalry officers, by including in his report of the expedition a careful description of the country he had traversed—the streams, fords, and roads; and he did not fail to note the availability of forage in the area.[40]

The cavalry of Buell's army, approximately equal in numbers to Pope's, had not yet been brigaded and did not perform as effectively as did Pope's horsemen.[41] Whatever the reason may have been, the records speak at considerable length of the accomplishments of Pope's cavalry but hardly mention Buell's. Indeed, the only report of any length concerning the latter is anything but flattering. On May 10, Colonel James B. Fry, Buell's chief of staff, asked Colonel James S. Jackson, who suddenly appears (and just as suddenly disappears) in the records as "Commanding Cavalry, Army of the Ohio," to express to his cavalrymen Buell's "disapprobation" of their conduct the previous day when, stationed in front of General Alexander McD. McCook's division of infantry, they were "approached by small parties of the enemy's skirmishers" and, as soon as the latter opened fire, "broke and fled in disorder and in a manner not at all creditable to themselves." In the grandiloquent language of overwrought indignation in which such accusations were invariably rebutted, Colonel Edward M. McCook denied that his 2nd Indiana behaved then or at any other time in the manner described by Colonel Fry. It then appeared that four companies of the 3rd Indiana might have been the culprits, but their Major J. W. Paramore insisted that "all the officers and men . . . [of his com-

---

39. *Ibid.*, 19; *Official Records*, Vol. X, Pt. 1, p. 731. On the previous day, the Iowans had charged a rebel camp and taken seventeen prisoners. Private J. Canfield brought in six, and Private R. M. Downer, three. Both men "had been reduced to the ranks from sergeants but a few weeks before, because they resented the tyranny of officers over them." Pierce, *History of the Second Iowa*, 19.

40. *Official Records*, Vol. X, Pt. 1, pp. 735–37.

41. On May 31, Pope had 2,522 cavalry "for duty," and Buell, 2,688. "Unattached" cavalry under Halleck belonging neither to Buell nor to Pope numbered 2,539. *Ibid.*, Pt. 2, p. 235.

mand] behaved with uncommon coolness and bravery, executing and obeying every order with promptness and good order." [42]

The historian of the 2nd Michigan noted the disastrous effect that the late spring and early summer heat of Mississippi was having on the troopers from the North.

Though we held the key to the North Mississippi country, yet the climate began to tell heavily on our troops, and out of 1,200 fighting men of six months before, the regiment could not muster over 450 to 500 effective men. The most healthy locations for camps were selected . . . where we might . . . recruit the shattered health of the men. . . . Near by were the field hospitals—long rows of large white tents spread beneath the few scattered trees, and from which more men were carried out to their long homes than had fallen upon the battle field; and as many more were sent away to the North as soon as they were able to creep from their cots upon which they had tossed for many weary days in the delirium of fever; or, moving about camp, living skeletons, around whose emaciated forms the coarse army clothing hung and flapped like emaciated scare-crows. . . . men were buried by the score. [43]

Those who were sent off to hospitals in the North, as was Webster Moses of the 7th Kansas, had to endure, if they could, a journey from Corinth to St. Louis that took as long as nine days, during which the sick and wounded were fed a diet of hardtack, raw bacon, and coffee. [44]

Beauregard's men were presumably inured to the heat; nevertheless, they had the same problems in Corinth as did the Federals outside the town. Beauregard had as many as eighteen thousand of his men, more than 30 percent of the total, on the sick list at one time, ill with typhoid, dysentery, or the measles. Among the wounded he had brought back from Shiloh, erysipelas was common, and eight of every ten amputees died of tetanus. [45]

Debilitating and frequently fatal illness was the worst of the trials the soldiers from the North experienced in their first summer in the Deep South, but it was not the only one. There were "lesser foes," as a regimental historian called them, all "strictly indigenous to the South-

42. Ibid., Pt. 1, pp. 831–33; Crofts, Third Ohio Veteran Volunteer Cavalry, 27–32.
43. Marshall P. Thatcher, A Hundred Battles in the West, St. Louis to Atlanta: The Second Michigan Cavalry with the Armies of Mississippi, Ohio, Kentucky, and Cumberland (Detroit, 1884), 58–59. The 7th Kansas, in camp near Rienzi, Mississippi, from the end of July on, lost nineteen of its men dead in two months in an epidemic of typhoid fever in which many more of its men were disabled. Starr, Jennison's Jayhawkers, 194.
44. Starr, Jennison's Jayhawkers, 211.
45. Horn, Army of Tennessee, 149.

ern country." The hardest of these to bear was "the voracious, the terrible ally to the rebel army," to wit, the "gray-back," or louse. The men discovered by bitter experience that "the speediest method of getting rid of . . . [gray-backs] was by boiling the clothes. Cold water washing only seemed to stimulate them; but at times when the camp kettle was not used for boiling beans or coffee, the boys would give their clothes a bath that would for the time thoroughly eradicate the pest. . . . The thumbnail slew its thousands, but boiling water its tens of thousands."[46] There were other insect pests besides the louse, and the soldiers of the Union had also to endure as best they could the fleas, the wood ticks, and the "serried millions . . . [of the] invisible jigger."[47]

"Jiggers" (or chiggers) were most commonly found in association with one of the major pleasures of a Mississippi summer, frequently recalled in regimental histories. During this period, the historian of the 2nd Iowa tells us, "Blackberries were in their prime, and surely no country on the globe can compete with Tishamingo county, Miss., in the production of this fruit. . . . we kept a supply of these berries constantly in our tents, and feasted on them to our heart's desire. The result of this was a marked improvement in the sanitary condition of the regiment." The more adventurous gastronomes in the ranks experimented with a variety of recipes that called for the succulent blackberry as their main ingredient. Much in favor with the 72nd Indiana Mounted Infantry (who decided that blackberries were "so conducive to health" that they "almost lived upon them") was a concoction, to feed a "mess" of eight troopers, consisting of a gallon of the berries covered with a gallon of water and brought to a boil, to which were then added three pounds of "broken" hardtack and a pound of sugar, well stirred in—"and the gods never ate a better dish," the historian added, doubtless smacking his lips in retrospect as he wrote the passage in his regimental chronicle.[48]

There were other delicacies in Mississippi besides blackberries for northern cavalrymen to enjoy. The troopers of the 8th Indiana, who did not fail to go out blackberrying every day, also found the local peaches very much to their taste. "It beats all for peaches here . . . that

46. Hartpence, History of the 51st Indiana, 29.

47. Vale, Minty and the Cavalry, 188–92.

48. Pierce, History of the Second Iowa, 26; Benjamin F. McGee, History of the 72nd Indiana Volunteer Infantry of the Mounted Lightning Brigade (Lafayette, Ind., 1882), 332.

I ever saw or heard of. They are as large again as any I ever saw before," one of them wrote his wife.[49]

A name that appeared in reports and dispatches with increasing
frequency and was receiving increasingly favorable mention was that
of the new commanding officer of the 2nd Michigan, Colonel Sheridan. On June 4, he joined in a reconnaissance in the direction of
Beauregard's new base at Tupelo, Mississippi, and was praised by
Granger for the "great skill and coolness" with which he directed the
operations of his regiment."[50] Two days later, in the course of another
reconnaissance, he met, "vigorously attacked," and "drove back" a
regiment of Confederate cavalry and an Independent Company of
mounted scouts from Georgia. It is worthy of note that in this action
Sheridan made full use of his advantage in firepower; he attacked the
Confederates with five of his companies, all armed with Colt's revolving rifles, dismounted.[51] On June 11, Washington Elliott, promoted to
brigadier general (the reward promised him by Halleck for his successful raid to Booneville), was taken from the cavalry by Pope to be his
chief of staff, and Sheridan, an infantry captain six weeks before, succeeded him in command of the Second Cavalry Brigade.[52]

Encamped with his brigade at an outpost just north of Booneville,
eight miles in advance of the nearest Federal infantry, Sheridan spent
the remainder of June scouting and mapping the area. On the morning of July 1, he was attacked by General James R. Chalmers, with, as
Sheridan reported, "between five and six thousand men."[53] Sheridan's
report of the "effective strength" of his two regiments at Booneville as
827 may be accepted as accurate, but his estimate of Chalmers' numbers, made with less than his usual assurance, appears to be grossly
exaggerated. If he was correct, as he probably was, in reporting that he
was attacked by six regiments and two odd battalions, Chalmers may
have had, at the outside, as many as 3,000 men, but a far more likely

49. Jacob W. Bartmess, "Civil War Letters," *Indiana Magazine of History,* LII
(1956), 64, 68; see also Hartpence, *History of the 51st Indiana,* 54.

50. *Official Records,* Vol. X, Pt. 1, p. 733. It must be noted, however, that Granger
praised in similar terms Lieutenant Colonel Hatch, whose 2nd Iowa also took part in the
operation.

51. *Ibid.,* 733.

52. Sheridan, *Personal Memoirs,* I, 153.

53. *Ibid.,* 156; Sheridan's account of the battle is in *Ibid.,* 156–65; other accounts
are in *Battles and Leaders,* II, 723; Pierce, *History of the Second Iowa,* 26–28; and
Richard O'Connor, *Sheridan the Inevitable* (Indianapolis, 1953), 65–68.

estimate is the 1,200 to 1,500 with which *Battles and Leaders* credits him, a numerical advantage that was offset, and perhaps more than offset, by the possession of Colt's revolving rifles by two battalions of the 2nd Michigan.[54]

Whatever Chalmers' numbers may have been, he delivered a series of vigorous attacks—at one point his men and Sheridan's fought hand to hand with the butts of their guns for weapons—which forced Sheridan to deploy in the fighting line every man he had. Completely in character, and prophetic of the Sheridan of 1864–1865, was the message he sent to General Asboth, commanding the nearest body of infantry: "I have been cut up some little, but am still strong."[55] On the ragged edge of being flanked on both sides and overwhelmed, he withdrew from the line two of the saber companies of each of his two regiments, a total of 90 men, ordered them to mount, and sent them under the command of Captain Russell A. Alger of the 2nd Michigan on a wide circuit on a "wood road" to charge the enemy's rear in column. At the same time he went over to the attack with the troops that had been fighting the enemy in the woods since morning. Readers of this chronicle have already met Captain Alger as the Colonel Alger who, in command of the 5th Michigan, on June 11, 1863, charged Wade Hampton's led horses, trains, and artillery caissons at Trevilian Station, Virginia. He would be met to their sorrow by the volunteers in the Spanish-American War, in his capacity as a singularly inept secretary of war. Alger's charge at Booneville did, however, accomplish its purpose, although he himself was not in at the finish, having been swept out of his saddle by an overhanging branch he had failed to see in time. Pressed front and flank by the attack of Sheridan's main body, frightened more than damaged by Alger's charge from the rear, the Confederates broke off the action and, so Sheridan has it, "ran in the utmost disorder over the country in every direction."[56]

54. Chalmers' strength is given as 1,200 or 1,500 in *Battles and Leaders*, II, 723; Pierce, *History of the Second Iowa*, 26, gives the figure of 4,000, and O'Connor accepts Sheridan's figure of 5,000. The present writer's reluctant guess that Chalmers *may* have had as many as 3,000 men is based on Sheridan's list of the Confederate regiments he fought, in *Official Records*, Vol. XVII, Pt. 2, pp. 65–66, and the statement in Thiele, "The Evolution of Cavalry," 348–49, that the average strength on April 13 of Beauregard's thirteen mounted regiments was 437. If Chalmers or any of his subordinates submitted reports of the action, they have not survived.

55. *Official Records*, Vol. XVII, Pt. 2, p. 62.

56. Sheridan, *Personal Memoirs*, I, 163.

Sheridan had a most gratifying little victory at Booneville. It meant little in terms of the war as a whole, but it had a most salutary effect on the morale of his small command; it reinforced the esteem, confidence, and even love of his men that Sheridan had already gained. It also led to the famous dispatch Rosecrans sent Halleck: "I have issued an order complimenting Sheridan and his command. More cavalry massed under such an officer would be of great use to us. Sheridan ought to be made a brigadier. He would not be a stampeding general."[57] Even more famous, and justly so, is the telegram sent to Halleck, who was by then in Washington as general-in-chief, by Generals Rosecrans, Granger, J. C. Sullivan, Elliott, and Asboth: "Brigadiers are scarce. Good ones scarce[r]. . . . The undersigned respectfully beg that you will obtain the promotion of Sheridan. He is worth his weight in gold."[58] Sheridan was duly promoted to brigadier general, and as a compliment to him on his Booneville victory, his commission bore the date of July 1, 1862.[59]

It is necessary now to leave the Union army sweltering in their woolen uniforms in hundred-degree heat in northern Mississippi and examine cavalry operations in the more salubrious climate of the Bluegrass region of central Kentucky.

A Confederate cavalryman whose performance in middle Tennessee and at Shiloh had attracted favorable notice was John Hunt Morgan of Lexington, Kentucky, a veteran of the Mexican War who had organized the Lexington Rifles, a gaudily uniformed company of militia, and after the collapse of Kentucky's hopeless endeavor to maintain its neutrality, had led them to join the Confederate forces at Bowling Green. Mounting themselves on horses obtained "by purchase or otherwise," Morgan's command turned itself into cavalry and eventually grew to a force of three companies.[60] Promoted to colonel, Morgan

57. *Official Records*, Vol. XVII, Pt. 2, p. 66. In reporting Sheridan's victory ("a brilliant affair") to Secretary Stanton, Halleck recommended his promotion to brigadier general "for gallant conduct" in the battle. *Ibid.*, 76.

58. *Ibid.*, 139.

59. On September 29 Sheridan was given command of the Eleventh Division of infantry in the Army of the Ohio. It is interesting to speculate on what the progress of the Union cavalry in the West would have been if he had remained a cavalryman.

60. Cecil F. Holland, *Morgan and His Raiders* (New York, 1942), 48. Some of the men who bought their horses did so with money Morgan lent them.

went to Beauregard following the Confederate retreat from the Shiloh battlefield to Corinth and proposed that he be sent on a raid deep into Kentucky to cut Halleck's principal supply line. Beauregard approved the plan, and as an expression of his confidence in Morgan, authorized him to add two companies to his command and gave him $15,000 for expenses.[61]

Departing on April 26, the raiders, 325 strong, reached Lebanon, Tennessee, on the chilly, rainy evening of May 4. There was a great deal of drinking to get warm and a consequent neglect of the most elementary security precautions; the sentries were sheltering in nearby farm houses when, just before daylight on May 5, a force of 600 Federal cavalrymen of the 1st Kentucky and the 7th Pennsylvania dashed into the town over the unguarded roads. The surprise was complete. About half of Morgan's men were killed or captured; the rest rode hell for leather, with the Federals in pursuit, toward the Cumberland River and safety, a ride known thenceforth as the Lebanon Races.[62]

Morgan himself escaped and at Knoxville set about reconstituting his command. He had the help of his brother-in-law, Basil Duke, recovered from the severe wound he had received at Shiloh, and of a British soldier of fortune, George St. Leger Grenfell, a man of fascinating antecedents. The latter tried to teach Morgan and his men as much as they were willing to learn of the rudiments of discipline and of the technique of cavalry operations that he himself had learned as an officer in the Anglo-Turkish Contingent in the Crimean War.[63] From a nucleus of those of his men who had escaped from Lebanon and new recruits, and with the addition of cavalry companies from Texas, Alabama, and Mississippi, Morgan built up a small regiment that was officially designated the 2nd Kentucky Cavalry.[64] In late June he was

61. Brown, *The Bold Cavaliers*, 54–55.

62. The fight at Lebanon is described by Tarrant, *Wild Riders of the First Kentucky*, 83, and Basil W. Duke, *A History of Morgan's Cavalry* (Bloomington, 1960), 159–63; see also Thomas F. Dornblaser, *Sabre Strokes of the Pennsylvania Dragoons in the War of 1861–1865* (Philadelphia, 1884), 65, and Brown, *The Bold Cavaliers*, 57–64. Colonel Frank Wolford of the 1st Kentucky was severely wounded in the fight. See Vol. I, pp. 83–84 of the present work.

63. Stephen Z. Starr, *Colonel Grenfell's Wars* (Baton Rouge, 1971), 51, 56–59. For Grenfell's career before he joined Morgan, see Stephen Z. Starr, "Colonel George St. Leger Grenfell: His Pre–Civil War Career," *Journal of Southern History*, XXX (1964), 278–97.

64. Duke, *History of Morgan's Cavalry*, 181.

joined by an equally small regiment of Partisan Rangers from Georgia, which raised his numbers to 876, about 200 of whom lacked arms. With this force Morgan set off on July 4 on what came to be called his "First Kentucky Raid," an enterprise that was to take him as far north as Cynthiana, within fifty miles of the Ohio River at Cincinnati.

In command of the exiguous forces in Kentucky when Morgan made his appearance there was General Jeremiah T. Boyle, an excitable individual, particularly in the language of his telegraphic messages to his military superiors and the officials in Washington. But he was much more shrewd and, given his severely limited resources, much more competent than he has been given credit for being. To oppose Morgan, he had nothing but hurriedly assembled, poorly armed, undisciplined home guards, "Fireside Rangers" as they were contemptuously called, and improvised battalions of convalescents from the military hospitals in Louisville, led by officers on their way to or from the armies in Tennessee and Mississippi, who were virtually kidnapped to command these *ad hoc* units.[65]

The only organized body of Federal troops Morgan encountered on the entire expedition was a four-company battalion of the 9th Pennsylvania, commanded by Major Thomas J. Jordan. A modern historian has stated that this "blackguard Major" (actually a respectable Harrisburg lawyer in his fortieth year, whose letters to his wife reveal him as a somewhat sententious, God-fearing family man) had threatened the ladies of Sparta and Celina, Tennessee, with rape if they did not promptly supply his men with home-cooked meals.[66] These "insults" were reported to Morgan, and in keeping with the spirit of the time and his own temperament, he decided that a detour was called for, to punish the recreant major. Having been alerted to Morgan's presence at Celina, where he was preparing to cross the Cumberland River, Jordan left his camp at Tompkinsville with his 230 officers and men to find and fight Morgan at Celina. But when he got there, Morgan had already left, and the prosouthern natives denied all knowledge of his whereabouts. Jordan returned to Tompkinsville, where, on the follow-

65. Starr, *Colonel Grenfell's Wars*, 66–67.
66. Brown, *The Bold Cavaliers*, 76; Rowell, *Yankee Cavalrymen*, 21. The wartime letters of Major (later Colonel) Jordan have been transcribed by his grandson, the late David L. Bacon, of North Haven, Connecticut, who kindly gave the author a copy of the transcript and permission to make use of it in the present work. It will be referred to hereinafter as Jordan Papers.

ing morning, he was attacked by Morgan. He had enough of a warning of Morgan's approach to have his men in position along the edge of a forest on the crest of a ridge, with open ground sloping away downhill for a distance of three hundred yards, below them.[67]

Some time before he reached Tompkinsville, Morgan detached a group of about 120 of his men to go on a wide circuit to attack Jordan from the rear when he made his frontal attack with the bulk of his command. It will be noted that on this occasion, as in all his subsequent operations in Kentucky, Morgan learned, from the same people claiming total ignorance of *his* whereabouts when questioned by the Federals, precise information about the location of any Federal force in the neighborhood. In an era in which the means of locating hostile troops were severely limited, it was an inestimable advantage to be able to rely on a friendly population eager to supply information about the enemy at the same time that they either pretended ignorance of one's own position, objectives, and numbers or misrepresented them to the enemy. It is not remembered as often as it should be that with the exception of General Lee's invasion of Pennsylvania, this was an advantage every Confederate force enjoyed, and a handicap every Union force had to contend against, throughout the war.

As Major Jordan faced the long line of Morgan's dismounted cavalrymen preparing to attack him, he thought he was outnumbered six to one. He was also being shelled by Morgan's two mountain howitzers, to which he had no artillery of his own to reply. After ten rounds from the howitzers, and seeing an outflanking movement developing on his left, Jordan ordered a retreat, which may or may not have been executed "with the precision of a parade, my men remaining perfectly cool and obedient to my orders," as the major, who was himself taken prisoner a short time later, described it.[68] A considerably different tale is told by Basil Duke. According to his account, Morgan's entire force, less R. M. Gano's squadron and the "notorious" C. P. Hamilton's company of Tennessee guerrillas (these being the troops he had sent to get into Jordan's rear), were dismounted, lined up at the foot of the hill, and advanced at a run against the Federals. They were met by three or

67. It is impossible to determine with certainty from the surviving reports and accounts whether Jordan's men fought mounted or dismounted; General Duke's account, however, strongly suggests the latter.

68. Major Jordan's report (which he wrote in December, 1862, after he had been exchanged and was about to return to duty) in Jordan Papers.

four volleys, but held their own fire until they were within sixty yards of the enemy. They then fired a volley of their own, and at the same moment, Grenfell "spurred his horse between the two lines, risking the fire of both, leaped a low fence behind which the enemy were lying, and began slashing at them right and left." Thereupon the Federals retreated or fled, leaving their camp, supplies, and wagon train to be captured by Morgan's men.[69]

The further course of Morgan's raid, cheered by a generally friendly populace and free of any serious opposition until he reached Cynthiana, provides no information of value on the course of Union cavalry operations in the West. Having decided to return to Tennessee on a line east of that he had followed on his way north, Morgan intended to cross from the west to the east bank of the Licking River at Cynthiana, which was garrisoned by a scratch force of about 340 made up of Kentucky and Ohio Home Guards, 75 raw recruits of the 7th Kentucky, and, manning a 12-pound howitzer, a squad of firemen from Cincinnati. After a totally needless fight in which Grenfell again greatly distinguished himself and in which (taking on faith each commander's report of his own casualties) a total of 25 were killed and 63 wounded, Morgan did get across the river and headed back to Tennessee via Paris, Crab Orchard, and Somerset.[70] General Boyle lacked the means for an effective pursuit.[71] He was authorized by Secretary Stanton on July 16 to raise a regiment of cavalry, but this was a mere forty-eight hours before the fight at Cynthiana and far too late to be of any use in the present emergency; equally useless was the permission wired him on the twenty-second to raise three regiments of cavalry for one-year terms of enlistment. The men for these regiments could be had, but Boyle lacked the necessary weapons. As for the horses he needed, he was directed to provide them "as far as possible by taking them from disloyal persons."[72]

69. Duke, *History of Morgan's Cavalry*, 184; Basil W. Duke, *Reminiscences of General Basil W. Duke, C.S.A.* (New York, 1911), 153; Major Jordan's report, Jordan Papers; Rowell, *Yankee Cavalrymen*, 64–67; Starr, *Colonel Grenfell's Wars*, 62–63; Brown, *The Bold Cavaliers*, 78–79; Holland, *Morgan and His Raiders*, 117–18. The Confederate accounts, and secondary works based on them, greatly exaggerate the number of Jordan's men taken prisoner, claiming many more than Jordan had altogether.

70. *Official Records*, Vol. XVI, Pt. 2, p. 756; Duke, *History of Morgan's Cavalry*, 199–202. General Duke, however, had doubled the size of the Federal force at Cynthiana.

71. *Official Records*, Vol. XVI, Pt. 1, pp. 733, 736, 746.

72. *Ibid.*, 743, 744, 749.

These directions to Boyle were the first indication—there were to be many others in the years ahead—that in the opinion of the wise men in the War Department, cavalry could be extemporized by providing a given number of men with whatever weapons happened to be available and with horses to ride; on no other theory could the enlistment of men for the cavalry service "for one year unless sooner discharged" have been justified.[73] Morgan's numbers had grown by the enlistment of eager recruits to 1,200, all of them fully armed with captures from the Federals and mounted on the best of the horses they had appropriated in a region famous for horseflesh. Boyle, lacking proper cavalry, had the hopeless task of trying to fight and catch Morgan with forces like those reported by General Clay Smith, namely 230 men of the 9th Pennsylvania, 165 of the 18th Kentucky Infantry, 100 Kentucky Home Guards, and 100 Cincinnati policemen.[74]

The First Kentucky Raid did something more than give Morgan a fully justified opportunity to gloat. After his arrival with his command at Livingston, Tennessee, at the end of July, he himself left for Knoxville, the headquarters of General E. Kirby Smith. His formal report of the raid, and doubtless his conversations with the general, in which he painted in glowing colors the prosouthern sentiments of Kentuckians, the weakness of the Federal forces in the state, the abundance of supplies available for feeding a large army and its animals, and the eagerness of large numbers of Kentuckians to enlist in the Confederate army if they could do so in safety, made a powerful impression and were to lead shortly to momentous consequences.[75] Before those consequences can be discussed, however, it is necessary to return to the hostile armies facing each other in northern Mississippi.

73. On the matter of weapons for Boyle's cavalrymen-to-be, see *Ibid.*, 741, 750, 752.
74. *Ibid.*, 759–60.
75. For Morgan's report, see *Ibid.*, 767–70.

IV

To War and Arms I Fly

EXCEPT FOR THE ACTIVITIES OF POPE'S CAVALRY, PREVI-
ously described, there was a pause in military operations following the
Confederates' evacuation of Corinth. Beauregard was dismissed on
June 20 from the command of the "Western department," including
that of the army at Tupelo, and Braxton Bragg was appointed in his
place. There were changes on the other side of the line as well. John
Pope was called east on June 15, and William Rosecrans, who had
commanded two divisions of Pope's right wing since May 27, succeeded him in command of the Army of the Mississippi. A more important change occurred on July 11 with the appointment of Halleck as
general-in-chief of the armies of the United States (to give him his full
title) with headquarters in Washington. A short time before, Halleck
had done away with the right wing–center–left wing–reserve scheme
of organization of his army, in effect in the campaign from Shiloh to
Corinth, and restored the military autonomy of the Armies of the Mississippi (Rosecrans), of the Ohio (Buell), and of the Tennessee (Grant).

When Halleck left for Washington, Grant, who had been at loose
ends as Halleck's nominal second in command, and in frustration had
removed his headquarters to Memphis, was elevated to the command
of the District of West Tennessee. The district, the headquarters of
which remained at Corinth, extended across the southwestern corner
of Tennessee at Memphis and across the northeastern corner of Mis-

sissippi as far east as Huntsville, Alabama, which had been occupied by a division of Buell's army under Ormsby Mitchel, West Point graduate, Cincinnati resident, and astronomer turned general. Rosecrans and his Army of the Mississippi, but not Buell, came under Grant's command pursuant to these arrangements.

No sooner did Rosecrans assume command of the Army of the Mississippi than he discovered that he did not have as much cavalry as he needed. There was considerable justification for his concern, as he had three divisions plus two brigades of infantry deployed in a long line from Corinth on the west nearly to Cherokee, Alabama, on the east, a distance of about thirty-five miles, exposed to irruptions by Confederate cavalry at any point.[1] His efforts to add to the cavalry he already had, cast an interesting sidelight on his personality and on the techniques and relationships of command in the early years of the Civil War.

Rosecrans' bombardment (for it was nothing less) of the authorities began on July 19 with a dispatch to the chief of the Ordnance Bureau in St. Louis, Colonel D. F. Callender. "Our cavalry is diminishing in numbers," Rosecrans wrote, "by contests with the superior rebel numbers on a front of 60 miles. . . . It is vitally important that they be mounted and armed well. . . . Twelve hundred and fifty Colt's army revolvers and 1,100 carbines or revolving rifles are required for the cavalry division. For the country's sake provide for this without delay. The cost and risk to which the Government is daily subjected for want of these arms are such that impossibility or imbecility alone could refuse or delay the supply."[2]

A few days later Rosecrans reported that his Fifth Division, commanded by Gordon Granger, consisted of six regiments of infantry and seven regiments of cavalry (7th Illinois, 2nd Iowa, 7th Kansas, 2nd and 3rd Michigan, 1st and 5th Missouri).[3] The other four infantry divisions of Rosecrans' army had no cavalry attached to them. With a long line to patrol and guard, Rosecrans had evidently decided to eke out the numbers of his cavalry (and to that degree to modify the pattern of organization of the cavalry that he had inherited from Pope) by giving

1. Which, however, Rosecrans represented to be 50 and 60 miles. *Official Records*, Vol. XVII, Pt. 2, pp. 24, 105.
2. *Ibid.*, 105.
3. *Ibid.*, 148.

Granger six regiments of infantry to add to his mounted troops, which, it will be noted, had grown since Pope's departure from four regiments to seven. Granger now had by far the largest cavalry organization assembled by the North in the Civil War up to that time. A week later, Rosecrans wired Halleck in Washington: "Please give our cavalry repeating rifles. It will double its force, for experience has shown that repeaters would double the power of an infantry regiment. A simple calculation will show what the peculiar economy of this would be to our army. Five hundred thousand dollars per day is a very fair interest on the difference between the price of repeating and common firearms. The calculation is simple, but the data are undoubted by practical men."[4] A hundred years later it was appropriate to assess the military effectiveness of weapons in economic terms—"a bigger bang for a buck"—but for the Civil War era, Rosecrans' approach was unconventional, to say the least.

Having tried on Halleck his skills as an advocate, Rosecrans next approached the secretary of war himself. "Our cavalry, in the face of the enemy," he telegraphed Stanton, "and in the best possible season for a campaign, are without arms. . . . One thousand breech-loading or revolving arms and 2,000 pistols are necessary to arm our cavalry, including recruits. Cavalry without arms anywhere is bad enough, but on a hostile frontier it is not only waste but murder. For Heaven's sake do something for us if you can."[5] It will be noted that Rosecrans was inclined to be both didactic and shrill in his dispatches to the War Department.

In response to the telegram to Stanton, Assistant Secretary of War P. H. Watson calmly listed the numbers of breech-loading carbines that had been "ordered to be sent . . . with dispatch" (which might or might not have been equivalent to "*were* sent") to nine different regiments, battalions, and companies in Rosecrans' command.[6] Whereupon Rosecrans protested that "profound disappointment followed the receipt of Mr. Watson's dispatch," which showed that the 2,750 carbines shipped or to be shipped were "all go[ing] to little detachments,

4. *Ibid.*, 154. The "repeating rifles" Rosecrans asked for were doubtless the sixteen-shot Colt's revolving rifles that his 2nd Michigan already had.

5. *Ibid.*, 281.

6. Watson listed as "ordered to be sent" 1,370 Sharps, 630 Smith, and 750 Burnside carbines, all "with accoutrements and ammunition complete." *Ibid.*, 282.

split up and performing picket duty in . . . [the] rear," instead of to the cavalry that were "massed and have had power to chastise and cow the rebel cavalry." It then appeared that the carbines had been consigned on the basis of directions given by "Col. Dickey, accredited by General Grant as chief of cavalry"—a sample of bureaucratic confusion and bungling not at all uncommon in wartime or in peacetime. Doing its utmost to demonstrate its cooperative attitude, the War Department promptly agreed to correct the maldistribution by sending additional carbines to the units Rosecrans would designate.[7]

During these late summer months, while Rosecrans was busily exchanging messages with Washington about the needs of his cavalry, his horsemen were just as busily scouting the roads and byways between their lines and the enemy camps at Tupelo. Since the Confederate cavalry was similarly engaged in the opposite direction, brushes between detachments of blue and gray cavalry were of daily occurrence. Granger complained that the enemy cavalry had his outnumbered five to one, that they knew "every cow-path and water-hole, and the country is filled with their friends, from whom they can obtain every kind of information as to our whereabouts, movements, and strength"; all of which, with the possible exception of his claim of the disproportion of numbers, was undoubtedly true. General Granger was equally correct in stating that "the small cavalry we have is not properly armed, and the extraordinary hard duty it is called to do is fast breaking it down. The way I am forced to use it on our present extended front through the terrible heat, dust, and want of water will in one month more dismount a large portion of it."[8] Notwithstanding these hardships, or perhaps even because of them, these operations were excellent training for the cavalry, especially for the company officers, the captains and lieutenants, who were usually in command of the scouting details and had to learn to cope with the sudden emergencies and surprises that occurred regularly in the wooded country in which these operations were conducted.

Taking the good with the bad, Rosecrans concluded that his cavalry

7. *Ibid.*, 284, 287, 290.

8. *Ibid.*, Pt. 1, pp. 40–41. Colonel A. L. Lee of the 7th Kansas reported after a scout from Rienzi to Marietta and Bay Springs, Mississippi, that "to fight small forces of the enemy in the region immediately below this point I consider impracticable unless they desire to fight. The posting and vigilance of their pickets is perfect, and their knowledge of the country enables them to evade an attack when evasion is desirable." *Ibid.*, 36.

was deserving of his commendation and would also benefit from a little friendly exhortation. In General Orders, therefore, after singling out Sheridan and Lieutenant Colonel Robert H. G. Minty, the British-born commander of the 3rd Michigan (and about to be promoted to colonel of the 4th Michigan) for special praise, he complimented Granger "for the signal services the cavalry under his command have been and are still rendering to this army, and [here came the exhortation] trusts that increasing ambition, care, watchfulness, and zeal for instruction, discipline, and order may add more to its efficiency and renown."[9]

One of the regiments of cavalry to which Rosecrans' General Orders were read at dress parade was the 7th Kansas, which had been transferred from Kansas to Mississippi at the end of May. Commanded by a fervent abolitionist, Lieutenant Colonel Daniel Read Anthony, since Colonel Jennison's resignation in a huff, the Jayhawkers had been a source of trouble from the day they crossed the Mississippi River.[10] Their march south through Tennessee was, as General Halleck reported, "marked by robbery, theft, pillage and outrages upon the peaceful inhabitants." A foraging detail of the regiment halted a funeral procession near Trenton, Tennessee, and, before they decided to allow Parson Koyle to keep his mules and buggy, broke open the coffin to satisfy themselves of the truth of the parson's claim that he was conducting a funeral. They were reported by the officer in command of the post at Bethel, Tennessee, as having not only "robbed the farmers of all their stock and in some cases of their watches and money," but, in one of the rare mentions of such incidents in the records, "in some instances attempted to force the women to cohabit with them when found at home alone." When on July 28, the Federal cavalry captured Ripley, Mississippi, west of Booneville, Sheridan reported that the troopers of the 7th Kansas, and on this occasion those of the 2nd Iowa as well, "were, through carelessness of their officers, permitted to break into and pillage some of the stores and private places."[11]

Nor were these the total of the Jayhawkers' misdeeds. Sharing the abolitionist sentiments of Colonel Anthony, they not only "jayhawked" slaves from their owners but also hid and protected runaway slaves

9. *Ibid.*, 18; General Orders No. 81, July 2, 1862.

10. Susan B. Anthony was Daniel Read Anthony's sister. The family resided in Rochester, New York, a hotbed of abolitionist sentiment in the 1850s.

11. *Official Records*, Vol. XVII, Pt. 2, pp. 77, 35, 53, 91, 94, 132.

who sought safety with them. They did so in defiance of the Fugitive Slave Law and of the army orders then in force, and any slaveowner who came to the Jayhawkers' camp to look for his escaped property did so at the risk of his life.[12]

Harassed by a stream of reports and complaints of the Jayhawkers' misdeeds, Halleck was at his wits' end as to what to do with the incorrigible Kansans. He told Secretary Stanton that he would do his best to reduce them to "proper discipline," but he added that he was "very doubtful of success, so long as bad officers, supported as they allege by political influence at Washington, encourage them in violating laws, regulations and orders." In another dispatch to the secretary, he was more specific; he expressed the fear that his efforts to bring the Jayhawkers to a state of order and discipline would be attributed by "Senator Lane and others . . . to political influences and will heap unmeasured abuses upon any officer who shall attempt to keep them in order."[13] Halleck himself left for Washington a few days after he sent this dispatch, leaving to his successor, Grant, the thorny problem of dealing with the unreformed and certainly unrepentant Jayhawkers.

Having bowed Beauregard out of Corinth, Halleck had to decide what to do next to carry the war to the enemy. One possible line of advance, greatly favored by the president, deeply concerned as he was to bring relief to the Unionist east Tennesseans, was to Chattanooga, more than two hundred miles away but connected with Corinth by the Memphis & Charleston Railroad. In favor of this line of advance was that it would block the only direct rail connection the Confederacy had between Richmond and the West and also that the Union army already had possession of two important points on this line of advance: Ormsby Mitchel's division was at Huntsville, and General George W. Morgan, also in Buell's command, held Cumberland Gap, within easy reach of Knoxville, with nine thousand effectives. By mid-July, Buell himself, ordered to move into and occupy east Tennessee, had reached

12. It is worthy of note that George H. Hoyt, who headed the corps of defense attorneys when John Brown was tried for treason at Charles Town for his Harpers Ferry Raid, commanded Company K of the 7th Kansas after the resignation because of poor health of John Brown, Jr., the first captain of the company.

13. *Ibid.*, 77, 91.

Stevenson, Alabama, forty miles from Chattanooga, with the main body of his army.

To sustain a Federal advance into east Tennessee, supplies could be sent by boat up the Tennessee River and by rail up the Memphis & Charleston. But the river was too shallow for navigation during much of the summer and early fall, and the railroad was vulnerable for its full length to raids by Confederate cavalry. An alternate strategy to avoid these difficulties had been foreshadowed by General Scott's Anaconda Plan, namely to concentrate resources on a push from Memphis down the Mississippi River to capture Vicksburg, form a junction with Federal forces pushing north from New Orleans, and thus open the Mississippi for its full length to navigation by the Union, at the same time cutting the Confederacy in two. This strategy would have given the lead role to Grant's army instead of Buell's. The risk inherent in either strategy was that it would leave open middle Tennessee and Kentucky, all the way north to the Ohio River, to a potentially devastating counterstroke if the Confederates were so bold as to abandon their defensive strategy long enough to risk mounting an invasion of their own.

Quite naturally, the Confederates, too, were groping for a strategy after what had been for their western armies a season of unrelieved disaster—Forts Henry and Donelson, Pea Ridge, New Madrid, Island No. 10, more questionably, Shiloh, and lastly, the loss of Corinth. The first suggestion of a desire to escape from the straitjacket of a defensive strategy came from General E. Kirby Smith, who held Knoxville with an army of about twelve thousand. Facing him on the northeast was George Morgan at Cumberland Gap, and more menacing, he was threatened by the advance of Buell, which, though slowed to a snail's pace by the need to repair the Memphis & Charleston as he moved eastward, had reached Stevenson by mid-July. Kirby Smith now proposed to Bragg that they join forces for an attack on Buell. On the foundation of this suggestion, Bragg erected a more ambitious structure: to take the offensive against Buell, gain his rear, drive him out of, or force him to withdraw from, middle Tennessee, and then invade Kentucky.[14]

14. Horn, *Army of Tennessee*, 160, 163. The invasion of Kentucky was an expansion, decided upon by Bragg in early August, of the initial project, which did not go beyond driving the Federals out of middle Tennessee. But see Grady McWhiney, *Braxton Bragg and Confederate Defeat* (New York, 1969), 267, 273–74.

It is generally believed that an important factor leading to Bragg's decision to invade Kentucky was Morgan's highly colored claims of prosouthern sentiment in the state, but there is no precise evidence leading directly from Morgan's reports to Kirby Smith's and Bragg's plans. Nevertheless, Bragg's decision to take along twenty thousand muskets to arm the Kentuckians whom he expected to come forward to enlist in his army certainly suggests the influence of the kind of optimism Morgan was capable of generating within himself and of communicating to others.[15]

There was, however, a more concrete contribution than the spreading of an aura of optimism that Morgan was able to make in furtherance of the Bragg–Kirby Smith project. On August 11, after a conference with Kirby Smith, Morgan moved out from his camp at Sparta and the next evening reached Gallatin, Tennessee. After capturing the 375-man garrison without firing a shot, Morgan set about the objective of the expedition: the wrecking of the tunnel, eight hundred feet long, of the Louisville & Nashville Railroad. This he did so effectively that the railroad—Buell's lifeline for food for his men, feed for his animals, munitions, and other supplies of all kinds—remained blocked until December.[16]

Well before Morgan's tunnel-wrecking exploit, Buell and his staff had tried to find ways to use their cavalry more effectively. Inspired perhaps by the accomplishments of such officers as Sheridan, Elliott, and Granger, all of the Army of the Mississippi, they searched for an officer to supply the magic spark. Their choice fell upon Brigadier General Richard W. Johnson, a Kentuckian by birth, ranked thirtieth in the West Point Class of 1849, assigned to the infantry upon graduation, transferred to the 2nd United States in 1855, and transferred again, to the 5th United States as captain in August, 1861. Johnson had arranged to be transferred from the Regular Army to the volunteer service, and after a two-month tour of duty as lieutenant colonel of the 3rd Kentucky, he was promoted to brigadier general on October 11,

15. See Morgan's dispatch of July 16 from Georgetown, Kentucky, to Smith: "Lexington and Frankfort . . . are garrisoned chiefly with Home Guards. . . . The whole country can be secured, and 25,000 or 30,000 men will join you at once." *Official Records*, Vol. XVI, Pt. 2, pp. 733–34; see also McWhiney, *Braxton Bragg*, 273–74, and Brown, *The Bold Cavaliers*, 103–104.

16. For Morgan's tunnel-wrecking technique, see Starr, *Colonel Grenfell's Wars*, 74–75.

1861. On July 24, 1862, Johnson was directed to assume command of three regiments, the 1st and 2nd Kentucky and the 2nd Indiana, and "operate actively" against any rebel force he could find around Columbia, Tennessee, south of Nashville.[17]

The 1st Kentucky was in clover when Johnson assumed command of the three regiments. It had been attached to General Negley's division and, broken up into detachments, was guarding the line of the Central Alabama Railroad from Nashville down to the Alabama line, a distance of nearly eighty miles. The work was "arduous," but it had its compensations. The regiment, so its historian has recorded, "was making a practical study of almost the entire geography of middle Tennessee"; at the same time, however, Negley had the whole regiment supplied with badly needed new uniforms and nine of its companies (three companies already had Sharps' rifles) rearmed with carbines, revolvers, and sabers, as a replacement for the "clumsy musket" with which they had served for a year.[18]

There are no reports to shed light on Johnson's activities in the three weeks following his new assignment, but a dispatch of General Nelson's suggests that as late as August 15, the three regiments he was to unite had not yet been assembled. Then, on August 18, after word of Morgan's Gallatin raid had reached Buell's headquarters, "the whole cavalry force, not otherwise engaged," was placed under Johnson's command. The regiments thus disposed of were the 2nd, 4th, and 5th Kentucky, the 2nd Indiana, and the 7th Pennsylvania; for reasons unknown, the 1st Kentucky of the original three was omitted from the list. The words *brigade* and *division* were conspicuously absent from the order; it was apparently intended that Johnson command an informal grouping of the five regiments. Equally strange was the absence from these orders of directions to Johnson to go after Morgan; he was told instead to "keep concentrated as much as possible" and, basing himself on Murfreesboro, to "protect the line of communications of the army with Nashville . . . and destroy the enemy's cavalry and guerrillas." If, as suggested by the chronology, it was intended that Johnson go

17. Cullum, *Biographical Register*, II, 245–46; *Official Records*, Vol. XVI, Pt. 2, p. 208.

18. Tarrant, *Wild Riders of the First Kentucky*, 92, 99. The Kentuckians' need for uniforms is demonstrated by the description of the trooper who was spotted by General Buell himself, wearing a "slouch hat, hickory shirt, two linen breeches, home-made gallowses, and two immense Texas spurs on his naked heels." *Ibid.*, 109.

after Morgan, these orders were puzzling, inasmuch as Murfreesboro was twenty-five miles southeast of Nashville, whereas Gallatin, where Morgan's cavalry had last been heard from, was the same distance northeast of Nashville. Quite possibly it was Forrest's cavalry, and not Morgan's, that Johnson was intended to "destroy"; indeed, an August 18 telegram of Buell's to General Thomas expressed the fear that Forrest, with a superior force, might be in pursuit of Johnson. It may not be a coincidence, in any event, that for the next two days, Buell had to inquire of Generals Thomas and Nelson and Colonel William B. Hazen, located at McMinnville, Nashville, and Murfreesboro, respectively, if they had heard anything of Johnson or knew his whereabouts. [19]

What Johnson had actually done is difficult to square chronologically with Buell's orders to him. On August 11, a week before the above-quoted orders of the eighteenth, he had assembled at McMinnville, thirty-five miles southeast of Murfreesboro, a force of 640 mounted troops, taken from the 2nd Indiana, the 7th Pennsylvania, and the 4th and 5th Kentucky, and started off to look for Morgan "in or near Hartsville," some eighty-five miles away. [20] It is to be noted that for a week Johnson was out of touch with Buell's headquarters, and they with him; on no other theory can one understand how the August 18 orders could have been issued to him. It is to be noted also that to assemble a force of 640 men, not much larger than the numbers of a single regiment after two or three months of active service, Johnson had to draw upon four regiments; the men selected were presumably the best armed and best mounted in their respective regiments.

On the morning of August 21, Johnson marched out from Hartsville in the direction of Gallatin to fight Morgan, at the same time that Morgan, with eight hundred men, marched out of Gallatin toward Hartsville to find Johnson. [21] When the forces came in sight of each other, Morgan would have preferred not to fight the Federals, but Basil Duke persuaded him to give battle. As nearly as can be determined, through a more than commonly impenetrable fog of war, the Confederates, most of whom Duke had ordered to dismount and take post

19. *Official Records*, Vol. XVI, Pt. 2, pp. 361, 364, 367, 371, 376, 379.
20. *Ibid.*, Pt. 1, p. 871. Another report gives Johnson's numbers as "some 767 men." *Ibid.*, 877.
21. Brown, *The Bold Cavaliers*, 111. There is a story, which may or may not be authentic, that on the day before his fight with Morgan, while having dinner in a Hartsville hotel, Johnson remarked that he would "catch Morgan and bring him back in a bandbox."

behind a roadside fence that gave them all the protection of the breastworks that became typical later in the war, were charged by the Federals with the saber across an open meadow three hundred yards across, wide enough to give Duke's men plenty of time to take good aim at the onrushing horsemen. Their first volley "seemed" to bring down two-thirds of the attackers and their horses. The survivors retreated to the far end of the meadow and, with far greater gallantry than good sense, charged again. The results were equally disastrous for the Federals; this time, facing the fire of the dismounted men behind their fence and attacked in flank by small bodies of mounted troops Duke had posted on the two wings of his line, they broke, and with organization lost, "at least half" of the survivors "precipitately fled, throwing away their arms, &c." Johnson succeeded in halting his men after a disorderly retreat of about three miles and formed a none-too-firm defensive line to face the pursuing enemy, but as Lieutenant Colonel Robert R. Stewart of the 2nd Indiana reported, the 5th Kentucky (presumably what was left of it), "in a style of confusion more complete than the flight of stampeded buffaloes," came crashing through the line and further disorganized it. With only seventy-five of the survivors left to him, the rest having "fled in every direction," Johnson surrendered.[22]

If the account of the battle by one of the officers of the 7th Pennsylvania is to be believed, Johnson used an outlandish tactical expedient in this battle. He ordered that regiment and the 2nd Indiana "to dismount, and *leading their horses,* to advance and engage the enemy with their revolvers! The movement was attempted, but failed, as its folly demanded it should."[23]

When he wrote his history of Morgan's command, General Duke tried to explain Johnson's defeat. He had no criticism of the Union rank and file. "They had been selected with great care from all the cavalry of Buell's army," he wrote, and when ordered to charge the dismounted enemy lined up behind their fence, did so "with spirit and without hesitation." As to the unfortunate Johnson, Duke had nothing but praise for his dispositions and for his "fine personal courage and

22. For Johnson's report, see *Official Records*, Vol. XVI, Pt. 1, pp. 871–73. See also the reports of Lieutenant Colonel R. R. Stewart, 2nd Indiana, Colonel George C. Wynkoop, 7th Pennsylvania, and Morgan, in *Ibid.*, 875–76, 877–78, and 879–81. See also *Ibid.*, 873. Morgan claimed that Johnson lost "some 180" killed and wounded, and 200 prisoners; his own losses he gave as 5 killed, 18 wounded, and 2 missing.
23. Vale, *Minty and the Cavalry*, 90.

energy," assuredly highly desirable qualities in a commander of cavalry. What then went wrong? General Duke thought he recognized Johnson's error. In the initial charge he ordered, his men could neither reach Duke's dismounted men with their sabers nor could they use their carbines. Johnson, in General Duke's opinion, "was evidently a fine officer, but seemed not to comprehend the 'new style of cavalry' at all."[24] The "new style of cavalry" General Duke spoke of was dismounted cavalry posted behind even minimum protection, making effective use of their firepower and their ability, given a field of fire of reasonable depth, to break up a saber charge before it could reach them.

There was another factor, not adverted to in Duke's comments on the fight, that contributed to Johnson's defeat. A command hastily thrown together, made up of men from a number of separate and independent organizations, cannot have the cohesion of a body of officers and men accustomed to working together; the element of mutual confidence, of support when needed taken for granted, is necessarily lacking. There was no need for this all-important factor in the excitement of the initial charges. But it became essential, and its absence fatal, after the charges had been repelled, and the Federals, their ranks riddled by casualties, had to reorganize on the defensive and withstand the attacks of a well led and aggressive enemy.[25]

Long before Morgan's Gallatin exploit, Buell had been complaining about his shortage of mounted troops. He wrote Secretary Stanton on May 12, "There is great and immediate need of more cavalry in Ken-

24. For General Duke's account of the fight, see his *History of Morgan's Cavalry*, 218–24. The account of the action in Vale, *Minty and the Cavalry*, 83–94 (the author was himself wounded and taken prisoner in the fight), is at variance at every point with Duke's and, for the most part, with the Federal reports. Vale is bitterly critical of Johnson: "He may have been a good infantry general, but certainly was utterly incompetent as a commander of cavalry." Vale's errors in identifying the Union regiments present and his more than doubling the numbers present on both sides, however, greatly weaken the reliability of his account.

25. In his report to Halleck of Johnson's defeat, Buell wrote: "The disaster is most unfortunate, as it costs us the services of a valuable officer and a large part of the small cavalry force I have. I was apprehensive that his force was insufficient, and sent instructions to him to strengthen himself with artillery and infantry and keep more within support." *Official Records*, Vol. XVI, Pt. 2, p. 387; see also *Ibid.*, 349. Such instructions, becoming common knowledge among the cavalry rank and file, were not likely to increase their self-confidence or their self-respect.

tucky and Tennessee. The warfare has already assumed a guerrilla character in Tennessee and it is to be renewed in Kentucky by marauding bands organized in the State, assisted by a few rebel troops. Kentucky ought to have at least three more regiments and Tennessee two more, if they can be spared from the East. I would recommend that they be sent immediately."[26]

Buell was told that the War Department "had no mounted cavalry at its disposal" but that new levies, part of which were destined for Kentucky and Tennessee, were being made.[27] This exchange occurred as Buell was complaining to Halleck that his cavalry force was limited, that the "little cavalry" he had in Tennessee was "broken down by constant hard work," and he begged for the return of a single regiment, the 1st Ohio, that Pope had "detained."[28] There were those who thought that lack of numbers was not the only source of Buell's difficulties; that, indeed, they were of his own making. In one cavalry veteran's opinion, Buell had "frittered away" his cavalry before Shiloh by attaching it by regiments to divisions of infantry, and when he tried to deal with Morgan's and Forrest's raid by organizing "independent cavalry commands," it was discovered that "the regiments had been demoralized by the character of their service, the officers selected to command were wanting in capacity, and the improvised brigades were powerless."[29] Nevertheless, Buell repeated to Stanton his plea for more cavalry; he telegraphed him on July 18, "The necessity for an increase in our cavalry force is imperative, and time is important." He reminded Halleck the same day that he had previously asked without success for eight more regiments of cavalry and that, with four hundred miles of railroad behind him to protect, he had to have sufficient mounted troops of his own to be able to cope with the swarms of enemy cavalry.[30]

Buell's subordinates, too, were pleading for more mounted troops. Ormsby Mitchel, who had the 4th Ohio attached to his division, reported after he entered Florence, Alabama, that his "great deficiency in cavalry had permitted the enemy to escape." General Morgan, at Cumberland Gap, wrote that he knew his line of communications to be

26. *Ibid.*, Vol. X, Pt. 2, p. 183.
27. *Ibid.*, 203.
28. *Ibid.*, Vol. XVI, Pt. 2, p. 9.
29. Harris, "The Union Cavalry," 351–52.
30. *Official Records*, Vol. XVI, Pt. 2, pp. 177, 360.

in danger, but having failed to get action on his request for two cavalry regiments to guard the line from Louisville to Nashville and two more between Lexington and Cumberland Gap, he was "powerless" to do anything about it.[31] From Columbia, Tennessee, General Negley reported that his cavalry was "insufficient to do the required patrolling and efficiently guard bridges and railroads." The same tale came from William Nelson at Murfreesboro; he professed to be able to "stop Morgan and Forrest" if he could have the cavalry he needed.[32]

Nelson's claim was doubly significant because John Morgan was not the only Confederate cavalryman making a name for himself in these summer months of 1862. Nathan Bedford Forrest was doing the same, with an exploit more meaningful militarily than Morgan's more showy feats. A wound Forrest received on April 8, while operating against the futile Federal pursuit after Shiloh, was sufficiently serious to immobilize any ordinary individual for months. Forrest, however, was back in action three weeks later, with a Federal bullet embedded in his back near his spine. Sent to Chattanooga and given command of a group of odds and ends of cavalry units to assemble into a brigade, he got his new command organized and on July 9 took it on a raid into middle Tennessee. At dawn on the thirteenth, he attacked Murfreesboro, the largest of Buell's posts guarding the Nashville & Chattanooga Railroad. Forrest's attack caught the garrison by surprise. Nevertheless, some units put up a stout fight, which he overcame with a "rare mixture of military skill . . . and bluff," and at the end of the day he had nearly 1,200 prisoners (including most of the men of four companies of the 7th Pennsylvania), artillery, a train of wagons with their teams and harness, and "a considerable quantity of much-needed cavalry equipment and small arms."[33] Colonel William B. Sipes of the 7th

31. *Ibid.*, Vol. X, Pt. 2, p. 206; Vol. XVI, Pt. 2, p. 150; see also *Ibid.*, Vol. X, Pt. 2, pp. 181, 182. In another dispatch, sent the same day as the one quoted, Morgan wrote Secretary Stanton: "I again respectfully state that my command is powerless from want of cavalry. . . . The enemy's cavalry is destroying everything in front and I have not the means to pursue it." *Ibid.*, Vol. XVI, Pt. 2, p. 150.

32. *Ibid.*, Vol. XVI, Pt. 2, pp. 173, 213.

33. Henry, *"First with the Most" Forrest*, 90; *Official Records*, Vol. X, Pt. 2, p. 602, Vol. XVI, Pt. 1, pp. 795, 798, 801, 810. Forrest claimed to have "captured the pickets without firing a gun," but Major J. J. Seibert, 7th Pennsylvania, reported that on the orders of Colonel Henry C. Lester, 3rd Minnesota Infantry, (who was dismissed from the service later in the year), five-man cavalry patrols were sent out every morning on each of the roads leading into the town, though no pickets were posted at night. *Official Records*, Vol. XVI, Pt. 1, p. 798. See also E. W. Sheppard, *Bedford Forrest: The Confederacy's Greatest Cavalryman* (Toronto, 1930), 65–66.

Pennsylvania remarked of Forrest's success at Murfreesboro: "The moral effect of this reverse was great, and for a time, demoralized the Union cause in middle Tennessee. The 7th felt the consequences in the depression that always followed defeat."[34] It will be noted that four companies only of the Pennsylvania regiment were at Murfreesboro; just the day before Forrest's attack, Buell had ordered the regiment divided between Murfreesboro, Nashville, Tullahoma, and Cowan.[35]

The detailed plans Generals Kirby Smith and Bragg worked out after they had agreed to collaborate in a campaign to eliminate the Federal threat to Chattanooga and east Tennessee required that Bragg move the bulk of his forces from Tupelo to Chattanooga. With the Memphis & Charleston Railroad, the only reasonably direct connection between the two towns, in Buell's possession, Bragg got his nearly 30,000 infantry (his cavalry and artillery marched by road) to Chattanooga by rail by sending them south to Mobile, then northeast via Montgomery to Atlanta, and thence northwest to Chattanooga, a roundabout journey of nearly eight hundred miles, making use of six railroads.[36] The original intention of the two generals was to join their forces for an invasion of middle Tennessee so as to get in Buell's rear, thereby cutting him off from his base at Nashville, which would force him to retreat north to Kentucky. But (and it is at this point that Morgan's eloquence may have influenced the course of events) Kirby Smith decided on a change: to mask and flank the Federal forces at Cumberland Gap and with the bulk of his army to invade Kentucky as far north as Lexington. Accordingly, he left Knoxville on August 14; on the thirtieth, at Richmond, Kentucky, he defeated and scattered to the four winds the army of green, untrained recruits commanded by William Nelson, whom Buell had sent north two weeks before to organize the defenses of Ken-

34. Sipes, *The Seventh Pennsylvania*, 19. The comment of Lieutenant Joseph Vale of the Pennsylvania regiment was even stronger; the Murfreesboro affair, he wrote, had "a demoralizing influence on the Seventh, almost destroyed the organization of the Third battalion, and for a time effaced the confidence infused in the regiment by the affair at Lebanon." Vale, *Minty and the Cavalry*, 78. "Many" of the Pennsylvanians were killed, wounded, or captured in their tents by the initial charge of the 18th Texas of Forrest's brigade, but 70 of them made their escape when Colonel Lester decided to surrender the garrison. Vale, *Minty and the Cavalry*, 75, 78.

35. *Official Records*, Vol. XVI, Pt. 2, p. 130.

36. McWhiney, *Braxton Bragg*, 268; Thomas L. Connelly, *Army of the Heartland: The Army of Tennessee, 1861–1862* (Baton Rouge, 1967), 203–204.

tucky.[37] On September 2, Kirby Smith entered Lexington, and there he remained for the rest of the month, waiting for Bragg, sending his cavalry meanwhile on raids in the direction of Cincinnati and Louisville.

Bragg had to change his plans when Kirby Smith, who as a department commander was not under his control, modified his. He set off on August 28 with upwards of 30,000 men in the direction of Louisville, planning so to regulate his march as to keep his army between Kirby-Smith at Lexington and Buell, who was expected to march north as soon as he had word of the Confederates' invasion of Kentucky. The northward progress of Bragg's and Buell's armies developed into a kind of footrace that Buell won, marching into Louisville on September 26.[38] Without question, Bragg should have been there before Buell, with incalculably serious consequences for the Union. It must not be forgotten that Bragg was "redeeming" Kentucky at the same time that General Lee was "redeeming" Maryland; consequently, and on the heels of Second Bull Run, Washington was in no position to rush troops from the East to Kentucky to help deal with Bragg and Kirby Smith. Whether Bragg *could* have been in Louisville before Buell or should have fought Buell at Bowling Green are much debated subjects, outside the scope of the present study.[39]

Bragg reached Glasgow, Kentucky, on his way north, on September 14. After a two-day rest, and preceded by Forrest's cavalry, he moved on toward the crossing of the Green River at Munfordville. A well-sited fort, manned by 4,000 infantry commanded by one of the most engagingly unconventional officers in the Union army, Colonel John T. Wilder of Indiana, guarded the crossing. Then followed the immortal

37. On the entire campaign, see Connelly, *Army of the Heartland*, 211–342. Nelson lost 206 killed, 844 wounded, and 4,303 captured or missing, plus 9 guns, 10,000 stand of rifles, and all his trains. Horn, *Army of Tennessee*, 164.

38. Buell had advance notice of Bragg's intentions. On July 27, Sheridan, whose brigade, reinforced by the 7th Kansas, was in camp at Rienzi, sent Colonel Hatch with the 2nd Iowa and the 7th Kansas to "cripple, if not capture" the Confederate outpost at Ripley. Hatch succeeded in driving the enemy out of Ripley (this was the occasion when, as mentioned previously, the two regiments got out of hand and plundered the town); one of their captures was a bundle of thirty-two private letters, doubtless taken from the post office, which disclosed that most of Bragg's army was being moved to Chattanooga. Sheridan at once grasped the significance of the information and sent the letters on to Granger, who presumably forwarded the letters or the information to Buell. Sheridan, *Personal Memoirs*, I, 171–72; *Official Records*, Vol. XVII, Pt. 2, pp. 91, 94.

39. Don C. Seitz, *Braxton Bragg: General of the Confederacy* (Columbia, S.C., 1924), 178–79; Horn, *Army of Tennessee*, 170–72; McWhiney, *Braxton Bragg*, 286–92.

episode in which Colonel Wilder, summoned to surrender to an overwhelming force by which he was surrounded and, as a mere volunteer, unsure of what military tradition and protocol required in such circumstances, took counsel with General Simon Bolivar Buckner of Bragg's army, confident that as a former Regular and a Kentuckian, Buckner would advise him correctly. Having satisfied himself by means of a guided tour of the Confederate army, as suggested by Buckner, that he was indeed surrounded by forces too large for him to be able to resist, he surrendered.[40]

Nothing of note was done by the Union cavalry in the Bragg–Kirby Smith invasion of Kentucky. Most of the cavalry Buell had left that was in a condition to fight after Johnson's defeat had to remain behind to guard the Nashville-Murfreesboro area and the railroad to the north. The "Light Brigade," a part-infantry, part-cavalry unit, the establishment of which has been mentioned, had been given the mission of "either destroying or driving off the cavalry under Morgan and Forrest." It now went into the discard after a mere one week of existence, and Buell ordered the organization of a cavalry division of two brigades, the First, under Colonel Edward M. McCook, consisting of the 2nd Indiana, the 1st, 3rd, and 4th Kentucky, and one battalion of the 7th Pennsylvania; the Second, under Colonel Lewis Zahm, of the 5th Kentucky and the 3rd and 4th Ohio. The whole was, from September 5 on, under the command of Colonel John Kennett.[41] In Kentucky, General Boyle was busy raising the additional cavalry he had been authorized to enlist in response to Morgan's raid into the state, and kept the wires to Washington humming with pleas for weapons and equipment for the men who were coming in. In one of his telegrams he complained that the Gallagher carbines he had been furnished were not "equal to a bar of iron"; in another, he repeated Buell's suggestion that he arm his cavalry recruits with shotguns, reported that he had none, and asked if they could be supplied to him by the ordnance people.[42]

40. Horn, *Army of Tennessee*, 168–69; but see *Official Records*, Vol. XVI, Pt. 2, p. 534. Four days before the entire Confederate army was in position before Munfordville, Colonel John C. Scott, 1st Louisiana, commanding Kirby Smith's advance, summoned Wilder to surrender. Wilder "peremptorily refused" and told Scott he would "fight anything that comes." *Official Records*, Vol. XVI, Pt. 2, p. 518.

41. For the organization of the "Light Brigade," see fn. 67, p. 23, above. *Official Records*, Vol. XVI, Pt. 2, pp. 430, 431, 438, 584.

42. *Ibid.*, 230, 254, 273, 343. At one point Boyle claimed: "I could put in the field

At some time near the end of September, General Ebenezer Gay was appointed chief of cavalry of Buell's department.[43] The October 1 returns, however, indicated a revival in the department of the old vice of scattering the cavalry, notwithstanding the organization in the previous month of John Kennett's cavalry division. Four companies of cavalry were now reported to be with Buell's Second Division, six with the Third, four with the Fourth, six with the Fifth, and five each with the Seventh and Eighth. It will be noted that none of the cavalry was assigned in regimental strength, compounding the vice of scattering. Buell also had six companies of cavalry at Nashville, and 1,296 of his mounted troops were "unattached." With the 3,032, rank and file, in Kennett's division, Buell had what would have been a mounted force of respectable size—about 7,000 men—and perhaps too of respectable effectiveness, had it been properly organized and led. But the absence of effective organization was not General Gay's only problem. He wrote that he had to estimate the numbers of his command, in the absence of the mandatory "morning reports" that he had failed to receive, inasmuch as "some of the regiments do not know what a morning report is, never having heard of such a thing, or a roll call."[44] Two of his regiments, the 9th Pennsylvania and the 2nd Michigan (the latter reduced to 300, rank and file), General Gay thought could be "depended upon"; the rest, the 6th, 7th, 9th, and 11th Kentucky and the 4th Indiana, had "never been drilled at all and . . . [were] perfectly raw."[45] Gay considered that if these regiments could have a few days' rest, he could "do a great deal toward organizing, arming and instructing them," but with the regiments "on constant duty nearly all the time," he had been unable to accomplish much toward improving them.

Bragg's proceedings in Kentucky following his capture of Munfordville make a fine cautionary tale for the instruction of army commanders but lie outside the scope of the present study. Buell's aggressive instincts were restored, and his numbers were greatly increased

---

4,800 cavalry if I had the arms. I have armed one regiment with Enfield rifles and American muskets. There are no arms except Prussian guns and some pistols." *Ibid.*, 301.

43. General Gay was a Regular, a captain in the 16th United States Infantry. His and other reports (for example, *Ibid.*, Pt. 1, p. 1037) indicate that, unlike the general run of chiefs of cavalry, he had command authority as well as administrative responsibilities.

44. *Ibid.*, Pt. 2, pp. 562–64. On ten companies of cavalry in his command, Gay had no information whatever. To arrive at the figure of 7,000, we have assumed that these ten companies had a strength equal to the average of the companies whose strength Gay was able to estimate.

45. *Ibid.*, 552–53.

after his safe arrival in Louisville, and he went over to the offensive. Bragg, on the other hand, after acting as master of ceremonies at the inauguration in Frankfort of Richard C. Hawes as governor of the non-existent Confederate Commonwealth of Kentucky, began to assemble his forces, and with nearly all the twenty thousand muskets with which he was to arm the Kentuckians who were expected to hasten to enlist in his army still in his wagons, he set off on his return march to Tennessee.[46]

The rear of Bragg's forces as he marched southward was protected by his cavalry, commanded by Colonel (later General) Joseph Wheeler of Georgia. Graduated nineteenth in the tiny twenty-two-man West Point Class of 1859, Wheeler was serving as a second lieutenant in the Regiment of Mounted Riflemen when the war broke out.[47] He resigned, joined the Confederate army, and was commanding an Alabama infantry regiment when, on September 14, 1862, he was called to the command of one of the two brigades of Bragg's cavalry and given the mission of operating on the left wing (nearest Buell) of Bragg's advance into Kentucky; Forrest, given command of the other brigade, operated on Bragg's right wing. On September 25, Forrest was sent back to middle Tennessee with orders to raise a new command and operate against the forces of General Negley, which Buell had left behind, by "cutting off supplies, capturing trains, and harassing them in all ways practicable"—in other words, by means of partisan warfare. With Forrest's former brigade added to the brigade he already had, Wheeler now had command of all the cavalry of Bragg's and Kirby Smith's armies, informally at first, and formally, as chief of cavalry, from October 13 on. This was not the mere administrative position held by nearly all chiefs of cavalry in both the Union and the Confederate armies at this stage of the war; the October 13 order that gave Wheeler the post authorized him "to give orders in the name of the commanding general" and directed that "all cavalry will report to him and receive his orders."[48] On the strength of these orders Wheeler began to refer to his command as the "Cavalry Corps."[49]

46. Connelly, *Army of the Heartland*, 273. Bragg wrote his wife that half the Kentuckians who enlisted (and whom he had presumably armed) had deserted. McWhiney, *Braxton Bragg*, 322.

47. Cullum, *Biographical Register*, II, 492.

48. Henry, *"First with the Most" Forrest*, 99, 102; *Battles and Leaders*, III, 17.

49. *Official Records*, Vol. XVI, Pt. 2, pp. 939–40. For Morgan's behavior and his absence from the rear guard on the retreat from Kentucky, see Starr, *Colonel Grenfell's Wars*, 80–81.

Except for one exploit, to be described in its proper place, Wheeler was not the equal of Forrest or even of the erratic Morgan as a leader of partisan cavalry. But when the occasion called for the use of cavalry in its traditional roles as the eyes of the army in an advance or as protection for its rear on a retreat, Wheeler could be relied upon to perform ably all that was expected of him. In Bragg's and Kirby Smith's retreat to Tennessee, with 3,000 men in his command, he covered the march of the two armies on two separate roads and provided escorts for Kirby Smith's train of 4,000 wagons, a long caravan of refugees, and a herd of 2,000 beef cattle.[50]

The autumn of 1862 was a season of an exceptionally severe drought in Kentucky. On the night of October 7, Gay's brigade of about 1,450 cavalry, made up of the 9th Pennsylvania, the 2nd Michigan, and the 5th Kentucky, leading Buell's advance, had a severe tussle in the darkness with Wheeler's horsemen, both sides trying to gain access to the only available water in the area, "the precious pools" in the nearly dry bed of Doctor's Creek, near the village of Perryville.[51] At daylight the next day, Gay moved forward and collided almost immediately with Confederate infantry in position and ready to contest his advance.[52] Checked by the enemy fire and forced on the defensive, Gay's troopers, particularly the men from Michigan with their Colt revolving rifles, broke up two or three charges that the enemy infantry launched against them.[53] Thereafter, the Union cavalry played a minimal role in the battle, which resulted in a tactical victory for the greatly outnumbered Confederates at a cost of 3,396 casualties, the Union casualties being 4,348.[54]

50. John W. DuBose, *General Joseph Wheeler and the Army of Tennessee* (New York, 1912), 105; Horn, *Army of Tennessee*, 188. On roads perfectly dry, the heavily loaded wagons averaged a mere five miles per day. *Battles and Leaders*, III, 18.

51. Horn, *Army of Tennessee*, 182; *Official Records*, Vol. XVI, Pt. 1, p. 1037. At the start of the campaign, the 9th Pennsylvania had 41 Sharps' and 13 Maynard carbines. The other approximately 450 men then in the regiment had only revolvers and sabers. Rowell, *Yankee Cavalrymen*, 85.

52. General Wheeler tells a different story. He states that *his* cavalry "was pressed forward at dawn on the 8th, and skirmished with the outposts of the enemy, until, on the approach of a Federal brigade of cavalry supported by infantry . . . [his own cavalry] charged, dispersing the cavalry, and, breaking through both infantry and cavalry, drove the enemy from their guns and took 140 prisoners." *Battles and Leaders*, III, 15.

53. Rowell, *Yankee Cavalrymen*, 89. The Union cavalry casualties, nearly all of the 2nd Michigan, were 4 killed and 17 wounded. *Official Records*, Vol. XVI, Pt. 1, p. 1036.

54. *Battles and Leaders*, III, 17.

On the Confederate side at Perryville, the cavalry of General John A. Wharton (who had succeeded Forrest as brigade commander) protected the right flank, and Wheeler the left. When in the afternoon the Confederates launched their full-scale attack, aimed at the Union left, their advance was led by Wharton's cavalrymen.[55] The Confederate left, including Wheeler's brigade, had little to do in the battle, but Wheeler's performance of his duties in the campaign as a whole caused Bragg to send him, a few days after the battle, his "most cordial thanks and congratulations" and to tell him that "no cavalry force was ever more handsomely handled and no army better covered."[56] No Federal cavalryman had been able to stake out a claim to a similar congratulatory letter from Buell. Gay had performed creditably with his three regiments at Doctor's Creek on the night of the seventh; aside from that, there was only one entry on the credit side for the Union cavalry, a minor triumph for the 2nd Indiana of Kennett's division just before Bragg began his retreat. Led by Lieutenant Colonel Stewart, at Elizabethtown, Kentucky, on September 29 the Hoosiers "surprised and captured the 3d Georgia at break of day, surrounded them, and captured the entire regiment, without the loss of a man or firing a single shot." Unlike many such reports, this one was evidently factual, for later in the year the commanding officer of the Georgia regiment was court-martialed and "sentenced to three months' suspension from rank and pay and to be reprimanded in orders by the general commanding."[57] On the other side of the coin of merit was a report by Colonel Hazen, who came up with the Confederate retreat after Perryville at Danville, Kentucky, and found the southerners drawn up in line of battle. He engaged them with the infantry of his brigade and praised their good conduct in his report, but not so the behavior of the two

55. On the battle of Perryville, see McWhiney, *Braxton Bragg*, 312–20; Connelly, *Army of the Heartland*, 262–66; Horn, *Army of Tennessee*, 180–86. An exceptionally interesting account of, and comments on, the battle and the campaign as a whole are in Duke, *Reminiscences*, 302–28.

56. DuBose, *General Joseph Wheeler*, 101. T. F. Thiele has expressed the opinion, with which the present writer agrees, that "of all the cavalry leaders in the period 1861–1863, Wheeler was undoubtedly the master of covering a retreat." Thiele, "The Evolution of Cavalry," 520.

57. *Official Records*, Vol. XVI, Pt. 2, pp. 1016, 1017. Also, on October 3, near Shepherdsville, Kentucky, Colonel Minor Milliken, with the 1st Ohio, trapped and captured 22 officers and men of the 6th Confederate (Regular) Cavalry, complete with their horses ("some of them good") and arms. *Ibid.*, Pt. 1, pp. 1018–19.

companies of the 1st Kentucky that led his advance. "At the first discharge of the enemy," he reported, the Kentuckians "retreated in disorder some half mile to a piece of wood and were with difficulty found."[58]

John Morgan's return to Tennessee "on his own hook" took him
past the rear of Buell's army and considerably west of the route followed by Bragg and Kirby Smith.[59] At first, the Federals thought he
was aiming for the Ohio River (he did, in fact, return north as far as
Lexington), and General A. J. Smith, eager to take off after him, wired
General Horatio G. Wright in Cincinnati, "O, a kingdom for four regiments of cavalry!" Needless to say, General Smith did not get the four
regiments. When Morgan's actual route was discovered—he was
marching south by way of Lawrenceburg and Bardstown—Gay, whose
brigade had evidently left Buell's army after Perryville, was asked to try
to intercept him. Colonel Minor Milliken, 1st Ohio, who commanded
the "Third Cavalry Brigade," which now makes a brief appearance,
was apparently given similar orders. Neither Gay nor Milliken succeeded in catching Morgan, who, after causing a modest amount of
damage, returned safely to Tennessee. Colonel Milliken thought it
necessary to excuse his lack of success and to explain the "somewhat
unintelligible and apparently unreasonable movements" of his brigade
with the claim that he had received no information or suggestions
from General Gay or anyone else. He went on to imply that it would
have done little good even if he had had proper guidance, because he
would have been unable to give Morgan a fight with the mere 575
"seasoned troops" of the 1st Ohio and the 1st Kentucky and the 600
"green troops, never under fire," of the 4th Michigan that made up his
brigade.[60]

Before considering cavalry operations in western Tennessee and
northwestern Mississippi in this eventful autumn of 1862, it will be of
interest to examine two raids at the year end, the first by the Union
cavalry under Brigadier General Samuel P. Carter, the other by the
Confederate cavalry under John Morgan.

58. *Ibid.*, Pt. 1, p. 1137. Not surprisingly, this incident is not mentioned in the regimental history.

59. See fn. 49, p. 91, above.

60. *Official Records*, Vol. XVI, Pt. 2, pp. 633, 647. There is a conflict of evidence on
the "greenness" of the 4th Michigan. The regimental historian states that the regiment
had had a brisk fight with Morgan on October 10 at Stanford, Kentucky. Vale, *Minty and
the Cavalry*, 100. It is of interest that the regiment, down to 600 men capable of making
a campaign in mid-October, had left Michigan 1,253 strong "fully armed, mounted and
equipped" on September 26. Vale, *Minty and the Cavalry*, 98.

Carter, who was now about to lead the first long-distance raid staged by the Union cavalry, an operation obviously inspired by Forrest's and Morgan's exploits in that line, was, like William Nelson, a navy lieutenant who had decided to do his fighting in the Civil War on dry land.[61] The forces for his raid were to consist of two battalions of the 2nd Michigan, one battalion of the 7th Ohio, and all of the 9th Pennsylvania, a disappointingly small (in Carter's opinion) total of 980 men, "a considerable portion [of whom] were in the field for the first time." This "considerable portion" could only have been the 230 men of the 7th Ohio, a quarter of the force.

The idea of the Carter raid came from General Granger, who had been promoted from his cavalry command to the command of the Army of Kentucky.[62] The purpose of the raid was to break the line of the East Tennessee & Virginia Railroad, a link in the chain of rail lines forming the most direct connection between the Confederacy's Atlantic coast and the West. If Granger, Carter, or anyone else had any misgivings about the hazards of an expedition launched in late December across a nearly trackless, practically uninhabited wilderness of mountains, they do not appear in the records.[63]

The raiders set out from Nicholasville, Kentucky, on December 20 with a few wagons loaded with rations, and a single howitzer; tents were left behind. Three days later, the rations were transferred from the wagons to pack mules. On December 26, the raiders' route lay in the steep-sided, narrow Red Bird Valley, on a trail—not a road—that followed what little level ground there was along the stream that zig-

61. Carter's grandfather was a pioneer in the area the grandson was about to invade. Samuel Carter attended Princeton for three years before his appointment to the Naval Academy, from which he graduated in 1846. After service in the navy afloat and at the Naval Academy as professor of mathematics, he was detailed in 1861 to the War Department and sent to organize Union volunteers in east Tennessee. He was made a brigadier general in 1862. Allen Johnson and Dumas Malone (eds.), *Dictionary of American Biography* (10 vols.; New York, 1957–58), II, Pt. 1, pp. 543–44. Cited hereinafter as *DAB*.

62. In his congratulatory telegram to Carter after the raid, Halleck called the operation "without a parallel in the history of the war" and proof of "the capacity of our cavalry for bold and dashing movements which I doubt not will be imitated by others." Quoted in Rowell, *Yankee Cavalrymen*, 95.

63. The only caveat was expressed by Rosecrans, who wrote General Wright: "I fear your expedition is too slight and feeble. . . . Can't you send more?" Wright replied: "The force is not only all I can spare, but I have already weakened too much the cavalry on your line of communication. . . . Granger has not, at this moment, 500 mounted men left." *Official Records*, Vol. XX, Pt. 2, p. 207.

zagged down the valley, first on one side and then on the other, necessitating forty-seven crossings of the stream. On the evening of the twenty-seventh the raiders crossed Pine Mountain, near Harlan, Kentucky, "marching single file along an old Indian trail." Late on the afternoon of December 28, they were at the northern foot of Cumberland Mountain, at Crank's Gap. Here the horses had their last full feed and the men their last hot food. The remaining rations—a scant day's feed for the horses and six days' half rations for the men—were issued, and the mule train was left behind.

Carter planned to reach the railroad where it crossed the triangular corner of Tennessee that separates Virginia and North Carolina, east of the main chain of the Alleghenies. The march to reach the railroad was unavoidably slow, as Carter explained, "owing to the roughness and narrowness of the roads (being mere bridle-paths along the banks of creeks and over steep and rugged mountains.)" He did, however, reach the railroad on the thirtieth at Union (now Bluff City), Tennessee, and with considerable difficulty, destroyed the rain-soaked covered bridge on which the tracks crossed the south fork of the Holston River, "a fine structure some 600 feet in length," as well as a wagon bridge near it. While this was being done, the 9th Pennsylvania was ordered forward to Carter's Depot, ten miles to the south, to destroy the three-hundred-foot railroad bridge at Watauga; for good measure, the depot building and "a large number of arms and valuable stores" were also destroyed. For entertainment, the Pennsylvanians ran a locomotive they had captured on the march to Carter's Depot onto the blazing bridge; it crashed through the fire-weakened timbers, taking with it what was left of the bridge as well as one of its piers.

Having accomplished his mission, Carter started for home. Other than bushwhackers (or partisan rangers) firing at them from the wooded hillsides, the raiders' only problems were hunger and the giving out of their horses. Although they appropriated "almost every serviceable horse on the route," many of them were marching along on foot, and all of them were half-starved, on January 8, when they reached a train of wagons carrying rations that had been sent forward to meet them.[64]

General Carter submitted a soberly factual report on his expedition,

64. *Ibid.*, Pt. 1, pp. 88–91. For details not in Carter's formal report, see the excellent description of the raid in Rowell, *Yankee Cavalrymen*, 95–109.

making no claims beyond what he actually accomplished. It is interesting nonetheless to have a report on the raid from a Confederate source. Major Isaac B. Dunn wrote a friend in Richmond:

The damage is small; nothing was interrupted except to take all the horses, watches, &c., of loyal citizens . . . destroy two bridges (worth probably $50,000 to construct them), with small amount of stores at each place, and . . . one . . . engine, run into the river at Watauga. The greatest injury is the confidence afforded to the Union sentiment in East Tennessee, for already they have commenced bushwhacking in Carter County, and several persons have been killed. . . . Our people are disappointed, for they see, with ample force in our midst, a Yankee army can invade us with impunity.[65]

It will be recalled that on September 25, Forrest was ordered to return to middle Tennessee to raise a new command for himself. In less than a month he was at the head of a cavalry brigade of four regiments. These regiments, and their commanding officers, all of whom will be heard of hereafter, were James W. Starnes's 4th Tennessee, George G. Dibrell's 8th Tennessee, Jacob B. Biffle's 9th Tennessee, and Alfred A. Russell's 4th Alabama.[66] Morgan, too, was back in middle Tennessee; he reached Gallatin on November 4 and was received by his friends there "with the warmest welcome."[67] On the very next day, on the orders of General John C. Breckinridge, who was occupying Murfreesboro with a small force, Forrest and Morgan staged a joint raid against Nashville, held by General Negley. The Louisville & Nashville Railroad was out of operation because of the blockage of the tunnel at Gallatin and the burning of a number of bridges by Morgan on the march he had just completed. As a result, about three hundred empty freight cars had accumulated in the yards at Edgefield, across the Cumberland River from Nashville. The plan for the joint Forrest-Morgan raid was that Forrest was to make a mock attack on Nashville with the greatest possible amount of noise; taking advantage of the distraction

65. *Official Records*, Vol. XX, Pt. 1, pp. 130–31.
66. Henry, *"First with the Most" Forrest*, 104. Basil Duke speaks of the organization of another 9th Tennessee Cavalry, which joined Morgan when he returned to Gallatin, and "became subsequently one of the very best in Morgan's command." Duke, *History of Morgan's Cavalry*, 294–95. Either R. S. Henry or General Duke has misnumbered the regiment or, what is more likely, each of the regiments was organized, and numbered in ignorance of the existence of the other.
67. Duke, *History of Morgan's Cavalry*, 293.

created by Forrest, Morgan was to swoop down on Edgefield from the north and burn the freight cars.

Forrest made his demonstration as scheduled (General Negley recognized it for what it was and paid little attention to it), and Morgan swooped as he had been ordered, but the Federal infantry guarding the freight yard put up a stout resistance—the fight of their pickets caused General Duke to note that he had "never seen men fight better than these fellows did." Morgan was repulsed; the dozen freight cars his men burned were a poor return for the five dead, the nineteen wounded, and the "stand of regimental colors" he had to leave behind when he called off the attack.[68]

On December 6, Morgan performed his most soldierly exploit. On a bitterly cold day, with deep snow covering the ground, he made a "ride and tie" march of about thirty miles with three of his regiments of cavalry and the two regiments of infantry that were lent him for the operation, to attack the 2,400-man Union garrison at Hartsville. Aided by the gross incompetence of the officer commanding the post, Morgan was able to effect a surprise, and after barely an hour of a listless defense, the garrison surrendered.[69]

A week later, Morgan, promoted to brigadier general by President Davis himself as a reward for his victory at Hartsville, married Martha Ready at her home in Murfreesboro and thereby made December 14, 1862, a red-letter day in Confederate folklore. Dressed for the occasion in the full-dress uniform of a general of cavalry, Morgan had for his ushers Generals Bragg, Breckinridge, William J. Hardee, and Benjamin F. Cheatham, and the marriage service was read by Leonidas Polk, wearing his vestments as bishop of the Episcopal Diocese of Louisiana over his uniform of a lieutenant general in the Confederate army.

Morgan allowed himself a week's honeymoon. Then, on December 22, with his command now swollen to nearly four thousand men in two brigades, the first made up of three regiments under Basil Duke,

68. *Official Records*, Vol. XX, Pt. 1, pp. 4–7; Duke, *History of Morgan's Cavalry*, 195–98; Henry, *"First with the Most" Forrest*, 106. Forrest's report refers to the enemy throughout as "the Abolitionists."

69. *Official Records*, Vol. XX, Pt. 1, pp. 43–72; Duke, *History of Morgan's Cavalry*, 309–14. The officer in command was Colonel Absalom B. Moore, 104th Illinois Infantry. He was recommended to be cashiered both by General Halleck and by Secretary Stanton, but he was able to muster enough political influence to escape.

the second of four regiments under Colonel William C. P. Breckinridge, plus a four-gun battery, he departed on what came to be known as his "Christmas Raid" to break once again the line of the Louisville & Nashville.[70] The tunnel at Gallatin that he had blocked in August had been reopened, and supplies from Louisville were arriving once again at Nashville. With the line from Bowling Green south protected by a chain of stockades thought to be too powerful to attack, Morgan and Bragg's staff decided that the most sensitive point on the line was the pair of trestles, each about five hundred feet long and eighty to a hundred feet high, at Muldraugh's Hill, just north of Elizabethtown and only eighteen miles south of Louisville. After a five-day march, much of it in the bad weather to be anticipated at that time of the year, the raiders reached the railroad bridge over Bacon's Creek, near Munfordville. On the chance that the Muldraugh's Hill trestles would be too strongly protected to be attacked, Morgan decided to destroy the Bacon's Creek bridge; he shelled the stockade guarding the bridge, forced its garrison to surrender, and destroyed not only the bridge but "several miles" of track as well.

On December 27, the raiders came to Elizabethtown; its six-hundred-man garrison was persuaded to surrender by a brief bombardment. The next morning, Morgan reached his objective and found each of the two trestles protected by a stockade manned by parts of the same regiment, the 71st Indiana Infantry. An hour's (by another account, two or three hours') bombardment caused both garrisons to surrender. The two trestles were then set on fire and destroyed. In a nearly unique instance of a raider underestimating the impact of his efforts, Morgan gave it as his opinion that the destruction of the trestles would halt traffic on the railroad for two months; actually, nearly three months were needed to rebuild the trestles and restore traffic on the road.[71]

The Union command knew as early as December 19 that Morgan

70. Duke, *History of Morgan's Cavalry*, 322–25; Holland, *Morgan and His Raiders*, 179–80. Duke, however, gives Morgan's artillery as one 3-inch Parrott and two mountain howitzers. The raid as a whole is described in Morgan's report in *Official Records*, Vol. XX, Pt. 1, p. 158; Duke, *History of Morgan's Cavalry*, 325–35; Brown, *The Bold Cavaliers*, 145–53; and Holland, *Morgan and His Raiders*, 179–83.

71. *Official Records*, Vol. XX, Pt. 1, p. 158; see also Brown, *The Bold Cavaliers*, 152. General Boyle thought it would "take four or five weeks to repair damage." *Official Records*, Vol. XX, Pt. 2, p. 296.

was "on his way to Kentucky," but Department Commander H. G. Wright was not unduly concerned: "Our troops must understand that they are expected to fight, and if they do half their duty they can whip Morgan's rascals."[72] A few days later, Wright assured Rosecrans that General Boyle had enough cavalry in Kentucky "to whip . . . [Morgan] if he can catch him." Catching Morgan was of course the rub, and as a hedge against the possibility that Morgan would not be caught in Kentucky, Wright promised to keep Rosecrans, in Murfreesboro, informed of developments so that he could "cut . . . [Morgan] off on his return." This communication caused Rosecrans, fertile in expedients always, to inquire of one of his subordinates, "How many pack and other horses can you raise, with saddles or bare backs, to put infantry on, to pursue . . . [Morgan] with, say, one-half ride, the others walk, and change horses—the infantry walking to start early, to be overtaken and take the horses, and go on to camp while the walking overtake them? Volunteers and picked men should go." Here in this poorly expressed "ride and tie" scheme was the unexpressed assumption once again that cavalry could be created instantaneously by mounting a foot soldier, however armed, on a horse—on a saddle if saddles could be had, and bareback if they could not. General Wright wrote to Halleck that with a command consisting mainly of infantry, he could "do little against cavalry raids except to hold important points" and asked for "authority to mount, say, 3,000 infantry, and to procure, by purchase, the necessary horse equipments for them, at not exceeding $30 the set"; with such a force, he thought, he could protect Kentucky.[73]

Morgan's return to Tennessee from Muldraugh's Hill was hampered more by the elements and the exhaustion of his men and horses than it was by the enemy. An attack on his rear guard at the Rolling Fork River near Bardstown caused some casualties. To confuse and evade pursuit, Morgan first went northeast to Bardstown; then, turning southeast through Springfield, he made a night march directly south around the Federal concentration at Lebanon that was expected to intercept him. The first day of the new year found the raiders at Columbia, Kentucky, and after another all-night march ("a dark, bitter

72. *Official Records*, Vol. XX, Pt. 2, pp. 204, 209, 239. As was almost always the case, the estimate of Morgan's numbers was a gross exaggeration. He was credited with a force of five to six thousand.
73. *Ibid.*, 239, 236, 297.

night and a terrible march," General Duke wrote) reached and crossed the Cumberland River on the second. Now the danger of pursuit was ended, and after a leisurely march, the raiders reached friendly territory at Smithville, Tennessee, on January 5.[74]

Colonel Wilder's brigade was stationed at this time at Glasgow. On January 1, the men heard firing to the northward and learned that Morgan was some distance to the east, marching past their position. Anxious to give chase but knowing that there was no hope of overtaking Morgan with his own men marching on foot, Wilder, taking a leaf out of Rosecrans' book, collected the mules of his brigade wagon train and ordered his men to mount. The silence of the regimental historian who tells the tale on the subject of saddles and implies that the men were to ride bareback, but the mules, "not more than one . . . out of six [of which] had ever had a man on its back," were firmly resolved not to be ridden at all. As fast as the men mounted, they were thrown. Colonel Wilder's scheme was a ludicrous failure, vastly entertaining in retrospect, but it left an idea in Colonel Wilder's mind: "It is said that this attempt to form a mule brigade to chase Morgan was the conception of the idea which resulted in Colonel Wilder having the brigade mounted some months afterwards. We had been chasing Morgan's force in mule wagons and on foot, and Colonel Wilder, seeing the futility of such chases, determined that he would try and have the brigade mounted so as to travel as rapidly as Morgan could."[75] This, if the historian's recollection may be trusted, was the genesis of the famous Lightning Brigade of Mounted Infantry, which came into being three months later.

74. Morgan's return march from Muldraugh's Hill is described in Duke, *History of Morgan's Cavalry*, 335–43; see also Brown, *The Bold Cavaliers*, 153–61. Morgan claimed "the capture of 1,877 prisoners . . . the destruction of over $2,000,000 of U.S. property, and a large loss to the enemy in killed and wounded." His own losses he reported as 2 killed, 24 wounded, and 64 missing. *Official Records*, Vol. XX, Pt. 1, p. 158.

75. McGee, *History of the 72nd Indiana*, 88–89. Contrary to the regimental historian's statement, this unsuccessful attempt to form a mule-borne brigade may actually have occurred at Bear Wallow (near the entrance to Mammoth Cave), twelve miles to the northeast of Glasgow and that much nearer Morgan's route.

V

Steed Threatens Steed

ON JANUARY 1, 1863, AS MORGAN AND HIS HORSEMEN WERE marching south from Campbellsville to Columbia, Kentucky, on their way back from their Christmas Raid, "all that day the roaring of artillery was distinctly heard by many men in the column."[1] The cannonading the men believed they heard was the sound of the battle of Stones River, or Murfreesboro, fought by the armies of Braxton Bragg and William Rosecrans. Of the 38,000 Confederates actually engaged in the battle, 10,266 became casualties; of Rosecrans' army of 43,000, a total of 13,249 were killed, wounded, or missing.[2] With a casualty rate of nearly 30 percent for the two armies, Stones River was thus a fitting introduction to what would prove to be the grand climacteric of the Civil War, the year of Chancellorsville and Gettysburg in the East and of Vicksburg and Chickamauga in the West.

After Halleck's departure for Washington, Grant had, for the first time in the war, an essentially independent command. He remained subject to Halleck's orders, but the newly appointed general-in-chief was nine hundred miles away, in telegraphic communication with the commander of the District of West Tennessee, to be sure, but no longer

1. Duke, *History of Morgan's Cavalry*, 342.
2. *Battles and Leaders*, III, 612, 611. The breakdown of Confederate casualties is 1,294 killed, 7,945 wounded, 1,027 captured or missing; of the Union casualties, 1,730 were killed, 7,802 wounded, and 3,717 captured or missing.

able to give that area his undivided attention, and Grant now had the opportunity to spread his wings. Authorized by Halleck to decide on his own strategy, he commanded from his headquarters at Jackson, Tennessee, an army of upwards of 45,000, half of whom, however, were needed to guard his lines of communication. Commanding the left wing of his forces was Rosecrans, at the head of three complete divisions of infantry and one partial one in the Corinth area; General Sherman, at Memphis, had the right wing, and General E. O. C. Ord, the center. Facing Grant, with forces totaling about 30,000, were Sterling Price at Tupelo and Earl Van Dorn at Vicksburg, the two commanders being independent of each other.

The events in northeast Mississippi in September and early October, 1862, and the actions of Grant's, Price's, and Van Dorn's armies hinged on the progress of Bragg's invasion of Kentucky. Price tried to prevent Rosecrans from reinforcing Buell; Grant at the same time tried to prevent Price from reinforcing Bragg. This led to the battle of Iuka on September 19. Subsequently, Price and Van Dorn joined forces for an attack on Corinth, "an exposed salient on Grant's extreme left," in the expectation that a success there would open the way to the recovery of west Tennessee for the Confederacy and to a possible invasion of Kentucky along a line to the west of Bragg's route.[3]

On September 7, anticipating a joint Price–Van Dorn attack on Corinth, Grant had Rosecrans evacuate the country to the east of the town, where his troops had been guarding the line of the Memphis & Charleston Railroad. This enabled Price to occupy the town of Iuka, on the railroad about twenty miles southeast of Corinth. Grant saw an opportunity to gobble up Price before he was joined by Van Dorn and, on the basis of Rosecrans' suggestions, planned a pincers attack on the town. Rosecrans, with about nine thousand men, was to attack Iuka from the south and southwest, at the same time that General Ord, with nearly eight thousand men, moved to Iuka by rail and attacked from the northwest.[4] Through a series of mischances, the pincers failed to

3. Quoted from Castel, *General Sterling Price*, 108. For the Union view of the strategic importance of Corinth, see *Battles and Leaders*, II, 739–40, 742–43.

4. Ulysses S. Grant, *Personal Memoirs of U. S. Grant* (2 vols.; New York, 1885), I, 408, 407. For the battle, see *Ibid.*, 408–13; *Battles and Leaders*, II, 730–36; Castel, *General Sterling Price*, 101–104; Catton, *Grant Moves South*, 309–12; Williams, *Lincoln Finds a General*, IV, 72–80; and William M. Lamers, *The Edge of Glory: A Biog-*

close; Rosecrans' attack was checked, Ord did not attack at all, and Price escaped during the night on a road Rosecrans had left unguarded. Grant blamed Rosecrans for the failure of the attack and for Price's escape.[5]

Present at Iuka and in the subsequent pursuit were the troopers of Colonel John K. Mizner's "Cavalry Division," which contained the 2nd Iowa, 3rd Michigan, 7th Illinois, and two companies of the 7th Kansas.[6] The cavalry, Rosecrans reported, "covered our flanks, reconnoitered our front, whipped the vastly superior numbers of [General Frank C.] Armstrong's cavalry under protection of their infantry, and kept them there during the battle and retreat," and he went on to "acknowledge the services of the able and indefatigable chief of cavalry," Colonel Mizner. To be noted are the absence from Mizner's command of Sheridan and his 2nd Michigan. After what was thought to be a violent altercation with Grant, who wanted him to stay, Sheridan left northern Mississippi for Louisville, taking the Michigan regiment with him.[7] His departure left vacant the command of what had been his brigade, reduced to two regiments by the departure of the 2nd Michigan. His replacement was Colonel Albert L. Lee of the 7th Kansas. General Granger having been transferred to Kentucky at the same time, Mizner moved up from the colonelcy of the 3rd Michigan to command of the cavalry division of Rosecrans' army.[8]

On the morning of September 19, the 2nd Iowa had a "short but brisk skirmish" at Peyton's (or Payton's) Mill with the 1st Mississippi

---

raphy of General William S. Rosecrans (New York, 1961), 103–30, a strongly pro-Rosecrans account.

5. Grant, Personal Memoirs, I, 413.

6. Official Records, Vol. XVII, Pt. 1, pp. 113–14. The roster of units present at Iuka in Battles and Leaders, II, 736, lists in addition the 5th Missouri and Captain Albert Jenks's independent company of Illinois cavalry.

7. Official Records, Vol. XVII, Pt. 1, p. 75; Sheridan, Personal Memoirs, I, 181–82.

8. As will be seen, Colonel Mizner did not have the makings of another Murat, but he more than made up for his shortcomings as a commander of cavalry with the verbose eloquence of his reports, of which the following is an example: "It is due to the cavalry to remark that, although the nature of their service in this wooded country is such that they are frequently denied a participation in general engagements, yet those whose praise and approbation is most to be desired do not lose sight of the invaluable services performed by them. No service is more arduous, yet, with patience and even a spirit of indifference to fatigue has their labor been performed. . . . The distance traveled, the labor performed, and the fatigue endured by the cavalry is almost incredible, and all this, so cheerfully performed and with such alacrity and spirit, entitle all to the highest commendation." Official Records, Vol. XVII, Pt. 1, pp. 244–45.

Partisan Rangers, commanded by Colonel W. C. Falkner, the great-grandfather of the novelist. The Iowans, as their regimental historian acknowledges, were much better armed than the Partisan Rangers and defeated them, inflicting twenty-two casualties against none of their own.[9]

It is impossible to arrive at an accurate account of the pursuit of Price's retreating army after Iuka. Grant, whose dislike of and hostility to Rosecrans is obvious throughout his account of the fight at Iuka and its aftermath, recalled that when he rode into the town shortly after it had been occupied by the Union infantry, he discovered that "the enemy was not being pursued even by the cavalry." He thereupon "ordered pursuit by the whole of Rosecrans' command and went on with him a few miles in person," presumably to make certain that his orders were obeyed, but, said Grant, soon after he himself left, Rosecrans called off the pursuit and went into camp.[10]

Grant's statement of Rosecrans' unhelpful role in the pursuit appears to be erroneous. It is not necessary to determine in the present study whether it is so intentionally or otherwise. It is sufficiently difficult to deduce from the contradictory reports of the two sides just what the cavalry pursuit, in which eight companies each of the 3rd Michigan and 2nd Iowa and two companies of the 7th Kansas were engaged, actually accomplished. Colonel Mizner asserted that his men, "striking for different points of the enemy's column," greatly retarded Price's march and harassed his troops until they were driven off by Price's artillery.[11] Colonel Hatch reported:

The enemy's skirmishers falling back rapidly . . . [our] men were drawn upon a masked battery, with a support of two regiments of infantry and a strong reserve of cavalry. . . . [The] men, being dismounted, dropped flat upon the ground, the guns and volleys of the enemy's infantry playing over them, not hurting a man. The enemy's cavalry charged the moment the firing ceased. The charge was repulsed, our men falling back fighting in the timber to my reserve of mounted men. Learning the enemy had run two of his guns up, [I] fell back. . . . I then formed four companies of my mounted rifles (to receive the cavalry charge) . . . when the enemy charged in force over the fields and

9. *Ibid.*, 113, 138, which give the enemy's numbers as 600. The Iowans' regimental historian gives the enemy numbers as 2,500. Pierce, *History of the Second Iowa*, 30. Both colonels, Hatch and Falkner, submitted reports; each claimed to have routed the other. *Official Records*, Vol. XVII, Pt. 1, p. 138.

10. Grant, *Personal Memoirs*, I, 413; but see Lamers, *The Edge of Glory*, 126–27.

11. *Official Records*, Vol. XVII, Pt. 1, p. 114.

was repulsed with loss, when the enemy again ran up his guns, forcing us back to another position. . . . Our infantry coming up rapidly, the enemy retreated.[12]

It would be difficult to deduce from this recital who the pursued were, and who the pursuers. Indeed, these operations had a far different appearance, viewed from the other side of the line by General Dabney H. Maury, who commanded one of Price's divisions of infantry: "The enemy followed us feebly, with cavalry chiefly, which was held in check all the time by the cavalry under General Armstrong. . . . the pursuing enemy was drawn into an ambuscade, admirably planned and executed by General Armstrong. . . . [The enemy] received the fire of the 2d Texas Sharpshooters; of Bledsoe's battery, with canister, at short range; were charged by McCulloch's cavalry, and were utterly routed. . . . During the remainder of the march they ventured within range no more."[13] Colonel Hatch reported that the enemy's sharpshooters, canister, and cavalry charge killed three horses and wounded six men; a modest return, surely, for a prodigious expenditure of effort and gunpowder.

The Federals' failure to "bag" Price at Iuka allowed him to join forces with Earl Van Dorn. Price had emerged from the affair at Iuka essentially unhurt—two only of his infantry brigades had done all the fighting on September 19—and on the twenty-eighth his troops and Van Dorn's united at Ripley, southwest of Corinth. Being the senior in rank, Van Dorn assumed command of the two brigades of cavalry and three divisions of infantry, a total of "about twenty-two thousand men, plus a sizable artillery train."[14] Price's contribution of 17,000 troops to the total was described as "well armed and equipped, well fed, well clothed, and well provided with everything that an army in the field needed . . . [and] thoroughly organized, drilled, and disciplined."[15] After some debate, Price and Van Dorn agreed to lead their troops on an immediate attack of Corinth, and they set forth on September 29.

In command of the Corinth defenses, a triple band of earthworks and artillery emplacements facing generally north and northeast, and

12. *Ibid.*, 139–40.
13. *Ibid.*, 137.
14. Castel, *General Sterling Price*, 106. Castel states that "most of the troops were veterans, well-armed and fully trained."
15. *Battles and Leaders*, II, 728.

of its garrison of "about 16,000 effective infantry and artillery . . . with 2,500 cavalry for outposts and reconnoitering," was Rosecrans.[16] Were it not for Chickamauga and Grant's hostility, Rosecrans' personal leadership at Corinth, the inspirational effect of his presence wherever the fighting was hottest and the danger greatest, would entitle him to be compared to Sheridan at Five Forks. The Confederate assaults on the Corinth defenses began on the morning of October 3 and were driven home with the utmost gallantry that day and the next, at great cost in casualties. On the morning of the fourth, the assaulting column of Price's army actually broke through the defenses into the streets of the town and captured Rosecrans' reserve artillery. But gallantry was not enough; in one of the most clear-cut demonstrations in the Civil War of the power of the defensive, the Federals drove off the attackers and inflicted 8,691 casualties upon them at a cost of 2,520 of their own.[17]

By the nature of the operation, Corinth was an infantry-artillery fight. Most of Rosecrans' cavalry was out on the flanks, "covering and reconnoitering."[18] The troopers of the 7th Kansas, however, were deployed dismounted and fought as skirmishers and sharpshooters on the evening of the third. In the severe fighting of the next day, six companies of the regiment were in the firing line to the left of Battery Robinette, in the Union center, helping to beat off the attack of General John C. Moore's brigade of four regiments of infantry and the 2nd Texas Sharpshooters of Dabney Maury's division, who "fought as hard as any Confederate troops anywhere fought during the whole war."[19] Four other companies of the Kansas regiment harassed the Confederate right flank, to the south of the battle zone. A number of individual Jayhawkers were detailed as orderlies, couriers, and dispatch riders at Rosecrans' headquarters; one of them, Sergeant Bayless S. Campbell, earned a battlefield commission for volunteering to carry an order through a belt of fire so intense that Rosecrans would not ask any of his aides or orderlies to cross it.[20]

16. *Ibid.*, 743, 744–45. These were Rosecrans' figures. Williams, *Lincoln Finds a General*, IV, 85, credits Rosecrans with forces totaling 23,000.

17. Lamers, *The Edge of Glory*, 154, 155. *Battles and Leaders*, II, 760, agrees with Lamers' figure of 2,520 Union casualties but shows only 4,838 Confederate casualties as against Lamers' figure of 8,691.

18. *Official Records*, Vol. XVII, Pt. 1, p. 167 (Rosecrans' report).

19. Castel, *General Sterling Price*, 117.

20. Starr, *Jennison's Jayhawkers*, 208. Company A of the 7th Kansas, separated for

For two consecutive nights, October 2 and 3, Rosecrans' men had been on the move, and for two days, October 3 and 4, they had been in constant action in temperatures well up in the nineties, short of water and short of food.[21] When late on the afternoon of the fourth, Van Dorn reluctantly decided that further attacks would be a useless waste of lives and began his retreat, Rosecrans was in no condition to pursue. Grant, whose brief description of the battle is a travesty of the facts, chastises Rosecrans for failing to follow up his victory despite Grant's "specific orders in advance of the battle for him to pursue the moment the enemy was repelled."[22] Doubtless Grant had forgotten, when he penned his condemnation of Rosecrans, his own far less excusable failure to pursue Beauregard after the battle of Shiloh.

When Rosecrans set off after the Confederates on the morning of the fifth (on the "wrong road," according to Grant), he had Colonel Mizner divide his cavalry into two flanking columns—one under Colonel Hatch marching to the north of the Chewallah Road, on which the Confederates were retreating toward the crossing of the Hatchie River, and the other under Colonel Lee to the south of the road. Both cavalry columns made "frequent dashes on the enemy's flanks" all the way to Ripley, where on Grant's orders and greatly to Rosecrans' disgust, the pursuit was called off.[23]

On October 16, a War Department order confirmed officially what had been a fact ever since Halleck's departure to Washington: it created the Department of the Tennessee, with Grant in command. A second order, eight days later, created another new department, that of the Cumberland, and gave the command to Rosecrans, whose relations with Grant had deteriorated in the days following the battle of Corinth

---

a time from the rest of the regiment, helped to defend Battery Phillips, on the left of the Union line. "Lying under cover of log breastworks and firing an average of eighty rounds per man [from their Sharps' carbines] they inflicted heavy punishment on Major General Mansfield Lovell's division." *Ibid.*, 209.

21. On the night of the third, with the worst of the fighting still ahead, the Federal garrison were "already weary almost unto death." Williams, *Lincoln Finds a General*, IV, 90.

22. Grant, *Personal Memoirs*, I, 416–17.

23. *Official Records*, Vol. XVII, Pt. 1, p. 243. See also Starr, *Jennison's Jayhawkers*, 210. If, as Grant claimed, Rosecrans took the wrong road, how was it possible for his cavalry to make these "frequent dashes on the enemy's flanks"?

to the point where Grant had "determined" that very day to relieve him of duty in his department.[24] Rosecrans' new appointment suggested that Halleck had more confidence in him (or a lesser fear of him as a possible rival) than Grant had. General Halleck, Secretary Stanton, and perhaps even the president would have been less than human if in the next two months they had not wondered from time to time if they had chosen wisely in placing in a position of authority an officer so restless and so insistently demanding.[25] The barrage of demands Rosecrans had laid down in previous months, for more cavalry, more weapons, more horses, more equipment, should have given Washington ample warning of what to expect from him, and it did not take long for the bombardment to begin anew.

Indeed, on October 30, the very day that Rosecrans formally entered upon his new responsibilities, he telegraphed General Halleck: "I find we have . . . eight regiments of cavalry. Would be able to do wonders under an able chief. Brigadier-General Stanley, besides being an able and indefatigable soldier, is a thorough cavalry officer. He can do more good . . . by commanding a cavalry than an infantry division. I beg you . . . to send him to me. You know the expense of cavalry and what the rebel cavalry has done. Stanley will double our forces without expense."[26] To comply with Rosecrans' request for Stanley, the War Department had to order or persuade Grant, under whom Stanley was then serving, to give him up. Both the War Department and Grant (the latter after a push in the direction of acquiescence by a couple of telegrams from Rosecrans direct) proved agreeable, and after only five

24. *Official Records*, Vol. XVI, Pt. 2, p. 642. One wonders what residue of hatred caused Grant to make this gratuitously derogatory statement in memoirs written thirty years after the event. In addition to command of the department, Rosecrans also received, in succession to Buell, command of the Army of the Cumberland.

25. To be strictly accurate, Stanton's name should not be included. He "had been strongly opposed to Rosecrans' appointment in the first place." Williams, *Lincoln Finds a General*, IV, 240.

26. *Official Records*, Vol. XVI, Pt. 2, p. 655. David S. Stanley, appointed from Ohio, graduated ninth in the West Point Class of 1852. He was assigned to the 2nd United States Dragoons and, after service in the Cavalry School for Practice at Carlisle Barracks and on the frontier in Texas, was transferred in 1855 to the 1st United States. In August, 1861, having been promoted to captain, he was transferred to the 4th United States and a month later was promoted to brigadier general in the volunteer service. Cullum, *Biographical Register*, II, 309–10. In January, 1862, McClellan, then general-in-chief, had written Halleck: "Can you spare Stanley to Buell as chief of cavalry, or should I look elsewhere to get him one? He [Buell] has not asked for him, but I know him to be a first-rate officer." *Official Records*, Vol. VII, 931.

more telegrams from Rosecrans to Halleck, Grant, and Stanton, all of which rang changes on his possession of "considerable cavalry in much confusion for want of a head" and his desperate need of such a head, General David Stanley did at length report to Rosecrans for duty and on November 24 was announced as chief of cavalry, with the command of all the cavalry in the department.[27]

It must be noted that in his pleas to the authorities for Stanley, Rosecrans made it clear that he wanted him to *command* his cavalry, and neither the War Department nor, apparently, Stanley himself questioned this departure from the concept prevailing earlier in the war, that the chief of cavalry was a combination administrative and staff officer and nothing more. It is equally important that Rosecrans spelled out the fact that he wanted Stanley to command a cavalry *division*. There had not been in October, 1862, nor would there ever be, to the end of the war, an official pronouncement defining and prescribing these fundamental changes in cavalry organization and leadership. They were tried, they seemed to work, and so the idea spread and was adopted first in one army and then in another, on empirical grounds and on a voluntary basis.

To find a brigadier general like Stanley, who was thought to have the talent for making cavalry an effective arm of the service, was relatively easy, though the officer so chosen did not always measure up to expectations. Far more difficult to satisfy was the second of Rosecrans' great wants, which he proceeded to spell out and reiterate in a lengthy series of telegrams to Halleck and Stanton. He pleaded for arms for his cavalry, which were "the eyes and feet of my army, and will be its providers." Typical of the content and tone of these messages are two telegrams, the first to the secretary of war on November 9: "If I have not worn out my welcome, I beseech you for the public service to send me revolving arms or breech-loading carbines for my cavalry. . . . They are half armed and two-thirds demoralized. We are wasting money on them at the rate of $10,000 per day for want of arms. . . . No promise of arms. What can you do for us?" The second went to General Halleck a week later: "General, we must have arms for our cavalry. Without arms we lose their services,

---

27. *Official Records*, Vol. XX, Pt. 2, pp. 5, 6, 27, 31, 33, 94, Vol. XVII, Pt. 1, pp. 467, 468. It is worthy of note, however, that John Kennett remained in command of Rosecrans' "cavalry division," but as a subordinate of Stanley's. In the November 24 orders, Lieutenant Colonel W. P. Hepburn, 2nd Iowa, was announced as inspector of cavalry.

and those of all the infantry absorbed in guarding trains and roads. Nothing but insurmountable obstacles can justify the present condition of things. Can you remedy it?"[28]

Two further messages sent the same day, one to Halleck and the other to the secretary, reverted to the proposal Rosecrans had made three months before, namely to mount infantry and arm them with revolving rifles.[29] To Halleck, who was presumed to be already familiar with the idea, Rosecrans wired simply: "I want to mount some infantry regiments, arm them with revolving rifles, and make sharpshooters of them. I cannot elaborate all the consequences that will flow from this, but they will be immense."[30] A more elaborate version of the same message went to the secretary:

It is a matter of great importance that we should arm some infantry with revolving rifles and use them as sharpshooters. I propose using saddles answering a double purpose for pack and riding saddles. This infantry is to be used as a very swift-moving body of light artillery, at the same time to be used against large moving columns of the enemy, to surprise and cut them to pieces. . . . at the mere cost of the arms and mounting, it will add to our force one or two regiments for every regiment we mount. Is it possible for you to carry out this measure by furnishing 4,000 revolving rifles? Prompt action . . . is called for.[31]

It speaks much for General Halleck's patience, and even more for that of the secretary, not generally credited with having any, that they both sent Rosecrans temperate answers. Halleck did remind him, and properly so, that "each army received its proportion of each kind of arms as fast as they can be prepared. This rule must be followed, for we cannot 'rob Peter to pay Paul.'" Stanton informed him that 1,600 revolving rifles, all that were then available, were being expressed to Louisville for issue to him and that he would receive the balance of the 4,000 he had requested "as rapidly as they can be made." But then came this tart reminder: "No effort shall be spared to supply what you ask for, but something is expected from you."[32]

When Stanley took on his new duties, he found more than just a

28. *Ibid.*, 31, 58. To make certain that General Halleck realized the urgency of his needs, Rosecrans wired him the next day, "Let me entreat you to give us cavalry arms." *Ibid.*, 59.
29. See above, p. 24.
30. *Official Records*, Vol. XX, Pt. 2, p. 58.
31. *Ibid.*, 57–58.
32. *Ibid.*, 60, 64.

shortage of numbers and of appropriate weapons amiss with Rose-crans' cavalry.[33] The first of the flaws that required correction, he decided, was that the cavalry had been "badly neglected. It was weak, undisciplined, and scattered around, a regiment to a division of infantry. To break up this foolish dispersal of cavalry, and to form brigades and eventually divisions, was my first and most difficult work. Generals commanding divisions declared they would not give up their cavalry regiments; but I insisted they should do so and General Rosecrans sustained me. I soon had three pretty substantial brigades formed, commanded by good officers."[34]

A radical by the standards of the day with respect to cavalry organization, Stanley was nevertheless a traditionalist in another respect. "Our cavalry," he wrote, "had been poorly instructed and depended upon their carbines instead of the sabre. I insisted on the latter. I sent for grindstones and had all the sabres sharpened. . . . This soon gave confidence to our men." Stanley's desire to have his men rely on "cold steel" ignored the fact that they had done so in the past on occasions when a saber charge seemed feasible. In an action in June at Jasper, Tennessee, for example, General Negley's escort, a battalion of the 7th Pennsylvania and a "portion" of the 5th Kentucky, charged a body of Confederate cavalry, "using their sabers with terrible execution. The narrowness of the lane and very open ground alone prevented the enemy from being totally destroyed." It was nevertheless true that this early in the war, before commanding officers learned better, they were apt to order odd and absurd tactics. The historian of the 1st Ohio re-

33. A regimental historian has written that of the 3,000 mounted troops Stanley was given to command, not more than 1,500 were "well disciplined cavalrymen." Thatcher, *A Hundred Battles in the West*, 293.

34. Stanley, *Personal Memoirs*, 120. Stanley was not alone in condemning the "foolish dispersal of cavalry." A regimental historian wrote that prior to Stanley's decision to form brigades and divisions, the cavalry's "proper organization for effective work . . . we had been attached in squads and battalions to various infantry brigades and divisions; not even a single regiment operating long enough as a unit to become an effective power; while, on sudden emergencies arising, these different detachments would be thrown together, placed under the nearest unemployed infantry colonel or brigadier general, and sent on scouts, or to engage the enemy; without having any opportunity to acquire that *esprit de corps* so necessary to successful military movements." Vale, *Minty and the Cavalry*, 107–108. The colonel of the 1st Ohio, Minor Milliken, "had always been very strongly in favor of organizing the cavalry into brigades and divisions, as he always claimed they could be of much more service massed than by cutting them up into detachments and having them attached to divisions of infantry by regiments and battalions." Curry, *Four Years in the Saddle*, 81–82.

minded his fellow veterans that "in the early part of our service it was usual to halt to receive the attack of the enemy, and attempt to fire from our horses, instead of dismounting to fight on foot, or drawing saber and charging him; all of which we learned before the close of the war." Even as late as the end of 1862, at Stones River, the 15th Pennsylvania made the "mistake," as the regimental historian realized it to be, of "attempting to charge at 'advance carbine.' To do it a soldier should have three hands, one to manage his horse and the other two to fire and load his carbine."[35]

Insofar as reliance on the saber represented an attitude, an expression of the "cavalry spirit," as it was called, Stanley's new charges were in favor of it. They were equally in favor of his desire that the cavalry play a more active role. "As he was very active and aggressive," wrote a regimental historian, "a long felt want in that arm of the service seemed to have been supplied. He was always on the alert for any duty required of his command, and he did not propose to settle down and wait for the enemy to come to him, but he went after the enemy, and usually found him."[36]

To anticipate by a few months, the day was to come within a year when Stanley would be glad to return to the infantry, after concluding that command of Rosecrans' cavalry was a "most unsatisfying and annoying" occupation. Stanley decided, as time went on, that "Rosecrans had no idea of the use of cavalry, and [future President] Garfield, his chief of staff, who became an 'Old Man of the Sea' on Rosecrans' shoulders, was everlastingly meddling. Rosecrans was in many respects a man of genius and disposed to do right, but he was easily influenced, and Garfield's blarney and deceitful tongue captured [him]."[37]

The "something" Secretary Stanton expected of Rosecrans was prompt and vigorous action against the enemy. Buell had been relieved of command and replaced by Rosecrans because of what Washington

35. Stanley, *Personal Memoirs*, 120–21; *Official Records*, Vol. X, Pt. 1, p. 904; Curry, *Four Years in the Saddle*, 18; Charles H. Kirk, *History of the Fifteenth Pennsylvania Volunteer Cavalry* (Philadelphia, 1906), 119.

36. Curry, *Four Years in the Saddle*, 82.

37. Stanley, *Personal Memoirs*, 158. Stanley was evidently a man of powerful dislikes, which he was not reluctant to voice. In 1873, he wrote about Custer, then lieutenant colonel of the 7th United States: "I have had no trouble with Custer, and will try to avoid having any; but I have seen enough of him to convince me that he is a cold blooded, untruthful and unprincipled man. He is universally despised by all the officers of his regiment excepting his relatives and one or two sycophants." *Ibid.*, 239.

considered the slow pace of his advance into east Tennessee. His army was still in Kentucky when the command change was ordered. Three weeks passed, and Rosecrans had progressed only as far as Nashville. Despite pressure from Washington to move on, there he remained, accumulating supplies, until the day after Christmas, when he put his army in motion toward Murfreesboro, where he expected to find Bragg. It has been suggested that a major reason for Rosecrans' reluctance to move against Bragg was the latter's great preponderance in cavalry.[38] No doubt the numerical superiority of Bragg's cavalry, actually between two and two and a half to one, but estimated by Rosecrans as four to one, was a factor in the latter's thinking, as it should have been. But the implication that he waited to move against Bragg until he knew that Morgan had departed on his Christmas Raid into Kentucky and that Forrest had taken his command on a raid, to be described later, against Grant's line of communications, smacks of *post hoc ergo propter hoc* reasoning.[39]

To keep Bragg off balance as long as possible, Rosecrans marched from Nashville in three columns. Thomas L. Crittenden's wing of three divisions, using the main Nashville-LaVergne-Murfreesboro Pike, was led by Colonel Minty's First Cavalry Brigade (3rd Kentucky, 7th Pennsylvania, 4th Michigan, and one company of the 2nd Indiana). General Thomas' two divisions, on the Franklin and Wilson Pike, were preceded by Colonel Zahm's Second Cavalry Brigade (1st, 3rd, and 4th Ohio). Minty's and Zahm's brigades formed Colonel John Kennett's Cavalry Division; Kennett's actual control over the two brigades appears to have been more a polite fiction than a reality. The three infantry divisions of General Alexander McD. McCook's wing, on the Nashville-Nolensville Pike, were shielded by a "reserve brigade" of three new regiments of cavalry (the 15th Pennsylvania and the 2nd and 5th Tennessee) plus four companies of the 3rd Indiana, all under the personal command of General Stanley, who also had overall com-

---

38. Edwin C. Bearss, "Cavalry Operations in the Battle of Stones River," *Tennessee Historical Quarterly*, XIX (March and June, 1960), 26; Lamers, *The Edge of Glory*, 198–99.

39. Rosecrans wrote Halleck on December 7: "Our great difficulties will come from . . . [the enemy's] numerous cavalry harassing us and cutting off our forage parties and trains. I am arming our cavalry, who are not more than one-fourth of their effective force, and much cowed from that fact and want of arms." *Official Records*, Vol. XX, Pt. 1, p. 41.

mand of the entire mounted force of some 4,400 sabers.[40] Morgan's
and Forrest's departure had not left Bragg denuded of cavalry; remaining with his army were about 5,000 horsemen, constituting the
brigades of Wheeler, John A. Wharton, John Pegram, and Abraham
Buford, the whole under Wheeler's command.[41]

When Rosecrans' army of about 44,000 "effectives" reached Stones
River just west of Murfreesboro, they found Bragg's army of about
38,000 in possession, deployed in a double line trending generally
northeast and southwest, in the dense cedar thickets, or "brakes,"
along the west bank of the stream.[42] With the two armies arrayed
against each other, the two commanding generals chose an identical
battle plan; each decided on using the infantry on his left wing to attack the enemy right. The battle developed as it did because Bragg
beat Rosecrans to the punch. At dawn on the last day of 1862, Hardee's
corps—the divisions of John P. McCown and Patrick R. Cleburne—
with Wharton's brigade of cavalry well out beyond their left flank, attacked McCook's corps, posted on the right, or southern, end of Rosecrans' position. As luck would have it, the division on the outer end of
McCook's line was commanded by Richard Johnson, who had been exchanged after his defeat and capture at Hartsville and given command
of a division of infantry; his fortunes were to be no better at Stones
River than they had been at Hartsville. The furious Confederate assault, pivoting on its right, drove back McCook's three divisions one
after the other, and then the two divisions of Thomas' corps, until at
about mid-day those of the men of these five divisions who had not
been killed, wounded, or taken prisoner formed a fairly coherent line
along the Nashville-Murfreesboro Pike, at right angles to the position
they had held at dawn.

All three of Stanley's cavalry brigades had had to fight their way
from Nashville to Stones River in skirmishes of more or less severity
with Wheeler's cavalry as well as with detachments of varying size of
Bragg's infantry.[43] The most severe fighting occurred on the twenty-

40. On December 31, Stanley reported 4,425 men in his three brigades. *Ibid.*, Pt. 2,
p. 283. For the tragic history of the 15th Pennsylvania, see Appendix I.
41. *Ibid.*, Pt. 1, pp. 176–77, 179, 182; Bearss, "Cavalry Operations," 27, 24.
42. For the numbers of the two armies, see *Battles and Leaders*, III, 613.
43. For the march of the Union cavalry to Stones River, see *Official Records*, Vol.
XX, Pt. 2, pp. 241, 245, 257, 266, 267, 268; Bearss, "Cavalry Operations," 30–32,
35–39, 41–42, 45–46; Vale, *Minty and the Cavalry*, 111–14; Kirk, *History of the Fif-*

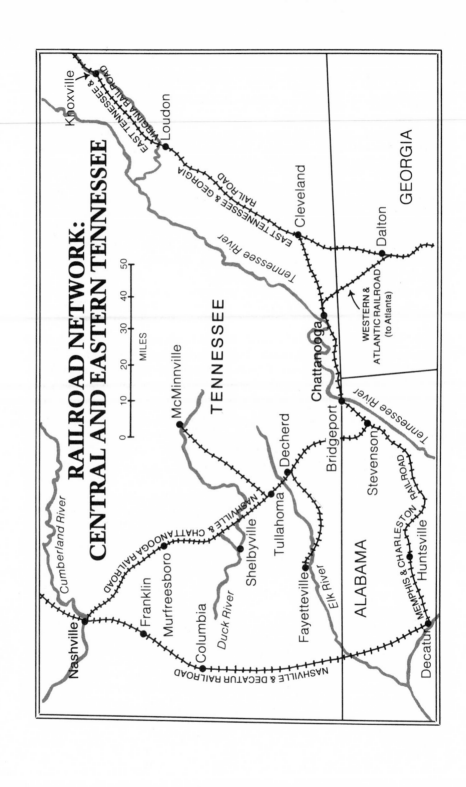

RAILROAD NETWORK: CENTRAL AND EASTERN TENNESSEE

ninth, when at the crossing of Wilkinson's Pike over Overall's Creek, the "reserve brigade," with the 15th Pennsylvania (often referred to as the "Anderson Cavalry" in the reports) in the van, drove Wharton's brigade across the creek and a mile and a half beyond it.[44] There, as General Stanley tells the story, the Pennsylvanians "fell upon two regiments of rebel infantry in ambush, and after a gallant struggle were compelled to retire, with the loss of Major Adolph G. Rosengarten and 6 men killed, and the brave Major Frank B. Ward and 5 men desperately wounded. With the loss of these two most gallant officers the spirit of the Anderson Troop, which gave such fine promise, seems to have died out, and I have not been able to get any duty out of them since."[45]

On the morning of the thirty-first, when the Confederate attack fell on the front and flank of Johnson's division, Colonel Zahm's brigade of three Ohio regiments, numbering a total of 950 rank and file, was posted as a "refused" wing facing south, a little more than a mile to the rear of the center of McCook's corps. The Ohioans were attacked by Wharton's cavalry, operating well out beyond the left flank of Hardee's infantry. Colonel Zahm reported that he saw Johnson's footsoldiers "scattered all over the fields," running toward his position, with "heavy lines" of Confederate infantry behind them; at the same time on his right Wharton's cavalry "were coming around in long columns" with the evident intention of attacking him in flank. Faced with this two-pronged threat, Zahm decided to retreat northward toward the Nashville Pike.[46]

Zahm's retirement was hastened by the shelling of Hardee's artillery and by the continuing pressure of the enemy infantry on his left

---

teenth Pennsylvania, 80–90; Curry, *Four Years in the Saddle,* 83; Crofts, *Third Ohio Veteran Volunteer Cavalry,* 59–60.

44. Wilkinson Pike was a main east-west road that joined the Nashville Pike just to the west of Murfreesboro; Overall's Creek was a northward-flowing stream that joined Stones River four miles north of what was to be the center of the battlefield two days later.

45. *Official Records,* Vol. XX, Pt. 1, p. 617. Major Ward's wound proved to be mortal. He was twenty years old when he died. Bearss identifies the "two regiments" that ambushed the 15th Pennsylvania as a "combat patrol drawn from the 10th and 19th South Carolina Consolidated Infantry," and for Stanley's "compelled to retire" he substitutes: "Panic-stricken by this sudden turn of events, the Pennsylvanians bolted for the rear." Bearss, "Cavalry Operations," 46.

46. *Official Records,* Vol. XX, Pt. 1, p. 635; Bearss, "Cavalry Operations," 119.

and what had now become his rear; Wharton continued to press forward on his right until his brigade was nearly surrounded. At this juncture an aide of General McCook's came on a gallop to Zahm and told him that the corps ammunition train was in danger of being captured by the enemy and that he must try to save it. It speaks well for the morale and discipline of Zahm's troops, and for his own leadership, that they maintained their cohesion and responded to his orders to form line to protect the ammunition train. But the long brigade line, mounted and at a halt, could not withstand the "furious charge of enemy cavalry, preceded by a shower of shells." Inevitably, there was a general stampede of all but Major James W. Paramore's battalion of the 3rd Ohio, on the left end of the brigade line.[47] Paramore was able to hold his position, and when Wharton's troopers veered away from the ammunition train to go after the more inviting target of Zahm's fleeing horsemen, he wheeled and, joined shortly by the 4th United States, charged upon the enemy rear "with terrible effect (scattering their rear columns in worse confusion, if possible, than they had just routed the balance of . . . [Zahm's] brigade)." Captain Elmer Otis of the Regulars reported that in this action, his men took more than 100 prisoners and also released "a large number" of Union cavalrymen the enemy had captured. Captain Otis made it a point to state that a "large majority" of his men were recruits who had transferred to the Regular cavalry from regiments of volunteer infantry; they had been mounted only five days before the battle.[48]

At dawn on this December 31, Colonel Minty's brigade was some distance to the northwest of Overall's Creek. General Stanley with the "reserve brigade" was even farther away, drawn to LaVergne by Wheeler's raid on Rosecrans' trains. When Rosecrans learned that McCook's infantry and Zahm's cavalry were being driven back, he sent orders to

47. With frankness unusual in the war, Zahm reported: "Three regiments skedaddled. . . . Tried hard to rally them, but the panic was so great I could not do it." *Official Records*, Vol. XX, Pt. 1, p. 637. General Stanley wrote that Zahm "contributed greatly by his personal example, to the restoration of order and confidence in that portion of the Second Brigade stampeded by the enemy's attack." *Ibid.*, 620, 966–67; see also Bearss, "Cavalry Operations," 120–22.

48. *Official Records*, Vol. XX, Pt. 1, pp. 637, 643, 649. General Stanley reported that the Regulars charged "with drawn sabers." *Ibid.*, 967. An example of the difficulty of unraveling the story of cavalry operations on this eventful December 31 is that the 4th Ohio also claimed credit for saving the McCook ammunition train. Wulsin, *Story of the Fourth*, 12.

Colonel Kennett and Stanley to collect all the cavalry they could find, and try to relieve the pressure on the army's right.[49] It would appear from the reports that Minty's brigade and the "reserve brigade" coalesced, but in the confusion, with the fields before them filled with stampeded infantrymen, batteries of artillery, and mounted and unhorsed troopers of Zahm's cavalry, all rushing to the rear, neither Kennett nor Stanley was able to bring all the cavalry together and make use of it as a coherent force. Minty, however, did manage to retain a considerable degree of control over his brigade. He ordered the 4th Michigan and part of the 1st Tennessee to dismount, deployed them in a skirmish line, and, with parts of the 7th and 15th Pennsylvania and the 3rd Kentucky mounted in support, sent them forward to face Wharton's oncoming cavalry.[50] With Wharton's 2,500 troopers (by Minty's estimate), some mounted and some on foot, charging them, the dismounted skirmishers and their mounted supports had already begun to retreat when they were charged in flank by a mass of Confederate infantry sweeping out of a cedar brake on their left. The flank attack "broke" the 15th Pennsylvania "and striking the left flank of the Seventh [Pennsylvania], now hard pressed by the rebel cavalry in front, forced it to fall back."[51] Seeing Minty's brigade in jeopardy, Stanley collected all the mounted men within reach: about 150 of the 15th Pennsylvania, two companies of the 4th Michigan, and Major William H. Jennings' battalion plus some oddments of the 7th Pennsylvania "formed column, mounted, and charged with drawn sabers directly upon the left flank of the rebel infantry; routing the enemy, taking one stand of colors, and creating a wild panic and demoralization for more than three fourths of a mile, into and along their left wing."[52]

49. Bearss, "Cavalry Operations," 123–24. Bearss indicates that Minty's brigade, too, was at LaVergne. This does not seem to square with Minty's own report.

50. *Ibid.*, 126. Bearss substitutes the 5th Tennessee for the 1st Tennessee in Minty's report.

51. Vale, *Minty and the Cavalry*, 115; *Official Records*, Vol. XX, Pt. 1, p. 624; Bearss, "Cavalry Operations," 127–28. The account in the 15th Pennsylvania's own regimental history is quite different; the regiment is forced at times to retreat, but it never breaks. It also suggests a greater degree of control of the cavalry by General Stanley than is indicated in other accounts. Kirk, *History of the Fifteenth Pennsylvania*, 90–95.

52. *Official Records*, Vol. XX, Pt. 1, p. 624. Minty reported that only 50 of the 15th Pennsylvania participated in the charge; the figure 150 is Vale's. Vale, *Minty and the*

As Stanley charged the Confederate horse in flank, Minty, ordering the 4th Michigan and 1st Tennessee to mount, "charged with the saber the two thousand five hundred cavalry in his front, drove the first line from the field; then, halting, reformed his command, under a terrific fire, and again charged their second line, posted on the opposite side of a lane, with two fences between him and them. The rebels waited only until they saw our men passing through the fences, when they broke, scattering in every direction, and were driven from the field in the wildest confusion."[53]

Shortly before Wharton's abortive attack on McCook's ammunition train, the 1st Ohio, led by Colonel Minor Milliken, retreated or fled, as one prefers, with the other regiments of Zahm's brigade. Now let the regimental historian take over:

The very acme of Colonel Milliken's ambition had been to have the regiment make a saber charge. His officers and soldiers were falling around him rapidly. . . . He must act at once, or his regiment would be stampeded and driven from the field, as they were being pushed and crushed by an overwhelming force of the enemy, flushed with victory. No officer of the brigade seemed to grasp the situation, no orders were given by the brigade commander, then Colonel Milliken, sending word to the commanders of the other regiments of the brigade to support his regiment in the charge, wheeled his regiment . . . giving the command, "Draw saber."

Spurring forward, the regiment followed their colonel in the charge, "cutting right and left . . . and there was a fearful struggle when the shock came and the melee was on, with its confusion, fighting, yelling, cursing, horses and men struggling in a confused mass and going down together."[54] The Ohioans were not supported in the charge by

---

Cavalry, 114–16. The latter writes, "It was, as is now known, this charge of the First brigade and the Fifteenth Pennsylvania cavalry, under General Stanley, which first arrested the triumphant sweep of the rebel army . . . released the pressure on Sheridan's line, and afforded time for General Rosecrans to re-form his lines, and thus hold his position along the Nashville and Murfreesboro' pike." The historian of the 15th Pennsylvania recalled that Stanley, "with his sword waving . . . ordered: 'Forward! charge! Use your pistols and sabers, boys!'" Kirk, *History of the Fifteenth Pennsylvania*, 54.

53. Vale, *Minty and the Cavalry*, 116. The historian adds that a sergeant of the 7th Pennsylvania, who was captured in this charge, said after he was paroled a few days later that the Confederate dead included "many officers and twenty men, that he knew of, from the sabers of the cavalry." *Ibid.*, 116–17.

54. Curry, *Four Years in the Saddle*, 83–85. In February, 1862, when Milliken, then senior major, was promoted to the colonelcy over the head of Lieutenant Colonel T. C. H. Smith, it caused "much dissatisfaction." The officers waited on Milliken in a body, asked

any other regiment of their brigade. Nevertheless, they were able to hack a wedge into the ranks of the enemy cavalry, but those on either side of the wedge held their ground, then closed in, and in a matter of minutes the 1st Ohio was surrounded. They then had to cut their way out, which they were able to do, but with the loss of 31 killed and wounded and about 100 taken prisoner. Among the killed was Colonel Milliken, shot in the neck by a trooper of the Texas Rangers.[55]

When the fighting ended in the early darkness of New Year's Eve, what was left of the Federal infantry, after the thousands of casualties it had sustained, occupied a fishhook-shaped position below the Nashville Pike, with McCook and Thomas facing southwest and Crittenden facing south and east. At the cost of crippling casualties, the Confederates had driven them to within an inch of total collapse.[56] Both sides were fought out, and when Rosecrans sought the opinion of his corps commanders on what he should do, Thomas and Crittenden evaded the responsibility of advising him; McCook and, surprisingly, Stanley recommended that he retreat.[57] Rosecrans, whose conduct that day in the most desperate circumstances was praised by no less a judge than Sheridan—whose own division had lost 40 percent of its 4,154 officers and men—demonstrated once again the validity of the military truism that victory and defeat are in the mind of the commander, and decided to stick it out.[58]

---

him to resign, and threatened to resign themselves if he did not do so. Eventually, however, Milliken won them over and the hostility to him evaporated. Smith was promoted to colonel when Milliken was killed, but was never mustered as such. *Ibid.*, 28, Appendix (Roster), 3.

55. *Ibid.*, 83–85; *Official Records*, Vol. XX, Pt. 1, p. 968. The Texan shot Milliken "in single combat."

56. For Confederate casualties, see Horn, *Army of Tennessee*, 208; Thomas L. Connelly, *Autumn of Glory: The Army of Tennessee, 1862–1865* (Baton Rouge, 1971), 62, 65; Williams, *Lincoln Finds a General*, IV, 274. Cheatham's division alone lost 36 percent of its effectives.

57. Lamers, *The Edge of Glory*, 235. Richard O'Connor, *Thomas: Rock of Chickamauga* (New York, 1948), 214, states that when asked for his opinion, Thomas "slammed his fist on the map table and boomed: 'This army does not retreat.'" Thomas B. Van Horne, *The Life of Major-General George H. Thomas* (New York, 1882), 97, and F. F. McKinney, *Education in Violence: The Life of George H. Thomas and the History of the Army of the Cumberland* (Detroit, 1961), 195, have essentially the same story. Neither Sheridan nor Crittenden, both of whom were present, mentions it.

58. Sheridan lost 1,633 officers and men; he writes that the number of his missing was "small and legitimate." Sheridan, *Personal Memoirs*, I, 241–42, 240. For his opinion of Rosecrans' conduct of the battle and leadership, see *Ibid.*, 232.

There was a day's lull in the fighting on January 1 and another costly Confederate assault the next day, ordered by Bragg over the objections of General Breckinridge, whose division had to do the fighting. On the evening of the third, Bragg retreated south, ultimately to Tullahoma and Shelbyville, and what had been a drawn battle with enormous casualties on both sides thereby became a Federal victory, or could be claimed as such. There was no pursuit worthy of the name; much of the Federal cavalry was unhorsed, and many more had to be employed to convoy the trains of wagons carrying the thousands of wounded back to Nashville and hauling ammunition and supplies back to the army. Not until the morning of the fifth did a portion of Stanley's horsemen take off after the retreating Confederates. Zahm's brigade followed General Polk in the direction of Shelbyville; Stanley himself, with another group of his command, pursued Hardee in the direction of Manchester. Wheeler commanded Bragg's rear guard, as he had done on the retreat from Kentucky. Stanley attacked Wheeler twice on the afternoon of the fifth, forced or persuaded him to disengage and take up new defensive positions a mile or two to the rear, and then called off the pursuit and returned to Murfreesboro.[59]

Partly because of the state of the roads and partly because of the Confederates' skillful delaying tactics, Rosecrans had needed four days to cover the thirty miles from Nashville to Stones River. On December 29, when the three columns of Federal infantry were still some distance from the site of the battle, Bragg sent Wheeler, with his brigade reinforced by the 1st Tennessee, C.S.A., thus giving him a total of three thousand mounted men, on an expedition north and west to cut across Rosecrans' line of communications and gobble up any of his supply trains that he might find. The possibility of such a raid had crossed Rosecrans' mind also, and he sent General John C. Starkweather's brigade of infantry north to Jefferson to block the crossing of

59. *Official Records*, Vol. XX, Pt. 2, p. 300. The Union cavalry casualties at Stones River were 357 killed, wounded, and missing, 8 percent of those present; incomplete Confederate reports give cavalry casualties as 11 percent of the 4,245 present. The Bearss account of the operations of the two cavalry forces is most helpful, but his unfavorable verdict on the performance of the Federal cavalry does not take into account its missions and the constraints these missions imposed on its freedom of action. Bearss, "Cavalry Operations," 142–44.

Stones River that raiders headed for the Union army's rear were likely to use.[60]

With a command already "badly jaded," Wheeler left on the raid at midnight on the twenty-ninth and, marching in a chill rain, reached Jefferson at daylight on the thirtieth. Starkweather's foot soldiers were already there, but the sixty-four wagons of his brigade supply train were just pulling into camp when Wheeler attacked. Held off by the Union infantry in a two-hour fire fight and capturing and destroying twenty of Starkweather's wagons, Wheeler decided to look for easier pickings elsewhere and set off for LaVergne, on the Nashville-Murfreesboro Pike, halfway back to Nashville.[61] At LaVergne, Wheeler found what he was looking for: the "immense supply trains," numbering about three hundred wagons, of the three divisions of McCook's corps, enjoying a midday rest. Escorting the train were about seven hundred infantry plus a company of the 2nd Indiana, the latter of which had escaped capture by Morgan at Hartsville only a few days before. Wheeler's attack, converging from three directions, caught the train guard by surprise, and there was practically no resistance. The escort was rounded up, and while the men's paroles were made out, the raiders looted the wagons of whatever took their fancy (officers' personal luggage was particularly favored), cut the mules' traces, and then set fire to the wagons. A Federal staff officer who reached the scene the next morning, wrote that the "turnpike, as far as the eye could reach, was filled with burning wagons. The country was overspread with disarmed men, broken down horses and mules. The streets were covered with empty valises and trunks, knapsacks, broken guns, and all the indescribable debris of a captured and rifled army train."[62] Flushed out of LaVergne by Colonel M. B. Walker's Federal infantry, Wheeler went on to Rock Spring and Nolensville, capturing and destroying smaller trains in both places and capturing on the way a number of Union foraging parties. On the morning of the thirty-first, having circled the rear of the Union army from left to right, he was

60. Bearss, "Cavalry Operations," 51–52, 110; Lamers, *The Edge of Glory*, 210.

61. Bearss, "Cavalry Operations," 110–12. Wheeler claimed to have destroyed all of Starkweather's wagons. *Official Records*, Vol. XX, Pt. 1, p. 958.

62. *Official Records*, Vol. XX, Pt. 1, p. 959; Horn, *Army of Tennessee*, 198–99; Bearss, "Cavalry Operations," 113–15; *Battles and Leaders*, III, 614n. The officer was Colonel G. C. Kniffen.

back at Stones River in time to join Wharton's brigade in its attack on the Federal right.

What did the raid accomplish? It kept out of the fight of the thirty-first two brigades of Thomas' corps and, until midmorning, two of Stanley's cavalry regiments that were sent to LaVergne to try to intercept the raiders; too late at LaVergne, the two regiments started back to Stones River early on the morning of the thirty-first and arrived in time to take part in the battle. Wheeler captured about a thousand Federals, most of whom he paroled, and he seized or destroyed supplies estimated to be worth nearly a million dollars. It cannot be said, however, that his exploit, whatever its value may have been in boosting the morale of his own men or of the Army of Tennessee in general, affected to an appreciable degree the outcome of the fight at Stones River or, even less, the outcome of the war as a whole. The loss of a million dollars' worth of supplies did not prevent Rosecrans from fighting the battle; it simply increased the size of the national debt that those of Wheeler's troopers who survived the war, and their descendants, had to help to pay off.[63]

63. Small-scale efforts to interrupt Rosecrans' communications with Nashville were made by Wheeler's cavalry after their return from the Jefferson-LaVergne raid. On January 1, a train of wounded, escorted back to Nashville by cavalry led by Colonel Zahm, was attacked at LaVergne by "Wheeler's brigade with two pieces of artillery." The Confederates attacked both the front and rear of the train. The 2nd Tennessee ran away "like sheep," and most of the 15th Pennsylvania "scampered off in most every direction." Nevertheless, Zahm reported, "not a wagon fell into the enemy's hands." He also reported on another attack by Wheeler two days later on a train carrying hospital stores and ammunition that Zahm escorted in the opposite direction; despite the Confederate attack, he was able to bring the train through "with but little damage." *Official Records*, Vol. XX, Pt. 1, pp. 634, 630; Crofts, *Third Ohio Veteran Volunteer Cavalry*, 60–61, 63–64, 69.

VI

The Weapons of War Perished

OCTOBER 16 AND 25, 1862, WERE IMPORTANT DATES IN THE calendar of Ulysses S. Grant's progress to the eminence of general-in-chief of the armies of the United States. On the former of these dates, the District of West Tennessee, which he then headed, was raised to the status of a military department, the Department of the Tennessee, and on the latter date, he formally assumed command of it. Grant now had direction of the war in northern Mississippi and in those portions of Tennessee and Kentucky that lay west of the Tennessee River. In a dispatch to General Halleck that he sent off the day after assuming command of the department, he proposed moving down the line of the Mississippi Central Railroad by way of Holly Springs, Oxford, Water Valley, and eventually Jackson, Mississippi; he would stay inland from the Mississippi River, force the evacuation of Vicksburg by the Confederates, and thereby gain control of the river for the Union.[1]

Grant was in a position to consider an aggressive campaign because his erstwhile subordinate, William Rosecrans, was expected to fight his way into east Tennessee and keep Braxton Bragg fully occupied. Moreover, Rosecrans' victory at Corinth on October 3–4, and the severe mauling he had administered to Van Dorn and Price, had also restored the initiative to the armies of the Union in the area em-

---

1. *Official Records*, Vol. XVII, Pt. 2, pp. 278, 294, 296; Sherman, *Memoirs*, I, 281.

braced in Grant's new department.[2] As his dispatch to Halleck indicated, Grant was eager to take advantage of the opportunity. There were, however, a number of problems to be overcome. First, the essentially defensive posture he had had to assume during the summer and early fall had made it necessary for him to scatter his forces, numbering about 45,000, from Memphis in the west all the way to Tuscumbia, Alabama, in the east, a distance of almost 150 miles; in addition, he had to protect the area in his rear, particularly his supply line, 85 miles of the single-track Mobile & Ohio Railroad from Columbus, Kentucky, on the Mississippi River, to his headquarters at Jackson, Tennessee. Every foot of this umbilical cord, without which the kind of inland campaign Grant had in mind would be impossible, especially in winter, was exposed to harassment and interruptions by Confederate cavalry of every degree, from the lone bushwhacker or guerrilla to groups of partisan rangers and large bodies of regularly organized cavalry, "saucy and active, and far superior to ours," as General Sherman called them.[3] And obviously, as he moved southward, each day's march added to the railroad mileage behind him that had to be guarded, garrisoned, and kept in repair: 70 miles of the Mississippi Central from Jackson to Holly Springs, another nearly 30 miles from Holly Springs down to Oxford, and so on.

The necessity of guarding his line of communications, and indeed the impossibility, given the geographic circumstances, of conducting an aggressive campaign without doing so, now raised in a new context what had been an old and chronic grievance of northern army commanders: Grant lacked the cavalry he needed. As far back as June 6, John McClernand, while protesting an order of Grant's that took from him three companies of Colonel Dickey's 4th Illinois, the only cavalry he had, and gave him in exchange "two small companies of German Cavalry poorly armed," made it clear that he needed more cavalry than he had, for "escort[ing] trains, scouting, accompanying expeditions, and picket duty."[4] Later in the month, Sherman, charged with the job of guarding the line of the Memphis & Charleston east of Memphis,

2. "The effect of the battle of Corinth was very great. It was, indeed, a decisive blow to the Confederate cause in our quarter, and changed the whole aspect of affairs in West Tennessee. From the timid defensive we were at once enabled to assume the bold offensive." Sherman, *Memoirs*, I, 264.

3. *Ibid.*, 258.

4. *Official Records*, Vol. X, Pt. 2, p. 267.

wrote that he "should have a good strong regiment of cavalry. . . . My cavalry is so used up that I cannot push them out more than 7 or 8 miles." Two months later, he told Grant that he "should have some cavalry. The Fourth Illinois is now a mere squad, and it is worse than [a] toothache to call upon them for hard work."[5] Grenville Dodge, in command at Corinth, who kept his nine hundred "effective" cavalry "on the move . . . with orders to wipe out guerrillas and cotton-burners [and] to disarm all known rebels in . . . all the country bordering the Obion swamps," asked for more cavalry, and if they could not be had, for a hundred saddles so that he could mount infantry "on contraband stock." When, two weeks later, Grant robbed Peter to pay Paul, as General Halleck would have called it, by sending him the 4th Illinois from Memphis, Dodge reported that they were "weak in men, horses, &c. I do not believe that they have 400 men in all told [sic] for duty." Another week passed, and General Dodge (having in the meantime mounted three companies of infantry) was begging for horses for his cavalry. In an effort to arouse the sympathy of the powers that be, he wrote that he "suffer[ed] every day for the want of them."[6]

In the end Grant himself had to join the chorus of his subordinates in asking for more cavalry. He telegraphed General Halleck on August 20: "The guerrillas are becoming so active in West Tennessee that a large mounted force is required to suppress them. Cannot a portion of General Curtis' cavalry [from Arkansas] be sent to me?" Halleck told him the next day that Curtis' cavalry could not be spared, but that Union Governor Andrew Johnson of Tennessee had been asked some weeks before to raise "some cavalry regiments to act against guerrilla bands" and that Grant would be sent more cavalry as soon as any more were available. Grant countered with the remark that his need for more cavalry was so great that he would have to mount infantry, "making secessionists furnish horses and forage."[7]

5. *Ibid.*, Vol. XVII, Pt. 2, pp. 39, 79. Sherman wrote that General Stephen A. Hurlbut had "about 300 cavalry without carbines and much used up" and that he himself had eight companies of the 4th Illinois, "now down to about 200 men, and they and horses much used up." *Ibid.*, 85. Despite his great need for mounted troops, Sherman, as he informed Grant, declined to provide his cavalry with horses until he succeeded in impressing them with "the importance of taking care of what they have." *Ibid.*, 202. At this same time, however, a company of the 4th Illinois was kept in Memphis "to assist the provost-marshal in the performance of his duties"—this when Memphis was garrisoned by three regiments of Indiana infantry. *Ibid.*, 31.

6. *Ibid.*, 104, 110, 180–81, 192, and Pt. 1, p. 55.

7. *Ibid.*, Pt. 2, p. 182.

The records do not disclose how it was done, but by November 10, eight days after his southbound campaign got under way, Grant had a respectable force of 5,530 cavalry present for duty, as part of his army of 61,000. The "Right Wing" of the army, under James McPherson, had the 2nd and 7th Illinois and a battalion of the 5th Ohio; the "Left Wing," under Charles Hamilton, had the 2nd Iowa, 7th Kansas, 3rd Michigan, 5th Missouri, and one company of the 11th Illinois. The whole of Hamilton's cavalry was commanded by Colonel Albert L. Lee. Sherman, at Memphis, had the 6th Illinois and Thielemann's Battalion. At Jackson, Tennessee, under General Hurlbut, there were the 4th and 11th Illinois (the last less one company), the 6th Tennessee, one company each of the 2nd and 12th Illinois and 4th Ohio, nine companies of the 5th Ohio, Hawkins' Horse, and Stewart's Independent Cavalry. The records do not show what cavalry, if any, had been assigned to General Thomas A. Davies at Columbus, Kentucky.[8]

The assignment of cavalry by regiments and parts of regiments makes it evident that as late as November, 1862, Grant was not ready to follow Pope's and Rosecrans' example by establishing brigades and divisions of cavalry; even the four regiments and the single company of a fifth in General Hamilton's "wing" are shown merely as led or commanded by Colonel Lee, but without being designated either a brigade or a division. Grant had dipped his toes into the water; his cavalry were no longer assigned to divisions and brigades of infantry, but he was not yet ready to take the plunge of creating an autonomous cavalry line.

Perhaps Grant's reluctance to consolidate his cavalry was due to his lack of confidence in the ability of any of his cavalry officers to provide effective leadership for mounted troops in units larger than a regiment. Gordon Granger and Sheridan were gone, and Stanley, commanding one of Hamilton's divisions of infantry, was about to leave to head Rosecrans' cavalry. Grant had had favorable reports from Sherman about Colonel Benjamin Grierson and from General McPherson about Colonel Lee. He himself made it a point to mention Lee in a dispatch to Halleck as "one of our best cavalry officers. I earnestly recommend him for promotion." In a message to Sherman a few days later he spoke of Lee as "one of the best cavalry officers I ever saw."[9]

8. For the numbers of Grant's cavalry, see *Ibid.*, 337–38; for its organization, *Ibid.*, 338–42.

9. *Ibid.*, 396, 331, 348, and Pt. 1, pp. 469, 486. It must be said, however, that the

Nonetheless, a week or so after praising Lee, when Grant finally bit the bullet and organized a cavalry division, the man he chose to head it was neither Grierson nor Lee, but the "generous, gracious, popular" Colonel T. Lyle Dickey, who had given no indication of outstanding abilities as a cavalryman.[10]

On November 26, Dickey assumed command of a three-brigade Cavalry Division, the First Brigade, under Lee, assigned to Hamilton's wing; the Second, under Colonel Edward Hatch, to McPherson's; and the Third, under Grierson, to Sherman's.[11] With each of the three brigades assigned to a separate wing of the Army of the Tennessee, the "Cavalry Division" was obviously that in name only. Moreover, with each of the three wings commanded by an officer who outranked not only the commanding officer of the cavalry brigade assigned to him but Colonel Dickey himself, it was evident that the operations of the cavalry would be controlled by the commanders of the wings, not by officers of their own. In fact, as the campaign unfolded, it was Grant himself who directed cavalry operations. On December 8, from Oxford, Grant wrote Halleck, "With the large cavalry force now at my disposal I will be able to have them show themselves at different points on the Tallahatchie and Yalabusha, and where an opportunity offers, make a real attack."[12] This was a far cry, indeed, from Sheridan, eighteen months later, leading an autonomous cavalry corps to pitch into Jeb Stuart; Grant's role in that operation was merely that of permitting Sheridan to go ahead with it.

But perhaps it was the cavalry itself, and not its commanding officers, that had failed to gain Grant's confidence. In November, when

language and tone of the dispatch in which Sherman sounded Grierson's praises make it seem like a conventional endorsement solicited by the subject of it rather than a spontaneous commendation. It must be noted also that Sherman had remarked in a report to Grant not too long before that his "cavalry have already made so many indefinite reports, which on examination proved unfounded, that I mistrust them." *Ibid.*, Pt. 2, p. 85.

10. The adjectives are those of Williams, in *Lincoln Finds a General*, IV, 190.

11. *Official Records*, Vol. XVII, Pt. 2, p. 263. In the First Brigade were the 7th Kansas, 2nd and 4th Illinois, and one battalion of the 2nd Iowa; in the Second, the 7th Illinois, 5th Ohio, and two battalions of the 2nd Iowa; in the Third, the 3rd Michigan and Thielemann's Battalion. It should be noted as a sign of progress that only one of the seven regiments was split up. Mizner's position under this new dispensation is an insoluble puzzle. On December 7, by which time he was serving under Grant, not Rosecrans, he is addressed as "Commanding Cavalry Division, XIII Army Corps"—the same position held by Dickey. *Ibid.*, 200, 245, 391.

12. *Ibid.*, Pt. 1, p. 474.

James Wilson, then a mere lieutenant in the Regular Army, arrived at Grant's headquarters to serve as his chief topographical engineer, he found the cavalry "green and badly organized," and volunteered to act as Colonel Dickey's adjutant. This was before the organization, just mentioned, of the cavalry division. His observation of the four regiments then under Dickey—the 4th Illinois, 2nd Iowa, 3rd Michigan, and 7th Kansas—caused Wilson to conclude that Grant's cavalry "were excellent material, but all untrained and badly deficient in discipline. In the advance they did well, but in the retreat they were entirely unmanageable. . . . The entire organization was lacking in coherence, cooperation, and steadiness. When Van Dorn and William H. Jackson [actually Forrest], a few days later, passed around Grant's army, capturing his 'rear headquarters' and his main depot of supplies . . . Dickey's raw and undisciplined cavalry, instead of following and harassing the enemy, turned tail and rejoined the infantry columns as soon as possible."[13] Wilson might not have realized it at the time, but he certainly could, and did, realize before too many months had passed, that Dickey's regiments lacked "coherence, cooperation, and steadiness" because they had never been given the opportunity to develop these desirable qualities.

Wilson noticed something else about the cavalry: that the slow pace of the army's advance, encumbered as it was with heavy trains, "gave plenty of time for straggling and plundering . . . which . . . seemed to have already become the habit with western troops" and which no one seemed to try very hard to stop.[14] At the very time when Wilson witnessed the straggling and plundering, a long series of orders issued by Hamilton, by Sherman, and by Grant himself exhorted the soldiers, horse and foot alike, to cease their "indiscriminate and extensive plundering," arson, and vandalism, threatened the guilty with dire punishment, and announced that regimental officers of whatever rank who failed to "use all their efforts to repress these gross outrages" faced imprisonment in the military prison at Alton, Illinois. Indeed, Grant went to the length of announcing that the cost of "depredations" committed would be charged against the pay owing to an entire division unless "the act . . . [could] be traced either to the individuals committing them or to the company, regiment, or brigade to which the

13. Wilson, *Under the Old Flag*, I, 143.
14. *Ibid.*, 142.

General Kenner Garrard
Courtesy U.S. Army Military History Institute

General David Stanley
Courtesy U.S. Army Military History Institute

General Edward M. McCook
Courtesy National Archives

General Washington L. Elliott
Courtesy National Archives

offenders belong." [15] Wilson himself was to learn when he reached a position of authority a few months later that no amount of orders from on high, no exhortations, and no threats were going to stop a practice the men in the ranks were unwilling to give up, and that line officers, many of them former enlisted men, were unwilling to risk their uncertain authority to try to stop it.

Grant's campaign got under way on November 2 and made good progress along the line of the Mississippi Central. By the eighth the army was at Grand Junction, where the Memphis & Charleston crossed the Mississippi Central and gave Grant an uncertain connection with Memphis, fifty miles to the west. Here Grant paused to repair the railroad behind him. [16] Colonel Lee's cavalry had led the advance. They had their first brush with the enemy on the eighth at the village of Lamar, twelve miles southwest of Grand Junction. The Jayhawkers, in the van, came upon Colonel W. H. Jackson's Confederate cavalry. Colonel Lee being in command of the brigade, command of the 7th Kansas had developed upon Lieutenant Colonel Thomas P. Herrick. As soon as he caught sight of the enemy, Herrick ordered a charge. Jackson, caught on the march, had no time to deploy before he was struck in flank by the Jayhawkers' attack; his men stampeded—one of the Kansans recorded in his diary that they "fled like sheep"—leaving dead, wounded, arms, horses, and prisoners, the last reported variously as 75, 103, 134, and "400 or 500," in the hands of the victorious Jayhawkers. [17] And, marvel of marvels, when the 7th Kansas returned to camp that evening, they were cheered by the infantry for their victory.

15. *Official Records*, Vol. XVII, Pt. 2, pp. 321, 326, 331, 359, 390. The 7th Kansas, which Wilson singled out for special censure, had been in trouble over its incorrigible plundering and vandalism ever since its arrival in Tennessee in the early summer and would continue to be in trouble over an endless chain of incidents of the same sort as long as it remained in Tennessee and Mississippi. *Ibid.*, 34, 52, 53, 77, 87, 91; Starr, *Jennison's Jayhawkers*, 186–89.

16. *Official Records*, Vol. XVII, Pt. 1, pp. 466–67; Grant, *Personal Memoirs*, 422–23. To Halleck, Grant announced Holly Springs as his objective, "and maybe Grenada," the latter being a hundred miles south of Memphis and the junction point of the Mississippi Central and the Mississippi & Tennessee railroads. By holding it, Grant would have a second supply line back to the Mississippi River. But Halleck warned him, "It is not advisable to put railroads in operation south of Memphis." *Official Records*, Vol. XVII, Pt. 1, p. 467.

17. Starr, *Jennison's Jayhawkers*, 219–20; *Official Records*, Vol. XVII, Pt. 1, p. 467.

The advance continued against weak opposition, and at daylight on November 13, Colonel Lee entered Holly Springs, Van Dorn's base after his defeat at Corinth six weeks before.[18] After another pause, longer than the one at Grand Junction, to repair the railroad behind him, Grant resumed his advance on the twenty-seventh. After what seemed to be a halfhearted effort to dispute the crossing of the Tallahatchie River, the Confederates withdrew to the south, and the next day Colonel Lee and his cavalry entered Oxford.[19]

To give Grant's campaign a boost, Halleck telegraphed General Samuel Curtis, in St. Louis, to concentrate a force of cavalry and infantry at Helena, Arkansas, and have it cross the Mississippi and raid the railroad junction at Grenada to interrupt the flow of supplies going north to the forces of General John Pemberton, which were contesting Grant's advance. The expedition, actually organized by General Frederick Steele, was made up of 1,925 cavalry (detachments varying in size from 92, the smallest, to 300, the largest, taken from ten regiments of Indiana, Illinois, Iowa, Missouri, Kansas, and Wisconsin cavalry) and "eight small guns" under the command of General Cadwallader C. Washburn, and a supporting force of 5,000 infantry and 14 guns under General Alvin P. Hovey. It disembarked at Delta, on the Mississippi side of the river, on November 27.[20] Setting off inland on the morning of the twenty-eighth, Washburn came to within seven miles of Grenada by the evening of the twenty-ninth. After causing insignificant damage to the railroad the following morning and thrashing about for three days thereafter with no indication of any coherent design behind his movements, Washburn had a skirmish on December 3 with the "First Texas Legion" and returned to Delta on December 6 or 7.

18. Grant decided to make Holly Springs his "dépôt of supplies and munitions of war." *Official Records*, Vol. XVII, Pt. 1, pp. 470, 488–89; Grant, *Personal Memoirs*, I, 427.

19. *Official Records*, Vol. XVII, Pt. 1, p. 492, Pt. 2, pp. 367–68. General Hamilton reported that Lee's advance had been "a continual skirmish." A newspaperman then with Grant noted, "Our advanced cavalry upon entering . . . [Oxford] and getting hold of some liquor, behaved scandalously and robbed the people right and left of everything they fancied." Sylvanus Cadwallader, *Three Years with Grant*, ed. Benjamin F. Thomas (New York, 1955), 27.

20. *Official Records*, Vol. XVII, Pt. 1, pp. 467, 528–41, Pt. 2, pp. 382, 388–94, 401–402, 408; Grant, *Personal Memoirs*, I, 428; Williams, *Lincoln Finds a General*, IV, 168–69.

There was another pause at Oxford in Grant's advance, to repair the railroad north of the Tallahatchie River and replenish supplies. In the meantime, however, the cavalry went forward, and by the evening of December 3, they were eight miles south of Oxford on the Coffeeville road, Lee on the right and Hatch on the left. Lee had crossed the Yocknapatalpha ("having driven the enemy from a burning bridge and repaired it") to reach this point. During the night Hatch, too, crossed the river and, shortly before noon on the fourth, marched into the village of Water Valley. As he was entering the settlement, he was attacked from his left rear by a force of enemy cavalry he estimated at eight regiments. "After a fierce fight" he drove them off "with considerable loss" to their side. Then, however, he was attacked by another group of Confederate cavalry, coming at him from his right rear. In order to redeploy to meet this new threat, Hatch had to retreat. Lee's brigade appeared on the scene just at this point, but inferring from what prisoners told him that Hatch had been beaten, Lee "advanced with great caution." This gave the Confederate cavalry time and the opportunity to disengage, cross the Otuckafola, and set fire to the two bridges (one of which the Federals were able to save) over the stream behind them.[21]

The following day—and be it noted that this was the first such occasion in a campaign now just over a month old—the three brigades of cavalry were united. With Dickey in command, they crossed the Otuckafola and, with Lee's brigade leading the way, took off after the Confederates. Just north of the town of Coffeeville, Dickey encountered an unpleasant surprise. General Mansfield Lovell, in command of a division of Confederate infantry, had learned from his scouts that there was a long gap between Dickey's cavalry and the supporting infantry of Hamilton's wing and decided to lay a trap for the overly confident cavalrymen. He posted his infantry in timber, a mile north of the town, on a ridge perpendicular to the road on which the cavalry were advancing. Behind the infantry he placed a four-gun battery, well screened by underbrush; three hundred yards behind the guns, on higher ground, he placed two long-range Parrott guns. Lovell withheld his fire until the Federals were within point-blank range of his guns. Then he sprang

21. Grant, *Personal Memoirs*, I, 428; *Official Records*, Vol. XVII, Pt. 1, pp. 500–501, 493–94; see also Pierce, *History of the Second Iowa*, 41–43.

the trap; at the same time that the six guns began shelling Lee's cavalry, Lovell's infantry opened on his "advanced dismounted skirmishers [four companies of the 7th Kansas] with rapid volleys, while heavy skirmishing was in progress on both flanks of the head of . . . [the] column," making it evident to Dickey that he had "encountered a heavier force than . . . [he was] able to combat under the jaded condition of . . . [his] men and horses." Dickey thereupon ordered a retreat, which was so well managed that General Lloyd Tilghman, who directed the Confederate attack, wrote that "the tactics of the enemy did them great credit."[22] Colonel Dickey described the retreat:

Colonel Lee was ordered to fall back steadily in the center and strong parties were at once sent to the support of our skirmishers on the right and left flanks. The column was faced to the rear and Colonels Mizner and Hatch were ordered to form successive lines of detachments on each side of the road to cover the retreat of our skirmishers and check the advance of the enemy on the main road. The enemy pressing hard on our retreating forces, the moving back of the led horses . . . and the reversal of wagons and ambulances occasioned considerable confusion, though no indications of a panic were at any time perceptible. Our flanks were repeatedly attacked by the enemy's infantry, but our flankers as often succeeded in repulsing them.[23]

The 7th Kansas had been forced to make a fast about-face from advance guard to rear guard by the first "withering volley" of Tilghman's infantry and thereafter were pressed steadily back. The fighting ranged over alternating bands of timber and cleared farmland. Forced back to the northern edge of a belt of timber, the Jayhawkers ran to their led horses, mounted, galloped across the clearing to the next patch of woods, dismounted, took position along its southern edge, and while the horse holders walked the led horses through the woods, the dismounted men held on in their skirmish line as long as they could, then ran through the woods to their horses, mounted, and repeated the process.[24]

Eight of the ten cavalrymen killed in this fight and forty of the sixty-three wounded were officers and troopers of the 7th Kansas. And

22. *Official Records*, Vol. XVII, Pt. 1, p. 505.
23. *Ibid.*, 494–95.
24. Starr, *Jennison's Jayhawkers*, 223–24. Private Christopher M. Ford of Co. A, 7th Kansas, was hit five times before he could be induced to leave the field. *Ibid.*, 224. For an account highly critical of Colonel Dickey, see Pierce, *History of the Second Iowa*, 43–44.

the regiment showed that Lieutenant Wilson's observation that Dickey's cavalry were "entirely unmanageable" in a retreat and lacked "coherence, cooperation, and steadiness," however true it may have been
of Dickey's cavalry in general, certainly did not apply to the Kansans.[25]

Dickey's retreat went on for about a mile and a half. There, with the
onset of darkness, the Confederate attacks ceased. Dickey and his men
did not know it at the time, but the advance of Grant's army along the
railroad had come to a halt.

It should have been apparent to Grant by December 3 that his three
brigades of cavalry were of considerable help to him in his advance,
but he was shackled by habit and could think of nothing better for
them to do than to raid the Mobile & Ohio, about fifty miles to the east
of his line of march. There is nothing in the records and no word in
Grant's *Personal Memoirs* to indicate what he hoped to accomplish
with an operation so eccentric in every sense of the word. After an initial message to Dickey on the subject, Grant did indicate, perhaps as
an afterthought, that if Dickey learned that Columbus, Mississippi,
was "only defended by conscripts it would be a great strike to get in
there and destroy the enemy's armories, machine shops, &c."[26] Additional messages on subsequent days further defined Dickey's objectives. He was "to select those of his cavalry whom he deem[ed] most
suitable for the expedition" but to leave behind about half his cavalry;
General Dodge would be ordered to move a brigade of infantry south
from Corinth as far as Tupelo to "cooperate" with him. And lastly,
Dickey was told, "The cavalry force you will have with you can subsist
on the country through which you pass. The plundering propensity
exhibited by some of the cavalry should be suppressed as far as practicable. This can be partially done by making a detail from each regiment and charging them with procuring rations and forage for their
regiments and replacing broken-down animals."[27] Colonel Mizner,

25. Wilson was present at this fight, but he wrote his reminiscences nearly fifty
years later. *Official Records*, Vol. XVII, Pt. 1, p. 495.

26. *Ibid.*, Pt. 2, pp. 379–80. Other language in the dispatch suggests that the idea
of the expedition may have come from Dickey. *Ibid.*, 385. Columbus was another thirty-
five miles as the crow flies beyond the railroad. K. P. Williams expresses the opinion that
Grant ordered the expedition "to give greater security to his left flank." *Lincoln Finds a
General*, IV, 174. There being no Confederate troops of any consequence on Grant's left
other than Bragg's army three hundred miles away, the theory has little to recommend it.

27. The dispatches setting the raid in motion will be found in *Official Records*,
Vol. XVII, Pt. 2, pp. 388, 391–92, 395, 399, 403, 410.

who was to command the portion of the cavalry Dickey was leaving behind, was ordered to move "to the south or southeast slowly, to cover the movement of Colonel Dickey," and if he detected any move of the enemy toward the raiders, to send word to Dickey or go to his assistance, as he thought best.[28]

Taking with him eight hundred men of the 2nd Iowa and 7th Illinois of Hatch's brigade, plus a small escort from Company F, 4th Illinois, Dickey took off on the morning of December 14. Marching much of the time in a "terrific rain storm," he reached the railroad at Saltillo, a short distance north of Tupelo, and spent the sixteenth and seventeenth "in hard labor, by which all the trestle work and bridges from Saltillo [south] to Okolona, a distance of 34 miles, and a large bridge south of Okolona, across a branch of the Tombigbee River, were thoroughly destroyed, as well as large quantities of timber lying along the railroad side for repairing purposes."[29] On the morning of the eighteenth, "before day," the raiders set off on their return march. At Pontotoc, later that day, Dickey saw a column of Confederate horsemen, "said to be 6,000 or 7,000," marching north.[30] As soon as the enemy force was out of the way, Dickey sent off couriers and an escort with dispatches to let Grant know of the northward-marching Confederate cavalry, but in the evening, on going into bivouac, he was mortified to discover that the couriers and escort "by a fatal misapprehension of . . . orders" had remained with the column. Dickey entrusted the dispatches to other couriers—two or more—but these messengers lost their way and after traveling all night "found themselves farther from Oxford than when they left camp."[31] Here, if ever, was Grant's opportunity to complain of "cavalry stupidity."

As Grant was about to learn, raiding, and raiding for a well-thought-

---

28. *Ibid.*, 411.

29. *Ibid.*, Pt. 1, p. 488.

30. Anticipating the inevitable questioning or criticism of his failure to attack the enemy, Dickey reported, "My horses were so worn down from long and hard marching that it was deemed imprudent to encounter an enemy so superior in numbers and mounted on fresh horses." *Ibid.*, 498; see also Cadwallader, *Three Years with Grant*, 35.

31. For Dickey's report on the expedition, see *Official Records*, Vol. XVII, Pt. 1, pp. 496–99. The historian of the 2nd Iowa reports that the railroad "was reduced to a complete wreck" and that at Okolona the raiders "burned ten thousand bushels of Confederate corn and a large amount of commissary stores, and captured thirty prisoners." The historian, who never has a good word for Colonel Dickey, writes that after the encounter with Van Dorn's force (which he puts at ten thousand) his own Colonel Hatch wanted to "harass and detain" the enemy "until notice could be given the garrison at Holly Springs of his approach and proper means of defense employed," but "Dickey

out purpose, was quite within the capabilities of his Confederate antag-
onists, for the horsemen Dickey had seen marching north were 2,500—
not 6,000 or 7,000—cavalry of John S. Griffith's and W. H. Jackson's
brigades (described as "small, ill-disciplined and poorly armed") and
Robert McCulloch's small brigade, on their way to Grant's main supply
base at Holly Springs.[32] The idea of the raid was proposed to General
Pemberton by Colonel Griffith "and other cavalry commanders" as the
best means of slowing down or stopping altogether the southward
progress of Grant's steamroller. Pemberton accepted the suggestion
and directed Earl Van Dorn, now his chief of cavalry, to take command
of the expedition, which was to be timed to coincide with Forrest's raid
on the Mobile & Ohio Railroad between Jackson, Tennessee, and Columbus, Kentucky. Starting from Grenada on the afternoon of December 17, Van Dorn used roads well to the east of the direct route to
Holly Springs, to create the impression that his destination was Tennessee. On the night of the eighteenth, after an almost continuous
march of more than thirty hours, the raiders bivouacked at New Albany. On the nineteenth, a participant in the raid relates, "the head of
the column was directed toward Holly Springs, and the precaution
was taken to arrest everybody going in that direction. . . . guards were
stationed at every house we passed, lest some one might undertake a
shorter route to get ahead of us and inform the enemy. . . . It was bitter
cold, those of us without coats suffered, although we had put on every
available shirt. This writer remembers he had on six."[33] Van Dorn's
precautions proved to be effective, and so did his carefully planned attack on the garrison and the town at daybreak on the twentieth, with
detachments charging from the northeast, east, south, and north.

What was the garrison doing in the meantime? In command at
Holly Springs was Colonel Robert C. Murphy, 8th Wisconsin Infantry,
at the head of fewer than 500 (by his account) infantry and six companies of the 2nd Illinois under Lieutenant Colonel Quincy McNeil.[34]

---

would not allow it. . . . The result of this blunder was the success of Van Dorn at Holly
Springs, and the consequent abandonment of the campaign of Gen. Grant." Pierce, *History of the Second Iowa*, 45. This is typical of the hindsight wisdom to be found frequently in regimental histories.

32. Thiele, "The Evolution of Cavalry," 360.

33. J. G. Deupree, "The Capture of Holly Springs, Mississippi, Dec. 20, 1862," *Publications of the Mississippi Historical Society*, IV (1901), 54.

34. Colonel Murphy's report is in *Official Records*, Vol. XVII, Pt. 1, pp. 508–509.
According to Grant, *Personal Memoirs*, I, 432, the garrison numbered 1,500.

Colonel Dickey, returning from his Mobile & Ohio raid and riding with his escort in advance of his main body, reached Oxford at 5:30 in the afternoon on the nineteenth and at once informed Grant of the "large rebel cavalry force" marching north from Pontotoc on the Ripley road that he had seen the previous day.[35] Grant's staff got off telegrams at once to all the major military posts to the north, including Holly Springs, to warn their commanding officers "to be prepared to meet . . . [the enemy] and to hold their respective posts at all hazards."[36] Colonel Murphy seems not to have taken any immediate action pursuant to this warning nor to a second he received before dawn on the twentieth, when a "contraband" brought him word that Van Dorn was only fourteen miles away with 5,000 cavalry and was expected to reach Holly Springs by daylight.[37] It is difficult to determine just what Colonel Murphy did, and exactly when, in response to these warnings; it does seem to be a fact that he did not alert his infantry and that the cavalry he reported ordering out to the east either did not receive timely orders or, if they did, failed to derive any sense of urgency from them. Grant, in any event, concluded that Murphy had failed to do his duty; on January 8, on his own authority and without the formality, customary in such cases, of a court-martial, he ordered Murphy dismissed from the service, stigmatizing his conduct of December 20 as "cowardly and disgraceful."[38]

Colonel Murphy's infantry were quickly overrun and captured in their camps by the raiders, and the colonel surrendered.[39] But the Illinois cavalrymen, encamped on the fairgrounds, some distance away, had sufficient warning to begin to saddle up, though not enough to organize a defense before the 1st Mississippi, their pistols blazing,

35. *Official Records*, Vol. XVII, Pt. 1, p. 499. Colonel Mizner reported to General McPherson earlier that day that "a heavy column" of cavalry had left Grenada for Pontotoc. *Ibid.*, Pt. 2, pp. 437, 438. Grant at first assumed this was cavalry sent north to intercept Dickey.

36. *Ibid.*, 439. It was at first assumed at Grant's headquarters that W. H. Jackson was in command of the raiders.

37. In his dispatch to Grant reporting the information the contraband had brought in, Murphy reported the enemy force as 5,000, but in his report on the capture of his post, he gives the size of the enemy force as 12,000. *Ibid.*, 444, and Pt. 1, p. 508.

38. *Ibid.*, Pt. 1, pp. 515–16, General Orders No. 4. Grant's orders were confirmed by the War Department on January 10. *Ibid.*, 516. See also Grant, *Personal Memoirs*, I, 432, 434, where he speaks of Colonel Murphy's "disloyalty" or "gross cowardice."

39. A paroled army surgeon told Colonel Mizner that "not above 40 shots were fired" before the infantry resistance ceased. *Official Records*, Vol. XVII, Pt. 2, p. 443.

came at them from all sides. Colonel McNeil and other officers of the regiment, Major Daniel B. Bush, Jr., Captain C. Carroll Marsh, Major John J. Mudd, Lieutenant Isaiah Stickel, and others, each led as many of their men as happened to be near them and, with sabers drawn, charged any group of Mississippians they were able to reach. Several of these detachments were able to hack their way through the encircling enemy cavalry and make their escape. A few escaped under Major Mudd; so did a group led by thrice-wounded Captain Marsh. Another group of about 70, after breaking through, rode all the way to Memphis, and Major Bush's detachment "forced the rebel lines on the northeast . . . and passed through town and back, fighting at every corner and recapturing . . . [the]camp and releasing many of . . . [the] prisoners."[40] A member of the 1st Mississippi wrote about the men from Illinois after the war: "They boldly drew sabres and charged upon us. . . . The 1st Mississippi met a foe worthy of their steel . . . [but] pistols in the hands of the Mississippians proved superior to sabres wielded by the hardy sons of Illinois, and the . . . Mississippians finally vanquished and drove from the field the rough riders of Illinois. . . . all in all, few of our regiment were killed, though many were wounded, most of them but lightly with sabre strokes."[41]

With the Federal garrison captured or driven away, the Confederates set about happily to fulfill the purpose of the expedition:

The sight of such an abundance of clothing, supplies of all kinds, blankets, provisions, arms, ammunition, medicines, etc., etc. . . . was overwhelming to thinly clad and hungry Confederates, who had never seen anything like it before. The depot buildings, the round-house, and every available place was packed full to overflowing. . . . A large brick livery stable was packed with unopened cases of carbines and Colt's army six-shooters. . . . After appropriating all we could use or arrange to carry away, the work of destruction was pushed with vigor. . . . Depots of provisions were first plundered and then burned . . . whiskey flowed in streams, causing more or less disorder. . . . On leaving Holly Springs, our entire command was the best equipped cavalry in the Confederate service. Every trooper had from two to six pistols, one or more carbines, one or more sabres, all the ammunition, rations, blankets, shirts, hats, boots, overcoats., his horse could carry.[42]

40. *Ibid.*, Pt. 1, pp. 512–14; Fletcher, *The History of Company A*, 68–71.
41. Deupree, "The Capture of Holly Springs," 55–56. The reader will note the difference between the breakouts described in the 2nd Illinois reports and the "drove from the field" in Deupree's.
42. *Ibid.*, 57–58. Before setting fire to the depots, the raiders invited the towns-

After sending off the warning telegrams on the evening of the nine-teenth, Grant ordered Colonel Mizner to "take all the available cav-alry . . . and take the most direct route to Rocky Ford. When you get on [Van Dorn's] trail follow him until he is caught or dispersed. [He] must be prevented from getting to the railroad in our rear, if possible."[43] Mizner had to confess that, having lost track of the 6th Illinois com-pletely and with many of the men of his other three divisions "out scouting, &c.," he could muster a force of no more than 1,200 to go after Van Dorn.[44] Grant told him to go ahead "without delay" with how-ever many men he had.

The records do not indicate when Mizner left Water Valley, but he aroused Grant's ire by going into camp at 6:30 on the evening of the twentieth at Abbeville, twenty-five miles north of his starting point but nine miles short of Waterford, where he was to join Colonel C. Carroll Marsh's infantry. From Waterford it was another nine miles to Holly Springs. Grant telegraphed Colonel Marsh the same evening that "if in the morning . . . [Mizner] shows any reluctance in the pursuit, arrest him and turn over the command to the next in rank."[45] After receiving word from Marsh on the twenty-first, apparently in the morning, that there was still no sign of Mizner, Grant telegraphed Mizner himself to turn over command to the next in rank and followed it up with an ex-planation: "Your apparent reluctance at starting . . . and the want of alacrity in complying with my orders has so shaken my confidence in you that no matter how well qualified you may be to command such an expedition as the one you have started on, I should feel insecure with you in command. My instructions to turn over the command to the next in rank will therefore be obeyed."[46]

---

people to share in the spoils. "People of all classes, without regard to previous condition of mastery or servitude, were free to walk up and help themselves, which they gladly did. Children, too, reveled in the pleasures of the occasion and grown people declared it was the grandest day Holly Springs had ever seen." J. G. Deupree, "The Noxubee Squadron of the First Mississippi Cavalry, C.S.A., 1861–1865," *Publications of the Mississippi Historical Society*, III (1918), 62. Van Dorn's own brief report of the capture of Holly Springs is in *Official Records*, Vol. XVII, Pt. 1, p. 503; Grant's, in *Ibid.*, 477–78.

43. *Official Records*, Vol. XVII, Pt. 2, p. 439. The message was sent when W. H. Jackson was still thought to be in command of the raiders.

44. In a message sent later, Grant told Colonel Marsh that Mizner had 2,000 men. *Ibid.*, 442.

45. *Ibid.*, 443.

46. *Ibid.*, 448. If Mizner was correct in claiming that he left his camp at 2 A.M. on

The officer to whom Mizner turned over command was Colonel Benjamin H. Grierson, 6th Illinois, who has been mentioned briefly earlier in this account and will play an increasingly important role in the operations of the Union cavalry in the West in 1863 and 1864. Colonel Grierson was born in 1826 in Pittsburgh, grew up in Youngstown, Ohio, where he learned to play the flute, clarinet, bugle, drums, piano, guitar, and violin and at the age of thirteen became the conductor of the town band. In 1851, he moved to Jacksonville, Illinois, where for the next ten years he divided his time between music, an unsuccessful mercantile business, and politics. When the Civil War broke out, he served for a short time as a "volunteer aide" on the staff of General Benjamin M. Prentiss at Cairo and was then appointed by Governor Richard Yates a major in the about-to-be-formed 6th Illinois. The regiment had even more than the common disciplinary problems under its first colonel, who was "compelled" to resign after the regiment, not yet provided with arms, had been moved to Kentucky; Grierson "formally applied" for the colonelcy and received the appointment on April 12, 1862. From early June, he and the regiment operated out of and near Memphis, being attached on July 21 to Sherman's command.[47] For a time, the 6th Illinois was the only cavalry Sherman had; he appointed Grierson his chief of cavalry and, as has been noted, seemed to think well enough of his performance to recommend him to Grant for promotion.[48]

His work of destruction at Holly Springs completed, Van Dorn departed on his journey back to his base. Instead of returning the way he had come, he went northeast along the railroad to Grand Junction and on into Tennessee as far as Bolivar, where he turned south and rode by way of Middleburg, Van Buren, Saulsbury, Ripley, and New Albany, to Pontotoc, where on December 26 the Federals called off their pursuit.

Colonel Grierson's report makes it evident that at no time was he

---

December 20, then his dismissal was unjustified. *Ibid.* Mizner was reinstated in command on the twenty-fifth. There is nothing in the records to explain why he was reinstated. *Ibid.*, Pt. 1, p. 519. See also *Ibid.*, Pt. 2, pp. 457, 465, 466, 475.

47. Bruce J. Dinges, "The Making of a Cavalryman: Benjamin H. Grierson and the Civil War Along the Mississippi, 1861–1865" (Ph.D. dissertation, Rice University, 1978), esp. p. 9.

48. Sherman wrote in his reminiscences that "Grierson, with his Sixth Illinois . . . made some bold and successful dashes at the Coldwater, compelling Van Dorn to cover it by Armstrong's whole division of cavalry." Sherman, *Memoirs*, I, 262.

ignorant of Van Dorn's whereabouts; indeed, from the time Grierson reached Bolivar late on the night of December 23 to the end of the pursuit, the pursuers and the pursued were frequently in touch. However, Grierson was never able to bring Van Dorn to a halt to defend himself, and his only trophies of the long chase were between sixty and seventy of the Confederates and an unreported number of horses, mules, and weapons captured, at the cost of two men slightly wounded and two others missing. Colonel Grierson blamed Colonels Lee and Mizner for the failure of the pursuit; he did not, he said, get Lee's "hearty cooperation," and Mizner declined to approve a night attack on Van Dorn on the twenty-fifth that Grierson had proposed.[49] It may have been regimental loyalty to Colonel Lee, but the troopers of the 7th Kansas, who by the end of 1862 had developed a tactical sense as keen as that possessed by most of their officers, were convinced that Grierson had failed to take advantage of two successive opportunities at and near Bolivar to bring Van Dorn to battle, and thus had allowed him to escape unscathed.[50]

It is worthy of notice also that the pursuers had left their camps with two days' rations. They were out for nine days, on the move every day from long before daylight until after dark, and in the last five days in an almost continuous bone-chilling rain. This was cavalry service minus its supposed glamor.

While Grant was fighting his way south, Braxton Bragg wired General Pemberton on November 21, apparently in response to the latter's plea for help, that he was sending "a large cavalry force under Forrest to operate in the enemy's rear and create a diversion in . . . [Pemberton's] favor."[51] When Forrest received Bragg's orders for the operation on December 10, he had a force of 2,100, about half of whom were armed with the shotguns and squirrel rifles they had brought from home; many of the other half were in no better case, one regiment, for example, being "armed" with four hundred flintlock muskets, pattern of

49. *Official Records*, Vol. XVII, Pt. 1, p. 520. Grierson's report is in *Ibid.*, 518–20.

50. Starr, *Jennison's Jayhawkers*, 228.

51. *Official Records*, Vol. XVII, Pt. 2, p. 755. In a longer message the same day to Adjutant General Samuel Cooper, Bragg wrote, "I send a large cavalry force under Forrest to create a diversion by assailing . . . [the enemy's] rear and communications in West Tennessee." *Ibid.*, 755.

1812.[52] Forrest's pleas for additional arms elicited the reply that the Confederacy had none to give him and that he must arm his troops with weapons captured from the enemy.

Notwithstanding the state of his arms, Forrest followed orders, and on December 15, began crossing the Tennessee River westward at Clifton, about thirty miles north of Pittsburg Landing. By the seventeenth, all his men were across and marching in the direction of Jackson, Tennessee, where the Mississippi Central branched off from the Mobile & Ohio. Rosecrans had early notice of the intended raid and sent a warning to Grant on the very day that Forrest left his camp. Then on December 15, General Jeremiah C. Sullivan, in command at Jackson, learned that a force, "supposed to be Forrest's cavalry, said to be 3,000 strong," was about to cross the Tennessee at Clifton, and he telegraphed the information to Grant the same day. Grant later acknowledged that he had received "timely notice" of the raid, and reported that he then sent reinforcements to Sullivan and orders to forces in Corinth and at Forts Heiman, Henry, and Donelson to cooperate.[53] But in a day of uncertain and slow communications, knowing the location of a cunning cavalryman like Forrest, knowing the size of his force (about which he was careful to spread greatly inflated rumors), and even being able to deduce with a fair certainty his probable destination gave no assurance of being able to catch him, especially not with infantry, either before or after he had fulfilled the purpose of his raid.[54]

After sending off his warning telegram to Grant, General Sullivan had the "chief of cavalry on his staff," Colonel Robert G. Ingersoll, assemble all the cavalry within reach—Ingersoll's own 11th Illinois, a battalion of the 5th Ohio, and the 2nd Tennessee, a total of 778 rank and file—and ordered him forward toward Clifton to intercept the raiders. Ingersoll, who was to make a considerable name for himself in the postwar years as a politician, lawyer, orator, and anti-Bible, anti-Christianity lecturer, made the mistake of thinking that going on the defensive was an effective way of stopping Forrest. He met the raiders

52. Wyeth, *That Devil Forrest*, 90–91.
53. Catton, *Grant Moves South*, 336–37; *Official Records*, Vol. XVII, Pt. 2, p. 415.
54. In four dispatches to Grant, Sullivan gave Forrest's strength as 5,000–10,000, 10,000–20,000, 7,000, and 7,500, all on the basis of information he had received. *Official Records*, Vol. XVII, Pt. 2, pp. 436, 465, Pt. 1, pp. 551, 552.

east of the village of Lexington, Tennessee, and was promptly defeated and taken prisoner with 150 of his men (124, by his account); the rest of his command saved themselves by running away, led, it was said, by the cavalrymen from Ohio and Tennessee.[55] Having swept Ingersoll out of his way, Forrest continued toward Jackson and, after bluffing General Sullivan into trying to find him southeast of that town, circled around to the north and began to destroy the railroad and the telegraph in the direction of Columbus. The work of destruction went on with what appears to have been considerable thoroughness day after day, through Humboldt, Rutherford, Kenton, Trenton, and Union City, as far north as Moscow, within ten miles of Columbus; bridges, culverts, trestles, and miles of trackage were broken up or burned. "With one exception," a participant in the raid wrote, "there was not a bridge left on . . . [the Mobile & Ohio]. Not a yard of trestlework was standing, not a culvert was left undestroyed, and the rails over much of this distance had been ruined for further use."[56] Where the Mobile & Ohio intersected other railroads, the Memphis & Ohio at Humboldt and the Northwestern Railroad at Union City, the tracks of the intersecting railroad were broken up for some distance in both directions.

On Christmas Day, Forrest turned back. He planned to recross the Tennessee at Clifton, where he had hidden the two flatboats on which he had crossed the river westward ten days before. To get to Clifton, he followed roads well to the east of the ones he had used on his way north. On December 31, at Parker's Cross Roads, near Clarksburg, Tennessee, Forrest found Colonel Cyrus L. Dunham's brigade of Sullivan's division deployed and waiting for him. As best as can be determined from three nearly irreconcilable accounts, Dunham, outnumbered about two to one, had been roughly handled and was on the verge of surrendering when Colonel John W. Fuller's brigade of Ohio infantry, which had been sent north to reinforce Sullivan, arrived on the scene, directly in Forrest's rear and entirely to his surprise. By charging both Dunham and Fuller, Forrest pried open the jaws of the Federal pincers and extricated himself, losing in the process three

55. *Ibid.*, Vol. XVII, Pt. 1, pp. 560, 553–55; see also Wyeth, *That Devil Forrest*, 95–98. Colonel Ingersoll reported that the 200 men of the 5th Ohio Battalion were "raw recruits, never having been under fire and never drilled." The Tennesseans, he said, "were not very well equipped and had never before been under fire." *Official Records*, Vol. XVII, Pt. 1, p. 554.
56. Wyeth, *That Devil Forrest*, 102–103.

hundred of his men taken prisoner.[57] He reached the river without further mishap on New Year's Day, after brushing aside Lieutenant Colonel William K. M. Breckinridge's 6th Tennessee. He then retrieved from hiding his two flatboats and, after twelve hours of hard work, had his entire command, his recruits, prisoners, and booty back on the right bank of the river on January 2, 1863.[58]

The effects of Van Dorn's and Forrest's twin raids have been a subject of considerable debate. J. P. Dyer, for example, speaks of "the almost incredibly magnificent manner" in which Forrest conducted his raid but minimizes its effect; it "did little more" he writes, "than cause Grant to shift his base from Columbus to Memphis."[59] Even if one leaves aside the full implications of that shift of base, it alone, one would think, was quite a feat for a handful of ill-equipped cavalrymen to accomplish. Nevertheless, General Wilson held much the same view in his reminiscences.

While the capture of his depots was commonly regarded as fatal to Grant's campaign and as having compelled its abandonment, it really had but little effect in that direction. It had already become apparent that a campaign in midwinter over muddy roads and through a poor country was not feasible for the force then in the field. With a single line of railway several hundred miles long through a hostile region, nothing but dirt roads to march on . . . and with the farms already denuded of their supplies . . . the least experienced officers soon perceived that our advance into central Mississippi must necessarily be so slow that the enemy would have ample time to concentrate a larger force against us.[60]

The immediate physical result of the two raids was clear enough. The contents of the warehouses at Holly Springs, to the value of $400,000 in Grant's opinion or a far more likely $1,500,000 in Van

57. For Parker's Cross Roads, see Henry, *"First With the Most" Forrest*, 116–19; Wyeth, *That Devil Forrest*, 104–14. The Federal reports are in *Official Records*, Vol. XVII, Pt. 1, pp. 568–90; Forrest's, in *Ibid.*, 595–97. Illustrative of what seems to be a constant of warfare in all ages is Forrest's assertion that the Federal losses in the battle totaled 800 to 1,000 killed and wounded; they were reported by Dunham as 23 killed, 139 wounded, and 58 missing. *Official Records*, Vol. XVII, Pt. 1, pp. 584, 596.

58. *Official Records*, Vol. XVII, Pt. 1, pp. 590–91, 599.

59. J. P. Dyer, "Some Aspects of Cavalry Operations in the Army of Tennessee," *Journal of Southern History*, VIII (1942), 216.

60. Wilson, *Under the Old Flag*, I, 144.

Dorn's, were carried away or destroyed.[61] The damage to the telegraph lines and the railroad north to Columbus was less serious, apparently, than it was at first thought to be—Grant at Oxford had no telegraphic communication with the North for over a week and received no supplies for over two weeks, but General T. A. Davies reported from Columbus on January 9 that he had a "heavy construction train" at work and expected to have the Mobile & Ohio in running order by the fifteenth.[62]

The more meaningful effect of the two raids was their impact on Grant's thinking. As early as December 20, before he could have had any word of the extent of the damage Van Dorn and Forrest were causing, he realized that to try to capture Vicksburg by way of a midwinter march through central Mississippi, with a single-track railroad vulnerable for its full length to Confederate attack as the conduit from the North of the supplies he had to have, was militarily unsound. It is impossible to quarrel with the decision he acted on that day—to call off the campaign. To General McClernand he explained a little later that "raids to my rear by Forrest . . . and by Van Dorn . . . have cut me off from supplies, so that farther advance by this route is perfectly impracticable. The country does not afford supplies for troops, and but a limited supply of forage." In his reminiscences he added—and with the emphasis, apparently, on Forrest's raid as the primary cause—that the interruption of his communications and supplies "demonstrated the impossibility of maintaining so long a line of road over which to draw supplies for an army moving in an enemy's country. I determined, therefore, to abandon my campaign into the interior with Columbus as a base."[63]

Having made his decision, Grant ordered Colonel Hatch, in command of the only cavalry he had with him, to "break up all the cavalry camps" and send all equipment, ambulances, etc., back to Oxford.

---

61. For Grant's figure, see *Personal Memoirs*, I, 478; for Van Dorn's, see *Official Records*, Vol. XVII, Pt. 1, p. 503.

62. *Official Records*, Vol. XVII, Pt. 1, p. 549. In another dispatch, General Davies reported that the railroad was "greatly damaged, not so much in the woodwork as in the rails. They built fires upon the rails on one side, which expands the rails and throws the track, ties, and all out of place, and when the iron gets so hot that it can push no farther, the rail knuckles, and when it cools breaks the rails. I understand miles of the road are so destroyed." *Ibid.*, Pt. 2, pp. 493–94.

63. *Ibid.*, Pt. 2, p. 443; Grant, *Personal Memoirs*, I, 433.

Hatch was then to "take all the effective cavalry force south of the Yocknapatalpfa River and make a demonstration as far toward Grenada as . . . [he could] go without serious resistance" and finally retreat to Oxford, "destroying thoroughly on [his] return all bridges on railroad and wagon roads and all mills on the line of . . . [his] march."[64]

There can be no question of the soundness of Grant's decision. That being conceded, it becomes apparent that the twin Van Dorn—Forrest raids had a military importance out of all proportion to the monetary value, however large it may have been, of the damage they caused. Inducing the Federals to terminate a campaign already two months old, then to retreat and begin building up resources for an entirely different—both geographically and conceptually—campaign was a considerable accomplishment. Van Dorn and Forrest, and primarily the latter, deserve to be credited with conducting the only cavalry raids of the war that produced a strategically significant result.

Given the complexities of the situation, it is fortunate that the high-level military and political maneuvers and shenanigans, involving the president, Secretary Stanton, General-in-Chief Halleck, and at the end, Grant, concerning John McClernand's ambition to enlist an independent western army and lead it to the capture of Vicksburg and the opening of the Mississippi are beyond the purview of this study.[65] There is one point concerning it that will, however, bear mention here. On October 15, McClernand informed Stanton that he would need 27,000 infantry, sharpshooters, sappers, and miners, plus light and heavy artillery, plus 3,000 cavalry, for his project, and he received authority to raise them in Indiana, Illinois, and Iowa.[66] All went well but for the cavalry. On December 2, still short of his 3,000-man goal, McClernand proposed to the secretary a novel mode of reaching his manpower goal. He would, he said,

provide horses or mules with equipments complete to mount at least one-fifth of the whole infantry force of the expedition; or, if horses or mules cannot be

64. *Official Records*, Vol. XVII, Pt. 2, pp. 442–43.
65. For those interested, the highly involved story may be found in Catton, *Grant Moves South*, 325–27; Williams, *Lincoln Finds a General*, IV, 146–48, 176, 434–39; and Grant, *Personal Memoirs*, I, 426–27, 430, 432.
66. *Official Records*, Vol. XVII, Pt. 2, pp. 277–78, 332–34, 334–35.

purchased in time, I would seize such as might be found in the possession of disloyal citizens. . . . Inferior animals . . . would answer, if the best could not be had, as they would only be used occasionally to meet an emergency requiring the rapid conveyance of infantry from one place to another. Of course the men would dismount in action. . . . If it should be objected that such service would tend to demoralize the infantry . . . I would not charge them with the care of the animals except when using them. At all other times they should be cared for by slaves seeking refuge in my camp, or who had been impressed for that purpose. Thus mounted, the infantry would be prepared to perform the double duty of men on foot and on horseback. . . . If an example was required of the soundness of these views I might refer to the success of the enemy in capturing our forces at Murfreesborough . . . [and] in overrunning Kentucky.[67]

By no stretch of the imagination can McClernand be considered one of the major military intellects of the Civil War, but it is not without significance that having come into the war as a volunteer officer without doctrinal preconceptions, using his eyes and his brains, he drew some of the right conclusions from Forrest's and Morgan's successes and as early as the winter of 1862 was advocating in a crude, incomplete, and in some respects absurd form the ideas that were to produce by the end of the following year the highly unorthodox, but highly effective, Federal mounted infantry.

67. *Ibid.*, 375. McClernand was not alone in advocating the establishment of regiments of mounted infantry. While Forrest was still working his way toward him, General Davies telegraphed General Halleck from Columbus: "In October last I applied to General Grant to mount the Second Division with such material as could be taken from the country in Mississippi. . . . I think we require mounted infantry, and if the authority can be given for such a force, it can be done and these raids effectually prevented." *Ibid.*, 462. Clearly, the "mounted infantry idea" was very much in the air by the end of 1862.

VII

Waving Banners and Glittering Steel

WE HAVE LEFT THE ARMIES OF GENERALS PRICE AND VAN Dorn, "almost disorganized and without discipline, staff departments defective, and supplies deficient," huddled at Van Buren, Arkansas, after the severe mauling they had received at the hands of Samuel Curtis' Federals at Pea Ridge, or Elkhorn Tavern, on March 6–8, 1862.[1] A month after the battle the two forces, numbering about twenty-two thousand, were ferried across the Mississippi to Memphis, and sent forward to reinforce Beauregard at Corinth. The story of their subsequent fortunes and misfortunes in northern Mississippi and Tennessee appears in Chapter V.

The departure of Price's and Van Dorn's troops left Arkansas without the protection of organized Confederate forces of any consequence, but the lack was made good in short order by Thomas C. Hindman, dispatched to Arkansas by President Davis in June with instructions to raise an army. Hindman's methods for creating an army earned him the appellation of "military tyrant," but they were effective.[2] On his

1. E. V. D. Miller (ed.), *A Soldier's Honor with Reminiscences of Major-General Earl Van Dorn by His Comrades* (New York, 1902), 71; Castel, *General Sterling Price*, 84–85; Robert L. Kerby, *Kirby Smith's Confederacy: The Trans-Mississippi South, 1863–1865* (New York, 1972), 31.

2. Hindman rounded up "thousands of stragglers that were skulking in all directions" and also organized workshops to manufacture arms, gunpowder, shot, clothing, and other supplies for his army. *Battles and Leaders*, III, 444–45; Kerby, *Kirby Smith's Confederacy*, 32.

own authority he imposed martial law on the entire state, blanketed it with recruiting officers and provost marshals, enforced the conscription laws without mercy, "kidnapped" five Texas regiments en route to reinforce Beauregard, executed "scores" of deserters, and conducted an intensive propaganda campaign. By these means he succeeded in raising an army of eighteen thousand men, backed by a further seven thousand "unorganized draftees."[3] He also succeeded in creating the impression in the minds of Generals Samuel Curtis, still at Pea Ridge, and John Schofield, in Missouri, that he disposed of an army of from forty thousand to as many as seventy thousand. It may be noted that Hindman organized his roughly six thousand cavalry as an autonomous cavalry division under General John Sappington Marmaduke, an invariably unsuccessful commander who capped a career of undistinguished futility by being taken prisoner by the Federals at Mine Creek in Kansas, on October 25, 1864. The two brigades making up Marmaduke's division were Jo Shelby's Missourians and Colonel Charles A. Carroll's Arkansas regiments.

General Curtis decided in early May that his 12,400-man "Army of the Southwest" at Pea Ridge was in an isolated position and hence in jeopardy. He thought it prudent, therefore, to move it eastward across Arkansas to Batesville, ninety miles north of Little Rock. He made a tentative move in the direction of Little Rock on the way but thought better of it. To establish a more secure line of communications with his base of supplies in St. Louis, he moved his army farther east to Helena, on the Mississippi River south of Memphis, where he established himself in mid-July. Hindman, in the meantime, persuaded General Theophilus H. Holmes, then in command of the Confederate Trans-Mississippi Department, to allow him to invade western Missouri. Facing Hindman was Schofield's Army of the Frontier of 11,000 men, later reinforced to 16,000, and described by Hindman as "Pin Indians, free-Negroes, Southern Tories, Kansas jayhawkers, and hired Dutch cutthroats."[4] Commanding a division of this army was General

3. Kerby, *Kirby Smith's Confederacy*, 32. Hindman's numbers are also given as 20,000 "armed men" in early July, as 18,000 infantry "effectives" and 6,000 cavalry in August, and as a "field army" of 13,100 in October. *Battles and Leaders*, III, 445–46; Stephen B. Oates, *Confederate Cavalry West of the River* (Austin, 1961), 48.

4. *Battles and Leaders*, III, 446–47; *Official Records*, Vol. XXII, Pt. 1, p. 83. Hindman went on, "These bloody ruffians have invaded your country; stolen and destroyed your property; murdered your neighbors; outraged your women; driven your children

James G. Blunt, a native of Maine, a physician by training, and a veteran of Bleeding Kansas days; another division was commanded by Pennsylvania-born Francis J. Herron, "wealthy, handsome and vain," a brigadier general at twenty-five.[5]

Colonel Joseph O. "Jo" Shelby, whose cavalry brigade had led Hindman's advance into Missouri, was a native of Lexington, Kentucky. He emigrated to Missouri in 1852 and became in short order one of the wealthiest young men in the state and a leader in the Border Ruffian attacks on the free-state settlers in Kansas.[6] When the Civil War broke out, Shelby raised a company of cavalry made up of fellow veterans of the border wars, whom he mounted and equipped at his own expense. He fought Sigel at Carthage, Missouri, and at Wilson's Creek; then, after campaigning against the Federals east of the Mississippi with Price's forces, he was sent back to Missouri to recruit a regiment of cavalry. At the head first of this regiment and then of a brigade of cavalrymen notorious for their "laxity of behavior and discipline" and for their looting propensities, Shelby displayed leadership qualities and talent as a commander of partisan cavalry similar to those of his fellow Lexington townsman and friend, John Hunt Morgan.[7] It will be seen that he remained a thorn in the sides of Union commanders in Arkansas and Missouri to the end of the war. If for nothing else, Shelby would deserve to be remembered for his reports in the *Official Records*. Although bearing his name, these reports were nearly always written by his adjutant, John N. Edwards, editor before the war of a Lexington, Missouri, newspaper, "one of the most modest and lovable of men, a student, a poet, and a gallant soldier," and the perpetrator of prose so purple as to be sui generis even in an age in which a highly charged, ornate vocabulary and elaborately convoluted diction were considered the essential ingredients of literary skill.[8] Of such writing Edwards was the enthusiastic practitioner and undisputed master.

---

from their homes, and defiled the graves of your kindred." The "Pin Indians" were the pro-Union Cherokees of Chief John Ross; their "badge" was "two pins crossed in the lapel of the coat or hunting shirt." M. W. Anderson, *Life of General Stand Watie* (Pryor, Okla., 1915), 12.

5. Jay Monaghan, *Civil War on the Western Border, 1854–1865* (Boston, 1955), 257.

6. Daniel O'Flaherty, *General Jo Shelby* (Chapel Hill, 1954), 4, 11. Shelby was one of the Border Ruffian leaders in the "Wakarusa War" in November, 1855, and in the "Sack of Lawrence" in May, 1856.

7. *Ibid.*, 6.

8. *Ibid.*, 116. Albert Castel holds that Edwards' reports of Shelby's exploits "are ab-

On October 4, Hindman being temporarily absent from his army, his cavalry was attacked and driven out of Newtonia, Missouri, and back into Arkansas by Schofield's forces. The Confederate retreat continued, even after Hindman resumed command, until his forces were back at Fort Smith, on the Arkansas River. It was now mid-November; Schofield decided that the lateness of the season would interdict further operations and returned to St. Louis, leaving Blunt in command of the Army of the Frontier. Blunt himself, with his own First Division of "some 7000 or 8000 men," was at Fayetteville, Arkansas; the Second and Third Divisions, under General Herron, were at Yellville, Arkansas, 110 miles to the east.[9]

The Federal cavalry had learned that campaigning in Arkansas was beset with difficulties. For one thing, guerrillas seemed to be far more plentiful than forage, and the summer climate, particularly in the lowlands along the eastern edge of the state, was deadly to troops not accustomed to the damp heat. While in camp in Helena, the 9th Illinois "suffered terribly from disease; often there were not enough men in camp to care for the sick and properly look after the horses"; in mid-August, when the regiment was ordered to furnish an escort for a forage train, "there were but 70 soldiers fit for duty."[10] The lack of proper weapons was another source of difficulty. The 9th Illinois had arrived in Arkansas in early May with a saber and a Colt's Navy or Remington revolver for each man, and one hundred of the notorious Hall's carbines to do for the entire regiment. In a fight with Confederate cavalry in June, a part of the Illinois regiment had an opportunity to use its sabers; four companies "rode forward with drawn sabers and made the

---

surdly exaggerated, even at times utterly fictitious." Castel, *General Sterling Price*, 161. Typical of Edwards' prose is his evocation of Springfield, Missouri, "on the last day of December, 1862, when the old year was dying in the lap of the new, and January had sent its moaning winds to wail the requiem of the past. . . . 'Twas a bright and beautiful scene. There lay the quiet town, robed in the dull, gray hue of the winter, its domes and spires stretching their skeleton hands to heaven, as if in prayer against the coming strife, and, drawing near and nearer, long black lines came gleaming on, while the sun shone out like a golden bar, uncurling its yellow hair on earth and sky, stream and mountain, and lent the thrilling picture a sterner and fiercer light." *Official Records*, Vol. XXII, Pt. 1, pp. 199–201.

9. *Battles and Leaders*, III, 447, 449. General Herron wrote General Curtis at this time: "You have here a good, reliable army, but there are some officers that must be cleared out. They are worse than worthless." *Official Records*, Vol. XXII, Pt. 1, p. 105.

10. Davenport, *History of the Ninth Regiment*, 52.

finest cavalry charge" Colonel Albert G. Brackett, a Regular, had ever witnessed.[11] This, however, was an extremely rare event; generally the cavalry had to fight in woods, swamps, and canebrakes, where sabers and even horses were a hindrance, and the troopers had to dismount and fight as infantry, with carbines if they had them or with infantry firearms that in many cases were the none-too-reliable makeshifts issued to western cavalry in the summer and fall of 1861. The 1st Wisconsin, for example, was armed with "Belgian rifles and Springfield muskets."[12]

Cavalry in the Kansas-Missouri-Arkansas area was organized in a variety of ways. It was in some instances attached by battalions or regiments (the latter either singly or in groups of two or three) to brigades or divisions of infantry, or joined together to form all-cavalry brigades or, in one case, organized into a full-fledged three-brigade cavalry division. An example of an independent cavalry brigade is that of Colonel George E. Waring, made up of the 4th Missouri, 1st Wisconsin, and four companies of the 13th Illinois and joined with two divisions of infantry to form the Army of Southeastern Missouri. The cavalry division was that of General C. C. Washburn, made up of regiments from Arkansas, Indiana, Kansas, Wisconsin, Iowa, and Missouri, and four regiments (plus an independent company) from Illinois.[13]

As a department commander, Schofield was unique at this stage of the war in not complaining of a shortage of cavalry and not begging for more. This was because Missouri, in addition to furnishing what may be called regiments of "regular" cavalry to the Federal service (the 1st and 4th Missouri, for example), also enlisted regiments of Missouri State Militia Cavalry—nine by the end of 1862—armed, equipped, and paid by the national government, which were placed by Governor

11. *Official Records*, Vol. XIII, 122; Davenport, *History of the Ninth Regiment*, 23, 27, 40–42. Concerning this charge, the regimental historian comments, "Had this affair occurred a year or two later the manner of fighting would have been different, for the men would have been dismounted while advancing on the enemy, and should have sought all convenient shelter, doing much greater execution with much smaller loss than we suffered at this time." Davenport, *History of the Ninth Regiment*, 42.

12. *Official Records*, Vol. VIII, 61, 69, Vol. XIII, 65, 205. The 1st Wisconsin had been sent to garrison Cape Girardeau, Missouri. In violation of his orders Colonel Edward Daniels "abandoned the district . . . and, with nearly his entire regiment, moved into Arkansas and joined the command of General Curtis at Helena." *Ibid.*, Vol. XIII, 16; E. B. Quiner, *The Military History of Wisconsin* (Chicago, 1866), 882–83.

13. *Official Records*, Vol. XXII, Pt. 1, pp. 889, 832.

OPERATIONS IN ARKANSAS AND LOUISIANA

H. R. Gamble under Schofield's command and, as he reported, "became a real addition to the effective force in the department." [14]

There were no operations by the Federal cavalry deserving of detailed notice in Arkansas in 1862. Early in November, an infantry officer—Colonel William Vandever, 9th Iowa Infantry—commanded a 1,200-man cavalry force, made up of detachments from seven regiments from Illinois, Indiana, Iowa, Kansas, Missouri, and Wisconsin, on a three-day scout from Helena to Moro, Arkansas. Later in the same month General Herron sent a "cavalry expedition" to Yellville, Arkansas, to destroy the arsenal and storehouses there and the saltpeter works in its vicinity. [15] The expedition, led by a cavalryman—Colonel Dudley Wickersham, 10th Illinois—and unlike many such forays, made up of two complete regiments (1st Iowa and 10th Illinois) and a battalion of a third (2nd Wisconsin) instead of detachments from a half dozen or more regiments, accomplished its mission and returned to camp with sixty prisoners and over a hundred "good horses." [16]

The defeat of his army by Schofield did not cause Hindman to give up his intention of invading Missouri. To do so, however, he had first of all to drive Blunt out of his way. In defiance of orders to bring his troops to Little Rock preparatory to being transferred across the Mississippi to make up Van Dorn's and Price's losses at Corinth, he sent Marmaduke with his division of mounted troops north to Cane Hill, fifteen miles southwest of Fayetteville, while he himself, taking a more easterly route with the rest of his forces, marched to get behind Blunt. Hindman expected that, attacked by Marmaduke in front and by himself in the rear, Blunt would inevitably be defeated and his forces scattered. This would open the way for an attack on Herron, with the odds greatly in the Confederates' favor. Unfortunately for Hindman, however, the "competent and pugnacious" (to which one may add shrewd) Blunt had his own idea of what to do. Drawing the correct inferences from the information his spies and scouts brought him, he hastened

14. *Ibid.*, 13 and Vol. VIII, 632, Vol. XIII, 396, 442, 506; Davenport, *History of the Ninth Regiment*, 52.

15. *Official Records*, Vol. XIII, 349, Vol. XXII, Pt. 1, pp. 38, 794.

16. The 2nd Wisconsin had been recruited by C. C. Washburn, who was succeeded as colonel by Thomas Stephens, who "had been a soldier in the British army and was an expert broad-swordsman. . . . He had no fault except the lack of ability for discipline and command." E. A. Calkins, "The Wisconsin Cavalry Regiments," MOLLUS, Commandery of Wisconsin, *War Papers*, (3 vols.; Milwaukee, 1891–1903), I, 177–78.

south with five thousand of his troops, horse and foot, before Hindman began his march north, and at Cane Hill, at dawn on November 28, attacked Marmaduke and drove him into a "running retreat" across the Boston Mountains to Van Buren.[17] Two Kansas cavalry regiments, the 2nd and 6th, played a prominent role in the fight; the 6th Kansas in addition performed one of the traditional functions of cavalry by hounding the retreat of the beaten Confederates, "cutting and shooting them down with sabers, carbines and revolvers."[18]

Four days before his victory at Cane Hill, as soon as he learned of Hindman's advance, Blunt sent orders to Herron to join him as quickly as possible. Herron did so with two thousand cavalry and four thousand footsoldiers, marching 110 miles to Cane Hill in three days.[19] He was just in time, for Hindman, not at all discouraged by Marmaduke's discomfiture on the twenty-eighth, decided to go ahead with a variant of his original plan. He left Van Buren on December 2 with nine thousand infantry (lack of shoes and weapons prevented him from taking more) and twenty-two guns, with Marmaduke's two thousand cavalry in the lead.[20] As before, Hindman intended to get his army between Blunt's and Herron's, each of whom he outnumbered two to one, but this time he proposed to "smash Herron, and then turn to defeat Blunt."

17. *Official Records*, Vol. XXII, Pt. 1, p. 43; Oates, *Confederate Cavalry*, 91–98; O'Flaherty, *General Jo Shelby*, 141–43. Considering that the action at Cane Hill lasted all day, casualties were amazingly light; Blunt's were 4 killed and 36 wounded, 4 mortally. *Official Records*, Vol. XXII, Pt. 1, p. 46. Colonel Carroll claimed that of his 1,700-man brigade of Arkansas cavalry, he had only 200 "effective men for duty" at Cane Hill, the horses of the rest being unusable because of overuse and lack of forage and horseshoes. *Official Records*, Vol. XXII, Pt. 1, p. 43.

18. Colonel Carroll reported, "The confusion . . . of our retreating men was disgraceful, and every effort made by officers to halt them futile, the cry extending down the line that our friends had gorged the road and were being sabered mercilessly by the enemy." *Official Records*, Vol. XXII, Pt. 1, p. 540.

19. *Battles and Leaders*, III, 449. For a description of the march, see Henry C. Adams, "Battle of Prairie Grove," MOLLUS, Commandery of Indiana, *War Papers* (Indianapolis, 1898), 452–54. Herron's cavalry (2nd Wisconsin, 1st Iowa, 10th Illinois, and 8th Missouri) reached Blunt on the evening of December 6. An exception was the 1st Arkansas, whose colonel, M. LaRue Harrison, was duly castigated by Blunt. Harrison had reported late on the evening of the sixth, Blunt wrote, when he was still eight miles short of Cane Hill, "that his horses and men were so tired that he did not think he could move farther until Monday the 8th. Whether his regard for the Sabbath or the fear of getting into a fight prompted him to make such a report . . . I am unable to say; but, judging from his movements he was not a man upon whom to place much reliance on the battle-field." *Official Records*, Vol. XXII, Pt. 1, p. 72.

20. *Official Records*, Vol. XXII, Pt. 1, pp. 138–39.

Hindman's dispositions for, and conduct of, the ensuing battle, fought at Prairie Grove, halfway between Cane Hill and Fayetteville, were poorly adapted to carry out the plan he was reported to have had in mind. He had succeeded in getting his forces where he wanted them, between Blunt and Herron, while the two Federal commanders were still twelve miles distant from each other. To clear the way for Hindman's infantry, Marmaduke had driven two regiments of Herron's cavalry back to the shelter of their infantry but was then driven back in his turn.[21] Hindman now brought up his infantry, but instead of attacking Herron according to plan, he deployed them in a good position and waited for the Federals to attack him. This Herron proceeded to do as soon as his men reached the Confederate lines.[22] Hindman's decision to allow the Federals to attack him gave Blunt, who rushed north as soon as he heard the sound of Marmaduke's fight with Herron, time to join in the battle. Hence, instead of beating the two Federal forces in detail, Hindman had to fight a defensive battle against their united strength, with all the advantages—numbers, "organization, arms, artillery, and leadership"—on their side. When the fighting ended in the evening darkness, Hindman had managed to hold his position but at the cost of 1,317 casualties (Blunt's and Herron's were 1,251). His army was fought out, and he was left with no choice but to retreat in the night, abandoning his 4,000 sick and wounded. Eventually he retreated as far south as Little Rock, which he reached in mid-January with the remains of his shattered army.[23]

Schofield, one of the more mean-spirited officers of the Union army, had, or professed to have, a poor opinion of Blunt. He wrote in his reminiscences, "Although I had at first esteemed General Blunt much more highly than he deserved . . . I became satisfied that he was

21. Captain Amos L. Burrows of the 1st Missouri reported that "a large body" of the 1st Arkansas and 7th Missouri were "on the retreat" after Marmaduke's attack and that the efforts of himself and his men to halt the fugitives were "of no use." *Ibid.*, 137; see also Adams, "Battle of Prairie Grove," 455.

22. Some of Herron's regiments lost heavily in these attacks; the 20th Wisconsin Infantry lost 217, the 19th Iowa Infantry 190; the 26th Indiana Infantry lost 204 of the 445 officers and men it had in the battle. Adams, "Battle of Prairie Grove," 457–59.

23. *Official Records*, Vol. XXII, Pt. 1, pp. 72–77, 83, 86, 111, 113, 137, 138, 149; *Battles and Leaders*, III, 449–50; Oates, *Confederate Cavalry*, 99–112; O'Flaherty, *General Jo Shelby*, 149–57; Kerby, *Kirby Smith's Confederacy*, 36; Adams, "Battle of Prairie Grove," 461. To cover his retreat, Hindman had campfires kindled "all along the ridge to fool the enemy, and blankets were wrapped around howitzer wheels to muffle their noise." Oates, *Confederate Cavalry*, 112.

unfit in any respect for the command of a division of troops against a disciplined enemy." This derogatory reference was doubtless the penalty Blunt was made to pay for winning a battle while his department commander was enjoying the wintertime amenities of his headquarters in St. Louis. Blunt, on the other hand, even after his victories at Cane Hill and Prairie Grove and notwithstanding the lateness of the season, saw an opportunity to carry the war to the enemy. Hindman had paused on his retreat after Prairie Grove at Van Buren, on the Arkansas River. On December 28, Blunt dashed into Van Buren at the head of a small mounted force and performed an extraordinary feat. He found at Van Buren "three large steamers, heavily laden with Government supplies" doubtless intended for Hindman's tatterdemalion forces. Warned of Blunt's approach, the ships got up steam and tried to escape downriver, but they "were pursued by the cavalry five miles and brought to by the fire of their carbines" and forced to return to Van Buren, where they were duly destroyed.[24]

The old year 1862 was not to be allowed to die "in the lap of the new," in Major Edwards' words, without one last military exploit. After Prairie Grove, Marmaduke's division was the only part of Hindman's forces to remain in being as a reasonably cohesive military organization. In an effort to force the Federals to retreat from northern Arkansas, Hindman sent Marmaduke on a raid to their base at Springfield, Missouri. Marching north on December 31 with an all-Missouri command of 2,370 men—the brigades of Shelby and J. C. Porter and Emmett McDonald's battalion—Marmaduke reached his objective on January 8. His troopers, it is said, "shot their way down the streets of Springfield, hoisted a rebel flag over a girl's finishing school, and shot their way out through the opposite side of town."[25] Enduring thereafter the hardships to be expected in a midwinter expedition, destroying some bridges, and committing the customary acts of arson and pillage on the way, the raiders reached their base at Batesville, Arkansas, on January 25. It is claimed, on exceedingly slender evidence, that the raid was a strategic success, in that it caused the Federals to evacuate

24. John M. Schofield, *Forty-Six Years in the Army* (New York, 1897), 63; *Official Records*, Vol. XXII, Pt. 1, p. 167; *Battles and Leaders*, III, 450. According to Adams, "Battle of Prairie Grove," 462, four ships, not three, were destroyed at Van Buren.

25. Kerby, *Kirby Smith's Confederacy*, 36. Oates, however, states in *Confederate Cavalry*, 115, that Marmaduke assaulted Springfield and was beaten off with the loss of 20 killed and 12 wounded.

Fort Smith and withdraw "most of their forces to the relative security of Missouri."[26]

One of the few units the Federals left behind in Arkansas when, in January, 1863, they withdrew the bulk of their forces to Missouri was Colonel M. LaRue Harrison's command, now expanded to a brigade, of his own 1st Arkansas and the 10th Illinois.[27] As the winter turned to spring, Harrison reported that the Arkansas regiment was at nearly full strength, notwithstanding that ordinarily Arkansas troops stationed in their home state were greatly given to desertion, or, more euphemistically, to "going home." Their "destitute condition" provided at least a plausible excuse for going home; as of the beginning of April, the 1st Arkansas had not "received any clothing for three months and only a small supply since November."[28] The command was in an even worse condition for mounts. There were only 154 serviceable horses for about 850 "effective" men, and there was little hope of improvement; forage was lacking, and as late as mid-April there was not enough grass to keep the animals fed.[29]

Notwithstanding such problems and difficulties, the enterprising Harrison kept his "Arkansas Feds" busy. He and they knew that they could make no move, "no matter how cautious or secret . . . [they] endeavor[ed] to be," without having their numbers and destination reported to the enemy; they also knew, or thought, that "the principal messengers . . . [were] women."[30] Nevertheless, as soon as the roads became passable, Harrison sent his men across the Boston Mountains and as far south as the Arkansas River "wrecking steamboats, demolishing bridges, cutting wires, raiding villages, pillaging stores, collecting cotton, burning barns, [and] killing livestock."[31]

While Harrison was making his forays in western Arkansas, John Marmaduke, who had wintered in the Batesville area, seventy-five

26. Kerby, *Kirby Smith's Confederacy*, 36.

27. *Official Records*, Vol. XXII, Pt. 1, p. 890.

28. *Ibid.*, Pt. 2, pp. 149, 192. The regiment's numbers, as reported by Harrison, were 1,032.

29. *Ibid.*, 192, 209. The 1st Arkansas' shortage of horses had not been remedied as late as August 10, four months later. *Ibid.*, 440.

30. *Ibid.*, Vol. XXXIV, Pt. 1, p. 147. This difficulty, however, cut both ways. In the hill country of northwestern Arkansas, the predominantly pro-Union population kept Harrison informed of the movements of Confederate troops.

31. Kerby, *Kirby Smith's Confederacy*, 124.

miles north of Little Rock, persuaded Generals Holmes and Kirby Smith to allow him to make another raid into Missouri. This time eastern, rather than western, Missouri was to be raided, with the important Federal supply depot at Cape Girardeau, on the Mississippi, as the principal objective. Marmaduke moved out of his camps on April 19 with 5,000 men, half of them conscripts he took along only because he believed that they would desert if he left them behind. Nine hundred of his men lacked mounts, which reduced the pace of the march and the distance covered each day to the capabilities of men marching on foot. In addition, 1,200 of the men were unarmed. Given these handicaps, it is not surprising that the raid was an unmitigated failure. The raiders reached Cape Girardeau on April 26 (their "lawless, undisciplined, and un-Christian" behavior on the march was later castigated by no less an authority on such conduct than General Sterling Price) and on Marmaduke's orders, delivered a completely futile, foredoomed assault on the fortifications protecting the town. Late in the night of the same day, the Federals attacked Marmaduke's camp and forced him into an immediate retreat to save his command.[32] A part of the rationale for the raid was Marmaduke's expectation that secessionist Missourians would "flock to his standard" as soon as he appeared in the state; those who actually flocked numbered 150. Marmaduke's losses in killed, wounded, and missing totaled 210.[33]

Major changes in the Confederate high command in Arkansas were made in the spring of 1863. Hindman, a failure as a commander of troops in the field, was transferred to Vicksburg. General Holmes was replaced as department commander by E. Kirby Smith, whom we have last seen commanding part of the forces in the Bragg–Kirby Smith invasion of Kentucky. Holmes was demoted to command of the District of Arkansas and its 25,000 troops, "low in morale, poorly equipped, inadequately fed . . . 'without shoes or hats, and clothed in

32. Marmaduke was pursued by cavalry commanded by General John McNeil, who had been a highly successful St. Louis hatter in civil life. Colonel John M. Glover, whose regiment was a part of McNeil's command, "asserted that he intended to charge . . . [Marmaduke's] scoundrels . . . with the 3d Missouri, his . . . regiment, as they had good sabers, and he wanted them to have an opportunity of trying them." *Official Records*, Vol. XXII, Pt. 1, p. 362.

33. *Ibid.*, 285; Oates, *Confederate Cavalry*, 124–30; Kerby, *Kirby Smith's Confederacy*, 125–27; John N. Edwards, *Shelby and His Men; or, The War in the West* (Cincinnati, 1867), 161.

rags.'" Sterling Price, back in Arkansas after his tribulations in Mississippi, was given command of a division of about 8,500 troops at Little Rock.[34]

The primary objective assigned to the troops in Arkansas by Confederate strategy in the late spring of 1863 was to do their utmost to relieve the pressure of Grant's forces on Vicksburg. The most convenient target for such an operation was the Federal base at Helena. In early 1863 the Helena garrison was a melange typical of Federal posts in the West: two regiments plus a detached company of infantry, a battery of artillery, and, for cavalry, three companies each of the 2nd Arkansas (a Negro regiment) and the 1st and 10th Missouri, six companies each of the 3rd and 4th Iowa, and four companies of the 10th Illinois. This, in the opinion of the commanding officer, Colonel Cyrus Bussey, was too small a force to guard the "several large warehouses filled with Government property, and other valuable stores," as well as a huge herd of 5,000 horses and mules entrusted to his care. Later in the spring, General Benjamin M. Prentiss, who had held the "Hornet's Nest" at Shiloh, took command of the post, the garrison of which had grown to seven regiments of infantry of the XIII Army Corps and Colonel Powell Clayton's cavalry brigade of the 1st Indiana and the 5th Kansas, giving General Prentiss a total of some 4,100 effectives.[35] The position was protected by a chain of bastions sited on the steep hills west of the town and by the monster 8-inch guns of the gunboat *Tyler.*

Not until a month after Grant reached the Vicksburg fortifications did Kirby Smith and Theophilus Holmes commit themselves to doing something concrete in the way of a diversion to help the beleaguered forces of General Pemberton. On June 16 Kirby Smith approved Holmes's proposal to attack Helena, which, Holmes assured him, he believed he could capture. It took Holmes the rest of the month to assemble the troops to make the attack—the infantry of Price's division and of James F. Fagan's Arkansas brigade plus Marmaduke's and General L. M Walker's cavalry, a total of just under 7,700 men—and to march them through the swamps to Helena under con-

---

34. Castel, *General Sterling Price,* 137, 139–40; Kerby, *Kirby Smith's Confederacy,* 53. According to General Kirby Smith, Price had "less than 8,000 effective men, of which a large portion were indifferent and ill-armed cavalry." *Official Records,* Vol. XXII, Pt. 1, p. 25.

35. *Official Records,* Vol. XXII, Pt. 2, pp. 65, 39; *Battles and Leaders,* III, 460.

ditions so grim that he needed ten days to cover a distance of sixty-five miles.[36] Not until July 3, the day before Vicksburg surrendered, did Holmes come within reach of the Helena fortifications and concert with his subordinates the attack to be mounted the next day. The assault, poorly planned and badly botched in the execution, was a disastrous and costly failure. By midmorning, by which time Holmes had already incurred the major portion of the 1,636 casualties the assault was to cost (21 percent of the attacking force), he realized that he was up against a hopeless proposition, called off further attacks, and ordered a retreat.[37]

The capture of Port Hudson, twenty miles above Baton Rouge, by General Nathaniel P. Banks, followed by four days the capture of Vicksburg by General Grant. Then, indeed, President Lincoln was justified in proclaiming, "The Father of Waters once more flows unvexed to the sea." Then, too, the return to Schofield of the 8,000 troops he had sent as reinforcements to Grant for the Vicksburg campaign enabled him to plan a campaign for the conquest of Arkansas.[38] The effect of the capture of Vicksburg and Port Hudson by the Union was to cut off from the main body of the Confederacy the Confederate troops west of the Mississippi. These forces might, perhaps, have been left to wither on the vine; hence the strategic wisdom of conducting major operations against them in Arkansas was somewhat questionable. Nevertheless, Schofield decided to use the troops Grant returned to him and the cavalry division he had previously organized, "to break up Price and occupy Little Rock."[39]

The Arkansas operation Schofield projected was to be based on Helena and commanded at Schofield's specific request by spade-bearded General Frederick Steele; the cavalry component of Steele's forces was to be commanded by General John W. Davidson.[40] Steele

---

36. *Battles and Leaders*, III, 461; Castel, *General Sterling Price*, 145.
37. *Battles and Leaders*, III, 460–61. The Union casualties totaled 239. The entire operation is described in *Ibid.*, 456; Castel, *General Sterling Price*, 144–52; and Kerby, *Kirby Smith's Confederacy*, 130–34.
38. *Official Records*, Vol. XXII, Pt. 1, pp. 13–14. The initial purpose of the campaign, which was ordered by Halleck from Washington, was to forestall a major invasion of Missouri that Price was believed to be organizing. Kerby, *Kirby Smith's Confederacy*, 225.
39. Schofield had previously sent Davidson's division to eastern Arkansas, presumably as a counter to Holmes's anticipated attack on Helena. *Official Records*, Vol. XXII, Pt. 2, p. 350.
40. Steele, a native of New York, graduated thirtieth in the thirty-nine-man West

began the campaign with two divisions of infantry, about 12,000 rank and file "for duty."[41] Davidson's cavalry (the 1st, 2nd, 3rd, 7th, and 8th Missouri, the 10th and 13th Illinois, the 1st and 3rd Iowa, and the 32nd Iowa Mounted Infantry), numbering "something less than 6,000 present for duty," was divided into three brigades.[42] As an anomaly surviving from an earlier day in the war, Colonel Powell Clayton's two-regiment cavalry brigade, now reduced to fewer than 500 men "for duty," was appended to one of the divisions of infantry instead of being incorporated in the cavalry division, as it should have been.

A number of points about General Davidson's command are worthy of notice. First, we learn that the 3rd Iowa was united as a regiment for the first time for the Arkansas Campaign, after being scattered in detachments over a large portion of Missouri. Not thought worthy of mention in the records, this was probably true of others of his regiments as well. Having regiments operate as regimental units (however reduced in numbers they may have become), no less than the setting up of a cavalry division, was a significant step forward in the creation of effective cavalry forces west of the river. Second, the presence in Davidson's division of a regiment designated as "Mounted Infantry" is not without significance. By the spring of 1863, the tactical functions of mounted troops of the Union armies in the West had already evolved quite far in the direction of the concept of mounted infantry. It is of interest to note that the as yet imperfectly sensed facts of tactical evolution were beginning to gain recognition, slowly and perhaps reluctantly, in the symbolically sensitive area of nomenclature. The name

---

Point Class of 1843 and was assigned as a 2nd lieutenant to the 2nd U.S. Infantry. After receiving two brevets in the Mexican War, he served in California and the Northwest and rose to major in the 11th U.S. Infantry. He fought in the battle of Wilson's Creek and then transferred to the volunteer service as colonel of the 8th Iowa Infantry. He was promoted to brigadier general and then to major general, and served in the Vicksburg Campaign from the Chickasaw Bluffs attack under Sherman to the surrender on July 4, 1863. Davidson, a Virginian by birth, received an at-large appointment to West Point and graduated twenty-seventh in the forty-one-man Class of 1845. He was posted as a 2nd lieutenant to the 1st U.S. Dragoons, with whom he served on the frontier against the Jicarilla Apaches and in California, Kansas, and Missouri. As major in the 2nd U.S. Cavalry, he served in the Peninsula Campaign, and was promoted to brigadier general in the volunteer service on February 3, 1862. Cullum, *Biographical Register*, II, 92–93, 128–29.

41. Steele was later reinforced by a 2,300-man brigade of infantry sent him by General Hurlbut from Memphis. Kerby, *Kirby Smith's Confederacy*, 229.

42. *Battles and Leaders*, III, 461; *Official Records*, Vol. XXII, Pt. 1, pp. 470, 475, Pt. 2, pp. 432–33.

mounted infantry was on its way to acceptance as a substitute for the time-honored word *cavalry*. An interesting sidelight on this evolutionary process is provided by an occurrence a few weeks after the start of the Steele-Davidson Arkansas campaign. In the pursuit of Price after the capture of Little Rock, Colonel Lewis Merrill, in command of the pursuit, held the 1st Indiana in reserve "*to act as cavalry*," inasmuch as they had "fresh horses and poor fire arms."[43]

General Davidson is entitled to considerably more credit as a cavalryman than he has received. Schofield had given him command of a newly organized cavalry division, which he had the foresight to train in tactics best suited to his men's capabilities no less than to the limited amount of time at his disposal for training of any kind. He wrote General Grant from Arkansas on August 1: "You should know the character of my force. I have three batteries, and my regiments are dragoons, taught by me to use the carbine dismounted when necessary, and after a march of 300 miles from Pilot Knob to this point, are better fitted— men, horses and transportation—to strike the enemy than when they started."[44]

Steele marched out of Helena with his infantry on August 11 and met Davidson, and the brigade of infantry sent to him from Memphis, at Clarendon, on the seventeenth.[45] The next day he crossed White River with his united forces and led them toward Little Rock, forty-five miles to the west. To oppose Steele, Price had at Little Rock about 7,700 men, half infantry and half cavalry. His lack of numbers was matched by his men's lack of morale, understandable enough after what they had undergone at Prairie Grove and Helena.[46] The best Price could do was to set his infantry to digging rifle pits on the north bank of the Arkansas a short distance to the east of Little Rock and to

43. *Official Records*, Vol. XXII, pt. 1, p. 498; emphasis added.
44. *Ibid.*, 430.
45. Davidson reached Clarendon after cleverly bypassing Marmaduke, who then had his command at Jacksonport. For this, Davidson was criticized by Schofield, who had wanted him to attack Marmaduke to prevent the latter from raiding into Missouri. After the Confederate defeat at Helena less than three weeks before, raiding into Missouri was the last thing Marmaduke wanted to do, or was capable of doing, at that moment. *Ibid.*, 424, 426.
46. *Battles and Leaders*, III, 461; *Official Records*, Vol. XXII, Pt. 1, p. 25. Indicative of the low morale of Price's command was his proclamation of September 4 "threatening both his own troops and the citizens of Pulaski county with military arrest and summary execution for desertion, unauthorized absence from places of duty," *etc.* Kerby, *Kirby Smith's Confederacy*, 230.

send Marmaduke and his cavalry eastward to burn bridges in Steele's path and delay his advance as much as possible without risking the safety of his own command.

On September 2, Steele reached the Arkansas opposite Little Rock, but instead of accommodating Price by attempting to storm the rifle pits manned by his infantry, he had Davidson scout Price's flanks both above and below Little Rock. On the strength of the information Davidson brought back, Steele ordered him to cross the river with his cavalry downstream from the town, sweep Price's right flank out of the way, and occupy Little Rock. The plan worked to perfection. On the morning of September 10, Davidson laid a pontoon bridge across the Arkansas at Terry's Ferry, ten miles below the town, had his men across the river by ten o'clock, and after being delayed briefly by Marmaduke's cavalry at the Bayou Fourche, a tributary of the Arkansas, marched into Little Rock, which Price had ordered evacuated as soon as he had word that the Federal cavalry had crossed to his side of the river.[47] Both in his official report on the campaign and in a later dispatch to General Halleck, Steele spoke highly of the "energy, perseverance, intelligence, and gallantry," deserving of "the highest commendation," with which Davidson and his troopers had handled their role in the campaign.[48]

The pursuit of Price's retreating forces was a less commendable performance. Led by Colonel Lewis Merrill, commanding the First Brigade of Davidson's division, it did not get under way until the morning following the capture of Little Rock and does not seem to have been pressed with the requisite energy. Steele, at any rate, reported that it had not been as vigorous as he had expected it to be. As is customary in such cases, Merrill's excuses were even more feeble than his pursuit had been. The road taken by the enemy, he reported, ran through country that made "successful pursuit exceedingly difficult, affording numerous strong defensive positions"; his men, moreover, were still "weary" from their exertions of the previous day. So, after following in the tracks of the retreating Confederates for sixteen miles "through thickets and heavy timber," Merrill called a halt to what could not have been an excessively strenuous day's effort. The second day's pursuit, if it can be called that, was even less energetic. Given the

47. *Official Records*, Vol. XXII, Pt. 1, pp. 476, 487, 14; see also *Battles and Leaders*, III, 456–57; Castel, *General Sterling Price*, 154–58; Kerby, *Kirby Smith's Confederacy*, 224–31.
48. *Official Records*, Vol. XXII, Pt. 1, pp. 480, 477.

state of morale of Price's command as they made their way to Arkadelphia, fifty miles southwest of Little Rick, it may be assumed that a more vigorous pursuit would have added nothing—other than more dead bodies, more wounded, and more captives—to what the Federals already had. Merrill reported that he had "scarcely left the suburbs of . . . [Little Rock] before . . . [his men] began to find the debris of a retreating and demoralized army—broken wagons, arms and equipments, partly destroyed, ammunition upset into small streams and mud-holes, and deserters and fagged-out soldiers in numbers continually brought in by . . . [his] advance and flankers."[49] General Holmes, who accompanied Price on the doleful march to Arkadelphia, remarked to Marmaduke, "Steele will make no effort to pursue. . . . *we are an army of prisoners and self-supporting at that*"—a most apt description of the sad state of Price's forces.[50]

While Steele was preparing to move against Little Rock, Blunt was making western Arkansas secure for the Union. The base he proposed to use for his operation was Fort Gibson, the westernmost Union post on the Arkansas River, located in Indian Territory ("The Nations," as it was commonly called) sixty miles northwest of Fort Smith. The post had been captured for the Union in January by Colonel William Phillips and his Indian Brigade. Indicative of the difficulty of maintaining posts or conducting operations in these sparsely settled areas is that merely to sustain the Fort Gibson garrison, a regular service of commissary trains of as many as two hundred wagons was needed. The trains, departing from Fort Scott in Kansas, had to have large escorts of cavalry, infantry, and artillery, going and coming, to protect them from bands of Confederate Indians and (in the summer of 1863) from General William Cabell's brigade of Arkansas cavalry.[51]

Blunt arrived at Fort Gibson on July 11, bringing cavalry reinforcements with him, and started his campaign four days later. After defeating and scattering Douglas Cooper's brigade of Choctaws, Chicka-

49. *Ibid.*, 497.

50. Castel, *General Sterling Price*, 158. At least a thousand, and perhaps as many as two thousand, of Price's men deserted on the way, and of those who remained, two thousand were unarmed. Kerby, *Kirby Smith's Confederacy*, 232.

51. A train of two hundred wagons that left Fort Scott in mid-July had for an escort four companies and two mountain howitzers of the 3rd Wisconsin and a two-hundred-man battalion of the 13th Kansas Infantry. A train making the return trip at the same time was guarded by six companies of Kansas infantry. *Official Records*, Vol. XXII, Pt. 2, p. 379.

saws, Creeks, and Cherokees at Honey Springs, he drove General William Steele (a cousin of Frederick Steele's) and his brigade of demoralized Arkansas cavalry 110 miles south to Red River. To Colonel William Cloud of Kansas, whose part-infantry, part-cavalry brigade had just joined him, Blunt assigned the job of taking Fort Smith, defended by Colonel William Cabell's cavalry brigade of Arkansas conscripts. Blunt's and Cloud's principal problem was not the enemy but the midsummer heat; Blunt complained that he was losing his horses in temperatures that rose as high as ninety-eight degrees in the shade, faster than he could replace them. Nevertheless, Cloud reached Fort Smith, drove Cabell out of his way, captured the post, and, leaving his infantry behind to demolish the fortifications, chased Cabell, whose numbers shrank by the hour because of straggling and desertion, toward Arkadelphia, on the Ouachita River. With Fort Smith now in possession of the Union, hundreds of Arkansans who had been conscripted into the Confederate army turned up there singly and in groups ("Mountain Feds" was Cloud's name for them) to take the loyalty oath and in many cases to enlist in the Union army. In a brush with Cabell's remnants at Dardanelle, Arkansas, Cloud and the 2nd Kansas were assisted by "three officers and about 100 men" formerly of Cabell's brigade, who had changed their allegiance and, still wearing their gray uniforms, fought side by side with the blue-clad Kansans.[52]

In the autumn of 1863, the only Confederate troops left in Arkansas that still retained some measure of an aggressive spirit were the Missourians in Shelby's and Marmaduke's cavalry commands. Within a week of the loss of Little Rock, Shelby requested authority to take his men on a raid into Missouri. His proposal having been approved by Generals Marmaduke, Price, Holmes, and Kirby Smith, he departed from Arkadelphia on September 22, a day when, as he (or actually Major Edwards) reported, "the weather was propitious, and the glorious skies of a southern autumn flashed cheerily down upon waving banners and glittering steel as we marched proudly by the white-haired chieftain, General Price, and his hearty benediction was solemnly prophetic of my entire success."[53] Starting out with 600 men, selected from the three regiments of his brigade, Shelby's numbers were dou-

52. *Ibid.*, 463, and Pt. 1, pp. 599, 603.
53. *Ibid.*, Pt. 1, p. 671. General Schofield claimed that Shelby was joined also by the guerrilla bands of Quantrill, Sidney D. Jackman, and others, "with all the guerrillas in Western Missouri." *Ibid.*, 16.

bled by the accession on the way of the partisan battalions of Colonels
DeWitt C. Hunter and John T. Coffee.[54] If Major Edwards' accounts
are to be believed, the main activity of the command on its way north
via Neosho, Sarcoxie, Humansville, Warsaw, and Tipton, to Boonville
on the Missouri River, was slaughter and pillage. A "band of Confederate deserters and Union jayhawkers . . . desperate villains" numbering
200, was attacked; 79 of the gang were killed in the attack, and 34
were captured; 31 of the 34 were "tried by military commission and
shot." Another "jayhawking band was . . . utterly destroyed"; its 54
members were killed to a man, "and none wounded or taken."[55] The
town of Oregon, or Bowers' Mill, "a notorious pest spot for the [Union]
militia . . . was sacked and then swept from the face of the earth, to
pollute it no more forever."[56] In Calhoun, the raiders were reported to
have "murdered two citizens . . . and robbed the town of everything in
it."[57] And of course the raiders took every horse they could find; "good
Union steeds were changed into rebel chargers," in Edwards' amiable
terms.[58]

As far north as Boonville, which was surrendered to Shelby on October 11, the raid had been a risk-free and eminently profitable excursion in pleasant autumn weather, but rather too slowly paced for ultimate safety. General Egbert B. Brown, in command of the District of
Central Missouri, had time to collect his widely scattered troops (five
regiments of Missouri State Militia Cavalry, plus the 1st Arkansas) and
on October 12 pitched into Shelby at Boonville and drove him northwestward toward Marshall, thirty miles away. As Shelby marched west
from Boonville, with Brown dogging his footsteps, General Thomas

54. Oates, *Confederate Cavalry*, 134.
55. Edwards, *Shelby and His Men*, 199, 201. On the other hand, when Lieutenant
Colonel Bazel F. Lazear and his 1st Missouri State Militia Cavalry entered Tipton and
found two stragglers from Shelby's command "in the act of knocking down and robbing
citizens," they killed them out of hand. *Official Records*, Vol. XXII, Pt. 1, p. 629.
56. *Official Records*, Vol. XXII, Pt. 1, p. 672.
57. *Ibid.*, 629. Major Emory S. Foster, 7th Missouri State Militia Cavalry, captured
three of the raiders at Calhoun. "I did not shoot them," the major apologized, "because
the enemy have possession of several of our men." *Ibid.*, 647.
58. *Ibid.*, 673. While at Tipton, on October 8 and 9, Shelby sent out a "cloud of
scouts" to destroy the Pacific Railroad in both directions from the town. He reported that
for "30 miles either way rails were torn up, ties burned, bridges destroyed, wire carried
off, and cattle-stops and water tanks obliterated." *Ibid.*, 673. It seems hardly possible that
a knowledgeable officer would actually believe that a few dozen "scouts" could injure
seriously sixty miles of railroad.

Ewing, Jr., William Tecumseh Sherman's foster brother and brother-in-law, with the thousand men he had hastily collected from the garrisons of the numerous posts in his District of the Border, came marching east. On October 13 the three forces met at Marshall. Shelby found himself hemmed in between Brown and Ewing and had to fight his way out. After a two-hour fire fight followed by a charge all along the line and after his artillery of two guns had swept "the crowded streets [of Marshall] with fearful slaughter," he did manage to extricate himself, but he had been considerably mauled.[59] Another account of the fight at Marshall has it that Shelby's forces were split in two by the Federals and were able to escape only by breaking up into small detachments and shedding arms, trains, ambulances, and ammunition wagons on the way south.[60] Not until November 3 did the raiders, "frostbitten, emaciated, and exhausted," reach their base at Washington, Arkansas, forty-five miles southwest of Arkadelphia. The claim has been made that this raid of Shelby's was a "brilliant demonstration of the power of a column of cavalry operating strategically."[61] A colorful exploit the raid assuredly was, and the stuff of legend—the excesses of the raiders were, for a Missouri operation, relatively modest—and the brigadier general's stars Shelby received for it had been bestowed frequently in both armies for considerably lesser achievements, but to claim that the operation had any strategic purpose, value, or effect is to deprive the word *strategic* of any meaning whatever. The raid signified nothing and accomplished nothing.[62]

59. *Battles and Leaders*, IV, 374–75; *Official Records*, Vol. XXII, Pt. 1, p. 675. Since General Brown reported thirty-one of his men killed and wounded in the entire campaign, the slaughter at Marshall could not have been as fearful as Shelby thought.
60. Oates, *Confederate Cavalry*, 136–37; *Official Records*, Vol. XXII, Pt. 1, p. 628. Joining in the pursuit were the commands of John McNeil, Ewing, and Colonel William Weer. Schofield claimed that Shelby lost more than half his command on the retreat. *Official Records*, Vol. XXII, Pt. 1, p. 16.
61. Oates, *Confederate Cavalry*, 139.
62. A "prominent Confederate Missourian" wrote President Davis that "the plundering which had accompanied Shelby's . . . [raid] had made the Southern uniform more feared in Missouri than the Northern." Castel, *General Sterling Price*, 161. It should be added, in the interest of fairness, that when in late August, 1863, the 3rd Missouri State Militia Cavalry and a detachment of the 1st Missouri made a scout from Cape Girardeau to Pocahontas, Arkansas, Colonel R. W. Woolson of the militia regiment reported several cases of highway robbery and theft committed by troopers of the 1st Missouri. He was satisfied, the colonel wrote, that "some of that detachment stole horses, watches, money, anything they could lay their hands on, from citizens and prisoners." *Official Records*, Vol. XXII, Pt. 1, p. 570.

One final operation in Arkansas in 1863 remains to be recorded. In late October, Marmaduke decided to follow Shelby's example but on a less ambitious scale; he set out to attack the Federal post at Pine Bluff, on the south bank of the Arkansas, forty-five miles south of Little Rock. Commanding the post for the Union was Colonel Powell Clayton; the garrison was his cavalry brigade of the 5th Kansas and the 1st Indiana, a total of some 550 men. Warned of Marmaduke's approach, Powell proceeded to turn the town into a fortress by means of the only material he had, namely bales of cotton, with which he "had all the streets leading into the court[house] square completely and very formidably fortified." After posting his artillery "so as to command every street leading into the square," he set all the Negroes in the town to hauling water up from the river to fill all the barrels they could find so that he would have a two-day supply of drinking water should the enemy cut him off from access to the river.

Marmaduke reached the town on October 24 with a force Colonel Clayton thought numbered 2,000 and, after a four-hour bombardment that "burned part of the city and destroyed considerable public and private property," staged an assault in due form; he deployed his men in three columns and charged the garrison from three directions. The attack was repulsed; Marmaduke decided to withdraw and did so after he "plundered every house he could get to, and stole every horse and mule from the citizens that he could lay his hands on." But he also left, according to Clayton, "a great portion of his wounded and dead on the field." The Federals estimated Marmaduke's loss as upward of 130; he admitted to 40, the same number the defenders lost.[63]

Operations against guerrillas contributed little or nothing to the development of cavalry doctrine in the Civil War. Nevertheless, in some theaters, notably in Missouri, on the Kansas-Missouri border, and in Arkansas, they were a major preoccupation of the Union cavalry and therefore call for brief mention.

After the excursions and alarums of the first nine or ten months of the war, Missouri and the Kansas-Missouri border became military backwaters, disturbed by military operations of any magnitude only by

63. *Official Records*, Vol. XXII, Pt. 1, pp. 723, 730, Pt. 2, p. 680.

the Confederate cavalry raids already described. The war had moved south, to Indian Territory and to Arkansas. What did remain in Missouri and on the border were guerrilla operations on a scale and of a ferocity unknown elsewhere. General Schofield remarked in September, 1863, that waging a guerrilla war amounted to a "passion" with "Western people" and that guerrillas would give the Union forces stationed in the area "more serious trouble than the organized rebel armies have done."[64] It is a reasonably safe guess that in Missouri, and perhaps also in Arkansas, the loss of life and the destruction of property incident to guerrilla warfare were at least as great, and may well have been much greater, than the casualties and the damage inflicted by organized and uniformed forces in their operations against each other. The brutalities practiced by one side against the other were commonly excused—when an excuse was thought to be needed—as justifiable retaliation for the equally heinous acts committed by the other.

However valid retaliation may have been as an excuse in some cases, there can be no possible justification for the pathological savagery of the Lawrence, Kansas, Massacre perpetrated by Quantrill and his hyenas on July 21, 1863 (Quantrill ordered his men to "kill every man big enough to carry a gun"); the Baxter Springs Massacre on October 6, 1863, another Quantrill exploit, with its toll of seventy-nine dead, many of whom were finished off after being wounded; and the Centralia Massacre on September 24, 1864, in which "Bloody Bill" Anderson's gang halted a North Missouri Railroad train and, after robbing the passengers, lined up and killed ("mustered out") twenty-four of the twenty-five unarmed, homeward-bound Union soldiers on the train.[65]

64. *Ibid.*, Pt. 2, p. 541. Captain Robert McElroy, 3rd Missouri State Militia Cavalry, reported that in the area of Pilot Knob, Alton, and Doniphan, in southeast Missouri, "the women . . . [were] even more daring and treacherous, and, in fact, worse than the men." *Ibid.*, Pt. 1, p. 744.

65. For Lawrence, see *Ibid.*, Pt. 1, pp. 14, 583–90, and Pt. 2, p. 479; and Richard S. Brownlee, *Gray Ghosts of the Confederacy* (Baton Rouge, 1958), 121–25. For Baxter Springs, see *Official Records*, Vol. XXII, Pt. 1, pp. 688–99, 781–82, 791, and Brownlee, *Gray Ghosts*, 128–31. For Centralia, see *Official Records*, Vol. XLI, Pt. 1, p. 417, and Pt. 3, p. 420; and Brownlee, *Gray Ghosts*, 216–18. Confederate General Henry E. McCulloch, be it said to his credit, wrote that Quantrill's mode of warfare was "but little, if at all, removed from that of the wildest savage. . . . we cannot, as a Christian people, sanction a savage, inhuman warfare." *Official Records*, Vol. XXVI, Pt. 2, p. 348.

The result of these incidents and of many more of the same kind was that bushwhackers and guerrillas (the terms were used interchangeably), especially those wearing some part of the Federal uniform, as many of them did, could expect no quarter. Order after order issued by regimental, brigade, division, army, and area commanders directed that (to quote a typical example) "all enemies found wearing the uniform of the United States Army will be immediately shot, and all guerrillas will be treated in a similar manner."[66] Inspector General R. B. Marcy (whom readers will recognize as George B. McClellan's father-in-law and, in 1862, his chief of staff) reported in March, 1864:

It has been the custom in many parts of the department [of the Missouri] for officers and soldiers, when operating against Guerrillas, to immediately put to death all who fall into their hands, even after they have thrown down their arms and asked for mercy, and colonels, lieutenant-colonels and other officers have told me that they habitually give orders to their scouting parties "to bring in no prisoners.". . . The existing practice enables evil-disposed persons to rob and murder loyal and inoffensive citizens under the plea that they were acting as bushwhackers, and it unquestionably tends greatly to demoralize troops.[67]

General Ewing directed the commanding officer at Cape Girardeau to instruct his subordinates that the guerrillas "swarming all around" his post, "killing and robbing," were "not to be captured under any circumstances, but to be killed when found." He went on to point out that when such people were brought in as prisoners, then tried and convicted, the only result was to put "the Government to the expense of boarding and lodging . . . [them] during the war, as the President rarely approves a sentence of death. It is therefore best to take few prisoners."[68] A special case were the guerrillas caught in arms after they had taken the oath of allegiance. On one occasion in September, 1862, the same Lewis Merrill who was to conduct the half-hearted pursuit of Price's army after the capture of Little Rock a year later, then in command of the Northeast Division of Missouri, had a batch of four-

---

66. *Official Records*, Vol. XXXIV, Pt. 2, p. 617. Other such orders will be found in *Ibid.*, Pt. 2, pp. 243, 775, Pt. 4, pp. 96, 218, and Vol. XXII, Pt. 1, pp. 224, 226, Pt. 2, p. 222, and Vol. XLI, Pt. 4, p. 928. The number of prisoners reported in the records as shot and killed "while trying to escape" strains the laws of probability and the reader's capacity for belief. See, for example, *Ibid.*, Vol. XXXIV, Pt. 2, p. 57, Pt. 4, p. 234, and Vol. XLVIII, Pt. 1, p. 195.

67. *Ibid.*, Vol. XXXIV, Pt. 2, pp. 775–76.

68. *Ibid.*, Pt. 4, p. 260.

teen of such unfortunates executed by firing squads "with due form and ceremony."[69]

It would be difficult to find in the reports of the hundreds of scouts, raids, and expeditions aimed at ridding a given area of bushwhackers and guerrillas any indication that they enhanced the military competence of the Union cavalry in Missouri and Arkansas. Nor, one may add, the moral standards of the troopers. Not surprisingly, some of the men came to enjoy guerrilla hunts; Corporal William O. Gulick, 1st Iowa, wrote his parents from Clinton, in west central Missouri, that he liked hunting in general, but that hunting guerrillas was "the best game I ever saw. . . . I have not much mercy for them dont beleive I would take many prisoners."[70] The records are nearly totally barren of indications that any conscious effort was made by commanders at any level to develop techniques for tracking down the elusive guerrilla. General Curtis reported in August, 1863, that Lieutenant J. B. Pond, 3rd Wisconsin, had "greatly distinguished himself during the past six months . . . in fighting guerrillas, fighting them at all times in their own style, principally at night, by watching the crossings of streams, suspected houses, &c."[71] Doubtless other regiments had their Lieutenant Ponds and by the usual process of trial and error developed their own more or less satisfactory methods of combating guerrillas.

Unfortunately, but not unexpectedly, the example of guerrilla misconduct was contagious. The 6th Missouri committed "outrageous excesses" in their own state, near Sikeston, Missouri; they killed one man "in his own house" and shot at another man and robbed his store. Colonel J. B. Rogers, commanding at Cape Girardeau, reported that "many citizens are killed and robbed by" the 6th Missouri. In August, 1862, the 6th Kansas, on an expedition to Independence, Missouri,

69. *Ibid.*, Vol. XIII, 660–61; see also p. 282. In the latter case the oath breaker's house and the houses of members of his gang were burned down, and the entire neighborhood was rounded up to witness his execution.

70. Guyer, "Corporal William O. Gulick," 402, 407. A little later, a regimental order directed that two of the 1st Iowa's prisoners were to be shot for every member of the regiment shot by guerrillas. There is no indication in Gulick's letters that the order was actually carried out.

71. *Official Records*, Vol. XXII, Pt. 2, p. 478. Not all the officers of the Wisconsin regiment were as devoted to duty as was Lieutenant Pond. General Blunt suggested to Schofield that the colonel and lieutenant colonel be given leaves of absence "until after the termination of the war," they being "entirely worthless as officers." *Ibid.*, 526.

burned the houses, outbuildings, and harvested crops of two individuals, one of whom they identified, perhaps correctly, as a "notorious
rebel and infamous scoundrel." After occupying Independence, the
Kansans arrested the editor of the local "secession paper," the *Border
Star*, a "lying, dirty sheet," and destroyed his type and press. A year
later, a detachment of the same regiment "entered Johnson and Henry
Counties [in Missouri] and robbed and plundered indiscriminately almost every citizen in their line of march."[72]

The 4th Missouri State Militia Cavalry burned down the village of
Sibley.[73] Just as the homes and farm buildings of known or suspected
guerrillas and of those suspected of harboring them were burned down
by Federal or Unionist Missouri state troops, so the homes and farm
buildings of Unionist Missourians were burned down by Shelby's and
Marmaduke's raiders, by guerrillas, or by their secessionist neighbors.
As early as the autumn of 1862, "all that was left [around Indepen-
dence] to remind one that the country had previously been inhabited
were a few fence rails, orchards, and the old-fashioned chimneys that
stood to mark the places where the planters' houses had been."[74] And
in the western counties of Missouri generally, "the troops might march
a day on some of the main roads without seeing a house or a fence
standing, where they saw only standing chimneys to mark the places
where the houses had been burned."[75]

Killing guerrillas did not stop the guerrilla war. There were too
many guerrillas to be killed, they were too difficult to track down, and
there were always more guerrillas to take the places of those eradi-
cated. Many schemes besides killing were tried, but none of them
worked. Burning the homes of guerrillas and of those harboring them
(some of whom did so under compulsion) accomplished nothing. Levy-
ing fines on the "disloyal inhabitants" of a given area was equally fruitless.[76] Just as ineffective was the expulsion from their homes of families

72. *Ibid.*, 542, and Vol. XIII, p. 255, Vol. XXII, Pt. 2, p. 722.
73. *Ibid.*, Vol. XXII, Pt. 1, p. 377; see also *Ibid.*, Vol. VIII, 357–58.
74. Isaac Gause, *Four Years with Five Armies* (New York, 1908), 63. Conditions
along the border became so intolerable that in desperation Schofield begged in October,
1863, for either a regiment of Kentucky cavalry or a regiment of Regulars to patrol the
border and relieve the area of the mutual atrocities committed by Kansas cavalry in Missouri and Missouri cavalry in Kansas. *Official Records*, Vol. XXII, Pt. 2, pp. 589, 597.
75. Wiley Britton, *The Civil War on the Border* (New York, 1891), 207.
76. *Official Records*, Vol. XIII, 800. Of the $15,000 levied on the pro-southern in-
habitants of Jackson County, Missouri, in November, 1862, half was to go to "subsist"

known or thought to have been "feeding and harboring" guerrillas.[77]

Following the Lawrence Massacre, General Ewing, whose District of the Border embraced the two westernmost tiers of counties of Missouri south of the Missouri River, wrote General Schofield about this area: "About two thirds of the families . . . are of kin to the guerrillas, and are actively and heartily engaged in feeding, clothing and sustaining them. The presence of these families is the cause of the presence there of the guerrillas. I can see no prospect of an early and complete end to the war on the border . . . so long as those families remain there."[78] And Ewing went on to propose the draconian remedy of the forcible removal of nearly the entire remaining population of Johnson, Cass, and Bates counties and of the northern half of Vernon County. Issued with Schofield's approval, Ewing's General Order No. 11 directed that these families be removed within fifteen days.[79]

As the war was about to enter its fourth year, the secessionist guerrillas of Missouri, and to a lesser degree those of Arkansas, remained an ever-present and deadly reality. The pitiless enforcement of General Order No. 11, recorded for posterity (with embellishments for propaganda purposes) by the painter George Caleb Bingham, failed to end the guerrilla war, with its mutually inflicted atrocities, even in the three and a half counties directly affected. It served only to add to the bitterness and hatred engendered by the war.

---

the pro-Union Missouri militia and half "to the relief of the destitute families of the soldiers engaged in active service and to relieve temporarily destitute refugees who have been driven from their homes by rebels or guerrillas."

77. *Ibid.*, Vol. XXII, Pt. 1, p. 547.

78. *Ibid.*, Pt. 2, p. 428; see also pp. 471–73.

79. *Ibid.*, p. 473. The counties listed were those along the Kansas border between the Missouri River on the north and Fort Scott, Kansas, on the south. The people to be removed were those living more than a mile from the nearest Union military post.

VIII

'Twas a Famous Victory

BOTH OF THE MAJOR EFFORTS MOUNTED BY THE UNION IN 1862 to capture Vicksburg by approaching it from the northeast ended in failure. Grant's march down the line of the Mississippi Central got as far south as Oxford, Mississippi, where it was brought to a halt in late December by the twin raids of Van Dorn and Forrest on his line of communications, which forced him to retreat. Then, on December 29, Sherman's direct assault on the high ground northeast of Vicksburg from the Chickasaw Bayou swamps was beaten off with ease. That same day, far to the east of Vicksburg, Rosecrans' advance south from Nashville reached the Confederate position protecting Murfreesboro, and two days later the battle of Stones River began. Technically a Union victory, the battle nonetheless served to check Rosecrans' progress south; not until six months later, at the end of June, did he resume his advance.

Thus, the major Union initiatives in the area between the Alleghenies and the Mississippi had ground to a halt by the end of 1862. On what may be called the "Vicksburg Front," Grant, in the midst of administrative problems, had to excogitate some new design for getting at the Confederate fortress, to take the place of the plans that had failed. The plan that eventually did the trick, evolved after a number of others had been tried and had failed, was to have the army march south on the Louisiana side of the river along the waterways, bayous, and oxbow lakes that seamed the lowlands from Milliken's Bend to New Carthage. The troops were to be met at Grand Gulf by Admiral David Porter's gunboats and transports, which were to have run the Vicksburg batteries. Ferried across the river by the navy, the army would be in a position to reach Vicksburg from the high ground to the east of the fortress. The plan, however, was subject to extreme hazards. When Grant discussed the idea with Admiral Porter, the latter made it clear that having run the batteries in a downstream direction with the aid of the current, he could not take the vessels upstream against the current to load up with supplies for the army and risk a second run downstream past the batteries. Nor would the waterlogged route the army was to use from Milliken's Bend down to Grand Gulf do for hauling supplies; it was found that teams of from twelve to eighteen horses were needed to drag a single gun through some stretches of what passed for the road.[1] Hence, to make the campaign Grant would have to cut loose from his base. Nevertheless, against the advice of some of his subordinates, including the normally aggressive Sherman, Grant went ahead with the operation. Porter ran the batteries successfully with his gunboats on the night of April 16 and with his transports six nights later, and on April 30 the transports began ferrying the army, which ultimately numbered 53,000, across the Mississippi.

As a preliminary to a direct attack on Vicksburg, Grant chose to move against Jackson, the capital of Mississippi, as a means of interdicting the possibility of reinforcements, munitions, and supplies reaching Vicksburg from the East, as well as forestalling attacks on the rear of his own army as it settled down to an investment of the Confederate fortress. On May 14 the Federals gained possession of Jackson. Leaving Sherman behind to destroy the railroads, "the arsenal, a foundery, the cotton-factory . . . etc., etc.," Grant fought and won on May 16 the battle of Champion Hill and the next day another battle at the crossing of Big Black River.[2] By the evening of May 18, Pemberton's army of some 28,000 was penned up in the Vicksburg defenses,

1. Bruce Catton quotes the remark of an unnamed gunner, presumably of the 16th Ohio Light Battery, to the effect that "a hike which took a fortnight could have been made in two days if there had been good roads, dry ground, and a few bridges." Catton, *Grant Moves South*, 419.

2. Sherman, *Memoirs*, I, 321. There are strong indications that the "etc., etc." destroyed by Sherman's men greatly exceeded in value that of the more strictly military installations they destroyed.

which ran in an irregular arc about six miles long through exceedingly rough terrain from the Mississippi above the town to the river below it.[3] Counting more than he should have on Confederate demoralization after the defeats they had sustained at Champion Hill and Big Black River, Grant mounted a full-fledged assault all along their defenses on the nineteenth. Made at a cost of 157 officers and men killed and 777 wounded, the assault was a failure.[4] Another assault three days later failed also and led to the removal of John McClernand from the command of the XIII Army Corps.[5] After May 22, the operations against the fortress became a siege conducted by all the traditional rules, and came to an inevitable conclusion six weeks later with the surrender of the starving garrison by General Pemberton on July 4.

Whether the cause was the nature of the terrain from Milliken's Bend south to the Mississippi—a crazy quilt of tangled watercourses and swamps—or Grant's inability, not to be outgrown for another year, to recognize and exploit the potential of his mounted force, there was little scope for the Union cavalry in the Vicksburg Campaign. On the march south from Milliken's Bend, a portion of the 2nd Illinois joined with the 69th Indiana Infantry on March 31 to capture Richmond, Louisiana. The cavalrymen, "dismounting from their horses, sprang into the small boats brought along on wagons, and paddling them across [Roundway] Bayou with the butts of their carbines, hastened to occupy the town."[6] The exploit added nothing to the corpus of cavalry tactics, but it demonstrated, if only in a minor way, the resourcefulness of midwestern volunteers.

On May 10, having crossed the Mississippi, Grant asked General Banks to send him the 6th and 7th Illinois, the two regiments, with a combined strength of between 900 and 950 officers and men, that had reached Baton Rouge eight days before, at the conclusion of Grierson's

3. *Battles and Leaders*, III, 550. Grant claimed that Pemberton's forces numbered "over sixty thousand." *Ibid.*, 519.

4. *Official Records*, Vol. XXIV, Pt. 2, p. 154. One of the wounded was General Albert L. Lee, former colonel of the 7th Kansas, later promoted to the command of a brigade in General Osterhaus' division of infantry. He was wounded by a musket ball that entered his right cheek and passed out at the back of his neck. Four days after he was wounded, he wrote or dictated his report of the assault. *Ibid.*, 231.

5. McClernand was replaced by General E. O. C. Ord.

6. *Official Records*, Vol. XXIV, Pt. 1, p. 139. Richmond, Louisiana, not to be found in modern maps, was located ten miles southwest of Milliken's Bend and a short distance below the line of the Shreveport & Vicksburg Railroad.

Raid, about to be described. The two regiments, Grant wrote, would be "of immense service" to him. But there was no chance that Banks, about to begin his investment of Port Hudson and as shorthanded for cavalry as was Grant, would give up the two veteran mounted regiments that, like manna, had dropped out of the skies into his domain.[7]

In mid-June, three regiments of cavalry—the 5th Illinois, 3rd Iowa, and 2nd Wisconsin—were brought across the river and, with the 4th Iowa, the single mounted regiment Grant already had, were "thrown into a provisional brigade" under Colonel Cyrus Bussey of the 3rd Iowa.[8] Until then, the mounted component of Grant's forces for the Vicksburg Campaign were the 4th Iowa as the only complete regiment, plus five companies of the 2nd Illinois, four of the 3rd Illinois, and seven of the 6th Missouri, as well as the two-company "battalion" of Thielemann's Illinois Cavalry and the single-company Kane County (Illinois) Independent Cavalry.

On the campaign from Bruinsburg and Grand Gulf (Grant's landing places on the east bank of the Mississippi) to Jackson and thence west to the Vicksburg fortifications, the fragments of Union cavalry then with the army were attached some to General Peter J. Osterhaus' Ninth Division of the XIII Corps, leading the Union advance, and some to General James B. McPherson's XVII Corps. On the morning of May 5, Osterhaus reported, his advance was halted east of Rocky Springs and Big Sandy Creek by Confederate infantry. He ordered the companies of the 2nd Illinois, attached to his division, to charge the enemy; led by Lieutenant Isaiah Stickel, they did so "boldly . . . with drawn sabers and drove them 5 miles, killing and wounding 12 and taking 30 prisoners." Osterhaus generously described the charge as "without doubt one of the most brilliant cavalry engagements of the war" and Lieutenant Stickel as deserving of "the highest praise for skill and bravery."[9] Ten days later, the three-company detachment of

7. *Ibid.*, Pt. 3, p. 289. A second request by Grant on May 25 for the two regiments was equally fruitless. *Ibid.*, 347.

8. *Ibid.*, Pt. 2, pp. 150, 152–53, 155, 158; Scott, *Story of a Cavalry Regiment*, 115. The regimental historian adds, however, that "for some time . . . the brigade organization was not much felt or seen . . . and the regiments were encamped at some distance from each other." Scott, *Story of a Cavalry Regiment*, 116. General Sherman, to whose corps the Thielemann cavalry was attached, wrote, "I cannot call [them] cavalry, rather mounted orderlies." *Official Records*, Vol. XXIV, Pt. 3, p. 4.

9. *Official Records*, Vol. XXIX, Pt. 2, p. 12.

the 3rd Illinois, numbering ninety men and commanded by Captain J. L. Campbell, led Osterhaus' march westward toward Champion Hill, but the terrain—"a chaos of ravines and narrow hills, sloping very abruptly into sink-hole like valleys diverg[ing] in all directions . . . [and] covered densely by trees and brush"—was impassable for men on horseback, and Osterhaus ordered Captain Campbell's small command withdrawn.[10]

After the Vicksburg operation became a siege, the cavalry, limited in numbers until the arrival of the three additional regiments a month later, was kept busy patrolling the area to the rear of the Union lines and carrying orders and messages from one end of the long line to the other. The work was arduous enough. General Osterhaus called attention on May 30 "to the very weak number" of his cavalry, which was "pretty much run down" by the "very hard service" they had to perform. He asked for reinforcements for them, partly to give the "overworked men and horses" a chance to rest and partly to "look a little closer after" the Confederate mounted infantry that lurked about his lines and camps. His plea for cavalry reinforcements was evidently fruitless, for a week later he repeated his "opinion that the cavalry force at . . . [his] disposal . . . [was] utterly inadequate to guard against and repel any attack the enemy might attempt." Since the enemy cavalry was thought to be a force of 4,000 under Forrest, assembling to the east of Big Black River, the threat was not to be taken lightly, and, as has been mentioned, three additional regiments of cavalry were brought across the river in mid-June.[11]

The effect of hard service before and apparently even after the arrival of reinforcements was recorded by the historian of the 4th Iowa. Before the three additional regiments arrived, he wrote, his regiment and the detachment, numbering about 150, of the 6th Missouri,

were relied upon to furnish all the cavalry pickets . . . and all scouting and reconnoitering parties. . . . From the 1st of May till the 1st of July scarcely an hour of rest was possible. Fifty-four days within those two months the effective force of the regiment, or a large part of it, was in the saddle; many of the

10. *Ibid.*, 13–14, 28. An *ad hoc* cavalry battalion of 162 men, commanded by Captain John S. Foster, 4th Independent Company, Ohio Cavalry (General McPherson's escort), worked with the XVII Army Corps at Champion Hill, some of them serving as orderlies, "some for driving up stragglers, and the remainder to watch the movements of the enemy." *Ibid.*, Pt. 1, pp. 735–36.

11. *Ibid.*, Pt. 2, pp. 213, 217, 223.

nights, too, were partly or wholly spent there. . . . The heavy work and insufficient food told severely upon the horses, too. Many hundreds were broken or worn out by their incessant trials, and . . . none could be got from the quartermaster's department to supply the deficiency. So that there was, from the beginning of the siege, a steady and rapid decline in the effective strength of the regiment . . . and when the fall of Vicksburg came, barely three hundred men, out of the eight hundred then on the rolls, could be mounted for duty.[12]

The same historian added in another account that his regiment "had that to do which should have employed six or eight regiments of cavalry," and that the excessive labor the men had to perform resulted in a "great many cases of sickness, and, in time, a number of deaths from sheer fatigue."[13]

The most significant cavalry operation connected with the Vicksburg Campaign got under way at dawn on April 17 from LaGrange, Tennessee, just north of the Mississippi-Tennessee border. On the preceding night, some two hundred miles to the southwest, Admiral Porter's gunboats had successfully run the batteries at Vicksburg.

As early as February 13, while Grant, as the New York *Times* editorialized, was still "stuck in the mud in northern Mississippi, his army of no use to him or to anybody else," he had written General Hurlbut, commanding the XVI Army Corps at Memphis, to suggest (but not to order) that Benjamin Grierson be sent on a long raid south at the head of 500 men, all of whom should be volunteers for an exceedingly risky operation, to cut the Vicksburg & Jackson Railroad.[14]

At the end of January, Hurlbut had had at his disposal a "Cavalry Division" without a divisional commander. (Not until April 3 was General C. C. Washburn appointed to the post; he assumed command six days later.) It was made up of Colonel Grierson's First Brigade (6th and 7th Illinois, 2nd Iowa) and General Albert L. Lee's Second Brigade

12. Scott, *Story of a Cavalry Regiment*, 96–98. On June 23 the Iowans (who, General Sherman thought, "must have been off their guard") were attacked by Wirt Adams' cavalry and got the worst of it. They were "forced to fly" and lost 8 killed, 12 wounded, and "about 20" missing. *Official Records*, Vol. XXIV, Pt. 2, p. 246.

13. Ingersoll, *Iowa and the Rebellion*, 422–23.

14. The New York *Times* comment is quoted in Earl Schenk Miers, *The Web of Victory: Grant at Vicksburg* (New York, 1955), 106. Grant's dispatch to Hurlbut is in *Official Records*, Vol. XXIV, Pt. 3, p. 50. On March 9, Grant repeated his wish that the raid be made.

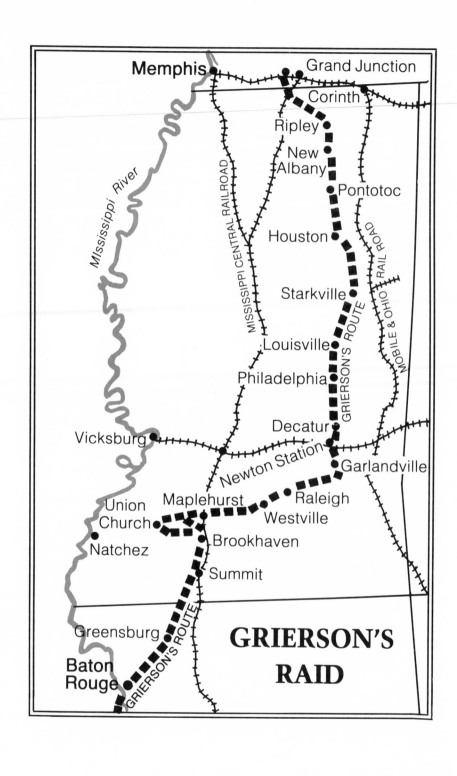

Memphis • •Grand Junction

Corinth

Ripley

New
Albany

Pontotoc

Houston

Starkville

MISSISSIPPI CENTRAL RAILROAD

Mississippi River

GRIERSON'S ROUTE

MOBILE & OHIO RAILROAD

Louisville

Philadelphia

Decatur

Vicksburg

Newton Station •Garlandville

Maplehurst   Raleigh
Westville

Union
Church
Brookhaven

Natchez

Summit

Greensburg

GRIERSON'S ROUTE

Baton
Rouge •

**GRIERSON'S
RAID**

(4th Illinois, 7th Kansas, 5th Ohio), plus odd companies and battalions of Stewart's Illinois Cavalry, 3rd United States, 5th Iowa, 2nd Illinois, 15th Kentucky, 4th Illinois, and 10th Missouri, scattered hither and yon in posts and forts in southwestern Kentucky and western Tennessee. At the end of February, Grierson's brigade numbered 2,002 "present for duty"; Lee's, 1,115. About half of Grierson's men, he later reported, were armed with Union and Smith's carbines, neither of which was a fully reliable weapon.[15]

In common with every other area and army commander in the Union army everywhere and at all times, Hurlbut's main problem with his cavalry was a shortage of horses. In late March, he asked the Quartermaster Bureau in St. Louis for 1,500 remounts, which suggests that nearly half his horsemen were dismounted. A week later, he complained that lack of shipping to transport the horses down the river from St. Louis to Memphis prevented his getting the remounts he needed. That difficulty was apparently overcome, for on April 4, Hurlbut received a shipment of 350 animals, but that helped him not at all. In company with General George Thomas, who happened to be in Memphis at the moment, he inspected the horses and found that they were "worthless." He wired Colonel Robert Allen, chief of the Quartermaster Bureau in St. Louis, "to send no more of that sort, but to send forward 1,500 good cavalry horses for immediate use." General Hurlbut's justified indignation failed to produce the results he demanded, for on April 14 he complained to Grant that he was "still horribly crippled for want of horses, by the gross neglect of quartermasters in St. Louis." Indeed, when Grierson departed on his raid three days later, some of his men were mounted on horses taken from the wagon trains.[16]

It was under such circumstances that Hurlbut had to deal with his commanding officer's request that he send a cavalry expedition to sever Vicksburg's railroad connection with the East. To Grant's March 9 dispatch, he responded on April 1 by proposing a somewhat different operation. If he could have another regiment of cavalry—"a good regiment with good horses"—for General Grenville Dodge, he would send

15. *Official Records*, Vol. XXIV, Pt. 3, pp. 169, 182, 26–28, 74–75, and Vol. XXVI, Pt. 1, p. 134.
16. *Ibid.*, Vol. XXIV, Pt. 3, pp. 106, 129, 174, 193; Thiele, "The Evolution of Cavalry," 455.

off one regiment from Corinth to cut the Mississippi Central Railroad, a second to cut the Mobile & Ohio near Okolona, and a third, the 6th Illinois under Grierson, taking advantage of consternation created by the other two, "to proceed by forced marches to Selma or Meridian."[17] How this fanciful project, and the confusion of successive orders issued by General Hurlbut in the days that followed, became transmuted into the plan actually adopted does not appear in the records.[18] It does seem to be beyond dispute, however, that Grant conceived of a cavalry expedition coming down from the north as an integral part of his campaign to capture Vicksburg. It was to serve the dual purpose of diverting the Confederate command's attention from the banks of the Mississippi where Grant planned to cross the river and of cutting the only rail connection of Vicksburg with the East. Since the raiders would be in hostile territory throughout the full course of their operation, the Confederate command could have been expected to learn quite early (as in fact they did) that they were faced with nothing more serious than a hit-and-run cavalry raid. As a diversion to facilitate Grant's crossing of the Mississippi, the expedition did not accomplish its purpose. General Pemberton seemed not to be distracted in the least; he decided as early as April 20 that he had "a mere raid" to deal with.[19]

In his final orders to Grierson, Hurlbut took pains to remind him, quite unnecessarily, that "rapidity" was to be the key ingredient of his proceedings. He also told Grierson that when he struck the Mobile & Ohio, his men were to destroy "wires, &c., and use up as much of the track as they can, and do it thoroughly; break up all provisions depots they can find, burn tanks, and do all the damage possible. . . . they and their horses must live on the country, and horses, of course, will be taken whenever advantageous."[20] As to the last point, it may be said

17. *Official Records*, Vol. XXIV, Pt. 1, p. 27.
18. *Ibid.*, Pt. 3, pp. 185, 193. In a dispatch of May 5 to General Halleck, Hurlbut took credit for the plan of the operation. "As the spring opened," he wrote, "I was daily more and more impressed with the feasibility of a plan, long entertained, of pushing a flying column of cavalry through the length of Mississippi, [and] cutting the . . . [Vicksburg & Jackson] Railroad. By consent and approval of General Grant, I prepared a system of movements along my entire line from Memphis to Corinth for the purpose of covering this cavalry dash." *Ibid.*, Pt. 1, p. 520.
19. Grant, *Personal Memoirs*, I, 489; Dee A. Brown, *Grierson's Raid* (Urbana, 1962), 59, quoting *Official Records*, Vol. XXIV, Pt. 3, p. 770.
20. *Official Records*, Vol. XXIV, Pt. 3, p. 196. The dispatch was actually addressed to General Sooy Smith, Grierson's immediate superior.

now that the 950 men who made the march all the way to Baton Rouge seized by Grierson's count 1,000 horses and mules; the 500 men of Colonel Edward Hatch's 2nd Iowa, whom Grierson detached from the main column and sent back to LaGrange, collected an additional 600 horses and mules, "with about 200 able-bodied negroes to lead them." For much of the way back to LaGrange the Iowans had to cross or skirt "the large swamps in which Central Mississippi everywhere abounds. These swamps were filled with horses and mules which had been run there by the affrighted citizens, and placed in charge of their most trusty servants, to keep them from the hated Yankees. . . . Now that we were where these fellows could claim our protection . . . [they] came hurrying to us, [and] proferred their services as guides to the coverts of these animals, gladly accepting our offer of the privilege of accompanying us and leading our captured stock."[21]

Early in March, Grierson had performed a highly creditable feat of arms, or at least a feat, as one may suspect, that he contrived to make appear highly creditable in his report. He left his camp at LaGrange on March 8 with the two Illinois regiments of his brigade on an expedition against Colonel Robert V. Richardson's 1st Tennessee Partisan Rangers. After "a forced march of 35 miles in seven hours, over roads almost impassable from the recent heavy rains," Grierson came upon Richardson's camp near Covington, Tennessee, thirty-five miles northeast of Memphis, and at once attacked "and completely routed him, killing 22, wounding and capturing over 70 . . . also taking and destroying his camp and equipage, commissary and quartermaster stores, his train, ammunition, and records." Colonel Richardson admitted that he had been driven out of his camp but claimed that he had a mere 150 men "engaged" and that his losses came to 2 men killed, 5 wounded, and 8 taken prisoner.[22] Shortly after this affair, Grierson departed on

21. Pierce, *History of the Second Iowa*, 52. The same historian describes the method used by his regiment to cross the Tippah River, after it had been forced to make a long detour because the ford they had intended to use was held by the enemy: "Here [Colonel] Hatch found some flood-wood lodged against a fallen tree; with this he constructed a rude foot-bridge, and we unsaddled our horses and each trooper carried his saddle across the bridge on his back. The bank on the side from which the horses must enter was about six feet above the stream and very nearly perpendicular. Three or four troopers would seize each horse and throw him into the stream, when they would, by the aid of long poles, compel him to the opposite bank, where two men stood hip-deep in water to aid him up the bank. In this way the entire command was crossed in safety . . . [on] as dark a night as I ever experienced." *Ibid.*, 51.

22. *Official Records*, Vol. XXIV, Pt. 1, pp. 423, 426, Pt. 3, p. 106.

leave and did not rejoin his brigade until just three hours before the dawn of April 17, when it was to leave on its raid. Had Grierson's return been delayed, command of the brigade, and hence of the raid, would have gone by seniority to Colonel Hatch.

The raiders left their camps on the morning of April 17. On the fifth day out, they had covered nearly a hundred miles, marching through Ripley, New Albany, Pontotoc, and Houston, and were approaching Starkville. There, Colonel Hatch and the 2nd Iowa left the main column. On the previous day, at Pontotoc, the command had been inspected, and about 175 of the men, and those of the horses deemed unfit to make a long march, were weeded out and sent back to LaGrange.[23] The orders given to Colonel Hatch on the twenty-first were to march his regiment due east, partly to confuse and draw off from pursuit of the main body the Confederate cavalry of General Daniel Ruggles and partly to destroy as much as he could of the Mobile & Ohio at West Point, Mississippi, and thence as far south as Macon, Mississippi. At Macon, or as near to it as Hatch could get, he was to turn north to Columbus, Mississippi, capture the town and destroy the government workshops located there, and, after breaking up on the way another stretch of the Mobile & Ohio near Okolona, return as best he could to LaGrange.[24] To fulfill this assignment to the letter, Hatch would have had to make a march of about eighty-five miles through hostile country with a regiment reduced to half strength.[25] There were no major Confederate forces in the area, but on the very first afternoon of his independent operation, near the settlement of Palo Alto, Hatch had a brisk fight with Colonel Clark R. Barteau's 2nd Tennessee, J. F. Smith's Mississippi Partisan Rangers, and W. M. Inge's newly raised 12th Mississippi Battalion of militia cavalry, the whole, Hatch reported, under the command of General Samuel J. Gholson. The Iowans, aided by the fire of the single two-pounder gun that represented their artillery and fighting dismounted to gain maximum advantage of the firepower of their Colt's revolving rifles, drove off the

23. Grierson described the men and horses weeded out as "the least effective portion of the command." *Ibid.*, Pt. 1, p. 523. They were given the responsibility of taking to LaGrange all the prisoners, led horses, and "captured property."

24. *Ibid.*, 523.

25. The regiment was down to "about 500 men." Pierce, *History of the Second Iowa*, 49.

enemy. Nevertheless, finding his way eastward blocked by the 2nd Alabama Mounted Infantry, Hatch decided to forgo any attempt to reach either West Point or Columbus and headed north toward Okolona. For the next three days his progress was slowed by the need to stop from time to time to repel Confederate attacks on his column's rear at the same time that "all the citizens in the country, armed with shot-guns and hunting rifles," were keeping his flanks under a constant fire. Neither form of attack was particularly effective, for Hatch lost "but 10 men killed, wounded and missing" on the march back to LaGrange.[26]

While Hatch was marching north, Grierson, with the 950 men of the two Illinois regiments left him after Hatch's departure, resumed his march south. At Starkville the raiders, as a doubtless biased Mississippi newspaper reported, "robbed the inhabitants of horses, mules, negroes; caught the mail boy and took the mail, robbed the postoffice, but handed back a letter from a soldier to his wife, containing $50.00, and ordered the postmaster to give it to her."[27] On April 22—the sixth day out—Captain H. C. Forbes, with 35 men of his Company B, 7th Illinois, was detached with orders to march east and strike the Mobile & Ohio near Macon; he was to create as much of a disturbance as possible on the way, to attract the enemy's attention while the main column continued its march southward. Forbes's diversion proved highly successful. News of his approach to Macon with a force whose size rumor magnified to 5,000 caused General Pemberton to send 2,000 infantry from Meridian to protect the place. By going fifty-odd miles north to protect Macon against a nonexistent threat, these troops became unavailable at the point where their presence would have been of value: at Newton Station on the Vicksburg & Jackson Railroad, some twenty-five miles west of Meridian. Grierson reached Newton after a laborious march through a succession of swamps, by way of Louisville and Philadelphia. The village and two trains, one eastbound and one westbound, were captured early on the morning of the

26. Hatch's report is in *Official Records*, Vol. XXIV, Pt. 1, pp. 530–31; see also Pierce, *History of the Second Iowa*, 49–55, and Brown, *Grierson's Raid*, 67–69. Colonel Barteau, in his report, accused Hatch of burning down the hospital at Okolona. *Official Records*, Vol. XXIV, Pt. 1, pp. 535–36. Of Hatch's 10 casualties, 1 was killed by a guerrilla, 4 were wounded, and 5 were taken prisoner in the fight at Palo Alto.

27. Undated report in the Columbus, Mississippi, *Republic*, quoted in Brown, *Grierson's Raid*, 75.

twenty-fourth by a battalion of the 7th Illinois commanded by Lieutenant Colonel William Blackburn. When the rest of the raiders reached Newton, Grierson set them to work destroying bridges, culverts, trestles, the telegraph line, and the track, on both sides of the station, as well as the station buildings and the two captured trains. Having fulfilled to some degree at least one of the primary objectives of the raid, Grierson could have turned around at Newton and gone back to La-Grange by one of a number of routes available to him. He decided instead to "move south . . . and then return to LaGrange through Alabama; or make for Baton Rouge as . . . [he] might thereafter deem best."[28]

For the next four days, until April 28, the command rode southwest, through piney-woods country, by way of Montrose, Raleigh, and Westville, across the Pearl River to Hazlehurst, and across the New Orleans, Jackson & Great Northern Railroad as far as Union Church.[29] Captain Forbes's detachment, its numbers reduced by one, a trooper killed near Philadelphia on the twenty-fourth, rejoined the main body at the crossing of the Pearl River on April 27. Misled by the confusing reports he was getting of Captain Forbes's marches and countermarches on his way back to the main column, General Pemberton concluded that Grierson had turned east and was trying to escape northward along the Mobile & Ohio through Okolona, on the route Colonel Hatch had taken. Grierson's intention this day was to feint far enough southwestward to make the Confederates think that Natchez was his objective, and then march due west forty miles to join Grant at Grand Gulf.

On the following day, the twenty-eighth, Pemberton took the sensible step of giving Colonel Wirt Adams command of the widely scattered bodies of Confederate cavalry hunting the raiders, which he had tried to direct himself from his headquarters at Jackson. He began to suspect at the same time that Baton Rouge, several days' ride to the south, might be the raiders' destination. And indeed, it was on April 29 that Grierson decided against trying to reach Grant and Grand Gulf. He sent the 6th Illinois on a feint in the direction of Fayette and Natchez, where Adams was waiting for him, and then headed south,

28. Brown, *Grierson's Raid*, 85, 107–13; *Official Records*, Vol. XXIV, Pt. 1, pp. 523–24, 525.
29. The New Orleans, Jackson & Great Northern became a part of the Illinois Central System.

along the line of the New Orleans & Jackson Railroad by way of Brook-haven toward Baton Rouge.

After following the railroad toward New Orleans as far as Summit, Grierson veered westward and, evading the pincers that Wirt Adams and Colonel Richardson (the same Richardson whom Grierson had beaten in Tennessee in early March, who had then turned up in Jackson and been given command of the 20th Mississippi Mounted Infantry) were trying to clamp on him, he headed toward Liberty. Near that settlement, on May 1, the raiders were ambushed by Major James DeBaun's command of three companies of cavalry. DeBaun was routed after a brief fire fight but not before he had inflicted the only loss of any consequence suffered by Grierson in the raid: three wounded (including Lieutenant Colonel Blackburn, wounded mortally) and five taken prisoner.[30] Later that day, the raiders reached the Louisiana line and at midnight crossed the Amite River, the only remaining major obstacle between themselves and Baton Rouge, on a bridge left unguarded by the Confederates. After an all-night march, on the afternoon of May 2, the sixteenth day after their departure from LaGrange, Grierson and his two regiments made a ceremonial entry into Union-held Baton Rouge.[31]

The Grierson Raid was the first long-range expedition by the Union cavalry into enemy territory. Jeb Stuart, John Morgan, Earl Van Dorn, and Bedford Forrest had set the example and shown the way. Grierson's losses were minimal; three killed, seven wounded, five taken ill and left behind to be cared for by farmers along the way, and nine missing; the loss of horses was more than made good by captures from enemy farms and plantations along the way. His command, Colonel Grierson reported, had marched more than six hundred miles through enemy territory, "killed and wounded about 100 of the enemy, captured and paroled over 500 prisoners . . . destroyed between 50 and 60 miles of railroad and telegraph . . . over 3,000 stand of arms, and other army stores and other Government property to an immense amount."[32] The raiders also fed themselves and their animals on supplies taken from

---

30. Brown, *Grierson's Raid*, 201; *Official Records*, Vol. XXIV, Pt. 1, pp. 526–27.

31. On April 29, thinking that Grierson might be trying to return north and would need help, Hurlbut mounted the 6th Iowa Infantry and, with the 2nd Iowa, sent them off "to relieve Grierson." *Official Records*, Vol. XXIV, Pt. 1, p. 519. For Confederate reports concerning the raid, see *Ibid.*, 531–53.

32. *Ibid.*, 528.

farms, large and small, along the way, and as was commonly the case in such situations, probably wasted as much as they consumed. They also deprived the enemy of the labor of the three hundred Negroes who followed them into Baton Rouge.

Grierson deserves high marks for his intelligent and skillful management of the expedition and for the resourceful way in which he adapted his plans from day to day to changing circumstances. It should not detract in any way from the credit due him to point out that earlier in the year Pemberton had been deprived of most of his cavalry, which had been sent to Tennessee by General Joseph E. Johnston. As soon as Pemberton received news of the raid, he begged Johnston for the return of his mounted troops, but to no avail; they and their commanding officer, Earl Van Dorn, whose presence in Mississippi might well have made a difference in the fate of the raid, remained where they were.[33] Forrest, whose absence from Mississippi Grierson should have counted as a major stroke of luck, was even then in pursuit of the unfortunate Colonel Abel D. Streight, whose command of mule-mounted infantry he captured on the day Grierson arrived in Baton Rouge.

Grierson's exploit was deservedly praised, both at the time and later. General Hurlbut described it in a dispatch to Washington as a "gallant exploit . . . unequaled in the war."[34] Grant, in a dispatch to General Halleck, called it "the most successful thing of the kind since the breaking out of the rebellion. . . . The Southern papers and Southern people regard it as one of the most daring exploits of the war." In another dispatch five days later he added: "He had spread excitement throughout the State, destroying railroads, trestleworks, bridges, burning locomotives and railway stock, taking prisoners, and destroying stores of all kinds. To use the expression of my informant, 'Grierson has knocked the heart out of the State.'"[35] General Banks invited Halleck's and the War Department's attention "to the valuable services rendered . . . by that excellent officer, Col. B. H. Grierson . . . and the

33. For Pemberton's dispatches describing his lack of cavalry and pleading for the return of the division that had been taken from him to reinforce Bragg in Tennessee, see *Ibid.*, 253–55.

34. *Ibid.*, 521.

35. *Ibid.*, 33–34. In his reminiscences, Grant called the raid "a complete success" and said that it "was of great importance, for Grierson had attracted the attention of the enemy from the main movement against Vicksburg." Grant, *Personal Memoirs*, I, 488–89.

6th and 7th Regiments of Illinois Cavalry under his command . . . by the most brilliant expedition of the war. . . . The moral effect of that remarkable expedition upon a wavering and astonished enemy, and the assistance rendered us in breaking up the enemy's communications . . . can hardly be overestimated. . . . I trust the services of Colonel Grierson and his command will receive at the hands of the Government that acknowledgement which they so eminently deserve."[36] Grierson's feat was widely reported in the press, both North and South, and it served notice to both sections—and to the Union cavalry east of the Alleghenies as well—that the Confederate cavalry no longer had a monopoly on the ability to conduct raids deep into enemy territory and that, indeed, the time had come when the hitherto despised Union cavalry was to be taken seriously, at least in the West.

An early historian of the United States Cavalry wrote, "This was a noble raid, and is without an equal in the annals of the cavalry service." A present-day historian has echoed this opinion: "Over a year before Sherman proved it, Grierson demonstrated that the Confederacy was a hollow shell."[37] The measurement of intangibles like morale is risky, even with the aid of modern sampling and survey techniques, but so far as can be determined from contemporary evidence, the raid did have a depressing effect on morale in the South, particularly in the large geographic area more or less directly affected.

A special and most remarkable aspect of the raid was pointed out by Grierson himself. In responding to a reception tendered him in New Orleans on May 6, he spoke of his command as being from the West, and not from the North.[38]

With the capture of Vicksburg by the Union, followed by the capture of Port Hudson four days later, the Mississippi Valley became of secondary importance as a theater of war. The center of attention of both combatants in the West shifted northeastward, to central and northeastern Tennessee, which was to become in the latter half of 1863 the area in which was played out a long duel between the antag-

36. *Official Records*, Vol. XXIV, Pt. 2, p. 366. The portions of the dispatch here omitted praise the subsequent services of Grierson and his cavalrymen in the siege and capture of Port Hudson.

37. Brackett, *History of the United States Cavalry*, 298; Thiele, "The Evolution of Cavalry," 458.

38. Brown, *Grierson's Raid*, 232, quoting B. H. Grierson's privately printed *Record of Services Rendered the Government, 1863*.

onists of Stones River, Generals Rosecrans and Bragg, and later a new cast that included the names of Grant, Sherman, Hooker, Burnside, and Longstreet. At no time, however, from July, 1863, to the very end of the war did military operations wholly cease along the Mississippi, sometimes on one side of the river, sometimes on the other.

Colonel Hatch had not been back at LaGrange for long after completing his modest share in the Grierson Raid before General Hurlbut sent him off on another expedition. He was to take his own 2nd Iowa, the troopers of the 6th and 7th Illinois whom Grierson had sent back to LaGrange as unfit to go on the raid, plus the 6th Iowa Mounted Infantry, "to beat up the rebel General [James R.] Chalmers' quarters and disperse his forces, collecting stock and provisions and destroying forage." Hatch left his camps on May 21 and was joined at Byhalia by Colonel LaFayette McCrillis, 3rd Illinois, with the Second Cavalry Brigade (3rd, 4th, and 9th Illinois). Being the senior, McCrillis took command of the expedition. Two days later he found the enemy, 1,500 strong, in "a very strong position" in the swamps of Senatobia Creek and in a three-hour fight put them to flight, at the cost of 5 men wounded. Hatch reported the loss of many of his horses due to the heat and dust, but he replaced his losses with captures and collected and took back to camp 400 mules in addition.

The expedition was marred by the usual "depredations," which Hatch, not surprisingly, blamed on McCrillis' brigade and which McCrillis neglected to mention in his brief report. A store at Byhalia was fired "on the windward side" either by McCrillis' men or by "some citizen scouts who happened to be with the brigade at the time."[39]

General Hurlbut obviously believed in keeping his horsemen occupied, and in the middle of June he sent his chief of cavalry, Colonel John K. Mizner, with 1,900 men of the 2nd Iowa, 3rd Michigan, 3rd, 4th, 9th, and part of the 11th Illinois, under Hatch and McCrillis, on an expedition from LaGrange to below the Tallahatchie River, to break up the Mississippi & Tennessee Railroad south of Panola, drive off Chalmers' cavalry (which had evidently recovered from its defeat by

39. *Official Records*, Vol. XXIV, Pt. 2, pp. 427–28, 429; Pierce, *History of the Second Iowa*, 57–58. Pierce claims that the brigade brought back to camp 600 horses and mules, as well as 400 Negroes.

McCrillis only three weeks before), and "sweep the country of horses, mules, negroes and the new crop of wheat."[40] Hurlbut was able to report to Grant on June 25 that the expedition had been an "eminent success," that by "breaking up the railroad, destroying crops, and bringing off horses and mules," Mizner had "succeeded in placing a wider belt of difficult country between the head of the railroad and . . . [Hurlbut's] line, and in depriving the enemy of large supplies of wheat, now just harvested."[41] There was no serious opposition, but in a skirmish the 11th Illinois lost 26 men taken prisoner by the enemy; Lieutenant Colonel Bazil D. Meek reported that "almost all the men who fell into the hands of the enemy were mounted on mules, and dismounted by the mules at the discharge of musketry by the enemy."[42]

Even before the surrender of Vicksburg had been completed by the paroling of the garrison and the gathering up of their arms and equipment, Grant sent Sherman with the IX, XIII, and XV Army Corps, plus one division of the XVI, to drive out of Mississippi the forces General Johnston had collected in the hope of breaking up the siege. As soon as Johnston heard of Pemberton's surrender, he retreated to Jackson, with Sherman at his heels. After sustaining a bombardment for six days, Johnston evacuated the city, which was then entered by General Frank P. Blair, Jr.'s division, with orders to protect private property.[43] Colonel Cyrus Bussey, whose "cavalry forces" (5th Illinois, 4th Iowa, six com-

40. *Official Records*, Vol. XXIV, Pt. 2, p. 485. Between these expeditions the 2nd Iowa "constructed a nice camp, building comfortable shades over all the tents of the men as well as over the stables," and with "all that skill could do to render . . . [their] camp agreeable" added to a naturally healthy, well-watered camping ground, the Iowans "here spent a very happy summer." Pierce, *History of the Second Iowa*, 59.

41. *Official Records*, Vol. XXIV, Pt. 2, p. 487. See also *Ibid.*, 490–93. Mizner's orders of June 20 to his subordinates directed them to "take all horses, mules, cattle, and means of transportation; destroy or bring away all subsistence and forage. Fences enclosing flourishing crops will be burned; leave no animals behind; if any give out, shoot them. Rout and capture all roving bands of guerrillas, and make the work thorough and complete, rendering it impossible for the enemy to subsist on the country." *Ibid.*, 492.

42. *Ibid.*, 499; see also Pierce, *History of the Second Iowa*, 60–61. Pierce states that "the country thus doomed was of great wealth, and the amount of property destroyed . . . immense. Millions of dollars worth of cotton, grain and meat, together with many miles of fencing and thousands of out buildings, fell before the circling flames." Taken back to camp were "1,000 head of horses and mules, and as many negroes."

43. *Official Records*, Vol. XXIV, Pt. 2, p. 539.

panies of the 3rd Iowa, and seven companies of the 2nd Wisconsin) were "temporarily attached" to the IX Corps, led the advance of the infantry to Jackson and was then sent north to Calhoun and Canton, partly to forestall an attack (which did not materialize) on Sherman's trains by William H. Jackson's 3,000-man cavalry division and partly to destroy the railroad as far out as forty miles north of Jackson. Bussey had numerous skirmishes with the enemy, but he also destroyed five locomotives, forty cars, "extensive machine shops and railroad buildings," an "extensive manufacturing establishment used by the Confederate Government . . . [and] every dollar's worth of public property found" and also took a few prisoners. But the most noteworthy aspect of the operation (which had kept his men "in the saddle every day for a month"), Colonel Bussey was pleased to report, was the "decided improvement in the discipline of . . . [his] whole command."[44]

In the following month, Sherman sent Colonel Edward F. Winslow, 4th Iowa, with 800 men of his own regiment, the 3rd Iowa, and the 5th Illinois, on an expedition to collect and take to Memphis the "immense number" of locomotives and cars of the Mississippi Central Railroad (Sherman called it the "Great Central Railroad") that had been trapped north of Grenada by Colonel Bussey's destruction of the road between Jackson and Canton.[45] Winslow was to employ "or, if necessary, compel," southern locomotive engineers and conductors to run the equipment to Memphis.

In the light of the behavior of Union forces in Mississippi in the preceding year, it will be of interest to note Sherman's instructions to Colonel Winslow on how he was to deal with enemy civilians on his march:

> You carry money with you, and it is now to the interest of our Government that all plundering and pillaging should cease. Impress this on your men from the start, and let your chief quartermaster and commissary provide liberally and fairly for the wants of your command by paying.
> Union people and the poorer farmers, without being too critical as to politics, should be paid . . . but where the larger planters and farmers have an abundance to spare you can take of the surplus, giving . . . a simple re-

44. *Ibid.*, 553–54.
45. The numbers were reported to be 70 locomotives and "near 500" cars. *Ibid.*, Vol. XXX, Pt. 1, pp. 6–7. The orders to Winslow ended: "I enclose you the best map we are able to compile. Add to it as you progress, and on your return I shall expect it to be filled with roads and names of localities not now on it." *Ibid.*, 7.

ceipt. . . . Also, when your horses break down, you can take a remount, exchanging the broken-down animal and giving a certificate of the transaction—the boot.

Deal firmly but fairly with the inhabitants. . . . Much importance is attached to this branch of the subject, and you will see that every officer and man is informed of it. Punish on the spot with vigor any wanton burning of houses or property without your specific orders.[46]

Colonel Winslow's reports fail to reveal how well or how poorly these directions were obeyed. Nor did he disclose how many locomotives and cars he was able to gather up; he did report, however, that Lieutenant Colonel James J. Phillips, 9th Illinois Mounted Infantry, who had been sent out from Memphis on an errand similar to his, destroyed fifty-seven locomotives, "upward of 400" cars, plus depot buildings, machine shops, and ordnance, and took back with him, as he did himself, a considerable number of railroad men, thus depriving the Confederacy of their services.[47] Perhaps Colonel Winslow would have been more successful had it not been for the questionable competence of many of his officers. General McPherson reported to Grant a short time later that "Winslow himself is a very good officer, though somewhat lacking in spirit and dash, but many of his subordinate officers are of no account whatever; even the horses have caught the timidity of the men, and turn around involuntarily and break for the rear as soon as a cannon shot is fired."[48]

It was in the course of this operation—described as a "great raid" by the historian of the 4th Iowa—that Winslow's command, a brigade in name for some weeks past, actually operated as such for the first time, and the troopers composing it "first felt . . . [themselves] to be a part of an organized body of cavalry. . . . Then . . . [they] learned . . . [their] first lesson in supporting and receiving the support of other cavalry, and first experienced the satisfaction and realized the value of such support."[49] This was a vitally important lesson for any body of soldiers to learn, and especially so for an arm of the service still in search

46. *Ibid.*, 7.

47. Winslow's reports are in *Ibid.*, 7, 8; the reports covering the Phillips expedition are in *Ibid.*, 11–24.

48. *Ibid.*, Vol. XXXI, Pt. 1, p. 748. General McPherson's comment clearly refers to Winslow's entire command, not to the 4th Iowa alone. He did end, however, with the statement "Winslow is doing his best to get the cavalry in shape."

49. Scott, *Story of a Cavalry Regiment*, 116.

of a place in the sun. It was a pity, but perhaps unavoidable, that the opportunity to do so was not available to the Union cavalrymen in the West until the third summer of the war.

A novel note was introduced into cavalry operations in Mississippi at this time by the organization and employment of three unusual units. The first was the 3rd United States Colored Cavalry, "a very successful regiment," commanded by an energetic and active officer, Colonel Embury D. Osband, and largely officered by men promoted from the 4th Illinois.[50] The second unit was the "1st Mississippi Cavalry (African Descent)," a detachment of which was reported on a later occasion as "of incalculable benefit . . . as scouts, &c."[51] Because of its truly peculiar character, the third, the Mississippi Marine Brigade, deserves more extended attention.

A type of military organization that enjoyed a degree of favor on both sides in the first year of the war was the "legion," combining infantry, cavalry, and artillery in varying proportions under a single commander in the same oversized organization. Well-known examples are the Hampton Legion of South Carolina and, on the Union side, the Sherman Brigade of Ohio. Only a short exposure to the demands and stresses of active campaigning was needed to demonstrate that the legion was neither flesh, fish, nor fowl, and the legions soon broke up into their component parts, each of which served thereafter as (or as part of) a regiment of infantry or cavalry, or a battery of artillery.

After Admiral David Porter assumed command of the flotilla of Union gunboats on the Mississippi, he was faced with the problem of trying to deal with the guerrillas who, hidden in the canebrakes and woods lining the banks of the river, picked off the crews of his ships with rifle and light-artillery fire. He asked the Navy Department to send him a force of marines whom he proposed to embark in "suitable vessels accompanying . . . [his] gunboats, and to be landed at points where the parties of guerrillas were wont to assemble. The gunboats alone could not break these parties up, and it was therefore necessary to have trained soldiers to chase and annihilate them."[52] The admiral's

50. Avery, *History of the Fourth Illinois*, 152; see also *Official Records*, Vol. XXXI, Pt. 1, p. 566, Pt. 3, p. 104.
51. *Official Records*, Vol. XXXII, Pt. 1, p. 318. The unit is also mentioned in *Ibid.*, Vol. XXXI, Pt. 1, p. 566.
52. Warren D. Crandall and Isaac D. Newell, *History of the Ram Fleet and the Mississippi Marine Brigade in the War for the Union on the Mississippi and Its Tributaries*

request resulted in the commissioning on November 1, 1862, of Alfred W. Ellet to "organize a Marine Brigade for service on the Mississippi River, to consist of one regiment of Infantry, four squadrons of Cavalry, and one Battery of Light Artillery . . . [to] be called the Mississippi Volunteers."[53]

The forty-two-year-old Ellet thus commissioned was a member of a numerous family of brothers and cousins who fought for the Union on the Mississippi and its tributaries. The founder of the dynasty, Charles Ellet, Jr., the sixth of fourteen children of a Pennsylvania farmer of the Quaker faith and a self-taught, highly gifted engineer, conceived the idea of a steam-driven ram to destroy the Confederate gunboats on the river. Authorized by Secretary Stanton to assemble, equip, and command a fleet of rams and commissioned a colonel in the army, he bought and rebuilt a fleet of nine vessels, one of which he captained himself; another was commanded by his nineteen-year-old son, and the other seven by an assortment of Ellet brothers and nephews. On June 6, 1862, at Memphis, with a fleet made up of five gunboats and four of his rams, Charles Ellet destroyed a Confederate flotilla of eight vessels. Ellet himself was the only Union casualty in the fight, suffering a leg wound from which he subsequently died. Memphis was surrendered to the Union immediately after this fight. On February 2, 1863, the Ellet ram *Queen of the West* successfully ran the Vicksburg batteries and, by showing that it could be done, opened the way for Grant's ultimately successful strategy for capturing that city.

Commissioned to raise the "Mississippi Volunteers," Alfred Ellet did most of his recruiting in St. Louis, Louisville, Nashville, Cincinnati, and New Albany, Indiana. His recruiting posters proclaimed:

MISSISSIPPI MARINE BRIGADE
SOLDIERING MADE EASY!
NO HARD MARCHING!
NO CARRYING KNAPSACKS!
There will be but very little

(St. Louis, 1907), 249, quoting Admiral Porter's "Naval History" (*sic*; presumably his *Incidents and Anecdotes of the Civil War*). For the kind of attack on river traffic the force envisaged by Admiral Porter was intended to punish, see *Official Records*, Vol. XXIV, Pt. 2, p. 501.

53. Crandall and Newell, *History of the Ram Fleet*, 252.

marching for any of the troops.
They will be provided on the
Boats with good cooks and bedding.

Even more irresistible, if possible, were Ellet's handbills, which announced:

The proposed service is especially attractive to old
soldiers. It has the following advantages:
   1. There are no trenches to dig.
   2. There are no rebel houses to guard.
   3. There is no picket duty to perform.
   4. There is no danger of camps in the mud,
      but always a chance to sleep under cover.
   5. There is no chance of short rations.
   6. The command will always be kept together.[54]

With such inducements at his command, Colonel (later Brigadier General) Ellet had the ranks of his unit filled in short order; indeed, he was able to assemble a brigade, exceptionally large for the time, of about two thousand, rank and file.[55] Shortly after muster-in, the infantry component was mounted, and the unit as a whole became known thereafter as "Ellet's Horse Marines" and were distinguished visually from the common run of mounted troops by caps "made with full, round tops, broad, straight visors, and a wide green band with trimmings of gold lace."[56]

It may be taken for granted that a military organization enjoying and boasting of the marine brigade's amenities would, deservedly or not, be in bad odor with other branches of the army not similarly pampered. The historian of the 4th Iowa wrote of the Horse Marines: "It was the hope of their imaginative inventor that some day they would be landed somewhere just in the nick of time to do something dreadful to the enemy. But, if history has not neglected their deeds, they permitted their enemies to live in peace and die from natural causes. The soldiers ridiculed them on land and the sailors spoke of them disrespectfully on the water."[57]

54. *Ibid.*, 256.

55. Francis Vinton Greene, *Campaigns of the Civil War, VIII: The Mississippi* (New York, 1882), 118. As early as July, 1863, however, Admiral Porter reported the brigade down to an "effective force" of about five hundred, too small to be useful to deal with "the bodies of guerrillas which infest the Mississippi." *Official Records*, Vol. XXIV, Pt. 3, p. 565.

56. Crandall and Newell, *History of the Ram Fleet*, 258.

57. Scott, *Story of a Cavalry Regiment*, 175. An obviously hostile Confederate wit-

In the summer of 1863, Lieutenant Colonel Samuel J. Nasmith, 25th Wisconsin Infantry, reported after his return from an expedition to Greenville, Mississippi, for which he had been reinforced by a hundred of the Horse Marines, that the latter "proved to be entirely worthless. . . . They failed me altogether when most wanted, and instead of being [of] any assistance . . . they were, to use no harsher language, a positive injury to the expedition."[58] Two months later, in a dispatch to Adjutant General Lorenzo Thomas, Grant urged "on account of the great cost of maintaining the Brigade, and the slight service it renders," that it be taken off its boats and "transferred to the land service." Grant's proposal was turned down; he was directed instead to "assume command of this brigade, and take proper measures to reduce it to discipline."[59]

There was general agreement on one aspect at least of the brigade's performance. With their boats providing convenient facilities for storing and transporting plunder, Ellet's men established an unenviable reputation for their "depredations." One of their squadrons raided the Louisiana plantation of one John Routh, to whom they declared that they were "freebooters, independent of the United States, with booty their only pay," and robbed him of $15,000 worth of silverware and $10,000 worth of table and house linen.[60] No doubt, in keeping with the nearly universal custom in such cases, Routh grossly exaggerated the value of his loss, but his was only one of many such complaints against the Horse Marines, causing Admiral Porter to write to General Sherman:

I have just received a notice from the Secretary of the Navy that the Marine Brigade . . . was turned over to General Grant. . . . The general and myself came to the conclusion long since, that the brigade should be broken up, the vessels used as transports, and the officers and men put on shore. I cannot tell you of all the reports made to me against the brigade. Its robberies and house-

---

ness wrote: "Floating about in the vicinity of the Confederate field of operations was what was known as the brigade of Marine Cavalry. . . . This worthy band of warriors was wont to travel on steam-boats, horses and all, and by making their appearance at unexpected points, capturing noncombatants, frightening women and children, stealing cotton, and an unlimited use of bravado, had managed to impress the country people with an exaggerated idea of their prowess." Edwards, *Shelby and His Men*, 370.

58. *Official Records*, Vol. XXIV, Pt. 2, p. 517. In command of the marine brigade detachment was Major James H. Hubbard.

59. *Ibid.*, Vol. XXX, Pt. 3, pp. 24, 25, 144, 183; Crandall and Newell, *History of the Ram Fleet*, 315, 317.

60. Crandall and Newell, *History of the Ram Fleet*, 315.

burning are shameful. . . . They are now doing nothing. . . . these brigade vessels are idling away at great expense. I do hope you will break up the whole concern as General Grant intended to do. The country will be served by so doing.[61]

Due to legal qualms, administrative inertia, or political influence exerted in the right quarters, the marine brigade was allowed to remain in being until the latter part of 1864. Its effective strength dwindled to 613 "mounted infantry," despite which it tied down as its means of transportation "six large steam transports, three tow-boats, three small steam tugs, two small rams, and [for its horses] six barges." It was eventually ordered disbanded, its enlisted men reassigned or discharged, and its officers mustered out. Not that it had experienced in the meantime a reformation of its conduct or morals. It had been taken along on General Banks's Red River Campaign in early 1864; on March 26, it was ordered to return to Vicksburg. General Charles P. Stone, in the midst of his travails as Banks's chief of staff, took time to inform General McPherson, then in command of the Department of the Tennessee, that "the Marine Brigade is reported . . . to have stopped at every landing thus far on its way out of Red River, solely for the purpose of pillaging and the destruction of private property."[62]

For those along the Mississippi and its tributaries who had the misfortune of being visited by the marine brigade, the existence of this singular organization was not a source of entertainment, however amusing the anomaly of "Horse Marines" may seem in retrospect. The existence of Ellet's strange command was one of the many expressions in the Civil War of the "try anything" spirit that, in its less outlandish manifestations, helped to preserve the Union.

61. Admiral Porter also complained that "the Ellets have been guilty of some very dirty underhand work toward myself." *Official Records*, Vol. XXXI, Pt. 1, p. 783.
62. *Ibid.*, Vol. XLI, Pt. 2, pp. 535, 712, Vol. XXXIV, Pt. 2, pp. 735, 768.

IX

Be Ye Men of Valour

THE FOCUS OF NATIONAL ATTENTION IN THE SPRING AND
early summer of 1863 was divided between the Rappahannock, where
Generals Hooker and Lee faced each other, and the Mississippi, where
General Grant was searching for a way to reach the Confederate
stronghold at Vicksburg. There was, however, a third major area of operations, which was quiescent at the moment and hence out of the
news but which nevertheless did not fail to engage the attention of the
authorities in Washington and Richmond. This was middle Tennessee,
where the Union Army of the Cumberland and the Confederate Army
of Tennessee faced each other across a wide no-man's-land.

After the battle of Stones River, Braxton Bragg had retreated southeast across a chain of high hills known as the Highland Rim to the
valley of Duck River. His army settled down on a line sixty miles long
running along the south bank of the river from Sparta in the northeast
to Shelbyville and Columbia in the southwest, but vulnerable, as the
events of the summer were to show, to a flanking thrust through one or
more of the numerous gaps through the Highland Rim—Hoover's
Gap, Gillie's Gap, Liberty Gap, and Guy's Gap—to cut in behind the
Confederate army and, by a threat to its communications with Chattanooga, force it either to retreat or to fight the Federal army in the
open. Bragg established his own headquarters at Tullahoma, thirty
miles from Rosecrans' headquarters at Murfreesboro. With no Federals

to fight, and "suffering from the beginnings of a nervous and physical breakdown," he proceeded to do battle with his own subordinates.[1]

William Rosecrans basked in the euphoria engendered by the complimentary messages on his Stones River victory that descended upon him from all quarters, from the president, the general-in-chief, and even his erstwhile enemy the secretary of war. There were, too, the congratulatory resolutions of Congress and of the legislatures of Ohio and Indiana. On his recommendations, seven of his subordinates—Sheridan and David Stanley among them—were promoted to major general. His requests for reinforcements resulted in the transfer of fourteen thousand men (including four regiments of cavalry) to him from the Department of the Ohio.[2] And lastly, in February he acquired a new chief of staff, thirty-one-year-old Brigadier General James A. Garfield.[3]

The popular acclaim and the eager compliance of the administration with Rosecrans' wishes and recommendations, however pleasing, did not solve his most serious and pressing military problem, a difficulty that was to embitter his relations with the War Department. The problem stemmed from the task of feeding a hundred thousand men and fifty thousand horses and mules in an area stripped nearly bare of supplies, with 212 miles of railroad constantly broken by enemy action, and 250 miles of roads nearly impassable in wintertime, as the alternate supply lines from the army's base in Louisville.[4]

Rosecrans' supply problems could in his judgment be solved by providing his lines of communication with additional protection from the enemy's cavalry, which, he insisted, outnumbered his own, four to one. This was the point of departure for a long series of dispatches he sent off to Washington. Even before he began his advance toward Murfreesboro, and all through the months of November and Decem-

1. For the geography of the Tullahoma position, see Connelly, *Autumn of Glory*, 112–13, 116; for Bragg's troubles with his subordinates, see *Ibid.*, 71–77; Horn, *Army of Tennessee*, 222–24; and Seitz, *Braxton Bragg*, 271–76.

2. The cavalry regiments transferred to Rosecrans were the 2nd Michigan, 9th Pennsylvania, and 6th and 9th Kentucky. *Official Records*, Vol. XX, Pt. 2, p. 342. The 1st Tennessee had been sent to Rosecrans previously from the Department of the Ohio. *Ibid.*, 302. The 2nd Michigan, assembled (or reequipped and remounted) in Louisville, were shipped from there to Nashville by rail, starting February 3. *Ibid.*, Vol. XXIII, Pt. 2, p. 42.

3. Lamers, *The Edge of Glory*, 245–47.

4. *Ibid.*, 248–49.

ber, 1862, he had kept the telegraph lines to Washington busy with pleas for General Stanley to be sent him as his chief of cavalry, for more and better arms (especially revolving rifles) for the cavalry he already had, for additional regiments of cavalry, for equipment to allow the conversion of infantry to mounted infantry, and so on. The telegraphic bombardment of the War Department on this general theme resumed shortly after the start of the new year. On January 14, Rosecrans wired Secretary Stanton that the Confederate cavalry, operating in masses and outnumbering his four to one, was "doing great mischief"; he believed they could be dealt with by using forces equally powerful.[5] He requested authority to buy horses and saddles to mount five thousand infantry. The following day he told General Halleck that he had to have cavalry or mounted infantry and complained that the saddles he had previously asked for were being delivered too slowly. He explained that "with mounted infantry I can drive the rebel cavalry to the wall and keep the roads open in my rear. Not so now," and he repeated his request for authority to purchase five thousand horses and saddles to mount infantry.[6] General Meigs, who had evidently been called on the carpet over Rosecrans' shortage of horses, pointed out that no one in the War Department had bothered to tell him that the latter had been authorized to mount five thousand of his infantry; he added that to collect so many horses was a major undertaking that would take time, especially since the Quartermaster's Department was as usual short of funds and "largely in debt." Rosecrans' next effort was a request to the secretary for five thousand revolving rifles. "Each rifle," he explained, "will add a man to my strength, and for the service for which I wish them they will add two men for each gun." Stanton responded the same day with the assurance that all the available revolving rifles ("all . . . that are manufactured in this country") had been sent to Rosecrans and that "more would be sent as fast as they can be procured." He ended the dispatch by authorizing him to buy whatever horses and saddles he could find locally.[7]

Having previously wired Stanton and Halleck, Rosecrans also wired General Meigs; in this message he raised his sights by 60 percent, in-

5. *Official Records*, Vol. XX, Pt. 2, p. 328.
6. *Ibid.*, 326; see also Halleck to Meigs, Meigs to Rosecrans, Halleck to Ripley, and Ripley to Rosecrans, *Ibid.*, 328, 329.
7. *Ibid.*, 326, 330, 331.

forming Meigs that he needed horses "to mount about 8,000 infantry in cases of emergency," to "smash up" all the enemy cavalry, whom he credited with a strength of 10,000 or 12,000.[8] Rosecrans' information was right on the mark in this instance, for Bragg had 8,707 cavalry in January, and the 3,400 Earl Van Dorn brought him on February 20 increased his mounted force to 12,000.[9] General Meigs responded with word that Rosecrans would receive 2,000 horses from Indianapolis and asked why he did not send his "infantry in wagons for forced marches to intercept cavalry," thereby laying himself open to the tart but not inappropriate rejoinder that Rosecrans had no wagons to spare, that even if he had them, they were too cumbersome for the narrow roads of middle Tennessee and of course could not travel cross-country. Wagons, he said in conclusion, "would do well on Pennsylvania avenue" but not in Tennessee.[10]

It would be tiresome for the reader, as it doubtless became to the authorities in Washington, to have to plow through the endless succession of Rosecrans' requests for additional regiments of cavalry, for additional cavalry firearms, for additional saddles and horse gear, and for more horses. They were sent in an unbroken stream throughout the first five months of 1863 and right up to the start of the Tullahoma Campaign on June 26. Rosecrans used every possible tone in these dispatches; he begged, he pleaded, he lectured, he exhorted, he hectored. When he heard of a cavalry regiment that the army grapevine reported as unassigned or not fully employed, he asked for it; he asked for the 2nd and 10th Ohio (accounting for the exchange of nine messages), the 4th Missouri, 1st Wisconsin, 8th and 9th Michigan, 3rd Kentucky, and, from the Army of the Potomac, Merrill's Horse. The need for weapons led to eleven messages, of which the following to General Halleck, on January 30, was typical: "It is of the first moment to have cavalry fire-arms. . . . Words are not needed to explain to you that if we cannot arm our cavalry, we had better disband it. I declare to you, upon my honor, the loss to the Government from this want alone, in this de-

8. *Ibid.*, 331.

9. Connelly, *Autumn of Glory*, 106; Thiele, "The Evolution of Cavalry," 138. By March 20, the number of Bragg's mounted troops increased to nearly 17,000 present for duty, but its effectiveness was reduced by the great variety of its armament, much of it unsuitable for use by cavalry. Thiele, "The Evolution of Cavalry," 152. See also *Official Records*, Vol. XXIII, Pt. 2, p. 31.

10. *Official Records*, Vol. XX, Pt. 2, pp. 332, 333.

partment . . . can be counted by millions of dollars."[11] Horses, too, were needed, and the messages on this vexing topic involved not only Washington but also the quartermaster officers in Louisville, who were charged with the duty of buying horses and mules for Rosecrans' army. As one might expect, this correspondence included the inevitable disagreement on just how many horses Rosecrans had actually received.[12]

The replies from Washington to this stream of messages were remarkably temperate. On only one occasion did General Halleck display an irritation wholly excusable under the circumstances. He wired Rosecrans on April 28:

I regret very much to notice the complaining tone of your telegrams in regard to your supply of horses. You seem to think the Government does not do its duty toward your army. You have been repeatedly informed that every possible authority has been given to the quartermaster of your army, and to all quartermasters in the West, to purchase all the animals they possibly can for you. . . . The authorities here have done all in their power to supply your wants. . . . you now have a larger number of animals in proportion to your forces than any other general in the field.[13]

Sent by the general-in-chief to a subordinate, this was an amazingly gentle reproof, but one that the recipient failed to heed, for a month later, Halleck had to tell him: "I have only to repeat what I have so often stated, that there is no more cavalry to send you. We have none, and can get none, until a draft is made."[14] Both these messages were antedated by the following well-earned snub:

11. *Ibid.*, 22.

12. *Ibid.*, 274–84, 288–90, 300, 320, 351. Rosecrans reported the numbers of his dismounted cavalrymen as 1,000 on February 2, as 3,500 on April 17, and as 2,000 on May 21. *Ibid.*, 34, 245, 521.

13. *Ibid.*, 284. General Meigs, who had been drawn into the disputes about the supply of horses for Rosecrans' army, wrote him on May 1 a remarkable letter that, were it not for its length (it occupies nearly four pages in the *Official Records*), would demand quoting in full. The War Department would have been well advised to distribute copies of it to every army commander and every cavalry officer in the Union army, for it is a strikingly able dissertation on the proper employment of cavalry. *Ibid.*, 300; see also Weigley, *Quartermaster General of the Union Army*, 262–66.

14. *Official Records*, Vol. XXIII, Pt. 2, p. 351. It should be said that Rosecrans did not neglect self-help to increase his available mounted force. He ordered (but not until May 17) that "to economize . . . cavalry," footsoldiers were to replace cavalrymen as orderlies at brigade and division headquarters, that only corps commanders were to have companies of cavalry assigned to them as escorts and orderlies, and that all other cavalry were to return at once to the chief of cavalry for duty. *Ibid.*, 336.

My attention has frequently been called to the enormous expense to the Government of your telegrams, as much or perhaps more than that of all the other generals in the field. . . . the habit with you seems to be increasing, and is really injuring you in the estimation of the Government. I feel it my duty to you as a personal friend to call your attention to the matter. . . . you repeat again and again the same thing. . . . you have telegraphed at least a dozen, and perhaps twenty times in the last few months that you require more cavalry. The Government is fully aware of your wants, and has been doing all in its power to supply them.[15]

While Rosecrans did battle with the authorities in Washington, his cavalry conducted expeditions into the wide stretch of country separating his army from that of the enemy. Some of these expeditions were hunts for forage—General Stanley led one such, made up of parts of three brigades of cavalry escorting a train of four hundred wagons—while others were probes for information of the enemy's whereabouts and activities. Many of Rosecrans' cavalry regiments and their commanding officers were now veterans with nearly two years of combat experience under their saber belts, and in their encounters with the enemy they gave a good account of themselves as often as not. Rosecrans wrote the secretary of war on Washington's Birthday that his cavalry had many "spirited skirmishes" every week with the enemy, which "terminate[d] well" for his horsemen.[16]

Indeed, there seemed to be a sound basis for Rosecrans' note of self-satisfaction. One of the "spirited skirmishes" he spoke of occurred in the course of a scout from January 31 to February 13 from Murfreesboro in the direction of Versailles, Middleton, and Unionville. Colonel Robert H. G. Minty, 4th Michigan, in command of detachments from his own regiment, the 7th Pennsylvania, 3rd Kentucky, 4th United States, and 2nd and 3rd Tennessee, totaling 1,328 rank and file, met, charged (the charge, "in the most gallant style," was made by 175 men of the 7th Pennsylvania, led by Captain W. H. Jenkins), and routed the

15. *Ibid.*, 255. Rosecrans was also inordinately fond of lecturing General Halleck. He wrote him on March 21, "You will observe from our tri-monthly [return] how utterly inadequate is our effective cavalry force—not half of what is allowed by writers for the proportion to the other arms." *Ibid.*, 154–55. And he took the trouble to inform General Meigs that "money is thrown away buying the kind of horses we have bought. . . . Cheap horses for service . . . is the worst possible plan, and this is tenfold worse when service is military. The cost of feeding poor horses and bringing them here is as great as that for good ones." *Ibid.*, 271.

16. *Ibid.*, Pt. 1, p. 48.

enemy, taking 49 unwounded and the same number of wounded prisoners; all but one of the latter were wounded with the saber.[17]

The permission granted to Rosecrans by the secretary of war to
mount 5,000 of his infantry had an important albeit incidental result.
The reader has already met Colonel John T. Wilder, first, commanding
the 17th Indiana Infantry, which he had organized at the outbreak of
the war; then, leading an infantry brigade made up of three Indiana
regiments, one from Illinois, and an Indiana battery; next, commanding the defenses of Munfordville; and lastly, engaged with his footsoldiers in the fruitless pursuit of John Morgan's fast-moving cavalry
on their return from their December, 1862, raid into Kentucky. A native of New York State, Wilder had moved West, first to Ohio and then
to Greensburg, Indiana. He was another of the large breed of self-
taught, self-confident, superbly competent engineer-entrepreneurs
who produced the explosive growth of American industry in the latter
half of the nineteenth century. Drawing the proper conclusion from
the failure of his infantry brigade to catch Morgan, Wilder proposed to
Rosecrans that he be permitted to convert his command of footsoldiers
to mounted infantry by "pressing" horses from the farms and plantations in the neighborhood of Murfreesboro.[18] The men of the 75th Indiana Infantry decided to continue as infantrymen, and their place in
what in time came to be known as the Lightning Brigade of Mounted
Infantry was taken by the 123rd Illinois Infantry. As has been mentioned in Volume I of the present work, the men of this brigade, whom
Wilder equipped with hatchets attached to two-foot handles in place of
sabers, were sufficiently enamored of their identity as mounted infantry to go to the trouble of removing from their uniforms the yellow trim
that would have identified them as cavalry.[19]

The genesis of the Lightning Brigade is an appropriate preface to
one of the classic errors in prognostication in the Civil War. The prog-
nosticator was General Halleck. After telling Rosecrans that cavalry
arms and horse equipments would be sent him "as fast as they can be

17. *Ibid.*, 25–26, 28.
18. McGee, *History of the 72nd Indiana*, 88–89.
19. *Ibid.*, 88, 108–109; S. C. Williams, *General John T. Wilder* (Bloomington, 1936),
11–13; John W. Rowell, *Yankee Artillerymen: Through the Civil War with Eli Lilly's Indiana Battery* (Knoxville, 1975), 53, 60–61. Lilly's battery remained attached to the brigade when it was converted to mounted infantry.

procured," Halleck cautioned him against weakening his army by converting too many of his infantry regiments to mounted infantry, for, he said, "Mounted infantry are neither good infantry nor good cavalry."[20] The regiments of mounted infantry in the West, where the mounted infantry concept flourished, and the four regiments of Colonel Wilder's brigade in particular, were to show that given reliable weapons and competent leadership, mounted infantry could be both good infantry and good cavalry—the latter, however, of an unconventional variety.

The story of the Spencer seven-shot repeater (originally a rifle, then also a carbine), its development by a Connecticut mechanic named Christopher Spencer, the resistance he encountered in trying to sell the weapon to the Army Ordnance Bureau, and the intervention of President Lincoln in his favor is too well known to require repetition here.[21] By the end of 1862, Spencer and his backers had organized the Spencer Repeating Rifle Company and had begun to manufacture the new weapon in a facility in Boston. To circumvent the Ordnance Bureau's opposition to its gun, the company sent Spencer west in early 1863 "to explain the proper use of his gun to troops which already carried it and to the commanders of troops not yet so fortunate."[22] One of those to whom Spencer demonstrated the gun was Colonel Wilder, who at once recognized its advantages and determined to obtain Spencers for his Lightning Brigade. Unable to get a commitment from the Ordnance Bureau to provide the guns, he borrowed from his hometown banks on his personal notes the substantial sum needed to buy the guns directly from the manufacturer. When the guns and ammunition (heavy brass cartridges a half inch in diameter) arrived on May 15, he issued them to his men, who covenanted to reimburse him in installments with money to be deducted from their pay.[23] Eventually,

20. *Official Records*, Vol. XXIII, Pt. 2, p. 155.

21. J. O. Buckeridge, *Lincoln's Choice* (Harrisburg, 1956), 4–25; Robert V. Bruce, *Lincoln and the Tools of War* (Indianapolis, 1956), 113–16, 203–204, 252–53. The president of the army board appointed at George B. McClellan's urging to evaluate the Spencer was Alfred Pleasanton. Buckeridge, *Lincoln's Choice*, 17. General Ripley, head of the Ordnance Bureau, objected to the Spencer as too expensive, too heavy, and too wasteful of ammunition.

22. Bruce, *Lincoln and the Tools of War*, 253; Buckeridge, *Lincoln's Choice*, 32–33.

23. McGee, *History of the 72nd Indiana*, 115, 121. The men's opinion of their new gun was expressed by this regimental historian: "This [gun], to our mind, was so nearly perfect that after using it for two years, our brigade had not a single change to suggest. . . . *It never got out of repair*. It was put together with screws, and anybody who had sense enough to be a soldier could take one all to pieces and put it all together. . . . It would shoot a mile just as accurately as the finest rifle in the world." *Ibid.*, 121.

the War Department took over the obligation to pay for the guns and reimbursed both Colonel Wilder and his men.

Wilder was not alone in pressing forward with a concept that, in its ultimate development, gave the Union armies in the West in the last year of the war a large force of mounted infantry. As early as 1862, to meet an occasional emergency, commanding officers (Rosecrans for one) would mount small bodies of their infantry on draft horses or mules and send them armed with their infantry rifles after the enemy. The emergency over, the horsemen *pro tem* reverted happily to their true trade of infantrymen. A scheme somewhat along these lines but on a much larger scale and a more permanent basis was proposed by General Lovell H. Rousseau, who commanded the First Division of Thomas' corps at Stones River. Rosseau visited Washington during the winter and, perhaps on Rosecrans' inspiration, "laid before the War Department the immense advantages of having a large mounted force to operate against the rebels in . . . [central Tennessee]." As Rosecrans wrote in a July 26 dispatch to General Halleck, operations in the spring and early summer of 1863 had made it evident that "the increasing area covered by our operations, the extension of our lines of communication, as well as the great advantages to be reaped from the proper use of cavalry on the enemy's lines of communication, his supply trains, and foraging parties, render an increase of our mounted force more than ever desirable. It is also essential to enable us to command the forage and subsistence which the country can furnish."[24]

Rousseau had a solution that he thought had been looked upon with favor when he spoke of it in the course of his Washington visit. Now, at the end of July, Rosecrans sent him back to Washington to try to sell the idea. On his arrival in the capital, Rousseau set forth his proposal in a lengthy communication to the secretary of war. In essence, he urged the enlistment of a corps that, naturally, he himself would command, of ten thousand "infantry or riflemen . . . [to] be mounted on mules, and 2,000 cavalry," the mules and horses, and presumably the remounts when needed, to be bought by the corps' own quartermaster. The infantry component of the corps was to be armed with Sharps' and Spencer carbines, and the cavalry with sabers and pistols.[25] The proposal was supported by a strong endorsement from

24. *Official Records*, Vol. XXIII, Pt. 2, p. 559.
25. *Ibid.*, 598–99. Rosecrans' dispatch, in which he announced that he was sending Rousseau to Washington, included a point omitted from Rousseau's submission to

Rosecrans based on the premise that if he had had an adequate cavalry force, he could have obtained control of middle Tennessee "with all its forage, horses, cattle and mules" without fighting the battle of Stones River.[26]

General Halleck was unimpressed; he saw "no advantages in . . . [the] project over the usual plan of enlisting for existing organizations. It greatly increases the number of officers, already out of proportion to the men. . . . it resembles those independent organizations which have caused so much discontent and trouble whenever the exigencies of the service require them to be employed in a different way." Over-ruling the objections of the general-in-chief, Stanton gave the scheme his blessing on August 17. That Stanton should have gone contrary to the advice of the professional head of the army is not surprising, but it is distinctly so that the normally sagacious General Meigs should have expressed himself in favor of Rousseau's proposal. He gave it as his judgment that the scheme was "practicable" and told Stanton that five thousand mules "suitable for the purpose required" could be had in six weeks at a price of $125 each. He was directed on August 18 "to purchase the mules . . . as speedily as possible."[27] But the scheme was overtaken by the exigencies of Rosecrans' Chattanooga Campaign, and perhaps, too, there were some in the War Department who remembered the sad fate, a scant three months before, of Colonel Abel D. Streight's mule-mounted infantry raid and as a result dragged their feet or sabotaged action on the plan. In another month, Rosecrans' loss of the battle of Chickamauga gave everyone concerned more urgent and important problems to think about, and the scheme quietly died.[28]

It would be difficult to find another operation in the Civil War that was—or that deserved to be—snakebit to the same degree as Colonel

---

Stanton, namely that enlistments in the new corps would be sought among "the large number of disciplined troops recently mustered out of the service in the East." *Ibid.*, 560.

26. *Ibid.*, 599–600; see also *Ibid.*, 559.

27. *Ibid.*, 599, and Vol. XXX, Pt. 3, pp. 62, 71.

28. The desire among army commanders to extemporize mounted troops never disappeared entirely. At the very time that Rousseau's proposal was being considered by the War Department, Grant asked for three thousand sets of horse equipments to be sent to Vicksburg so that he could mount infantry in an emergency. On the previous day, Halleck had wired him: "In your contemplated operations . . . [in Arkansas and north-

Streight's ill-fated raid of April and May, 1863. The idea of the raid was
Streight's. He was colonel of the 51st Indiana Infantry, then a part of
the Army of the Cumberland, and was described as "a man of great
courage and activity."[29] The scheme, adopted with great enthusiasm
by General Garfield and by Rosecrans himself, was to take four infantry regiments, the 51st and 71st Indiana, 3rd Ohio, and 18th Illinois,
plus two companies of Unionist Tennessee cavalry, whose troopers had
actually been recruited in northern Alabama—a total of two thousand
officers and men—mount the men on mules, and starting from Eastport, on the Tennessee River in the northeastern corner of Mississippi,
cross northern Alabama from west to east through the sparsely inhabited, barren, rugged belt of country lying twenty to forty miles south of
the Tennessee River, break the Western & Atlantic Railroad (the rail
link between Atlanta and Chattanooga) south of Dalton, Georgia, and,
as a secondary objective, destroy the Confederate arsenals in Rome,
Georgia.[30] The purpose of breaking the Western & Atlantic (the line of
the Andrews raiders and of the "General") was to force Bragg to retreat
from east Tennessee.[31] Streight's movement was to be aided by an advance along the line of the Memphis & Charleston from Corinth by
General Grenville M. Dodge with a force that eventually numbered
6,000 infantry and 1,500 mounted infantry and cavalry, later reinforced by the 7th Kansas. The purpose of Dodge's massive operation
was to draw upon himself the attention of the Confederate forces in
the area so that Streight would have a clean start.

Streight's woes began in Nashville, where he expected to receive
the mules to mount his command. He was issued 800, which was
1,200 fewer than he needed, but 800 mules was all the Nashville quartermasters had. Unless these mules have been maligned by Colonel
Streight, they "were nothing but poor, wild, unbroken colts, many of
them but two years old, and . . . a large number of them had the horse

---

west Louisiana] you will probably require additional cavalry. You are authorized to
mount any of your infantry regiments, making requisitions on the proper departments
for horses and equipment." *Ibid.*, 129; see also pp. 131, 147, 109.

29. Wyeth, *That Devil Forrest*, 166. Wyeth also calls him "the lively Hoosier."
Ibid., 167.

30. For Streight's orders, see *Official Records*, Vol. XXIII, Pt. 1, p. 282. In fairness to
Garfield, it should be said that he asked Rosecrans to allow him to command the raid,
but Rosecrans refused. Lamers, *The Edge of Glory*, 257.

31. The Western & Atlantic is called the Atlanta & Chattanooga in some reports.

distemper; some 40 or 50 were too near dead to travel, and had to be left. . . . 10 or 12 died before we started, and such of them as could be rode at all were so wild and unmanageable that it took us all that day and a part of the next to catch and break them."[32] Another hundred of the miserable animals gave out and were abandoned on the cross-country march from Palmyra to Fort Henry, where the expedition re-embarked for a journey by boat up the Tennessee to Eastport, where they arrived on April 19, already four days behind schedule.[33] That night brought another installment of Colonel Streight's tale of disasters. Some of Philip Roddey's Confederate cavalrymen made their way into Streight's encampment and stampeded the mule herd, with the result that another day and a half was lost while the men scoured the countryside for the missing animals, 200 of whom they were unable to find.[34] Streight was down to well under 500 for his nearly 2,000 infantrymen; hunting for mules and horses after the local farmers had had ample time to hide their animals produced few mounts and served only to wear out the mules and horses the raiders already had. General Dodge helped out by turning over to Streight "some 600" horses and mules that he took from his trains and mounted infantry.[35] Colonel Streight's and General Dodge's grasp of numbers fell victim to these embarrassments, for when the former, having weeded out 500 of his men as not sufficiently robust to be taken along on the raid, departed at long last from Tuscumbia at 11 P.M. on April 26, only 150 of the men, he said, had to follow the column on foot; 1,350 of the men had mounts of some sort—good, bad, or indifferent. As the march went on to its sad denouement, the number of mounts captured along the way balanced, with a little to spare, those that gave out.[36]

32. *Official Records*, Vol. XXIII, Pt. 1, p. 286. See also Gilbert C. Kniffin, "Streight's Raid Through Tennessee and Northern Georgia in 1863," MOLLUS, Commandery of the District of Columbia, *War Papers*, No. 82 (Washington, D.C., 1887–), 3–4.

33. In one of its infrequent attempts at military utility, the Mississippi Marine Brigade escorted Streight's command on their voyage up the Tennessee. *Official Records*, Vol. XXIII, Pt. 1, p. 282.

34. Wyeth, *That Devil Forrest*, 168–69; H. Harvey Mathes, *General Forrest* (New York, 1902), 111; *Official Records*, Vol. XXIII, Pt. 1, p. 286.

35. *Official Records*, Vol. XXIII, Pt. 1, p. 248. Streight says that General Dodge gave him only 200 mules. *Ibid.*, 287.

36. Streight reported that when he left Tuscumbia, 150 of his men, in addition to the 150 who had no mounts at all, had mules that "were unable to carry more than the saddles" and hence had to slog through the darkness and the mud on foot. *Ibid.*, 287.

Colonel Streight's difficulties over his mules caused a total and ultimately fatal delay of between five and five and a half days. On April 23,
two days beyond the date when the raiders should have left Tuscumbia, only Colonel Roddey's small command of about 1,200 cavalry was
in the area to try to cope with Streight's and Dodge's forces. On the
evening of that day, however, Forrest, stationed with his brigade of four
regiments of Tennessee cavalry and John Morton's battery at Spring
Hill, Tennessee, ninety miles as the crow flies north of Tuscumbia,
was handed orders from General Bragg to move at once to the Tennessee River, find and join Roddey, take command of the combined
forces, and block Dodge's advance.[37] Forrest started south at once. He
reached and crossed the Tennessee on the twenty-sixth, and two days
later joined Roddey and had an all-day artillery duel with Dodge's cavalry at Town Creek, a southern tributary of the Tennessee some twenty
miles east of Tuscumbia.

The Federal cavalry at Town Creek was commanded by Colonel
Florence M. Cornyn, who at the start of the war had exchanged a surgeon's scalpel for a cavalryman's saber and the colonelcy of the 10th
Missouri.[38] In the present operation, Cornyn led Dodge's advance to
Tuscumbia, in the course of which he had a number of skirmishes,
described in lavish detail in his report, with Roddey's cavalrymen.[39] He
had begun the campaign with a brigade that, owing to almost daily
changes in its composition, had never had the chance to jell as an organization and was therefore a brigade in name only. Initially, the brigade consisted of Cornyn's own 10th Missouri, the 15th Illinois, the
1st Alabama, and the 9th Illinois Mounted Infantry. Then the 1st Alabama was taken from the brigade and replaced sometime later by the

37. Henry, *"First with the Most" Forrest*, 142, 144; Wyeth, *That Devil Forrest*,
170–71.
38. *Official Records*, Vol. III, 96.
39. Cornyn had scraps with Roddey at Great Bear Creek, Buzzard Roost, and
Leighton. *Ibid.*, Vol. XXIII, Pt. 1, pp. 251–56. For the fight at Leighton, see also Starr,
Jennison's Jayhawkers, 261–64. On April 17, just to the east of Great Bear Creek,
Cornyn got too far in advance of the infantry and gave Roddey the opportunity to get
behind him and capture a section of two pieces of artillery and its escort of two companies of mounted infantry. Hearing the firing in his rear, Cornyn sent back the 1st Alabama, commanded by Captain James C. Cameron, to charge the enemy and retake the
guns. The Alabamians, "new recruits and poorly drilled," armed "with muskets only and
those not loaded," nevertheless made the charge (in which Cameron was killed) and recaptured one gun and one caisson. *Official Records*, Vol. XXIII, Pt. 1, p. 247.

7th Kansas (down to 400, rank and file); on the following day, the Illinois mounted infantry regiment was taken from the brigade.[40]

At dusk on April 28, a scout of Roddey's named James Moon brought word to Forrest that Streight's column (the strength of which Moon estimated at 2,000) was marching from Mount Hope in the direction of Moulton and was therefore well to the south and rear of Forrest's position at Town Creek.[41] With the flair that made him the great cavalry commander that he was, Forrest concluded that Dodge's advance, which he had been opposing at Town Creek, was a blind and that the real threat was the force that Moon had seen. Leaving Roddey and Colonel James H. Edmondson's 11th Tennessee to block any reinforcements Dodge might try to send to Streight, he himself prepared to take off after the raiders.[42] Following his regular practice, Forrest, in the words of his biographer, did not "leave the details of preparation to any subordinate. . . . He selected the best horses and harness, and double-teamed his artillery and caissons. He even stood by to see the ammunition carefully distributed. . . . He saw to it that the farriers were busy shoeing the horses and tightening the shoes which were loose. Three days' rations were cooked, and shelled corn issued for two days' forage." And the biographer concludes with a rhetorical question: "At the bottom of . . . [Forrest's] remarkable and almost unbroken series of brilliant achievements, may not this patient attention to the smallest detail explain in part the wonderful measure of his success?"[43]

At 1 A.M. on April 29, Forrest, with Jacob B. Biffle's and J. W. Starnes's regiments, a section of two guns of John Morton's battery, and Ferrell's Georgia Battery of six guns, took off after the raiders. On the evening of the same day, Streight had reached the western foot of Day's Gap, "a narrow and winding defile" leading to the summit of Sand Mountain; he had not only made a creditable day's march of thirty-five miles over "rough and muddy roads" but had also swept the countryside for miles on either side of his route for horses and mules to

40. *Official Records*, Vol. XXIII, Pt. 1, pp. 254–55; see also Starr, *Jennison's Jayhawkers*, 242–43.

41. Henry, *"First with the Most" Forrest*, 145; Wyeth, *That Devil Forrest*, 171.

42. There is some confusion in the reports on Forrest's pursuit, for Roddey, represented in some accounts as left behind to prevent Dodge and Streight from reinforcing each other, is also reported as present with Forrest at Day's Gap and in the Sand Mountain attack on Streight on April 29.

43. Wyeth, *That Devil Forrest*, 173.

replace the worst of the animals he had and to provide mounts for nearly all of the men who had none.[44] Forrest, however, had done even more. With two breaks of an hour each to rest and feed his animals, he had marched fifty miles in twenty-three hours and, when he went into bivouac at midnight, was a mere four miles behind Streight.

A year after these events, having had ample time to think over the history of his "ill-fated expedition," Streight concluded that he would have succeeded if, instead of "poor, young mules," he had been given 800 good horses at Nashville or if General Dodge had been able to detain Forrest just one day longer. There is no question that the poor quality of the animals issued to Streight's inexperienced men was a nearly fatal handicap, both directly and indirectly, and the main cause of the delay in starting that made it possible for Forrest to engage in the pursuit. There was, however, another major ingredient—one which Streight failed to realize—in the causes of his failure. *Effective* cavalry, or even effective mounted infantry, simply could not be improvised overnight. The historian of the 72nd Indiana Mounted Infantry could have told Streight what to expect. After his regiment received its horses—not unbroken mules—the infantrymen learned, as the historian put it, that "while we were well drilled as infantry, on our undrilled horses we were little less than a mounted mob for a little while."[45]

On the night of April 29, notwithstanding the proximity of Forrest's cavalry, the raiders, exhausted and suffering from saddle sores as they undoubtedly were, did have a good night's rest, the last they were to have for the next ninety-six hours. Early the next morning they climbed Day's Gap and reached the top of Sand Mountain, a wide plateau intersected by watercourses. But now Streight knew that Forrest was right behind him and that he must lose no time to find a good defensive position to resist the inevitable attack. This Streight did, and from it his men repulsed attacks by Roddey's and Edmondson's troopers led by Forrest in person. In fact, in a well-timed counterattack they captured the two guns and caissons of Morton's battery.[46]

44. *Official Records*, Vol. XXIII, Pt. 1, p. 287; Henry, *"First with the Most" Forrest*, 146.
45. McGee, *History of the 72nd Indiana*, 115.
46. *Official Records*, Vol. XXIII, Pt. 1, pp. 288–89; Wyeth, *That Devil Forrest*, 178–79; Henry, *"First with the Most" Forrest*, 147.

Resuming his march after this check to the pursuit, Streight had to halt again six miles farther on at Hog Mountain and deploy for another fight. He was attacked this time by Biffle's and Starnes's cavalrymen "about one hour before dark," and the attacks were repeated time and again until the combatants were fighting by the light of a full moon.[47] Again the raiders were able to hold their own, with the aid this time of the two pieces of artillery they had captured from the enemy earlier in the day. When, however, the attacks ceased, Streight made the only decision open to him: as soon as he could collect his men, who by then had marched and fought without a break for nearly eighteen hours, he resumed his march.

From this point on, until Streight was compelled to surrender on the morning of May 3, near Gaylesville, just west of the Alabama-Georgia border, the pursued and pursuers were engaged in a contest of sheer endurance, physical and moral. Streight's tactics were to move on as rapidly as the steadily deteriorating state of his horses and mules and the desperate weariness of his men (who, "being unaccustomed to riding, had become so exhausted from fatigue and loss of sleep that it was almost impossible to keep them awake") allowed, "until his rear was too hard pressed, and then, whenever a suitable position offered, to ambush his adversary, and thus discourage direct assault."[48] As a matter of course, he had the road behind him blocked with felled trees wherever possible and destroyed all bridges. At last, on the morning of May 3, with the way to a questionable safety beyond the Coosa River at Rome, Georgia, blocked, the unfortunate infantrymen were attacked once again. But now they could do no more; "nature was exhausted, and a large portion of . . . [the] best troops actually went to sleep while lying in line of battle under a severe skirmish fire."[49] Streight had no choice but to surrender. Forrest's bag of prisoners numbered about 1,150; as best as Streight was able to estimate, he had also lost 145 officers and men killed and wounded and about 200 men whose mounts had given out and who, unable to keep up with the column on foot, had fallen behind and were picked up by the enemy.[50]

47. Henry, *"First with the Most" Forrest*, 148. Forrest "in person led his men again and again in the assault, with seeming desperation." Wyeth, *That Devil Forrest*, 181.
48. *Official Records*, Vol. XXIII, Pt. 2, p. 292; Wyeth, *That Devil Forrest*, 180. The endlessly repeated romantic tale of Emma Sanson and the "lost ford" across Black Creek will be found in Wyeth, *That Devil Forrest*, 186–90.
49. *Official Records*, Vol. XXIII, Pt. 1, p. 292.
50. There is the usual discrepancy of numbers here; Forrest claimed 1,446 pris-

In his account of the raid, Colonel Streight commented thus on the travails of his command: "I will here remark that my men had been worked very hard in scouring so much of the country, and unaccustomed as they were to riding, made it still worse; consequently, they were illy prepared for the trying ordeal through which they were to pass."[51] In the light of that ordeal, it is not inappropriate to quote the diary entry for April 28, and hence not written with the benefit of hindsight of a knowledgeable veteran of the 7th Kansas: " We think that mounted infantry, with a cumbersome pack train, is a poor outfit for a raid. It is our opinion that our best cavalry should have been sent."[52] General Stanley, who did have the benefit of hindsight and whose judgments on fellow officers of high rank seldom erred on the side of charity, was positively scathing on the subject of this raid in his reminiscences. Streight's raid, he wrote,

was the most senseless thing I saw done during the war to waste men and material. Streight worked on Garfield . . . [who] had no military ability, nor could he learn anything, yet he persuaded Rosecrans that, with four regiments of mounted infantry, one could ride through the Confederacy, burn all their bridges, destroy their foundries, and then surrender—the immense damage done compensating for the loss of the four regiments. . . . Never had such a fool's plan been approved by a general commanding an army. . . . Indeed, Streight's raid was a contemptible fizzle from beginning to end. . . . We lost four fine regiments, mounted, one hundred loyal Alabamians, who were liable to be shot if taken prisoner, and nothing to show for it but the vainglory of the charlatan Streight.[53]

General Stanley's strictures on Colonel Streight—who handled his forces with commendable skill and determination in his encounter with one of the greatest commanders produced by the war—are far too harsh. Streight was not by any means the only victim of Forrest's great ability and fierce energy. He, and Generals Garfield and Rosecrans with him, may be censured for undertaking a visionary, patently impractical project with unsuitable means. But one must hasten to add that the desire and willingness to experiment, to try anything, was

---

oners. Streight and his officers were kept in Libby Prison in Richmond until February 9, 1864, when Streight and four of his officers escaped; they reached Washington three weeks later. *Ibid.*, 295, 292. For Streight's account of the treatment of the wounded he was forced to leave behind by Forrest's troopers, see *Ibid.*, 293.

51. *Ibid.*, 288. Each time the raiders dismounted to fight as infantry, they gave a good account of themselves.

52. Fletcher Pomeroy, "War Diary," quoted in Starr, *Jennison's Jayhawkers*, 242.

53. Stanley, *Personal Memoirs*, 131–32.

very much a part of the mid-nineteenth-century American spirit. This was no less true of the enterprises, tactics, and tools of a war fought mainly by hastily uniformed civilians than it was of the self-taught engineers and manufacturers who provided these amateurs of warfare with the novel weapons and paraphernalia that helped win the war.

As the spring of 1863 turned into summer, a new and ominous note began to creep into General Halleck's dispatches to the Army of the Cumberland. Three months, then four months, then five elapsed following the Battle of Stones River. Throughout those months, as has been noted, Rosecrans' harassment—for it was nothing less—however justified it may have been, of his superiors in Washington for more cavalry, more and better cavalry weapons, and more horses went on relentlessly. On January 26, in asking that the 2nd and 10th Ohio be transferred to him, Rosecrans sounded a theme that he was to repeat with regularity in the months ahead. He told General Halleck, "A sufficient force of cavalry is all I require to make an advance. . . . I wish to have cavalry enough to destroy the enemy's cavalry, and, this done, I can occupy this whole country with my forces."[54] A few days later, Halleck countered by telling Rosecrans that it was "exceedingly important" that he keep Bragg "occupied" in order to prevent the transfer of troops from the latter's army to Vicksburg and Port Hudson.[55] Realizing, perhaps, that the state of the roads at that time of the year and the precarious state of Rosecrans' supply lines made an immediate campaign impractical, Halleck did not again urge him to move until March 25, when he telegraphed, "It is exceedingly important at the present time that you give the enemy in your front plenty of occupation." There was little comfort for the general-in-chief in Rosecrans' reply: "Dispatch received. Rebels appear to me just now engaged in giving me occupation. . . . I do not think it prudent or practicable to advance . . . until I am better or differently informed. Will know soon." What Rosecrans knew "soon" (actually two weeks later)

54. *Official Records*, Vol. XXIII, Pt. 2, p. 14.
55. *Ibid.*, 23. Halleck went on, "Should the enemy succeed in holding your army in check with an inferior force while he sends troops to the Mississippi River, it is greatly to be feared that the time of many of our troops will expire without our having accomplished any important results."

and communicated to General Halleck was that he needed "only" battery and cavalry horses and the return of the army's "spare baggage" to be ready to move. At the same time, however, he expressed the hope that the Streight raid, then about to get under way, would, if successful, drive Bragg out of Tennessee into Georgia without, one may assume, Rosecrans having to incur the hazards of another battle like Stones River.[56]

Another five weeks passed, and on May 21 Rosecrans told Halleck that if given 6,000 additional cavalry plus 2,000 remounts for the cavalry he already had, he "would attack Bragg within three days" but that an advance without these increases in his mounted strength would in the opinion of his corps commanders and his chief of cavalry hazard "more than the probable gains." It was in response to this message that Halleck sent the previously quoted telegram to the effect that the government had no more cavalry that it could send to Rosecrans. Then, on June 3, by which time Rosecrans had built up a respectable stock of supplies at Murfreesboro, and five months after the battle of Stones River, Halleck tried an indirect approach; he wired Rosecrans: "Accounts here indicate that Johnston is being heavily reinforced from Bragg's army. If you cannot hurt the enemy now, he will soon hurt you."[57]

Throughout this period, Rosecrans claimed repeatedly that he was greatly outnumbered in mounted troops by the enemy. On February 1 he reported, correctly, the arrival in his front of Earl Van Dorn's cavalry, which, he said, would increase the number of Bragg's mounted troops to 15,000.[58] On February 12, he credited Bragg with an "enormous" cavalry force; Van Dorn, he said, was reported to have brought 6,000 to 7,000 mounted troops from Mississippi, in addition to which Bragg said to be mounting 4,000 infantry. A month later, Rosecrans passed on to Halleck an informant's report crediting Bragg with more than 30,000 cavalry; he obviously considered this figure to be believable, for he contended a week later that his own "utterly inadequate . . . effective cavalry force" amounted to "not one fourth, perhaps not one-sixth," of the enemy's. After the lapse of a month, he

56. Ibid., 171, 282.
57. Ibid., 351, 353.
58. Ibid., 31; see also Connelly, Autumn of Glory, 106, and Thiele, "The Evolution of Cavalry," 138.

asserted that Bragg's army was able to collect the resources of the area because its cavalry outnumbered his own, five to one.[59]

There are no grounds for questioning Rosecrans' good faith in making these statements to the War Department; so far as one can tell 120 years after the event, Rosecrans believed these figures. All the same, and presumably unknown to him, Bragg's margin of superiority in mounted troops was never so great as he thought. Van Dorn had brought only 3,400 troopers from Mississippi, not 6,000 to 7,000, and his orders were to remain with Bragg only "until it may appear that he can render more service elsewhere"; in fact, in early May, after the success of Grierson's Raid, a "delegation of influential Mississippians" persuaded President Davis to order him back to their state to reinforce Pemberton.[60] There were other reductions, entirely apart from absences, legitimate or otherwise, from the colors, of large numbers of individual cavalrymen. Late in the spring, Philip Roddey's small brigade was sent to northern Alabama, and in June, John Morgan disappeared over the horizon, and ultimately into captivity, with nearly 2,500 of his (and Bragg's) troopers. Bragg's cavalry was never so numerous as Rosecrans thought; nor was the Union cavalry ever outnumbered six to one or even four to one, but strictly with respect to numbers, the odds in the Confederates' favor were sufficiently great, as shown by the following tabulation of official strength reports.

There were, however, factors at work to reduce at least partially the impact of the Confederates' numerical superiority in mounted troops, even in the period when they had it. Bragg had his cavalry divided nearly half and half, with Van Dorn at Columbia guarding the left of his line and Wheeler at McMinnville, nearly a hundred miles by road from Columbia, guarding the right. More importantly, perhaps, Wheeler, from January 22 on "in command of all cavalry in Middle Tennessee, did not have the cordial support of several of his subordinates."[61] Morgan and Forrest resented having to take orders from the twenty-four-year-old West Pointer. After the bloody failure of the attack in early February on Fort Donelson and the town of Dover, di-

59. *Ibid.*, 59, 154–55, 290.

60. *Ibid.*, 646; Joseph E. Johnston, *Narrative of Military Operations During the Late War Between the States* (Bloomington, 1959), 160–61; Connelly, *Autumn of Glory*, 106. Van Dorn was killed on May 7 by a jealous husband.

61. *Official Records*, Vol. XXIII, Pt. 2, p. 614. Wheeler had been appointed chief of cavalry on October 13, 1862.

Union and Confederate Cavalry Strength in Middle Tennessee,
January–July, 1863

Date	Present for Duty Union[1]	Present for Duty Confederate[2]	"Effective Strength" Confederate[3]
January 31	4,549	8,707	7,980
February 20		11,610	10,717
February 28	5,040	9,101	7,466
March 10		9,661	8,848
March 20		16,618	15,892
March 31	6,289		
April 10		15,164	14,214
April 20		15,167	14,096
April 30	4,961	15,125	13,981
May 10		15,193	13,914
May 20		15,096	14,113
May 31	4,961		
June 10		13,868	12,703
June 30	10,560		
July 20		9,089	8,265
July 31	10,883		

1. The Union numbers for January, February, March, April, May, and July are in *Official Records*, Vol. XXIII, Pt. 2, pp. 29, 93, 197, 298, 378, 573; for June, in *Ibid.*, Pt. 1, p. 410 (the accuracy of the June 30 figure, as it appears in the records, is suspect). Up to and including May, the numbers are those of a cavalry division; in June, of a cavalry command; in July, of a cavalry corps. Note also that the numbers of the 15th Pennsylvania (between 460 and 490), of Wilder's brigade of mounted infantry, and doubtless of other mounted infantry units as well were regularly omitted from the totals.

2. The Confederate numbers are in *Official Records*, Vol. XXIII, Pt. 2, pp. 622, 643, 654, 680, 718, 749, 779, 806, 829, 846, 873, 920.

3. The term *effective strength* is not defined in the records; it may be assumed to mean the number of fully armed and equipped mounted men present with the colors.

rected by Wheeler and made over Forrest's objections, Forrest said to Wheeler, "I will be in my coffin before I will fight again under your command."[62] It is worthy of note also that Bragg had a poor opinion of Morgan's and Forrest's capabilities; neither, he thought, was anything more than a raider.[63] Even as early as the spring of 1863, Forrest had already demonstrated uncommon gifts as a commander of mounted

62. Dyer, "Some Aspects of Cavalry Operations," 222; Wyeth, *That Devil Forrest*, 126–32; *Official Records*, Vol. XXIII, Pt. 1, pp. 31–41; Connelly, *Autumn of Glory*, 124.

63. Bragg wrote to General Johnston on March 2, "I fear Morgan is overcome by too large a command; with a regiment or small brigade he did more and better service than with a division." *Official Records*, Vol. XXIII, Pt. 2, p. 656.

troops, which Bragg should have had the insight and the willingness to recognize. Unfortunately for the Confederacy, Bragg remained unimpressed, perhaps because Forrest was not a West Pointer or even a gentleman. Wrong as he may have been about Forrest, Bragg was certainly right about Morgan, as the events of June and July, 1863, were to demonstrate.

Fortunately, John Hunt Morgan's militarily insane Indiana-Ohio Raid need not be discussed in a history of the Union cavalry.[64] Contrary to his usually level-headed appraisal of Morgan's operations, General Duke, who was a participant in the raid, calls this disastrous aberration of his brother-in-law's "incomparably the most brilliant raid of the entire war." The raiders, 2,460 strong, began on July 2, when Morgan crossed the Cumberland River into Kentucky. Six days later, Morgan crossed the Ohio at Brandenburg, Kentucky, and marched northeast along the river through Indiana and then, after skirting Cincinnati, east through southern Ohio (his men looting stores in Corydon and Salem, Indiana, and Jackson, Ohio, on the way) until he and the remnant of his command not previously captured were forced to surrender near Lisbon, Ohio, on July 26. All or parts of six regiments of Union cavalry (4th United States, 14th Illinois, 9th Indiana, 1st Kentucky, 9th Michigan, and 2nd Ohio) joined some Union infantry and numerous home-guard units in the pursuit of the raiders and sustained casualties of 5 killed and 5 wounded while doing so.[65]

64. The full story will be found in *Ibid.*, Pt. 1, pp. 632–818, and Pt. 2, pp. 502, 514, 519, 520, 521–23, 536, 541, 542, 544, 548, 552. It is told in narrative form in Brown, *The Bold Cavaliers*, 177–226; Duke, *History of Morgan's Cavalry*, 409–62; and Holland, *Morgan and His Raiders*, 222–49.

65. Duke, *History of Morgan's Cavalry*, 458; Brown, *The Bold Cavaliers*, 179; *Official Records*, Vol. XXIII, Pt. 1, p. 637.

X

Feats of Broil and Battle

DESPITE THE PROBLEMS AND DIFFICULTIES THEY SHARED with all other armed forces of the Confederacy and despite other problems—military, organizational, and in some cases personal—peculiar to the Army of Tennessee, both Wheeler and Forrest performed creditably in the early months of 1863. Wheeler had at his headquarters a British soldier of fortune, "Colonel" George St. Leger Grenfell, who had spent the summer and autumn of 1862 as John Hunt Morgan's adjutant general and, after leaving that post, was appointed by Bragg inspector (or inspector general) of his cavalry. No doubt he described for Wheeler what he had learned about the technique of cavalry operations as a captain in the mounted component of the "Anglo-Turkish Contingent" in the Crimean War; doubtless, too, some of these ideas found their way into the manual of cavalry tactics Wheeler compiled at this time and published later in the year.[1] At the same time, however, Wheeler, criticized for lack of ability in long-range planning and for being "more intent on leading the traditional Rebel cavalry dash against

1. For Grenfell, see Starr, *Colonel Grenfell's Wars*, 95–100. For Wheeler's tactics (published as *A Revised System of Cavalry Tactics for the Use of the Cavalry and Mounted Infantry, C.S.A.*) see J. P. Dyer, *"Fightin' Joe" Wheeler* (Baton Rouge, 1941), 101–102. Dyer suggests that a full-fledged attack by Forrest on the Louisville & Nashville, Rosecrans' lifeline, might have prevented the Union conquest of middle Tennessee. Dyer, "Some Aspects of Cavalry Operations," 217.

targets of lesser importance," added to Rosecrans' apprehensions with a raid behind the Federal camps at Murfreesboro. He burned some bridges on the Nashville & Chattanooga Railroad and marched north as far as Harpeth Shoals on the Cumberland River, where on January 19 he captured "four large transports; destroyed three, with all the supplies. . . . He was hotly pursued by a gunboat, which he attacked and captured, and destroyed her with her whole armament."[2]

A month later, Wheeler again rode around Rosecrans' army with his own brigade plus one regiment of John Pegram's. He attacked the Federals' "trains, their guards, and numerous stragglers. He succeeded in capturing several hundred prisoners and destroying hundreds of wagons loaded with supplies and baggage."[3] In April, he made another dash on the Nashville & Chattanooga Railroad; a detachment of 500 "picked men" of his, under Lieutenant Colonel S. C. Ferrill, intercepted a passenger train at Antioch Station, twelve miles southeast of Nashville, drove off the train guard (6 of whom were killed and 12 wounded, 3 mortally) and "took possession of the train, capturing most of the passengers, releasing some 43 [Confederate prisoners], plundering the mail and express packages, and robbing the passengers of money, watches, clothing, boots and hats, and setting fire to and destroying seven cars." A second group of Wheeler's raiders circled Nashville, planted their artillery on the south bank of the Cumberland, and at a distance of 250 to 300 yards (or by another account, 700 yards) shelled the "very large locomotive" of the first southbound Louisville & Nashville train that came into view across the river. The gunners made excellent practice; their very first shot "knocked off the dome of the locomotive, the next went through the boiler. . . . Thirty-five shots were fired, and nearly all of them struck the train," killing some of the horses "and other stock" with which its eighteen cars were loaded.[4]

Militarily, such raids were mere annoyances. Of somewhat greater significance was a fight on March 4 and 5. On one side were an 1,845-man brigade of infantry, an Ohio battery of six rifled Rodman guns, and about 600 cavalry, mainly of the 9th Pennsylvania, beefed up with

2. *Official Records*, Vol. XX, Pt. 1, p. 983 (Bragg's report of the operation, which he concluded by recommending Wheeler for promotion).

3. *Ibid.*, 663.

4. *Ibid.*, Vol. XXIII, Pt. 1, pp. 215–21. For the attack at Antioch Station, see esp. p. 216.

detachments from the 2nd Michigan and the 4th Kentucky; on the other side were Van Dorn's Cavalry Corps of about 6,300 rank and file, consisting of the two divisions he had brought north from Mississippi, and Forrest's brigade.[5] In command of the Federal force was Colonel John Coburn of the 33rd Indiana Infantry; Colonel Thomas J. Jordan of the 9th Pennsylvania commanded the cavalry. Orders from Rosecrans' headquarters directed Coburn to make "a reconnaissance in force" from Franklin as far as Spring Hill, thirteen miles to the south, to locate the enemy.

At the same time that Coburn marched south pursuant to these orders, Van Dorn marched north on a mirror image of Coburn's assignment. Advance detachments of the two forces bumped into each other on March 4, less than four miles south of Franklin. In a dispatch that evening to General C. C. Gilbert, in command of U.S. forces in Franklin, Coburn reported that he had "repulsed a force of about 2,000 to 3,000 rebel cavalry" who were nevertheless still on his left flank. "What shall we do?" the colonel asked.[6] Without waiting for a reply, however, he resumed his advance the following morning. He had dismounted cavalry, deployed as skirmishers, in the lead, and they pushed the enemy "handsomely across the fields and over the hills."[7] Unfortunately for Coburn, he was being led into a trap, which was duly sprung at Thompson's Station, on the Alabama & Tennessee Railroad, nine miles south of Franklin. With Van Dorn's two divisions in a strong position blocking farther progress south, Forrest's four regiments of cavalry and Captain S. L. Freeman's battery attacked Coburn's left flank and rear. Coburn's infantry put up a stout fight but were eventually forced to surrender. Notwithstanding Coburn's recital of other factors—a shortage of ammunition, the disappearance of his cavalry and artillery—he implies that the primary cause of his defeat and surrender was Forrest's skillful and aggressive handling of his forces, and his remorseless attacks on, and threats to, Coburn's flank and rear.

Coburn is particularly harsh, but seemingly without justification,

5. *Ibid.*, 84. In his report the Federal commander stated that he had 2,837 officers and men and estimated Van Dorn's strength at 15,000. *Ibid.*, 86, 90.

6. *Ibid.*, 78. Gilbert, who was severely criticized for failing to go to Coburn's aid the next day, sent an officer of the 2nd Michigan to check on Coburn's "condition." The officer reported on his return that Coburn was "in a good deal of doubt as to the intentions of the enemy and not over-confident." *Ibid.*, 79. Gordon Granger faulted Coburn for "not approaching the enemy with sufficient caution." *Ibid.*, Pt. 2, p. 112.

7. *Ibid.*, Pt. 1, p. 87.

concerning the role in his discomfiture of his own cavalry and their commander. The reader will recall that Jordan, then a major, was defeated and captured by Morgan at Tompkinsville, Kentucky, in July, 1862. Exchanged in December, he returned to the regiment and became its commanding officer in January, 1863. On the second day of the march, when Coburn learned of the threat developing to his left by Forrest's advance, he ordered his infantry to retreat and directed Jordan "to bring two companies of his cavalry to support the regiments [of infantry] as they retired." Jordan "went off," Coburn reported. "I saw him no more. I saw . . . [the cavalry] no more, although I sent for them." Later in his report, he makes the explicit charge that the cavalry and the Ohio battery left the field "without orders, and against orders . . . at the very moment when they should have put forth their greatest exertions to repel the enemy rushing upon us" and thereby left the infantry with no alternatives other than "a disgraceful and fatal flight, or [to] fight till further resistance was vain."[8]

Needless to say, Colonel Jordan's report tells a tale quite different from Coburn's. He was ordered by Coburn, Colonel Jordan wrote, "to call in . . . [his] cavalry and form it in such position as to cover . . . [Coburn's] retreat." This, Jordan said, he proceeded to do, but his efforts came to naught, because the infantry retreated "in a directly opposite direction from the point . . . he was holding to cover its retreat." Colonel Jordan's account appears to be the more reliable of the two.[9] There was in any event no palliation of the fact that Coburn, who should have been alerted by the fight of the first day to the possibility of serious trouble ahead, failed to use his cavalry, or even a part of it, to scout well ahead of his infantry to try to learn the composition and size of the enemy force facing him. He blundered ahead blindly on the morning of the second day, and Forrest, with his alertness and combative flair, saw to it that he paid the penalty for his rashness. The Union loss that day was 48 killed, 247 wounded, and 1,151 taken prisoner.[10]

8. *Ibid.*, 88, 89, 90.
9. *Ibid.*, 81–82; see also Rowell, *Yankee Cavalrymen*, 114–21. Captain Charles C. Aleshire, commanding the 18th Ohio Battery, reported that "the conduct of the cavalry . . . during the whole time, and particularly in the retreat, was unexceptionable. Had it not been for their repeated efforts to drive back the enemy, neither my battery, nor the wagon train could possibly have been saved." *Official Records*, Vol. XXIII, Pt. 1, p. 115.
10. *Ibid.*, 75. The cavalry's share of these casualties was 5 killed, 16 wounded, and

A week later, it was the Federals' turn. In mid-January, on the strength of rumors, later proved to be unfounded, that James Longstreet's corps was being transferred from the East to reinforce Bragg, General Horatio G. Wright collected in his Department of the Ohio the 14,000-man reinforcement for Rosecrans mentioned previously, and sent them off under Gordon Granger's command to Nashville.[11] On March 6, Granger, then at Franklin, was asked by Garfield how soon he could be ready to attack Van Dorn and was then admonished by Rosecrans himself, "Now lay your plans well, and clean those fellows out thoroughly, if possible."[12] Since neither Granger nor Van Dorn reported formally on their operations of the next few days, the exact course of events is somewhat unclear, although it can be deduced from a number of dispatches and subsidiary reports. Under heavy pressure from 2,500 of Granger's infantry and General Green Clay Smith's Fourth Cavalry Brigade (2nd Michigan, 9th Pennsylvania, 4th, 6th, and 7th Kentucky), supported from March 9 on by an advance on their left of Philip Sheridan's division of infantry and of "the brave Colonel Minty," as Rosecrans called him, with the 4th Michigan, 7th Pennsylvania, 3rd Ohio, 4th Indiana, and 4th United States, Van Dorn evacuated Spring Hill and retreated first across Rutherford Creek, and, when Minty's men succeeded in crossing the creek, to the south bank of the unfordable Duck River.[13] The operation, however, had no lasting effect.

---

17 missing. Confederate losses were 56 killed, 289 wounded, and 12 missing. *Ibid.*, 119. For other accounts of the fight, see Henry, *"First with the Most" Forrest*, 129–31, and Wyeth, *That Devil Forrest*, 135–44.

    11. Lamers, *The Edge of Glory*, 250.

    12. *Official Records*, Vol. XXIII, Pt. 2, pp. 112–13. For the ensuing operations, see *Ibid.*, 113, 114, 119, 120, 129, 130, 132–33, 136, 677, 678, 681, 684, 685, 687, and Pt. 1, pp. 127, 130–31, 132–33, 134; Rowell, *Yankee Cavalrymen*, 122–24; Wyeth, *That Devil Forrest*, 145–46; Henry, *"First with the Most" Forrest*, 131–32.

    13. On March 1, at Bradyville, Tennessee, the 3rd and 4th Ohio, led by Stanley, "charged the enemy in front and flank, routing him, and sending his horses flying in all directions." The enemy was mainly the 2nd Kentucky, C.S.A. (Morgan's old regiment). The Ohioans charged "with sabers and pistols" and took prisoner 83 of the Kentuckians. *Official Records*, Vol. XXIII, Pt. 1, pp. 65–69. Four days later Minty fought "about 600 rebel cavalry" at Unionville, Tennessee. Minty attacked, with the 7th Pennsylvania in the lead, and captured 51 of the enemy, "13 of whom were severely wounded, having received saber cuts about their heads." *Ibid.*, 127–28, 129–30. In a fight on March 9 against Armstrong's brigade and Starnes's regiment, the 7th Pennsylvania charged once again and captured 109 of "the flying, scattered" enemy, "of which 58 were wounded by saber cuts. . . . Not a shot was fired by the 7th in this affray, the saber only being used." Sipes, *The Seventh Pennsylvania*, 54–55. Such reports contradict the statements of for-

Unable to get across Duck River, the Federals turned back and were followed by Forrest with his own division and Frank C. Armstrong's brigade, and on March 15 the Confederate cavalry, not at all "cleaned out," was back in its old quarters at Spring Hill.

Following the return to Spring Hill, Forrest performed outpost duty for the most part. On March 25, however, he led the two brigades of his division on an expedition against the Union garrisons at Brentwood and at the stockade guarding the Nashville & Franklin Railroad bridge over the Harpeth River. He captured both garrisons—a total of 751 officers and men of two infantry regiments, one from Wisconsin, the other from Michigan—together with their equipment, trains, and supplies. It does not appear that either garrison, summoned to surrender subject to Forrest's usual threat of no quarter if they did not do so, put up a very strenuous resistance. Alerted to Forrest's presence in the area, Granger sent out Green Clay Smith with 600 or 700 men of his brigade to deal with the raiders. Forrest had already started back to his base when Smith attacked and routed the 4th Mississippi and 10th Tennessee, C.S.A., in Forrest's rear, the escort for the wagons he had captured. Smith recaptured the wagons, but he was then attacked himself on both flanks by the rest of Forrest's men and forced to retreat. Forrest carried off his prisoners (whose guns armed or rearmed those of his men who were unarmed or had inferior weapons) and all the Federals' wagons that Smith had not retaken.[14]

On April 10, David Stanley, Rosecrans' chief of cavalry, arrived at Franklin to take personal command of the Federal cavalry, which was now reorganized into a First Division, commanded by General Robert B. Mitchell, and a Second Division, commanded by Russian-born General John Basil Turchin (originally Ivan Vasilevich Turchininoff), one of the strangest of the numerous foreign-born officers in the Union army.[15] The four brigade commanders, Colonels Archibald P. Campbell

---

eign observers, such as the one by Captain Edward Hewett of the British army that the Union cavalry were "merely mounted infantry. They are not taught to use the sword at all, and indeed several regiments can muster but few swords anyway." Quoted in Jay Luvaas, *The Military Legacy of the Civil War* (Chicago, 1959), 28.

14. For Forrest's Brentwood operation, see *Official Records*, Vol. XXIII, Pt. 1, pp. 176–94; Wyeth, *That Devil Forrest*, 146–56; Rowell, *Yankee Cavalrymen*, 125–28; Henry, *"First with the Most" Forrest*, 132–36. General Smith absurdly overestimated Forrest's numbers (5,000) and casualties (400–500). *Official Records*, Vol. XXIII, Pt. 1, pp. 180–81.

15. For Turchin's career, see John Beatty, *Memoirs of a Volunteer, 1861–1863*, ed.

and Edward M. McCook in the First Division and R. H. G. Minty and Eli Long in the Second, were to make their mark as cavalry commanders of outstanding merit in the remaining years of the Civil War.[16] The two divisions were made up of twenty-two regiments of cavalry, an unattached regiment of Indiana mounted infantry, and three batteries of artillery.

David Stanley faced a difficult situation. He had little respect for Rosecrans' ability to use his cavalry effectively; he was to write in his reminiscences that Rosecrans (and for good measure, he added Sherman and Grant) never "understood the true uses of cavalry. Each of these commanders was given to sending cavalry upon aimless raids, invariably resulting in having their cavalry used up and accomplishing nothing." Then, of his twenty-two regiments, ten, raised in Kentucky and Tennessee, were novices. In a dispatch to Rosecrans he credited Van Dorn with 12,000 cavalry (about twice Van Dorn's actual strength) and then wrote: "With one of our old divisions we could whip them out of their boots. I do not know whether it would be judicious to attack with this green force, but if you think 'the game is worth the candle' we will slap away at them. . . . Van Dorn is in a strong position, and must be approached with judgment and in force." And lastly, despite the fact that (as Colonel Thomas Swords, in charge of horse procurement in Louisville, reported to General Meigs on April 29) 14,976 horses had been supplied to the Army of the Cumberland "since November," Stanley reported that 2,000 of his men—nearly 25 percent of his command—were dismounted. He was thereupon ordered to take his dismounted men to Louisville and "make arrangements" to have them mounted "as speedily as possible."[17]

Harvey S. Ford (New York, 1946), 120*n*. "General Turchin, as a cavalry officer, was not a success. He was personally brave, and had a good deal of dash in his mental makeup, but was physically out of place on horseback, the circumference of his body being equal to his height. His failure as a commander of cavalry was due, more than anything else, to the fact that he marched with too long a tail, his staff, orderlies and escort numbering nearly four hundred." Vale, *Minty and the Cavalry*, 196. Another member of Turchin's division commented that his "training in the strict military schools of Russia rather disqualified him for American volunteer service, where soldiers are always men, never willingly becoming machines or menials." Sipes, *The Seventh Pennsylvania*, 78. When Turchin was replaced by George Crook, a Regular, a member of Stanley's staff wrote: "Turchin was relieved this morning. Good!" *Official Records*, Vol. XXIII, Pt. 2, pp. 567–68.

16. Not included in Stanley's command was the Wilder brigade of mounted infantry.

17. Stanley, *Personal Memoirs*, 132; *Official Records*, Vol. XXIII, Pt. 2, pp. 226, 246, 253.

It is a truism that there was never a moment in the life of the Union cavalry, in the East or the West, when it was not beset by these or similar problems. Part of the burden of commanding officers at every level of authority was to make the best use they could of their advantages— and they had some of those, too—at the same time that they overcame as best they could their disadvantages. Stanley and his subordinates, his commanders of divisions, brigades, and regiments, were about to show how well they had learned this eternal constant of warfare, for Rosecrans' proudest achievement, the Tullahoma Campaign, was about to get under way.

As has been mentioned, the Confederate army under Bragg, numbering at the end of June approximately 33,000 infantrymen and gunners and 14,000 cavalry, had spent the six months following Stones River deployed in a hundred-mile arc along Duck River.[18] Its two flanks extended and protected by cavalry, the army's right-hand corps, under General William J. Hardee, lay at Wartrace, and the left-hand corps, commanded by General Leonidas Polk, at Shelbyville. Both corps' positions were protected by wide belts of well-sited and well-constructed field fortifications. Rosecrans had at this time an effective force under his immediate command of 44,000 infantry and artillery and 7,000 cavalry, backed by Gordon Granger's "Reserve Corps" of 12,575 of all arms.[19]

After some preliminary moves in early June and following another firm hint from Halleck that it was high time for him to get started, Rosecrans swung into action on the twenty-fourth. The ensuing campaign, concluded on July 3, is generally, and justly, thought to be a strategic masterpiece.[20] Apart from the fights of the Union cavalry with their Confederate opposite numbers, mainly in the early stages of the operation, the campaign was nearly bloodless.[21] At little cost, Rosecrans maneuvered Bragg out of a naturally strong defensive position, "covered by the defiles of Duck River—a deep, narrow stream, with

18. *Battles and Leaders*, III, 635. Rosecrans' remarkably accurate estimate of Bragg's numbers credited him with "about" 30,000 infantry and artillery and "probably" 8,000 effective cavalry. *Official Records*, Vol. XXIII, Pt. 1, p. 404.

19. *Battles and Leaders*, III, 636.

20. President Lincoln praised it as "the most splendid piece of strategy I know of." For his, Halleck's, Stanley's, and Henry Villard's equally high praise, see Lamers, *The Edge of Glory*, 290.

21. Total Union casualties were 84 killed, 473 wounded, and 13 captured or missing. *Battles and Leaders*, III, 637.

but few fords or bridges— . . . [and] a range of high, rough, rocky hills," which the Confederates had had six months to strengthen with extensive field fortifications.[22] Tullahoma, Bragg's headquarters, located to the south of the center of the Confederate defense line, was turned into "a large entrenched camp, with formidable breastworks . . . screened by an abatis of felled trees, 600 yards wide," behind a wide and dense "black jack thicket."[23]

A downpour that was to last for seventeen days began on June 24 and turned the entire region over which the armies were to operate into a "quagmire," making any movement so difficult that General Thomas L. Crittenden's XXI Army Corps, on the left wing of Rosecrans' advance, needed three days to negotiate a distance of seventeen miles. The rain and mud prevented the accomplishment of Rosecrans' ultimate purpose, to force Bragg to leave his fortified lines and fight a defensive battle in the open with the odds greatly in the Federals' favor.[24] Bragg did, however, have to vacate his defense lines and retreat, first from the Shelbyville-Wartrace line to Tullahoma, then from Tullahoma across the Tennessee River to Chattanooga, where he had his back against the Georgia border.[25] Middle Tennessee belonged thenceforth to the Union.

On the evening of June 23, when Rosecrans issued his orders for the first day's operations, Stanley and the cavalry were already at Triune, fifteen miles due west of Murfreesboro. For reasons Rosecrans has not explained, he gave Gordon Granger, also at Triune with his Reserve Corps, what appears to have been supervisory authority over Stanley and the cavalry. Rosecrans may have become disenchanted with Stanley's performance as an adequately aggressive cavalry com-

22. *Official Records*, Vol. XXIII, Pt. 1, p. 404. "The Duck River describes an irregular arc, flowing from Manchester by Tullahoma . . . [and] Shelbyville . . . and is distinguished for its deep bed and rocky sides. . . . it runs nearly the whole distance through a rocky gorge from twenty to fifty feet deep, and from two hundred to three hundred yards wide." Vale, *Minty and the Cavalry*, 170.

23. Lamers, *The Edge of Glory*, 276.

24. *Battles and Leaders*, III, 636. "Horses and mules, floundering in the mud, were unhitched, and artillery and ammunition wagons dragged through deep morasses by the infantry. In some places mules perished in the mud, unable to extricate themselves." *Ibid.*, 637. Crittenden was told by Rosecrans "to lighten up . . . [his] trains . . . [and] throw out everything but rations, forage and ammunition." *Official Records*, Vol. XXIII, Pt. 2, p. 470.

25. For Rosecrans' report of the campaign, see *Official Records*, Vol. XXIII, Pt. 1, pp. 403–409.

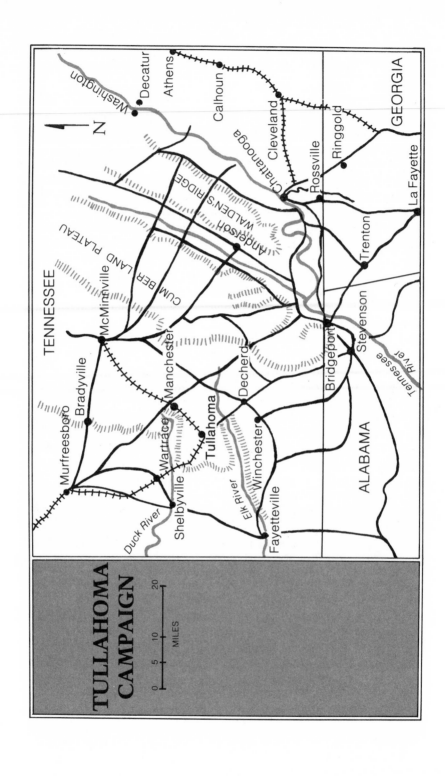

TULLAHOMA
CAMPAIGN

MILES

0   5   10   20

mander, a feeling he was to express in no uncertain terms to Stanley himself a few weeks later, or he may have decided that it would be convenient to have the commander of the infantry corps with which the cavalry was to work, control the operations of all three arms. In any event, Granger had experience as a cavalryman; the reader will recall that he preceded Sheridan as colonel of the 2nd Michigan. It is of course possible that nothing more than the relative seniority of the two officers was responsible for the arrangement.

Rosecrans' plans took into account not only the location of Bragg's forces, and the defenses, both natural and man-made, behind which they sheltered, but also of the topography and the nature of the road network behind them. Accordingly, the campaign was to begin with a feint in sufficient strength to be interpreted by the enemy as the principal attack, directly south from Triune toward General Polk's lines at Shelbyville, carried out by Mitchell's cavalry division and Granger's corps. This diversionary attack was to set the stage for Alexander McD. McCook's (not to be confused with Edward M. McCook, the cavalry brigade commander) and George Thomas' corps, and Crittenden's corps well out to their left, to march southeast along the Murfreesboro-Manchester and Murfreesboro-Shelbyville pikes. Then, having gotten behind both Hardee and Polk and forced them to vacate their fortified positions, they would compel Bragg to fight the Army of the Cumberland in the open to avoid being cut off from his base at Chattanooga.[26]

Pursuant to Rosecrans' overall plan and Granger's orders, General Mitchell's cavalry left its camps on June 23, a day in advance of the rest of the army. With the 9th Pennsylvania of the First (Campbell's) Brigade leading the way, the division marched south of the Triune-Shelbyville road through Eagleville. A short distance below that settlement, the Pennsylvanians, later relieved by the 2nd Michigan, had a "brisk skirmish" with enemy cavalry, whom they drove southward eight miles, taking a few prisoners, until they bumped up against Confederate infantry and artillery manning an outpost of the Shelbyville defenses. After fighting off a Confederate flank attack, its men exhausted ("the weather being exceedingly hot and the ground advanced over being covered with thick undergrowth exceedingly difficult of penetration"), the brigade retraced its steps and went into

26. After marching south on the Shelbyville Road, McCook was to turn left, seize and hold Liberty Gap, and then support Thomas' right flank. *Ibid.*, 405.

bivouac a short distance north of the village of Rover.[27] At 1 A.M. that night, the rains that were to turn the entire operation into a nightmare began to fall.

There seemed to be a failure in advance planning of the cavalry phase of the campaign, or at least in the logistical support for it, for General Mitchell reported on the evening of the twenty-fourth that the horses of his division had had "nothing to eat, except what the men brought on them, since yesterday morning. . . . There is nothing in the country for the horses to eat. Everything is cleared out."[28]

At daybreak on June 24 the cavalry advance resumed. It was now the turn of the Second (McCook's) Brigade to lead. Orders were to march by way of Versailles to Middleton, in the direction of the Nashville & Chattanooga Railroad.[29] Having learned of Mitchell's fights of the twenty-third—which were evidently reported as more serious than they had actually been—Stanley detached Minty's brigade from Turchin's division and led it to reinforce Mitchell, who in the meantime had driven a force of Georgia and Alabama cavalry out of Middleton.[30] Mitchell's and Minty's commands then remained in a drenched bivouac, in a state of acute discomfort, until the morning of the twenty-seventh. The pause gave Colonel Jordan of the 9th Pennsylvania the opportunity to write his wife: "It has rained steadily for four days & we have not had a tent to cover us. Wet to the skin all the time, we lie down in the water & sleep comfortably, but two or three are daily sent to the rear sick." The historian of the Minty brigade noted that "it rained every day and every night . . . in successive, constantly recurring tremendous showers, at from ten minutes to three hours intervals. Thus . . . the men were compelled to 'slop around' in wet clothing, to wade and fight through the mud by day and sink to sleep in the mud at night."[31] Cavalry on the march in this constant downpour was described by another member of Minty's brigade.

27. *Ibid.*, 543, 547; Rowell, *Yankee Cavalrymen*, 134–35. Colonel Jordan of the 9th Pennsylvania wrote his wife just before the campaign began that "with all . . . [the] hard duty the men have remained healthy. Indeed they have not time to get sick." Letter of June 21, 1863, in David L. Bacon (comp.), *Wartime Letters of Gen. Thomas J. Jordan to His Wife Jane, 1861–1865* (Privately printed, 1978), hereinafter cited as *Jordan Letters*.

28. *Official Records*, Vol. XXIII, Pt. 1, p. 532.

29. *Ibid.*, 548.

30. Not mentioned in any of the reports are the orders to the cavalry on June 24 to build a long chain of campfires behind their bivouacs to make the Confederates believe that a large body of infantry was behind the cavalry. Lamers, *The Edge of Glory*, 278.

31. Letter of June 26, 1863, in *Jordan Letters*; Vale, *Minty and the Cavalry*, 188.

A photograph of . . . the . . . Union cavalry . . . splashing the mud all over themselves and everybody near them, with the rain coming down on their heads in a torrent, would certainly have made an excellent picture and exhibition of real active service in the field in time of war. Each man with his head stuck through the center of his poncho, part hanging in front and part behind, the brim of his hat turned so as to shed the pouring rain, and bending low so as to cover as much of the body as possible with the poncho. In this condition we would come into camp, or rather make a stop somewhere on the road, rain still pouring down and nothing but water overhead and mud underfoot. Hence no fire could be built. . . . the horses were not unsaddled, partly to keep the saddles out of the mud, but also for the sake of keeping the horses' backs warm. . . . The men's efforts to get a little sleep on such nights would furnish another fine model for the artist.[32]

The sad fate of the single brigade (Eli Long's) remaining under General Turchin's control after Stanley took away Minty's brigade may have been part of the reason for Stanley's poor opinion of Rosecrans' ability to make effective use of his cavalry. Turchin's assignment in the first four days of the campaign was to cover the outer (left) flank of Crittenden's corps. On June 28, he was ordered to Manchester and, beginning with the afternoon of that day, received a series of orders to send sometimes one, sometimes two, battalions to do picket duty in front of the XIV and XXI Corps. "In this manner," poor Turchin reported, "the whole brigade was scattered by battalions, under command of majors and lieutenant-colonels, on the front of two army corps, the regimental commanders and the brigade commander remaining in camp with twelve companies of different regiments, and at the head was the division commander himself," with, he might have added, no division to command. The approximately five hundred men remaining with Turchin eventually met their own First Brigade and Mitchell's division at Elk River, on the road to Decherd, on July 2, the next to last day of the campaign.[33]

The feint of Generals Mitchell and Granger toward Shelbyville accomplished its purpose. Not only did it cause Bragg to think that General Polk's corps would have to bear the brunt of the Federal attack, but it also caused Wheeler to draw in toward Shelbyville from his position on the right flank of the army. He left only one regiment, the 1st Ken-

32. James Larson, *Sergeant Larson, 4th Cavalry*, ed. A. L. Blum (San Antonio, 1935), 170–71. The writer had been a sergeant in the 4th United States, of Minty's brigade.

33. *Official Records*, Vol. XXIII, Pt. 1, pp. 552–56.

tucky, C.S.A., to guard Hoover's Gap ("a four-mile-long pass between eleven-hundred-foot ridges . . . [and] so narrow that two wagons could hardly pass side by side"), through which passed the road to Manchester and the rear of Bragg's army. Hoover's Gap was therefore the geographic key to the success of Rosecrans' operation. Furthermore, Wheeler left behind only a single brigade to cover the large area from the southern foot of Hoover's Gap to that of Liberty Gap, five or six miles to the south by road.[34]

On the morning of June 24, Wilder's mounted infantry brigade rushed Hoover's Gap and drove the garrison out of the gap itself and beyond its southern foot for a distance of two miles. Early in the afternoon, news that the Federals had gained possession of the gap reached the two brigades of Confederate infantry—William C. Bate's and Bushrod Johnson's of Hardee's corps—in camp four miles away. An attack to recapture the gap was quickly organized. Colonel Wilder received word from his pickets of the approach of the Confederate infantry and deployed the 72nd Indiana, the 123rd Illinois, and Lilly's battery just below the southern entrance to the gap to meet the attack, posting his other two regiments in reserve. Horses were sent to the rear, and the men, their Spencer rifles loaded, waited for the approach of the enemy. Major James A. Connolly, 123rd Illinois Mounted Infantry, described the ensuing action.

The enemy opened on us a terrific fire of shot and shell, from five different points, and their masses of infantry, with flags flying, moved out of the woods . . . in splendid style. . . . Our regiment lay on the hill side in mud and water, the rain pouring down in torrents. . . . Presently the enemy got near enough to us to make a charge on our battery, and on they came; the men are on their feet in an instant and a terrible fire from the "Spencers" causes the advance regiment to reel and its colors to fall to the ground, but in an instant their colors are up again and on they come, thinking to reach the battery before our guns can be reloaded, but they . . . didn't know we had the "Spencers," and their charging yell was answered by another terrible volley, and another and another without cessation, until the poor regiment was literally cut to pieces, and but few men of that 20th Tennessee that attempted the charge will ever charge again.[35]

34. Connelly, *Autumn of Glory*, 126, 118. There is a conflict in the records as to whether the 1st or the 3rd Kentucky garrisoned Hoover's Gap. Liberty Gap was captured on the evening of the twenty-fourth by August Willich's brigade of Richard W. Johnson's division, in what Rosecrans described as a "very gallant and creditable" operation. *Official Records*, Vol. XXIII, Pt. 1, p. 406.

35. J. A. Connolly, *Three Years in the Army of the Cumberland* (Bloomington, 1959), 91–92.

Four regiments of Bate's brigade charged the 17th Indiana, one of the regiments Wilder had posted in reserve, on a hillside to the right of the 123rd Illinois. These regiments met the same deadly reception as did the 20th Tennessee Infantry; they had to face head on a stream of bullets from the Spencers of the Indiana regiment and were also raked from one flank by Captain Lilly's rifled Rodmans, firing double charges of canister, and from the other by the volleys of the 98th Illinois, the second of Wilder's regiments in reserve.[36] Wilder's casualties in this action were 13 killed and 47 wounded, one mortally; General Bate's, 19 killed and 126 wounded—over 22 percent of the 650 officers and men he led into action.[37]

The Wilder brigade was held in reserve behind the infantry the next day; on the twenty-sixth they rode along the flank of the XIV Corps infantry toward Manchester, which they entered shortly after daylight the next day "before the few rebels there knew of . . . [their] approach."[38] They were then sent to break the railroad to Chattanooga behind Bragg. They were "impeded by the streams flooded beyond all precedent" by the incessant rains. The men were half starved, and the horses were "almost entirely without forage"; nevertheless, they made their way to the railroad at Decherd, "an important rail and supply center" twenty miles behind the Confederate army then at Tullahoma, and destroyed the depot buildings, "well filled with commissary stores," and about three hundred yards of track.[39] Wilder then led the brigade by devious paths "through the mountains, without guides . . . over a very rocky and steep road" back to Manchester, which they reached

36. *Official Records*, Vol. XXIII, Pt. 1, pp. 457–59; Rowell, *Yankee Artillerymen*, 76–82; McGee, *History of the 72nd Indiana*, 130.

37. *Official Records*, Vol. XXIII, Pt. 1, pp. 459, 613–14. After the action ended, General John J. Reynolds, Wilder's division commander, sent his adjutant with orders for the brigade to retire to the north of the gap. Although threatened with arrest, Wilder refused, remaining where he was until he was relieved by Reynolds' infantry. Rowell, *Yankee Artillerymen*, 82.

38. *Official Records*, Vol. XXIII, Pt. 1, p. 459.

39. *Ibid.*, 460–61; Connelly, *Autumn of Glory*, 130. General John Beatty, a brigade commander in the XIV Corps, wrote that the damage caused by Wilder at Decherd delayed the movement of trains by a mere two hours. Beatty, *Memoirs of a Volunteer*, 224. On the other hand, a participant wrote: "In actual damage done to the enemy [the] expedition [to Decherd] was a failure, but in unifying the brigade and giving each man confidence in himself and his officers it was a grand success. The rebels had hitherto had it all their own way in raiding railroads; this expedition demonstrated that we were just as competent in raiding rebel railroads as the rebels were to raid Union railroads." McGee, *History of the 72nd Indiana*, 135.

just ahead of Forrest, who attempted to intercept them with nine regiments of cavalry and a section of artillery.[40]

The whereabouts of Forrest had been a cause of concern for the Union cavalry command from the beginning of the campaign.[41] The death of Van Dorn on May 7 had produced a command vacancy; Bragg had to appoint someone to command the cavalry on his left wing. Forrest's pursuit and capture of Streight and his raiders had clearly caused his stock to rise in Bragg's estimation, for on May 13 he was received by Bragg with "unwonted warmth and cordiality," given command of what had been Van Dorn's corps, and told that he would be recommended for promotion to major general. After a reorganization necessitated by the return of William H. Jackson's small division to Mississippi, Forrest's new command consisted of the divisions of Frank C. Armstrong and James W. Starnes. In a disgraceful brawl with a disgruntled lieutenant of artillery of his command (an event treated in a gingerly manner by Forrest's admiring biographers), Forrest was gravely wounded by a pistol shot; he was still bedridden eleven days later when he received word of the advance of the Federal cavalry toward Shelbyville. Ignoring his still unhealed wound, Forrest started off at once toward Shelbyville with his entire command. Using roads north of Duck River, it was clearly his intention to strike in flank the Federal forces working their way toward General Polk's lines. But by the afternoon of June 27, two days later, when he approached his destination, Polk had already evacuated the Shelbyville defenses. Wheeler and his cavalry, still north of Duck River, were being pressed back toward the Skull Camp Bridge across the stream. Notified of Forrest's approach, Wheeler hoped to hold the roads to the bridge until Forrest arrived, so that they could unite their forces, cross the river, and act as rear guard for Polk's infantry and trains as they retreated to Tullahoma. The Union cavalry, however, proved to be more than Wheeler could handle that day; he was driven into and across the stream. Judging

40. Major Connolly noted in his diary that between June 24 and July 4, the brigade "used up" 500 horses; there had been "no feed except grass." Connolly, *Army of the Cumberland*, 99.

41. Stanley expressed his apprehension in a June 26 dispatch to Rosecrans: "no news from Forrest's force yet." At 11 P.M. the same day, Granger wrote Rosecrans: "We are keeping a portion of the cavalry midway between . . . [Christiana] and Murfreesboro, watching the movements of Forrest, whose whereabouts I am unable to ascertain. He will yet turn up at some unexpected place." *Official Records*, Vol. XXIII, Pt. 2, pp. 459–60, 461.

from the sound of the gunfire that the Federal cavalry had blocked access to the bridge, Forrest turned back downstream and eventually found a place to cross, four miles below the town.[42]

On June 30, Bragg decided to give up Tullahoma and retreat across Elk River and the Tennessee to Chattanooga. Until Rosecrans called off the pursuit of the retreating Confederates, Forrest had the job of protecting the flanks and rear of Bragg's infantry and trains as they made their way southward across the Cumberland Plateau. On July 6, the Confederate army, horse and foot, was across the Tennessee River. It spent the next two months licking its wounds. During this period of recuperation, Forrest and his cavalry were posted around Kingston, on the Tennessee River, about seventy miles northeast of Chattanooga.[43]

As has been mentioned, Wheeler moved with the bulk of his cavalry to the Shelbyville area when the Federal advance began, and left less than sufficient forces behind to guard the right wing of his army. In the absence of any formal report by Wheeler (the *Official Records* contain only a small number of his dispatches for the period July 1–4 and none for the last ten days of June) or by his principal subordinates, his operations north of Shelbyville until June 27 cannot be reconstructed with complete certainty.[44] It may be taken for granted that he endeavored to block the advance of Stanley's cavalry and Granger's infantry; it is known in any case that for a time he held Guy's Gap, in the range of hills north of Shelbyville, through which passed the Murfreesboro-Shelbyville turnpike. There was a change on the twenty-seventh, however, in what he had to do. That morning, General Polk began evacuating the Shelbyville defenses, pursuant to orders he had received from Bragg late on the night of the twenty-sixth. Having been

42. Henry, *"First with the Most" Forrest*, 160, 164–66.

43. Throughout the campaign the 15th Pennsylvania, which because of its past (see Appendix) was not brigaded with Stanley's cavalry, "was used for special scouting and courier duty. . . . the wings of the army were frequently so far separated that the courier line was forty or fifty miles in length. Five or six men would be stationed at posts at intervals of six or eight miles, one always being ready, night and day, to mount and receive the dispatch . . . and carry it at a gallop or trot, as might be indicated on the envelope, to the next post. . . . the couriers had many exciting and dangerous rides across mountains, through forests and country infested with rebel guerrillas, when the nights were so dark they could not see the road and had to depend upon their horses to follow it. A courier's imagination was apt to be very vivid when he was riding by himself on a dark night . . . and expecting every minute that the enemy would pounce upon him." Kirk, *History of the Fifteenth Pennsylvania*, 204.

44. His dispatches (or presumably those that survived) for those four days are in *Official Records*, Vol. XXIII, Pt. 1, pp. 615–17.

driven out of Guy's Gap by Stanley's cavalry, Wheeler now had to act as rear guard for Polk's corps as it began its slow march under a continuing downpour and through the bottomless mud to Tullahoma, twelve miles distant.

On this occasion, rear guard duty turned out to be exceptionally hazardous. Stanley had received orders from Rosecrans that morning to "dislodge" the enemy from Guy's Gap. After learning from his scouts that the gap was held by cavalry alone, Stanley obtained Granger's permission to make "a direct attack" on the position.[45] The attack was made by the 4th United States and the 1st Tennessee (called sometimes the 1st Middle Tennessee) of Minty's brigade. It forced the Confederates to evacuate the gap and retreat in some haste toward Shelbyville. Three or four miles north of the town, sheltered by the field fortifications vacated that morning by Polk's infantry, Wheeler's cavalrymen—William T. Martin's division and a part of John A. Wharton's—attempted to make a stand. Minty, who earned in full measure this day the high praise he was to receive in Rosecrans' report on the campaign, moved forward with three regiments of his brigade. A battalion of the 7th Pennsylvania dismounted as skirmishers was in the lead, and the 4th Michigan was swung well to the right and the "western battalion" of the 3rd Indiana to the left, to break through the entrenchments and flank the enemy; meanwhile the other two battalions of the 7th Pennsylvania, led by Lieutenant Heber S. Thompson, in column of fours, mounted, charged straight ahead, and right behind them was the regiment of Regulars.[46] The charge and the threat to their flanks caused the enemy to break and run, with the loss of 300 men taken prisoner.

When the charging troopers, joined now by the flanking detachments, came within a quarter mile of Shelbyville, they saw before them four pieces of artillery "well posted in the town." Minty then demonstrated how far the officers of the Union cavalry had come in

45. *Ibid.*, 539. Except where noted otherwise, the account of Minty's operations on June 27 is based on his own and on Stanley's reports in *Ibid.*, 556–58, 539–40. See also the reports of regimental commanders in *Ibid.*, 559–65, and Vale, *Minty and the Cavalry*, 174–80 (the last not entirely reliable). A member of Minty's staff wrote that Mitchell's division, originally in the advance, gained only a half mile in two hours, causing Minty to rage "like a chained lion." Stanley, too, was angered, and ordered Minty to take the advance. Vale, *Minty and the Cavalry*, 175.

46. Six companies of the 3rd Indiana served in the East throughout the war, and four companies in the West. See Starr, *Union Cavalry*, I, 239.

learning the tricks of the cavalryman's trade. He sent for Captain Charles C. Aleshire's 18th Ohio Battery and had the captain place two of his guns hub to hub on the turnpike and the other two on either side of the road. He then lined up 150 men of two battalions of the 7th Pennsylvania in column of fours on the road, with Captain Charles C. Davis at their head, ready to charge, and ordered Captain Aleshire to fire his guns in a salvo. "At the moment . . . [the guns] were fired, the Seventh Pennsylvania . . . passed between the guns, and with a yell rushed upon the enemy."[47] Thought too obvious, perhaps, to require mention in the report of Colonel William B. Sipes, 7th Pennsylvania, was the fact that his men were momentarily hidden in the dense cloud of powder smoke produced by the discharge of the four guns. This reduced the duration of their exposure to the fire of the enemy battery. The Confederate gunners had time to fire their pieces only once, killing one trooper and two horses, before the charging Pennsylvanians, their sabers swinging, were upon them.[48] Behind Captain Davis and his men rode the regiment of Regulars and Lieutenant Colonel Robert Galbraith's 1st Tennessee, but the "True Glory" of this dramatic feat of arms belonged to the Pennsylvanians.

General Stanley, who rode with Minty but did not interfere with the latter's handling of his command, witnessed Captain Davis' charge. He would write, many years after the war: "On the part of the Union soldiers there can scarcely be instanced a finer display of gallantry than the charge made by the 7th Pennsylvania Cavalry, backed by the 4th U.S. I have read of nothing more admirable. To face a battery ready loaded and waiting, supported on either side by riflemen, to ride at the muzzles of the guns, and through them, is no baby's play, and this was done by a regiment of Pennsylvania blacksmiths. . . . Their small loss in this charge only illustrates how superior nerve unnerves an enemy." General Mitchell, in a generous tribute to an officer and troops who did not belong to his division, wrote in his report: "I cannot refrain from expressing . . . my admiration of the conduct of Colonel Minty and his brigade. Though not under my command, they came under my imme-

47. The figure of 150 men in the charge appears in Colonel Sipes's report, in *Official Records*, Vol. XXIII, Pt. 1, p. 565. A second account gives the number as 274. Vale, *Minty and the Cavalry*, 179.

48. Colonel Sipes reported that the enemy gunners fired three times. If (as all accounts agree) the charge was over a distance of a quarter mile, it is most unlikely that the gunners would have had the time to fire more than once.

diate observation. Before the gallantry and skill of this commander and the dashing bravery and skill of his troops, all efforts of the rebels to withstand his advance were ineffectual."[49]

The reader will not fail to note that on this occasion the men of a Union cavalry regiment—the fact that it was an eastern regiment may or may not be of significance—performed with spectacular bravery and skill one of the principal functions of the cavalry of tradition, a thundering charge with the saber, the "arme blanche" of cavalry orthodoxy. And they did this after a battalion of their own regiment had demonstrated comparable skill as dismounted skirmishers, performing one of the important functions of mounted infantry.

Colonel Sipes felt obliged to give a properly restrained account in his formal report of the charge of his regiment at Shelbyville (in which he participated), but many years after the war, when he wrote its history, he quoted at length from an 1898 article by John A. Wyeth, a biographer of Forrest's who had himself been ridden down in the charge. Wyeth described it as "the most brilliant cavalry manoeuver" he had ever seen. "On either side of the highway," he wrote, "in columns of fours, they advanced at a steady gallop. . . . The Union troopers, with sabers high in the air, made no sound whatever, beyond the rumbling tattoo which their horses' hoofs played upon the ground. . . . No more gallant work was ever done by any troops than was done this day by the Seventh Pennsylvania."[50]

The charge carried the brigade into the streets of the town. The four enemy guns were captured after the gunners and supporting troops, defending themselves with clubbed muskets, had been driven off or taken prisoner. Colonel Sipes wrote that "many prisoners were taken; how many is not known, because no one had time to count them, but the number certainly ran into the hundreds."[51] Those who were able to escape—mainly Wheeler's cavalrymen—made their way across Skull Camp Bridge to the south bank of Duck River.[52]

49. Stanley, *Personal Memoirs*, 147–49; *Official Records*, Vol. XXIII, Pt. 1, p. 545.
50. Sipes, *The Seventh Pennsylvania*, 64–65. A minor point to illustrate the difficulty of reconstructing the past: Wyeth has the Pennsylvanians making "no sound whatever" in their charge. Vale has the men "yelling like demons." Vale, *Minty and the Cavalry*, 179. Both Wyeth and Vale wrote as eyewitnesses.
51. Sipes, *The Seventh Pennsylvania*, 65.
52. The only mention of a second bridge ("the upper bridge") at Shelbyville appears in General Stanley's reminiscences. None of the other accounts or reports of the fighting

Now Wheeler, who was one of those who had managed to get across the bridge, performed a gallant action. He had escaped destruction, and was safe south of the river. By remaining on the south side of the river and destroying the bridge behind him, he could have ensured his own safety, as well as the safety of the huge train of wagons crawling its way toward Tullahoma carrying the supplies of Polk's corps, and that is what he intended to do. But just as his men were about to set fire to the bridge, Major G. V. Rambaut of Forrest's staff arrived with word that "his commander with two brigades was within sight of Shelbyville and advancing rapidly to secure a crossing."[53] Wheeler of course realized that if he destroyed the bridge, Forrest would ride into a trap, with an unfordable river on one side and a greatly superior body of Union cavalry on the other. He decided therefore to recross with two pieces of artillery and about 500 men of Martin's division and try to retain possession of the bridge and its approaches until Forrest arrived. But this was simply not his day; it was the day of the Union cavalry. General Mitchell had sent Colonel Campbell's brigade on a circuit to the left, and Campbell, with the 9th Pennsylvania leading, came charging into the town and onto Wheeler's right flank, at the same time that Minty charged him head on.[54] Wheeler must have ordered the two guns back across the bridge at this point, but in the excitement one of the caissons overturned and blocked access to the bridge. Everyone on the south bank of the stream was now trapped. After a four-day downpour, Duck River was a roaring torrent, with its crest fifteen feet below the level of the streets of Shelbyville and with a nearly vertical drop from the riverbank to the water below. Wheeler, "saber in hand, shouted to his men that they must cut their way through and swim the river, ordered the charge, and, with General Martin, led in the desperate venture."[55] Those who had the courage, and apparently many did, followed Wheeler and Martin, spurred their mounts to leap from the bank into the river, and then struggled to get

---

on June 27 speak of it. There may well have been a railroad bridge as well as the highway bridge at Shelbyville. Stanley, *Personal Memoirs*, 147.

53. Wyeth, *That Devil Forrest*, 208.

54. General Stanley states that Campbell had been sent to the left to seize the "upper bridge." There is no mention of that fact in Colonel Campbell's own report. Stanley, *Personal Memoirs*, 147; *Official Records*, Vol. XXIII, Pt. 1, p. 547.

55. Wyeth, *That Devil Forrest*, 208.

across the rushing waters to the far bank. The two generals were successful in their desperation attempt, but many of their men were not. The number of cavalrymen who drowned in Duck River that evening is not known; the lowest estimate was "some forty or fifty."[56] There is a fair measure of agreement on the number of Confederate prisoners, the accounts varying from "more than 500" to 600.[57] Whatever Wheeler's exact losses may have been, there is no question but that he had sustained a severely damaging defeat, administered by a Union cavalry whose officers and troopers had become as competent as were his own. General Stanley may well have been justified in believing that the effect of this fight at Shelbyville "was very disastrous to the Confederates. The actual loss in killed, wounded and prisoners has never been correctly stated, but it must have been at least a thousand. . . . but the most disastrous loss was in morale. The Confederate cavalry never recovered from the demoralizing effect which it experienced that day of being ridden down by the Union cavalry."[58]

The Army of the Cumberland followed the retreating Confederates in easy stages and came to rest with the bulk of its infantry encamped on a line from Winchester northeast as far as McMinnville. Rosecrans established his headquarters, doubtless with a full realization of the propaganda value of doing so, at Tullahoma, where Bragg's headquarters had been. The cavalry was pushed forward to Huntsville, Alabama.

Rosecrans' brilliant strategy had forced Bragg to seek safety south of the Tennessee River in Chattanooga, a railroad and communications center it was vitally important for the Confederacy to hold and equally vital, in terms of the further prosecution of the war, for the Union to capture. As Rosecrans was to write in his report on what came to be

56. *Ibid.*, 209. Colonel Jordan said that "at least 50 or 60" drowned. Letter of July 1, 1863, *Jordan Letters*. Granger, Stanley, and Mitchell lumped the drowned with those killed or wounded, and reported that the total was "at least 200–225," "as high as 200," and "upward of 175 or 200." Minty reported that those who tried to escape by swimming the river "perished by scores." *Official Records*, Vol. XXIII, Pt. 1, pp. 509, 539, 545, 558.

57. *Official Records*, Vol. XXIII, Pt. 1, pp. 537, 539, 558. Lieutenant Colonel Robert Klein, 3rd Indiana, reported that 15 of the prisoners taken by his battalion were wounded with the saber. *Ibid.*, 559.

58. Stanley, *Personal Memoirs*, 148. Joseph G. Vale wrote that "the finest cavalry of the rebellion . . . found a grave in the mud and slime of Duck river. They never recovered from this defeat and its attendant horrors." Vale, *Minty and the Cavalry*, 180.

called the Chickamauga Campaign, Chattanooga was the logical and necessary goal of his next operation, because the town—notwithstanding that it had fewer than 3,000 inhabitants at the time—was a junction point of railroad lines radiating to all points of the compass. It commanded "the southern entrance into East Tennessee, the most valuable if not the chief sources of supplies of coal for the manufactories and machine-shops of the Southern States, and . . . [was] one of the great gateways through the mountains to the champaign counties of Georgia and Alabama."[59]

The essential preliminary of a campaign from the northwest to take Chattanooga was to restore the line of the Nashville & Chattanooga Railroad, together with its bridges, culverts, trestles, and all its appurtenances, which had been destroyed by Bragg on his retreat. Rosecrans needed the railroad to haul from his base at Nashville the forage and subsistence to fuel his advance to Chattanooga, which he could not hope to transport by wagon over the "horrible roads" of the region. The railroad was essential also to enable him to accumulate the large stocks of additional subsistence and forage the army would need before it could strike off into the mountainous area south of the Tennessee River for a campaign against Chattanooga, and perhaps beyond. The rebuilding of the railroad and the subsequent replenishment of the army's stocks of supplies were to take until mid-August. This delay of a forward move by the Army of the Cumberland while the weeks of the most favorable campaigning weather went slipping by, however justified and necessary it may have seemed to Rosecrans, became a daily irritant to the War Department and served to embitter further their already mistrustful relations with him.

59. *Official Records*, Vol. XXX, Pt. 1, p. 47.

XI

Clouds of Dust . . . in All Directions

AN AUGURY OF THE CONTINUING DETERIORATION OF ROSE-
crans' relations with the War Department was Secretary Stanton's in-
excusably tactless telegram notifying him of the Union victories at
Gettysburg and Vicksburg and ending: "You and your noble army now
have the chance to give the finishing blow to the rebellion. Will you
neglect the chance?"[1] Not a word of commendation, not even an ac-
knowledgment, of Rosecrans' feat—strategically more important in its
ultimate consequences than Meade's victory at Gettysburg and perhaps even Grant's capture of Vicksburg—of forcing Bragg's retreat
from middle Tennessee in a fast and nearly bloodless campaign. Rosecrans would have had to be more than human, and considerably wiser
than he was, to ignore the implied slur; nor did he do so. His reply,
which Stanton was not likely to forgive or forget, read the secretary a
lesson. "You do not appear," Rosecrans wrote, "to observe the fact that
this noble army has driven the rebels from Middle Tennessee, of which
my dispatches advised you. I beg on behalf of this army that the War
Department may not overlook so great an event because it is not written in letters of blood."[2]

Curiously enough, the desire of the administration, expressed in a

1. *Official Records*, Vol. XXIII, Pt. 2, p. 58.
2. *Ibid.*, 518.

telegraphic harassment by Halleck of the unfortunate Rosecrans, seemed to be based not on their grasp of the strategic possibilities that possession of Chattanooga by the Union would open up—possibilities that would be exploited by Sherman in 1864—but on a desire to deliver from Confederate oppression the Unionist population of east Tennessee. Whatever the exact motivation of the Washington authorities may have been, they obviously kept the pressure on General Halleck, who in turn kept the pressure on Rosecrans with a long string of exhortations, both official and personal. The first of these went off on July 23, twenty days after the end of the Tullahoma Campaign; Halleck asked for a report on the position of Rosecrans' army, information Rosecrans sent him the same day. The following day's messages, one official and one "Private and Confidential," were brusque. "You must move forward immediately," Halleck wired. "Unless you can move more rapidly, your whole campaign will prove a failure." In the unofficial message Rosecrans was told: "I have deemed it absolutely necessary, not only for the country, but also for your own reputation, that your army should remain no longer inactive. The patience of the authorities here has been completely exhausted, and if I had not repeatedly promised to urge you forward, and begged for delay, you would have been removed from the command. . . . the pressure for your removal has been almost as strong as it has been in . . . [Buell's] case."[3]

The Washington authorities may have been crying for Rosecrans' scalp, but he had the admiration of his subordinates, and he retained it even after the disaster of Chickamauga. The normally carping David Stanley called him "a man of genius"; Colonel Thomas Jordan wrote that he was "the man to command an army"; Major James Connolly, 123rd Illinois Mounted Infantry, thought him the "*beau ideal* of a leader . . . the light and life of this army."[4] The flaws in his personality showed up most prominently in his dealings with superiors. Nevertheless, difficult and exasperating as he was to deal with, his record up to August, 1863, had been one of unbroken success, and even if it had not been, no army commander should have been exposed to so wounding a campaign of nagging and threats as he was. Messages similar in tone and content to those just quoted showered down upon Rosecrans

3. *Ibid.*, 550, 551, 552.
4. Stanley, *Personal Memoirs*, 158; letter of July 1, 1862, *Jordan Letters*; Connolly, *Army of the Cumberland*, 134.

on August 3, 4, 7, and 9. The two-sentence telegram of August 4 was particularly blunt. "Your forces must move forward without further delay," he was told and was ordered to report daily the "movements of each corps" until he was across the Tennessee.[5] To Rosecrans' query "I wish to know if your order is intended to take away my discretion as to the time and manner of moving my troops?" Halleck replied that the orders to move were "peremptory."[6]

It is impossible to tell, at the astronomical distance of 120-odd years that separates us from the summer of 1863 in terms of the means of moving an army's supplies and paraphernalia, if Rosecrans could have moved sooner than he did. To restore service on the Nashville & Chattanooga turned out to be a formidable undertaking. Rosecrans told Halleck that a bridge 450 feet long had to be built to get the track across Elk River, to replace the bridge destroyed by Bragg on his retreat.[7] Not until July 25 was the road in operation all the way to Bridgeport, on the Tennessee, and another three weeks were to elapse before Rosecrans was satisfied that his stores had been built up to a point that made it safe for him to resume his advance.[8] At last, on August 16, the army began to move.

Rosecrans' plan for attacking Bragg was controlled by the peculiar topography of the area between the two armies. Bragg, at Chattanooga, was protected in front by the usually unfordable Tennessee River, its bridges broken. The dominant geographical feature was not the river (which, nevertheless, the Federals had to cross to get at

5. *Official Records*, Vol. XXIII, Pt. 2, pp. 554, 590, 597, 601, 592.

6. *Ibid.*, 592. In addition to the messages from Halleck, Rosecrans also received two letters, courteous and kindly in tone, from President Lincoln, urging him forward. Lamers, *The Edge of Glory*, 297–98.

7. *Official Records*, Vol. XXIII, Pt. 2, p. 529. Rosecrans' delay was partly due to the time needed to repair the one-of-a-kind locomotive that had been built to negotiate the sharp curves of the branch line to Tracy City, where he decided to establish a secondary supply base. Lamers, *The Edge of Glory*, 294–95; F. F. McKinney, *Education in Violence: The Life of George H. Thomas and the History of the Army of the Cumberland* (Detroit, 1961), 217.

8. The Nashville & Chattanooga actually ended at Stevenson. From there to Bridgeport and Chattanooga, it and the Memphis & Charleston shared a common track. The Nashville & Chattanooga was rebuilt by the 1st Michigan Engineer Regiment. *Official Records*, Vol. XXX, Pt. 1, p. 50. It is reported that a daily delivery of 28 carloads (225 tons) of forage (grain only) was needed to feed the horses and mules of the army, and another 32 carloads (257 tons) to feed the men. The ten-day reserve Rosecrans thought necessary was the equivalent of 600 carloads. *Ibid.*, Vol. XXIII, Pt. 2, p. 601; see also McKinney, *Education in Violence*, 217.

Bragg) but a series of parallel, steep-sided, high ridges, a part of the Appalachian chain, trending northeast to southwest. With the success of his complicated maneuvers in the Tullahoma Campaign in mind, Rosecrans planned an equally complex series of moves behind the curtain of the ridges between the two armies, to befuddle Bragg with feints here, there, and everywhere while he accomplished his real intention of crossing the Tennessee below Chattanooga. Having crossed the river, Rosecrans' forces were to march across Sand Mountain (the continuation, south of the Tennessee, of Walden's Ridge) and Lookout Valley, to reach the western foot of Lookout Mountain well to the south of Chattanooga and be in a position to march eastward from there to cut the lines of the East Tennessee & Georgia Railroad and the Western & Atlantic, which were Bragg's means of communicating with, and getting supplies from, the East.[9]

Rosecrans did not expect to have to rely entirely on his own army for success. General Ambrose Burnside, given command of the Department of the Ohio after his disastrous failure at Fredericksburg, was intended to cooperate with Rosecrans by marching his Army of the Ohio through southeastern Kentucky to Knoxville and thereby threaten to envelop Bragg's forces from the northeast at the same time that Rosecrans attacked him from the southwest. Knoxville was held at that time by General Simon Bolivar Buckner with about five thousand "badly disciplined and poorly armed" infantry.[10]

General Halleck's involvement in these highly promising plans points up a major weakness in the high-level command structure of the Union armies: the lack of unquestioning obedience to orders by department and army commanders, a reflection partly of the intrusion of politics into army administration and partly of the absence at the top of a general-in-chief whose orders (such as those of Chief of Staff George C. Marshall in World War II) carried with them not only the authority of rank and position but the more important authority of a

9. Rosecrans described Lookout Mountain as a "vast palisade of rocks rising 2,400 feet above the level of the sea, in abrupt, rocky cliffs, from a steep, wooded base. Its eastern sides are no less precipitous. Its top varies from 1 to 6 or 7 miles in breadth, is heavily timbered, sparsely settled, and poorly watered." *Official Records*, Vol. XXX, Pt. 1, p. 48. The only practicable roads across the mountain were one skirting its nose in the north, and two others, 26 and 42 miles to the southwest, respectively. They were described as "extremely bad." Beatty, *Memoirs of a Volunteer*, 244.

10. *Official Records*, Vol. XXIII, Pt. 2, p. 529; Connelly, *Autumn of Glory*, 149.

dominating personality. On July 13, Halleck had to confess his impotence by wiring Rosecrans that "General Burnside has been frequently urged to move forward and cover your left by entering East Tennessee. I do not know what he is doing. He seems tied fast to Cincinnati." He wired Burnside the same day: "I must again urge upon you the importance of moving forward into East Tennessee, to cover Rosecrans' left. Telegraph what you are doing toward this object." The telegram to Burnside failed to elicit a response, for eleven days later, Halleck wired him again: "You have not yet replied to my dispatch in regard to your movements toward East Tennessee. You will immediately report the position and numbers of your troops organized for that object. There must be no further delay in this movement. It must be pushed forward immediately." This time Burnside did deign to reply. He explained that it was the absence of his cavalry, then pursuing Morgan across southern Ohio, that was the main impediment.[11] Morgan was captured on July 26, but not until August 8, after another prod from Halleck, did Burnside inform Rosecrans that he would be ready to march for Knoxville in three or four days with seven thousand infantry and five thousand cavalry.[12] On the same day Burnside appointed as his chief of cavalry General Samuel D. Sturgis, whose undistinguished performance in that post might have been predicted from his lackluster career in the Civil War prior to July, 1863.[13]

A week after Burnside had officially started his march to Knoxville, he wired Rosecrans from Crab Orchard, Kentucky, "We have had a

11. *Official Records*, Vol. XXIII, Pt. 2, pp. 531, 553.

12. *Ibid.*, 593, 600. On August 9, in response to a query from Halleck, Burnside reported that he expected to have "a mounted force . . . [of] 8,000 men as soon as all of the organizations are perfect, which will be in a very few days." *Ibid.*, 603. No doubt Burnside had to leave behind 3,000 of the 8,000 troops because, as he had previously explained to Halleck, "Rosecrans' line of railroad has to be guarded as well as the line of the Cumberland and to its mouth, and the whole of the Eastern Kentucky line." *Ibid.*, 553.

13. *Ibid.*, 600. Sturgis, a Pennsylvanian by birth, graduated thirty-second in the West Point Class of 1846 (George Stoneman was thirty-third in the same class). He served in the Mexican War and with the 1st Dragoons on the frontier, in California, Missouri, and Kansas. Promoted to captain in the 1st Cavalry in 1855, he was stationed at Fort Leavenworth at the time of the Kansas-Missouri border wars. He fought in the battle of Wilson's Creek and assumed command of the Union army after General Lyon was killed. Promoted to brigadier general, he commanded the District of Kansas for a short time, then was moved east and fought at Second Bull Run, South Mountain, Antietam, and Fredericksburg. He was transferred to Kentucky in April, 1863. Cullum, *Biographical Register*, II, 159–60.

serious delay in mounting the cavalry and accumulating forage and subsistence, but all the columns are in motion."[14] There is a dreary sameness about these excuses for delay.

Aside from the time needed to build up an adequate backlog of supplies and subsistence and to wait for Burnside to draw Bragg's attention in the direction of Knoxville, Rosecrans was also delayed (as he told Halleck) by the lack of an "adequate cavalry force to combat that of the enemy, and keep up our line of communications. I could not obtain horses enough to mount the men I actually had." This hackneyed argument evidently failed to impress Halleck, for in his report on these operations, he wrote, "General Rosecrans had complained of his inadequate cavalry force, but the stables of his depots were overcrowded with animals, and the horses of his artillery, cavalry, and trains were dying in large numbers for want of forage."[15] On August 20, Rosecrans reported an "Aggregate Present" of cavalry numbering 12,511 and "Present for Duty" 10,400.[16] If dismounted men account for the total difference of 2,111 between the two figures—an unlikely assumption, inasmuch as those *not* "Present for Duty" doubtless included men absent because of illness and of the innumerable "details" that were a constant drain on the fighting strength of the cavalry at all times and in all places, as well as the men lacking weapons—it was still stretching the facts for Rosecrans to claim, as he did, that lack of horses made it impossible for him to move. Whatever the exact situation may have been, General Meigs reported to Stanton that in the five months from December 1, 1862, to April 27, 1863, Rosecrans had received "by transfer, capture, or purchase 18,450 horses, and 14,607 mules." From April 27 to August 17, the Louisville quartermasters had sent him an additional 12,383 horses and 5,789 mules, making a total for the 8½ months of 30,833 horses and 20,396 mules.[17]

A grim tale told by the historian of the 72nd Indiana Mounted Infantry indicates the callous disregard of the welfare of their animals on

14. *Official Records*, Vol. XXX, Pt. 3, p. 72.
15. *Ibid.*, 110, and Pt. 1, p. 37.
16. *Ibid.*, Vol. XXIII, Pt. 2, p. 607. Included in these figures are the numbers of the 15th Pennsylvania, but not those of Wilder's brigade or of the 39th Indiana Mounted Infantry.
17. *Ibid.*, Vol. XXX, Pt. 3, pp. 62–63, 72. A later report stated that 18,957 horses and 16,477 mules had been furnished the Army of the Cumberland from January 2 to August 29, 1863. These figures did not include animals bought in Tennessee. *Ibid.*, 356.

the part of the men that accounts at least in part for Rosecrans' lack of horses. The Wilder brigade, of which this regiment was a part, had been "constantly picking up loose horses, until each company had from 10 to 50 more horses than men." The extra horses were looked after and herded on the march by the Negroes who had attached themselves to the brigade. It may be mentioned incidentally that such horses were at times the basis of a profitable but illegal commerce; they were bought by officers for a fraction of their real value from the men who had captured them, and then shipped North. A gunner of the 18th Indiana Battery recorded that the Lightning Brigade had "authority to keep themselves supplied with horses from off the country, consequently the officers speculate considerably in horses."[18] In the course of the Tullahoma Campaign, the brigade had accumulated a surplus of 700 mounts. As a result of the usual process of swapping, the surplus came to consist of "convalescent horses" the brigade did not want to take along when the campaign resumed on August 16. "So," the historian relates, when the brigade was about to start out, the men "hauled rails and fenced in a pasture of 100 acres, turned out horses into it, and left them. We supposed, of course, that they would be sent back to Nashville and cared for. But it seems that when we moved, the whole army moved, and those horses were left in the pasture, had eaten up every green thing, and had died of starvation. We counted 200 carcasses inside of two acres of ground."[19]

The end of the Tullahoma Campaign found the Lightning Brigade at Decherd. General Stanley's cavalry was at Huntsville, Alabama, whence it moved a few days later to Fayetteville, Tennessee, a few miles north of the Alabama-Tennessee border, in order to "control lawless elements of the population," that is, bushwhackers. A brigade order of Colonel McCook's directed that all captured bushwhackers be hanged and, in areas where bushwhackers had attacked his soldiers,

18. Rowell, *Yankee Artillerymen*, 89. The officers of the Lightning Brigade were not alone in engaging in this activity. At Memphis, at the other end of Tennessee, a XVI Army Corps order of August 20 announced that "the practice of shipping horses and mules . . . to the North having been found to encourage a system of robbery and stealing, both from the government and citizens, [it] must be put a stop to," and so the order forbade such shipments thereafter. *Official Records*, Vol. XXX, Pt. 3, p. 82.

19. McGee, *History of the 72nd Indiana*, 208, 212. The brigade had returned to camp at Rowesville, Tennessee, on July 21, after a "seven-day scout" with "over 800 horses and mules and nearly 300 negroes." Connolly, *Army of the Cumberland*, 108–109.

that all "property" be destroyed.[20] There was doubtless the usual connection between this flare-up of guerrilla activity and the conduct of
Stanley's cavalrymen in the Huntsville-Fayetteville area, "scouting
over the country . . . gathering all kinds of army supplies—forage,
horses, cattle, mules, negroes." This cause-and-effect relationship was
clear enough to perceptive officers. General Garfield wrote to Stanley
in connection with the Huntsville-Fayetteville operation, "The lawlessness of which you speak on the part of our soldiers on foraging parties will make bushwhackers faster than any other thing."[21]

The men of the Union cavalry had other problems besides the
strain of living with the daily and nightly fear of a bushwhacker's bullet. Camping in the swampy lowlands of the valley of the Tennessee
and its tributaries sent dozens of troopers to the morning sick calls
with chills and fever and the dreaded malaria.[22] Then there was a serious difficulty with the saddles furnished the cavalry by the Ordnance
Department: exposure of the saddles to rain—presumably they were
made of untanned leather—caused "rapid wear." Rosecrans coupled a
request for two thousand saddles with an unnecessary lecture to General Ripley, telling him that "worn-out saddles are ruining our horses'
backs. As horses are much more expensive and hard to replace, I beg
you will send us a supply at once." Despite General Ripley's assurance
the next day that the saddles would be sent, Rosecrans repeated his
request a week later and doubled the number he wanted, explaining
that the increase was to give him enough to issue saddles to returning
"convalescent soldiers, recruits and conscripts, and the enlistments in
the Tennessee regiments."[23]

A major change in the organization of the cavalry occurred on
July 30 with the replacement of General Turchin by George Crook in
command of the Second Division. Born in Ohio, Crook graduated
thirty-eighth in the West Point Class of 1852; Sheridan and David

20. Colonel McCook reported two weeks later that the "country had been pretty
well cleared of bush whackers since he had issued these orders." *Official Records*,
Vol. XXX, Pt. 3, p. 106.
21. Crofts, *Third Ohio Volunteer Cavalry*, 105; *Official Records*, Vol. XXIII, Pt. 2,
p. 527.
22. *Official Records*, Vol. XXX, Pt. 3, p. 53.
23. *Ibid.*, 111, 27, 33; see also Vol. I, p. 124 of the present study. General Ripley
wired back within a day that four thousand "sets of horse equipments" would be forwarded to Nashville "as fast as possible." *Ibid.*, 131.

Stanley were among his classmates. After graduation he served, as did Sheridan, in the 4th Infantry on the West Coast. When the Civil War broke out, he was appointed colonel of the 36th Ohio Infantry and on September 7, 1862, was promoted to brigadier general. After serving in the Army of the Potomac and participating in all its battles in 1862, Crook was sent to Tennessee. One of his subordinates, Colonel William B. Sipes, was to write of him: "Crook was an excellent officer. He 'put on no frills'; was always ready to share hardships and dangers with his men, possessed and exhibited the most untiring energy, and was very popular, because of these traits, with the rank and file."[24]

On August 15 Rosecrans was at last ready to move; orders were issued that day for the army's advance to begin the following morning. The bulk of Rosecrans' forces—the XIV Army Corps less the Lightning Brigade, the XXI Army Corps less one division, the XX Army Corps, and the Reserve Corps—were to cross the Cumberland Plateau into the Sequatchie Valley and proceed thence south to the Bridgeport-Stevenson area, downstream from Chattanooga, where Rosecrans intended to cross the Tennessee. Minty's brigade, supported by Horatio P. Van Cleve's division of infantry, taken from the XXI Corps, was to form the left wing of the elaborate operation to cause Bragg to think that the crossing would be attempted upstream from the town and to keep him pinned down in Chattanooga while the Union army marched around his left rear. The right wing of this feint was the Lightning Brigade, whose mission was to "make a demonstration on Chattanooga and Harrison's Landing," the latter being about twelve miles upstream from the town.[25]

Minty's brigade had spent the weeks following the end of the Tullahoma Campaign in "clearing the country between Columbia, Tennessee, and Huntsville, Alabama . . . of small bodies of rebels." On August 1, it was detached from the Cavalry Corps, moved to McMinnville, and placed under the orders of the XXI Corps for the forthcoming campaign. While waiting for the campaign to get under way, Minty kept up the fighting edge of his command by leading two expeditions against Colonel G. G. Dibrell's 8th Tennessee, C.S.A., of Forrest's division, encamped on Dibrell's own plantation near Sparta, Tennessee,

24. Cullum, *Biographical Register*, II, 329–30; Sipes, *The Seventh Pennsylvania*, 78.
25. *Official Records*, Vol. XXX, pp. 35–38.

twenty-six miles from McMinnville. The first expedition, on August 4, failed when an alarm by Dibrell's pickets (14 of whom were captured by the 3rd Indiana) frustrated Minty's intention of surprising Dibrell's camp.[26] The second expedition, five days later, resulted in casualties heavy for the numbers engaged, and two utterly irreconcilable reports. Dibrell had "not over 300 men present," according to his own report, and according to Minty's, "between 800 and 900," outnumbering Minty's own 774. Dibrell claimed to have chased Minty's command eighteen miles after repulsing his attack; Minty, on the other hand, asserted that "the rebels, although outnumbering us and holding a strong position, difficult of access, would not wait for the attack, but scattered in every direction."[27]

The campaign began for Minty's brigade at 2 A.M. on August 17, when, 1,200 strong, it moved out toward Sparta, whence it was to march southeast toward Pikesville and the Tennessee River. The fight with Dibrell eight days before, whatever its course may have been, had not had a lasting effect on the latter, for on the afternoon of the seventeenth the first Confederate troops encountered by Minty were Dibrell's pickets. They seemed to have nothing more than a watching brief, however, for they fought the advancing Federals with "widely detached skirmishing parties . . . from hill to hill and stream to stream" and retreated steadily; the following morning, "no trace of the rebels could be found." The brigade reached the Tennessee without incident and thereafter, by means of vigorous patrolling, did their best to suggest that they were the forerunners of an attempt by the Union army to cross the river somewhere between North Chickamauga Creek and Kingston.[28] This was no light task, for Minty had to maintain maximum visibility and create a show of force here, there, and everywhere on a front of sixty miles, with a brigade that was now down to 1,100 men.[29]

The Lightning Brigade had been strengthened by the addition of a fifth regiment armed with Spencer rifles, the 92nd Illinois Mounted Infantry. They moved camp to Normandy, north of Tullahoma, in "a

26. Vale, *Minty and the Cavalry*, 195; *Official Records*, Vol. XXIII, Pt. 1, p. 845.
27. *Ibid.*, 846, 847; Vale, *Minty and the Cavalry*, 201–202; Wyeth, *That Devil Forrest*, 213–14. The casualty figures in the two reports are as impossible to reconcile as are their accounts of the action.
28. *Official Records*, Vol. XXX, Pt. 1, pp. 920, 921; Vale, *Minty and the Cavalry*, 206–207, 210–15; Sipes, *The Seventh Pennsylvania*, 77–78.
29. *Official Records*, Vol. XXX, Pt. 3, p. 316.

very pleasant little valley," where they enjoyed "plenty of vegetables . . . [and] fruit," especially apples and blackberries, and where the horses, too, had plenty of forage after feeding on nothing but wheat straw for several days during the campaign just ended.[30]

On August 2, the brigade moved south to Decherd, the scene of their none-too-effective railroad-breaking exploit of a month before. Two weeks later, carying ten days' rations, they left camp and climbed the "extremely steep, slippery, and winding" road to the top of the Cumberland Plateau, on the way to Tracy City ("three houses and a depot"). On the afternoon of the nineteenth, after crossing the plateau in a northeasterly direction, the brigade descended into the Sequatchie Valley. Up to that point, there had been only bad roads, lack of water, and an abundance of rattlesnakes to contend with. But then, near Dunlap, the brigade had their first encounter with the enemy; the scouts of the 72nd Indiana surprised and captured a group of 14 Confederates not otherwise identified, who were making preparations to hang 5 Union soldiers they had taken prisoner. The Union captives were liberated; the records are silent on the fate of their former captors.[31]

On August 20, the column crossed Walden's Ridge and entered the valley of North Chickamauga Creek, fifteen miles above Chattanooga. The next day, Colonel Wilder began to make good on his primary mission of misleading the enemy. He sent two of his regiments north to Harrison's Landing to protect his rear, while he marched with the rest of the brigade downstream to Chattanooga. August 21 was a Sunday, which, in the aftermath of Gettysburg and Vicksburg, had been designated by President Davis as a day of fasting and prayer for the success of Confederate arms. Services were under way in the Chattanooga churches when Wilder's three regiments and two sections of artillery reached the riverbank opposite the town. Captain Lilly unlimbered his guns and began to shell the houses across the river, and it was doubtless with considerable glee that the troopers and gunners watched the people and troops in the town in a state of "great consternation, running in all directions." After Lilly silenced a number of guns that re-

30. Rowell, *Yankee Artillerymen*, 88–89. Major Connolly noted on July 11, "There are more blackberries and finer ones here than I ever saw, and I have eaten so many of them that I don't think I shall ever want any more." Connolly, *Army of the Cumberland*, 103.

31. Rowell, *Yankee Artillerymen*, 93; *Official Records*, Vol. XXX, Pt. 1, p. 445.

plied to his fire, destroyed the steamer *Paint Rock*, disabled another steamship lying at the Chattanooga landing, and sank a number of Bragg's pontoons, he limbered up his guns and rode away.[32]

For the two following weeks, Wilder divided his attention between observing and reporting Bragg's activities, on the one hand, and, on the other, discharging his main responsibility of making a show of an imminent crossing of the river above Chattanooga. His frequent reports to his immediate superior, General J. J. Reynolds, and to Rosecrans' headquarters are models that any officer, American or European, trained in the cavalry tradition, might well have imitated. It is to be noted that these reports and the observations on which they were based were the work of a man who had had no cavalry training whatever, who had, so far as is known, never read a cavalry manual and relied wholly on his native good sense in deciding what to look for and what to transmit to his superiors. The precision and directness of the language of his dispatches are as noteworthy as was their content.

While his guns were bombarding Chattanooga, Wilder wrote General Reynolds: "A pontoon bridge is lying in the stream on the opposite side, all laid ready to swing across the stream. . . . Clouds of dust are now rising in all directions south of the river. I can see no camps. Citizens, prisoners, and deserters say that Bragg has about 30,000 men, including the cavalry. . . . Prisoners . . . say that Polk's corps is stationed at or near Chattanooga. Hardee's old corps, now commanded by D. H. Hill, said to be at or near Tyner Station." Wilder had the good judgment to indicate in each instance the source of the information he reported, to enable Reynolds and the staff officers at army headquarters to decide how much credence to attach to their statements. Wilder wrote General Garfield the next day: "I believe the rebels are leaving Chattanooga. I distinctly saw two locomotives leave there drawing eight other locomotives to-day. . . . There does not appear to be as many troops in the vicinity as there was yesterday." And later the same day, he sent word to Garfield that he thought "the rebels have one corps of two divisions at Chattanooga and vicinity—D. H. Hill's. . . . Polk's corps is reported to be down the road toward Bridgeport. None of this information is very well founded, being made up from reports from deserters, negroes, and citizens. There is no rebel force

32. *Official Records*, Vol. XXX, Pt. 1, p. 445, Pt. 3, p. 100.

north of the river except bushwhackers on the mountains."[33] And lastly, on the twenty-fourth: "Last night thirteen trains of cars came into town apparently empty, and five went out loaded, at least the noise made by them indicated such to be the case. . . . They are strengthening their position with rifle-pits to-day. All the fords above are defended by rifle-pits and guns in works. Two of my regiments went to Sale Creek yesterday . . . where they found Colonel Minty, who reports Forrest 20 miles above with 5,000 cavalry."[34]

Equally worthy of imitation was Wilder's performance of his mission to mislead the enemy. His recital of his efforts in that respect is deserving of quotation in full:

> We then commenced making feints as if trying to cross the river at different points for 40 miles above the town, and succeeded in so deceiving them as to induce them to use an entire army corps to prevent the execution of such a purpose, they working every night fortifying the south bank of the river at every feasible crossing for miles above. Details were made nearly every night to build fires indicating large camps, and by throwing boards upon others and hammering on barrels and sawing up boards and throwing the pieces in streams that would float them into the river, we made them believe we were preparing to cross with boats.[35]

This campaign of ingenious mystification was kept up until September 8, the day Bragg evacuated Chattanooga. Wilder, as well as Rosecrans' staff, thought that Bragg was evacuating the city but were not certain that he was doing so. Wilder made it his business to find out. He sent the 17th Indiana to Friar's Island, eight miles upstream from Chattanooga, on the evening of the eighth; on the following morning, after waiting for the autumnal river-valley fog to lift, he rushed the 98th Illinois across the river, drove off the Confederate cavalry guarding the southern bank at that point, and rode forward toward Chattanooga. He would have been the first to enter the city, had not one of his own regiments beaten him to it. The 92nd Illinois had been de-

33. *Ibid.*, Pt. 3, pp. 100, 119, 122.

34. *Ibid.*, 151. One possible source of information about the enemy is alluded to in Major Connolly's diary entry for September 5, "across the river from Chattanooga": "Colonel James W. Monroe [123rd Illinois Mounted Infantry] and myself have crossed the river several times in a canoe and spent several hours talking and playing cards with rebel officers under the shadow of Lookout mountain and they have as often crossed to our side and talked and played with us. We find them intelligent gentlemen and good fellows." Connolly, *Army of the Cumberland*, 117–18.

35. *Official Records*, Vol. XXX, Pt. 1, pp. 445–46.

tached from his brigade some days earlier and sent to operate with General Thomas' XIV Corps. A scouting party of that regiment returned to camp on the evening of the eighth with the news that the Confederates had marched out of the town that morning, and it was the 92nd Illinois that was the first to enter Chattanooga "and unfurl the national colors" on the morning of the ninth.[36]

The reader will have noted that the preliminaries of the capture of Chattanooga involved primarily Colonel Wilder's brigade, which until October 18 was actually part of an infantry division. On that date, the brigade was transferred to the cavalry, and starting with October 31, the "Mounted Infantry Brigade" appears in reports as part of the Cavalry Corps.[37] It will be proper to refer hereafter to Colonel Wilder's men as "troopers"; their reaction to the change has not been recorded.

Only to a lesser extent did the preliminaries to the campaign to recover Chattanooga for the Union involve the cavalry, properly so called. The diversionary role assigned to Minty's brigade was of lesser importance than the same role performed by the mounted infantry. The duties given General Stanley and the bulk of the cavalry—five of the six brigades of the Cavalry Corps—go a long way to justify Stanley's previously quoted opinion that Rosecrans "had no idea of the use of cavalry"; the initial orders for the campaign merely told him that he should "follow general headquarters" with his "reserve brigade" (a mysterious entity that does not appear anywhere in the Tables of Organization of the army) and that he would receive "special instructions for the remainder of the cavalry . . . [from] the general commanding."[38] Coming from an army commander who for eight months had been clamoring for more cavalry, this was perfunctory treatment indeed, for in essence it consigned the cavalry to the uninspiring role of keeping out of the way while the infantry dealt with the Confederate army. The work the cavalry was given to do from August 16 to September 4, the day the last of the Union infantry crossed the Tennessee, was completely inconsequential. Stanley was ordered to picket the

36. *Ibid.*, Pt. 3, pp. 465, 450, Pt. 1, pp. 450, 454.
37. *Ibid.*, Pt. 4, p. 464, and Vol. XXXI, Pt. 1, p. 809.
38. Stanley, *Personal Memoirs*, 158; *Official Records*, Vol. XXX, Pt. 1, pp. 46–47, Pt. 3, p. 37. On August 31, each of the two divisions of the corps consisted of three brigades; Minty's being detached left three brigades of the First Division (Edward M. McCook in command, in the absence due to illness of General Mitchell) and two of the Second under Stanley's immediate command. *Official Records*, Vol. XXX, Pt. 1, pp. 274–75.

river in front of a brigade of Sheridan's division, to establish a courier line, to send a regiment across the river to "drive bushwhackers away from the other side," and to mark with buoys one of the fords across the river.[39]

Not until September 3 was the cavalry given an assignment that provided them with an opportunity to play a worthy role in the campaign. Stanley was sent orders that day to move from the river to Rawlingsville, Alabama, and thence in two columns, Crook on the left and himself with Mitchell's division on the right, toward Rome, Georgia, to cover the right wing of the infantry advance on a southeasterly line across Sand Mountain, Lookout Valley, and Lookout Mountain to the village of Alpine, located at the eastern foot of Lookout Mountain about forty-five miles south of Chattanooga. It would be his responsibility also "to ascertain the position and intentions of the enemy." The force he sent forward from Alpine in the direction of Rome was to "push forward with audacity, to feel the enemy strongly, and [to] make a strong diversion in that direction." Of special interest is a request Garfield sent to Stanley two days later. "Our maps are very imperfect," Garfield wrote. "Do all you can to correct and extend them."[40] Many of the dispatches exchanged from the time the Army of the Cumberland crossed the Tennessee until the battle two weeks later attest to the fact that commanding officers at all levels frequently lacked accurate information on distances, roads, and the location of settlements and of the gaps through the mountains.

On September 6, Stanley was given an additional task. Rome was fifty miles from his point of departure at the western foot of Lookout Mountain. Bragg's rail connection with Atlanta, the Western & Atlantic, ran south through Kingston, Georgia, fifteen miles to the east of Rome. Stanley was ordered to "strike the railroad" if possible. He was told that since Forrest and a part of Wheeler's cavalry had been located near Chattanooga, he could "attack with impunity any mounted force the enemy may have in the direction of Rome and the Railroad."[41] The distance and the nature of the terrain to be traversed made success of the venture questionable, and to make it even more so, it appeared that

39. *Official Records*, Vol. XXX, Pt. 3, pp. 141, 193, 204, 240.
40. *Ibid.*, 322, 374.
41. *Ibid.*, 379. The cavalry was expected to strike the railroad between "Resaca bridge and Dalton." *Ibid.*, Pt. 1, p. 53.

Stanley's regiments had "no clawhooks, crowbars, or any other means for tearing up railroad track . . . [or] any torpedoes . . . for blowing up railroad bridges, culverts, &c." Stanley demurred for the further reason that his force—"thirteen small regiments . . . reduced by battalions guarding the [Nashville & Chattanooga]"—was "entirely inadequate to the work to be performed."[42] He was urged to try anyway. "Even should you fail in thoroughly breaking the railroad," Garfield told him, "you would at least make a strong diversion in that direction. . . . The severing of the enemy's railroad communication with Atlanta will be the most disastrous to him."[43]

On September 8, before it was known with certainty that Bragg was abandoning Chattanooga, a dispatch from Stanley to Garfield and one from Rosecrans (unquestionably written by himself) to Stanley, crossed in transit. Stanley informed Garfield that he had been unable to start out on the raid to Rome and the railroad that morning from his camp at "Winston's," a farm about thirty-five miles south of Chattanooga at the western foot of Winston's Gap over Lookout Mountain, "on account of deficiency of horseshoes."[44] His reassurances to headquarters were not only lame but were also too late. "I am in pretty good trim now," he wrote, "and gain 600 men by delaying." But Rosecrans had sent him in the meantime a well-earned rebuke. "I learn from . . . [a messenger]," Rosecrans wrote,

that your command lies at the foot of the mountain on this side, intending to move in the morning. I am sorry to say you will be too late. It is also a matter of regret to me that your command has done so little in this great movement. If you could do nothing toward Rome, nor toward the railroad, you might at least have cleared the top of Lookout Mountain. . . . you had peremptory orders to move, which were reiterated yesterday. . . . It appears the enemy has sent a large infantry and cavalry force to Alpine. Your cavalry ought to have full patrol from your position to that place. This you do not appear to have done. Had you gone according to orders you would have struck the head of their column, and probably inflicted on them irreparable injury. So far your command has been a mere picket guard for our advance.[45]

42. *Ibid.*, Pt. 3, pp. 375, 431. One wonders what Colonel Wilder would have done under such circumstances.

43. *Ibid.*, 432.

44. *Ibid.*, 468.

45. *Ibid.*, 467–68. Nor did Rosecrans forget his dissatisfaction. In his report on the campaign, he wrote: "The cavalry for some reason was not pushed with the vigor nor to the extent which orders and the necessities of the campaign required. Its continual

It is quite evident in the light of after knowledge, and it certainly should have been evident to Rosecrans and his staff, that Stanley was not one to decide for himself what needed doing by the cavalry within the framework of the army's general objectives and then to go ahead and do it. To act, he needed orders, and those given him prior to September 3 had in fact made him "a mere picket guard." Clearly, this does not excuse his failure to act on the "peremptory orders to move," but criticism on that score, however justified it may have been, came with ill grace from Rosecrans, of all people.

The orders Stanley had failed to execute were overtaken by events. On learning that Bragg had evacuated Chattanooga, Rosecrans sent him new orders. "In view of the uncertainty of the enemy's route," Garfield told him, "the general commanding leaves your operations to your own discretion, with the general direction to cover our extreme right flank and move upon Rome or such other point as shall do the enemy most serious harm. If their retreat can once be turned into a rout, your command can do them immense injury."[46]

There was a second scolding for Stanley a few days later. He had failed to set up a courier line to ensure the speedy transmittal of dispatches between his own headquarters and those of the commanding general. Always ready to lecture, Rosecrans had his aide-de-camp remind Stanley that "there is no military offense, except running from the enemy, so inexcusable as a neglect to keep up communications with headquarters." He was ordered to remedy the situation "at once."[47]

Having moved at last, Stanley gained possession of Alpine on September 9. He was able to report that the Confederates were at LaFayette and that their cavalry were at Summerville and on their way to LaFayette to join the rest of their army, which (as Stanley reported a few days later) had been reinforced by troops that had been with Johnston in Mississippi in July. Whatever else Rosecrans may have expected of

---

movement and the absence of Major-General Stanley . . . have prevented a report which may throw some light on the subject." *Ibid.*, Pt. 1, p. 52. Stanley never submitted a report, but three months later Rosecrans had changed his mind, or professed to do so, about both the cavalry and Stanley. His reappraisal will be cited later.

46. *Ibid.*, Pt. 3, p. 506. Orders to Crook on September 8 directed that "his dismounted men, with suitable number of commissioned officers, be sent back with the train to-day to Stevenson carrying their arms and horse equipments with them. . . . they will proceed to Nashville for a remount, the horses being now there." *Ibid.*, 470.

47. *Ibid.*, 588.,

Stanley, the information-gathering part of his duties he seems to have performed fairly effectively.[48]

Stanley, unfortunately, had a legitimate excuse for failing to come up to Rosecrans' expectations. He wrote Garfield on September 12 that he had anticipated Rosecrans' orders to try to ascertain the strength and position of the enemy around LaFayette by sending Crook with his two brigades "to drive into LaFayette and see what they have at that place"; but, he added, "My dysentery, which has been working on me for a week, has completely prostrated me, so that I am not able to be out of bed but a few minutes at a time."[49] It might have been wise if, struck with a debilitating disease at a time when all his energy was needed, Stanley had stepped aside, but his desire to retain command while in the midst of a major campaign is certainly understandable. Nevertheless, on September 14, when General Mitchell returned from sick leave, Stanley wrote Garfield: "I am still confined to my bed, and have had to ride in an ambulance to-day coming over the mountain. Unless I get better I shall have to turn over the command to General Mitchell and go where I can have rest and quiet." He had to report the next day: "I am so prostrated that I am not able to sit up, and I will this morning turn the command over to General Mitchell. . . . I desire to go to Nashville for treatment."[50]

Later the same day General Mitchell sent his first dispatch as temporary commander of the corps. ("Columns of dust could be seen in the valley moving toward Rome," he said.) He reported that Stanley ("He is very sick, and I am fearful that he will have a serious time") was leaving, and he asked "for specific directions with regard to cavalry movements," which he evidently had been unable to get from Stanley. He added that the cavalry were "badly used up, both men and horses," and that he had three hundred men sick, whom he had to send to the rear.[51]

While the Army of the Cumberland was maneuvering to reach and then cross the Tennessee, General Burnside set off on his campaign to recover east Tennessee for the Union. He started on August 21 from

48. *Ibid.*, Pt. 1, pp. 887–90.
49. *Ibid.*, Pt. 3, pp. 589, 551. Minty had crossed the Tennessee and was about to join the Cavalry Corps.
50. *Ibid.*, 637, 653.
51. *Ibid.*, 653.

central Kentucky with two divisions of infantry, a division of mounted troops, and an "Unattached Cavalry Brigade," all forming parts of General George L. Hartsuff's XXIII Army Corps.[52] The two divisions of infantry were made up entirely of regiments from the western states. The division of mounted troops, commanded by General Samuel P. Carter, who had led the cavalry raid of December, 1862, into eastern Tennessee, was an amalgam of cavalry and mounted infantry units. Colonel Robert K. Byrd's First Brigade included one regiment of cavalry and three of mounted infantry. Colonel John W. Foster's Second Brigade had two regiments and parts of two others of cavalry, and one regiment of mounted infantry. General James M. Shackelford's Third Brigade consisted of three regiments of cavalry and a regiment of mounted infantry. There is nothing in the records to suggest that this mixing of the two types of mounted units in the same brigade had a motivation grounded in tactics; it may well have been the accidental result of an attempt to make the three brigades roughly equal in numbers and possibly also to accommodate the three brigade commanders with congenial regimental commanders. The "Unattached Cavalry Brigade" was commanded by Frank Wolford, colonel of the 1st Kentucky; it included another regiment of Kentucky cavalry, plus nine companies of a third, besides his own.[53]

One of the regiments in General Shackelford's brigade was the 2nd Ohio, which the reader has already met as part of the Cavalry Corps of the Army of the Potomac. After its reorganization and reequipment following service in Kansas and in Indian Territory, the regiment consisted of two veteran battalions, and a third battalion of recruits assembled in the fall of 1862. Just before leaving on the march for Knoxville, the regiment had taken part in the pursuit of Morgan on his Indiana-Ohio raid; in the course of it the troopers learned the meaning of the expression "light marching order": it meant "one blanket, one

52. *Ibid.*, Pt. 2, p. 577. The First Division of the corps was made up of the foot, horse, and gunners manning fifteen posts in Kentucky; these troops did not take part in the Knoxville Campaign. Hartsuff's corps was followed to Knoxville by the IX Army Corps, reduced to six thousand, rank and file, sent on from Vicksburg via Cincinnati. They arrived in Knoxville in installments from September 25 to October 1. Fifteen of the twenty regiments of infantry and both batteries of artillery in the corps hailed from the East. *Ibid.*, 551–53, 574–75.

53. *Ibid.*, 555. The August 31 trimonthly return of Burnside's command (officially the Department of the Ohio) shows 6,578 "cavalry" (which may be assumed to include the mounted infantry) "Present for Duty, Equipped." *Ibid.*, 557.

poncho, one change of underwear, one hundred rounds of ammunition, one pair of horseshoes with nails . . . three days' rations, and three days' forage for the horses."[54] The last—three days' forage—was a counsel of perfection. There were to be long periods in the operations about Knoxville in the fall and winter of 1863 when even one's day's forage would have been a life-saving boon for the starving animals of the 2nd Ohio.

The march of the XXIII Corps over the steep hills, through the narrow valleys, and across the frequent watercourses of southeastern Kentucky was uneventful. Wolford's brigade had the job of guarding the supply and ammunition trains. Neither they nor General Carter's division met any resistance worth mentioning, and had only the "steep rugged mountains, bad roads, and short forage" to contend with. Kingston, the first objective, was reached and occupied on September 1. Colonel Foster's cavalry entered Knoxville the following day. There was no opposition, for General Buckner's garrison had been ordered to evacuate the town and had withdrawn westward to Loudon before the Federals arrived. On September 9 Burnside forced the surrender of the Confederate garrison, numbering about 2,500, of Cumberland Gap. Thereafter he was pulled in two directions. Halleck urged him to concentrate on his primary mission to hold east Tennessee for the Union, support the pro-Union population of the area, and prevent the transit of reinforcements to Bragg from Virginia over the direct rail line through Knoxville. But as early as September 10 he was also being pulled in the opposite direction; Rosecrans asked him (through General Crittenden) to move his cavalry southwest to "occupy the country recently covered by Colonel Minty."[55] And Rosecrans wired Halleck the same day: "I did not, in my last telegram, lay enough stress on uniting Burnside's cavalry with mine. The two combined can control the country far into the interior, and prevent the enemy from gathering the crops."[56] In a dispatch to Burnside direct, Rosecrans struck a more urgent note: "The enemy never retreated farther than LaFayette, and it appears is concentrating his forces . . . and massing all his cavalry.

54. Gause, *Four Years with Five Armies*, 130.
55. *Official Records*, Vol. XXX, Pt. 2, pp. 550, 549.
56. *Ibid.*, Pt. 3, p. 507. Colonel McCook reported to General Stanley a possible means of increasing the numbers of the cavalry. He wrote that "a party of citizens from the mountains want to be mustered into service for six months as partisans . . . furnishing their own horses and arms. What shall I do with them?" *Ibid.*, 61–62. An answer, if there was one, to this dispatch, is not in the *Official Records*.

Every indication now is that he feels able to give us battle. It is highly desirable—I may say of the utmost importance—that all your cavalry should come to our relief as quickly as possible."[57]

Indeed, Rosecrans' instinct gave him accurate signals. His antagonist did not evacuate Chattanooga with the intention of running away to Atlanta or even to Rome. He meant to give the Yankees a fight. Rosecrans' elaborate plan to circle Chattanooga to the south and get his army across Bragg's rail connection with Atlanta, at the same time that Burnside, at Knoxville, barred his direct connection with the Virginia seaboard, had a serious flaw as a consequence of the nature of the terrain. To swing far enough south to gain easy access to the Western & Atlantic and to get his large army and its trains across the mountains (Lookout Mountain in particular) in a reasonable time, Rosecrans had to parcel out his troops among a series of gaps through the mountains.[58] As a result, Thomas' corps, crossing Lookout Mountain into McLemore's Cove by way of Cooper's and Stevens' Gaps, was twenty-six miles away from Crittenden's corps in Chattanooga and twenty miles from McCook's corps to the south, the latter having crossed Lookout Mountain by way of Winston's Gap.[59] The cavalry, after preceding McCook through Winston's Gap, swung farther to the right (or south) in the direction of Alpine and on the most direct route across Broomtown Valley and Taylor's Ridge to Rome, which positioned them between ten and fourteen miles to the southeast of McCook and just about sixty miles from Crittenden. In terms more representative of the realities of 1863, Thomas was separated by one and a half days' march from Crittenden in one direction and two and a half to three days' march from McCook in the other.[60] At the moment, Bragg's and Rosecrans' armies were of roughly equal size, but whereas the latter was scattered over a wide expanse of mountainous terrain, the former was concentrated in a central position in and around LaFayette, nearer to two of Rosecrans' corps than they were to each other and athwart the only good direct road over which they could unite quickly.

57. *Ibid.*, 618.
58. A single division of Thomas' corps, with its trains, needed two days to cross Lookout Mountain. *Ibid.*, Pt. 1, p. 53.
59. McLemore's Cove is a V-shaped valley, with its apex to the south, between Lookout Mountain on the west and Pigeon Mountain (which branches off Lookout Mountain) on the east.
60. McKinney, *Education in Violence*, 223.

Braxton Bragg did not lack intelligence, whatever his temperamental and emotional failings may have been. Mainly because of a faulty placement of his cavalry and Wheeler's failure to obey orders, he had misread Rosecrans' plans for crossing the Tennessee. But now, when he became aware of the dispersion of the invader's forces and worked out excellent plans to beat them in detail, his subordinates failed him; his "command structure collapsed," and his plans failed.[61] Not only did Bragg's plans miscarry, but the movements of his forces alerted Rosecrans to his peril. He now realized that Bragg was not retreating to Rome, as he had assumed, and that, on the contrary, Bragg intended to take the offensive and make a fight for the possession of Chattanooga.

The alarm bell was rung by General Alexander McD. McCook from Alpine on September 12. He realized that if Bragg had his army concentrated at LaFayette and was not retreating toward Rome, then he himself was in an exposed position and in grave danger. He wrote General Thomas: "[Bragg's] object will be to oppose his whole force to our fractions. . . . All citizens here, both Union and Secession, say that he will fight, and with the advantages he has, I think so also."[62] The Lightning Brigade was at the moment attached to General Crittenden's corps; advancing southward, toward Lee and Gordon's Mills, they ran into powerful opposition at Tunnel Hill, near Ringgold. This was another straw in the wind.[63] Rosecrans had also been led to believe by "an accumulation of evidence," all of it false, that troops detached from the Army of Northern Virginia had reached Atlanta on September 1 and were about to join Bragg. These reinforcements, two divisions of just under twelve thousand men of James Longstreet's corps, did not in fact leave Orange Courthouse, Virginia until September 9, and because of Burnside's capture of Knoxville, they had to take a roundabout, time-consuming route through the Carolinas and Georgia, over the badly deteriorated railroads of the South, to reach Bragg. The first three brigades of Longstreet's command did not detrain at Catoosa Station, near Ringgold, until September 17.[64]

61. Connelly, *Autumn of Glory*, 163–64, 189.
62. *Official Records*, Vol. XXX, Pt. 3, p. 570.
63. *Ibid.*, Pt. 1, p. 446. The opposition was John S. Scott's and George G. Dibrell's brigades of Forrest's cavalry. Henry, *"First with the Most" Forrest*, 179.
64. Connelly, *Autumn of Glory*, 152. Longstreet's actual strength was 11,716 officers and men. *Battles and Leaders*, III, 676.

On the basis of all the evidence Rosecrans had, he decided, wisely, that it was "a matter of life and death" to concentrate his forces and lost no time doing so. By the eighteenth he succeeded in getting Crittenden, Thomas, and McCook joined in a more or less continuous line above the west bank of Chickamauga Creek, Crittenden on the north with his left at Lee and Gordon's Mills, Thomas in the center in McLemore's Cove, at the foot of Stevens' Gap, and McCook on Thomas' right, a position he reached after a three-day march of fifty-seven miles that included two crossings of Lookout Mountain.[65] Granger's Reserve Corps moved down from Chattanooga to Rossville, where he was within about eight miles of Crittenden's left. The cavalry was recalled from Alpine and posted at Crawfish Springs (presently called Chickamauga) on McCook's right, to guard the large field hospital there as well as the crossings of the Chickamauga upstream from the hospital; it was to operate under McCook's orders.[66]

The Lightning Brigade, less the 92nd Illinois, which had been detached to man a courier line on Lookout Mountain, was ordered on September 12 to join Reynolds' division of the XIV Corps. Marching along the Ringgold-LaFayette road, the brigade ran into a hornet's nest. They struck the pickets of John Pegram's division of Forrest's corps, who led them into a trap at Leet's Tan-yard. Pegram's main body was "posted Indian fashion behind trees" to their front; Frank Armstrong's cavalry brigade on their left; John S. Scott's cavalry in the rear; and General O. F. Strahl's brigade of infantry, backed by the rest of Polk's corps, across the road from Lee and Gordon's Mills and the Union infantry of the XXI Corps.[67] The brigade lost thirteen killed and nineteen wounded in driving Armstrong and Pegram out of their way, but an indication of the effectiveness of Spencer rifles in the hands of Wilder's men is General Pegram's admission that the loss of his command alone in this fight, which "for a time . . . was almost literally hand to hand . . . was

65. Chickamauga Creek, so called in this and all other accounts of the battle, is actually *West* Chickamauga Creek. It joins *East* Chickamauga Creek near Chattanooga. Called *South* Chickamauga Creek beyond the junction of its two branches, it flows into the Tennessee from the south nearly opposite the mouth of *North* Chickamauga Creek, which flows into the Tennessee from the north.

66. *Official Records*, Vol. XXX, Pt. 1, pp. 54–55.

67. This was the same Colonel Scott whose dispatch on September 22 to General B. F. Cheatham, commanding a division in Polk's corps, is a classic of high-level Confederate indiscipline. See Vol. I, 226n of the present work, or *Official Records*, Vol. XXX, Pt. 2, p. 530.

about 50 killed and wounded, numbering some of . . . [the] most valu-able young officers."[68]

Forcing the Confederate cavalry out of the way was not the end of Wilder's difficulties. He had still to find a way around the infantry blocking his route to Lee and Gordon's Mills, and to forestall a con-centric Confederate attack on his brigade while he did so. At dusk, therefore, he resorted to the time-honored dodge of building campfires over a large area, deployed three of his regiments and his artillery to meet a possible attack, and set the 17th Indiana to hunt for an escape route, which the Hoosiers did by collecting "all the old inhabitants to act as guides, threatening them with death if they failed to lead them out of the trap." A way was found around the northern end of Strahl's position, and the brigade set out "across . . . fields, over ditches, hol-lows, fences, stumps and everything in the way of obstructions. . . . [They] crossed and recrossed roads, followed cow paths &c." and at midnight, after an eight-mile march, reached Crittenden's lines with-out the loss of a man and "with greatly relieved [sic] minds."[69]

While the Wilder brigade operated on what appeared to be a roving commission, joined now to one infantry division or corps, now to an-other, Minty's brigade, again numbering 1,200 effectives, marched south on September 13 from Chattanooga to Lee and Gordon's Mills. Under the orders of General Crittenden (a situation that seemed not to meet with Colonel Minty's approval) they spent the next four days picketing and scouting, mainly in the neighborhood of Reed's Bridge, "a narrow, frail structure . . . planked with loose boards and fence rails," across Chickamauga Creek, downstream not quite two miles from Wilder's brigade at Alexander's Bridge and five miles from Lee and Gordon's Mills.

On the evening of the fifteenth, Minty reported to General Crit-tenden that Longstreet was at Dalton, Georgia.[70] The information was

68. *Official Records*, Vol. XXX, Pt. 2, p. 528; Rowell, *Yankee Artillerymen*, 106–109.

69. *Official Records*, Vol. XXX, Pt. 1, pp. 447, 450–51, 454–55; Rowell, *Yankee Artillerymen*, 108–109. The statement in Colonel Wilder's report that to make his escape he decided to "cut [his] way through" and accordingly "charged Strahl's com-mand, driving back his left, and opening the road," is not borne out by any of his subordi-nates' reports, nor by the journal of one of his men, quoted in Rowell, *Yankee Artil-lerymen*, 109.

70. *Official Records*, Vol. XXX, Pt. 1, pp. 921–22; Vale, *Minty and the Cavalry*, 216–17, 219–20.

premature and Crittenden placed no faith in it. Obviously, however, word of Longstreet's transfer from Virginia to reinforce Bragg preceded his arrival in Tennessee, and the fact that Minty's scouts were able to pick up the information demonstrated once more the woeful lack of security about military movements in the Confederacy. Despite the inexcusable publicity his transfer to Tennessee received, Longstreet's people were able to take their place in the Confederate line of battle along Chickamauga Creek, and to play a decisive part in the defeat of the Union army on September 20.

XII

The Battle to the Strong

THE SEVENTEENTH OF SEPTEMBER SAW THE PRELIMI-
naries of "The Great Battle of the West," the battle of Chickamauga.
Bragg had been unable to take advantage of the opportunity to attack
Rosecrans' corps and divisions while they were scattered over the land-
scape. Now, when they had been collected and deployed in line behind
the left bank of Chickamauga Creek, facing east, Bragg prepared to
attack them. The terrain over which the ensuing battle of Chickamauga was fought is exceptionally broken and complex, even after the
currycombing it has received at the hands of the National Park Service; in 1863 it was a nightmarish tangle of barely penetrable forest
and underbrush, with visibility in many places limited to a few yards.
It is therefore understandable that Bragg's approach march from LaFayette carried his right wing well to the north of the northern end of
Crittenden's position at Lee and Gordon's Mills. This was potentially a
piece of good fortune for Bragg, for it presented him with the opportunity of cutting Rosecrans off from Chattanooga and of driving him at
the same time southward into the cul-de-sac of McLemore's Cove to be
destroyed or captured.

Bragg's orders for the eighteenth called for Bushrod R. Johnson's
3,600-man division to cross the Chickamauga at Reed's Bridge and
turn left, General W. H. T. Walker's "Reserve Corps" of two divisions
(5,000 men) to cross at Alexander's Bridge and also turn left, and two

divisions of Buckner's corps to cross at Thedford's (or Tedford's) Ford, three quarters of a mile upstream from Alexander's Bridge, and join Johnson and Walker in a grand sweep left toward what was thought to be the northern flank of Rosecrans' line.[1]

Had Bragg's design succeeded, he would take rank with Generals Lee and Jackson in the Confederate generals' pantheon, instead of being the favorite whipping boy of every analyst of Confederate defeat in the West. The failure of the plan was certainly not due to any lack of soldierly qualities in the rank and file of his army. Indeed, they played their part with unexampled drive and devotion; they attacked and kept on attacking regardless of losses, until all they could see of the enemy was the flashes of their guns in the darkness. They, and the Union infantry who fought under Thomas on Snodgrass Hill on September 20, made Chickamauga one of the hardest-fought and most costly battles of the war, in which the Army of Tennessee and the reinforcements James Longstreet brought from Virginia sustained nearly 18,500 (or 28 percent) casualties.

There were several reasons for the failure of Bragg's plan; the first, as he pointed out in his report, was the stout resistance put up by Minty's brigade at Reed's Bridge, and Wilder's at Alexander's Bridge. Bushrod Johnson, joined in the afternoon by three brigades of John Bell Hood's division from Virginia, was delayed in his approach to the bridge by having to use "bad and narrow country roads," but he was then held up well east of the bridge by Minty's brigade. On the evening of the seventeenth, Minty had been near enough to Ringgold to hear the chuffing of locomotives on the Western & Atlantic; the brigade historian claims that "almost hourly" Minty sent dispatches to General Crittenden to report that "train after train was arriving at Ringgold from the South."[2] Crittenden, so the historian states, decided that what Minty heard was the noise of trains hauling off some of the stores Bragg had had to leave behind and that there was nothing but dismounted cavalry facing Minty. Colonel Minty was sure that he was right and, by daylight the next morning, had large patrols of the 4th

1. *Official Records*, Vol. XXX, Pt. 2, p. 31; *Battles and Leaders*, III, 649. General Polk, at Lee and Gordon's Mills, was to cross there or over one of the fords downstream from it. Wheeler's assignment was to hold the gaps through Pigeon Mountain, protect the left and rear of the army, "and bring up stragglers."

2. Vale, *Minty and the Cavalry*, 224. These "almost hourly" dispatches are not to be found in the *Official Records*, nor are they mentioned by Minty in his report.

United States, 4th Michigan, and 7th Pennsylvania, out toward Ring-gold and Leet's Tan-yard to bring timely word of the Confederate advance that he was sure was about to strike him from that direction. Within an hour word came back from the patrols that the Confederates were approaching in heavy force. He immediately notified Colonel Wilder, and Generals Granger, Crittenden, and Thomas J. Wood, the latter in command of the left-wing division of Crittenden's corps. Aided by two regiments of the Wilder brigade and a section of Captain Lilly's battery, which Colonel Wilder sent in response to Minty's request for help, he made a fighting retreat across Pea Vine Creek and Pea Vine Ridge to the Chickamauga, which he reached far enough ahead of the Confederate infantry to give him time "to mask" his artillery, a section of the Chicago Board of Trade Battery, in the scrub trees and bushes on the right bank of the Chickamauga a short distance below the bridge.

When the head of the column of Johnson's infantry, "moving at the double-quick as steadily as if at drill," came charging toward the bridge, Minty's artillery opened on them with canister from the flank at point-blank range. This brought the charge to a halt, and as the foot-soldiers, aided by Forrest with a few hundred men (dismounted) of his command, began to deploy from column into line, they were charged with the saber by the 7th Pennsylvania and the 4th Michigan. But the horsemen were greatly outnumbered, and the Confederate infantry on the flank of the units directly facing the charge by the two cavalry regiments pivoted on their left and came running toward the bridge. "For several moments it looked as though the whole [of Minty's] brigade east of the creek would be captured or annihilated; the enemy . . . artillery raking every foot of the space between the little line of mounted men and the bridge," and raking the bridge as well.[3] The 4th Michigan, followed by the 7th Pennsylvania, in column of twos (the bridge was too narrow for the normal column of fours), crossed the bridge at a trot; a desperation charge with the saber by a single squadron of the 4th United States, led by Lieutenant Wirt Davis, bought the time needed for the men from Michigan and Pennsylvania to get across the bridge and for the artillery to ford the stream to safety. Lieutenant Davis did even more. As he retreated across the bridge after charging the enemy, he and a few of his men dismounted, and "though [the

3. *Ibid.*, 226.

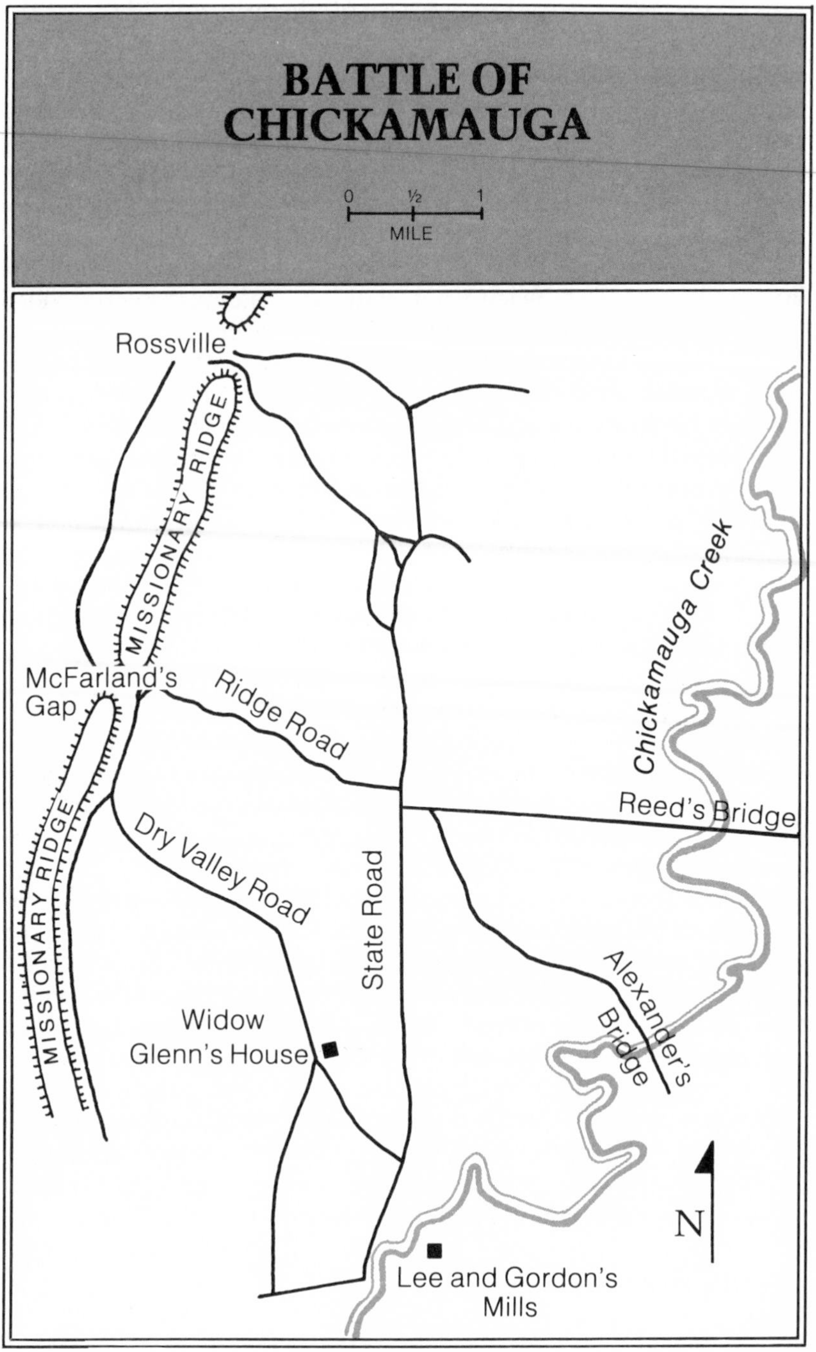

BATTLE OF
CHICKAMAUGA

0   ½   1
MILE

Rossville

MISSIONARY RIDGE

McFarland's Gap

MISSIONARY RIDGE

Ridge Road

Dry Valley Road

State Road

Chickamauga Creek

Reed's Bridge

Alexander's Bridge

Widow Glenn's House

Lee and Gordon's Mills

N

bridge] was then raked by every discharge from the rebel artillery," tore up the flooring and made the bridge impassable.[4]

Driven across the stream, Minty deployed his men and his guns on high ground to the west and for another two hours held off the Confederate infantry, now commanded by General Hood. Minty reported that it was not until he had word that Wilder had been driven back from Alexander's Bridge that he himself retreated to Lee and Gordon's Mills, where he joined the Wilder brigade. He had his men dismount and help Wilder and an infantry brigade of General Van Cleve's division repel a late-evening Confederate attack. He claims in a tone of obvious self-satisfaction that at Reed's Bridge his brigade of 973 men "had disputed the advance of 7,000 rebels from 7 o'clock in the morning until 5 in the evening."[5]

It is apparent from the reports, as well as from the fact that Wilder was able to send two of his four regiments and two of his six pieces of artillery to help Minty, that he was less severely pressed at Alexander's Bridge than was Minty two miles downstream. He was attacked by a single brigade of Walker's corps in the morning and three brigades in the afternoon but repulsed both attacks with ease.[6] At about five in the afternoon, Wilder withdrew from his position at the bridge and joined Crittenden's corps to the south.

The historian may choose between a number of explanations of Colonel Wilder's late-afternoon retreat. His own explanation is that he withdrew after his pickets brought him word that a "strong force" of enemy infantry had reached the rear of his position facing the bridge, but he does not say how they got there. Colonel Miller of the 72nd Indiana has the enemy forcing a passage over a ford halfway between the two bridges, and with communications between the Wilder and Minty brigades cut, it was deemed advisable for Wilder's regiments to fall back on the Union infantry at Lee and Gordon's Mills. Captain Lilly explains that Wilder withdrew after Minty's brigade was driven back

4. John B. Hood, *Advance and Retreat* (New Orleans, 1880), 61.

5. *Official Records*, Vol. XXX, Pt. 1, p. 923, which also describes the action. See also Vale, *Minty and the Cavalry*, 224–27, and Sipes, *The Seventh Pennsylvania*, 79–80.

6. *Official Records*, Vol. XXX, Pt. 1, p. 447. The historian of the 72nd Indiana claims that the attacks were repelled by a single company, Company A, of his regiment. "No artillery was used at all; only the repeating Spencers, in the hands of brave, cool men, who knew how to use them. . . . It was one company defeating a whole division, and the rebels were shown what fearful execution a few determined men could do with such rifles in their hands." McGee, *History of the 72nd Indiana*, 171.

from Reed's Bridge. Colonel James Monroe, 123rd Illinois, says simply and bluntly that the Lightning Brigade was "driven back" from the bridge. General Walker, whose men attacked Wilder at the bridge, reports that General Edward C. Walthall's brigade "after a sharp and short encounter took the bridge, which was torn up by the enemy, making it necessary for the command to cross at Byram's Ford."[7]

It is of interest to note a significant foretaste of the future that occurred after the fighting stopped late in the evening of the eighteenth. The historian of one of Wilder's regiments recalled, "We knew the value of hastily constructed defenses, and we all dropped our guns and went vigorously to work piling up rails and logs and by the time the sun was up we had a line of works from which Longstreet's whole corps failed to drive us that day."[8]

Fighting on the nineteenth began with cavalry in action—Confederate cavalry on this occasion—Pegram's division and Dibrell's brigade, dismounted, and led by Forrest himself, distinguished by the long linen duster he wore, attacking the northernmost unit of Thomas' corps, a brigade of infantry commanded by John T. Croxton, who was to make his mark in command of a brigade of cavalry in James H. Wilson's Selma Campaign.[9] At Chickamauga, Croxton performed a notable feat; he not only brought Forrest's attack to a halt but also drove him back on his infantry.[10] The fighting on Thomas' left wing intensified as more and more of the Union infantry of McCook's and Crittenden's corps marched north to reinforce the endangered left wing of the army.

An incidental result of the northward shift of Rosecrans' forces was that Wilder's brigade, which had been on the left wing of the army on the evening of the eighteenth, found itself constituting the right wing on the nineteenth. Wilder now had the assignment of protecting from the attacks of Bragg's infantry the army's right flank, which had moved to a point nearly two miles downstream from Lee and Gordon's Mills.

7. *Official Records*, Vol. XXX, Pt. 1, pp. 447 (Wilder), 451 (Miller), 466 (Lilly), 460 (Monroe), and Pt. 2, p. 239 (Walker).

8. McGee, *History of the 72nd Indiana*, 173–74. The mounted infantry were not alone in learning the usefulness of such impromptu defenses. General D. H. Hill wrote that the ringing of axes could be heard in the Union lines all night, and by morning the four divisions of Union infantry facing him were protected by "substantial breastworks of logs." *Battles and Leaders*, III, 654, 654n.

9. See Vol. I, pp. 31, 33, 33n of the present work.

10. *Battles and Leaders*, III, 649; Henry, *"First with the Most" Forrest*, 184; Wyeth, *That Devil Forrest*, 223–26.

He accomplished this by frequent shifts of position and front, seeking always to be in a position from which his men could deliver an enfilading fire from their Spencers and from the guns of Lilly's battery on the closely massed columns of the infantry of Bragg's left wing.[11]

Minty's brigade rested on the nineteenth. Relieved by infantry at daybreak, the brigade moved to the rear, where the troopers fed their horses and ate breakfast—the first food the men had had since daybreak of the previous day—then marched north as a guard for the trains moving toward Chattanooga, and camped for the night near Rossville. The rest of the Union cavalry—the First Division (less Minty's brigade), commanded by Colonel McCook, and George Crook's Second Division—were ordered to assemble at Crawfish Springs, where they protected the southern end of Missionary Ridge and the "spare trains" of the army. Except for skirmishes with the enemy, which at times were severe enough, the cavalry saw no action on the nineteenth. In the evening, Rosecrans ordered General Mitchell to detail one of his regiments to deliver water in buckets to their colleagues of the infantry, who had spent the day under a hot sun in the firing line. The 39th Indiana Mounted Infantry also played the role of Good Samaritans; they gathered up a thousand canteens, filled them at Crawfish Springs, and on their way north to join Wilder passed them out to the thirsty infantry.[12]

When the firing ceased on the evening of September 19 after a day of heavy casualties for both sides, neither Rosecrans nor Bragg could claim a victory. On balance, however, the strategic advantage seemed to incline in Rosecrans' favor. He had not only succeeded in uniting his army but had also thwarted Bragg's design of cutting him off from Chattanooga and driving him to destruction in the mountains. As night fell, the two armies lay facing each other on a north-south line, well to the west of Chickamauga Creek, preparing as well as they were able for a renewal of the battle the next day.

In the belief that he was greatly outnumbered by Bragg, Rosecrans intended to fight a defensive battle on the twentieth. Bragg's plan, on the other hand, was to continue the offensive. He intended to attack

11. *Official Records*, Vol. XXX, Pt. 1, pp. 447–48. Wilder reported that his artillery had fired "over 200 rounds of double-shotted 10-pounder canister at a range varying from 70 to 350 yards, and at the same time kept up a constant fire with our repeating rifles, causing the most fearful destruction in the rebel ranks." *Ibid.*, 448.

12. *Ibid.*, 923, 893, 57, and Pt. 3, p. 744; Rowell, *Yankee Artillerymen*, 121.

the Union left flank at daybreak and, as each of his divisions took up the attack in succession from north to south, they were to pivot on their left and drive the Union army toward and into McLemore's Cove, as Bragg had intended them to do on the previous day. Bragg planned for the attack on the Union left to be delivered at dawn, but it did not come until sometime between 9 and 10 A.M. John C. Breckinridge's division was the spearhead, with Forrest's cavalry, again dismounted, on its right. Despite large losses, Breckinridge and Forrest fought their way through and well to the rear of the left flank of Thomas' line, held by General Absalom Baird's division, but were then driven back by re-inforcements rushed northward by Rosecrans, and by the timely arrival of Gordon Granger's Reserve Corps, marching to the sound of the guns. The Confederates kept attacking but were checked and driven back each time by the reinforcements, sometimes a brigade, sometimes only a regiment or two, hurried to the threatened point by General Thomas himself.

Thomas' left flank was under attack at the same time that Longstreet's divisions on Bragg's left moved in succession to attack Crittenden and McCook in their front. These attacks, and the continuing need to send reinforcements to shore up Thomas' hard-pressed left flank, combined with a poorly worded order and a disgruntled subordinate (General Thomas J. Wood) to produce a wide gap, vacated by Wood's division of the XXI Corps, through which Longstreet drove eight brigades of his infantry. The five brigades of Alexander McD. McCook's corps (including Sheridan's division) and a brigade of Crittenden's, caught on the move beyond the break, were driven off the field with losses McCook estimated at 40 percent. But the far more serious damage to the Union army came about as a result of Longstreet's (or Hood's) decision to ignore Bragg's wishes; instead of turning south after breaching the Union line, he had his men wheel to the right to deliver a murderous attack on the open south (right) flank of Crittenden's corps. Longstreet's men, many of whom were to die before that day was over, sensed a great victory as they rushed northward from beyond the gap, "shouting, yelling, running over batteries, capturing trains, taking prisoners, seizing . . . [Rosecrans'] headquarters . . . until they found themselves facing the new Federal line."[13] This new line,

13. *Battles and Leaders*, III, 657–58, 688; Hood, *Advance and Retreat*, 63–64; James Longstreet, *From Manassas to Appomattox: Memoirs of the Civil War in America* (Philadelphia, 1896), 449.

General Gordon Granger
Courtesy National Archives

General John T. Croxton
Courtesy National Archives

Colonel John T. Wilder
Courtesy Archives, Eli Lilly and Company

on a horseshoe-shaped ridge named Snodgrass Hill, was hastily organized by Thomas and Granger and manned by every soldier they could collect from the wreckage of the army. Thomas was everywhere in evidence, and the magnificent stand made by his troops in the face of the equally magnificent attacks that came at them time after time, earned him the name of The Rock of Chickamauga.

One of the commanding officers of the Union army to come out of the battle with an enhanced reputation (there were not many) was Colonel Wilder. On the morning of the twentieth his brigade was posted on Missionary Ridge, on the right rear of McCook's corps and about two miles southwest of Rosecrans' headquarters at the Widow Glenn's house. Shortly after noon, as he was in the process of moving to close up to McCook's right, the Union line was breached, and Wilder saw on his left "a column of rebels, five lines deep," charging the Union infantry to the north of the break, "driving them by weight of numbers in great confusion into the woods in their rear."[14] This gave Wilder his opportunity. His brigade, which had been joined by the 39th Indiana Mounted Infantry, was squarely on the flank of the attacking troops—Arthur M. Manigault's brigade of Hindman's division—and was deployed in line of regiments, which made it possible for two regiments, the 17th Indiana and the 123rd Illinois, to fire into the enemy with their Spencers at the murderous range of less than fifty yards. The first volley caused Manigault's men to break and run, but they reassembled in a patch of woods to the rear and charged again past the sheet of fire of Wilder's Spencers. Driven back again, they reassembled and charged for the third time and, unbelievably, tried twice more, losing altogether 66 officers and men killed, 426 wounded, and 47 missing.[15] The rest of Wilder's brigade having come into line, he led them in an attack on the rest of Hindman's division, driving them back to the State Road running south to Lee and Gordon's Mills and capturing two of their guns while doing so. So continuous was the fire of his brigade's Spencers that it caused Longstreet to think (as he told Wilder after the war) that he was under attack by an entire army corps, and it held up his deployment against Thomas just long enough to enable the latter to extend his lines on Snodgrass Hill to meet Longstreet's attack when it came.

14. *Official Records*, Vol. XXX, Pt. 1, p. 448. Wilder cites the time as 11:30 A.M. in his report.

15. *Ibid.*, Pt. 2, pp. 291, 342, Pt. 1, p. 448; *Battles and Leaders*, III, 658–59n.

In the chaos of an obvious Union defeat, with the woods "full of . . . fugitives, running in every direction, ambulances filled with wounded, the drivers frantically urging the horses on, they knew not whither; artillerymen . . . trying to get their guns away, in many cases with but a single span of horses. Caissons, limber chests, guns, ambulances and men . . . wandering in confusion over the hills and knobs like sheep without a shepherd," the Lightning Brigade held together. Wilder was talked out of his intention to join General Thomas on Snodgrass Hill, first by General McCook's chief of staff, who "advised" (or "ordered") him to fall back to Lookout Mountain; then by the uncalledfor interference of a panic-stricken civilian, Assistant Secretary of War Charles A. Dana, who told Wilder that the army had suffered "a worse rout than Bull Run" and "strongly advised . . . [him] to fall back and occupy the passes over Lookout Mountain, to prevent the rebel occupancy of it"; and lastly by Sheridan, who did not have one of his better days at Chickamauga and sent word to Wilder that he had "better fall back to the Chattanooga Valley." This Wilder proceeded to do, marching off "in good order," his "command in good condition except . . . [the] horses . . . [and] bringing off wagon trains, ambulance trains, a supply of recaptured ammunition, and stragglers from Generals Sheridan's, Davis', and Van Cleve's commands."[16]

Two months later, General Thomas, Rosecrans' successor in command of the Department and Army of the Cumberland, transmitted Wilder's report of the operations of his brigade from August 16 to the end of the battle of Chickamauga, with the following endorsement: "For his ingenuity and fertility of resource in occupying the attention of an entire corps of the rebel army while our army was getting around its flank, and for his valor and the many qualities of a commander displayed by him in the numerous engagements of his brigade with the enemy before and during the battle of Chickamauga, and for the excellent service rendered by him generally, I would . . . recommend him . . . for an appointment as brigadier-general." Rosecrans, whose recommendations after Chickamauga counted for very little, nevertheless added his encomium to that of Thomas. He spoke of the "brilliant part" played by Wilder's brigade in attracting Bragg's attention up-

16. *Official Records*, Vol. XXX, Pt. 1, p. 449, Pt. 3, p. 751. Major Connolly wrote after the battle: "We got through the three days of fighting without losing many men. We think our Spencers saved us, and our men admire them as the heathen do their idols." Connolly, *Army of the Cumberland*, 127.

stream from Chattanooga while the army was preparing to make its crossing downstream, of his "bold and successful" fight at Leet's Tanyard, and of his "noble stand" at Alexander's Bridge and urged that Wilder be promoted to brigadier general as a reward "for his many gallant services."[17]

Unfortunately, these words of praise and recommendations came too late. Wilder's health broke down. Two days after the battle he had to turn over command of the brigade to the senior colonel, Abram O. Miller of the 72nd Indiana Mounted Infantry, and on September 22 he went home on sick leave.[18]

Rosecrans wrecked his career with an impulsive error of judgment at Chickamauga. So overwhelming was the impact on his mind and judgment of Hood's breakthrough, so shocking the rout of Davis', Sheridan's, and Van Cleve's divisions that Rosecrans decided that the battle was lost beyond recovery, and he rode to Chattanooga to organize a last-ditch defense instead of joining Thomas on Snodgrass Hill. It has been well said that "his nerve and will seem to have collapsed."[19]

Late in the afternoon the attacks on Thomas slackened sufficiently to enable him to withdraw, a division at a time, from Snodgrass Hill to Rossville. There, during the night, Thomas organized his infantry in a defensive line stretching from Missionary Ridge on the left to Chattanooga Creek on the right. General Mitchell, at Crawfish Springs, learned late in the afternoon of the disaster on the Union right; he therefore decided to leave his now isolated position. He started his trains, and ambulances loaded with all the wounded in the Crawfish Springs hospital able to be moved, up the Chattanooga Valley toward the town and followed them with his cavalry. On the way north his men collected two pieces of artillery abandoned by General McCook's gunners, and "about a regiment of stragglers from the same command," and bivouacked for the night to the right of Thomas' infantry.

On the next day, September 21, Mitchell kept his men in line of battle and had frequent skirmishes with the enemy.[20] Among the at-

17. *Official Records*, Vol. XXX, Pt. 1, pp. 444, 79.
18. *Ibid.*, Pt. 3, pp. 779–80, 804; Williams, *General John T. Wilder*, 39.
19. McKinney, *Education in Violence*, 264.
20. *Official Records*, Vol. XXX, Pt. 1, p. 893. There was no interference with Mitchell's retreat on the twentieth, because Wheeler had been kept on the right (east) bank of Chickamauga Creek and was not ordered until 5 P.M. to pursue the retreating Federals. Connelly, *Autumn of Glory*, 225–26.

tackers were four hundred men of the Confederate cavalry led by Forrest and General Armstrong. This was the occasion when Forrest climbed to a treetop observation platform that had been built by Union signalmen, from which he could see "Chattanooga and every thing around." In a message to General Polk marked "Please forward to Gen Bragg," he reported: "I think they are evacuating as hard as they can go. . . . I think We ought to push forward as rapidly as possible."[21] Forrest was, however, mistaken. Rosecrans had recovered his nerve and had no intention of leaving Chattanooga. In the next forty-eight hours, his men worked furiously to improve the defenses that Bragg had left behind and to build new ones, and at the end of that time they had constructed a secure position for themselves. After some hesitations and controversy on what should be done, the Confederates, in possession of Lookout Mountain on the west and Missionary Ridge on the east, and therefore able to interdict the flow of supplies into Chattanooga, settled down to besiege and starve out the Union army.

Notwithstanding some claims to the contrary, the Army of the Cumberland had taken a severe drubbing at Chickamauga. In addition to casualties amounting to more than a quarter of the army, they lost 51 guns, 24,000 small arms, many wagons and ambulances, and large quantities of supplies.[22] But in some respects this was a most peculiar defeat. The men in the ranks knew they had been beaten but seemed not at all disheartened. Infantry General John Beatty wrote on the evening of the twentieth, "We have been badly used during the day; but it does not occur to us that our army has been whipped." Two weeks later he still felt the same way: "[The enemy's] long lines of campfires almost encompass us. But the campfires of the Army of the Cumberland are burning also. Bruised and torn by a two days' unequal contest, its flags are still up and its men still unwhipped." General Rousseau, given the job on the morning of September 21 to "sort out" the disorganized troops and send the men back to their units, "found the task comparatively easy, the men separated from their regiments being in

21. Wyeth, *That Devil Forrest*, 236.

22. *Battles and Leaders*, III, 673. Granger lost 1,788 men killed, wounded, and missing, nearly 50 percent of his total force of 3,700. Bragg's losses, too, were severe. The total was nearly 18,000, of whom 2,389 were killed; twelve of Bragg's regiments sustained losses of more than 50 percent. *Ibid.*, 667, 675–76; Connelly, *Autumn of Glory*, 226. "In percentage of losses, Chickamauga's casualties were heavier than those of any other Civil War battle." McKinney, *Education in Violence*, 261.

high spirits and not at all cowed. . . . I find the troops in fine spirits and ready to reenter the fight."[23] Major Connolly of Wilder's brigade wrote, "We are *somewhat* whipped but will get over it"—not an observation reflecting discouragement.[24] The one exception was the commanding general, who wired both Halleck and Burnside on the afternoon of the twentieth, "We have met with a severe disaster." The president thought it well to reassure him: "Be of good cheer. We have unabated confidence in you and in your soldiers and officers. . . . We shall do our utmost to assist you."[25]

Whatever comfort Rosecrans may have derived from the president's message, or from the dispatches Halleck sent him to let him know of the reinforcements being rushed to him from the North, the West, and the East, may well have served to disguise the bitter fact that, in the eyes of the administration in Washington, his usefulness as commanding officer of the Army of the Cumberland was ended. The decision to relieve him was made at the beginning of October and was effected in two steps: the War Department's announcement on October 16 of the establishment of the Military Division of the Mississippi, to embrace the Departments of the Ohio, Cumberland, and Tennessee, with Grant in command; and the replacement of Rosecrans on October 20 by George Thomas in command of the Department and Army of the Cumberland.[26]

Once the position at Chattanooga was stabilized, Rosecrans', then Thomas', overriding problem was to get enough food for their men and forage for their animals into the town. The Confederates on Lookout Mountain and on Raccoon Mountain, its neighbor to the west, blocked all direct access to Chattanooga from Nashville and the northwest generally, by rail, river, and road. Supplies could be hauled by rail as far as Bridgeport, but from there to Chattanooga to avoid the Confederate artillery they had to be wagoned on a triangular course more than 60 miles long, northeast up the Sequatchie Valley through Jasper and then on mountain trails southeast over Walden's Ridge to the pontoon

23. Beatty, *Memoirs of a Volunteer*, 251, 256; *Official Records*, Vol. XXX, Pt. 3, p. 782.

24. Connolly, *Army of the Cumberland*, 123. General Meigs reported on September 27 that "the men [are] vigorous, hearty, cheerful, and confident." *Official Records*, Vol. XXX, Pt. 3, p. 890.

25. *Official Records*, Vol. XXX, Pt. 1, pp. 142, 146.

26. *Ibid.*, Pt. 4, p. 404, and Vol. XXXI, Pt. 1, p. 669.

bridge across the Tennessee to Chattanooga. The roads and trails the wagon trains had to use were so poor that it took a loaded wagon ten days to make the sixty-mile journey, and on one occasion, five hundred wagons and their teams were stalled on the road. For a time, the troops in Chattanooga were on half rations. The area traversed by the road had long since been stripped bare of forage, and feed for the army's horses and mules had a low priority on the list of supplies to be hauled. As a result, the army is said to have lost ten thousand animals by starvation.

On September 24, Captain Chris. Beck reported on his inspection of the 2nd and 4th Indiana and 1st Wisconsin, forming the Second Brigade of the First (Edward McCook's) Division of the Cavalry Corps. It is probably safe to assume that Captain Beck's findings in these three regiments held good for the corps as a whole. The brigade, with an effective force of 1,068 officers and men, plus an amazingly small number of 58 dismounted men, was not, in the captain's opinion, "in a very efficient condition," owing to "the arduous duties" it had recently performed. "The horses are very much run down principally from a want of forage, which, under the circumstances, could not be had. Quite a large number of the men reported [fit] for duty are hardly so, but which a little rest and medical attention will soon remedy. The arms are in serviceable condition, and the command is fully supplied with ammunition . . . [but] is very much in need of clothing, especially boots."[27] Three days later, Colonel Louis D. Watkins, commanding the Third Brigade of the division, reported that the four Kentucky regiments (4th, 5th, 6th, and 7th) that made up his command numbered an aggregate of only 905 men, which certainly justified his comment that the brigade was "in a very bad condition, having been cut up at Crawfish Spring[s] on the 21st instant, losing one-half of their effective force in the engagement."[28]

In addition to guarding against a direct attack on his defenses at Chattanooga, Rosecrans also had to be concerned about the possibility that Bragg would cross the Tennessee above or below the town, break the Nashville & Chattanooga Railroad behind his army, and, with no major Union forces nearer than Memphis and Vicksburg to stop him,

27. *Ibid.*, Vol. XXX, Pt. 3, pp. 833–34.
28. *Ibid.*, 900. The "21st instant" date should be "20th instant." Mitchell's division had left Crawfish Springs on the afternoon of the previous day.

have a nearly unobstructed march to the Union base at Nashville. This was in fact the course of action Longstreet claimed to have urged Bragg to adopt.[29]

To forestall as best he could such a move by Bragg, on September 23 Rosecrans sent Crook and his division, numbering about two thousand "effective men," to guard the fords across the Tennessee for a distance of fifty miles upstream from Chattanooga, an impossible assignment for so small a force, for, as Crook explained, "The roads leading to the different fords and ferries were in many cases 5 miles apart. Between these points there were practicable fords almost every half mile."[30] Six days later, as part of a poorly coordinated cavalry attack on Rosecrans' communications, to be described later, Wheeler was ordered to take the divisions of Martin and Wharton of his own corps, and General D. H. Davidson's division of three brigades of Forrest's corps, a total of between five thousand and six thousand men, to raid the Sequatchie Valley–Walden's Ridge route Rosecrans' wagon trains had begun to use. The three brigades of Davidson's division numbered a mere five hundred men each, described as "badly armed . . . [with] but a small supply of ammunition, and their horses . . . in horrible condition. . . . The men . . . worn out and without rations."[31] With these forces Wheeler crossed the Tennessee over one of the "intermediate" fords George Crook had referred to and was unable to guard, and headed northwest.[32]

Wheeler crossed the Tennessee on the night of September 29. On October 1, Crook was ordered to pursue with all the mounted units he could collect; he set off with Minty's and Long's brigades and the Chicago Board of Trade Battery. The Lightning Brigade joined him on Walden's Ridge.[33] At the same time, Colonel McCook, guarding the ferries and fords in the Bridgeport area, was ordered to march at once up the Sequatchie Valley to Anderson's Cross-Roads (thirty-nine miles

29. Longstreet, *From Manassas to Appomattox*, 461; but see Connelly, *Autumn of Glory*, 229–30.

30. *Official Records*, Vol. XXX, Pt. 2, p. 684.

31. *Ibid.*, 723; see also *Ibid.*, Pt. 4, p. 719.

32. *Ibid.*, Pt. 3, pp. 952, 953. The crossing was made near Cottonport, forty miles from Chattanooga. It was opposed unsuccessfully by a battalion of the 4th Ohio. Francis T. Miller (ed.), *The Photographic History of the Civil War: The Cavalry* (New York, 1957), 160.

33. A fourth of the brigade had to be left behind "because of unfit horses." Rowell, *Yankee Artillerymen*, 127.

distant) "to protect . . . wagon trains."[34] This McCook proceeded to do with the three regiments of his division actually at hand, and he sent orders to Colonel Archibald P. Campbell at Pump Springs, Alabama, to follow him by forced marches with his brigade.

Shortly after crossing the river, Wheeler divided his forces. He himself, with about 1,500 of his men, crossed Walden's Ridge and rode down the Sequatchie Valley toward Dunlap and Jasper; the rest of his forces crossed the valley near Pikeville and rode westward toward McMinnville.[35] On the morning of October 2, at Anderson's Cross-Roads, south of Dunlap, Wheeler saw before him the head of an immense wagon train, its numbers given variously as from 800 to as high as 1,000 six-mule wagons "heavily loaded with ordnance, quartermaster's, and commissary stores," plus 40 or more sutlers' wagons.[36] Guarded by a mixed force of about 600 infantry and cavalry, the train occupied ten miles of road, end to end. After driving off the guard (the size of which is greatly overstated in Wheeler's report), the Confederates went to work on the train. The best of the mules and horses were unhitched, to be taken along by the raiders; many of the rest were sabered or shot. The wagons were looted of everything immediately usable—clothing and footwear were especially favored—and some number, given as from 300 to 500, were burned. The sutlers' wagons were of course the prime target for the hungry troopers and were thoroughly looted of their contents.[37]

While the raiders were still rioting among the burning wagons, Colonel McCook, coming up the valley, saw the column of smoke and increased his pace from a walk to a trot. He deployed the 1st Wisconsin and the 2nd Indiana side by side in column of battalions, charged the

34. *Official Records*, Vol. XXX, Pt. 4, p. 21. Two days earlier, McCook asked "if possible, to have four days' rest . . . and in this time [I] can, I think, have the command in as good a condition as when it left Triune last June. I can get horses and horse equipments enough at Stevenson to mount all my dismounted men, and can procure overcoats for the command there." *Ibid.*, Pt. 3, p. 920.

35. *Ibid.*, Pt. 4, p. 21. In reporting Wheeler's crossing of the Tennessee to General Halleck, Rosecrans could not resist adding, "As I have often advised, more mounted force will be needful to cover our advance, or even hold our own." But he did go on to make a well-justified request for an able cavalry commander "inasmuch as both Stanley and Mitchell were much disabled." The man he asked for was John Buford. *Ibid.*, 9.

36. On the way to Anderson's Cross-Roads, the raiders captured and destroyed a small train of 32 six-mule wagons. *Ibid.*, Pt. 2, p. 732.

37. For the destruction of the train, see *Ibid.*, 723; Miller (ed.), *Photographic History*, 160–64; Rowell, *Yankee Artillerymen*, 126–27.

raiders, and drove them back "with considerable loss." The Wisconsin regiment, with the loss of only 3 men wounded and 1 captured, claimed to have killed and wounded 37 of the enemy and to have taken 42 prisoners; "nearly all the wounds were inflicted with the saber," Colonel Oscar H. LaGrange reported.[38]

While Wheeler and his part of the raiding force were busy destroying the Federal wagon train, the rest of the raiders, under General Wharton, marched across Walden's Ridge, "over a road the most execrable I ever traversed," as Colonel George B. Hodge, commanding one of General Davidson's brigades, described it. Wheeler and his detachment joined the Wharton command at the northern foot of the Cumberland Plateau.[39] Crook was then fourteen hours behind Wharton, but he tried to narrow the gap by taking a shortcut called Robinson's Trace across the Cumberland Plateau and caught up with Wharton's rear guard, Colonel J. M. Crews's brigade of Davidson's division, at Thompson's Cove at the northern foot of the Plateau.[40] The terrain being "rocky and brushy, no place for cavalry to operate," Crook attacked with the Lightning Brigade, dismounted. They succeeded in surrounding Crews's small brigade, but by the time they had done so it was dark, and Crews was able to break through the encirclement and escape.[41]

The historian of one of the regiments of the Lightning Brigade had his own tongue-in-cheek explanation of the inability of Crook's cavalry to charge the enemy. The nature of the terrain was not the cause; in Thompson's Cove, he wrote, "we found our cavalry all massed in column . . . and the rebels in line of battle stretched across the mouth of the cove to receive us. The 4th U.S. Cavalry, of Minty's brigade, had the advance, and were urged to make a saber charge and drive the

---

38. *Official Records*, Vol. XXX, Pt. 2, pp. 683, 675–76. Another account gives Wheeler's loss as "120 killed and wounded (60 killed, chiefly with the saber) and 87 prisoners." *Ibid.*, 696. The conduct of Wheeler's men toward their captives (including civilians) and of the troopers of the Indiana and Wisconsin regiments toward theirs, became the subject of heated controversy. *Ibid.*, 819–21.

39. *Ibid.*, 726. The chronology of the raid from October 1 on is in a state of confusion, the Union and Confederate reports being in disagreement by one day. The present account follows the chronology in *Ibid.*, 663, but without full confidence in its accuracy.

40. The "trace," covered with loose stones, was so bad that 25 men had to be assigned to each caisson to help the horses drag it up the plateau. The two-mile uphill march took six hours. Rowell, *Yankee Artillerymen*, 128.

41. *Official Records*, Vol. XXX, Pt. 2, pp. 685, 693.

rebels out. The cavalry formed line and made ready, but for some cause did not charge. We afterwards learned that it was because they were barefooted, having traded their boots off over at . . . Washington [Tennessee]: and . . . we remembered that, as we came up the valley, we noticed all the women wore boots."[42]

On the morning of the fourth, the united commands of Wheeler and Wharton marched east to McMinnville, garrisoned by a green regiment, the 4th Tennessee Infantry, commanded by Major Michael L. Patterson. Summoned to surrender, Patterson did so "without making any resistance," according to General Crook, or, according to himself, not until after he had repulsed three charges by the enemy and lost seven of his men killed and thirty-one wounded and missing.[43] Wheeler claimed to have captured at McMinnville, in addition to the garrison, "an enormous supply of quartermaster's and commissary stores"; or, as General Crook reported it, he "sacked" the town, "destroying a great deal of public and private property."[44]

Just what Wheeler intended to do next is unclear. He moved out from McMinnville on the fifth to "make a demonstration" on Murfreesboro, but if, as stated in the Federal reports, the entire Union Cavalry Corps and the Lightning Brigade were at his heels and in actual contact with his rear guard, what did he hope to gain from a "demonstration"? Equally mystifying are the movements of Crook's command. On the evening before Wheeler captured McMinnville, the Lightning Brigade had the fight, mentioned above, with his rear guard. Approximately eighteen hours later Wheeler captured McMinnville, and then spent nearly eighteen undisturbed hours, from shortly after noon on October 4 until the morning of October 5, destroying government stores, a locomotive, a train of cars, and a bridge in the town. Not until he had left the town, and his rear guard was two miles beyond it, was he attacked by Crook.[45] Where was Crook, and what was he doing, from the evening of the third to the morning of the fifth?

Before Crook was joined by the First Division near Murfreesboro, he was outnumbered by Wheeler by two and a half or three to one and

42. McGee, *History of the 72nd Indiana*, 197.
43. *Official Records*, Vol. XXX, Pt. 2, pp. 685, 723, 726–27, 709–11.
44. *Ibid.*, 685.
45. *Ibid.*, 669, 723–24. The attack was made with the saber by the 2nd Kentucky, led by their Colonel Thomas P. Nicholas and brigade commander Eli Long. It drove the rear guard five miles onto Wheeler's main body. *Ibid.*, 685.

therefore may not be blameworthy for adopting the role of merely escorting the raiders, doing nothing more than to keep them moving by attacking their rear guard from time to time. Even after Crook and McCook joined forces and had the benefit of having their movements coordinated by the corps commander, General Mitchell, their pursuit did not prevent Wheeler from turning south to Shelbyville on the fifth and sacking and plundering the town.[46] Not until October 7, at Farmington, fourteen miles due west from Shelbyville, did the pursuers come to grips with the raiders.

The events of October 7 on the approaches to Farmington, except for the eventual outcome—an unmitigated defeat of Wheeler's forces—are, as usual, shrouded in a fog of conflicting reports and claims. What appears to have happened grew out of Wheeler's decision on the evening of the sixth to have his command, divided into three segments, camp north of the Shelbyville-Farmington road—Davidson's three brigades three miles west of Shelbyville, Martin's division two miles west of Davidson, and Wharton another two miles west of Martin. Wheeler does not explain why he chose to have the three units camp so far from one another. The reason may have been nothing more than the availability of water and forage; on the other hand, the men of the Lightning Brigade may well have been right in suspecting that he was setting a trap for the pursuers by vacating the road so that they could march far enough westward without hindrance to give Wharton the opportunity to attack them in front, Martin on their right flank, and Davidson in the rear.[47]

In the event, the plan (assuming it existed) miscarried, and Wheeler claimed that Davidson's failure to follow orders was the reason. As the Federals moved out on the seventh, with the Lightning Brigade leading, Colonel Miller learned of Davidson's whereabouts; he left the road and marched cross-country toward the enemy camp. He was met by John S. Scott's brigade, which he charged, first on horseback and then on foot, and routed. In this instance at least, the word *routed* was not the usual hyperbole of exaggerated or mendacious action reports. Davidson, alerted by the attack on Scott, got his men mounted and on the

---

46. *Ibid.*, 670, 727; Curry, *Four Years in the Saddle*, 137. Henry Campbell, bugler of the 18th Indiana Battery, noted that "ten or twelve" stores in the town were completely destroyed. Rowell, *Yankee Artillerymen*, 132. It is to be noted that Confederate troops behaved in this way in what was officially Confederate territory.

47. *Official Records*, Vol. XXX, Pt. 2, p. 724; Rowell, *Yankee Artillerymen*, 133.

move toward Farmington. Colonel Hodge, in obedience to orders to form a rear guard with his brigade, was taking his men to the rear at a gallop when, as he reported, he "encountered the whole of Scott's brigade crowded in frightful and horrible confusion, wild and frantic with panic, choking the entire road and bearing down upon me at racing speed. It was too late to clear the way; they rode over my command like madmen, some of them stopping only . . . when they reached the Tennessee."[48] General Davidson and Colonel Hodge succeeded in stopping enough of the fugitives to form a sketchy defense line, which, however, was pressed steadily back. "For five hours and a half, over 7 miles of country, the unequal contest continued," Hodge wrote; his brigade was "cut to pieces and slaughtered" by the unrelenting attacks on foot of the Lightning Brigade, alternating with "most gallant saber charge[s]" by the Second Brigade, led by Colonel Long, in one of which Long himself was wounded.[49] One of Long's troopers wrote after the war that this had been "a 'red letter day' for Crook's command. It was 'up and at them, boys' all day. No time to think of being tired and exhausted. It was 'mount and dismount,' then on to find the enemy and hit him another hard blow." A final charge just outside Farmington by Colonel Miller's brigade, dismounted, drove the Confederates through the village and captured four of their cannon and some wagons.[50]

Strangely enough, Colonel Minty, who normally tried hard to be in the forefront of any cavalry action, was not involved in the fighting between Shelbyville and Farmington on October 7. Having sent Minty orders when the enemy was first met in the morning to move forward to flank them on the right, Crook believed that if his orders had been followed, "a large portion" of Wheeler's force, "together with all his artillery and transportation," would have been surrounded and captured before they reached Farmington. General Mitchell, riding out from Shelbyville to join McCook's division, found Minty and his brigade resting peacefully in camp. Minty claimed that he had received no orders from Crook to move out. Guided by simple military common sense, which on this occasion seemed to have deserted the colonel,

48. *Official Records*, Vol. XXX, Pt. 2, p. 727. Wheeler reported, "Most of the troops fought most nobly; others acted shamefully." *Ibid.*, 666.

49. *Ibid.*, 728, 686, 691, 693–94, 695; Curry, *Four Years in the Saddle*, 137–38; Wulsin, *Story of the Fourth*, 45–46. The account in Wulsin is a transcript of a talk given by Captain William L. Curry, 1st Ohio, to the Ohio MOLLUS on April 1, 1908.

50. Wulsin, *Story of the Fourth*, 46; *Official Records*, Vol. XXX, Pt. 2, p. 687.

Mitchell ordered him "to move at once and join his command."[51] Minty did as he was told, but it was too late. By the time he reached Farmington, the day's fighting was over and the enemy gone. Quite properly, Crook placed him under arrest and turned over command of his brigade to Colonel Sipes of the 7th Pennsylvania. It is a great pity that General Crook's remarks to Minty on this occasion were not preserved, to brighten a page in the history of the Union cavalry.[52]

As the Lightning Brigade advanced toward Farmington on the heels of the retreating raiders, they saw "the road and the fields on each side . . . literally covered with dead and wounded rebels," and "stolen goods, abandoned arms," and northern uniforms strewn everywhere. In a dispatch to Bragg that the Yankees captured, Wheeler wrote that "many men were allowed by their officers to throw away their arms to bring out private plunder," much of which they had to throw away to stay ahead of their pursuers.[53] Nevertheless, the saddles of many of the horses captured by Crook's men "were completely covered with bundles of Calico[,] Clothes, Boots & everything conceivable in the way of plunder," and the dead, the wounded, and the prisoners, many of them wearing plundered civilian clothes or all or parts of the northern uniform, were relieved of the watches, money, hats, boots, and other plunder they had acquired in McMinnville and Shelbyville. Those wearing parts of the northern uniform ran a special risk, for Crook had ordered that such men were not to be taken prisoner. It is said that "a number" of them who tried to surrender were killed.[54]

On the morning of the eighth, pursuit of the Confederates, who had turned southwest through Pulaski, Tennessee, was resumed. By this time all the cavalry of the Army of the Cumberland was in the chase, most of them under General Mitchell, who rode with the First

51. *Official Records*, Vol. XXX, Pt. 2, pp. 687, 670.

52. *Ibid.*, 668, 687. Crook placed Minty in arrest partly for his behavior that day and partly for his "disposition manifested during the whole expedition to frustrate . . . [Crook's] dispositions in a covert manner." Minty asked for a court-martial or a court of inquiry, which was eventually granted. In February, 1864, he was tried on charges of "disobedience of orders" and "conduct subversive of good orders and military discipline," and acquitted. He was then restored to his command. *Ibid.*, 668*n*, and Pt. 4, p. 291, and Vol. XXXI, Pt. 1, p. 844.

53. Rowell, *Yankee Artillerymen*, 133–34; *Official Records*, Vol. XXX, Pt. 2, p. 666.

54. Rowell, *Yankee Artillerymen*, 134. The order directing the killing of Confederate cavalrymen wearing northern uniforms is, not surprisingly, absent from the *Official Records*. The passage concerning the order in question is quoted by Rowell from W. H. H. Benefiel, *History of Wilder's Brigade* (Pendleton, Ind., *ca.* 1913), 22.

Division, and some under General Stanley, who had returned to duty but had apparently not yet resumed command. Crook had left behind 500 dismounted men at Murfreesboro, and his numbers had been reduced further by the men killed or wounded in the fight at Farmington. He was nearest the enemy in the pursuit beyond Farmington. Wheeler evidently marched his men most or all of the night of the seventh and managed thereby to outdistance the pursuit, but his retreat had become a rout. He was shedding stragglers and deserters, broken wagons, baggage, broken-down horses, hats, canteens, coats, and weapons along the way.[55] General Crook reported that one entire enemy regiment, the 4th Alabama, C.S.A., "deserted and scattered through the mountains."[56] Wheeler arrived at the Tennessee River ahead of the pursuers, and the last of his men reached safety on the south bank of the river at Muscle Shoals just as the 7th Pennsylvania, leading the pursuit that day, arrived at the north bank.

The ten-day campaign, in which Crook's division and the Lightning Brigade together lost 14 killed and 103 wounded, was over.[57] Wheeler had succeeded in destroying much of a huge wagon train loaded with supplies badly needed in Chattanooga, but he was (or seemed to be) kept on the run thereafter by Crook and not given time to inflict major damage on the Nashville & Chattanooga, which would have been far more injurious to the Union than was the destruction of a single supply train, however large. For this accomplishment, Wheeler paid with the loss of a large number of his men—no fewer than 2,000 of them, in General Crook's opinion, or between 2,000 and 3,000 in General Mitchell's—killed, wounded, taken prisoner, or deserted.[58] If these estimates were reasonably close to the mark, Wheeler's command was very nearly wrecked. Nor should the loss of morale caused by defeat be forgotten.

Crook's cavalrymen, encamped on the night of October 9 at Rogersville, just north of the Tennessee River, after what they decided in retrospect had been "the hardest continuous ten days' riding and fighting in which . . . [they] participated during the war," looked forward to getting a few days of badly needed rest. But that night, as one of them

55. *Official Records*, Vol. XXX, Pt. 4, p. 371; Wulsin, *Story of the Fourth*, 47.
56. *Official Records*, Vol. XXX, Pt. 2, p. 688.
57. Nearly all of these losses fell on the Lightning Brigade: 13 of the killed and 79 of the wounded. One of the killed was Colonel James Monroe of the 123rd Illinois. *Ibid.*, 673, 696.
58. *Ibid.*, 688, 673.

recorded in his diary, "Hundreds of campfires are burning . . . the camp is ringing with shout and song, the boys all feeling happy over the success of the campaign."[59] General Mitchell, less carefree, as he had to be, than his troopers, reported that the command was "badly used up. Hard marches, scarcity of [horse]shoes (although each man carried two at starting), and miserable, worthless saddles that never should have been bought by the Government, or put on a horse's back after they were bought, have ruined many of the horses."[60]

Mention should be made of the fact that Wheeler's raid was intended by Bragg to be the right-hand branch of a three-pronged attack on Rosecrans' communications. The left-hand branch was to be a raid by General Stephen D. Lee from Alabama on the Duck River and Elk River crossings of the Nashville & Chattanooga. The center prong was to be an attack on the Federal wagon road in Sequatchie Valley by General Philip Roddey's 1,000-man division from northern Alabama. In the event, Lee, with 2,000 men, marched north as far as the Tennessee, decided not to cross, and marched back to his base. Roddey did cross the river, but before he could accomplish anything, he learned of Wheeler's retreat and recrossed the river.[61]

In his "Special Field Orders" issued just before he gave up command of the Army of the Cumberland, Rosecrans praised and thanked his cavalry, "and particularly General Crook, with the officers and soldiers of his division," for driving Wheeler across the Tennessee, and complimented them on "inaugurating the new practice of coming to close quarters without delay."[62] The last phrase may have been a backhanded apology for his bitter criticism of the cavalry on September 8. Rosecrans may well have decided that his strictures had been too severe and that an amende honorable was called for. In transmitting, as addenda to his earlier report on the battle of Chickamauga, the reports of General Mitchell and Colonel Wilder, he said this about the cavalry:

I cannot forbear calling . . . special attention . . . to the conspicuous gallantry and laborious services of this arm. Exposed in all weather, almost always mov-

59. Wulsin, *Story of the Fourth*, 48.

60. *Official Records*, Vol. XXX, Pt. 2, p. 673. In a dispatch to Rosecrans on October 15, he wrote, "My men are destitute of provisions and clothing; are very much in need of clothing and rest." *Ibid.*, Pt. 4, p. 397.

61. *Ibid.*, Pt. 1, pp. 671, 677–78, 695, Pt. 4, pp. 371, 444, 713, 717, 724, 728, 748, 764; Connelly, *Autumn of Glory*, 268–70; Rowell, *Yankee Artillerymen*, 137; Rowell, *Yankee Cavalrymen*, 154–55.

62. *Official Records*, Vol. XXX, Pt. 2, p. 667.

ing, even in winter, without tents or wagons, operating in a country poorly supplied with forage, combating for the most part very superior numbers, from the feeble beginnings of one year ago . . . it has become master of the field, and hesitates not to attack the enemy, wherever it finds him. The great change . . . has been greatly promoted by giving them arms in which they have confidence, and by the adoption of the determined use of the saber.

To Maj. Gen. D. S. Stanley is justly due great credit for his agency in bringing about these results, and giving firmness and vigor to the discipline of the cavalry.[63]

The determination of the administration to hold Chattanooga despite the defeat of Chickamauga was expressed in a flurry of activity.[64] Grant, now in command of the Military Division of the Mississippi, moved to Chattanooga; the XI and XII Army Corps, the whole commanded by Joseph Hooker, were rushed from Virginia to Tennessee in a classic of the effective use of railroads in war. General William T. Sherman was ordered on September 22 to ready first one, and then two more, of his divisions for an immediate move to Chattanooga; then Grant decided that Sherman himself should accompany these three divisions. General Meigs was rushed West from Washington to coordinate and speed up the replacement of all the matériel expended or lost at Chickamauga. Nor was Rosecrans' cavalry forgotten. Even while the corps was engaged in the pursuit of Wheeler, General Meigs arranged to have 2,000 horses delivered to Nashville, to be there until the railroad to Chattanooga was back in service.[65] General George Stoneman, head of the Cavalry Bureau in Washington, sent Rosecrans a wire on October 11, the like of which the latter had not seen for many a day, if ever; it told him that if he had not received from General Meigs all the horses he needed, he could have 2,000 horses from Chicago at "any time . . . [he] wished."[66]

There were of course other shortages besides those of horses and "horse equipments." General Crook reported that the chase after Wheeler had left his division and the Lightning Brigade "in terrible condition," with a "great many of . . . [the] men . . . nearly naked" and many of the horses without shoes and "worn out." A few days later he

63. *Ibid.*, Pt. 1, pp. 79–80.
64. They were "thoroughly stampeded" in General Sherman's opinion. Sherman, *Memoirs*, I, 346.
65. *Official Records*, Vol. XXX, Pt. 4, p. 246.
66. *Ibid.*, 280. It was determined ten days later that at least 3,000 horses and the same number of sets of horse equipments were needed. *Ibid.*, Vol. XXXI, Pt. 1, 685.

added that his horses were "badly used up for want of shoes and the hard service they have done the last month."[67] Whatever else may have been lacking, the want of horses was, as always, the crucial problem. In a message to General Mitchell, Crook wrote that if he were ordered to move out of his encampment at once, he could muster only a thousand "effective men" and would have to abandon at least seven hundred broken-down horses.[68] The First Division was in an equally calamitous state, reduced to about 1,400 effective men because of a lack of horses fit for service. General Mitchell, after repeating (and expanding on) his bitter criticism of the saddles furnished by the government (which, he said, "simply murder horses; it is a sure ruin to a horse to put one on his back"), proceeded to give a revised estimate of his needs; he required, he said, "at least 3,000 horses and 3,000 or 4,000 horse equipments immediately."[69] Even General Meigs, who in the past had been prone to blame the enormous wastage of horses on the cavalry, recognized that the animals of the Army of the Cumberland had been "almost destroyed" by hard work, exposure, insufficient grain, and a total lack of hay and would need three months' rest "to become serviceable."[70]

The difficulty of getting supplies to the Union forces in Chattanooga was solved, to all intents and purposes, with the opening on October 27 of the "Cracker Line," the shortcut across the Tennessee at Brown's Ferry and then across the neck of Moccasin Point, which avoided the Confederate artillery on the northern end of Lookout Mountain. The Cracker Line was a makeshift, but it eliminated the horrors of the haul, lined with the carcasses of horses and mules, up the Sequatchie Valley and across Walden's Ridge. For thousands of the army's animals in and around Chattanooga the opening of the Cracker Line would have come too late in any event. Hauling subsistence for the men took precedence over feed for the animals on the single-track,

67. *Ibid.*, Vol. XXX, Pt. 4, pp. 463–64, Vol. XXXI, Pt. 1, p. 708. See also Crook's October 25 dispatch to Grant: "the cold drenching rains we have had . . . have so completely used up my horses that there are scarcely any of them fit for service." *Ibid.*, Vol. XXXI, Pt. 1, p. 836.

68. *Ibid.*, Vol. XXXI, Pt. 1, p. 835. Two days later, Grant, who had arrived in Chattanooga, wired Halleck for 4,000 sets of horse equipments for the Department of the Cumberland. *Ibid.*, 752.

69. *Ibid.*, 835–36.

70. *Ibid.*, 729. Regiments patrolling the river above Chattanooga reported on October 22 that unless something could be done quickly to get forage to them, "their horses must perish." *Ibid.*, 697.

badly dilapidated rail link between Nashville and the western terminus of the Cracker Line at Bridgeport; as a result, as much as a month after the Cracker Line was opened, Assistant Secretary of War Dana "requested" (why, with the area swarming with high-level army officers from Grant on down, it should have been necessary for a civilian observer to make such a request is difficult to understand) that, to save the starving animals, the cavalry be moved to some point where they would not have to depend on the railroad for hay and grain to keep their animals alive and could forage for themselves.[71] But military exigencies made such a solution impossible, for now General Burnside in Knoxville needed help, and it had to come from the Army of the Cumberland.

Rosecrans' kind words about his cavalry were written as it was about to undergo top-level command changes. It will be recalled that General Mitchell's return from sick leave coincided with General Stanley's illness and departure. Barely a month after Mitchell's return to duty, his health broke down again. On October 14, on his return from the chase after Wheeler, he wrote General Garfield, "I am as near a dead man on horseback as you ever saw." Four days later, he ended a report to Rosecrans on his efforts to improve the material condition of his command with this statement: "As soon as possible I wish to be relieved from duty in the cavalry command, as I cannot, if I have any regard for my health, continue longer in it." He told Rosecrans that General Robert S. Granger, commanding the post at Nashville, was "very anxious to be assigned to the cavalry command," and recommended him for the job. The post, however, went to a Regular, Washington L. Elliott, who had gone from a captaincy in the 3rd United States to the colonelcy of the 2nd Iowa and was later promoted to brigadier general of volunteers. On October 24, Mitchell's wish was granted; he was relieved of duty as commanding officer of the First Division of Cavalry and was replaced by Elliott. By virtue of his seniority, Elliott also assumed command of the Cavalry Corps, in the continued absence of David Stanley; Edward M. McCook, as senior colonel, took command of the First Division.[72]

71. McKinney, *Education in Violence*, 275; *Official Records*, Vol. XXXI, Pt. 3, p. 161.
72. *Ibid.*, Vol. XXX, Pt. 4, pp. 371, 462, Vol. XXXI, Pt. 1, pp. 693, 717.

On October 31, the cavalry of the Army of the Cumberland embraced two divisions, Wilder's brigade, and the unattached 15th Pennsylvania, and numbered 10,145 officers and men "present for duty." After some organizational shifting about ordered on November 8 and 10, the corps had a First Division, made up of the brigades of Colonels Campbell, LaGrange, and Watkins, and George Crook's Second Division, containing the brigades of Colonels W. W. Lowe (Colonel Minty being under arrest), Eli Long, and Wilder.[73]

The second major change in the cavalry command occurred on November 12. On that date, General Stanley was relieved of his post of chief of cavalry of the Army of the Cumberland and transferred to the command of a division of infantry in the IV Army Corps. On the nineteenth he turned over command of the cavalry to Elliott, and the next day, after issuing the customary farewell circular, departed without regret, having found duty under Rosecrans and General Garfield, his chief of staff and "Old man of the Sea" (as Stanley called him), a "most unsatisfying and annoying" experience.[74] What qualifications General Elliott was thought to possess to make him a suitable successor to the command of a cavalry corps do not appear in the records.

While these command changes were taking place, one of the rising lights of the Cavalry Corps, Eli Long, was ordered on November 17 to take his brigade, its numbers increased to 1,500 by detachments from the 4th Michigan, 4th Ohio, and the 17th Indiana and 98th Illinois Regiments of Mounted Infantry, to the north of the Tennessee, on a loop eastward to Cleveland, Tennessee, to break up the Eastern Tennessee & Georgia Railroad behind Bragg. After destroying stores and facilities—flour, tanbark, corn, grain sacks, rockets and shells, 85 wagons, 11 ambulances, the only copper rolling mill in the South, and a number of railroad cars—and breaking up several miles of track, Long returned to Chattanooga on November 27 or 28 with 233 prisoners. He, his men, and his horses were given little time to rest. On the twenty-ninth they were on the march again, with orders to join Sherman, who was advancing with his infantry to the relief of Burnside at Knoxville. Capturing on the way two droves of hogs, one numbering 300, the

73. *Ibid.*, Vol. XXXI, Pt. 1, pp. 801, 809, Pt. 3, pp. 89, 109. On November 30 the corps numbered 10,744, but on December 31, after a month of hard campaigning in atrocious weather by the First Division, the corps was down to 9,720 officers and men. *Ibid.*, Pt. 3, pp. 291, 548.

74. *Ibid.*, Pt. 3, pp. 126, 436, 204; Stanley, *Personal Memoirs*, 158.

other 500, "belonging to the Confederate Government," Long reported to Sherman, who sent him to Loudon to secure Longstreet's pontoon bridge across the Tennessee, an operation to be described later.[75]

Elliott himself, after moving his headquarters and the First Division to Alexandria, Tennessee, forty-three miles east of Nashville, was ordered to take LaGrange's and Campbell's brigades of the division to Kingston, Tennessee, eighty miles from Alexandria, to "harass" Longstreet's forces and to join Burnside "if unable to find Longstreet." Elliott marched out from Alexandria on November 28 but did not reach Knoxville until December 16. He got himself into trouble with Grant and with the War Department for taking nearly three weeks to march a distance he should have covered in four days or at most five. He blamed the delay on "impassable streams, bad roads, and scarcity of forage (he did in fact lose seven men of the 2nd Indiana by drowning, when the ferry on which they were crossing unfordable Caney Creek "foundered"), but he neither explained nor even mentioned the week's halt at Sparta, Tennessee, to await the arrival of a wagon train from Nashville, "loaded with clothing and stores" for his men, however badly the clothing and stores may have been needed.[76] This was hardly an auspicious start for a newly appointed chief of cavalry, but somehow or other, Elliott retained the post.

75. *Official Records*, Vol. XXXI, Pt. 2, pp. 560–62, 33, 70, 71, 91, Pt. 1, p. 436.
76. *Ibid.*, Pt. 1, pp. 437, 264, 265, Pt. 3, pp. 378–80, 96.

XIII

All the Business of War

THROUGHOUT 1863 AND UNTIL THE AUTUMN OF 1864 THE
Civil War passed Kansas by, except for the loathsome interlude of the
Lawrence Massacre on the morning of August 21, 1863, in which a
gang of 450 guerrillas led by Ohio-born William C. Quantrill killed in
the name of southern independence between 150 and 180 men and
boys, all civilians, burned down 182 homes and buildings, and robbed
the survivors, male and female, of money, watches, jewelry, and all
portable valuables.[1]

A month before the Lawrence Massacre, Governor Thomas Carney
had obtained War Department authorization to organize the 15th Kansas. He offered the colonelcy of the regiment to Charles R. Jennison,
who, in the year following his resignation as colonel of the 7th Kansas,
had been occupied with Republican politics and murky activities involving the sale in Kansas of livestock and other readily marketable
valuables "jayhawked" in Missouri, which were to make him a wealthy
man by the end of the war. The 15th Kansas and their colonel had
their own interpretation of the meaning of their mandate from Governor Carney to protect Kansas "at all hazards . . . to avenge the lawless
sacking of Lawrence, and to punish the rebel invaders of the State."[2]
The regiment was mustered in 1,015 strong on October 17. There was

1. Starr, *Jennison's Jayhawkers*, 254–55, 255n.
2. *Ibid.*, 255.

no lack of men willing to enlist in a regiment headed by Jennison, but as usual, horses were in short supply. The quartermaster at Fort Leavenworth was unable to furnish the horses the regiment needed, even after an urgent request from Governor Carney that he do so. It was reported in the Kansas press that "a number of men in different parts of the state have recently been caught stealing horses, and reported themselves as belonging to the 15th regiment; and one party is said to have remarked that the regiment was to get horses in this way."[3]

The system adopted by the valiant 15th Kansas in its home state to obtain mounts was a fair omen of what its behavior was to be to the end of its career. In February, 1864, General Egbert B. Brown reported that the "citizens of Kansas City and other towns on the border . . . [were] under apprehension of danger" should the 15th Kansas be stationed nearby, and a month later, General Samuel R. Curtis, in command of the Department of Kansas, ordered the officer commanding a company of the regiment that he was not to cross the line into Missouri unless specifically ordered to do so by General Curtis' own headquarters or unless he was "in close pursuit" of the enemy.[4] Notwithstanding these orders, a battalion of the 15th Kansas, led by Lieutenant Colonel George H. Hoyt, also an alumnus of the 7th Kansas, did cross the line into Missouri for a scout along the Little Blue, south of Kansas City. Presumably with good reason, it was ordered that if members of the regiment "commit[ted] depredations upon Union men," the "guilty parties" be arrested. A short time later, Hoyt's attention was called to the fact that the practice by his officers of "running around loose . . . [had] prevailed to an alarming extent"; it may be assumed that he was expected to put a stop to it.[5] It will be seen later that in November, 1864, the "depredations" committed by this regiment with the knowledge, and perhaps even the connivance, of Colonel Jennison,

3. Unidentified clipping from a Kansas newspaper, in Jennison Scrapbook, Kansas State Historical Society, Topeka, Kan., quoted in *Ibid.*, 259. In May, 1864, seven months after the regiment was mustered in, General Curtis reported that he needed horses for it. *Official Records*, Vol. XXXIV, Pt. 3, pp. 466, 488.

4. *Official Records*, Vol. XXXIV, Pt. 3, p. 398, Pt. 2, p. 686. The citizens of the Missouri counties adjacent to Kansas had good reason to be apprehensive. Exactly a month before, a group of 40 to 60 men of the 11th Kansas "made a raid through . . . [Jackson] county for no other purpose than to rob and plunder. . . . [They] robbed quite a number of men of money, clothing, watches. . . . They committed a great many other outrages too numerous to mention." *Ibid.*, Pt. 2, p. 150.

5. *Ibid.*, Pt. 4, p. 445, Pt. 3, p. 16.

became so outrageous that 16 of its officers signed and presented him with a "protest against the indiscriminate pilfering and robbing of private citizens, and especially of defenseless women and children. . . . If soldiers are permitted to rob and plunder . . . the result must be demoralization of the men and disgrace to the officers and the service, in which we are unwilling to share."[6]

Horses for the 15th regiment were not the only shortage to beset the Federal troops in Kansas. The state, and the troops in it, were very nearly at the end of the geographic chain of distribution that had its starting point on the eastern seaboard and inevitably yielded weapons and supplies of all kinds in inverse proportion, both in quantity and quality, to the distance from Washington. Thus, General Curtis wrote Halleck on February 27, 1864 (the same day he appointed Major B. S. Henning, 3rd Wisconsin, chief of cavalry of the Department of Kansas), that he was in need of carbines and revolvers "to arm cavalry regiments which are mustered, and have been for months almost useless for want of arms." Two months later, a part of the 11th Kansas at Fort Riley, far enough west to keep them away from the western counties of Missouri, were given "arms of various kinds, cavalry and infantry . . . unfit to issue to either except in case of emergency."[7]

Unaccountably, and despite these shortages, only two weeks later Halleck reported to the secretary of war that of the 5,500 troops "effective for duty" of an aggregate force of 5,988 present in the Department of Kansas, nearly 5,000 were cavalry.[8] The only possible explanation for such a report is that viewed from Washington, any soldier in Kansas wearing a cavalryman's uniform could be considered as "effective for duty" even if he lacked a horse and was armed with previously condemned infantry weapons.

The primary military problem for the Union army in Missouri in 1863 and 1864, as it had been from the beginning of the war, was the Confederate guerrilla and bushwhacker. Despite the hypocritical and fraudulent claims of a patriotic motivation made by or on behalf of these people, most of them were no better than the feuding gangsters of a later era.[9] On occasion they fought with what their opponents rec-

6. *Ibid.*, Vol. XLI, Pt. 4, p. 591.
7. *Official Records*, Vol. XXXIV, Pt. 2, pp. 446, 447, Pt. 3, p. 425.
8. *Ibid.*, Pt. 3, p. 660.
9. One ex-guerrilla wrote in his unrepentant old age, "Desperate and remorseless

ognized as "valor, discipline, and skill," but for the most part they relied on hit-and-run tactics and operated in small, constantly changing, and totally undisciplined groups.[10] By preference they engaged in their own version of economic warfare against Union supply trains, undefended settlements, and patrols of the Missouri State Militia Cavalry. At sunrise on June 14, 1864, "about 75 bushwhackers" attacked the town of Melville, plundered and burned down the town, and killed "several men, mostly citizens." A detachment of the 6th Missouri State Militia Cavalry that pursued the gang surprised their camp on the following morning as they "were selling off at auction to one another the goods they had stolen at Melville before they burned the town." The militiamen charged the camp, killed 7 of the guerrillas, and recaptured "almost all the goods they had stolen, together with about 15 horses."[11]

Six weeks after the Melville incident, it was the turn of the settlement of Steelville, near Rolla. At daylight on August 31, Steelville was attacked by "Thomas Lennox's gang," who plundered the village and killed a "Baptist preacher named Butler" and the 5 militiamen who came hurrying to Steelville on word that it had been attacked. Not often, nor by choice, did such gangs tackle organized bodies of troops, but they were willing to do it when the numbers were obviously in their favor or when they could catch the troops by surprise. In September, 1864, when Boone and Howard counties were reported "swarming with guerrillas," they surprised and killed all 12 members of a detachment of the 3rd Missouri State Militia Cavalry. When in the same area Major Reeves Leonard in turn killed 6 members of "Bloody Bill" Anderson's band, he found a total of 30 revolvers on the 6 bodies.[12]

An enemy who by choice attacked by night or from ambush and wore either civilian clothes or the uniform or overcoat of the Union army was dealt with by the national and state troops in Missouri with

---

as he undoubtedly was, the guerrilla killed in the name of God, and his country, and saw shimmering down on his pathway a luminous patriotism." Thomas F. Berry, *Four Years with Morgan and Forrest* (Oklahoma City, 1914), 170.

10. *Official Records*, Vol. XXXIV, Pt. 1, p. 1007. One gang of a hundred guerrillas took four carloads of horses from a North Missouri Railroad train at Centralia, on September 7, 1864. *Ibid.*, Vol. XLI, Pt. 1, p. 745. Over a ten-day period in mid-June, General Brown, in the Central District of Missouri, lost 23 of his men killed and wounded by guerrillas (21 of them in a single ambush) compared to 27 guerrillas killed and mortally wounded by his men. *Ibid.*, Vol. XXXIV, Pt. 1, pp. 996–99.

11. *Ibid.*, Vol. XXXIV, Pt. 1, pp. 1006, 1010.

12. *Ibid.*, Vol. XLI, Pt. 1, pp. 734, 740.

the same merciless brutality with which he himself treated his victims. Perhaps unnecessarily, numerous orders directed that bushwhackers, and especially those wearing the northern uniform, were not to be taken prisoner and, if captured, were to be tried by drumhead court-martial and shot. "Take no prisoners. Kill the villains wherever caught in their hellish practices," read one order. "You will not capture, under any circumstances, any man known to be a guerrilla or acting with them. They will be killed when and where found," read another.[13]

Dispatches setting forth the chapter and verse of compliance with such orders were not likely to be written. At best, executions were reported under the convenient euphemism of "shot while trying to escape." Examples of such strikingly good marksmanship were the fate of two "notorious bushwhackers and horse thieves" caught by a detachment of the 5th Missouri State Militia Cavalry, and of three men who had been harboring the guerrilla gang that killed a certain Mr. Hicks and were caught by a cavalry detachment sent out from Cape Girardeau.[14] Colonel J. B. Rogers, in command of that post, more cautious or perhaps less perceptive than most, notified General Ewing that his troops had caught John F. Bolin, head of the "Bolin gang," and asked the general to tell him if he should have Bolin shot out of hand "or try him by drum-head court and muster him out."[15] Most officers knew what to do and did not bother to ask questions. General Brown, for instance, simply reported the "summary trial" of three bushwhackers and the execution of two of them who, in his opinion, had "forfeited their lives by law, human and divine," and had been caught wearing the Federal uniform besides.[16]

The guerrilla practice, at least as much from necessity as for the purpose of deception, of wearing the northern uniform, and the oppor-

13. *Ibid.*, Vol. XXXIV, Pt. 3, p. 216, Pt. 4, pp. 96, 218, and Vol. XLI, Pt. 4, p. 928.

14. *Ibid.*, Pt. 2, p. 57, Pt. 4, p. 234. A bushwhacker who had been wounded and thrown from his horse in a skirmish with the 1st Missouri State Militia Cavalry was later found and "executed on the spot." *Ibid.*, Pt. 3, p. 709.

15. In a later dispatch Rogers reported that Bolin had "commanded at the Round Pond massacre . . . [and was] guilty of many cold-blooded murders of citizens." Rogers also wrote General Clinton B. Fisk that his men had captured seven of Bolin's men, all of whom claimed to be "regular soldiers in the rebel army." *Ibid.*, Pt. 2, pp. 243, 248.

16. *Ibid.*, Pt. 3, p. 32. General Brown also publicized a special order to the effect that "upon the first overt act of lawlessness committed by . . . [Shumate's] or any other band of guerrillas or bushwhackers" in his district, "the prisoner John Wilcox, a member of the said Shumate's band . . . will be immediately shot." *Ibid.*, Vol. XLI, Pt. 2, pp. 8–9. For another instance of his use of hostages, see *Ibid.*, Vol. XXXIV, Pt. 4, p. 564.

tunity it gave them of catching their enemies in the Union army un-
awares, were much on General Brown's mind. His solution was a requisition for sky-blue forage caps for his men so that they could be
distinguished at a glance from disguised Confederates. He supported
his request with the statement, which may well have been substantially true, that when Shelby raided Missouri in the fall of 1863, "he
had an advance guard of about 200 men, all dressed in our uniform,
and in many cases deceived our troops and the people."[17] His request
was turned down, with the suggestion that he supply his men with a
badge of "conspicuous colors" to be worn on the cap or coat and to be
changed from time to time, a solution that did not commend itself to
the general. This, it must be remembered, was the heyday of secret
societies, with elaborate ceremonies of initiation, grips, and signs of
recognition, and the resourceful General Brown announced the following recognition signals for his troops for the month of April: "The challenging party will ride forward, take off his hat or cap, and hold it verti-
cally above his head. The challenged party will answer by taking off his
hat or cap and holding it down by his right side. If near enough to speak,
challenging party will call out 'Who are you?' answer 'Rosecrans.'
Then the challenged party will call out 'Who are you?' answer 'Babes
in the wood.'"[18]

Shelved for three months following his removal from the command
of the Army of the Cumberland, Rosecrans was appointed on January
28, 1864, to the command of the Department of the Missouri. From his
predecessor, John Schofield, he inherited forces numbering 16,983
officers and men "present for duty"; a department bordered on three
sides by loyal states in which there were no organized bodies of enemy
troops; the same equipment shortages that plagued General Curtis in
Kansas; and lastly, the problem of trying to handle the ubiquitous
guerrillas, which, unfortunately for him, seemed much less of a problem to his superiors in Washington (at least one of whom, General Halleck, had had the same problem to deal with in 1861–1862 and should

17. *Ibid.*, Vol. XXXIV, Pt. 2, p. 777. The use, as an advance guard or lead unit of a
Confederate raiding party, of men wearing Union army overcoats was a stratagem commonly used in the East as well as in the West.

18. *Ibid.*, 777, and Pt. 3, pp. 92–93. When, however, he sent orders to Colonel
James McFerran to scout the area of Snibar Creek, near Warrensburg, he directed
McFerran to have his men wear fastened around their hats or caps "a strip of red cloth
until Monday . . . [May 30] when it will be replaced by white, to be worn during the
week ending June 5." *Ibid.*, Pt. 4, p. 22.

have known better) than it did to him. Worst of all, he took to St. Louis with him the burden of his own difficult personality and the hostility of Grant, about to be promoted to general-in-chief. The depth of Grant's dislike was expressed later in the year, when Rosecrans was relieved of the Missouri command and Grant replied to a query from Secretary Stanton about Rosecrans' next assignment: "Rosecrans will do less harm doing nothing than on duty. I know of no department or army commander deserving such punishment as the infliction of Rosecrans upon them." [19]

The guerrillas of Missouri, alive to the advantages of mobility, operated nearly always on horseback, sometimes as cavalry, with revolvers taking the place of carbines and sabers, and sometimes as mounted infantry. Conventional wisdom had it that in an area like Missouri, still predominantly rural (where it was not an even more primitive undeveloped wilderness) in 1863–1864, only mounted troops could cope with the fast-moving guerrillas. That theory led to the organization of nine regiments of Missouri State Militia Cavalry, a "mere scouting force," Rosecrans called them, which nevertheless represented the bulk of his 9,500 cavalry.

As he had done in Tennessee, Rosecrans began almost as soon as he arrived in Missouri to plead for more cavalry. Bypassing his military superiors, he asked the president to send him "at least one good mounted regiment" from the East to be stationed in north Missouri. [20] A short time later, Rosecrans tried his luck with Grant, with a request for "two or three good cavalry regiments" and for permission to muster those of the Missouri State Militia Cavalry who were willing to enlist in the United States service and to disband the rest. Both requests were disapproved. In July, to deal with what he considered an "immediate threatening emergency for more troops for temporary duty . . . in destroying dangerous and formidable bands of organized guerrillas," he in effect kidnapped two veteran regiments of cavalry, the 1st Missouri and 1st Iowa, passing through St. Louis on their way to join General Frederick Steele in Arkansas. [21]

As might have been expected, Rosecrans' efforts to increase his mounted force aroused the anger of General Halleck, who wrote to

19. *Ibid.*, Vol. XLI, Pt. 4, p. 742.
20. *Ibid.*, Vol. XXXIV, Pt. 3, p. 65, Pt. 2, p. 682.
21. *Ibid.*, Pt. 3, pp. 62, 106, 136, and Vol. XLI, Pt. 2, p. 175.

Grant that Rosecrans, as well as General Curtis in Kansas, were "flooding" the president and members of Congress with "stampeding telegrams" in their efforts to increase their forces to 20,000 "to oppose 2,000 guerrillas."[22] At this very time, however, Rosecrans declared to General Clinton B. Fisk at St. Joseph, in northwest Missouri: "I do not like mounted men to hunt bushwhackers; they make too much noise, are too conspicuous, commit too many depredations, and are too helpless . . . . all the infantry you have mounted would merely overrun the country and leave the guerrillas hidden to laugh as they passed by." And yet he countered an order from Halleck to transfer the 2nd Colorado to Kansas with the statement that the regiment, "now out after guerrillas," would be sent not immediately, as Halleck had ordered, but "as soon as it can be relieved"; he added, "The subdistrict occupied by . . . [the regiment] cannot be abandoned without fearful injury to the inhabitants and the public interest."[23]

At the same time that Rosecrans tried to get more mounted troops assigned to his department, he also tried to obtain horses and weapons for the cavalry he already had. As usual, the demands upon the government from every point of the compass were far in excess of the supply. In April there were between 4,000 and 5,000 cavalrymen in St. Louis, members of regiments returning from veterans' furlough, waiting for horses and weapons before going on to the armies in Tennessee and Arkansas.[24] On March 25, when the veterans of the 7th Kansas arrived in St. Louis on their way back to Tennessee, they found six regiments ahead of them in line to receive horses, which were coming in at the rate of about a hundred a day. Not until May 11, six weeks later, did the Jayhawkers receive their horses; then they had to wait five more days for sabers and another week after that for carbines.[25] As much as four months later, when Rosecrans transferred to Missouri the 17th Illinois, which in some strange way had been assigned the

22. *Ibid.*, XXXIV, Pt. 4, p. 504. In March, 1864, General Curtis begged to be allowed to retain in Kansas the 7th Kansas, then at home on veterans' furlough, but his request was denied. *Ibid.*, Pt. 2, p. 606.

23. *Ibid.*, Vol. XLI, Pt. 3, pp. 32, 45, Vol. XXXIX, Pt. 2, p. 307.

24. Scott, *Story of a Cavalry Regiment*, 221–22.

25. Starr, *Jennison's Jayhawkers*, 297–300; *Official Records*, Vol. XXXIV, Pt. 3, p. 80. The sabers issued to the regiment were the new "Light Cavalry Saber, Model 1860," shorter and lighter than earlier models. See Stephen Z. Starr, "Cold Steel," *Civil War History*, XI (1965), 142–59. This article was reprinted in John T. Hubbell (ed.), *Battles Lost and Won* (Westport, Conn., 1975), 111–12.

duty of guarding the military prison in Alton, Illinois (and were "festering in service without cavalry arms or horses," Rosecrans wrote), he had to beg General Halleck for 500 horses for the regiment, without which, he said, it would go to ruin.[26] Meanwhile, Colonel J. H. Ford at Kansas City, with "over three counties full of brush to guard," was begging plaintively for horses for his nearly 400 dismounted men, and the only way 300 recruits for the 3rd United States, on their way to join their regiment in Little Rock, could be armed and equipped was to take "arms and accoutrements and ammunition" from the 12th Missouri.[27] On July 22, Rosecrans wrote Stanton: "I want more cavalry arms here. Those now in the hands of troops are thrice condemned. To support troops and lose a large percentage of their numerical fighting power by bad arms is a military and economical error of the gravest character. Five thousand complete sets of arms and horse equipments should be sent here for issue." The reply, sent by Assistant Adjutant General E. D. Thompson and not by the secretary, told Rosecrans that the 5,000 sets of cavalry arms and equipment he had requested were "ordered to be forwarded [to him] immediately." But he was told also that his reference to the "defective and thrice condemned" arms in the hands of his cavalry was the first notice of that fact the secretary had received, and he was directed, in carefully restrained language, to "forward a copy of any report, telegram, or communication which . . . [he had] heretofore made on the subject . . . in order that the matter may be inquired into."[28] Not surprisingly, there is no indication in

26. *Official Records*, Vol. XLI, Pt. 3, p. 28. The regiment had had no arms at all from February 2 until, on May 15, it was given "infantry arms to enable it to do duty at Alton." *Ibid.*, Vol. XXXIV, Pt. 3, p. 611. To anticipate somewhat, an inspection report of January 21, 1865, said this about the regiment, which had in the meantime been moved to Arkansas: "The affairs of the 13th Illinois Cavalry are in the utmost confusion. Serious charges have been made against every field officer. . . . The quartermaster has been found guilty of selling Government property and appropriating the proceeds; the company kitchens . . . are filthy, the rations squandered . . . arms and equipments were in a dirty and disorderly condition; discipline bad; personal cleanliness dirty." *Ibid.*, Vol. XLVIII, Pt. 1, p. 600. On September 19, Rosecrans was begging for 700 horses for the 13th Missouri, a veteran regiment for which he had arms and equipment. *Ibid.*, Vol. XLI, Pt. 3, p. 249. Rosecrans himself had organized the regiment from "veterans of the Missouri State Militia force and from such of the non-veterans of that force who chose to reenlist." The latter were required to enlist for three years or the duration of the war and were to receive a bounty of $100. *Ibid.*, Pt. 2, p. 234.

27. *Ibid.*, Vol. XXXIV, Pt. 3, pp. 442, 611.

28. *Ibid.*, Vol. XLI, Pt. 3, pp. 332, 358. Colonel Thompson, on the secretary's direction, also told Rosecrans that he was to make his wants known thereafter to General

the *Official Records* that any such material was ever sent to the War Department.

A change in Rosecrans' official family at this time was to have a significant effect on military events in Missouri in the latter part of 1864. On April 11, Alfred Pleasonton was announced as second-in-command of the Department of the Missouri, with headquarters in St. Louis.[29] The records do not indicate on whose initiative the appointment was made, but the reader will recall that only two weeks before the announcement Pleasonton had been replaced by Sheridan in command of the Cavalry Corps of the Army of the Potomac.[30] Clearly, Pleasonton's new post was a thinly disguised form of military exile.

By the end of 1863, all of Arkansas down to a narrow belt just north of the Louisiana border was held by the Union. Fort Gibson, Fort Smith, Little Rock, Pine Bluff, Arkadelphia to the south, and a wide strip along the west bank of the Mississippi for its full length contiguous to the state, were in the hands of the Union army. In command of the area was General Frederick Steele. His Confederate opposite number, with headquarters in Camden, was that hardy perennial, General Sterling Price, commanding the corps of General Thomas Churchill and the divisions of Generals J. F. Fagan and J. S. Marmaduke.

Steele commanded a force of just under 21,000 of all arms "present for duty" as of April 30, 1864. Included in the total was General Eugene A. Carr's "Cavalry Division" of 3,929 officers and men, a 499-man "Cavalry Brigade" under Colonel Powell Clayton, and lastly, "Cavalry not brigaded" numbering 1,440. Nominally, therefore, Steele had at his disposal mounted troops numbering just under 6,000.[31] But, as was the case with mounted troops throughout the war, particularly so with those in the West, sheer numbers signified very little. Early in the year, when a campaign by Steele south to Camden or to Shreveport, Louisiana, in cooperation with General Banks's Red River Campaign,

---

Edward R. S. Canby, who was in charge of the Military Division of West Mississippi, to which the Department of the Missouri now belonged.

29. *Ibid.*, Vol. XXXIV, Pt. 3, p. 154.

30. See Vol. II, pp. 73–74 of the present work.

31. *Official Records*, Vol. XXXIV, Pt. 3, p. 370. It will be of interest to note that on the same date Rosecrans had 15,266 of all arms (including the Missouri militia) present for duty, and General Curtis, 3,814. *Ibid.*, 371.

was under discussion, Steele wrote to Grant that his cavalry had not "had a remount for a year. Many of them are dismounted and most of the horses now on hand are in poor condition." Reports from individual regiments and posts make it clear that General Steele did not exaggerate the situation, which continued to deteriorate. In April, the 1st Nebraska and 11th Missouri, in Batesville, northeast of Little Rock, had not been receiving sufficient forage (owing to causes unknown to the commanding officer) with the result that 1,150 of the aggregate of 1,750 cavalry at the post were dismounted. At Pine Bluff, to the south, the situation was equally bad; Colonel Powell Clayton reported that of his 1,350 cavalrymen (the 7th Missouri, seven companies of the 1st Indiana, and ten companies of the 5th Kansas), 650 were dismounted. From Fort Smith, on the western border of the state, General John M. Thayer reported in July that his mounted troops were "almost useless as cavalry, for the want of serviceable horses," a particularly dangerous state of affairs because the organized Confederate troops in the area, estimated by Thayer as numbering 5,000 to 7,000, were nearly all mounted and, in addition, the region was swarming with guerrillas.[32]

From Little Rock, where the bulk of Steele's forces were concentrated, he reported that "more than one-half" of his cavalry were dismounted.[33] In late August, 1864, when General Joseph R. West, whose yeoman work in rebuilding the effectiveness of the Federal cavalry in Arkansas will be discussed shortly, tried to catch Jo Shelby after one of his raids north, he reported that the task was hopeless, for Shelby could march three miles to his two. "Upon this expedition," West reported, "as upon a previous one made earlier in the month, the miserable plight of animals that had at any time for months back only been partially foraged, and sometimes left entirely without any, rendered any rapid movement an impossibility." A few months earlier, General Nathan Kimball, speaking also of the cavalry at Little Rock, had put it more succinctly: "My cavalry," he said, "is nothing." And when additional regiments were sent from Missouri, ostensibly to reinforce the cavalry in Arkansas, they arrived without horses, as did the 10th Illinois in April and the 3rd Michigan at the end of May.[34]

32. *Ibid.*, Pt. 2, p. 646, Pt. 3, p. 181, Pt. 1, p. 772, and Vol. XLI, Pt. 1, p. 24, and Vol. XXXIV, Pt. 3, p. 49.

33. *Ibid.*, Vol. XXXIV, Pt. 3, p. 634; see also *Ibid.*, Pt. 4, pp. 108, 122, 231, Pt. 3, p. 281, and Vol. XLI, Pt. 2, p. 944.

34. *Ibid.*, Vol. XLI, Pt. 1, pp. 297–98, and Vol. XXXIV, Pt. 3, pp. 133, 281, Pt. 4, p. 108.

Rather than multiply specific instances, it will be useful to cite a report of Lieutenant Colonel John M. Wilson, assistant inspector general of cavalry in the Military Division of West Mississippi. Speaking of the situation in September, 1864, Colonel Wilson wrote:

The condition of the cavalry at this time was most deplorable. For sixty days the horses had received no hay and only one-half rations of grain, while occasionally for a week at a time they received nothing, and subsisted on what could be picked up. From January 1 to September 1 the supply of forage averaged about one-third rations. In August . . . a recuperative and remount camp was organized at Devall's Bluff, and soon after Captain [Horace G.] Loring, in charge of it, reported that the horses were dying at the rate of fifty-six a day . . . not from disease, but from poverty [sic] brought on by actual starvation before reaching the camp. . . . From January 1 to October 1 the number of horses reported officially as dead . . . was 5,000, nine-tenths of which died by starvation.

As if this information had been insufficiently shocking, it was discovered that neither at Memphis nor at St. Louis were there any requisitions from Arkansas for forage, notwithstanding that there were ample supplies in both places, and transportation to get forage to Arkansas was readily available. The quartermaster officer sent to Memphis who made this discovery was able to get off a four-hundred-ton shipment the very day he arrived, and a second shipment of five hundred tons the next day.[35]

Unfortunately, starvation was not by any means the only cause of the truly scandalous loss of horses. Colonel Wilson's findings merely underscored the conviction expressed earlier by General Francis J. Herron that the poor state of the cavalry in Arkansas was due "first, [to] want of forage which could and ought to have been had; second, [to] overwork and indiscreet use of this arm of the service, by sending out unnecessarily large scouting parties, &c.; [third, to] bad management in the use of cavalry for pickets, the number being at least one-third too large, and much done by cavalry that could be done by infantry." A fourth factor, as destructive, perhaps, as all the others besides starvation, was a combination of neglect and abuse of the horses. An inspection in September disclosed the existence of "much gross ne-

---

35. *Ibid.*, Vol. XLI, Pt. 4, p. 570. Three days before the date of this report, the 2nd Arkansas reported from Fayetteville, Arkansas, that its horses were "in bad condition and were five days without forage." *Ibid.*, 547. In August, the daily feed allowance of the cavalry horses in Little Rock averaged three pounds of hay and six pounds of grain, a little over a third of the prescribed daily ration. *Ibid.*, Pt. 2, p. 649.

glect on the part of commissioned officers to attend regular stable calls and to give personal attention to stable police. Private soldiers have been left to feed and groom their horses at pleasure." In the 9th Kansas, the inspector found "not one commissioned officer . . . present at the stables. No stable call had been sounded. Most of the horses had been fed; many had not. . . . When I inquired of a private soldier whether the officers were in the habit of attending stable calls, he laughed. . . . Others stated that officers did not attend stable calls. Men seem to feed and groom their horses when they are ready." [36]

General West sent C. S. Clark, colonel of the 9th Kansas, a copy of this inspection report, with a scorching covering note of his own. "As commanding officer," General West wrote, "you are responsible for the shameful condition of affairs, and how you can reconcile it with a proper sense of your obligations as a regimental commander I am at a loss to conceive. . . . Should a subsequent inspection—and it will be made soon—disclose further inattention on your part, or that all the duties of officers and men in your command are not thoroughly and promptly performed, a recommendation for your summary dismissal from the service will be submitted to the department commander." [37] Had there been more such reprimands, and had they in fact led to more summary dismissals of colonels and officers of lesser rank from the service, the Union cavalry in the West would doubtless have achieved a high estate in the service much earlier than it did.

When the need for cavalry horses in Arkansas at length led to action, the quartermasters in St. Louis were ordered in early June to ship "all cavalry horses in Saint Louis . . . to the Department of Arkansas." An inspection report two months later revealed that horses were shipped downriver from St. Louis closely packed on the decks of open barges "without any covering, or anything to feed from other than the deck of the barge. By this fully one half of the grain is wasted by becoming mixed with the filth made by the animals. . . . Some days the animals were not watered at all." [38]

A significant sidelight on the neglect and mistreatment of what were called "public animals" is that the horses of the 15th Illinois,

36. *Ibid.*, Pt. 3, p. 504.
37. *Ibid.*, 504. Two months earlier, "great complaints had been made against [the] Ninth Kansas Cavalry" by the people of Lewisburg, Arkansas. The Kansans, they reported, "robbed men and women, friend and foe, indiscriminately." *Ibid.*, Pt. 1, p. 14.
38. *Ibid.*, Vol. XXXIV, Pt. 4, p. 265, Vol. XLI, Pt. 2, p. 650.

which were owned by the men until they were bought at this time by the government, were reported to be "in fine condition."[39]

Second only to horses as essentials to the making of an effective cavalry were weapons, and in this respect, too, the situation in Arkansas was considerably less than satisfactory. A majority of the 1st Nebraska had in April, 1864, only pistols and sabers. When the regiment had been organized three years before, carbines were unavailable, and the men were given Springfield rifled muskets; many of these had been worn out or damaged by three years of use and had become unserviceable but had not been replaced.[40] The 10th Illinois, whose arrival in Arkansas without horses has been mentioned, was without arms also. The 15th Illinois, stationed in Helena in August, 1864, was "almost entirely unarmed"; the regiment possessed a total of 185 carbines, "most of which . . . [had been] condemned."[41]

John N. Edwards, the devoted hagiographer of Jo Shelby, recorded that in the summer of 1864 conditions in Confederate Arkansas were in a sorry state. "The people got tired at last," Edwards wrote. "The soldiers had been disgusted long before. No order, no system, no fighting, no anything except incessant wrangling, orders and counterorders, proclamations and protocols." The condition of the Union cavalry in the state, according to Edwards, was scarcely better. "So notoriously inefficient and cowardly were . . . [Steele's] cavalrymen," Edwards wrote, "that their fighting became a byword and a reproach among the Confederate ranks."[42] However biased and exaggerated Edwards' comment may have been—and exaggeration was a rhetorical device he was greatly addicted to when he took pen in hand—there was more than a little justice in his unflattering report.

On June 6, 1864, General John W. Davidson was relieved of duty with the Cavalry Bureau and on the twenty-fourth was announced as chief of cavalry of the Military Division of West Mississippi.[43] The order announcing his appointment to the latter post stated that in addition to the largely staff responsibilities he was to discharge as chief of cavalry,

39. *Ibid.*, Vol. XLI, Pt. 2, p. 714.
40. *Ibid.*, Vol. XXXIV, Pt. 3, p. 41. The regiment was also short of ammunition. *Ibid.*, 181.
41. *Ibid.*, 281, and Vol. XLI, Pt. 2, p. 714.
42. Edwards, *Shelby and His Men*, 318, 267.
43. On hearing of General Davidson's appointment, General Steele wrote General Canby from Little Rock: "I hope General Davidson will not be sent to this department. We cannot serve together in harmony." *Official Records*, Vol. XXXIV, Pt. 4, p. 483.

he was also to exercise "command of the cavalry forces when concentrated and in the field."[44] This was an advance of the greatest importance over the status of a chief of cavalry in the early years of the war, both in the East and in the West, when the holder of the post had had only administrative and staff responsibilities, and operational orders to the cavalry had come from commanders of divisions or corps of infantry or from an army commander. Davidson's expanded role gave him the same kind and scope of authority that Sheridan had already received in the Army of the Potomac and that James H. Wilson was about to be given by Sherman in the Military Division of the Mississippi.

Six weeks after Davidson received his appointment, General Joseph R. West was appointed chief of cavalry of the Department of Arkansas and stepped into the midst of a formidable array of problems.[45] He wrote General Davidson that his task was nothing less than that of "resurrecting the cavalry of this department from a state of utter chaos."[46] In a second letter a few days later he wrote that he found himself "in the very unpleasant position of sacrificing a reputation in a department where it . . . [was] impossible to do anything with the . . . [existing] staff organization." The "utter supineness and inefficiency" of the cavalry then in the department, he went on, would bear witness to the accuracy of his opinion, and, he concluded, "The prospects of improving the cavalry much here are gloomy in the extreme."[47] Nevertheless, he set out to try, as he was duty-bound to do.

A few of the outward symptoms of the difficulties with which General West was compelled to deal, other than the previously mentioned state of the horses and arms, were the desertion in March of sixty troopers of the 14th Kansas from Fort Smith;[48] excessive mortality among the men attributed to a lack of "vegetables and . . . [commissary stores] of an anti-scorbutic character";[49] an "open mutiny" of the

44. *Ibid.*, 241, 531.
45. General West's appointment is dated August 20, 1864. *Ibid.*, Vol. XLI, Pt. 2, p. 782.
46. *Ibid.*, Pt. 3, p. 81. One of the necessities West lacked was qualified staff officers. More were to be found in Little Rock, "and selections from the line . . . [were] rendered very difficult by the absence of qualifications among the scanty number of officers serving with their regiments." *Ibid.*, 81.
47. *Ibid.*, 200.
48. *Ibid.*, Vol. XXXIV, Pt. 2, pp. 706–707. In reporting the incident, Thayer mentioned that he had to send detachments as far out as forty to sixty miles to find forage.
49. *Ibid.*, Vol. XLI, Pt. 2, p. 220. The 3rd Michigan buried six men and the 11th

1st Arkansas, apparently the result of an effort by Lieutenant Colonel Hugh Cameron to put a stop to the "irregular trading" of horses; and the threatened mutiny at Little Rock of more than three hundred troopers of the 1st Iowa, whose three-year terms of enlistment had expired and who were angered by the delay in being discharged.[50] The root cause of these troubles, in General West's opinion, which General Davidson shared, was improper organization. Most but not all the cavalry in Arkansas was brigaded (that lesson, at any rate, had sunk in throughout the army by the summer of 1864). With one exception, however, these cavalry brigades were attached to infantry organizations. The regiments not brigaded were shifted about from one infantry command to another as their services were thought to be needed. Moreover, prior to General West's appointment, the department had no chief of cavalry "or anyone whose particular duty it . . . [was] to attend to the wants of or correct the faults that may exist in" the cavalry.[51] These organizational shortcomings, or perhaps General Steele's inclinations, caused him (or in his own judgment, compelled him) to keep most of his cavalry "out in detachments all the time" to watch the movements of the enemy, with the result that it was being "frittered away without any apparent result in mere skirmishes."[52]

General Davidson pointed out in no uncertain terms that the joining of brigades of cavalry to divisions of infantry was wrong. "No such organizations," he wrote, "are authorized in our armies by regulation or sound custom. . . . any such organization . . . would have to be broken up on the march and on the field of battle. It injures the esprit de corps of the mounted arm." And he concluded by "urgently" recommending that the divisional organization of the cavalry in the Department of Arkansas be ordered forthwith.[53]

Three weeks later General West proposed grouping the cavalry in the department into a division of four brigades, the First, at Pine Bluff

---

Missouri seven on a single day. One inspection report spoke of "much sickness among the men from the neglect of officers." *Ibid.*, Pt. 4, p. 570.

50. *Ibid.*, Pt. 2, pp. 361, 474.

51. *Ibid.*, 649. In September, 1863, the cavalry in Arkansas had been formed into a division commanded by Davidson, but after he was reassigned the division was broken up into its constituent brigades. *Ibid.*, Pt. 4, p. 569.

52. *Ibid.*, Pt. 3, p. 82.

53. *Ibid.*, Pt. 2, p. 740. General Davidson named Generals West and Cyrus Bussey as qualified to command the division.

(1,890 present) to include the 13th Illinois, 5th Kansas, 7th Missouri, and 1st Indiana; the Second, at Little Rock (2,856 present), the 1st Iowa, 1st and 3rd Missouri, 3rd United States, and 4th Arkansas; the Third, at Austin (2,964 present), the 2nd, 8th, and 11th Missouri, 9th Iowa, and 10th Illinois; and the Fourth, at Huntersville (3,348 present), the 1st Nebraska, 9th Kansas, 3rd Wisconsin, 3rd Michigan, and 3rd Arkansas. Special Orders No. 223 of September 15 established the division West proposed, and he himself was named to its command.[54] It should be added that notwithstanding the discouraged tone of his dispatches, including one (quoted previously, sent on the very day his divisional scheme was approved) in which he spoke of sacrificing his reputation within two or three weeks of his taking charge, inspectors not in his chain of command spoke of progress already being made, of the construction of "recuperating stables" in the cavalry depot he established in an "excellent location" at Devall's Bluff, and of the encampment in the same location of 1,200 dismounted men ready to ride recuperated horses back to their units. In general, these inspectors spoke in terms of admiration of General West's performance and attributed to his efforts the fact that "a new vigor has been instilled in officers and men."[55]

On December 14, 1862, General Nathaniel Banks, Massachusetts politician turned soldier, victimized earlier in the year by Stonewall Jackson in the Valley Campaign, arrived in New Orleans to take command of the Department of the Gulf. He took over from another Massachusetts politician, General B. F. Butler, 31,253 northern troops stationed in and near New Orleans. Included in that number, and as its only mounted component, were 432 Louisiana unionists embodied in three troops of cavalry by Butler and given the designation the 1st Louisiana. As early as October, 1862, Godfrey Weitzel, who had been promoted from lieutenant of engineers to brigadier general of volunteers on Butler's recommendation and sent to drive General Richard Taylor's forces out of the LaFourche district southwest of New Orleans, re-

---

54. *Ibid.*, Pt. 3, p. 199. Sometime later, but before November 15, their horses were taken from the "worst" of these regiments, the 4th Arkansas, 9th Kansas, and 3rd Wisconsin, and distributed among the dismounted men of the "efficient" regiments of the division. *Ibid.*, Pt. 4, p. 570.

55. *Ibid.*, Pt. 4, pp. 504, 570.

ported that this small body of cavalry had been "of invaluable service" in the operation and that he wished that he could have had four times as many as his mere three companies.[56] This comment of General Weitzel's may be taken as the *leitmotif* of military operations on the Gulf Coast until the end of the war. No one ever had enough cavalry. Within ten days of his arrival in New Orleans, Banks wrote General Halleck that he "suffer[ed] very greatly from the want of cavalry" and that he was "extemporizing" additions to the little he had by mounting companies of infantry. In mid-January, 1863, Banks reported that "the almost total deficiency in cavalry" made him "almost helpless either for offensive or defensive operations."[57] In March, reporting to Halleck on operations around Port Hudson, Banks wrote: "The want of cavalry, which I have so frequently and so strongly represented, is felt almost hourly in every movement. Large detachments of infantry are required to do slowly and uncertainly what a small party of cavalry could accomplish speedily and accurately. We must use a brigade to hold a road which a squadron could patrol. I cannot but regret that any consideration of economy should have prevented the Government from sending . . . all the cavalry which it could control."[58] Whether Banks could have used cavalry effectively if he had had it may be open to question, but he deserves credit for being convinced that the mounted arm could be of benefit in his operations.

A month later, by which time the arrival from the North of portions of the 2nd Rhode Island and the 2nd Massachusetts Battalion had increased the numbers of Banks's cavalry to 730, he wrote Halleck again: "I beg leave, at the risk of being considered importunate, to repeat my earnest request that more cavalry may be sent to this department. Every day but confirms the experience that our operations are seriously crippled by want of it."[59] The manner, obviously, was quite different from Rosecrans'; the matter, however, was the same.

---

56. *Battles and Leaders*, III, 584; *Official Records*, Vol. XV, 169. General Taylor was no better off for cavalry. "One or two companies of mounted men, armed with fowling pieces . . . and Colonel Ed. Waller, Jr.'s battalion of mounted riflemen . . . recently arrived from Texas" and armed with "worthless" altered flintlocks, was all the cavalry he had. Richard Taylor, *Destruction and Reconstruction* (New York, 1879), 110.

57. *Official Records*, Vol. XV, 619, 647.

58. *Ibid.*, 259; see also *Ibid.*, 362, 652, 694.

59. *Ibid.*, 702–703, 712–13; see also *Ibid.*, Vol. XXXIV, Pt. 2, p. 269, Vol. XXVI, Pt. 1, pp. 699, 701. The "2nd Massachusetts Battalion" is not to be confused with the 2nd Massachusetts *Regiment* of Cavalry, which was active in the defenses of Washington and then with Sheridan in the Shenandoah Valley.

Banks's plan of "extemporizing" cavalry faced a grave handicap; horses were not nearly as plentiful in the portion of Louisiana then under Federal control as they were farther north. As Major Harai Robinson, commanding officer of the 1st Louisiana, explained:

The district of Louisiana in possession of the United States forces is not a stock-raising country. On the large plantations mules are exclusively used for farming and . . . the poor non-slaveholding population have only Texan and Mexican mustang ponies, which are all unfit for cavalry purposes. A few race horses and the horses used by the planters and overseers . . . would . . . be about the only animals fit for military purposes, and most of this class were driven off by the rebels, and the few remaining have been already taken by the first United States forces occupying the country.[60]

Direct contact of the Delta with the North via the Mississippi River was of course closed until midsummer, 1863, when Vicksburg and Port Hudson were captured. The only means until then of adding to Banks's cavalry was to send him eastern regiments, men, horses, weapons, and equipment, by ship down the Atlantic coast, around the Florida peninsula, and on to the mouth of the Mississippi. In this way two Rhode Island regiments—the 2nd and 3rd—were sent to the Department of the Gulf, followed over a period of time by the 2nd Maine, 3rd Maryland, 6th Massachusetts, 2nd New Hampshire, and the 2nd, 11th, 14th, and 18th New York.[61] Later, after the North gained control of the Mississippi for its full length, a number of western regiments moved down to Louisiana: the 6th Missouri, the 2nd, 3rd, 12th, and 15th Illinois, the 16th Indiana, and the 87th and 118th Illinois and the 4th and 17th Wisconsin Regiments of Mounted Infantry.

The exposure of men from the North to the heat and humidity of the Delta produced at times disastrous results. The 11th New York, campaigning in the summer of 1864 in "low, humid, swampy and malarious country along the Mississippi, reported "the hand of death . . . laid on one man in every four and . . . scarcely a man escaped the fever. Although the bullet claimed but few victims . . . the remains of nearly three hundred men of the regiment, the victims of disease, lie in those swampy lowlands." In July and again in August, the regiment

60. *Ibid.*, Vol. XV, 1104; see also *Ibid.*, 694, 1102, 1103.
61. *Ibid.*, Vol. XXXIV, Pt. 4, pp. 29–30. The 11th New York made the journey south "on several different sailing ships (one took 31 days for the voyage) and on two steamers." Thomas W. Smith, *The Story of a Cavalry Regiment: "Scott's 900," Eleventh New York Cavalry* (Chicago, 1897), 131.

had nearly five hundred of its men "unfit for duty," and most of those had to be hospitalized.[62]

There can be no question that the Gulf climate had a crippling effect on men not acclimated to it and not accustomed to coping with it. But after General B. S. Roberts, one of the long line of chiefs of cavalry in the department, noted the "remarkable contrasts in the sick reports of the division at Baton Rouge and the brigade at Morganza," the former reporting 16 percent of its men on the sick list, the latter only 10 percent, it should not have surprised him that the difference was due to "the care, supervision, and discipline of company and regimental commanders over their men." "If company commanders," General Roberts concluded, "are required by commanders of regiments to attend personally to the cooking at the messes, to the police of camps, [and] the cleanliness and habits of the men," the sick lists and mortality among the men would be greatly reduced.[63]

It may not be unfair to lay at least part of the blame for the failings of cavalry officers noted by General Roberts to the frequent turnover of chiefs of cavalry in the Department of the Gulf. At the start of Banks's command of the department, as of January 15, 1863, his cavalry amounted to only one-eightieth of his forces, and he did not have enough mounted troops to justify the appointment of a chief of cavalry. By late August, 1863, however, notwithstanding that the numbers of his cavalry had not yet increased appreciably, Banks had "the hope of organizing a sufficient number of regiments . . . as soon as . . . [he could] get control of a portion of the country adjacent," and he asked that "an efficient cavalry officer" be sent him "to take charge of that arm of the service." He had in mind for the post Colonel Horace Binney Sargent, 1st Massachusetts, and for good measure asked "on public and on personal grounds" for Sargent's regiment as well.[64] Unable to get the colonel, who, strangely enough, was on leave in Europe in the midst of the war, Banks appointed as his chief of cavalry General

62. Smith, "Scott's 900," Eleventh New York, 137, 153, 156. On July 9, 1864, the 2nd Maine at Thibodaux had 105 men sick out of the 1,075 present. Official Records, Vol. XLI, Pt. 2, p. 95.

63. Official Records, Vol. XLI, Pt. 4, p. 685.

64. Ibid., Vol. XXVI, Pt. 1, pp. 699–700. On September 8 General Halleck wrote Banks that he would receive all the cavalry Grant could spare, a large quantity of horse equipments (8,000 sets to be divided between him and Grant), and as many horses as possible from St. Louis, but that he should not expect to receive any cavalry regiments

Albert L. Lee, former colonel of the 7th Kansas, latterly in command of a brigade of infantry and wounded in the taking of Port Hudson. Not until a month later did Banks's cavalry number 2,845; nevertheless, these troops were announced as constituting a division, to be commanded by Lee, who was charged with the responsibility for the "efficiency and discipline" of the cavalry and was further directed to take personal command of as much of it as was then in the field.[65]

At the time of General Lee's appointment, the division he was to command consisted of two brigades. The First Brigade, under Colonel John G. Fonda, had the 118th Illinois Mounted Infantry, nine companies of the 1st Louisiana, seven companies of the 6th Missouri, and six companies of the 14th New York. The Second Brigade, under Colonel John J. Mudd, was made up of one company each of the 1st and 4th Indiana, seven companies of the 2nd Illinois, five companies of the 3rd Illinois, and one company each of the 15th and 31st Illinois Regiments of Mounted Infantry. A month later, a Third Brigade was added to the division; commanded by Colonel Charles J. Paine, it was made up of the 2nd Louisiana Mounted Infantry and one company each of the 1st and 4th Indiana and of the 15th Illinois Mounted Infantry, seven companies of the 6th Missouri, and six of the 14th New York.[66]

As has been indicated, General Lee combined the administrative post of chief of cavalry with command of that arm in the field until the Union defeat (and his own) at Sabine Cross-Roads in the Red River Campaign. Thereafter, chiefs of cavalry came and went in rapid succession. General Richard Arnold, chief of artillery, was given the cavalry post on April 26; on June 25 he was succeeded by Colonel John P. Sherburne, 11th New York.[67] Next came General B. S. Roberts on October 27. On December 30, the post of chief of cavalry at the depart-

---

from the North. "The great losses in that arm in recent battles," Halleck wrote, "and by the discharge of two years' and nine months' men, and the difficulty in procuring cavalry recruits, places this matter beyond question or discussion. Requisitions are received almost simultaneously with yours from nearly every other department for additional cavalry, some 20,000 or 30,000 being urgently asked for, it being alleged in many cases that operations cannot be continued without them. . . . I have not a single man to supply these demands." *Ibid.*, 719.

65. *Ibid.*, 722, 725, 770. The cavalry became a division in name only, because the detachments posted in various locations in the state or "serving with other commands" were left undisturbed. *Ibid.*, 725.

66. *Ibid.*, 336, 376.

67. *Ibid.*, Vol. XXXIV, Pt. 3, p. 294. The records do not indicate if General Arnold

mental level was abolished entirely, and all its duties involving equipment, supplies, and inspections, but not military movements, were
assigned to Captain C. J. Walker, 2nd United States, as part of his job
of special inspector of cavalry.[68] General Lee, in the meantime, after a
short spell in the military wilderness following the collapse of the Red
River Campaign (he had the job of reorganizing the cavalry depot in
New Orleans), was restored to the command of the 3,000-man division
of cavalry at Baton Rouge on General Davidson's recommendation and
remained in that post until December 28, when he was replaced by
General Joseph Bailey, who had been promoted to that rank from the
lieutenant colonelcy of the 4th Wisconsin Infantry for his spectacular
achievement of floating the Union fleet at Alexandria.[69]

One condition affecting the cavalry was peculiar to the Department
of the Gulf. In no other theater was the conversion of infantry regiments to cavalry, of cavalry regiments to infantry, and of the same regiment from one arm to the other more than once, practiced with the
same abandon as in that department. No doubt there were reasons,
thought to be adequate by those who had the decision to make, for
these changes, but it is impossible to think that such changes contributed anything to the morale or efficiency of the men directly affected.
In the light of the difficulty of sparing cavalry regiments for Louisiana
from the North, it is understandable that as horse equipments and cavalry arms were shipped to New Orleans, infantry regiments would be
converted to cavalry, as were the 17th Wisconsin and 30th Massachusetts Regiments of Infantry. This, however, does not account for the
31st Massachusetts Infantry's metamorphosis into the 6th Massachusetts, and then back again into the 31st Massachusetts Infantry, nor
for the 41st Massachusetts Infantry's being transformed into the 3rd
Massachusetts, then reverting to its original footsoldierly state and
designation, and finally, after being shipped north, becoming the 3rd
Massachusetts once again, greatly to the delight of its members.[70] The

was relieved from his post of chief of artillery on his appointment as chief of cavalry or if
he combined the two posts.

68. *Ibid.*, Vol. XLI, Pt. 4, pp. 266, 963–64.

69. General Davidson cited in Lee's favor the fact that he had had more cavalry experience than any other brigadier general in the department, that he knew "how to provide for and take care of" cavalry as well as how to fight it, and that cavalrymen had
great faith in him. *Ibid.*, Vol. XLIV, Pt. 2, p. 948, Vol. XLI, Pt. 2, pp. 591–92, 596.

70. *Ibid.*, Vol. XXVI, Pt. 1, pp. 273, 782, 811, 899, Vol. XXXIV, Pt. 4, p. 559; James K.

18th New York and the 3rd Rhode Island were first dismounted and then remounted. The 4th Wisconsin Infantry became the 4th Wisconsin in September, 1863, and was rearmed as infantry in May, 1864. Two months later, the 3rd Maryland was converted to infantry.[71]

The degree to which these changes of status contributed to the difficulties of the cavalry in the department is impossible to determine. In mid-1863 Banks made the general observation that his cavalry lacked "efficiency, owing to defective organization and discipline and want of instruction." The more specific complaints made by others seemed usually to concern regiments affected by these changes in status. In July, 1864, the 18th New York was reported as being "in a very badly demoralized condition and should be taken back to camp of instruction. All the field officers and part of the line officers are in arrest, and it is lacking in arms, accoutrements, virtue, and discipline, and sorely needs an energetic and high-minded commander."[72] A year earlier, the 17th Wisconsin Mounted Infantry, having been converted previously to that status, were recalled from the pursuit of a Confederate raiding force, being "considered entirely insufficient for any successful pursuit, as they are badly armed and mounted, and of very little use for any purpose whatever."[73]

In August, 1864, General Davidson discovered that not a single officer of the 6th Missouri knew his drill (none "could countermarch a squadron or form line faced to the rear from column") and recommended that "a board of examination be appointed for the officers and the ignorant and inefficient be discharged."[74] The 3rd Rhode Island had been recruited mainly in New York and "was mostly composed of men entirely beyond control. Their depredations and robberies were frightful. . . . They were wholly worthless as soldiers." Following the resignation of their officers because of their inability to control their

---

Ewer, *The Third Massachusetts Cavalry in the War for the Union* (Maplewood, Mass., 1903), 79–80, 98–99, 190, 236–67.

71. *Official Records*, Vol. XLI, Pt. 2, pp. 69, 799, Pt. 3, pp. 183, 185, 265, Vol. XXXIV, Pt. 4, p. 516; Quiner, *Military History of Wisconsin*, 507; Calkins, "Wisconsin Cavalry Regiments," 187–88.

72. *Official Records*, Vol. XXVI, Pt. 1, p. 572, Vol. XLI, Pt. 2, p. 328.

73. *Ibid.*, Vol. XXVI, Pt. 1, p. 315. In the same month the 1st and 2nd Louisiana were ordered consolidated, and to weed out the unfit, the officers of both regiments were ordered to go before an examination board. *Ibid.*, Vol. XLI, Pt. 2, p. 847.

74. *Ibid.*, Vol. XLI, Pt. 2, p. 681.

men, the consolidation of the regiment with the 1st Louisiana was ordered, whereupon the enlisted men mutinied. The mutiny was put down by the conviction of the two ringleaders by a drumhead court-martial and their execution within a half hour of the verdict.[75]

The Rhode Island regiment had made a bad name for itself for marauding before the mutiny occurred, but it was not alone in that respect. On a scout from Napoleonville to Bayou Pigeon in September, 1864, a portion of the 12th Illinois broke open houses, took money and clothing from the citizens, and "commit[ted] depredations." The pickets of the cavalry stationed in Baton Rouge were permitted by their officers "to leave their posts, wandering about at will, and helping themselves without stint to whatever could be found."[76]

But as always, the picture was not wholly bleak. An inspection of the 2nd Illinois showed the regiment "unequaled by any of the regiments of the same arm" for "military bearing and efficiency."[77] After inspecting General Lee's division and Colonel Edmund J. Davis' brigade in November, 1864, General Roberts reported the arms "good and . . . kept in excellent serviceable condition." Of the 1,200 carbines he had personally inspected, only one was not "clean and in excellent condition." The horses of Davis' brigade were "conditioned for active and hard service . . . [and] well and thoroughly groomed," and the men's discipline and instruction were good. Despite the fact that Lee's division had just returned from a "hard raid," the men's arms, horses, and equipments were "in better order than might have been expected, and . . . in condition for further active service."[78]

For all of Banks's concern to have an "adequate" force of cavalry, in 1862 there was really very little for cavalry to do in the department. Mounted troops were used mainly in small detachments for patrolling

75. *Ibid.*, Vol. XXVI, Pt. 1, pp. 262–73. The personal appearance of the men of the 2nd Rhode Island was described as "bad" and the condition of their arms such "that they cannot be used. They appear not to have been cleaned since issued." *Ibid.*, 264. Two months later, at Bayou Bourbeau, six men of the 1st Louisiana deserted from a picket reserve and went over to the enemy. The report does not indicate if the men were Louisianians or if they had originally been members of the 2nd Rhode Island. *Ibid.*, 360.

76. *Ibid.*, Vol. XLI, Pt. 1, p. 82, Pt. 2, p. 780.

77. *Ibid.*, Pt. 4, p. 530.

78. *Ibid.*, 685. Lee reported on this raid as he was returning to Baton Rouge: "I shall arrive to-night. Have captured 200 prisoners, 25 commissioned officers. Had a strong fight at Liberty. Whipped them badly. . . . Have from 600 to 800 head of horses and mules. . . . Destroyed immense stores." *Ibid.*, 638.

the countryside, on roads and through swamps often "belly deep" in water and requiring the crossing of bayous ten to twenty feet deep and thirty to fifty yards across by swimming the horses.[79] Guerrillas and bushwhackers were present, but unlike in Mississippi, Tennessee, and Missouri, they were only a nuisance rather than a constant danger.[80] There was an occasional raid for the Union cavalry to conduct, in one of which General Lee surprised the camp of the 7th Tennessee, C.S.A., and returned with prisoners and captured horses and arms. In another raid the surprised party was a detachment of the 1st Louisiana Mounted Zouaves, C.S.A.[81] There was an occasional expedition by a sizable body of infantry in which the cavalry participated in brigade strength. Colonel Grierson, with his two regiments (which Banks would have been happy to keep in his department) backed by a large body of infantry, marched on May 13 from Baton Rouge toward Port Hudson. In the absence of any opposition, Grierson destroyed three hundred yards of the Port Hudson–Clinton Railroad and on the return march captured a herd of two hundred beef cattle.[82] When Banks laid siege to Port Hudson, Grierson covered the rear of the army, protected its foraging parties, and dispersed the groups of enemy cavalry hovering about behind the lines of investment, work that in General Banks's opinion "contributed to a great degree to the reduction of the post."[83] Noteworthy also was the contribution of the 3rd Massachusetts to the success of the siege. On June 15, in response to a request by Banks for volunteers to form a storming column of a thousand men, twenty-nine members of the 3rd Massachusetts volunteered. At their head were Colonel Thomas E. Chickering, Captain Francis E. Boyd, and Lieutenants William T. Hodges, Henry S. Adams, David P. Muzzey, and Charles W. C. Rhoads; their names deserve to be recorded.[84]

Banks's forces marched into Port Hudson on the morning of July 9.

79. *Ibid.*, Vol. XV, 268.

80. On November 24, 1864, the 2nd Illinois, whose pickets outside Baton Rouge had been fired on at night by guerrillas, caught and hanged two of them. "For two days the bodies were left there as a warning to their associates, when they were cut down and buried. The example was a gruesome one . . . but it proved effectual, for it practically ended the shooting of our pickets." Fletcher, *The History of Company A*, 144–45.

81. *Official Records*, Vol. XXVI, Pt. 1, pp. 369, 370; see also *Ibid.*, 377.

82. *Ibid.*, Vol. XV, 409–11, Vol. XXVI, Pt. 1, p. 137.

83. *Ibid.*, Vol. XXVI, Pt. 1, pp. 16, 138. In mid-July, Grierson left the Gulf command to return to Grant. *Ibid.*, 644, 645.

84. *Ibid.*, 56–57, 61.

A month later, Halleck informed Banks, "There are important reasons why our flag should be restored in some point of Texas with the least possible delay." In a second dispatch four days later Halleck explained that the movement was "urged by . . . [Secretary of State] Seward," and suggested that the best and safest way to accomplish the objective was "a combined military and naval movement up the Red River to Alexandria, Nachitoches, or Shreveport," an operation that had evidently been proposed sometime earlier by Banks himself.[85] And let it be said, to the credit of an officer who has had very little, that Banks set to work on the project with the utmost energy. But neither as to time, nor, certainly, as to its outcome, did the ensuing Red River Campaign match his or his government's expectations.

85. *Ibid.*, 172, 673.

XIV

Amidst the Ranks of War

ON THE EVENING OF OCTOBER 23, GRANT, "LAME, WET AND dirty," reached George Thomas' headquarters in Chattanooga. His star in the ascendant after Vicksburg, Grant had a few days before been given command of the newly created Military Division of the Mississippi, embracing the Departments of the Mississippi, Cumberland, and Ohio. His host, The Rock of Chickamauga, now had command of the Department and Army of the Cumberland, the latter reinforced by the arrival of the XI (Oliver O. Howard) and XII (Henry W. Slocum) Army Corps from the Army of the Potomac, under the command of Joseph Hooker. Four days after Grant's arrival, the Cracker Line to Chattanooga was opened, and the threat of actual famine for the Union army was thereby removed. On November 23, Sherman and three divisions of his own and one of the XVII Army Corps arrived across the river from Chattanooga after a slow march from Memphis.

With supplies for the army assured, Grant's and Thomas' principal objective became the breaking of the Confederate ring around Chattanooga and the Union army.[1] Hooker's two corps lay in Lookout Valley, bounded by Raccoon Mountain on the west and Lookout Mountain on the east, and Sherman's four divisions were on the right bank of the Tennessee, upstream from Chattanooga. The bulk of Grant's forces—

1. Not until mid-January, however, were the men back on full rations. McKinney, *Education in Violence*, 280.

the Army of the Cumberland proper—was hemmed in between Longstreet's two divisions atop Lookout Mountain on one side and the Army of Tennessee atop Missionary Ridge as far south as Rossville on the other, with part of the latter posted across Chattanooga Valley to make contact with Longstreet's troops to the west. Eventually, the Federal forces available to break the encirclement grew to eighty thousand. Making their success inevitable was Bragg's acceptance of a scheme proposed originally by President Davis, to send Longstreet with his twelve thousand infantry and E. Porter Alexander's artillery to join Wheeler's cavalry and General C. L. Stevenson's division of infantry, for the purpose of driving Burnside, who had advanced gingerly along the Tennessee to help Thomas, back to Knoxville.[2] Longstreet's departure left Bragg with thirty-six thousand infantry to oppose Grant's eighty thousand.

In the climax of a three-day battle, November 23–25 the siege of Chattanooga was broken and the Confederate army driven southeast into Georgia. The fighting began with the capture by the Army of the Cumberland of Bragg's outworks on Orchard Knob. On the twenty-fourth, Hooker attacked the Confederates on the northern foot of Lookout Mountain ("The Battle in the Clouds") and cleared the way for his advance into Chattanooga Valley. On the afternoon of the third day, after the failure of Sherman's elaborately planned attack southward along the crest of Missionary Ridge, the men of Sheridan's and T. J. Wood's divisions, with fifty-three regimental flags in the van, charged headlong up the steep, in places nearly vertical, face of Missionary Ridge; they reached the crest, first singly, then by dozens, and ultimately by regiments. In one of the totally inexplicable incidents of the war, the center of Bragg's line gave way, then panicked and fled. Three days later, on a cold, rainy day, the Army of Tennessee, "more a milling, frightened mob than an army," thousands of the men weaponless, reached what they hoped was safety in Dalton, Georgia.[3] On that day, Bragg sent in his resignation.

At the beginning of what came to be known as the Knoxville Campaign, Ambrose Burnside had under his command in and near Knoxville 11,952 infantry and artillery, a garrison of 4,994 at Cum-

2. Connelly, *Army of the Heartland*, 255; *Official Records*, Vol. XXI, Pt. 1, pp. 455–56. One of the many handicaps Longstreet had to contend with in the subsequent operation was the lack of reliable maps.

3. Connelly, *Army of the Heartland*, 276.

berland Gap, and a "Cavalry Corps" of 8,673.[4] The latter, called "temporary," had two divisions, and was commanded by General James M. Shackelford. The First Division, under General William P. Sanders, was made up of the brigades of Colonels Wolford, Robert K. Byrd, and Charles Pennebaker. Colonel Samuel P. Carter's Second Division consisted of the brigades of Colonels John W. Foster (not to be confused with General John G. Foster) and Israel Garrard.[5]

In September, before the onset of autumnal bad weather with its rains and raw winds, troopers capable of responding to the beauty of nature saw spread before them some of the most magnificent scenery in the eastern half of the United States. When the 14th Illinois crossed Clinch Mountain in the middle of the month, "Our road over the mountain," their historian wrote, "was rugged and serpentine and verged, in places, steep declivities. The scenes were highly romantic. Precipices and cliffs, ravines and running brooks, the varying foliage of many species of trees and shrubs, the charming songsters of the forest warbling their morning songs, all conspired to make us forget the toil of ascent. At the summit we paused to survey the lovely scene, over which the Mountain Deities seemed to preside."[6]

By October, however, commanding officers of Shackelford's cavalry had no time or thought to spare for the beauties of nature. Their days were filled with the difficulties of their commands, problems that by the latter part of 1863 had acquired the patina of tradition. Colonel Wolford's brigade had at least six, and perhaps more, different firearms—Sharps', Henry, and Enfield rifles, and Burnside, Smith, and Union carbines—requiring several different types and calibers of ammunition, all of which, the colonel reported, his troopers were "most entirely out of."[7] In early November, General Sanders reported that the horses of his division were "in a very bad condition" with "the scratches, or sore heel"; being without "horse medicines of any kind," he could do nothing for the afflicted animals. Furthermore, the men of one of his brigades had neither blankets nor tents.[8] Lack of remounts

4. The numbers are as of November 30, 1863. *Official Records*, Vol. XXXI, Pt. 1, p. 267.

5. *Ibid.*, Pt. 3, p. 35.

6. W. L. Sanford, *History of the Fourteenth Illinois Cavalry and the Brigades to Which It Belonged* (Chicago, 1898), 67.

7. *Official Records*, Vol. XXXI, Pt. 1, pp. 682, 688.

8. *Ibid.*, Pt. 3, p. 110. In June, 1863, Sanders, then a colonel, had led a force of

was another problem; in early November, General Shackelford reported that for the 2,500 of his men whom he classified as "effective," he had only 1,800 serviceable horses.[9] Remounts—broken-down animals supposedly "recruited up by good care and rest" in the government corrals in Nashville—were an uncertain resource; of the 92 such horses issued to the 12th Kentucky after dark on November 10, two died before they reached camp that evening.[10]

Feed for the animals and rations for the men caused difficulties almost from the start of the campaign. The problem grew progressively worse as roads became "one continuous mudhole" and as foraging in the relatively sparsely settled and poor area west of the mountains became less and less productive, more and more chancy. Quite typical was the experience of the 14th Illinois:

> (October 19): Get fresh beef and mutton without salt and one hardtack per man; forage scarce.
> (October 20): No bread; fresh beef without salt our entire fare.
> (October 21) Same fare as yesterday.
> (October 22): Same fare.
> (October 24): Usual starvation fare . . .
> (November 2): Our fare for some days has been flour without meat or salt, or anything else but water. We have had no sugar, coffee or tea for weeks.[11]

On November 3, Grant queried Burnside whether his cavalry was in condition to raid the railroads *east* of Atlanta, behind Bragg. A strangely visionary scheme, this, even for Grant in his dealings with the cavalry. Just to reach the Georgia Railroad, which connected Augusta, Georgia, and Atlanta and was the nearest to Knoxville of the lines Grant had in mind, would have meant a round trip of at least four

---

1,500 mounted men (made up of detachments from Ohio and Kentucky regiments of cavalry and Ohio and Tennessee regiments of mounted infantry) to raid the East Tennessee & Virginia Railroad. From near Knoxville eastward to Strawberry Plains he "destroyed all the small bridges and depots" on the road and, most important, the "splendid bridge over the Holston River, over 1,600 feet long, built on 11 piers. The trestle work included, this bridge was 2,100 feet in length." General Buckner reported to Richmond that he would have all the damage repaired and the bridge over the Holston rebuilt in two weeks. *Ibid.*, Vol. XXIII, Pt. 1, pp. 386–88, 390.

9. *Ibid.*, Vol. XXXI, Pt. 3, p. 78.

10. Sanford, *History of the Fourteenth Illinois*, 75–76; *Official Records*, Vol. XXX, Pt. 3, p. 117.

11. Sanford, *History of the Fourteenth Illinois*, 83, 85.

hundred miles in wintry weather on roads deep in mud, and two crossings of the Alleghenies. Nevertheless, Burnside replied that he could send off 1,200 picked men ("as large a force as seems . . . advisable to send through the mountains") and "a few pieces of artillery" on the raid.[12] Then the idea quietly—and rightly—died.

In his query about the raid Grant also asked Burnside if he had "the right sort of commander for such an expedition"; taking it for granted that he did not, Grant proposed as "a cavalry commander of daring, judgment, and military experience" a choice of either General William Sooy Smith or a member of his own staff, Colonel of Engineers James Harrison Wilson. Burnside hastened to reassure Grant that he already had "a first-rate cavalry commander" in the person of General Sanders.[13] It is, however, difficult to judge the caliber of Burnside's cavalry commanders. It may well be that Grant's query was based on suspicion or knowledge that does not appear in the records. It is a fact that on October 20, Colonel Wolford's brigade, at Philadelphia, Tennessee, southwest of Knoxville, was surprised (a bit of information absent from the colonel's reports) by the Confederate cavalry of Colonels George G. Dibrell and J. J. Morrison, thoroughly beaten, and chased eight miles as far as Loudon, which he reached with the loss of all his artillery (six mountain howitzers), numerous wagons and ambulances, many weapons, much "camp equipage," and worst of all, 447 officers and men captured by the enemy, in addition to 32 killed and wounded.[14] The Confederates, too, sustained losses—15 killed, 82 wounded, 3 missing—which indicates that at least initially, Wolford's men put up a good fight; indeed, they were credited by the enemy with "stubborn resistance" and a "gallant fight."

A scant three weeks later, on November 6, at Rogersville on the Clinch River northeast of Knoxville, Colonel Israel Garrard, with his own 7th Ohio and the 2nd Tennessee Mounted Infantry, was surprised and routed by the cavalry brigades of Colonel Giltner and General William E. Jones, the latter, better known as "Grumble" Jones, an exile

12. *Official Records*, Vol. XXXI, Pt. 3, pp. 35, 45, 63, 105. Perhaps Grant had in mind an expedition like Streight's, from which the raiders were not expected to return.

13. *Official Records*, Vol. XXXI, Pt. 3, pp. 35, 45.

14. *Ibid.*, Pt. 1, pp. 5–8; see also Tarrant, *Wild Riders of the First Kentucky*, 226–31. Inspired perhaps by state loyalty, Roger Hannaford wrote that what little good repute the Wolford brigade had it owed to the presence in its makeup of the 45th Ohio Mounted Infantry. Roger Hannaford, "Reminiscences," the Cincinnati Historical Society, Cincinnati, 18(d).

from Jeb Stuart's Cavalry Corps of the Army of Northern Virginia. In a refreshing departure from normal practice in such cases, Colonel Garrard reported without beating about the bush that he had been "totally defeated." The defeat was total indeed: the enemy captured Garrard's 4 guns, 60 wagons, 1,000 horses and mules, nearly all the Tennesseans, and about half of the Ohio regiment, a total of more than 700 men.[15]

Longstreet's infantry and artillery, hampered by a shortage of transportation, crossed to the north bank of the Tennessee at Loudon and approached the outskirts of Knoxville on November 18. On that and on the previous day, General Sanders, with his 700-man brigade, and Colonel Pennebaker, with two regiments of mounted infantry, delayed as best they could the advance of Longstreet's veterans, an operation in which Sanders (an "intimate" friend at West Point of Confederate Colonel Alexander), exposing himself to encourage his men, who fought dismounted behind the uncertain protection of a rail fence, was mortally wounded.[16] The resistance put up by these two small commands gave Burnside's infantry—who themselves only reached Knoxville at daybreak on the seventeenth—two days in which to dig a continuous line of "infantry parapets" and trenches, anchored on Forts Sanders and Huntington Smith and surrounding the town from the Holston River upstream from it to the river downstream.

On November 13, Longstreet had detached Wheeler, with three of his brigades, to remain south of the Tennessee and march to Maryville, fifteen miles due south of Knoxville. He was to surprise and cap-

15. *Official Records*, Vol. XXXI, 551–66. For General Jones (not to be confused with General Samuel Jones, Confederate commander of the Department of Western Virginia and Tennessee) see Vols. I and II, *passim*, of the present work.

16. *Battles and Leaders*, III, 737–38, 747; Tarrant, *Wild Riders of the First Kentucky*, 246–48; *Official Records*, Vol. XXXI, Pt. I, p. 275. Sanders, a native of Kentucky, but appointed from Mississippi, graduated forty-first in the rather undistinguished West Point Class of 1856. Commissioned a second lieutenant in the 1st Dragoons, he later transferred to the 2nd Dragoons and served on the frontier. He was commissioned colonel of the 5th Kentucky, then served for two months as chief of cavalry, Department of the Ohio, and was commissioned brigadier general a month before his death in action. Cullum, *Biographical Register*, II, 442. As nearly as can be determined, Sanders' force consisted of the 8th Michigan, 1st, 11th, and 12th Kentucky, and the 112th Illinois and 45th Ohio Regiments of Mounted Infantry. Sanders was succeeded in command of the division by Colonel Wolford, and he in turn in command of his brigade by Lieutenant Colonel Silas Adams, 1st Kentucky. For encomiums on Sanders, see Tarrant, *Wild Riders of the First Kentucky*, 248–49, and *Battles and Leaders*, III, 738. A group of 20 men of the 112th Illinois Mounted Infantry captured by the enemy on this occasion were taken to Andersonville, where 11 of them died. A twelfth "died a few days after his exchange of a disease contracted in prison." Thompson, *History of the 112th Regiment*, 136.

ture the brigade of Union cavalry reported to be stationed there and then take possession of the high ground overlooking Knoxville.[17] The Maryville garrison, which Wheeler inflated in his report to consist of "Sanders', Shackelford's, Wolford's, and Pennebaker's brigades, with one battery of rifled guns, all being commanded by General Sanders," actually consisted of two companies of Colonel Felix W. Graham's command, whose camp Wheeler overran and most of whom he captured. General Sanders, who seemed to be everywhere in the course of these operations, learned of the attack on Graham and moved out in hot haste to restore the situation. The 1st Kentucky, leading his advance, was "driven back in confusion" by the enemy, but Sanders was able to rally "a portion of them" and, with the aid of his second regiment, the 45th Ohio Mounted Infantry, succeeded "in driving . . . [the enemy] slowly." Wheeler's claim that his attack had broken the lines of the Union cavalry, whose "entire mass . . . swept on toward Knoxville in the wildest confusion . . . [and] dashed over their pontoon in their fright into the city, creating the greatest confusion," is rendered suspect by the fact that Sanders remained on the south bank of the Holston until he was recalled two days later to delay Longstreet's advance, which, as has been mentioned, he succeeded in doing at the cost of his life.[18]

It may be noted, in connection with these operations, that Assistant Secretary of War Dana, who visited Knoxville just before Longstreet laid siege to it, reported to his chief that Burnside's "position seem[ed] safe except for Longstreet's great superiority in cavalry." Dana credited Wheeler with between seven thousand and nine thousand men, whereas Burnside could muster no more than about three thousand without giving up the cavalry outposts he maintained northeast of the city in the area from which he drew the bulk of the supplies he was able to collect in the countryside.[19] James H. Wilson, who accom-

17. For this operation, see *Official Records*, Vol. XXXI, Pt. 1, pp. 456, 540–42, 420–21. The numbers of the Maryville garrison were variously reported by Wheeler as 500 to as many as 4,000. Union casualties in the action were 6 killed, 9 wounded, and 86 captured or missing. *Ibid.*, 540, 288.

18. *Ibid.*, 420–21, 541.

19. *Ibid.*, 260. Wheeler actually had about five thousand men at this time. *Battles and Leaders*, III, 746n. Wilson defined the area from which Burnside drew most of his "bread, meat and forage" as "the rich country between the Clinch River, Rogersville, and the Great Smoky Mountains." *Official Records*, Vol. XXXI, Pt. 1, p. 265. See also Thompson, *History of the 112th Regiment*, 152, concerning foraging south of the Holston for hay and grain for the horses.

panied Dana to Knoxville, made no recommendation of his own, but did quote Burnside's assertion that for active operations against the enemy, four thousand or five thousand cavalry, transferred from the Army of the Cumberland, would be useful.[20]

The siege of Knoxville began on November 18 and lasted until the departure eastward of Longstreet's forces on the night of December 4. It was a failure for Longstreet and his army, but a failure made memorable by the desperate gallantry of the charge with the bayonet by three brigades of Georgians and Mississippians of General Lafayette McLaws' division, in a hopeless attempt to capture Fort Sanders, the northwestern anchor of the Union position. The attack went in after a few moments of artillery preparation at first light on Sunday, November 29. Colonel Orlando M. Poe (who had been General Sanders' classmate at West Point), Burnside's chief engineer, had had the duty of building or strengthening the defenses of the city. He chose to rely for the defense of Fort Sanders primarily on a ditch twelve feet wide around its star-shaped, partially completed perimeter. The ditch varied in depth from six to eight feet, "depending upon the accidents of the ground," and formed, with the outer face of the parapet or "scarp" of the fort behind it, a high, continuous forty-five degree slope, nearly impossible to climb without ladders. The attackers got as far as the ditch, and into it, where they were raked by enfilading fire. A few of them— color bearers and officers—actually succeeded in getting to the top of the parapet, where they were immediately gunned down. The attack lasted forty minutes and cost Longstreet 129 killed, 458 wounded, and 226 taken prisoner; the Union loss was "only about 20."[21]

Two days after Longstreet pulled up stakes and moved away toward Virginia, the omnipresent Dana was back in Knoxville. He reported to Secretary Stanton that Burnside had "fully twenty days' provisions, much more, in fact, than at the beginning of the siege." The loyal population of the area, he explained, had done their utmost to keep supplies moving to Knoxville, floating flatboats down the Holston and French Broad rivers and using the road (which Longstreet failed to block) from Sevierville.[22] One wonders about the source of Dana's in-

20. *Official Records*, Vol. XXXI, Pt. 1, p. 267.
21. *Ibid.*, 270, 277–78, 460–61; *Battles and Leaders*, III, 741–44, 747–50. See also Donald B. Sanger and Thomas R. Hay, *James Longstreet* (Baton Rouge, 1952), 232–34.
22. *Official Records*, Vol. XXXI, Pt. 1, p. 263; see also Sherman, *Memoirs*, I, 368.

formation. He had evidently not talked to Roger Hannaford of the 2nd Ohio, who had been in the "Asylum Hospital" in Knoxville throughout the siege, recovering from a severe flesh wound in his right arm. Hannaford could have told him that the sick and wounded in the hospital were reduced to two meals a day, each consisting of "fresh fat pork" and a kind of bread made of bran held together by sorghum, the latter a cause of chronic diarrhea, which carried off as many men as did the complications and infections of their wounds.[23] And even if Dana's eyes and nose had failed to record the information, he could have learned from Sergeant Tarrant, 1st Kentucky, what the latter wrote in his regimental history: "Our rations, at best not calculated to tempt fastidious appetites, had almost played out. At first, the horses slaughtered or dying from other causes, were hauled away from camp; but now they died so numerously, and surviving teams became so weak, that they could not be removed. About a dozen or more dead horses lay within a few feet of brigade headquarters. . . . Starvation was already staring us in the face. How long we could hold out was not now a question of days or weeks, but a question of hours."[24]

The division of cavalry and some six-month regiments of Indiana infantry stationed at Tazewell, northeast of Knoxville, were no better off than those in and near the city. They, too, were short of food; besides, the horsemen, without tents, had nothing but their horse blankets for protection from the cold and were "all ragged, many barefoot." As Roger Hannaford, a trooper of the 2nd Ohio, noted, in December, when eligible regiments had to decide whether or not to reenlist as veterans, "many Regts. vetranized . . . more from a desire to get out of E. Tenn that winter than for anything else, our own among the number."[25]

23. Hannaford, "Reminiscences," 20(d). Hannaford noted that 5 or 6 bodies were carried out of the hospital every day and buried in mass graves. *Ibid.*, 19(a). See also *Official Records*, Vol. XXXI, Pt. 1, p. 287. General John G. Foster reported in December that forage for the animals "had become nearly exhausted, and had to be sought at distances varying from 10 to 40 miles." *Official Records*, Vol. XXXI, Pt. 1, p. 287.

24. Tarrant, *Wild Riders of the First Kentucky*, 265; see also 257–58.

25. Hannaford, "Reminiscences," 25(a), 23(b). One of the inducements to veteranizing was a thirty- to thirty-five-day furlough at home. Hannaford's opinion of six-month regiments is worthy of notice. "I object to 6 mos. soldiering," he wrote; "you are out just long enough to learn all the most disagreeable parts yet not long enough to get inured & learn the better features of camp life. [I]f a soldier is every homesick it is during the first 6 months, if ever sick in 9 out of 10 cases it is during the same time, for 6 months will generally harden or kill him, beside[s] a man whose time is nearly out is apt

Nearly as great a hardship as the shortage of food was the interruption of mail. On January 27, the 3rd Ohio received its first mail in two months. The historian of another Ohio unit wrote after the war: "During all our army life, whether in camp or on the march, nothing was looked forward to with a keener interest than the arrival of the mail. Sometimes we could get none for weeks at a time and then it would come by the wagonload. Each division, brigade and regiment had its postmaster. At brigade headquarters the mail was sorted for the various regiments. In each of the latter the cry 'orderlies for your mail' always provoked a yell and a scramble for letters." [26]

With the administration's, and especially the president's, anxiety about east Tennessee firmly in his mind, Grant had laid plans to send troops from Chattanooga to "relieve" Knoxville as soon as Bragg had been driven off Missionary Ridge. Gordon Granger, with the IV Army Corps reinforced to twenty thousand men, was to start for Knoxville at once, but Granger, already in Grant's black books as a trifler, delayed his departure, and on November 29 Grant decided to send Sherman to Knoxville also. [27] Granger eventually got under way with two divisions and with a shallow-draft steamer loaded with provisions chuffing up the Tennessee abreast of his marching men. Sherman, who had pursued Bragg as far as Dalton, marched his entire command cross-country toward the Tennessee. He crossed the Little Tennessee on a bridge 240 yards long constructed by General (as he had now become) James H. Wilson "with only such tools as axes, picks and spades . . . partly with cut wood and partly with square trestles (made of the houses of the *late* town of Morgantown)." [28]

On December 2, Sherman ordered Colonel Eli Long with his brigade (the cavalry that had been assigned him for the Knoxville expedi-

---

to be particularly careful of himself in battle." *Ibid.*, 16(d). For Burnside's opinion see *Official Records*, Vol. XXXI, Pt. 1, p. 259.

26. Crofts, *Third Ohio Veteran Volunteer Cavalry*, 126; Wilbur F. Hinman, *The Story of the Sherman Brigade* (Alliance, Ohio, 1897), 374.

27. Grant, *Personal Memoirs*, II, 89, 91–92; Wilson, *Under the Old Flag*, I, 303–307; Sherman, *Memoirs*, I, 379–80. In a December 1 dispatch, Sherman wrote Grant in his inimitable way: "Recollect that East Tennessee is my horror. That any military men should send a force into East Tennessee puzzles me. Burnside is there and must be relieved; but when relieved I want to get out, and he should come out too." *Official Records*, Vol. XXXI, Pt. 3, p. 297.

28. Sherman, *Memoirs*, I, 381. The bridge was built in water 3½ feet deep and "too cold for infantry." Wilson, *Under the Old Flag*, I, 313–14.

tion) to move ahead of the infantry to rush, and if possible capture, Longstreet's pontoon bridge across the Tennessee at Loudon, guarded by General John C. Vaughn's brigade of infantry. Long moved fast enough to surprise and capture Vaughn's pickets, but Vaughn also had "artillery in position, covered by earthworks" to protect the bridge "and displayed a force too respectable to be carried by a cavalry dash." Before any of Sherman's infantry could reach the scene to lend the cavalry a hand, Vaughn decamped, but not before "destroying the pontoons, running three locomotives and forty-eight cars into the Tennessee River," and also leaving behind four pieces of artillery and "much provision."[29] His plan to cross the Tennessee at Loudon foiled, Sherman resumed his march eastward, along the south bank of the river. First, however, he sent his aide, Major Joseph C. Audenried, forward to Loudon, to explain to Long "how all-important it was that notice of . . . [Granger's and Sherman's] approach should reach Burnside," whose poorly worded dispatch of November 23 to Grant had given the impression that if the siege was not lifted in ten to twelve days, he would either have to surrender or abandon Knoxville and take his chances on trying to escape. With only one day left before Burnside's deadline, Audenried was to order Long "to select the best materials of his command, to start at once . . . push into Knoxville at whatever cost of life and horse-flesh" and let Burnside know that help was on the way. The distance Long had to cover was forty miles, "and the roads villainous." Before daylight on the third, Long and his troopers were on the road, and they reached Knoxville early on the morning of the fourth.[30]

Long need not have hurried, for Longstreet had learned in good time of the numerous Federal relief columns of horse and foot converging on Knoxville. In addition to the forces of Granger and Sherman, General John G. Foster was coming from Kentucky via Cumberland Gap, and General Washington L. Elliott marched from Alexandria, Tennessee, at the head of the First and Second Brigades of the First Division of Cavalry, with orders "to harass Longstreet's . . . force, and,

29. Sherman, *Memoirs*, I, 380; *Official Records*, Vol. XXXI, Pt. 1, pp. 264, 435. Long's brigade was made up of the 2nd Kentucky, 1st, 3rd, and 4th Ohio, plus, in December, the 98th Illinois and 17th Indiana Regiments of Mounted Infantry and detachments of the 4th Michigan and 3rd United States.

30. Grant, *Personal Memoirs*, II, 92; Sherman, *Memoirs*, I, 380; *Official Records*, Vol. XXXI, Pt. 1, pp. 435, 436, Pt. 2, pp. 562–63.

if unable to find him, to report to Burnside." Wisely, Longstreet decided to end the siege. "As our position at Knoxville was somewhat complicated," he said in his report, "I determined to abandon the siege and to draw off in the direction of Virginia." He issued orders accordingly, and on the night of December 4, his infantry, preceded by its trains and followed by the cavalry of Generals William T. Martin and "Grumble" Jones as rear guard, marched away from Knoxville in the direction of Rogersville.[31]

The Knoxville Campaign was at an end, and for General Burnside it ended in more senses than one. In October, he had written the president that he was "quite ill" and "might be forced to ask to be relieved of the command of the department." To his evident surprise, he learned "some days" before December 7 that he had been taken at his word and that War Department orders dated November 16, which had not previously been communicated to him, directed that he turn over command to General John G. Foster, who was even then on his way to Knoxville to take over. It cannot be said that Burnside's departure was a loss to the army—indeed, it is a pity that he was later given another command and the opportunity to be partially responsible for the Petersburg mine fiasco—but he had given a good account of himself in the defense of Knoxville, for which he and his troops were voted the thanks of Congress. Still, whatever his shortcomings, he did not deserve the underhanded way in which his removal was effected—a maneuver in which it may not be unfair to detect the hand of the secretary of war himself.[32] A regimental historian has recorded the fact that on December 10, "a meeting of all the officers of the cavalry corps was held . . . and resolutions of confidence and respect were unanimously adopted, and several speeches made, highly eulogistic of Gen. Burnside, which were heartily endorsed by all present."[33]

General Foster took over from Burnside on December 12. Soon afterward, Foster's horse fell with him on "a ledge of rock," opening an imperfectly healed leg wound he had sustained in the Mexican War. Unable to ride and confined to quarters from time to time, Foster had

31. *Official Records*, Vol. XXXI, Pt. 1, pp. 436–37, 408, 462, 546; Longstreet, *From Manassas to Appomattox*, 510–11; Sanger and Hay, *James Longstreet*, 235–37.
32. *Official Records*, Vol. XXXI, Pt. 1, p. 281, Pt. 3, pp. 166, 384. The orders transferring command from Burnside to Foster are dated December 11.
33. Thompson, *History of the 112th Regiment*, 170.

to give up the command on January 28, 1864, and was replaced by John M. Schofield, transferred to Knoxville from the Department of the Missouri.[34]

General Foster's dispatches and reports, written during his brief tenure of the command of the Department and Army of the Ohio, suggest a confident, clear-eyed, level-headed officer with an orderly administrative mind.[35] On his arrival in Knoxville he reported to General Halleck that he found the

commissariat of the department very destitute, there being only a few days' supplies of the most requisite parts of the rations, which are now, and have been for a long time, issued in half and quarter rations. Beef and pork only are issued in full rations. Nearly all the breadstuffs have been drawn from the surrounding country, and all the forage for the animals. . . . The rains of the past three days have made the roads so nearly impassable that it will be impossible to make a campaign . . . [against Longstreet] in the present destitute condition of the men and animals.[36]

He went on to voice an interesting observation on the kind of troops best adapted to operate in his mountainous domain.

I found that the mounted force is in this broken and extended country the most in demand for all operations except a general engagement. This kind of arms is very much inferior in numbers to that of the enemy, and must be increased. I am satisfied that mounted infantry, for which service the Western troops are specially adapted, can be used to more advantage in this country than any other arm. I have, therefore, ordered all the troops, which General Burnside had enlisted for the purpose, to be organized and mounted, and have tendered inducements to the six-month volunteers [of Indiana infantry] to reenlist for the same purpose. All these are to be armed with the carbine or rifle. I also require one first-rate cavalry regiment, armed with the saber and revolver.[37]

Foster informed Halleck that he had chosen General Samuel D. Sturgis to take command of his cavalry, which he intended "to keep together as the cavalry corps of the department." He did not explain

34. *Official Records*, Vol. XXXII, Pt. 1, pp. 251, 322, and Vol. XXXI, Pt. 3, pp. 529, 571.

35. General Halleck called Foster "a good officer and a live man." *Ibid.*, Vol. XXXII, Pt. 2, p. 80.

36. *Ibid.*, Vol. XXXI, Pt. 1, pp. 281–82. This dispatch was written within a week of Dana's reporting that Burnside had "full twenty days' provisions."

37. Foster wrote in the same dispatch that the IX and XXIII Army Corps were down to a total of 10,000 men "able to march and fight" and that the vacant buildings in Knoxville were full of the sick, for whom he had no medicines. *Ibid.*, 282–83.

why he had decided not to retain General Shackelford, General Burnside's appointee, in that post. The establishment of the corps, and Sturgis' appointment to command it, were formalized in orders dated December 12 and 14.[38] Sturgis was to write sometime later—and there is no reason to doubt his accuracy—that when he assumed command of the cavalry, "the arms . . . [were] in a sad condition and of every possible caliber, the equipments . . . incomplete and worn out, currycombs and brushes a novelty, &c.; the demoralization and want of discipline complete."[39]

General Foster's initial orders to Sturgis were to operate with the bulk of his forces (including his dismounted men) in the area between the Little Tennessee, French Broad, and Holston rivers checking any advance by the enemy cavalry from the south or east, his main objective being to keep "the enemy as far from . . . [Knoxville] as possible, and to subsist . . . [his] men and horses." Given the decrepit state of his command, the lack of supplies for the men and forage for the horses, and the state of the roads, this alone was as much as Sturgis could have been expected to accomplish, even with Elliott's command added to his own. Grant, however, asked for more. He urged Foster to "move forward and attack Longstreet" as soon as he could, and he asked, "Can you not now organize a cavalry force to work its way past Longstreet . . . to get into his rear and destroy railroad and transportation?"[40]

On December 1, while Knoxville was still under siege and Sherman still on his way there, Grant propounded a scheme typical of his notions of the proper use of cavalry that he was not weaned away from until Sheridan did it in March, 1865. He suggested that Sherman collect 1,200 or 1,500 of Foster's or Thomas' cavalry (or some from each) and, with George Crook or J. H. Wilson in command, have them "move, without transportation" and living "entirely on the country," to "strike through into South Carolina to destroy their east and west roads . . . burn stores accumulated along with them . . . take all the

38. Shackelford had reported on December 13 that he had been "quite sick for two or three days," which may have been why he was replaced. The historian of the 1st Kentucky notes that Shackelford "obtained leave of absence and departed for Kentucky" but does not say if the leave of absence led to, or was caused by, Sturgis' appointment. *Ibid.*, 415, and Pt. 3, pp. 394, 401–402; Tarrant, *Wild Riders of the First Kentucky*, 276.

39. *Official Records*, Vol. XXXII, Pt. 3, p. 30.

40. *Ibid.*, Pt. 2, pp. 138–39, 153, 193.

good horses they find," and return by whatever route was handiest.[41]
Fortunately for all concerned (including Grant himself), Grant told
Sherman that he did not insist on this moonstruck project, the nearest
intellectual equivalent of which was John Morgan's Indiana-Ohio Raid
of the previous summer, but left it up to Sherman to decide whether to
go ahead with it. Like the sensible subordinate that he was, Sherman
did not argue about the suggestion; he quietly ignored it and allowed it
to sink out of sight of its own weight.

Judging by the first few orders Sturgis thought it necessary to
issue, he most certainly took over a sadly disorganized command.
Plundering was and remained a major problem, notwithstanding that
Sturgis' cavalrymen operated in an area overwhelmingly Unionist in
sentiment. Infantry General M. D. Manson reported from Strawberry
Plains, Tennessee, that there were in the area several hundred dismounted cavalrymen, as well as stragglers and large wagon trains belonging to the Cavalry Corps, with no officers in charge, "and the consequence is that the soldiers . . . [were] marauding and pillaging, and
the animals attached to the trains . . . [were] not properly cared for
and supplied with forage."[42] It should be said to Sturgis' credit that
he thought it a pity that his men should be compelled "to entirely exhaust the country of these loyal people. If we remain here long they
must suffer, and it will be impossible for them to raise anything next
year. . . . It is distressing to witness the sufferings of these people at
the hands of friends for whom they have been so long and so anxiously
looking." And he emphasized the fact, known to every commanding
officer after three years of war, that "the necessity for pressing supplies
leads so immediately to plundering that soldiers find no difficulty in
taking the step from the one to the other," despite anything commanding officers could do to stop it.[43]

When Sturgis penned the foregoing dispatch, he had already issued stringent and sensible regulations that "strictly prohibited" foraging by individuals ("as it only leads to pillaging and plunder") and directed that foraging be done on a brigade basis, under the supervision
of "energetic and intelligent" officers. This order, essentially identical

41. *Ibid.*, Vol. XXXI, Pt. 3, pp. 297–98.

42. *Ibid.*, 520. General Manson commanded the Second Division of the XXIII Army
Corps.

43. *Ibid.*, Vol. XXXI, Pt. 1, pp. 114–15.

to hundreds on the same subject issued in all theaters from the beginning of the war until well past its formal end, was no more effective than any of the others. Less than four weeks later, Sturgis had to "listen hourly to the complaints of loyal citizens of the cruel treatment they receive at the hands of . . . soldiers . . . [who] are permitted to wander away from their camps alone or in squads, with no intent but to plunder and rob helpless families," and he threatened to punish any soldier found a mile away from his camp without a written pass.[44] One may wonder if he realized that neither such orders, nor threats of punishment (especially threats that were seldom if ever carried out) would have any effect on men who, as he himself reported, had had to live "for nearly two months . . . mainly on parched corn, most of which has been gathered at a distance of from 6 to 15 miles."[45]

In mid-December, General Elliott and his 2,800 cavalry reached Knoxville and were ordered by General Foster to join the Department of the Ohio cavalry, which had been greatly reduced in numbers (Wolford's entire division mustered a mere 800 to 900 mounted men) and was operating in the rear of Longstreet's camps. Elliott was as badly off for supplies as was Sturgis; in fact, he had to ask Sturgis for "relief" in the way of subsistence and was promptly but courteously turned down, Sturgis explaining that his own men were "entirely dependent on the country for what . . . [they] can pick up from day to day."[46] Captain Eli Lilly's 18th Indiana Battery was now attached to General Elliott's cavalry; greatly to the displeasure of its gunners, it had been separated from its friends in the Lightning Brigade on November 17 and reassigned to Elliott's division.[47]

44. *Ibid.*, Vol. XXXI, Pt. 3, pp. 440–41.
45. *Ibid.*, Vol. XXXII, Pt. 2, p. 27, Pt. 1, p. 138. Sturgis wrote in this dispatch, "The weather at times has been intensely cold, and the suffering very great[,] most of . . . [the men] being without shelter of any kind." On another occasion about the same time he reported: "The question of forage is becoming a very serious one with us. We now send 10 and 12 miles for it, and have difficulty obtaining sufficient even then. Besides, it is ruining our horses, for when they return to camp, they have traveled some 20 or more miles over bad roads and their backs and saddles are ruined by the packing of the load." *Ibid.*, Pt. 2, p. 53.
46. *Ibid.*, Pt. 1, pp. 132, 626, and Vol. XXXI, Pt. 3, pp. 440, 441; Tarrant, *Wild Riders of the First Kentucky*, 279.
47. When Lilly's battery marched away to join their new command, "all regiments of Wilder's brigade were assembled . . . and cheered when the artillerymen rode by"; Rowell, *Yankee Artillerymen*, 143. The Civil War was fought by men on both sides who had the capacity to sing, cheer, yell, and even cry.

Before Christmas day, Longstreet's infantry crossed to the south bank of the Holston and began building winter quarters at Russellville and Morristown. Despite the weather, the state of the roads, and the decrepit condition of his troops, short as they were of ammunition, shoes, clothing, rations, and even medicines and "hospital stores," General Foster felt it incumbent upon him to try to push Longstreet (whose men were just as badly off as his own) out of east Tennessee.[48] To accomplish this goal, he sent Sturgis and Elliott across to the south bank of the Holston also, to operate against the cavalry shielding Longstreet's infantry camps. Sturgis, by virtue of his seniority in the rank of brigadier general, commanded Elliott's cavalry as well as his own. At 3 A.M. on December 24, he sent forward Archibald P. Campbell's brigade of Edward McCook's division, Colonel Israel Garrard's brigade of the Department of the Ohio cavalry, and two sections of Lilly's battery, from New Market, east of Knoxville, toward Dandridge, ten miles to the southeast.[49] Sturgis hoped to get between Colonel A. A. Russell's Confederate cavalry at Dandridge and the rest of General Martin's forces "in the vicinity of" Morristown and then, presumably, beat the two commands in detail. Sturgis, too, divided his forces. Campbell and the artillery marched directly on Dandridge and were expected to get there by daybreak. Meanwhile Garrard, making a circuit by way of Mount Horeb, was to get into a position to intercept Russell after he had been driven out of Dandridge by Campbell. The operation, which appears to have been disjointed and was either misdirected or undirected, did not work out as Sturgis intended. Campbell's attack at Dandridge, General Martin reported, was "unexpected" and threw the Russell brigade into momentary "confusion," but Russell's men "rallied and repulsed the enemy." And General Martin also had a trick up his sleeve. He sent Charles C. Crews's small brigade of about 600 men (1st, 2nd, 3rd, and 6th Georgia) to get behind Campbell. Led by Major A. F. Bale ("a fine looking young man with a commission of Col in his pocket," who was killed in the ensuing action), the Georgians captured two of Lilly's guns, but they were then driven off, and the guns recaptured, by a charge of the 2nd Michigan.[50]

48. *Official Records*, Vol. XXXI, Pt. 1, p. 287.
49. Sturgis' plans and the fighting in and near Dandridge on December 24 are covered in *Ibid.*, 437, 547, 632, 635–37; and Rowell, *Yankee Cavalrymen*, 160–61. Campbell's brigade was made up of the 2nd Michigan, 9th Pennsylvania, and 1st Tennessee.
50. Rowell, *Yankee Artillerymen*, 155.

Garrard's brigade, which was to have completed the success of the operation by intercepting Russell's retreat, was itself attacked and had to ask for help. Receiving orders from Sturgis to return to New Market, Campbell found himself "surrounded by the enemy, one brigade in front and one in . . . [the] rear," and sent to Garrard for help, which the latter, himself under attack, was unable to furnish. Campbell eventually escaped by the skin of his teeth. He sent his ambulances, artillery, and led horses on paths through the woods while his fighting men held off the enemy. The 2nd Michigan, dismounted, used their Colt rifles to hold the enemy in check while the 9th Pennsylvania and 1st Tennessee charged them with the saber. Colonel Campbell lost one of the Indiana battery's guns (it was spiked and abandoned after its axle broke) and caissons, and 56 men killed, wounded, and missing; he estimated that the enemy lost not fewer than 150 killed and wounded.[51]

Mossy Creek was the name of both a minor watercourse and a town and station on the East Tennessee & Virginia Railroad, four miles east of New Market.[52] Early on the morning of December 29, both the Union and the Confederate cavalry were on the move.[53] Sturgis had been told on the night of the twenty-eighth of the presence of a brigade of Confederate cavalry at Dandridge, and he sent John W. Foster's and Frank Wolford's divisions to drive them out. He then posted Colonel Oscar H. LaGrange's brigade of McCook's division at Bay's Mountain, where it could support either the troops attacking Dandridge or those remaining at Mossy Creek. At 9 A.M. on the twenty-ninth, however, the whole body of Martin's cavalry, whose numbers Sturgis greatly overestimated at 6,000 (General Martin stated that he had 2,000 men), crossed Mossy Creek from the east, delivered a sharp attack on the left of Sturgis' forces (Archibald Campbell's cavalry and Colonel Samuel R. Mott's brigade of infantry), and forced them back. The attack was eventually checked by the fire of Mott's infantry and Lilly's guns and by a mounted charge by Colonel James P. Brownlow's 1st Tennessee. In the early afternoon, after Colonel LaGrange's brigade came up from the south to reinforce the Union right, Sturgis went over to the attack.

51. *Official Records*, Vol. XXXI, Pt. 1, pp. 635, 637, 638; Rowell, *Yankee Cavalrymen*, 160–61; Rowell, *Yankee Artillerymen*, 154–57.

52. The damming of rivers in east Tennessee by the TVA and the formation of large lakes behind the dams make it difficult to trace on present-day maps some of the geographic landmarks of 1863–1864.

53. For the fight at Mossy Creek, see *Official Records*, Vol. XXXI, Pt. 1, pp. 547–48, 646–61, 648, Pt. 3, pp. 388–90, 504–506; and Rowell, *Yankee Artillerymen*, 159–65.

By the time darkness fell and ended the action, the Confederates had been driven (or had retreated) back across Mossy Creek. Union casualties, including those of the infantry, totaled 110; Confederate losses were estimated (and doubtless exaggerated) at not less than 250 and perhaps as many as 500.[54] In his report on the action, General Elliott took special pains to single out for praise Lilly's battery (which, he said, had been "so admirably served") and Colonel McCook's cavalry.[55]

While Sturgis and Martin dueled in the area between the main bodies of Longstreet's and Foster's armies, Wheeler's cavalry, whom Longstreet had previously sent back to the Army of Tennessee, attacked a wagon train at Calhoun, Tennessee, northeast of Chattanooga, on December 28. Escorting the train, which was carrying supplies from Chattanooga to Knoxville, were 2,000 or 3,000 infantry, mainly convalescents returning to duty, under the command of Colonel Bernard Laibolt, 2nd Missouri Infantry. He reported that Wheeler, with a force reputed to number 1,500, attacked the train as it was crossing the Hiwassee River. Laibolt formed his footsoldiers in line of battle to hold off Wheeler long enough to allow the train to complete the crossing of the river. Then he "charged with the infantry in double quick on the astonished rebels and routed them completely," whereupon he ordered Eli Long, who had joined him with the 150 troopers he had in camp at the moment, to charge the Confederates and "give them the finishing touch." Unfortunately, Laibolt reported, Long's handful was not sufficient for "an effective pursuit"; hence Wheeler got away, but did so minus the 131 officers and men he left as prisoners in Colonel Laibolt's hands. Colonel Long, for his part, reported that Wheeler had attacked the train with 1,200 to 1,500 cavalry and mounted infantry. Laibolt's footsoldiers' stout defense did indeed cause Wheeler to "give way," and Long and his 150 pursued, concentrating their attention on a body of from 400 to 500 who had become separated from the rest. A "vigorous use of the saber" caused this group to scatter "in every direction . . . throwing away large numbers of arms, accoutrements, &c.," and losing as prisoners to Long 121 (not 131) officers and men Colonel Laibolt claimed as his own. In reporting this

54. *Official Records*, Vol. XXXI, Pt. 1, pp. 650, 653, 655.
55. *Ibid.*, 653. One of Lilly's gunners wrote that Mossy Creek had been "the hottest we ever had as a battery." Of the 50 men the battery had in action, it lost 10 killed or wounded, an unusually high casualty rate for artillery. Rowell, *Yankee Artillerymen*, 160, 164.

scrap to General Halleck, General Thomas wrote, "For this and many other gallant acts of Colonel Long . . . I earnestly recommend him for promotion to brigadier-general of volunteers."[56]

The old year 1863 ended in east Tennessee with the assertion of a peculiar brand of egalitarianism by the troopers of the 9th Pennsylvania. As December 31 drew to a close with the temperature falling rapidly, ushering in what came to be remembered in the South for many years thereafter as "The Cold New Year's Day," some of the troopers of the Pennsylvania regiment, encamped east of Mossy Creek, became disgruntled over having to spend the bitter cold night in the open, wrapped in their blankets and lying as close as they dared to huge bonfires of fence rails while Colonel McCook and his staff officers sheltered in a nearby house. So they set fire to the house and thus derived whatever satisfaction there was in knowing that for the rest of the night their divisional commander and his staff were just as uncomfortable as they were.[57]

From the end of the Mossy Creek fight until April 7, when Longstreet was ordered to leave east Tennessee and rejoin the Army of Northern Virginia, operations along the Holston and the French Broad continued in a desultory fashion, with both sides, but Longstreet in particular, hampered by a lack of supplies.[58] There were fairly frequent skirmishes and scraps of varying degrees of severity, a fight once again at Dandridge on January 16–17, another at Fair Garden, or the Middle Fork of the Pigeon River, on January 27. In the fight on the seventeenth, Sturgis faced all of Longstreet's cavalry plus three brigades of his infantry.[59] Sturgis apparently had the worst of the encounter, especially Wolford's division, reported as "in full retreat, galloping away from the enemy," but the setback could not have been serious, for, unlike the customary phraseology to describe an enemy defeat ("fled

56. *Official Records*, Vol. XXXI, Pt. 1, pp. 435, 641–44.

57. Rowell, *Yankee Cavalrymen*, 165; Starr, *Jennison's Jayhawkers*, 282.

58. *Official Records*, Vol. XXXII, Pt. 3, p. 756. For the state of the roads, described by Colonel McCook as "the worst I ever saw," see *Ibid.*, Pt. 2, pp. 154, 162, 174. The food situation in Knoxville was not helped by the capture on January 23 by "enemy cavalry" of a "carelessly driven" herd of 800 beef cattle. The escort, a company of the 10th Michigan, "retired without firing a shot." *Ibid.*, Pt. 1, p. 42.

59. For the fighting of January 16–17, brought on by a Confederate advance, see *Ibid.*, Pt. 1, pp. 33–34, 80–94. Sturgis' casualties totaled 83. *Ibid.*, 81. See also Rowell, *Yankee Artillerymen*, 170–71; Rowell, *Yankee Cavalrymen*, 166–67; and Tarrant, *Wild Riders of the First Kentucky*, 283.

in confusion" and the like), Sturgis' retreat was described as "made somewhat hastily and not in very good order." General Longstreet, who used that expression in his report, added: "Our infantry was not in condition to pursue, half of our men being without shoes. Our cavalry is almost as badly off for want of clothing, and the horses are without shoes, or nearly half of them."

The fighting on the twenty-seventh, unlike that ten days before, was an all-cavalry affair.[60] It actually began late the previous afternoon, with Wolford's division of "at most 900 men" being driven back two miles from Fair Garden in the direction of Sevierville, by an advance of the two divisions (Armstrong's and Morgan's) of General Martin's cavalry.[61] Sturgis ordered McCook to counterattack at first light the next day. The counterattack, made in a dense fog by Colonel Campbell's brigade, dismounted, struck Morgan's command, which had become separated from Armstrong's division in the previous day's Confederate advance. In a "stubborn" fire fight lasting until midafternoon, Campbell, supported by Lilly's battery, pressed Morgan's division back about two miles. Then, at four o'clock, just as Morgan was preparing to move his artillery to the rear to rescue it from a dismounted charge by Campbell's brigade, Colonel LaGrange, whom Sturgis had sent off on a circuit to the left to get on Morgan's flank, saw his chance. With detachments of the 2nd and 4th Indiana, mounted, LaGrange charged the enemy ("a magnificent and gallant saber charge," Colonel McCook called it), sabered the gunners and their supports, and captured two 3-inch Rodman rifled guns with their teams, one caisson, 800 stand of small arms, 112 prisoners (including 2 regimental commanders and 7 other officers), and General Morgan's battle flag and body servant. In Sturgis' words, LaGrange "routed . . . [the enemy], horse, foot and dragoon." Colonel LaGrange showed in this fight that he was worthy of the terms Sturgis had previously used about him—"an exceedingly energetic, valuable officer."[62]

60. The action is described in reports and dispatches in *Official Records*, Vol. XXXII, Pt. 1, pp. 130–50. See also Tarrant, *Wild Riders of the First Kentucky*, 285–89; Rowell, *Yankee Artillerymen*, 175–82; and Rowell, *Cavalrymen*, 167–69.

61. One of the 18th Indiana Battery gunners wrote about the Wolford division, "the whole Div. was disgracefully routed   they came rushing back . . . every man for himself, part of them throwing away their arms so badly were they scared. The whole Div. is a disgrace to the army anyhow. they never did accomplish anything." Rowell, *Yankee Artillerymen*, 175. A battery that had worked with the Lightning Brigade for a year was not likely to have much charity for lesser mortals.

62. *Official Records*, Vol. XXXI, Pt. 1, p. 630.

On January 28, on receiving word that three brigades of enemy infantry were crossing the French Broad to his side of the river, Sturgis sent LaGrange to support Wolford, who was guarding his distant left flank. Before LaGrange's brigade could reach the scene, the Confederate infantry had had time to establish themselves in "dense woods" behind breastworks of rails and logs. LaGrange was moving up to the attack when a sad incident occurred. Lieutenant William D. Stover, 2nd Indiana, who had led his company to a jump-off position sixty yards from the Confederate breastworks, was killed, "it is believed . . . shot accidentally by some of our own men in his rear." Describing the event, Colonel LaGrange added the bitter comment: "Thousands of rounds were fired in this skirmish by men who did not see the enemy. The habit of allowing cowards to fire over the heads of their own party from a safe distance in the rear is one of the most reprehensible, and officers who cannot prevent it ought to be shot themselves." LaGrange did not accuse anyone of responsibility for the lieutenant's death, but Colonel McCook took pains to point out in a covering note that the "our men" LaGrange spoke of were not members of McCook's division. Left unsaid was the clear implication that they could only have belonged to Wolford's division.[63]

In his report of the fight of the twenty-seventh to Richmond, General Longstreet wrote that the Union cavalry, "greatly increased by the cavalry from Chattanooga"—that is, General Elliott's command—was superior in numbers to his own men, and he asked not only for reinforcements but also for a chief of cavalry. Evidently, General Martin's performance in that post did not meet with his approbation.[64]

Mention has been made previously of the fact that with rare exceptions, regiments of infantry welcomed the opportunity to become "cavalry," or more accurately, mounted infantry, and resented being turned back into footsoldiers when the shortage of mounts or the exigencies of the service required it. An exception was the 112th Illinois Infantry. It had been mounted in April, 1863, and had fought through the east Tennessee campaign as a mounted infantry component of Wolford's division.[65] If the regimental historian represented correctly the opinions

63. *Ibid.*, Vol. XXXII, Pt. 1, pp. 145, 142.
64. *Ibid.*, 150.
65. The regiment was armed initially with "old Harper's Ferry muskets" but was rearmed with Enfield rifles in July, 1863. Thompson, *History of the 112th Regiment*, 33, 63.

of his fellow soldiers, they welcomed the change when in April, 1864, the regiment was ordered dismounted, and to be "equip[ped] . . . for service in the field as 'flat-footed' infantry." The "mounted service," the historian wrote,

in which the 112th had been engaged had been detrimental to the discipline and morale of the regiment. Attached to an inferior force of cavalry, it had been compelled to do double duty, scouting and skirmishing as cavalry, and fighting, dismounted, as infantry; always at a disadvantage, as compared with regular infantry, as it required every fifth [sic] man to hold the horses, while many men were left in the rear on account of disabled and broken down horses. . . . Company and battalion drills and dress parades and reviews had been unknown during the East Tennessee campaign.[66]

On January 23, a change had taken place in the command of the Union cavalry in east Tennessee. By an order of General Foster's, Washington Elliott was relieved of duty in the Department of the Ohio "at his own request" and was directed to report for duty to General Thomas in Chattanooga, in his old post as chief of cavalry of the Department of the Cumberland.[67] He departed without the farewell order customary in such cases. Elliott's reasons for asking to be relieved—if, indeed, the initiative was his—do not appear in the records. As Thomas' chief of cavalry, he received his orders directly from the department commander, and he may well have resented having to take orders by reason of an accident of seniority from Sturgis, whose dispatches to him, however, were invariably courteous in tone. The inflated egos of young lieutenants and captains of the Regular Army, jumped overnight to brigadier or major general of volunteers, were as important a factor in the command relationships of the Union army as was ever the prickly "cavalier spirit" of Confederate officers in their army.

No sooner was the siege of Knoxville lifted than Grant came under intense pressure from Washington to drive Longstreet out of east Tennessee. In dispatch after dispatch Halleck rang the changes on the idea that the "holding of East Tennessee" was of the utmost importance for

66. *Ibid.*, 196. The historian had this to say about his regiment's 1863 Christmas dinner: "Roast turkey, plum puddings and pumpkin pie were not to be obtained. Instead . . . [the men] dined on parched corn, or cornbread baked in ashes. Canteens were split open and made into graters by punching holes with a bayonet, and the corn grated . . . and the meal, mixed with nothing but water, made into bread." *Ibid.*, 175.

67. *Official Records*, Vol. XXXI, Pt. 1, pp. 83, 629, and Vol. XXXII, Pt. 2, p. 171; Rowell, *Yankee Artillerymen*, 174.

the Union and that "the expulsion of the enemy from East Tennessee" was the primary concern of the secretary of war and of the president himself.[68] To some degree the preoccupation of the administration with the situation in east Tennessee, and their desire to have Longstreet driven out of it, were due to the inactivity of the Army of the Potomac following the Bristoe and Mine Run campaigns in October and November. Unable to persuade General Meade to move against the enemy, they concentrated their attention on Grant and east Tennessee. To an extent, Grant was himself to blame for the unrelenting pressure he was under, because he had told Halleck repeatedly, sometimes in cocky tones most uncharacteristic of him, that he intended to drive Longstreet out of the state.[69] Eventually he visited Knoxville to see for himself the condition of Foster's troops and realized that an aggressive campaign was beyond their capabilities. He informed Halleck accordingly, not forgetting, however, to make it clear that the "oversight" of having "ever permitted Longstreet to come to a stop within the State of Tennessee after the siege [of Knoxville] was raised" was General Burnside's fault and most definitely not his own ("my instructions were full and complete on this subject") nor General Sherman's.[70]

Lacking the capability for an immediate major operation against Longstreet, but with the desire (for whatever reason) to do something, Grant suggested to General Foster that he organize a cavalry expedition to Abingdon and Saltville, to start from eastern Kentucky. He suggested that Colonel August V. Kautz, 2nd Ohio (whom the reader has met as a brigadier general commanding the cavalry of the Army of the James in the summer of 1864), "a most excellent officer," command the raid. Whether it was pursuant to Grant's suggestion or for some other reason, Kautz was ordered to proceed to Camp Nelson, Kentucky, "to organize" the East Tennessee mounted troops there and at Camp Burnside.[71] Nothing came of the Abingdon-Saltville project at this time, but on January 30, General Foster sent Sturgis elaborate orders to collect his best-mounted men up to a total of two thou-

68. *Official Records*, Vol. XXXI, Pt. 3, pp. 396, 454, 472, 496, Vol. XXXII, Pt. 2, p. 126.

69. For example, see *Ibid.*, Vol. XXXI, Pt. 3, p. 458, and Vol. XXXII, Pt. 2, pp. 99, 192.

70. *Ibid.*, Vol. XXXII, Pt. 2, pp. 43, 99, 149–50.

71. *Ibid.*, 27–28, 38; Vol. II, pp. 176–207 of the present work.

sand, cross to the north bank of the Holston, march via Cumberland Gap, Jonesville, Stickleyville, and Stillville to Carter's Depot on the Watauga, then to Union or Zollicoffer on the Holston, then to Abingdon, wrecking as many bridges as possible on the way, and finally to Saltville, where he was to try to destroy the saltworks, which were of vital importance to the Confederacy. Having accomplished all this, or if he was checked at any point in his advance, he was to retreat across the mountains into Kentucky. He was told, lastly, that if he had not a subordinate in whom he had sufficient confidence to assign to the command of the raid, he was to command it himself.[72]

Nothing came of this ambitious, probably overly ambitious, project.[73] On February 3, the day John Schofield was ordered to take over the East Tennessee command, Sturgis was ordered—once again there is no trace in the record of the reason or reasons—to dismount one of the two divisions of the cavalry of the Army of the Ohio, turn over the horses to mount the other, and proceed himself with the dismounted division to northeast Kentucky to get it remounted, equipped, and armed as rapidly as possible. So far as one can tell, this was a thinly disguised sentence of exile to Siberia for Sturgis.[74] In lengthy dispatches written two months later, Sturgis apologized for, and tried to explain, the unconscionable delay in getting the division in condition to take the field, but to all intents and purposes, his connection with the Army of the Ohio and with operations in east Tennessee had effectively ceased.[75]

72. *Official Records*, Vol. XXXII, Pt. 2, pp. 262–63. Sturgis suggested an alternative route. *Ibid.*, 307. Readers will recall that the bridge over the Watauga at Carter's Depot had been the objective of General Samuel P. Carter's raid in December, 1862.

73. At about this time (the order is not in the *Official Records*), Colonel McCook was ordered to send LaGrange's brigade on an "expedition toward Virginia." He reported on February 13 that "as yet . . . [he] had been unable to procure the necessary horseshoes," and added: "I regard the expedition as utterly impracticable at this season of the year. Without horseshoes and imperfectly provided in other respects, it is likely to result in a failure, possibly a sacrifice of the command." There is no further mention of this plan, and it may therefore be assumed that it was dropped. *Ibid.*, 386–87.

74. *Ibid.*, 322. Another paragraph of Grant's order assigning Schofield to command the Department of the Ohio sent George Crook to the Department of West Virginia for duty. Crook had been ordered to West Virginia in August but either failed to receive the orders or chose to ignore them. General Thomas tried to keep Crook but when his request was turned down, asked for either James H. Wilson or Colonel Wilder to replace him. He was unable to get either. *Ibid.*, Vol. XXX, Pt. 3, p. 65, Vol. XXXII, Pt. 2, pp. 130, 132, 154, 166. Schofield arrived in Knoxville and took over on February 9. *Ibid.*, Vol. XXXII, Pt. 2, p. 356.

75. *Ibid.*, Pt. 3, pp. 30–31, 181–84. Schofield wrote in a long report to Grant on

Another warrior whose connection with operations in east Tennessee and indeed with the Union army ceased at this time was Colonel Frank Wolford. The colonel had gone north to Kentucky with his division. While Sturgis struggled with the manifold difficulties of remounting and reequipping Wolford's division, the colonel enjoyed the comforts of home. On March 10, in a speech accepting the gift of a jeweled saber, sash, pistols, and spurs from admiring fellow Kentuckians, he charged the president of "wantonly trampling upon the Constitution, and crushing under the iron heel of military power the rights guaranteed by that instrument." Such language from a serving officer was not to be tolerated. Wolford was ordered in arrest and on March 24 was dishonorably discharged from the army by order of the president.[76]

Under the new commander of the Department of the Ohio, the department's cavalry would shortly acquire a new commander: General George Stoneman, former commander of the Cavalry Corps, Army of the Potomac, and latterly the first head of the newly established Cavalry Bureau.

February 22: "At present I am unable to determine what can be done by Sturgis' cavalry. I am informed it is now scattered all over Kentucky and Sturgis gone north. I am making every effort to get it together and prepare it for service." *Ibid.*, Pt. 2, p. 447.

76. Hambleton Tapp, "Incidents in the Life of Frank Wolford, Colonel of the First Kentucky Union Cavalry," *Filson Club History Quarterly*, X (1936), 91–92; *Official Records*, Vol. XXXII, Pt. 3, pp. 88, 146; Tarrant, *Wild Riders of the First Kentucky*, 303–309.

XV

The Flinty and Steel Couch of War

GRANT'S CAPTURE OF VICKSBURG, A SPECTACULAR FEAT OF military skill, settled perhaps the major strategic problem of the Civil War, namely the question whether the Confederacy or the Union would control the Mississippi. But no sooner had the Union infantry taken possession of the Vicksburg bluffs overlooking the river than their commander and his superiors in Washington had to give thought to what Grant and the Army of the Tennessee should do next. More or less independently of one another, Sherman, General Banks in Louisiana, and Grant himself, came up with the same idea: a campaign to capture Mobile. The scheme, however, evaporated over the administration's desire to establish a strong United States military presence in Texas to counter the capture of Mexico City by the French on behalf of Emperor-to-be Maximilian.[1] Before any firm decision was reached on any plan, the summer wore away, Rosecrans was defeated at Chickamauga, Grant was ordered to Chattanooga as commanding officer of the Military Division of the Mississippi, and Sherman joined him there a month later.

The main focus of military activity on the Mississippi in the summer and autumn of 1863 lay along the river north of Memphis and in the country inland from the river as far east as General Grenville M.

---

1. See pp. 330–31 above.

Dodge's domain at Corinth. In command of the District of Memphis, and of the XVI Army Corps, was General Stephen A. Hurlbut. General Richard J. Oglesby, commanding the inland "left wing" of Hurlbut's forces, centered about LaGrange, Tennessee, forty-five miles due east of Memphis, had under him a major portion of Hurlbut's cavalry. On June 9, he organized it "temporarily" into a division under Colonel John K. Mizner, to relieve himself "of much detail" and, he hoped, to "make the cavalry more effective." Included in the division were the brigades of Colonels LaFayette McCrillis (3rd, 6th, and 9th Illinois) at Germantown, Tennessee; Edward Hatch (2nd Iowa, 3rd Michigan, 1st West Tennessee) at LaGrange; and Florence M. Cornyn (10th Missouri, 7th Kansas, battalions of the 5th Ohio and 15th Illinois) at Corinth; and of Lieutenant Colonel Bazil D. Meek (11th Illinois, 2nd West Tennessee, and detachments of the 6th and 7th Illinois) at Saulsbury, Tennessee.[2]

On June 11, Colonel William H. H. Taylor, 5th Ohio, was announced as chief of cavalry of the XVI Army Corps.[3] Taylor's tenure of the post was brief, for on July 24 Benjamin Grierson succeeded him and was promoted to brigadier general, the rank appropriate to his new responsibilities. Grierson's rise owed much to the success and fame of his raid in April, but it owed at least as much to his persistence as a promoter. No other officer of cavalry was so assiduous an inspirer of testimonials to his own merit addressed to higher authority, the language of which (reminiscent in tone of the hair-restorer testimonials of the day) suggests a common source, whoever the actual signers may have been.[4]

James H. Wilson, for one, did not respond with favor to the Grierson testimonials. He wrote his friend General Rawlins that he considered Colonel Hatch "Grierson's superior" and cited as proof the state of Hatch's regiment, the 2nd Iowa, which he had just inspected; though it was not, he wrote, "all that cavalry should be, it . . . [was] by far the best cavalry regiment in the Department of the Tennessee, and . . .

2. *Official Records*, Vol. XXIV, Pt. 3, pp. 386–98.
3. *Ibid.*, 405. But during Taylor's tenure of the post, Colonel Mizner was also referred to at times as chief of cavalry, *e.g.*, *Ibid.*, Pt. 2, p. 499. Two months earlier, on April 9, General C. C. Washburn had been announced as in "command of the cavalry in West Tennessee." *Ibid.*, 182. There is no indication in the records as to how, or indeed if, he actually exercised command.
4. For example, *Ibid.*, Vol. XXIII, Pt. 1, p. 243 (Hurlbut), Vol. XXIV, Pt. 3, pp. 366–67, and Vol. XXIV, Pt. 3, p. 511 (Colonel Thomas Kilby Smith).

Hatch . . . the best officer." Shortly after taking over as chief of cavalry, Grierson reorganized the command into a three-brigade division.[5]

A second cavalry force along the river was Colonel Edward F. Winslow's brigade (4th, 5th, 11th Illinois, 4th Iowa, 10th Missouri), listed as belonging on October 31 to General Frank P. Blair, Jr.'s XV Army Corps, but spoken of by General James B. McPherson in a letter of October 26 to General Grant in terms that imply that Winslow's brigade belonged to his XVII Army Corps.[6] Evidently that was the case, for the brigade appears as attached to the XVII Army Corps in reports later in 1863 and in early 1864.

On October 31, General Grierson's cavalry numbered 5,191 officers and men present for duty. Colonel Winslow's brigade, its strength not shown separately from that of the infantry division to which it was attached, numbered approximately 1,500.[7] Colonel Embury D. Osband had a cavalry regiment officially designated "First Mississippi Cavalry (African Descent)" operating out of Vicksburg, and the Mississippi Marine Brigade was credited officially with a battalion of cavalry, but by the latter part of 1863 its infantry component was probably mounted also. Thus the mounted forces of the Union in this large area, in which numerous and active Confederate mounted units, large and small, seemed to roam at will, numbered something over 7,500. General McPherson, who was not an alarmist, thought that the Confederates had a much larger total of mounted men in Mississippi than he had previously believed, perhaps as many as 10,000, at least some of them well armed with "short Enfield rifles, with sword bayonets, an excellent weapon for fighting on foot or on horseback."[8] And what General McPherson did not yet know when he wrote this letter was that the character, and certainly the intensity, of cavalry operations in the northern Mississippi–western Tennessee area were about to un-

5. *Ibid.*, Vol. XXX, Pt. 3, pp. 664, 82.
6. *Ibid.*, Vol. XXXI, Pt. 1, pp. 819, 748–49. The 11th Illinois is listed as part of Mizner's division in the XVI Army Corps and part of Winslow's brigade in the XV Army Corps. This may be a clerical error, or it may be (although the records do not so indicate) that Grierson had the 11th Illinois Mounted Infantry and Winslow the 11th Illinois Cavalry. There is a similar confusion concerning the 10th Missouri, which appears both as a part of the brigade of Colonel Cornyn (whose regiment it was) and as a part of Winslow's brigade.
7. *Ibid.*, 817, and Vol. XXX, Pt. 2, p. 802. It is not inappropriate to speak of "Grierson's cavalry," for he had both operational and administrative command of the division.
8. *Ibid.*, Vol. XXXI, Pt. 1, p. 449.

dergo a significant change—a change much for the worse from his point of view—with the transfer of Forrest from General Bragg's command to west Tennessee. Forrest arrived in northern Mississippi with an "effective total" of no more than 271 officers and men of his escort, Major Charles McDonald's Battalion, and Captain John W. Morton's battery, but confident of being able to raise a force of 5,000 on his home grounds.[9]

Hurlbut felt himself in danger after the departure of three of Sherman's divisions for the relief of Chattanooga and tried to minimize the peril by keeping his cavalry "in motion all the time." He had ample cause to be alarmed, for even before Sherman's departure, he had had to cope, not always with success, with the well-led, knowledgeable, and enterprising mounted forces of the enemy. In mid-June, Major John Henry, 5th Ohio, "allowed himself to be surprised and surrounded in camp [near Hernando] and his whole command was stampeded." "It is evident," General Hurlbut wrote, "that gross carelessness prevailed. The *morale* of the affair is very bad." The physical effect, too, was bad: a hundred of Major Henry's men taken prisoner and presumably a larger number of horses, weapons, and equipment lost. On July 7, "rebels" attacked General Dodge's corral holding unserviceable horses and mules and "drove off a large portion of the stock, which was so broken down that they left it along the road," but they took along as prisoners 30 of Dodge's men, presumably also their weapons and equipment.[10] A week later, it was the turn of Hungarian-born General Alexander Asboth, in command at Fort Pillow, who became the recipient of a reprimand and a lecture from Hurlbut: "I am much mortified at the surprise and capture of your force on outpost duty at Union City. It appears at this distance to be the result of criminal negligence. The system of breaking up cavalry into small squads is wrong, and proceeds from a desire to hold many minor points. . . . To send small bodies of cavalry to put at isolated posts is to give them away to the enemy. . . . when you move your cavalry move them in force."[11]

---

9. Forrest's transfer was authorized by an order dated November 14. *Ibid.*, Pt. 3, pp. 603, 645, 646, 694; Wyeth, *That Devil Forrest*, 241–50.

10. *Official Records*, Vol. XXXI, Pt. 3, p. 12, and Vol. XXIV, Pt. 1, pp. 485–86, Pt. 3, pp. 423, 486.

11. *Ibid.*, 512. To forestall a repetition of this incident, Colonel George E. Waring, Jr.'s entire brigade was moved to Union City.

These were isolated incidents, but early October brought on a more serious and larger-scale operation. To divert attention from General Stephen D. Lee's abortive move to join the Wheeler and Roddey raid on Rosecrans' supply line north of the Tennessee River, General James R. Chalmers was ordered to move north with his own and Robert V. Richardson's brigades and attack the line of the Memphis & Charleston Railroad at Collierville. On October 8, before Richardson joined him, Chalmers had a fight with McCrillis' brigade, reinforced by the 6th Tennessee, 7th Kansas, and 9th Illinois Mounted Infantry, a total of 1,250 officers and men.[12] Chalmers had either 850 or 1,200 men; he gives both numbers and also credits McCrillis with "not less than 2,000 men," a relatively modest exaggeration of enemy numbers. McCrillis gives Chalmers a force of 4,000. On October 9, Colonel Hatch reported that Chalmers had 6,000 men, including infantry and artillery. Having reported what they supposed to be the enemy's numbers, the Chalmers and McCrillis reports of their fight part company. Finding the Union cavalry "in a strong position immediately west of the town," Chalmers attacked them frontally and, he reported, "after three hours' hard fighting drove them from every position" and caused them to retreat "in disorder" with losses, on the testimony of "reliable persons," of 47 killed and 103 wounded, Chalmers' own loss being 1 killed and 27 wounded. Colonel McCrillis' report of what purports to be the same action has his men checking the enemy's repeated frontal assaults until, his men's ammunition nearly gone, he ordered a retirement, which was accomplished in good order, one regiment at a time moving to the rear and mounting. Not counting the 9th Illinois Mounted Infantry, which had failed to report its casualties, his losses were none killed, 2 men mortally and 8 others seriously wounded and 1 missing.[13]

There is one sentence in Colonel McCrillis' report that bears emphasis. He had in this fight, as nearly as it can be determined (his report is not as clear on this point as it might be), the three Illinois regiments of his own brigade, the Kansas and Tennessee cavalry regiments, a part of the 7th Illinois, and the 9th Illinois Mounted Infantry, for a total of six full regiments and part of a seventh. When he learned that "several" of

12. *Ibid.*, Vol. XXX, Pt. 2, pp. 745–46, 757–59, 735.
13. Union General Thomas W. Sweeny reported (at second hand) that McCrillis was "driven back on the railroad with considerable loss." *Ibid.*, 735.

his regiments "had exhausted all their ammunition," he could not order an equal division of what ammunition was left, because the men's guns were "of at least six different calibers."[14]

Although entirely unplanned, the most spectacular event of this Chalmers raid occurred at Collierville on Sunday, October 11. Having started his infantry on their way to Chattanooga, General Sherman, his staff, his headquarters orderlies and clerks, his escort—consisting of a 260-man battalion of the 13th United States Infantry commanded by Captain C. C. Smith—and the general's own horses and those of his staff boarded a special train to start their journey to the same destination. The subsequent events are described in Sherman's own report, which he submitted in the meticulous observance of the *Regulations for the Army of the United States* that he expected, but did not always get, from his subordinates. The Collierville garrison, 240 men of the 66th Indiana Infantry, was commanded by Colonel DeWitt C. Anthony, who had the kindness (and wisdom) to acknowledge in his report his great debt to General Sherman "for his valuable advice."[15]

As Sherman's special train pulled out of Collierville, "signs of danger" were observed; the train was stopped and backed to the depot. Just then a flag of truce appeared with a demand from Chalmers for the instant and unconditional surrender of the garrison. Sherman instructed Anthony "to return an emphatic negation." A perimeter defense was organized and, despite the four-to-one odds, held off the enemy until nearly dark, when Chalmers drew off on the approach of General Montgomery D. Corse's division of infantry. Notified of Sherman's peril before the Confederates tore down the telegraph wires, Corse had his men march the entire distance of twenty-six miles from Memphis at the double-quick.

One of the Confederates' successive charges on the right of Colonel Anthony's position got as far as the horse cars at the end of the train; when they were driven back, they took five of the horses with them, including Sherman's favorite mare, Dolly. Given the disparity of num-

---

14. *Ibid.*, 746.
15. For this second action at Collierville, see *Ibid.*, 731–33, 751–55, 759–61, 768–70; Sherman, *Memoirs*, I, 351–53. Chalmers mentions details of the 6th and 7th Illinois as present at Collierville. Colonel Anthony does not mention the 7th Illinois at all. As to the 6th, he writes that a company of that regiment, on temporary duty at Collierville, "made a hasty retreat to LaFayette . . . 5 miles distant, and reported that the garrison at Collierville had surrendered." *Official Records*, Vol. XXX, Pt. 2, pp. 760, 754.

bers, the Collierville garrison should have been overwhelmed, and Chalmers should have had the rare trophy of a captured major general to take back to Mississippi. One reason, Chalmers claimed, for his lack of success was the misconduct of Colonel John McGuirk's brigade of the 3rd Mississippi State Cavalry and the 1st Mississippi Partisans. In a flank attack northwest of the town, McGuirk struck what Chalmers called the "cavalry camp" and drove off the troops holding it, "but the delay occasioned . . . in collecting the stragglers, who were led from the ranks by the rich booty of the camp, was so great that the opportunity to take the town was lost." Indeed, "to prevent the demoralization of his men, Colonel McGuirk was compelled to burn the greater part of the property found in the . . . camp." Not mentioned in General Chalmers' report, nor in that of Colonel James A. Barksdale (in command of the 3rd Mississippi), is a fact mentioned by Colonel McGuirk, that he ordered the Union camp burned when he discovered that "liquors were being distributed by the stragglers there."[16]

On October 8, the day of McCrillis' fight at Salem, Colonel Hatch arrived at LaGrange from Memphis, with General Hurlbut's orders giving him command of the Cavalry Division. At daybreak on the eleventh, he marched out of LaGrange toward Salem at the head of two brigades of cavalry plus the 9th Illinois Mounted Infantry and supported by six regiments of infantry and two batteries of artillery, the whole constituting a force of 4,000, divided about equally between mounted troops and footsoldiers. In overall command was General Thomas W. Sweeny, commanding officer of the Second Division, XVI Army Corps. In the course of the morning, Hatch, leading the advance, learned that Chalmers had left Salem and was marching south toward Holly Springs. Misled by an incorrect report that the enemy were heading toward his own base at LaFayette, Sweeny halted, lost touch with his cavalry, and had no further part in the proceedings.[17]

Upon his arrival at LaGrange on the eighth, Hatch had "organized" the cavalry he found there (including the 9th Illinois Mounted Infantry) into two brigades, one under Lieutenant Colonel Jesse J. Phillips

16. *Official Records*, Vol. XXX, Pt. 2, pp. 760–61, 765. Anthony reported total Union casualities as 14 killed, 42 wounded, and 54 missing. Based on information from "citizens," Chalmers wrote that Anthony had 117 killed and 130 wounded; he also claimed to have taken 135 prisoners. *Ibid.*, 754–61.
    17. *Ibid.*, 736–38.

of the mounted infantry regiment and the other under Colonel Gilbert Moyers, 3rd Michigan.[18] On the eleventh, he led his command on Chalmers' tracks in the direction of Holly Springs. After a march of fifty-two miles in twenty-four hours, he found Richardson's brigade, which he outnumbered by more than two to one, three miles below Byhalia, a settlement about twelve miles south of Collierville.[19] The Confederates were "posted in a strong position" on a line of hills, behind the shelter of the swamps of Byhalia Creek. For the next several hours, the action was nothing more than a lively skirmish and an intermittent exchange of artillery fire. Strangely enough, it was not Hatch (whose handling of the affair displayed a surprising degree of caution and want of drive) but Richardson who then attacked, directing a "spirited" charge against the 7th Illinois and the 9th Illinois Mounted Infantry in the center of Hatch's line. Not until after this attack was repulsed did Hatch go over to the offensive; he attacked Richardson's left with the 7th Illinois and 7th Kansas, supported by the 6th Illinois, and drove the enemy back toward Hernando until late in the evening.[20]

Before daylight next morning, October 13, Hatch resumed his pursuit of the Confederates. Chalmers and Richardson had joined; protected by their rear guard, they made for the bridge across the Tallahatchie at the village of Wyatt, twenty miles to the south. The 3rd Mississippi State Cavalry had already crossed the bridge, but Hatch was so close on Chalmers' heels that in order to gain time to allow the entire command to escape across the river, the Mississippians were ordered to recross and help hold off the enemy and protect the bridge. On this occasion, too, Hatch failed to show the determination and energy to be expected of a topflight cavalryman. Chalmers' command had been reduced by "straggling and other causes" to 1,600, he was running short of ammunition, and only three of his artillery pieces were still functioning. Nevertheless, it was he who attacked time after time, and held the enemy at bay for seven hours. Not until nine o'clock in the evening, in pitch darkness, in the midst of a thunderstorm and in driving rain, did Hatch go over to the attack. Four of his regi-

18. *Ibid.*, 741. Strangely enough, there is no mention of McCrillis and his brigade in Hatch's report of his operations from October 11 on.
19. Chalmer's brigade had gone on toward Pigeon Roost Creek, farther south.
20. *Ibid.*, 741–42, 749, 761.

ments "charged the town . . . [drove] the enemy in confusion into the river and over the bridge *en masse*," and, in Colonel Hatch's words, "crossed the bridge with the enemy."[21]

On the morning following the fight at Wyatt, Hatch sent a battalion of his cavalry on a scout south of the Tallahatchie, but they found no sign of the enemy. Concluding that "they had fled to Oxford," Hatch turned about to march back to his base. That, however, was not the way General Chalmers saw it. His men, he wrote, "were drawn up in the intrenchments on the south side of the river to resist any attempt of the enemy to cross." They waited "some hours" hoping that the Yankees would do so, but they were disappointed, for the enemy showed no indication of a desire to cross.[22]

A mere three weeks after his retreat from Wyatt, General Chalmers had another go at the Federals. On the morning of November 3, he was back at Collierville with the brigades of Robert A. McCulloch and W. F. Slemons, seven regiments of Missouri, Tennessee, Mississippi, and Arkansas cavalry, as well as mounted Mississippi militia and a battery of six guns. The operation was ordered by General Johnston after he learned that Sherman was moving east; the aim was "to harass his rear and break the [Memphis & Charleston] railroad behind him."[23] As modified by Chalmers, the plan called for himself to make a demonstration in the direction of Collierville to "draw the enemy's cavalry from the road between LaGrange and Corinth" and for Colonel Richardson's brigade to break up the track somewhere in the stretch vacated by the Union cavalry in moving against him.[24] The garrison at Collierville had been changed since the fight on October 11. The post was now held by eight companies of the 7th Illinois, a fact reported to Chalmers by his scouts and confirmed by "citizens." Based on this information, Chalmers decided to charge the village and "take . . . [it] by assault." Unfortunately for him, however, Colonel Hatch, at Germantown, four miles to the east, with six mountain howitzers and eight companies of the 6th Illinois and 450 men of the 2nd Iowa, most of them armed with Colt revolving rifles, learned that Chalmers was crossing the Coldwater River on the road leading to Collierville. Moving west at a gallop, he

21. *Ibid.*, 742, 761–62, 770–71, 773, 776.
22. *Ibid.*, 739, 742, 762.
23. The reports covering the operation are in *Ibid.*, Vol. XXXI, Pt. 1, pp. 242–54, Pt. 3, pp. 31–33, 43, 56, 57. See also Pierce, *History of the Second Iowa*, 68–72.
24. *Official Records*, Vol. XXXI, Pt. 1, p. 247.

reached the village in time for the 2nd Iowa to deploy its "rifle companies" dismounted, lying in line on the ground, and the "saber companies" mounted, guarding their flanks, just as the Slemons brigade of Chalmers' command was moving to the attack. Then, the historian of the Iowa regiment reports,

the enemy came down upon us at full speed, their right led by Chalmers, and their left by Gen. [J. Z.] George, of the Mississippi Militia. The sight was truly imposing, for their course was across an open field where their entire line was visible. They kept their line remarkably well dressed, while the riflemen of the Second Iowa quietly awaited their approach. . . . Unfortunately they fired a moment too soon, and few fell from the balls thrown. Gen. George, who supposed he was charging single shooting carbines, now yelled to his men to "Come on, as they have now no loads in their guns, they will be ours before they can reload." These words were not out of his mouth, however, ere a second volley, more murderous than the first, apprised him of his error. . . . His lines waver, but still follow their dauntless chieftain; a third volley whistled past him with murderous effect upon his followers, who break in confusion.[25]

At the same time that General (or Colonel) George charged the Iowa regiment, McCulloch's all-Mississippi brigade charged the left and rear of Hatch's line. Anticipating the attack, Hatch moved the 6th Illinois around the rear of his line to meet the attack, and, he reported, "The charge of the enemy was received, broken, and repulsed."[26]

The resistance put up by Hatch, and perhaps also the fire of the 2nd Iowa, made Chalmers realize that he had been misled about the kind of opposition he would face at Collierville, and he therefore decided to withdraw, which he was able to do "easily and in good order, each brigade forming alternately in rear of the other until we were out of reach of the enemy . . . and crossed the Coldwater." Colonel Hatch reported, and doubtless believed, that Chalmers' withdrawal was hastened by the advance of the entire Federal line, the four mounted companies of the 2nd Iowa, "sabers charging."[27]

Colonel Hatch credited Chalmers with an orderly return march to

25. Pierce, *History of the Second Iowa*, 69. General George (called a colonel by General Chalmers) was taken prisoner after his horse was killed under him, by John M. Guild, Company G, 2nd Iowa. Colonel Hatch reported that "the regiment, lying on the ground, waited until the enemy's cavalry were within 50 yards, sprang to their feet, and, with cheers, poured in a severe fire from revolving rifles." *Official Records*, Vol. XXXI, Pt. 1, p. 245.
26. *Official Records*, Vol. XXXI, Pt. 1, p. 245.
27. *Ibid.*, 248.

and across the Coldwater but described his subsequent retreat of thirty-five miles south to Chulahoma, where he called off the pursuit, as "a perfect rout." Command conflicts between Hatch, Mizner, and McCrillis, and the speed of Chalmers' retreat (he had learned that McCrillis was moving through Holly Springs to cut him off from the crossings of the Tallahatchie) had made Hatch's victory less complete than it might have been.[28]

A minor item in Chalmers' plans for the raid was to destroy the railroad water tank at White's Station, nine miles from Memphis. To do this, he called on Major G. L. Blythe to join him with his command of partisan cavalry. Major Blythe let it be known that he would not obey General Chalmers' orders. This caused Chalmers to voice his opinion of the partisan ranger units that accounted for a large share of the Confederacy's military strength in the area of western Mississippi and Tennessee. "If," he wrote, "all the men were actuated by patriotism and a fixed determination to do a soldier's duty, these independent partisan organizations might be very serviceable; but when such organizations are made the receptacle of men seeking to avoid conscription merely, and who serve only when it suits their convenience, and who boast of their privileges in the presence of regular cavalry, they become essentially hurtful, and, furthermore, they often degenerate into mere bands of robbers, who steal indiscriminately from both friend and foe."[29]

A few days after Chalmers' defeat at Collierville, an order from General Grant's headquarters announced William Sooy Smith as chief of cavalry of the Military Division of the Mississippi.[30] It will be recalled that

28. *Ibid.*, 245, 244.
29. *Ibid.*, 249. In an age of steam locomotives, water towers to refill locomotive boilers were essential to railroad operations.
30. Smith was a native of Ohio who graduated 6th in the West Point Class of 1853, a class that also included McPherson, Schofield, Sheridan, and Hood. He was posted to the artillery but resigned within a year and taught and practiced as a civil engineer until Fort Sumter, when he reentered the army. He was promoted to brigadier general on April 15, 1862, and held a succession of divisional commands of infantry in the Army of the Ohio and in the Vicksburg Campaign. He was appointed chief of cavalry of the Army of the Tennessee on July 20, 1863, and of the Military Division of the Mississippi. Colonel George E. Waring, Jr., who served under him, described his as a "a young and handsome, but slightly nervous individual, who eschewed the vanities of uniform. . . . He

the Military Division, established a month earlier, embraced the Departments of the Ohio, the Cumberland, and the Tennessee; hence Smith's authority extended over the vast area between the Mississippi and the Alleghenies and north of General Banks's Department of the Gulf. Grant's instruction to Smith spelled out in language that left much to be desired with respect to precision, the scope of his authority, and what Grant expected him to accomplish. The commanding officers of the three departments under Grant were to retain operational control of their mounted forces ("Department commanders will locate the cavalry of their respective commands," in Grant's words) and when enemy appeared, "cavalry commanders" were to pursue at once, without waiting for (presumably Smith's) orders to do so. When, however, the cavalry forces of two or all three departments joined in an operation, Smith, "when practicable," was to take operational command in person.

Smith's major responsibility was "to endeavor to supply all deficiencies in arms, equipments and horses at the earliest moment and hold the cavalry always ready for active service." Horses were to be obtained (*i.e.*, seized) as much as possible "in the country traversed by the cavalry."[31]

The first thing Grant expected Smith to do was to acquaint himself "with the organization, location, and condition" of the three departmental cavalry commands, and that is what he spent the month after his appointment in doing. What he saw made a grim story. After inspecting the corral from which remounts were issued to the Department of the Tennessee cavalry, he wrote General Meigs that "not one-fourth of all the horses . . . are fit for cavalry service. Nothing but uniform failure can be expected of cavalry mounted upon them, and to accept and endeavor to use them, will only encumber the service, and perfect [sic] a shameful fraud upon the Government."[32] In a dispatch to General George Stoneman, then the head of the Cavalry Bureau in Washington, he repeated his conviction that purchasing quartermasters and inspectors were perpetrating a fraud on the government. "Many" of the horses he himself had inspected were over fifteen years old, some were

---

was vacillating in his orders . . . but . . . cool and clear-headed under fire." Cullum, *Biographical Register*, II, 337–38; George E. Waring, Jr., *Whip and Spur* (Boston, 1875), 108–109.

31. *Official Records*, Vol. XXXI, Pt. 3, pp. 122–23.
32. *Ibid.*, 176.

blind, others were badly spavined. He proposed that every inspector be required to brand an identification mark on a hoof of every horse he inspected and to post a bond against which the government could charge the cost of every unfit horse he passed. Smith ended the dispatch with the apt observation that "it is sufficiently difficult to compel volunteers to take care of good horses; those manifestly unfit . . . in the beginning they will kill as soon as possible."[33]

In a later dispatch to Stoneman, Smith complained that he was having "great difficulty" in equipping cavalry. There was not a saber belt or a holster to be found in the Nashville supply depot. "Scarcely any" cavalry arms were to be had, and those available were "of such inferior character as to be next to worthless." He had found detachments of cavalry in Nashville that had been there and out of action for as much as two months, waiting for arms and "equipments." He also noted a fact mentioned previously in this account, namely that the firearms supplied the cavalry were "so various in character that scarcely a single regiment is uniformly armed, and many of them have arms of three or four different calibers, making it difficult, if not impossible, to keep them properly supplied with ammunition."[34]

Not surprisingly, the most serious of Smith's difficulties was the shortage of horses. A mid-October dispatch of General Hurlbut's illustrates the extent of the wastage of cavalry mounts. He wrote Grant that with 5,700 "effective mounted men" in his command, he expected to need 2,000 remounts in the two months from November 1 to January 1, and 6,000 more in the six months after that. One, but only one, cause of the wastage was that despite the availability of the Mississippi for the hauling of bulk freight, the post of Vicksburg was without forage for six weeks beginning October 1. "There are over 3,000 animals in this command to-day," General McPherson reported, "with not a spear of hay or a grain of oats for issue." It turned out that Memphis, whence the supply of forage for Vicksburg should have come, had also "been entirely destitute of a supply to feed" its own animals. The excuse given by the quartermasters in St. Louis, whose responsibility it was to keep the downriver posts supplied with forage, was "the immense amount" required by the Army of the Cumberland, which evidently had first call on what supplies were available.[35] Hay and oats did

33. *Ibid.*, 254. Spavin is a family of disabling horse diseases affecting the hock joint.
34. *Ibid.*, 438.
35. *Ibid.*, Vol. XXX, Pt. 4, p. 472, Vol. XXVI, Pt. 1, pp. 907–908.

eventually reach Memphis, but not the remounts Hurlbut needed, for on January 2 he reported to General Sherman, who was now in command of the Department of the Tennessee, that 1,800 of his cavalry were dismounted and that he had not received any remounts against the estimates he had submitted in October. Only two weeks later, General Smith reported that Grierson's division (Hurlbut's cavalry), with 7,324 officers and men present for duty, needed 3,248 remounts to be fully mounted.[36] An incidental remark in this dispatch to Grant had a great deal of merit, but there is no indication that it was ever acted on, as it should have been. "I will ask a summary dealing," Smith wrote, "in the case of all officers reported for habitual neglect of their duties. A few dismissals from the service will have a magical effect upon the officers who are responsible for the killing up of the horses of their commands."[37]

General Dodge, at Pulaski, Tennessee, sixty-five miles due south of Nashville, seemed not to have any of the difficulties that filled the dispatches of his colleagues to the east and to the west. He wrote General Sherman near the end of November that his district was "loaded with corn, wheat, fodder and meat," enough for his own command and, with respect to forage, a surplus large enough to keep Sherman's entire command supplied. It was the same with respect to horses: Dodge "picked up"—a painless synonym for "confiscated"—enough "stock" to refit 350 teams, to mount one regiment and nearly mount two more regiments of infantry, and to accumulate 300 remounts besides.[38] But not every district commander had the drive and resourcefulness of Grenville Dodge.

And now, at the beginning of December, Hurlbut, Smith, and their subordinates were about to be faced by a problem of even greater complexity and menace. Its name was Nathan Bedford Forrest. On November 14, an order of General Joseph Johnston announced his appointment "to the command of West Tennessee," not otherwise defined, and directed that "he will, on arriving there, immediately proceed to raise and organize as many troops for the Confederate States service as he

---

36. *Ibid.*, Vol. XXXII, Pt. 2, pp. 13, 123, Vol. XXXI, Pt. 3, p. 564.

37. *Ibid.*, Vol. XXXII, Pt. 2, p. 123. In another dispatch, Smith wrote, "I must at once adopt some reformatory measures to secure better care of horses, and I am inclined to think that we will have to muster out of service a great many cavalry officers who are neglecting existing orders on the subject before the stupendous evil can be reached and corrected." *Ibid.*, 75. See also *Ibid.*, 241.

38. *Ibid.*, Vol. XXXI, Pt. 3, p. 235.

finds practicable."[39] This Forrest proceeded to do, crossing into West Tennessee (bounded by the Mississippi and the Tennessee) on December 2 at Saulsbury, through a gap in the cordon of Union cavalry protecting the Memphis & Charleston.[40] The expedition was a triumphant success. Forrest's name and energetic recruiting enlisted from 50 to 100 men a day—many from the kinds of organizations General Chalmers had criticized—and in addition to 3,500 men he also collected 40 or 50 wagonloads of bacon and other supplies and large numbers of beef cattle and hogs on the hoof. On December 6, Forrest got as far north as Jackson, and after a highly profitable stay of a little over two weeks, alerted by his scouts to the forces of Union cavalry moving toward him from every point of the compass, he decided that it was time to retreat.

As early as November 24, General Hurlbut knew that Forrest was at Okolona, reputedly with 7,000 men, and was "preparing for a dash into West Tennessee." He notified Halleck, Grant, and General Sooy Smith and told them that if Forrest came, he intended to follow him (Hurlbut recognized the obvious fact that he could not stop Forrest from getting into west Tennessee) with all his cavalry and as much infantry as he could spare.[41] Grant told General Halleck on December 18 that he was organizing a "heavy cavalry force to move against Forrest."[42] General Smith, at Columbus, Kentucky, at the moment, was to command a part of this force, but General Sherman thought that all this activity was

39. *Ibid.*, 694.

40. *Ibid.*, Pt. 1, pp. 576, 578, 580–81, 583–87; Henry, *"First with the Most" Forrest*, 302. General Hurlbut anticipated that if Forrest came with cavalry alone, he would cross the railroad at Saulsbury, as Forrest actually did. *Official Records*, Vol. XXXI, Pt. 3, p. 302. To distract the Federals, Generals S. D. Lee and Chalmers struck the railroad at Moscow and LaFayette and had a fight with Hatch's brigade and the Second Regiment, West Tennessee Infantry, African Descent, an action that earned the Negro regiment Hurlbut's commendation in General Orders for its "gallant and successful defense of the important position to which they had been assigned." *Official Records*, Vol. XXXI, Pt. 1, p. 577. In the midst of the fight, "Col. Hatch was shot through the right lung, a very dangerous wound. So engrossed in the battle was he, that he refused to give up the command or leave the field, though the ball had passed entirely through his body. Ordering an ambulance to the spot, he was placed therein and driven from point to point on the field, while he directed the movements of the men." Pierce, *History of the Second Iowa*, 77.

41. *Official Records*, Vol. XXXI, Pt. 3, pp. 242, 243.

42. Grant repeated the message in a different form a few days later. The cavalry force, "as large . . . as can be spared," was to move east from Savannah, Tennessee, and cooperate with Hurlbut's cavalry "in clearing out entirely the forces now collecting . . . under Forrest." *Ibid.*, 436, 473.

unnecessary. He would have been willing to allow Forrest to "rampage at pleasure in West Tennessee until the people are sick and tired of him, when the cavalry, as already ordered, can get on his heels and chase him to the wall." Sherman also thought that Sooy Smith was a poor choice to deal with the invader—he was "too mistrustful of himself for a leader against Forrest."[43] General Hurlbut, for his part, made the mistake of trying to direct a campaign against a wily and resourceful opponent from his headquarters in Memphis.[44] That was not the way to catch Forrest.

Lacking arms for many of his men and hampered by his animate and inanimate plunder, Forrest had to cross two unfordable rivers swollen by the December rains, the Hatchie and the Wolf. He had to fight, or try to elude, General A. J. Smith, coming south from Kentucky; General Joseph A. Mower, with Mizner's cavalry brigade, a brigade of infantry, and a battery, marching north from Corinth to Purdy, Tennessee; Sooy Smith from Nashville; George Crook from Huntsville, Alabama; and Grierson with his Second and Third Brigades moving north from LaGrange toward Bolivar. It should be noted that Grierson's Third Brigade was made up on this occasion of two regiments of infantry and a battery of artillery and was commanded by infantry colonel William H. Morgan. Making full use of his genius for befuddling his opponents by doing the unexpected, and with a minimum of actual fighting, Forrest crossed the Hatchie on the night of December 24 at Estenaula, after brushing aside Colonel Edward Prince's 6th Illinois, which had been sent north of Grierson "to watch all the crossings and destroy all the means of crossing that stream."[45]

Hurlbut assumed that Forrest would now head south by picking the relatively easy going over the high ground east of the headwaters of the Wolf, the same route, approximately, that he had used going north. Thus, Hurlbut deployed his infantry and Grierson's brigade to bar that exit. To make sure that Forrest took that route, he ordered all the bridges across the Wolf destroyed. The destruction of the bridge at LaFayette, entrusted to Lieutenant Sidney O. Roberts, 9th Illinois, was bungled. All but one span of the bridge remained standing, and word

43. *Ibid.*, 445. In a slip of General Sherman's (or a copyist's) pen, Forrest is called "Walker."

44. *Ibid.*, 450.

45. *Ibid.*, 568, 612–13; Wyeth, *That Devil Forrest*, 260–62.

of that fact was sent to Forrest, who decided to take advantage of the opportunity, notwithstanding that it took him almost within sight of Memphis. His advance detachment reached the bridge at daybreak on the twenty-seventh and had it repaired by the time the main body arrived an hour or two later. Forrest was across the bridge, then across the railroad at Collierville, and well on his way to Holly Springs before Colonel Morgan, whom Grierson ordered to LaFayette as soon as he learned that Forrest was there, reached the scene.[46]

General Hurlbut wired General Sherman that Forrest had "eluded Grierson" and escaped. Grierson blamed Colonel Morgan's unaccountable slowness and lack of enterprise for Forrest's escape, and Morgan denied the charge with indignation and at considerable length.[47] Outnumbered five to one by the numerous forces converging upon him, Forrest escaped with all his plunder, "a lot of prisoners," 3,500 recruits, and "regretting very much that . . . he had to leave West Tennessee so early," convinced that he could have doubled the number of his recruits had he been able to stay ten days longer.[48]

There were no major operations in the Department of the Tennessee in the January of the new year. Sherman returned to Memphis from east Tennessee after a brief visit to his home at Lancaster, Ohio, and began preparations for the campaign he had decided to conduct in February. His plan was to free the navigation of the Mississippi from harassment by the "considerable force of infantry and cavalry" that the Confederates still had in Mississippi and to do it by means of a campaign aimed at Meridian.[49] Sherman explained his plan to Grant and was authorized to proceed with it. In furtherance of the project, Grant ordered Sooy Smith to Memphis with 2,500 cavalry from middle Tennessee, to add to the 6,641 cavalry Hurlbut already had.[50]

46. *Official Records*, Vol. XXXI, Pt. 3, pp. 611–12, Pt. 1, pp. 608–609; Wyeth, *That Devil Forrest*, 263–65; Henry, *"First with the Most" Forrest*, 210–12.

47. Grierson ended his report with the statement that "if Colonel Morgan had evinced as much enterprise in pursuing and attacking the enemy as he has in making excuses for his tardy movements, success would undoubtedly have attended our efforts." *Official Records*, Vol. XXXI, Pt. 1, pp. 608–10, 615–20.

48. *Ibid.*, 620–21. A later report of Forrest's gives a good picture of the chaotic state of the Confederate military administration in the West, which accounted at least in part for the chronic manpower shortages of its armies. *Ibid.*, Vol. XXXII, Pt. 2, p. 512.

49. Sherman, *Memoirs*, I, 388; Grant, *Personal Memoirs*, II, 107; *Official Records*, Vol. XXXI, Pt. 3, p. 473. It was intended originally that General Banks should cooperate by conducting a campaign westward from the river.

50. Grant, *Personal Memoirs*, II, 108. Hurlbut's numbers given were as of Janu-

General Smith reached Memphis sometime between January 8 and 14. On the latter date he wired Colonel Hatch, who had taken charge of the Cavalry Bureau offices in St. Louis while recovering from the severe wound he had received less than six weeks before, "to hurry forward horses and equipments designed for this department as rapidly as possible. . . . give this department preference for the present. . . . Time is everything."[51] Smith had found Grierson's division "even worse off than the cavalry of Middle Tennessee." In addition to the previously mentioned need for 3,248 horses to fully mount the division, the serviceable horses the division already had "needed a great deal of shoeing" after their racing about after Forrest, and hay was needed to "recruit [them] up." Moreover, the cavalry regiments were "greatly scattered" and had to be brought together to be organized into brigades. A favorable factor was that the horses arriving from St. Louis were "of good quality, much better than those heretofore received." At the same time, however, General Smith wrote, recruits for Grierson's cavalry were arriving in Memphis "freely" and increasing the demand for mounts.[52]

On January 27, General Sherman issued orders giving Sooy Smith direct command of the cavalry of the Department of the Tennessee and sent him detailed instructions, to be described later, for his role in the forthcoming Meridian Expedition. Smith lost no time asserting his authority, with a bluntly worded order to Grierson to report the "precise condition" of his division, "particularly as regards its preparation for a long and rapid march."[53]

The opportunity to "veteranize," described in the second volume of

---

ary 31, 1864. For the XVII Army Corps cavalry see *Official Records*, Vol. XXXII, Pt. 2, pp. 297, 305. The cavalry Smith took to Memphis consisted of the 2nd, 3rd, and 4th Tennessee, 3rd and 5th Kentucky, 4th United States, and 28th Kentucky Mounted Infantry. *Official Records*, Vol. XXXII, Pt. 1, pp. 254–55.

51. *Official Records*, Vol. XXXII, Pt. 2, p. 97. Typical of the casual attitude of army officers toward the need for security was the opening phrase of the dispatch: "As our cavalry in West Tennessee and North Mississippi will be called upon for very active service within a few days . . ." Even worse was Smith's dispatch to George Crook two weeks later: "I start in about three days with 4,000 men to Meridian via Pontotoc." *Ibid.*, 250.

52. *Ibid.*, 123; see also 190. Smith had received 818 horses—not nearly enough—from St. Louis by January 27. *Ibid.*, 241.

53. *Ibid.*, Pt. 1, p. 182, Pt. 2, p. 250. Grierson's letter of January 14, sent directly to the secretary of war and not through channels, recommending Colonel Hatch's promotion to brigadier general, may have had something to do with the tone of Smith's January 27 dispatch to him. *Ibid.*, Pt. 2, p. 98.

the present work, was offered to the eligible regiments of the western armies in the closing months of 1863.[54] One of these was the 7th Kansas, reported to be without a tent and unable to get any. At the year-end, 340 of the Jayhawkers—all who had serviceable horses—were out on a scout toward Moscow and LaGrange. All day on December 31 the temperature was dropping, to introduce "The Cold New Year's Day," mentioned previously. After a bivouac in the snow and cold on New Year's Eve, the regiment started back to its base in Corinth on January 1, but it was so bitterly cold that the men could not ride for more than a few minutes at a time. They had to dismount and walk, leading their horses, to restore their circulation and keep from freezing. After a short march in nearly impossible conditions, the regiment went into bivouac long before dusk. Rails taken from a nearby field were used to build lean-tos, which were covered with the men's ponchos. A blazing fire of fence rails was built before each lean-to and kept the men alive through the night. The suffering of their horses is beyond imagination or description.

Under these conditions, in their New Year's Day bivouac, the 7th Kansas debated the question of reenlisting as veterans. Before the day was over, four-fifths of them signed up to do so, and the Jayhawkers became the first regiment in the XVI Army Corps to veteranize. One of the troopers wrote his bride-to-be: "The general opinion is that we will have about one year to serve or less[.] We think that the Confederacy is about *played out.* . . . the Most of Co. D have reenlisted and we wanted to go all together and want to see the war over and then we will come home to stay."[55] On January 15, the Jayhawkers were ordered to turn in their horses and weapons in preparation for going home on the thirty-day furlough they had earned by reenlisting.[56]

Another regiment to veteranize was the 3rd Michigan. They had been busy building their huts for the winter and, exceptionally, stables for their horses, when they made the decision to sign up. On January 26 they were ordered mustered in as veterans and to march to Memphis to

54. See Vol. II, pp. 45–46 of the present work.
55. *Official Records*, Vol. XXXII, Pt. 2, p. 15. Starr, *Jennison's Jayhawkers*, 281–84. Another regiment that spent New Year's under similar conditions was the 14th Illinois: "Reveille at 4:30 a.m. Commenced freezing at mid-night; cold increased until it was fearful—the coldest known for half a century. . . . We did not even have tents but lay out on the cold ground, scarcely half clad, as we had not drawn clothing for six months." Sanford, *History of the Fourteenth Illinois*, 135.
56. *Official Records*, Vol. XXXII, Pt. 2, p. 108.

go home for their veterans' furlough.[57] Those troopers of the two regiments who had decided not to veteranize, or were not eligible to do so (called "bobtails"), were turned over to the 2nd Iowa to serve with that regiment until their own returned to duty.[58]

General Sherman planned to accomplish the basic objective of his Meridian operation by means of a two-pronged campaign. A force of about 20,000 infantry, two divisions each from the XVI and XVII Army Corps, plus Colonel Winslow's brigade of 1,952 cavalrymen (of the 5th and 11th Illinois, 4th Iowa, and 10th Missouri), would march due east under Sherman's own command from Vicksburg to Meridian, 130 miles away. The footsoldiers, General Sherman wrote, were "to break up the enemy's railroads [the Mobile & Ohio] at and about Meridian, and to do the enemy as much damage as possible . . . to result in widening our domain along the Mississippi River, and thereby set the troops hitherto necessary to guard the river free for other military purposes."

General Sooy Smith was to have charge of the second prong of the campaign, with a command of three brigades numbering approximately 7,000 cavalry. Smith was to leave Collierville on February 1, march southeast to the Mobile & Ohio at Okolona and then south along the railroad to Meridian. On the way, he was to "destroy General Forrest, who, with an irregular force of cavalry, was constantly threatening Memphis and the river above, as well as . . . [the Union] routes of supply in Middle Tennessee."[59] The details of what Smith was to do were spelled out in a number of conversations between the two generals, as well as in a memorandum handed to Smith on January 27. With a cavalry force Sherman believed "to be superior and better in all

57. *Ibid.*, 68. The 2nd Iowa veteranized after their return from the Meridian Campaign. They did so on condition that they be allowed to conduct a new election of officers. They thought the condition had been agreed to and held the election (Major Coon was elected colonel), but not all those elected were commissioned. Pierce, *History of the Second Iowa*, 92–94.

58. *Official Records*, Vol. XXXII, Pt. 2, p. 229. The offer to reenlist as veterans was of course open to all arms of the service, and even the Regulars were offered a modified version of the plan. The drawback of an otherwise admirable scheme was voiced by General Sherman. It deprived the army for as much as four months of the services of many of its most effective veteran regiments. Sherman, *Memoirs*, I, 395.

59. *Official Records*, Vol. XXXII, Pt. 1, pp. 171, 172, 174, Pt. 2, pp. 174–75; Sherman, *Memoirs*, I, 394.

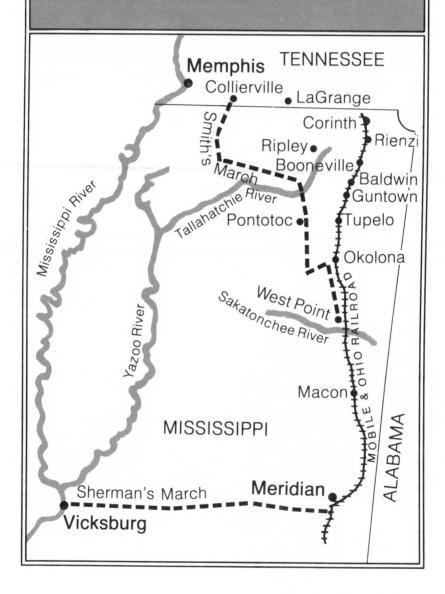

MERIDIAN EXPEDITION

MILES

0 10 20 30 40 50

respects than the combined cavalry which the enemy . . . [had] in all the State of Mississippi," Smith was to make the 250-mile march from Collierville in ten days, arriving in Meridian on about February 10. On his way south, he was to "disable . . . [the Mobile & Ohio] as much as possible, consume or destroy the resources of the enemy along that road, [and] break up the connection with Columbus, Miss." He was warned not to let the enemy draw him into "minor affairs." He was to sustain his command by taking "liberally" the forage and standing corn along the way, as well as all the horses, mules, and cattle his men could find. Dwellings and families were to be respected as "too sacred to be disturbed by soldiers," but "mills, barns, sheds, stables and such like things" were to be "used" for the "benefit and convenience" of his command.[60]

Two of Smith's brigades, Lieutenant Colonel William P. Hepburn's (previously Mizner's) Second (6th, 7th, and 9th Illinois and 2nd Iowa) and LaFayette McCrillis' Third (72nd Indiana Mounted Infantry, 5th Kentucky, 2nd, 3rd, and 4th Tennessee, and five companies of the 3rd Illinois), had been deployed along, or near, the Memphis & Charleston and were readily collected and organized for a departure from Collierville on schedule. Not so, however, Colonel George E. Waring, Jr.'s First Brigade (7th Indiana, 4th Missouri, 2nd New Jersey, 19th Pennsylvania, and five companies of the 2nd Illinois), stationed at Union City, near the northern border of Tennessee, one hundred miles as the crow flies from Collierville.

Waring left Union City at daybreak on January 22. It took his supply train until 2 P.M. that day to cover the first two miles of the journey, through the "almost impassable" Troy Bottom, which surrounded the town. This was an appropriate but relatively mild foretaste of the difficulties and delays Waring was to encounter on the entire march south. His report of the march is recommended to all who harbor notions of the glamor of service in the cavalry in the Civil War.[61]

By 10 A.M. on January 23, the brigade train, following the cavalry, was over the worst of the road, a stretch of about thirteen miles south of Union City. Ten miles farther on was Sharp's Ferry, across the swollen and still rising Obion River. When Waring reached the ferry, he found

60. *Official Records*, Vol. XXXII, Pt. 1, pp. 181–82. The memorandum of instructions ended: "We have talked over this matter so much that the above covers all points not provided for in my published orders of to-day."

61. *Ibid.*, 262–65; Waring, *Whip and Spur*, 105–108.

its rope broken and "the boat swamped in the ice, with which the river was entirely choked." The pioneer corps of the 4th Missouri (a St. Louis regiment, almost solidly German and called for that reason the "Vierte Missouri") somehow raised the boat, replaced the rope, and chopped a way through the ice across the river. A part of the cavalry, including the colonel himself and his staff, were able to cross. The river rose to such a degree during the night that on the morning of the twenty-fourth, when the 7th Indiana crossed, the water the horses had to step into at the ferry landing on the south bank was three feet deep.

The first three miles of the road south of the ferry ran through the flooded bottoms of the Obion, with water in the wide sloughs it crossed as much as two to four feet deep and "filled with large cakes of broken ice, which caused the horses and men to fall at every few steps." To add to the miseries of the march, there were "very heavy rains" on the nights of January 29 and 30, rendering the roads "almost impassable" and causing the washing away of the bridges across the many swollen streams and creeks Waring had to cross. This necessitated long detours to find passable roads and usable crossings over the streams. When, on February 8, Waring finally reached Collierville, he had marched an estimated 220 miles and been on the road eighteen days to make a journey that under normal conditions would have taken no more than six to eight days.

Three days of "great effort" were needed after Waring's arrival at Collierville to prepare Smith's "whole command" for the expedition south, and on February 11, the day after he should have reached Meridian, he got under way.[62] Smith did not explain what was done, or what had to be done, in those three days. Colonel Waring reported that the time was "occupied in arranging a pack train," and it is difficult not to agree with his comment that the train "might have been made ready in advance."

General Sherman's report of the campaign included a temperately worded but unequivocal condemnation of Sooy Smith's proceedings from start to finish. "I enclose herewith," he wrote, "my instructions to General Smith with a copy of his report, and must say it is unsatisfactory. The delay in his start to the 11th of February, when his orders contemplated his being at Meridian on the 10th . . . is unpardonable, and the mode and manner of his return to Memphis was not what I

62. *Official Records*, Vol. XXXII, Pt. 1, p. 255; *Battles and Leaders*, IV, 417.

expected from an intended bold cavalry movement. . . . I hope General Smith will make these points more clear to the general-in-chief."[63]

In a letter to Sherman ten years after the war, Smith claimed that in the conversations in which the details of the operation were hammered out, Sherman had replied to his query whether he should wait for Waring's brigade, should it be delayed in reaching him, with "Certainly; if you go without it, you will be too weak." This may have been so, but Smith was also aware of the timetable of the infantry phase of the operation, and he had Sherman's orders in writing that he was to be in Meridian "as near the date I have mentioned [February 10] as possible." This, assuredly, did not mean eleven days or more past the February 10 target date. Sherman wrote in his reminiscences: "Of course I did not and could not approve of . . . [General Smith's] conduct, and I know that he yet chafes under the censure. I had set so much store on his part of the project that I was disappointed, and so reported officially. . . . General Smith never regained my confidence as a soldier, though I still regard him as a most accomplished gentleman and a skillful engineer. Since the close of the war he has appealed to me to relieve him of that censure, but I could not do it, because it would falsify history."[64]

Two days before he left Collierville, Smith issued "Special Field Orders" to his all-cavalry, mainly veteran command, that are worthy of notice:

The strength of cavalry consisting to a great extent in its momentum, the attack must be made en masse, and with just such a rate of speed as is consistent with a maintenance of the organization of each command.

Our commands must never be permitted to receive a charge at a halt, but must meet charge with charge.

All officers of every grade are specially instructed to inculcate the idea that on favorable ground a saber charge of our forces upon the enemy, who have laid aside their sabers, must result in most signal and decisive success, if resolutely made.[65]

These copy-book exhortations were addressed to forces that still, on occasion, charged with the saber or pistol or both, but who, by the

63. *Official Records*, Vol. XXXII, Pt. 1, p. 175. Before March 7, the date of this report, Grant had been promoted to lieutenant general.

64. *Battles and Leaders*, IV, 417n; *Official Records*, Vol. XXXII, Pt. 1, p. 181; Sherman, *Memoirs*, I, 391–95.

65. *Official Records*, Vol. XXXII, Pt. 2, p. 358. Readers may recall one of Frederick

early months of 1864, and particularly so in the western theater, had come to rely more and more on their firearms in dismounted action, forces that in many cases had converted themselves from cavalry to mounted infantry.

Two of the three brigades of cavalry that made the Meridian Campaign belonged to Grierson's division, and Grierson himself went along in an indeterminate capacity. His brief report relates that by Smith's direction, he marched with the Second Brigade, but it tells practically nothing of what he did. The printed records contain only four messages sent by Smith to him in the course of the campaign and one sent by him to Smith. None of the five is of any significance. Grierson's own description of his role, "a sort of supernumerary," seems to be apt. His report also gives the crystal-clear impression of his desire to place as great a distance as possible between himself and the failure of the campaign. In contrast, however, Smith's reports on Grierson and his performance are nothing less than glowing; in a semiofficial letter to Sherman, he wrote that "Grierson behaved nobly, and is a man of more capacity than either you or I have credited him with."[66]

When Smith finally got away from Collierville, he used a brigade of infantry, lent to him for that purpose, to create the impression that he intended to cross the Tallahatchie at Wyatt, which enabled the cavalry to cross at New Albany "without firing a shot." Brushing out of their way a body of Mississippi state militia, a portion of the command rode south through Pontotoc toward Houston, while the main body veered eastward, toward Okolona and thence south to West Point. A short distance below West Point, on February 20, Smith halted. He was led to believe by "careful reconnaissances" that the roads through the streams and swamps to his left, as well as those directly before him and to his right (the Tombigbee, the Oktibbeha, and the Sakatonchee, in that order), one of which he had to cross to continue on toward Meridian, still eighty miles away, were "all . . . strongly held by the enemy, present in four brigades and to the number of about 6,000 or 7,000."[67] Smith had reports that Mississippi state troops and Stephen

---

the Great's regulations quoted previously (Vol. I, p. 51), that "any cavalry officer awaiting an attack will be cashiered."

66. *Ibid.*, Pt. 1, pp. 260–61, 254, Pt. 2, pp. 408, 409, 430, 431; *cf. Ibid.*, Pt. 1, p. 259; Pierce, *History of the Second Iowa*, 81.

67. *Official Records*, Vol. XXXII, Pt. 1, p. 256. General Smith's estimate of Forrest's *total* strength (actually 5,700) was remarkably close to the mark, but as Major Coon of

D. Lee with all or part of his cavalry were coming to reinforce Forrest's command, already facing him. His own force was hampered by its pack train of seven hundred mules and by the three thousand Negroes who had flocked from all sides to join the column. Even more important, seemingly, in Smith's analysis of his predicament, were two points he emphasized in his report: "The ground was so obstructed as to make it absolutely necessary that we should fight dismounted, and for this kind of fighting the enemy, armed with Enfield and Austrian rifles, was better prepared than our force, armed mainly with carbines. There was but one of my brigades that I could rely upon with full confidence. The conduct of the other two on the march had been such as to indicate such a lack of discipline as to create . . . the most serious apprehensions as to what would be their conduct in action."[68] And lastly, knowing that he was ten days late ("owing to the delay of Waring's brigade," as he put it), Smith had "every reason to believe" that Sherman had returned to Vicksburg with the infantry. In the light of all these factors, the sensible course seemed to him not to march into the "trap" set for him by the enemy but to "move back" and draw them after him, so that he could fight them on favorable ground of his own choosing. The decision was manifestly an expression of Smith's engineering logic and not at all of a "cavalry spirit," a quality he lacked and the absence of which was cited against him in General Sherman's report. His subordinates came to a conclusion not at all flattering to General Smith. As Colonel Waring later wrote, "All of us who were in a position to know the spirit with which we were commanded were conscious of a gradual oozing out at the finger-ends of the determination to make a successful fight."[69]

The lack of discipline on the march that disturbed General Smith was a course of arson and rapine in which his men engaged from the time they reached the "beautiful prairie region of eastern Mississippi" from Okolona southward, "the *bread basket*" of the South. Part of

---

the 2nd Iowa wrote in his report, facing Smith at the crossing of the Sakatonchee when he decided to turn back were no more than 2,000 men. *Ibid.*, 299.

68. *Ibid.*, 257. The advantage of the Confederates' rifles was their greater range. On the basis of all the reports and dispatches covering the campaign, it is evident that the two brigades Smith considered to be of doubtful value were Waring's First and McCrillis' Third. But by the early months of 1864, there was plenty of evidence Smith should have been aware of, that many regiments and brigades combined poor discipline on the march and in camp with bravery, reliability, and even discipline in a fight.

69. Waring, *Whip and Spur*, 116.

Smith's assignment was to destroy supplies of use to the Confederacy; he claimed in his report that he had done so to the extent of two million bushels of corn and two thousand bales of cotton burned, creating a "line of fire" from Okolona to West Point. The inevitable by-products of such operations (which also included the taking of three thousand horses and mules) were arson "of the most shocking kind" and robbery General Smith condemned and tried unsuccessfully to stop, ordering on one occasion to have shot the first man caught in the act and announcing a reward of five hundred dollars for his "detection."[70]

The Regulars of the 4th United States were far from squeamish about the taking of "enemy property," but what they saw on this march shocked them. Their Sergeant Larson wrote, "The behavior of some of the troops was rather disgraceful and not as we had been in the habit of seeing cavalry act in . . . [Tennessee]," which, he might have added, was bad enough at times.[71] And Colonel Waring wrote about this march after the war:

During the two days following our arrival at Okolona . . . the sky was red with the flames of burning corn and cotton. On a single plantation our flanking party burned thirty-seven hundred bushels of tithe corn. . . . no sooner was its light seen at the plantation houses than hundreds of negroes, who swarmed from their quarters to join our column, fired the rail-built cribs in which the remaining nine-tenths of the crop was stored. Driven wild with the infection, they set the torch to mansion house, stables, cotton gin and quarters until the whole village-like settlement was blazing. . . . The incidents of all this desolation were often sickening and heart-rending.[72]

A mile from West Point, Smith ran into the brigade of Colonel Jeffrey E. Forrest, the general's brother, and "drove [it southward] after a short, sharp fight."[73] With a complement of a thousand, rank and file, this was the smallest of the four brigades Forrest (a major general since December 4) now commanded. On February 20, the day Smith decided to turn back, only two of the four brigades—Jeffrey Forrest's and Robert McCulloch's, a total of 2,200 effectives—faced Smith's 7,000, where the road south to Meridian crossed Sakatonchee Creek.[74]

70. Battles and Leaders, IV, 417; Pierce, History of the Second Iowa, 81; Official Records, Vol. XXXII, Pt. 1, pp. 257, 252, Pt. 2, p. 431.

71. Larson, Sergeant Larson, 217.

72. Waring, Whip and Spur, 112–13; see also the tragic tale on 113–14.

73. Official Records, Vol. XXXII, Pt. 1, pp. 252, 256, 291; but see Ibid., 352.

74. Wyeth, That Devil Forrest, 272–73. The younger Forrest's and McCulloch's brigades were joined in an informal division under General James R. Chalmers.

General R. V. Richardson's brigade, 1,500 strong, and Colonel Tyree H. Bell's, with 2,000 officers and men, were upwards of ten miles away, one to the east and the other to the west.

Smith's retreat was to begin on the morning of the twenty-first. To cover it, he ordered the 2nd Iowa "to make a demonstration" with the Colt revolving rifles with which eight of its companies were armed, at the crossing of the Sakatonchee. After a noisy fire-fight of two hours, the Iowans withdrew at 10 A.M. in obedience to orders. Their commander, Major (later, and deservedly, Colonel) Datus E. Coon was "thoroughly convinced . . . that the Federal force was at least 4 to the enemy's 1."[75] Major Coon was a competent officer and a veteran; his disgust at General Smith's pusillanimous proceedings shows through the restrained language of his report. He resented the order to retreat.

Forrest, himself a master of such stratagems, seemed on this occasion to have failed to recognize Major Coon's demonstration for what it was. Not until after the Iowans had begun to withdraw did he organize a pursuit, but having begun, he gave the Federals no rest until it was too dark to see. Sending orders to Richardson and Bell to converge on Okolona, thirty miles to the north, he led the pursuit himself, at the head of his escort company and a portion of Colonel W. W. Faulkner's 12th Kentucky. Five miles north of the Sakatonchee, he attacked the Iowans' rear guard, commanded by Captain George C. Graves, Company D, who had to call for help. Major Coon dismounted and deployed four of his rifle companies; they checked the Confederates momentarily, but against a pursuit driven by Forrest, the fire of four companies was not enough. Coon had to dismount and put into line his other four rifle companies and post his saber companies, mounted, to protect his flanks. Under unremitting attack, "with the greatest difficulty" and with the aid of four companies of the 6th Illinois, he got his led horses, two howitzers, and lastly his men, across a swamp and through a belt of woods to safety. His riflemen, unaccustomed to long marches on foot, became "so completely exhausted that Major Coon was sure that half of them would fall behind and be taken prisoner."[76]

75. *Official Records*, Vol. XXXII, Pt. 1, pp. 300, 350, 352. On February 21, a Sunday, "the sun arose to a cloudless sky, shining forth 'mid all the beauty and grandeur of a lovely Southern spring day. The birds sang sweetly their morning lay from the budding trees, and all nature seemed to praise the God of its being." Pierce, *History of the Second Iowa*, 84.

76. Major Coon wrote, "Although I had given notice that my command was hard

Smith kept his command moving until midnight; indeed, some of the rearmost regiments did not reach the camp, three miles south of Okolona, until 2 A.M. The retreat was resumed at daylight on the twenty-second. In the rear this day were the Third (McCrillis') Brigade and the 4th United States. Forrest, like Smith, had allowed his men (he had been joined by his brother's and McCulloch's commands) only a short rest. He had them on the march before daylight and began the day's operations by driving the Federal pickets and the regiment of Regulars through Okolona. As Sergeant James Larson remembered, Okolona "was one of the few places where fights occurred in towns during the Civil War and gave ladies, children, and non-combatants a chance to be present. . . . The affair . . . took place . . . before the sun was up, all the windows in the upper stories were crowded with ladies, young and old, and some old men, too. The ladies appeared very interested in the affair. . . . they hung half out of the windows and waved small Confederate flags and handkerchiefs . . . to encourage their men to give those hateful Yankees Hail Columbia."[77]

On this January morning, the Confederate ladies of Okolona had something to cheer about. The 4th United States were driven through the town. "When we left Okolona," wrote Colonel Waring, "we left hope behind, for our road struck at once into a wooded, hilly country, full of by-ways and cross-roads known to the enemy but unknown to us, and we well knew that this movement would double Forrest's power and divide our own."[78]

From Okolona north for nine to twelve miles, Forrest, reinforced by the arrival of Tyree Bell's brigade (commanded by Colonel Clark R. Barteau, Bell being ill), attacked and kept on attacking the rear and both flanks of the retreating and at times disorganized and panic-stricken column, causing some regiments—nearly all those of the Third Brigade and one or two of the First, somewhat later—to break and run, stampeding with the contagion of their own panic any unit

---

pressed and that I was in great need of re-enforcements, I had been unable to get assistance." His brigade commander, Lieutenant Colonel Hepburn, who coincidentally was also Major Coon's immediate superior in the 2nd Iowa, claimed that "no calls for assistance or re-enforcements were made that were not at once responded to." The casualties of the 2nd Iowa were six killed, eighteen wounded, and eight missing. *Official Records*, Vol. XXXII, Pt. 1, pp. 300–301, 292; see also Pierce, *History of the Second Iowa*, 85–87.

77. Larson, *Sergeant Larson*, 22.
78. Waring, *Whip and Spur*, 118.

that had the misfortune to be behind them. The numerous Union reports of the day's fighting agree only in denying any misconduct on the part of the writer's own regiment or brigade, but there is no unanimity on the identity of the regiments that broke and fled. Most frequently named as "driven in" or "retiring in haste" are the Regulars and the 2nd Tennessee.[79]

Later in the day, Colonel Waring's brigade, which had been at the head of the column, formed a defensive line across the road and held it "until the Third Brigade had passed through, portions of it in such confusion as to endanger . . . [its own] morale." It then fell back to a stronger position about a mile to the rear, but had to abandon it, retiring "without unbecoming haste . . . and in perfect order" by one account, "overwhelmed by Forrest's irresistible onslaught" by a second, and carried backward by the stampede of the "immense train of pack mules and mounted contrabands" by a third.[80]

Smith, who had been at the head of the column, rode to the rear to try to retrieve an obviously desperate situation. At Ivey's Hill, about two miles behind what had been the second position of Waring's brigade, he formed up in three hours his retreating regiments and batteries as they arrived, on a "position of great natural strength, which commanded the road on which the pursuers had to advance."[81] Forrest

79. All the Union reports will be found in *Official Records*, Vol. XXXII, Pt. 1, pp. 251–315. The historian of the 72nd Indiana Mounted Infantry writes: "Just then the . . . [4th United States] were driven back on the 2nd Tennessee in some confusion, when the Tennessee regiment became panic stricken and broke like stampeded buffalo. . . . For four miles, it was a race for life . . . horses stumbling and falling; riders trampled to death; rebels riding promiscuously among us and cutting men down right and left; dismounted men running on foot and imploring help from their more fortunate companions; officers powerless, abandoning sick, wounded and footmen." McGee, *History of the 72nd Indiana*, 272, 278. See also Wyeth, *That Devil Forrest*, 286, quoting Lieutenant I. W. Curtis, 1st Illinois Light Artillery. Colonel Joseph Kargé, 2nd New Jersey (formerly lieutenant colonel of the 1st New Jersey; see Vol. I, 94–95, 285–86, 333n of the present work) wrote, "I saw the Fourth Regulars coming . . . in a rather disturbed condition, exhibiting marks of pretty severe handling." *Official Records*, Vol. XXXII, Pt. 1, p. 283.

80. *Official Records*, Vol. XXXII, Pt. 1, p. 268, 284, 353; Wyeth, *That Devil Forrest*, 285–87; Henry, *"First with the Most" Forrest*, 227, 229; Pierce, *History of the Second Iowa*, 87–91. It is to be noted that two of the regiments driven back, the 2nd New Jersey and 2nd Illinois, were armed with Spencers. If Sergeant Larson is to be believed, Smith took, or threatened to take, their Spencers from them as punishment for their behavior at Okolona. Larson, *Sergeant Larson*, 238.

81. Colonel Waring wrote that this was done "without orders" by portions of the First and Second Brigades. *Battles and Leaders*, IV, 417.

came up to Ivey's Hill and at once attacked with his brother's and McCulloch's brigades, which were down to a combined strength of about 1,200. Jeffrey Forrest was killed in this charge, and Colonel McCulloch painfully wounded. "Staggered" by the fire of Smith's dismounted cavalry, the Confederates "wavered and then halted." Meanwhile Bell's brigade arrived, and after sending a portion of his brother's brigade around to the left to attack the Federals' flank and rear, Forrest led the rest of it, as well as Bell's and McCulloch's men, in charges that eventually broke the Federal lines. In the forefront of the attack, as always, Forrest had two horses killed and a third wounded under him. "From this time the Federals offered no further resistance at any point. Discouraged and beaten they hurried on their weary journey toward Memphis," as the Confederate chronicler has it.[82]

Recourse must be had to Forrest's own report, and to those of General Smith and Colonel Waring, to learn what happened on Ivey's Hill. After Jeffrey Forrest's and McCulloch's charge was checked by the fire of Smith's dismounted men and the mountain howitzers of the 4th Missouri and the Confederates began to fall back, Waring begged Smith to order a saber charge against the retreating enemy. Smith agreed, and the charge was made by the 4th Missouri, six companies of the 7th Indiana, and, on the enemy's left flank, by the 3rd Tennessee. Forrest described it as "the grandest cavalry charge ever witnessed," but Colonel Waring had to be satisfied with its moral effect, because the main body of the enemy was found sheltered behind a high stake-and-rider fence that the charging cavalrymen were unable to break down or to breach. They had to sheathe their sabers and change to their pistols. They were then driven back by the "heavy firing at close range" of the enemy but were rallied by their officers and charged a second time.[83] Under the cover of these charges, which (and it may be assumed, exhaustion as well) halted Forrest's pursuit for the day, Smith resumed his retreat and that night got nearly to Pontotoc. To effect their own withdrawal and that of their artillery, two detachments of the 4th Missouri and a portion of the 7th Indiana made another "desperate and brilliant" charge.[84]

82. Wyeth, *That Devil Forrest*, 287–92; Henry, *"First with the Most" Forrest*, 229–31.

83. For a description of the charge, see Waring, *Whip and Spur*, 119–22.

84. *Official Records*, Vol. XXXII, Pt. 1, pp. 257–58, 268, 276, 279–80, 354; Thomas S. Cogley, *History of the Seventh Indiana Cavalry Volunteers* (Laporte, Ind., 1876), 86;

The crestfallen, disheartened, bedraggled expedition reached the line of the Memphis & Charleston and safety on February 26. It is difficult to tell how much of the comment on the state of mind of the command represents contemporary knowledge, and how much postwar wisdom, but we are told that the general opinion in the command was that the expedition had been mishandled. Their losses had been heavy—54 killed, 179 wounded, 155 missing or taken prisoner, as well as 6 cannon and 5 caissons left behind—and of course the men knew perfectly well that the objective of the operation had not been accomplished.[85] They had brought back 1,500 Negroes, whose labor was lost to the Confederacy, and 3,000 horses and mules, the loss of which was a blow to the agriculture of the region; they had destroyed thirty miles of the track of the Mobile & Ohio, burned huge quantities of corn and cotton, and taken for their own use or destroyed untold amounts of commissary and quartermaster stores.[86] Even the moral effect of their campaign of arson and pillage had its importance, for it demonstrated to the people of a hitherto unravished area that their own armies could no longer protect them.

Nevertheless, Smith's cavalry, officers and men, knew or suspected that the first two days of the retreat, unnecessary to begin with, had been an incompetently managed, costly muddle and that they had been exposed to defeat and humiliation by an enemy force much inferior to their own. Colonel Waring wrote about his brigade: "We were a worn and weary lot as we finally went into camp . . . sadly demoralized and almost dismounted. I lost fifteen hundred good horses and my men, who had been eager and ready for a successful campaign, were broken in spirit and sadly weakened in discipline." And he added,

Henry, *"First with the Most" Forrest*, 231–32. At Pontotoc, the next day, the 4th Missouri had an opportunity to charge as a regiment with the saber. Colonel Waring's dramatic description of the charge is quoted in Vol. I, p. 286 of the present work.

85. Waring, *Whip and Spur*, 125; *Official Records*, Vol. XXXII, Pt. 1, pp. 193–94; Pierce, *History of the Second Iowa*, 92. Forrest reported 27 of his men killed, 97 wounded, and 20 missing. If his figures were correct, this was one of the rare occasions in the Civil War when the losses of troops on the defensive exceeded those on the offensive by nearly three to one. Colonel Winslow's brigade, marching with the infantry, lost 9 killed, 26 wounded, and 9 missing. *Official Records*, Vol. XXXII, Pt. 1, p. 193.

86. General Grierson was to state two months later that less than 1,000 horses and mules (mostly mules) were brought back. On the other hand, Grierson wrote, "the road from West Point to . . . [Memphis] was literally strewn with dead and abandoned animals in consequence of the rapidity of the gait with which we returned, and hundreds of horses died after we reached . . . [Memphis]." *Official Records*, Vol. XXXIX Pt. 2, p. 14.

"The expedition filled every man connected with it with burning shame." General Hurlbut wrote with some bitterness in April that "the cavalry of Grierson, now at Memphis, is of little value. . . . All the dash and energy they ever had was taken out by Sooy Smith's misfortune." Not to be lost sight of is the fact that Smith's failure "strengthened Sherman's belief that as an instrument for achieving major results in war cavalry had been much overrated"; thereafter, he was to voice ever more bluntly, and unfortunately also act on, his distrust of the cavalry.[87]

87. Waring, *Whip and Spur*, 125; Mathes, *General Forrest*, 186; *Official Records*, Vol. XXXII, Pt. 3, p. 517; Lewis, *Sherman: Fighting Prophet*, 336.

XVI

War Is Cruelty

IN A CEREMONY IN THE WHITE HOUSE ON MARCH 9, 1864, President Lincoln handed Ulysses S. Grant his commission of lieutenant general. Orders published three days later placed him in command of the armies of the United States. Superseded "at his own request" as general-in-chief, General Halleck was consoled with the position of Grant's chief of staff and served as his representative in the War Department and his channel of communications with the authorities in Washington and the Union armies in the West and South. After a quick visit to General George C. Meade, Grant returned to Nashville to wind up affairs in the command he was leaving, preparatory to moving east and establishing his headquarters with the Army of the Potomac. On March 18, General Sherman formally took over from Grant command of the Military Division of the Mississippi and the next day traveled with him as far as Cincinnati, so that they could discuss on the way the campaign in the spring against the Army of Tennessee, now commanded by General Joseph E. Johnston, that Grant had planned to conduct but that now fell to Sherman to execute.

Notwithstanding the establishment in October of the previous year of the Military Division of the Mississippi, the three armies and departments east of the Mississippi composing it—those of the Tennessee, Cumberland, and Ohio—were virtually autonomous.[1] The lines of sep-

1. The fourth army and department embraced by the Military Division was General Frederick Steele's in Arkansas.

aration between them began to blur when three divisions of the Army of the Tennessee marched east to aid first the Army of the Cumberland in Chattanooga and then the Army of the Ohio at Knoxville; blurred further with the sending of Washington L. Elliott and one of his divisions of cavalry from the Army of the Cumberland to help the Army of the Ohio; and blurred still more with the appointment of William Sooy Smith as chief of cavalry of the Military Division, with a considerable degree of authority over the cavalry forces of all three armies. All of these armies—of the Tennessee under McPherson, of the Cumberland under George Thomas, and of the Ohio under John Schofield—were to make the Atlanta Campaign under Sherman. The events and activities of the two months following the collapse of Sooy Smith's expedition toward Meridian revolved mainly around preparations for the Atlanta Campaign, and for three months beyond that, they revolved around the protection of Sherman's line of communication through Chattanooga and Nashville all the way back to Louisville, his source for supplies like ammunition that he could not expect to capture from the enemy.

On February 29, Sherman had at his disposal a large mounted force. The Army of the Cumberland, under Washington L. Elliott as chief of cavalry, had the divisions of Edward M. McCook and of a newcomer, Kenner Garrard, a total of 10,832 officers and men present for duty.[2] The Army of the Tennessee, without a chief of cavalry, had 10,309 cavalry present for duty, 7,560 of them in Benjamin H. Grierson's division, attached to the XVI Army Corps. The Army of the Ohio had 5,282 cavalry present for duty in the divisions of Frank Wolford and Israel Garrard, under Samuel D. Sturgis as chief of cavalry.[3]

2. Kenner Garrard, a Kentuckian by birth, graduated eighth in the West Point Class of 1851. Assigned originally to the artillery, he transferred to the 1st Dragoons in 1852, had a tour of duty on the frontier, and served as instructor in the cavalry school at Carlisle and as instructor in artillery, cavalry, and infantry tactics at West Point. He became colonel of the 146th New York Infantry, was given a brevet for "conspicuous gallantry and efficiency" in the battle of Gettysburg, was promoted to brigadier general on July 23, 1863, and headed the Cavalry Bureau in Washington (in succession to Stoneman) from December, 1863, to January, 1864, before his assignment to command the Second Division of Cavalry of the Army of the Cumberland. Cullum, *Biographical Register*, II, 283–84.

3. *Official Records*, Vol. XXXII, Pt. 2, pp. 503–505. At the end of March the Cumberland cavalry had increased to 14,131, the Ohio to 5,511, but the Tennessee had decreased to 4,997 present for duty, Grierson's division alone dropping from 7,560 to 2,887, possibly because of the absence of large numbers of men on veterans' furlough. *Ibid.*, Pt. 3, pp. 208–10.

Despite his humiliating defeat in the Meridian Campaign, Sooy Smith retained his post of chief of cavalry of the Military Division until his resignation from the army, due officially to illness, on July 15, 1864.[4] He did not again command troops in combat, however, and it is not surprising that he was not taken on the Atlanta Campaign, notwithstanding the presence in Sherman's forces of the major portion of the cavalry of the three armies of the Military Division, for whom Smith was technically responsible. He was simply and deservedly relegated to the administrative functions that seemed to be more within his competence.

The most immediate of Smith's administrative problems, but one beyond his power to cure, was the shortage of manpower caused by the absence from the field of large portions of the veteran cavalry regiments. The thirty- (or in some cases thirty-five-) day veterans' furlough, with perhaps ten days added for travel, stretched in many cases into an absence of several months. One regiment for whom precise data are available, the 7th Kansas, was ordered on January 15 to leave for Memphis in preparation for muster as veterans and departure on furlough. The regiment arrived in Memphis on January 21; in the next four days it turned in its weapons and horses, was mustered as veterans and for pay, and left by steamboat for home. It arrived in Leavenworth on February 6, and after experiencing the rigors of an elaborate civic reception, the men scattered to their homes. They reassembled at Fort Leavenworth and on March 21 departed for St. Louis, where they were to receive weapons, equipment, and horses to replace those they had turned in before leaving Memphis. But St. Louis had neither weapons nor horses to give them, and the troopers of this veteran regiment cooled their heels for two months in a dismal camp on "Bloody Island" where there was neither shelter nor camp facilities of any kind when they arrived. The Jayhawkers and their horses finally left St. Louis in three installments as transportation became available on May 31, June 1, and June 6; on June 11, five months nearly to the day after being relieved of duty to go on a thirty-five-day furlough, they were reassembled, their "bobtails" back in their places, and were ready once again for active service.[5]

4. Cullum, *Biographical Register*, II, 338.
5. For the adventures of the 7th Kansas from January 15 to June 11, see Starr, *Jennison's Jayhawkers*, 284–301. The new sabers issued to the regiment measured just

As has been indicated, the 7th Kansas was not the only cavalry regiment stranded for months in St. Louis in the spring of 1864. In early April, General Grierson complained to the adjutant general of the army, General Lorenzo Thomas, that in addition to the 7th Kansas and the 3rd Michigan, both of which should have been back in Memphis in early March, six other regiments of his division, "the oldest and most experienced in the command," were on veterans' furlough and not expected back until the first ten days of May—an exceedingly optimistic estimate.[6] In a dispatch of May 2, Grierson spoke (but without naming them) of "three quarters of eight regiments and above one-half of a ninth of . . . [his] command absent upon veteran furloughs."[7] Two weeks later, he was able to report that two of the absent regiments, the 3rd and 9th Illinois, had just reached Memphis, and two more, the 6th Illinois and 2nd Iowa, were due back in another week or ten days. The four regiments returned "a part . . . mounted, and a part not."[8] Eventually, but not until the end of April, Sherman ordered that "all cavalry regiments at Saint Louis belonging to the sixteenth Army Corps be sent forward without any delay to Memphis. . . . until they obtain horses they can be of good service as garrison, and . . . the horses can follow as soon as practicable."[9]

---

under thirty-five inches overall, with a curved blade one inch wide at the hilt and slightly over thirty inches long. It was shorter, lighter, and more manageable than earlier models. Starr, "Cold Steel," in Hubbell (ed.), *Battles Lost and Won*, 111–12. The 4th Iowa, of Winslow's brigade, arrived in St. Louis in April on its return from veterans' furlough and was quartered in Benton Barracks to wait for its remount. "There were four or five thousand other dismounted cavalry men of other regiments in the barracks," wrote the historian of the Iowa regiment, "also waiting for horses, some having been waiting there for a long time; and the quartermasters then had on hand only about eight hundred good horses, which they were trying to distribute in small numbers in such a way as to satisfy the clamoring cavalrymen." Scott, *Story of a Cavalry Regiment*, 221–23.

6. *Official Records*, Vol. XXXII, Pt. 3, pp. 406–407. Grierson had gotten into the dangerous habit of taking his troubles directly to the authorities in Washington.

7. *Ibid.*, Vol. XXXIX, Pt. 2, p. 13. The other one quarter of the eight regiments, and half of the ninth, were the "bobtails."

8. *Ibid.*, 33. The 2nd Iowa had a more orderly experience than did their Kansas comrades. The 360 men of the regiment who veteranized were mustered in on March 28, left Memphis for Iowa on April 7, reached Davenport on the fourteenth, reassembled there on May 15, arrived at St. Louis on the twentieth, and after a wait of a mere six days for horses, were back in Memphis on May 29. But there they had to wait three weeks, until June 19, for their firearms, which, happily, were Spencers. Pierce, *History of the Second Iowa*, 95–97.

9. *Official Records*, Vol. XXXIX, Pt. 2, p. 4; see also *Ibid.*, Vol. XXXII, Pt. 3, pp. 536–37.

The records fail to disclose the extent to which the Armies of the Cumberland and the Ohio lost cavalry by the absence of regiments on veterans' furlough.[10] The 2nd Michigan, 9th Pennsylvania, 2nd Indiana, and 1st Wisconsin, all of the Army of the Cumberland, indicated their willingness to reenlist provided they could have their furlough, but were told that they could not be spared and were still with their army in early April.[11] Obviously, there was a considerable difference from one army to another in the way the problem was handled.

The Armies of the Ohio and the Cumberland, with fewer men absent on veterans' furlough than the Army of the Tennessee, had, however, large numbers of individual cavalrymen, entire regiments, and even a full division of cavalry absent to be reequipped or remounted or both. Mention has been made of General Sturgis' journey north to Kentucky to rehabilitate Colonel Frank Wolford's division. After inspecting it, Sturgis reported that "it was necessary to reorganize them . . . make out requisitions for almost every item required by a cavalry soldier, drill, and more than all, discipline them," a process he estimated would take from six to eight weeks. This was on March 6. At the end of March, he confessed himself frustrated by the "circumlocutions" of the staff departments with which he had to deal, which were causing him difficulties and delays at every step.[12] On April 14, General Stoneman, who had replaced Sturgis, reported that he had 2,720 men mounted ("a portion" of them without arms, however) and 2,746 dismounted ("a large portion . . . entirely unarmed"). He added that he was "trying in every direction to get horses" and hoped to have his entire force mounted, armed, and equipped by May 1, by which date these troops would have been absent from the Army of the Ohio for well over two months.[13]

Nashville was a convenient central point from which Sooy Smith could carry on his duties of chief of cavalry of three widely scattered armies. From Nashville he wrote on April 7 to General J. W. Davidson,

10. It is known, however, that the 2nd Ohio, which had gone home on veterans' furlough, was permanently lost to the Army of the Ohio.

11. *Official Records*, Vol. XXXII, Pt. 3, p. 256.

12. *Ibid.*, 30–31. Sturgis had suggested that the Second (and only other) Division of the Army of the Ohio cavalry be sent to Kentucky for the same purpose.

13. *Ibid.*, 361–99. General Stoneman added that "stores" (presumably equipment and arms) were arriving "almost daily in small lots" but that only 150 horses had been received in the preceding ten days.

head of the office the Cavalry Bureau had established in St. Louis, that there were "nearly 15,000 cavalry troops at . . . [Nashville] awaiting arms, equipments, and horses. The ordnance depot is drained of everything in the nature of supplies for cavalry, and I cannot learn that any considerable shipments are on the way." General Smith damaged his own credibility by writing four days later to General Wilson, head of the Cavalry Bureau in Washington, that "eight thousand enlisted men are now idle in this neighborhood alone for want of horses, arms and equipments."[14] Whatever the precise numbers may have been, it is an inescapable fact that there were thousands of cavalrymen in idleness in Nashville, just as there were in St. Louis, in Memphis, in the remount camp outside Washington, and doubtless in other places, men of no use whatever to the war effort for lack of mounts or arms or both.

It would be pointless to weary the reader with the dreary details of another tale of a lack of remounts, and of horses being destroyed as fast as they were supplied by the government. General Smith wrote the commanding officer of the 5th Tennessee, in response to the latter's request for horses to mount his regiment:

You have no idea of the demands made upon our Government for horses to remount our cavalry. No one Government—not all the Governments of the world—could keep so much cavalry mounted while animals are so recklessly destroyed. . . . Horses cannot be bought at the North at any reasonable rate, and but few can be had at any rate whatever. . . . Endeavor to feed well and insist upon the very best kind of grooming. Our cavalry will share in the coming campaign just in proportion to the nursing they will bestow upon their horses, for it is a question of horses, not men.[15]

A fundamental evil that underlay the procurement and distribution of horses to the mounted troops (and to a lesser extent, to the field artillery) was that at any given moment, no one knew how many horses were needed, or where. The army had a requisition system, whereby the needs of individual units were added up at successive levels of command and the totals transmitted for action by the purchasing officers of the Quartermaster's Department or the Cavalry Bureau. Anticipation of the demand was practiced to some degree. The entire system, however, worked imperfectly at best. Second, the army's procurement arrangements lacked the historical and statistical base and the

14. *Ibid.*, 287, 301.
15. *Ibid.*, 70.

degree of sophistication that would have allowed needs to be predicted and changes in demand anticipated to take into account the lengthy time lag between today's shortage in a given regiment, brigade, division, or army and deliveries several months hence. James Wilson, who prided himself on having put "the fear of God" into horse contractors after he became chief of the Cavalry Bureau at the beginning of the year, let contracts in January in four markets for a total of 11,500 horses. He was directed to have all 11,500 delivered to Nashville, where, Grant told him, "full 12,000 horses will be required," presumably for the Army of the Cumberland alone, which in the three months from October 1 to December 31, 1863, had received 22,911 horses and would presumably need a like number in the spring of 1864.[16] Grant said nothing about the needs of the other two armies in his Military Division. Yet on April 8, when Sooy Smith wrote Wilson that he had been unable "to procure estimates from department chiefs of cavalry for the horses, arms, and equipments that they require," and gave it as his own guess that each of the three needed 10,000 horses ("These wants are all immediate and pressing"), he incurred the wrath of both Grant and Sherman.[17]

The flaws in the mechanics of procurement were compounded by the lack of any system for allocating to individual regiments the horses that were delivered to the armies. The records provide no hint of a pattern, other than the impulse of the moment, for deciding who should get the horses that were received. A partial exception was Sherman's message to Wilson that with a "vast amount of dismounted cavalry" in his command, he wanted "the newly purchased cavalry horses to go to veterans, with a clear understanding if they fail to take proper care of them they will not again have a remount."[18] At the same time, Wilson submitted to the secretary of war a list of twenty-three veteran regiments—eighteen regiments of cavalry and five (including the four regiments of the Lightning Brigade) of mounted infantry of the Army

16. *Ibid.*, Pt. 2, pp. 330, 337, and Vol. XLV, Pt. 2, p. 558. In contrast with the nearly 23,000 horses General Thomas received in three months, Grierson, in Memphis, reported on March 31 that in the preceding nine months he had received "only about 1,500 horses." *Ibid.*, Vol. XXXII, Pt. 3, p. 205.

17. *Ibid.*, Vol. XXXII, Pt. 2, pp. 300–301, 398. Smith's guess that as many as 30,000 horses would be needed for the three armies was misunderstood by (or was misrepresented to) Sherman and Grant as a requisition for that many horses.

18. *Ibid.*, 255.

of the Cumberland—which he proposed to have remounted and returned to duty before any horses were supplied to "new" regiments. Wilson estimated that from 6,000 to 9,000 horses would be needed "to properly mount" these twenty-three regiments. The records do not indicate what action, if any, was taken on this proposal. It should be noted that Wilson wrote in the same memorandum that it was "advisable to discourage all mounted infantry regiments. Many of these regiments the Cavalry Bureau have no account of. They deprive the cavalry of their proper allowance of forage, pay no attention to stable duties, have neither curry-combs nor brushes, and General [Sooy] Smith remarks that if these infantry regiments were all dismounted they would furnish enough horses to mount all the cavalry of this [*i.e.*, of the Cumberland] department."[19]

The reader will recall that a standard reaction of the War Department to a request from commanders in the field for additional mounted troops was the suggestion that they mount regiments of infantry. An example is a Halleck dispatch of June 5 to Hurlbut, which reminded him that he had authority to mount as many troops as he could find horses for.[20] There is no hint of a realization by anyone of the obvious fact that the mounting of regiments of infantry simply added to the demand for remounts. The creation of these units of impromptu cavalry was wasteful of manpower and misguided enough, but the evil was compounded in the Department of the Ohio by the enlistment in Kentucky of eight regiments of mounted infantry to serve for one year, "by whose authority no one knows," General Wilson wrote. An inspection of these one-year units at Camp Nelson produced a shocking report: They were, the inspector wrote, "a disorganized, unavailable band . . . partially mounted—that is, one or two or more companies in a regiment, making in the aggregate about 3,000 horses. . . . The horses are used for pleasure and display, and are fast being destroyed by neglect and bad usage. I would . . . suggest that these twelve months men be all dismounted and the horses made available for

19. *Ibid.*, 257.
20. *Ibid.*, Vol. XXIV, Pt. 3, p. 386. But it should be mentioned that on at least one occasion the opposite was the case. Grant ordered McPherson on March 11 to "dismount . . . [his] infantry armed with cavalry arms as fast as their horses and arms are required for the purpose of equipping cavalry troops for service. This is rendered necessary from the impossibility of procuring horses and arms for the cavalry arm of the service and the necessity of getting it ready for service without delay." *Ibid.*, Vol. XXXII, Pt. 3, p. 53.

mounting active cavalry for military purposes."[21] If the 3,000 horses of these regiments of negligible military utility had been taken from them, there would have been enough animals to mount fully five or six regiments of veterans.

There seems to be no end to the grim catalog of avoidable and unavoidable difficulties that kept a large percentage of the Union cavalry dismounted at any given moment. In Memphis, there was a "prevalence of the distemper" among the newly issued horses of the 3rd and 4th Iowa.[22] Then there was the plague of political interference, which wormed its way at one time or another into every aspect of army administration. A particularly blatant practitioner of interference in military affairs was Military Governor Andrew Johnson of Tennessee.[23] The Wilson memorandum to Secretary Stanton, portions of which have been quoted previously, contained the statement that "regarding the efficiency of . . . Tennessee regiments there is but one opinion. With the exception of the First Tennessee they are all worthless." And Wilson proceeded to quote the report of Special Inspector Captain William R. Price, to the effect that "as the Tennessee regiments now organizing at Nashville are nearly all cavalry, I wish respectfully but earnestly to protest against giving them arms and equipments, as in my opinion it is prejudicial to all the interests of the cavalry service, to the prosecution of the war, and to the best interests of the State of Tennessee, and the dictates of humanity counsel against it." Captain Price's recommendation was approved by the secretary, and General Sherman was notified that orders had been issued that "no more horses be furnished to Tennessee regiments until all other demands are supplied."[24] But such

21. *Ibid.*, Vol. XXXII, Pt. 3, pp. 257–58, 79. A little research would have disclosed to General Wilson that these one-year regiments were being raised pursuant to an act of Congress passed in late 1863 authorizing the enlistment of 20,000 troops in Kentucky "to serve in the State unless the President orders them out." *Ibid.*, Vol. XXXI, Pt. 3, p. 465.

22. *Ibid.*, Vol. XXXIX, Pt. 2, p. 28. Horses landed at Memphis for distribution to regiments stationed inland from the river were "kept in bad condition and on short allowance, by which they . . . were injured." *Ibid.*, 147.

23. See, for especially crass examples, *Ibid.*, Vol. XXXII, Pt. 3, pp. 105, 268, 278, Pt. 2, p. 202.

24. *Ibid.*, Pt. 3, pp. 256, 206. General Smith had written in December, 1863, to General A. J. Smith: "I am not able . . . to fill your requisition for cavalry arms. I hardly think it desirable that the Tennessee regiments now in process of organization should be cavalry proper; They are wholly unfamiliar with the saber . . . and in fact, I am fully satisfied they will do better as mounted infantry." *Ibid.*, Vol. XXXI, Pt. 3, p. 385.

orders were of no consequence to Andrew Johnson. General Kenner Garrard reported that just before he had left the Cavalry Bureau, arrangements had been made to supply 8,000 horses to Grant's veteran regiments, but that Johnson announced that he wanted 5,000 horses—for which no provision had been made—for *his* regiments, and it was understood by the quartermasters in Louisville that Johnson would "probably be supplied first."[25] Nor was this the only incident of its kind. In mid-June, Sooy Smith reported that he had "fully mounted and equipped 4,000 Tennesseans" with horses taken mostly "from the country," which, one may assume, could have been used to mount veteran regiments if they had not been used to mount Tennessee regiments of mounted infantry.[26]

To conclude the tale of the Tennessee Unionist mounted troops, it is of interest to note that General Sherman had a poor opinion of the military utility of these regiments. He wrote in June, 1864, to General J. D. Webster in Nashville: "I have always regarded General [Alvan C.] Gillem's command as a refuge hospital for indolent Tennesseans. I . . . have never reckoned them anything but a political element." General Richard W. Johnson reported to General Sherman three months later that he had under his jurisdiction "several regiments of Tennessee cavalry claiming to be independent of General Sherman or any one else save Andy Johnson. These regiments violate safeguards, rob, and murder in open daylight and refuse to report the facts to any one except the Governor. I have refused to issue arms and equipments to them. . . . The withholding of these supplies may have some effect upon their conduct. Have I done right?"[27]

A somewhat more reasonable individual than Andrew Johnson was Governor Oliver P. Morton of Indiana, but he, too, had a contribution to

25. *Ibid.*, Vol. XXXII, Pt. 2, p. 436. At the same time, however, Colonel William B. Stokes of the 5th Tennessee found it necessary to "call the attention of the general commanding to the necessity of mounting . . . [his] command," over half of whom were dismounted, "having worn out their horses by constant duty." *Ibid.*, Pt. 1, p. 495.

26. *Ibid.*, Vol. XXXVIII, Pt. 4, p. 462.

27. *Ibid.*, Vol. XXXIX, Pt. 2, pp. 438–39. Johnson was assured that he had "certainly done rightly." *Ibid.*, p. 446. Only a few days before General Johnson's dispatch, however, General Robert H. Milroy, in command of the defenses of the Nashville & Chattanooga Railroad, who had under him the 5th, 10th, and 12th Tennessee, wrote of the three regiments: "I cannot speak too highly of the bravery, endurance, perseverance and patience of the Tennessee cavalry regiments. With proper discipline they could not be excelled by any troops." *Ibid.*, Vol. XXXVIII, Pt. 2, p. 493.

make to the problems of maintaining the Union cavalry in the West in operating condition. With every mounted unit already in the service clamoring for horses and arms, he proceeded to raise five new regiments of cavalry for whom neither he nor the government in Washington had horses. A lengthy tug-of-war then ensued. Grant first offered the five regiments to General Schofield, who declined to accept them. Sherman then wrote the governor that since the government could not possibly equip, mount, and arm the five regiments as cavalry, he would like to have them armed as infantry, "to be held in reserve" in Nashville. The governor did not need anyone to tell him that if he agreed, the "reserve" would in no time at all be doing duty as footsoldiers in the Army of the Tennessee. Hence he countered with the argument that to accept Sherman's proposal would be a breach of faith with men who had enlisted to serve as cavalry. But Sherman had covered his flanks: he had enlisted the help of Secretary Stanton, and that dextrous lawyer and politician "instructed" the governor that there was no question of a breach of faith and that the five regiments had to be sent forward on foot if they were not mounted. A week later, Assistant Secretary Dana negotiated a compromise acceptable to everyone. Mounts were found for 1,200 of the men; these were to be consolidated into a single regiment or "three detached battalions" of cavalry. The rest, about 4,300, were to serve as infantry until they, too, could be mounted.[28]

It is hardly a relief to turn from the frequently tragic story of cavalry mounts to the guerrillas in northern Mississippi, the northeast corner of Alabama, and Tennessee in 1863 and 1864. Colonel McCook reported that he had "pretty well cleared" his area of responsibility around Larkinsville, Alabama (about equidistant from Huntsville and Stevenson), of "bushwhackers" since ordering "them when caught to be hung and property destroyed in vicinity where they make attack." But two months later, in the same area, General Crook found it unsafe to set up a courier line to communicate with army headquarters, because "the country . . . [was] so badly infested with guerrillas."[29]

The railroads under Federal control were of course a prime target for guerrillas, and not always for military reasons alone. General

28. *Ibid.*, Vol. XXXII, Pt. 3, pp. 74, 76, 495–505, Vol. XXXIX, Pt. 2, p. 5.
29. *Ibid.*, Vol. XXX, Pt. 3, p. 106, Pt. 4, p. 463.

Thomas W. Sweeny sent a detachment of the 9th Illinois to LaFayette, near Memphis, with orders that if they found "the railroad bridge" (of the Memphis & Charleston) destroyed and could not find "the men who did it," they were to arrest "every man and lad in the vicinity" to be delivered to General Sweeny's headquarters and were then to "burn down every house in the vicinity." A few months earlier, a passenger train on the same line was "seized" near Moscow by twelve guerrillas. The twenty-five armed soldiers and three or five officers on the train offered no resistance and were carried off as prisoners, but not until after the guerrillas had relieved the civilian passengers of their valuables. General Hurlbut termed the failure of the soldiers and officers to "defend themselves or the public property" a "disgraceful incident."[30] At nearly the same spot a few months later, a train carrying the 52nd Indiana Infantry was fired into by "a party of guerrillas." "Several" of the soldiers were killed or wounded, and "some of the men who jumped or fell off the cars were captured and afterward murdered. Their bodies were recovered by a party of the 2d Iowa."[31]

In January, 1864, General Sooy Smith sent his friend Colonel Stephen G. Hicks, at Paducah, Kentucky, "a lot of prisoners . . . desperate characters . . . genuine guerrillas, most of them captured with arms in their hands. . . . I do not myself know just what the Government does with such prisoners."[32] General Smith may have been at a loss regarding the proper disposal of captured guerrillas, but other officers of the Union cavalry, and their men, were not; they knew just what to do. Lieutenant Colonel James P. Brownlow, 1st Tennessee, reported on a skirmish near Sparta, Tennessee, with Colonel John M. Hughs's command, which he said was made up of a number of guerrilla bands, that he "would take no prisoners."[33]

30. *Ibid.*, Vol. XXXI, Pt. 1, p. 783, Vol. XXIV, Pt. 1, p. 485.
31. *Ibid.*, Vol. XXXI, Pt. 1, p. 295.
32. *Ibid.*, Vol. XXXII, Pt. 2, p. 49. This dispatch was sent together with the prisoners captured in the course of Smith's march with 2,500 cavalry to Memphis. See above, p. 374.
33. *Ibid.*, Vol. XXXI, Pt. 1, p. 591. In July, 1864, Brownlow made a name for himself with an exploit that Colonel McCook called a "characteristic feat." "I had ordered a detachment to cross at Cochran's Ford," McCook reported. "It was deep, and he took them over naked, nothing but guns, cartridge boxes and hats. They drove the enemy out of their rifle pits, captured a non-commissioned officer and 3 men. . . . They would have got more, but the rebels had the advantage running through the bushes with clothes on." *Ibid.*, Vol. XXXVIII, Pt. 2, p. 761; W. R. Carter, *History of the First Regiment of Tennessee Volunteer Cavalry in the Great War of the Rebellion* (Knoxville, 1902), 169–72.

Colonel Brownlow's attitude was typical of that of his fellow Unionist Tennesseans'—"renegade Tennesseans," as Forrest called them.
Their cavalry regiments had little mercy for fellow Tennesseans who
were, or were thought to be, Confederate guerrillas or, worse still,
bushwhackers. The 6th Tennessee, ordered to march to Purdy "and
proceed to the destruction of all armed enemies to the United States
Government," obeyed so literally that Forrest declared Colonel Fielding
Hurst, his officers, and men "outlaws and not entitled to be treated as
prisoners of war" if they fell into his hands, citing as his justification
the fact that the regiment had been "guilty of house burning, [and]
guilty of murders, both of citizens and soldiers of the Confederate
States." Colonel William B. Stokes's 5th Tennessee, U.S.A., described
by General Lovell H. Rousseau as "neither well drilled, disciplined, or
equipped," and whose main function, as General Thomas understood,
was to operate at and around Sparta against the guerrillas who had
"infested that country since the war commenced," on a scout in early
February killed seventeen "of the worst men in the country . . . known
to have been engaged in murder, robbery, and rape; in fact, all were
accessory to the outrages committed throughout this country."[34]

In November, 1863, General Hurlbut sent Colonel Hatch and his
brigade, divided into a number of separate columns, on a sweep through
the area north of the line of the Memphis & Charleston, in the direction of Somerville, forty-five miles northeast of Memphis. Hatch's assignment, as spelled out by General Hurlbut, was "the absolute destruction of the guerrilla bands north of the railroad . . . and Colonel
Hatch will see to it that no misjudged clemency prevents such course."
Moreover, all "mills where guerrillas assemble" were to be destroyed.
In a raid through an area southwest of Nashville, Lieutenant Jordan W.
Creasy, 10th Tennessee, struck the trail of two notorious guerrillas,
Colonel Pointer and Lieutenant Buford, "pursued them o'er hill and
dale until he was finally upon them, they being concealed in a house of
ill fame, situated in a most secluded spot on the top of a large bluff. The
lieutenant, fearing escape on their part, dashed upon them alone, and
shot them both."[35]

Before leaving this unedifyng subject, it may be useful to glance at

34. *Official Records*, Vol. XXXII, Pt. 2, pp. 66, 268, 64, Pt. 3, pp. 664, 665, 118–19,
90, Pt. 1, pp. 416–17, 494–95.
35. *Ibid.*, Vol. XXXI, Pt. 3, p. 245, Vol. XXXIX, Pt. 1, p. 6.

the problem of guerrillas in Tennessee through the eyes of two of the most realistic, hardheaded commanding officers in the area. General Forrest had no illusions about the kind of people who made up the guerrilla bands. The inhabitants of the area above the Memphis & Charleston, as far north as Purdy, he wrote, "have been by the enemy and by roving bands of deserters and tories stripped of everything; they have neither negroes nor stock with which to raise a crop. . . . The whole of West Tennessee is overrun by bands and squads of robbers, horse thieves, and deserters, whose depredations and unlawful appropriations of private property are rapidly and effectually depleting the country." The devastation of the area and the sufferings of the inhabitants were the handiwork of their own people, who (with the exception of the "tories," *i.e.*, Unionist Tennesseans), as Forrest knew, made up the guerrilla bands. From the other side of the hill, General Sherman wrote: "In this department I pay but little attention to guerrillas. They have never attacked any place of note, and are chiefly engaged in harassing their own people, who merit little at our hands. Those will in time beg us to save them from their own irregular soldiery, and even then it will be well to let them continue to suffer the protection of Jeff. Davis—the protection the wolf gives the lamb."[36]

The early months of 1864 produced a greater than ordinary number of changes in the roster of cavalry commanders in the western armies. General Thomas seemed satisfied with the men he had; he wrote General Grant that he had "efficient colonels" commanding cavalry brigades and preferred keeping them to having brigadier generals sent him "who know nothing about cavalry service."[37] This comment was called forth by Grant's offer of General Thomas E. G. Ransom to take over the cavalry command vacated by George Crook's transfer to West Virginia. Grant thought Ransom suitable because he was "the best man . . . [he had] ever had to send on expeditions. He is a live man and of good judgment." Thomas had asked for James Wilson for the post

36. *Ibid.*, Vol. XXXII, Pt. 3, p. 664, Pt. 2, p. 115.
37. *Ibid.*, 142. In an earlier dispatch on the same subject, General Thomas spoke of his efficient colonels, whom he did not want to exchange for "worthless brigadiers." *Ibid.*, 141. In January, Thomas urged the promotion to brigadier general by brevet of five of his cavalry colonels—McCook, Long, Wilder, L. D. Watkins and Campbell—who had been commanding brigades for from five months to more than a year. *Ibid.*, 275.

but was told that Wilson was not available, since he was about to take charge of the Cavalry Bureau in Washington. The upshot was the arrival of Judson Kilpatrick, transferred in April from the Army of the Potomac to the Army of the Cumberland; Thomas gave him command of the Third Cavalry Division.[38]

The command changes in the Army of the Ohio followed a more complex pattern. On January 28, John Schofield was appointed to the command of the Department of the Ohio, to replace General Foster. On the same day, command of the XXIII Army Corps was given to General George Stoneman.[39] Thereafter the situation became more than ordinarily confusing. It will be recalled that Samuel Sturgis, as chief of cavalry of the Army of the Ohio, was sent to Kentucky to rehabilitate Frank Wolford's division. On April 4, James Wilson reported Schofield as complaining of "a great want of competent cavalry commanders in his department." On the same day, Stoneman's place in command of the XXIII Army Corps was taken by Schofield, who, however, retained command of the Department of the Ohio. The order announcing these changes stated that Stoneman was to be assigned "to the command of a special cavalry force" to be organized under instructions Schofield would receive from Sherman's headquarters. What that "special cavalry force" might have been never came to light, because the next day an order of Schofield's placed Stoneman in command of "the cavalry of this department," which he was to "organize . . . into brigades and divisions according to his judgment so as to place the most competent officers in command." He was to assemble at or near Lexington the regiments Sturgis had taken to Kentucky, and "prepare . . . [them] as quickly and as thoroughly as possible for active service in the field." Sturgis was disposed of by being "relieved from duty as chief of cavalry" and ordered to report to Stoneman for duty, but he did not remain in a subordinate position for long. A mere three weeks later he reappeared on the stage in Memphis, with an undefined command in, but not necessarily of, the cavalry of the XVI Army Corps, under the new commander of the District of Memphis, General Cadwallader C. Washburn, who had replaced Stephen A. Hurlbut in mid-April. Not surprisingly, Sturgis' appearance in Memphis was followed at once by

38. *Ibid.*, 131, 141, 142, and Pt. 3, pp. 375, 465, 498; Vol. II, pp. 75–76 of the present work.

39. *Official Records*, Vol. XXXII, Pt. 2, p. 251; see also pp. 322, 329, 359, 363, 365.

Benjamin Grierson's request, made, as he said, "with no other than the most earnest wishes to serve our country where . . . [he] could render the most efficient service," to be relieved from duty with the five under-strength regiments of cavalry remaining in Memphis and "ordered to Illinois and Iowa, for the purpose of reorganizing, arming, mounting, and equipping" the eight regiments of his division that were then absent in those states on their veterans' furloughs.[40] The records do not indicate how Grierson was talked out of his petulant request (if indeed the request was not simply ignored), but nothing more was heard of the absurd errand Grierson had proposed for himself, and he remained in Memphis as commanding officer of the Cavalry Division of the XVI Army Corps.

Grierson's hurt feelings may well have been caused by the uncertain terms of Sturgis' assignment to serve in Memphis. The printed records do not contain the customary "Assignment to duty" order spelling out the scope of Sturgis' authority and duties, and his dispatches do not carry the customary caption (*e.g.*, "Headquarters, Cavalry Division, Sixteenth Army Corps") to indicate his status and function. As a matter of fact, Grierson's dispatches show him as continuing in command of the cavalry division under Washburn. It may be assumed that Sturgis was given an undefined assignment, unknown to the regulations, to command Washburn's cavalry in campaign and battle, with Grierson retaining responsibility for administration, just the reverse of what the functions of chiefs of cavalry had been in the early years of the war. To make such an assignment in 1864 and, in particular, to do so without a formal order defining its place in the hierarchy of command, its scope, duties, and limits, does not speak highly of Sherman's (or possibly McPherson's) sense of organization.

General Sherman had a definite objective in having General Sturgis at the head of the cavalry—what there was of it—in Memphis and in having General Washburn replace Hurlbut, whose management of affairs, so Sherman thought, manifested a "marked timidity." The rationale of both changes was, in Sherman's words, to "whip Forrest . . . wherever he may go" or, as McPherson phrased it, to seize the horses

40. *Ibid.*, Pt. 3, pp. 256, 268, 269, 312, 397, 484, 502.

needed to mount all the cavalry in and about Memphis, and then go
out and "attack Forrest wherever he can be found." [41]

This new concern with Forrest was the outgrowth of a second
Forrest expedition into northwest Tennessee. Unlike his December
foray, the new campaign, which he was about to make at the head of
four brigades with a total complement of about 5,000 men, nearly all
of them armed, lacked a clear-cut purpose or objective. His formal orders from General Polk merely directed that he "make a short campaign in West Tennessee" with as much of his command as he thought
he needed, leaving behind his artillery and wagons. [42] Presumably the
primary purpose of the campaign was to keep the Federals on edge
while he collected the recruits and supplies he said he could have
brought out in December if he had had more time.

Forrest left his camps near Columbus, Mississippi, on March 15.
News of his advance was quick to reach General Hurlbut, who not only
warned Grierson on March 18 ("It is reported that Forrest with about
7,000 men was at Tupelo last night or night before, bound for West
Tennessee") and ordered him to "bring . . . [his] cavalry at once into
the best state of efficiency and watch him closely," but also made the
shrewd or lucky guess (or learned from his scouts) that Forrest was
aiming either for the Ohio River at Paducah or the Mississippi at
Columbus, Tennessee. General Grierson responded with a recital of
his weaknesses, reporting that he had at his disposal a mere 1,500
mounted men, nearly half of them in the 6th Tennessee. On March 30,
Hurlbut ordered him to "take all the available cavalry force at and near
Memphis and move as rapidly as possible to attack the force under
General Forrest. The march must be active and at the same time cautious. The enemy will be attacked at all hazards wherever met, and followed closely." [43] Grierson had no opportunity to demonstrate his ability
to reconcile the contradictory injunctions laid upon him. Indeed, he
confined his efforts to reporting that the numbers of his mounted force
had increased to 2,200, but, he hastened to add, "much of this force is
new and inexperienced, and not very reliable." [44] It was certainly true
that in the exuberance of their success in meeting the challenge of the

41. *Ibid.*, 381, 411, 415, 430.
42. *Ibid.*, 611, 586.
43. *Ibid.*, 91, 195.
44. *Ibid.*, 196. He wrote that he also had 1,000 dismounted cavalrymen.

veterans' reenlistment program, the district and the department allowed themselves to be stripped of cavalry, both in numbers and in experience, by the nearly simultaneous absence on furlough of eight of its best regiments. It is indeed a puzzle to account for the disappearance of the large number of animals these veterans had turned in when they departed on furlough. How did the approximately 7,000 mounts the Memphis cavalry was reputed to have had when Sooy Smith returned from his aborted Meridian Expedition at the end of February shrink to 1,500 less than a month later? [45] And while Forrest went rampaging about west Tennessee, Grierson, convinced that the enemy had "at least 7,000 mounted men, while at the same time the force of General S. D. Lee, at least 6,000 strong . . . [was] hovering . . . within striking distance of Memphis," confined his efforts to preparing elaborate explanations of the shrinkage of serviceable mounts available to him. [46]

On March 23, Forrest reached Jackson, Tennessee. The next day, Colonel W. L. Duckworth, 7th Tennessee, C.S.A., bluffed and frightened Colonel Isaac R. Hawkins, 7th Tennessee, U.S.A., into an unconditional surrender of the garrison, larger than Duckworth's command, of Union City. [47] It was a different story, however, at Paducah, on the twenty-fifth. There, Colonel Stephen G. Hicks, 40th Illinois Infantry, commanding a garrison that numbered 665, rank and file, and included 271 men of the 16th Kentucky and 274 of the 1st Kentucky Heavy Artillery (Colored), held Fort Anderson against Forrest himself. After his initial attack on the fort had been repulsed, Forrest sent in under a flag of truce a demand for the surrender of the garrison, couched in the language he usually employed—"If I have to storm your works, you may expect no quarter." Colonel Hicks declined to surrender, stood off another assault, and in the morning Forrest made the belated discovery that smallpox was "raging" in the town, broke off the siege, and departed. [48]

45. *Ibid.*, 204–205.
46. *Ibid.*, 204–205, 482–83.
47. J. P. Young, *The Seventh Tennessee Cavalry (Confederate): A History* (Nashville, 1890), 83–85; Henry, *"First with the Most" Forrest*, 238–39.
48. *Official Records*, Vol. XXXII, Pt. 3, pp. 547–49. Hicks had 14 killed and 46 wounded (numbers to be contrasted with Union casualties at Fort Pillow, to be discussed below) and made the absurd claim that Forrest had 300 killed and 1,000 to 1,200 wounded. Forrest's admiring biographer, Robert Selph Henry, quotes the words "to avoid

Two weeks later, General Abraham Buford was back at Paducah with his mounted infantry division of Kentuckians. It is said that his reason for returning was to collect the horses and whatever else of use to his troops he could find. It may be questioned if Buford really expected to find anything worth taking after Forrest's visit only two weeks before. Whatever his purpose may have been, he sent in the customary flag of truce, suggesting that Colonel Hicks arrange to have women, children, and noncombatants leave the town and announcing his willingness to grant an hour's grace for that purpose. Colonel Hicks thanked Buford for his "act of humanity," accepted the hour's grace, and closed his reply with the words: "After that time come ahead; I am ready for you." Under the protection of the white flag, so Colonel Hicks claimed, some of Buford's men got into the town and broke into houses, "robbing and plundering." Buford and the main body, without waiting for the grace period to expire, "commenced retreating," taking with them about forty "Government horses . . . which were taken during the pending of the flag of truce."[49]

Two days before these farcical proceedings at Paducah, there occurred one of the most horrible incidents of the Civil War, worthy to rank with Quantrill's Lawrence Massacre of the previous summer. About forty miles upstream from Memphis, and overlooking the Mississippi, lay Fort Pillow, garrisoned by about 550 men, divided equally between five companies of recruits for the 13th Tennessee on the one hand and the colored troops of a battalion of the 6th United States Heavy Artillery and of a battery of the 2nd United States Light Artillery on the other, the whole commanded by Major Lionel F. Booth. Forrest decided to capture the fort (built originally by the Confederates and named for General Gideon Pillow, under whom Forrest had served briefly at Fort Donelson) because, he reported, the garrison had "horses and supplies which we need."[50] He appeared at Fort Pillow at sunup on

the unnecessary effusion of blood" in Forrest's surrender demand, but (no doubt inadvertently) fails to quote the concluding words, "you may expect no quarter." Henry, *"First with the Most" Forrest*, 240.

49. *Official Records*, Vol. XXXII, Pt. 1, pp. 549–50. On April 13, Buford tried to panic Colonel William Hudson Lawrence, 34th New York Infantry, into surrendering the garrison of Columbus with a demand that ended with Buford's variant on the Forrest formula. "Should I," Buford wrote, "be compelled to take the place, no quarter will be shown to the negro troops whatever; the white troops will be treated as prisoners of war." *Ibid.*, 553.

50. *Ibid.*, 608–609. Forrest had written in the same dispatch, "I feel confident in

April 12 with 1,500 men of Tyree Bell's and Robert McCulloch's brigades, drove in the pickets, directed two assaults against the fort, both of which were repulsed, and in midafternoon sent in under a flag of truce a demand for the surrender of the garrison, using on this occasion a variant of his standard threat. "[I] can," he wrote, "take your works by assault, and if compelled to do so you must take the consequences."[51] Major Booth had been killed earlier in the day; Major William T. Bradford of the 13th Tennessee, who succeeded to the command, declined to surrender.[52]

Fort Pillow was then stormed, and an indiscriminate massacre of the garrison followed, which included the killing of the wounded and of men, both white and black, who had surrendered. Fortunately for the author and the reader alike, it is unnecessary in a history of the Union cavalry to describe in detail the sickening events in Fort Pillow on the evening and night of April 12 and the following morning. Forrest might not have intended it, but for once his "no quarter" language was taken literally by his men, who killed in hot blood and continued killing long past the time when they might have used "killing in hot blood" as an excuse.

Forrest himself reported that 500 of the garrison were killed and that his own losses were 20 killed and 60 wounded. One of his biographers, after sifting the evidence in his own way, arrived at a count of the dead as "not more than 231," which we may assume constitutes only a small massacre. The seriously wounded, he estimated, numbered 110 to 120.[53] But whether the dead numbered 231 or 500, and the wounded 110 or 120, for anyone familiar with the rate of casualties in what may be termed a "normal" Civil War fight, these numbers, and the disproportion between them and the number of Confederate casu-

---

my ability to whip any cavalry they can send against me . . . [and] can hold West Tennessee against three times my numbers."

51. A second note Forrest sent in later ended with the same words.

52. Major Bradford was taken prisoner. While being marched with other prisoners to Jackson by two companies of the 7th Tennessee, C.S.A., he was taken into the woods by an execution squad of five soldiers, and killed. But see the account, based on Forrest's self-serving statement (*Ibid.*, 557, 592) in Henry, *"First with the Most" Forrest*, 269.

53. *Official Records*, Vol. XXXII, Pt. 1, pp. 609, 610. Henry, *"First with the Most" Forrest*, 258–59. Quite typical of Confederate accounts of the massacre is to blame it on the "insane defense" of the fort by troops who "had been liberally dosed with liquor during the eight hours' 'investment.'" Mathes, *General Forrest*, 224, 227.

alties, makes the conclusion inescapable that there was indeed a massacre of prisoners and the wounded.[54]

Relaxing from their exertions at Fort Pillow, Forrest and his command marched back to Jackson. A few days later, on orders from General Polk he began a leisurely march south to Okolona with his main body. Forrest left a few small detachments around Memphis to distract and confuse Hurlbut and Grierson. Washburn and Sturgis now took over, with the assignment, in General Sherman's words, "to find and whip" Forrest or, in more restrained and more appropriate language, "to whale Forrest if you can reach him."[55]

But to try to reach Forrest with the means Washburn and Sturgis found when they reached Memphis was the crux of the problem. Washburn wrote to Secretary Stanton and to General Grant on the very day he arrived in Memphis that he found "only 1,800 mounted cavalry . . . and that very poor, 2,000 infantry, and 3,500 colored troops, entirely too weak . . . to move far aggressively, without leaving Memphis at . . . [Forrest's] mercy." Forrest's total force, Washburn believed, was "about 8,000 men, all well mounted."[56] Within twenty-four hours of his arrival, however, Washburn sent three steamers down to Vicksburg to bring up to Memphis whatever cavalry was there, and he informed General McPherson that he hoped to get together enough troops, mounted (many of them on horses he had seized in Memphis) and footsoldiers, to be sent out under Sturgis' command, to "whip" Forrest and "drive him from the State."[57] His representations about the state of

54. For reports on the capture of Fort Pillow and the affidavits of survivors (which do not make pleasant reading), see *Official Records*, Vol. XXXII, Pt. 1, pp. 518–40, 554–72, 594–619. See also Henry, *"First with the Most" Forrest*, 248–68; Wyeth, *That Devil Forrest*, 309–41; Andrew Lytle, *Bedford Forrest and His Critter Company* (New York, 1960), 276–81; Sheppard, *Bedford Forrest*, 172; and John Cimprich and Robert C. Mainfort, Jr. (eds.), "Fort Pillow Revisited: New Evidence About an Old Controversy," *Civil War History*, XXVIII (1982), 293–306. It may be mentioned that the Confederate Congress voted its thanks to Forrest and his command for their "brilliant and successful campaign," in which they were said to have gained "enduring fame." *Official Records*, Vol. XXXII, Pt. 1, p. 619.

55. *Official Records*, Vol. XXXII, Pt. 3, p. 441.

56. *Ibid.*, 462–63. Washburn described the cavalry he found at Memphis as "made up of odds and ends."

57. *Ibid.*, 484, 516. For Hurlbut's peculiar status after Washburn's arrival in Memphis see *Ibid.*, 517–18, 545–46, and Vol. XXXIX, Pt. 2, pp. 3–4. There is a hint in the records that addiction to the bottle was at least partially responsible for Hurlbut's removal. *Ibid.*, Vol. XXXIX, Pt. 2, p. 12.

his forces, and particularly the small number of mounted troops he expected to be able to scrape together, made enough of an impression on Sherman to cause him to caution Washburn through McPherson to "hold Forrest and as many of the enemy near him as he can, rather than to risk too much in his attack."[58]

By April 28, Washburn knew that he would receive only 575 men, mounted and equipped, from Vicksburg and another 230 dismounted men belonging to the 4th Iowa. General John McArthur, commanding the post after General McPherson's departure, wrote Washburn that Sherman's Meridian Campaign had "told severely on the horses" of Colonel Winslow's brigade, that he himself needed 2,500 horses and the same number of carbines to equip properly the cavalry at Vicksburg, and that he hoped that General Washburn would help him get them. Washburn could expect no help from St. Louis, where General John W. Davidson of the Cavalry Bureau had succeeded in mounting the 800 men of the 3rd Iowa and sending them on to Memphis, but it would have been impossible for them to arrive in time to be of use to Sturgis and Washburn. Another regiment, the 3rd Michigan, returning from veterans' furlough and mounted in St. Louis, was intercepted there and in effect kidnapped by General Rosecrans. Ten days earlier, Grant had ordered Rosecrans to send the 12th Missouri, 9th Iowa, and 13th Illinois to Cairo "without delay" and explained in a later dispatch that these regiments, and any other troops, horse or foot, that Rosecrans could send, were needed for use against Forrest. Grant's explanation was repeated in more detail by Sherman. The 9th Iowa, then actually in transit from St. Louis to Springfield, Missouri, was intercepted en route and hurried back to St. Louis by special train, but Rosecrans informed Grant that the 12th Missouri and 13th Illinois lacked mounts and would be sent only if Grant directed that "foot troops" also should be sent.[59]

Despite all these disappointments and difficulties, Washburn could wire Sherman on April 30 that he had been able to send out that day an expedition made up of 3,500 cavalry and 2,000 infantry and that he

---

58. *Ibid.*, 526, 527. McPherson himself added, "By [Washburn's] assuming the offensive-defensive—watching him [Forrest] closely and striking a blow whenever it can be put to advantage—he will be compelled to be on his guard, and will not, I hope, be able to inflict upon us any serious damage." *Ibid.*, 536.

59. *Ibid.*, 529, 503, 537, and Vol. XXIV, Pt. 3, pp. 183, 194.

was "confident that they will whip . . . Forrest and drive him from the State."[60] The object of all this attention and effort left Jackson on May 1, three days earlier than Washburn had anticipated. General Sturgis decided to try to intercept Forrest at or near Bolivar, but delayed by "very bad" roads and the need to repair or rebuild bridges, he did not reach Somerville, twenty miles from Bolivar, until May 2. Realizing that he was badly behind schedule, he sent Colonel Joseph Kargé forward to Bolivar with 700 "select men" of the 10th Missouri and the 2nd New Jersey to hold the crossing of the Hatchie. Kargé was met at the town by Forrest himself and 300 of his men. In a fight lasting until dark, Forrest kept Kargé away from the town and the bridge over the river while the Rebel wagon train and unarmed men, protected by Forrest and his 300 from an attack in flank, marched south toward Purdy on roads east of the river. Then Forrest destroyed the bridge to prevent Sturgis from crossing to follow the main body and, he himself staying west of the river, marched south toward Ripley. Prevented from crossing the river, Sturgis, too, marched south toward Ripley and reached the town on May 6, two days after Forrest's rear guard had passed through. Unable to find forage for his horses in the totally destitute forty-mile stretch between Bolivar and Ripley and with no hope of overtaking Forrest, Sturgis gave up the pursuit and consoled General Washburn (and perhaps also himself) with the observation, "Though we could not catch the scoundrel we are at least rid of him, and that is something."[61]

The only noteworthy feature of Sturgis' failed expedition is that it was made by a combined force of infantry and cavalry. The role of the footsoldiers was to provide a reliable backstop for a body of cavalry, half again as large but of uncertain reliability, to fall back on if it got into trouble. It seemed to occur to no one, as it should have in the fourth year of the war, that in a region of poor roads and seamed with watercourses, one of two things was likely to happen. The cavalry would either have to slow its pace to retain contact with the infantry or set overtaking the enemy as its prime objective, even if it meant becoming

60. *Ibid.*, Vol. XXXII, Pt. 3, p. 545. The cavalry was mainly Colonel Waring's brigade. The infantry was Colonel William L. McMillen's brigade. Sturgis also had a battery of field artillery and the four mountain howitzers of the 4th Missouri.

61. For the story of Sturgis' unsuccessful expedition, see *Ibid.*, Pt. 1, pp. 693–703, and Henry, *"First with the Most" Forrest*, 274–76.

separated from the infantry. In the first case, the cavalry would forfeit any possibility of overtaking and attacking a fast-moving enemy; hence there would be no fight and no need for an infantry backstop. In the second case, the cavalry having overtaken the enemy and engaged it in a fight, the infantry would have been too far in the rear to serve as a backstop; and perhaps even worse, should the cavalry have been defeated, the unprotected infantry would then have been exposed to the likelihood of being defeated in its turn. Sturgis chose the first of these equally unattractive alternatives. "I did not deem it safe to move forward the entire cavalry force until the infantry had arrived to within supporting distance," he reported, and as a result, he allowed an insurmountable two-day gap to open up between Forrest and himself.[62] This was not the way to catch Forrest or even a commander of Confederate cavalry possessing only a modest share of Forrest's energy and resourcefulness.

62. *Official Records*, Vol. XXXII, Pt. 1, p. 699.

XVII

Tipped with a Line of Steel

FOLLOWING THE BATTLE OF PERRYVILLE IN OCTOBER, 1862, and the return of Bragg's and Kirby Smith's forces to Tennessee, Kentucky ceased to be afflicted with military operations on a major scale, but the threat of Confederate raids into the state remained. The Commonwealth was exposed to forays from the southeast, from east Tennessee and Virginia over the many gaps through the mountains, and from the south, into the western counties of the state, lying between the Tennessee and the Mississippi. But the raids from outside the state, Morgan's (on his way to Indiana and Ohio) in the summer of 1863, and even Forrest's in April, 1864, were of little or no military significance. The essential strategic fact in 1863 and 1864 was Kentucky's geographic position, which made its rivers, roads, and railroads the key channels of communications between the North and its armies in Tennessee, Mississippi, and Georgia.

In the later years of the Civil War, Kentucky was kept in a state of turmoil not by the march of armies but by the feuds of Unionist politicians, fueled by the bitterness engendered by the Emancipation Proclamation and the enlistment of Negroes in the Union army. Inevitably, this bitterness carried over into the command and operations of the army in the state and into the relations of the military with the civil authorities. There were, besides, the activities of guerrillas and the machinations, real or suspected, of Copperhead organizations like the Knights of the Golden Circle.

After a short interregnum, Morgan's antagonist of 1862, General Jeremiah Boyle, was succeeded in February, 1864, in command of the District of Kentucky by General Stephen G. Burbridge, a native Kentuckian. Like every other area commander, Burbridge needed more cavalry than he had, to hunt guerrillas and keep them on the jump, to fight incursions into the state by Confederate cavalry, and to protect that most inviting of targets, the Louisville & Nashville Railroad. In 1863, the line had sustained damage to the extent of $543,000, inflicted mainly by John Morgan; in 1864, his place was taken by guerrillas, whose "constant attacks on the trains made it very difficult for the road to secure employees" and who in addition caused $120,000 worth of damage to the road and its appurtenances.[1]

General Horatio G. Wright, whose forces were "largely infantry," believed himself unable to do much against cavalry raids "except to hold important points" and proposed what had become the standard solution: he asked for authority to mount and equip 3,000 infantry, a force large enough, he thought, to protect Kentucky. A month later, General Quincy A. Gillmore, at Lexington, telegraphed General Wright that if he could have the "horse equipments" to mount his two regiments of infantry, he, too, "would feel much stronger." At Columbus, at the western end of the state, General Alexander Asboth was also in a state of poverty for mounted troops. He solicited the help of Adjutant General Thomas to prevent the threatened removal from his command of the 4th Missouri and asked to have another regiment of cavalry assigned to him.[2] A few months later, but still in 1863, came a cry of anguish from General Boyle. "The guerrillas overrun the border," he telegraphed, "and rob banks, sack towns, and pillage the people, all for want of horses, horse equipments, and arms. We have more than 3,000 [men] and can clear the country, if the men be mounted and equipped." These pleas for more cavalry and for facilities to create more mounted troops came at a time when cavalry and mounted infantry already in being were rendered nearly helpless by a lack of adequate equipment. General Julius White, in command of the Eastern

---

1. Robert S. Cotterill, "The Louisville and Nashville Railroad, 1861–1865," *American Historical Review*, XXIX (1924) 711–13. On July 22, 1864, James Guthrie, president of the road, asked the War Department for 300 repeating rifles to arm his employees. Guthrie said that "the increase in guerrilla bands has been such that unless those running the trains are armed, it will not be possible much longer to retain them in the service." *Official Records*, Vol. XXXIX, Pt. 2, p. 198.

2. *Official Records*, Vol. XX, Pt. 2, p. 297, Vol. XXIII, Pt. 2, pp. 42, 241.

District of Kentucky, wrote that the 10th Kentucky, "being armed only with pistols and sabers, is in this mountainous region comparatively useless, except for guard or outpost duty. The enemy, dismounting, take the steep, broken hillsides, which are inaccessible for cavalry, and, keeping out of pistol range, render light cavalry little more than spectators." Sent out on a scout to Burkesville, Kentucky (southeast of Glasgow), Lieutenant Colonel William E. Riley moved out with 150 men of his 11th Kentucky, "as many men of my command as are equipped with arms at all serviceable," and he added, "all . . . [his] officers and men . . . need to enable them to meet any foe, is . . . to be properly armed and equipped. They only had fifty-three guns on this occasion, and . . . the Savage pistol, with which they are armed, is worthless."[3]

As nearly as can be determined from incomplete and imperfect reports, there were on May 15, 1863, a total of 1,881 Union cavalry stationed in four posts in the District of Central Kentucky, most of them in Somerset, on the road to Knoxville, and 4,575 "present for duty," also in four localities, in the District of Western Kentucky, to keep the guerrillas under control and to deal with the recurring incursions of Confederate cavalry into the state.[4] The first of these raids in point of time was John Pegram's, from March 22 to April 1, 1863, with a 1,550-man brigade of cavalry and a three-gun battery, across the Cumberland River and ranging as far north as the Kentucky River, to collect beef cattle. Having collected 750 animals and started south, Pegram made a stand on Dutton's Hill, three miles north of Somerset, to give time for the cattle to be taken across the Cumberland, six miles behind him. Here he was attacked by General Gillmore, with a force of 1,250, made up of Wolford's 1st Kentucky, Israel Garrard's 7th Ohio, and the 45th Ohio and a portion of the 44th Ohio Regiments of Mounted Infantry. The battle, which began with a fire fight that caused little damage on either side and the usual maneuvers to attack the enemy in flank and rear, ended with Gillmore storming Pegram's position atop the hill and forcing him to flee "in confusion" towards the fords across the Cumberland.[5]

3. *Ibid.*, Vol. XXXI, Pt. 1, p. 750, Vol. XXIII, Pt. 1, pp. 196, 265–66.
4. *Ibid.*, Pt. 2, pp. 330, 333. There are no figures in the records for the District of Eastern Kentucky. See *Ibid.*, 379–80, for the manner in which the figures usually appear.
5. *Ibid.*, Pt. 1, pp. 165–75. In the fight at Somerset, Pegram lost "slightly over 200"

The second cavalry raid of some significance occurred from July 25 to August 6, again in brigade strength, and was led by Colonel John S. Scott, 1st Louisiana, C.S.A., who had also participated with his regiment in the Pegram raid. The object this time was "to cut the enemy's communications; to destroy their trains and supplies; to capture horses, mules, and arms; to send out cattle, if possible, and incidentally to make a diversion in favor of General Morgan."[6] Colonel Scott had in his brigade portions of his own regiment, the 2nd and 5th Tennessee, 10th Confederate Regulars, and the 5th North Carolina Cavalry Battalion, some or all of which General Simon Bolivar Buckner had in mind when he spoke in his report of "undisciplined cavalry, as is most in this department."[7] As was the case with most raids, and aided by the poor communications of the area, Scott was highly successful on his march northeast through Williamsburg, London, Richmond, and Winchester, driving off on the way a number of small Union garrisons. Scott met real opposition for the first time on July 28 near Richmond. Led by (then) Colonel W. P. Sanders, who was to lose his life outside Knoxville in October, the opposition was made up of the 2nd and 7th Ohio, detachments of the 10th and 14th Kentucky, and the 112th Illinois Mounted Infantry.[8] After thirty minutes' fighting, which could not have been severe, for Scott's losses were 3 killed and 10 wounded, he charged and drove back Sanders' horsemen, who, Sanders reported, "in falling back, became completely panic-stricken. . . . It was an unnecessary panic. Many men are cut off, captured, and some killed and wounded. . . . I will try and form them . . . but doubt whether I can do much with them. Ten miles has been a complete and disgraceful rout." The next day, however, with his numbers increased to about 2,400

---

killed, wounded, and captured, and Gillmore not over 30. Gillmore also claimed to have recaptured 300 or 400 of the beef cattle Pegram had taken.

6. *Ibid.*, 842. The reference to Morgan is to his Indiana-Ohio Raid, in which he crossed Kentucky diagonally from Burkesville northwest to Brandenburg, where he crossed the Ohio into Indiana on July 8 and was captured in eastern Ohio on July 26. Hence, insofar as the Scott raid was intended to help Morgan, it was too late and a failure.

7. *Ibid.*, 842.

8. Earlier in the month the 112th Illinois Mounted Infantry had finally been able to turn in the old Harper's Ferry muskets it had carried since its organization in 1862, and received in their place new Enfield rifles. Thompson, *History of the 112th Regiment*, 63. Two months earlier, the regiment had exchanged its "large camp tents" for shelter halves, much to the disgust of the men but enabling the regiment to reduce its wagon train from fifteen to one. *Ibid.*, 63, 40, 39.

with the addition of detachments from the 1st Kentucky, 8th and 9th Michigan, 5th Tennessee, and the 1st and 2nd Tennessee Mounted Infantry, it was Sanders' turn. He hung on Scott's rear, took prisoner a number of his men, and compelled him to abandon some of the wagons, horses, and mules he had captured on his march north. On the thirty-first Scott's retreat continued, under continuing pressure from Sanders. Near Lancaster, where Scott tried to make a stand, Sanders ordered Captain Frank E. Watrous to charge the enemy; the charge "was handsomely executed, capturing about 30 prisoners, and wounding a number of the enemy with the saber."[9] Later the same day, Sanders ordered a charge of all his "cavalry" (presumably of those of his regiments that were armed with the saber), which was also successful and resulted in the capture of more than 200 prisoners. Sanders kept up the pursuit until Scott crossed the Cumberland on August 1, leaving behind a part of his captures of wagons and animals.[10]

General Burbridge, like his predecessors, had to cope with an excess of guerrillas and a shortage of horses. As to the former, he was the recipient of one of the most striking of the many striking letters General Sherman wrote during the war. The acts "of the so-called partisans or guerrillas," Sherman wrote, "are nothing but simple murder, horse-stealing, arson, and other well-defined crimes, which do not sound as well under their true names as the more agreeable ones of warlike meaning. . . . you may order all your post and district commanders that Guerrillas are not soldiers but wild beasts unknown to the usages of war."[11] Thus encouraged, Burbridge more than took Sherman at his word. On July 16, 1864, he published his General Orders No. 59, the most significant portion of which was the announcement that "wherever an unarmed Union citizen is murdered, four guerrillas will be selected from the prisoners in the hands of the military authorities, and publicly shot to death in the most convenient place near the scene

9. *Official Records*, Vol. XXIII, Pt. 1, pp. 833, 835.
10. For the entire story of the raid, see *Ibid.*, 828–43. See also Tarrant, *Wild Riders of the First Kentucky*, 190–95.
11. *Official Records*, Vol. XXXIX, Pt. 2, p. 135. In an earlier dispatch, Sherman had written Burbridge: "Go on, raise the hue and cry, and don't mind the cost of money or horseflesh to hunt down every robber and guerrilla in your state. Make a clean job of it, and Morgan and all other such men will let Kentucky alone in all time to come." *Ibid.*, 115.

of the outrage." The order was not an empty threat: Within three days of its publication, two prisoners were taken from prison in Louisville to Henderson and shot in retaliation for the wounding of one James E. Rankin, and two others were executed in Russellville in retaliation for the killing of a citizen named Porter. Two more executions took place in Bloomfield, two others in Simpson County, four in Jeffersontown (for the murder of a Union soldier), two each in Georgetown and Louisa, and four more in early September at Brandenburg, where Morgan had crossed the Ohio River on his Indiana-Ohio Raid.[12]

Retaliation by northern soldiers for the killing of comrades was a commonplace event wherever they were the target of guerrilla and bushwhacker attacks, just as it was a common response by southern troops in east Tennessee, where the guerrillas and bushwhackers were Unionists. A typical example was the 72nd Indiana Infantry. Right after the regiment became mounted, two of its men, belonging to Company B, were captured by what their comrades believed were bushwhackers, tied to a tree, and shot. "After that barbarous atrocity," the regimental historian has written, "bushwhackers were turned over to Co. B . . . and the Provost Marshal's list [of prisoners] was never encumbered with their names."[13] Whatever one may think of such conduct by men in uniform whose lives were regularly at risk, there was an enormous difference between retaliation by men who had been shot at from the brush or in the night by men not recognized as soldiers, and the cold-blooded execution of hostages. Moreover, and not surprisingly, Burbridge's draconic policy did not work. Five months after it was instituted, in mid-November, Burbridge reported that he had five regiments of cavalry (11th Michigan, 12th Ohio, 11th Kentucky, and the 30th and 39th Ohio Mounted Infantry) scattered throughout the state, hunting guerrillas. As late as January, 1865, "Guerrillas attacked [a] cattle train twenty-two miles from Louisville." Near the end of March, with Appomattox only two weeks away, General John M. Palmer ordered General E. H. Hobson to organize an ex-

12. Robert Emmett McDowell, *City of Conflict: Louisville in the Civil War* (Louisville, 1962), 165–66; *Official Records*, Vol. XXXIX, Pt. 2, pp. 172, 203, 206, 339, 376.
13. McGee, *History of the 72nd Indiana*, 110–12. On May 9, General Hobson sent orders to Colonel Charles S. Hanson at Irvine, Kentucky: "I would prefer, and will insist, that no regular guerrillas be sent in as prisoners; direct your command to deal with such characters in a speedy and summary manner. The usages and customs of civilized nations when at war forbid the extension of clemency or quarters [*sic*] to guerrilla bands." *Official Records*, Vol. XXXIX, Pt. 2, p. 19.

pedition at once to "go for" guerrillas on the Louisville & Nashville near Glasgow. Hobson's response, sanctified by a Civil War tradition now four years old, was to ask for 500 sets of horse equipments to enable him to do the job and to "clean out" Metcalfe and Monroe counties as well.[14]

General Burbridge's military ambitions did not end with the hunting down of guerrillas. John Morgan gave him his first opportunity for greater things. After being captured on July 26, 1863, Morgan and his officers were confined in the Ohio State Penitentiary (not yet translated into a "correctional institution") in Columbus, from which he and six of his officers escaped under mysterious circumstances on the rainy night of November 26.[15] After getting to Cincinnati by train, Morgan crossed the Ohio and with the help of Confederate sympathizers rode across Kentucky and Tennessee to safety. With little help from the authorities in Richmond, he began in early 1864 to assemble near Wytheville, Virginia, across the mountains from Kentucky, a replacement for the command he had destroyed the summer before. By the end of May, he had collected between 2,000 and 2,500 men—some of them survivors of the glory days of 1862—and he took them on a raid into Kentucky to capture some of the 15,000 horses he said the Union army had in the state.[16] On the morning of June 8, he captured the small Union garrison at Mount Sterling, after which his men looted all the stores in the town and entered some private houses in search of food, clothing, and valuables. Women were stopped on the street and robbed of jewelry at gunpoint, and the bank was robbed of $80,000 in gold, silver, and currency.[17] So far, except for the physical hardship of a long and hurried march over primitive mountain roads, Morgan's progress had been trouble-free, but now his difficulties were about to begin.[18]

14. *Official Records*, Vol. XLV, Pt. 1, p. 929, Vol. XLIX, Pt. 1, p. 582, Pt. 2, p. 102.

15. Brown, *The Bold Cavaliers*, 237–45; Duke, *History of Morgan's Cavalry*, 468–91. But see Howard Swiggett, *The Rebel Raider: A Life of John Hunt Morgan* (Indianapolis, 1924), 166–91.

16. Morgan's own estimate of the size of his force, just before his departure, was 2,700, divided into the brigades of Colonel Henry L. Giltner (1,100 men), Colonel D. Howard Smith (700), and Lieutenant Colonel Robert M. Martin (800 dismounted men). Holland, *Morgan and His Raiders*, 318–19.

17. S. K. Smith, *Life, Army Record, and Public Services of D. Howard Smith* (Louisville, 1890), 116–18; Holland, *Morgan and His Raiders* 321–22; *Official Records*, Vol. XXXIX, Pt. 1, pp. 74–75, 77–82.

18. "We marched from twenty-two to twenty-seven miles per day, the dismounted

Three weeks before these events, Generals Halleck and Schofield had suggested to Burbridge that he make a diversion in Schofield's favor, and at the same time protect Schofield's left flank, by attacking the Confederate forces on the other side of the mountains, in Virginia.[19] Burbridge promptly organized an expeditionary force and was actually about to cross the mountains when he received word that Morgan, with a command represented as numbering 5,000, was crossing the mountains in the opposite direction, by way of Pound Gap. Ordering Colonel John Mason Brown, located on the Kentucky side of the mountains with the 45th and a detachment of the 39th Kentucky Regiments of Mounted Infantry to shadow Morgan, he himself turned around and, after an unbelievable march of ninety miles in twenty-four hours, joined Brown just to the east of Mount Sterling on the night of June 8. Morgan had left the town in the afternoon with D. Howard Smith's brigade to capture Lexington, which was practically undefended. He left behind at Mount Sterling the brigades of Henry L. Giltner and R. M. Martin "to destroy stores and mount the dismounted men upon the captured horses" and to join him in Lexington the next day. The posting of vedettes and pickets beyond the Confederate camps that evening was in keeping with the frivolity of the entire operation; the pickets were so near the bivouacs that when the Federals, led by Colonel Brown and the 45th Kentucky Mounted Infantry, attacked Martin's bivouac east of the town at 4 A.M. on the ninth, the attack was "a thorough surprise." The pickets were shot and the bivouac was overrun before Martin's men could roll out of their blankets.[20] Martin lost 250 men killed, wounded, and taken prisoner; the rest of his men made a fighting retreat through the town and joined Giltner. In the fighting that continued west of town, Martin lost 50 more men.

Morgan's advance detachment had reached Lexington at 2 A.M. on June 10 and were joined by the rest of the command later in the day. The excesses of Mount Sterling were repeated in Lexington. Stores,

making that distance over mountain passes that troops had never traveled before." Morgan's report, *Official Records*, Vol. XXXIX, Pt. 1, p. 68. Giltner's brigade lost 200 of its horses on the way.

19. *Ibid.*, 22.

20. Colonel Brown had learned that Martin's pickets were "very carelessly posted at the very verge of their camp . . . [and] concluded that a surprise by the whole division was perhaps possible." *Ibid.*, 44. See also Frank H. Mason, *The Twelfth Ohio Cavalry* (Cleveland, 1871), 40–41.

individuals and a bank were robbed, and several buildings were fired. Morgan also captured, he said, 2,000 horses in the government corrals, "and about 5,000 magnificent horses that had been sent from the country for protection."[21] How Morgan, with something over 2,000 men, each of whom already had a horse, managed to move off with 7,000 captured horses is something of a puzzle.

In the course of his day in Lexington, Morgan learned that there was a Union garrison at Cynthiana, twenty-four miles to the north, where he had had a successful fight with the Federals two years before. Collecting his men and his captured horses, however many of the latter there may have been, he left Lexington to march to Cynthiana. His report does not indicate why he did so; nor is there any hint of what his intentions may have been from Cynthiana on, if indeed he had formulated any such plan. The Cynthiana garrison was a 400-man detachment of the 168th Ohio Infantry, a militia regiment of hundred-day men, who had reported for duty with great reluctance, "very poor guns," and no ammunition. Morgan attacked and captured the lot and, in the process of doing so, burned down a "great portion" of the town because, Morgan explained, "The Federals took shelter in the houses, and the alternative (as we had no artillery) was to fire them."[22]

While this fight in the town was going on, General Hobson advanced toward Cynthiana by train from Cincinnati with another hundred-day militia regiment, the 171st Ohio Infantry, of about 600 men.[23] He was met and attacked a short distance north of the town by Colonel Giltner's brigade and fought them on more or less equal terms until Morgan led a battalion of cavalry on a swing to his rear. Attacked front and rear, he surrendered.

Against the advice of his officers, Morgan decided to stay in Cynthiana overnight. This gave Burbridge, who had followed the raiders to Lexington, ample time to overtake them. With Colonel Charles S. Hansen's Third Brigade (12th Ohio and the 37th, 40th, and 52nd Kentucky Mounted Infantry) in the lead, followed by Colonel David A. Mims's Second Brigade (11th Michigan, 39th Kentucky Mounted Infantry), he attacked Morgan (whose numbers were down to about 1,200) two miles south of Cynthiana at 2:20 A.M. on June 12. Behind

21. *Official Records*, Vol. XXXIX, Pt. 1, p. 68, Pt. 2, pp. 95, 96.
22. *Ibid.*, Pt. 1, p. 69.
23. This regiment appears in Morgan's report as a 1,500-man brigade. *Ibid.*, 69.

the shelter of stone walls and fences, the Confederates held their own for an hour but then began to break. Having been reinforced by Colonel Israel Garrard's brigade (9th Michigan, 7th Ohio), Burbridge outnumbered Morgan two to one. Advancing with some of his regiments mounted and some on foot, Burbridge drove the Confederates from the shelter of their stone walls and fences and into the town (Captain J. Bates Dickson, in his report to the governor of Kentucky, spoke of "our cavalry making several brilliant saber charges").[24] There, in Colonel Garrard's convoluted English: "The mass of them were come up with at the [Licking River]. . . . The River was crowded with men and horses struggling together in the deep water. Many were drowned and an opportunity was had for firing several hundred shots into them."[25] There is no count of the number of Morgan's men killed or drowned in this affair, but many of them were taken prisoner, 83 by the 9th Michigan alone.[26] Morgan himself, with the few hundred of his men who had been able to reach their horses, escaped in the direction of Flemingsburg and eventually got back to Virginia, with losses he estimated (and obviously underestimated) at 80 killed, 125 wounded, and 150 missing.[27] The looting at Mount Sterling and Lexington that had disgraced the advance of the raiders into their home state distinguished their retreat also, at Georgetown and Sardis in particular.[28] Typical of the warped sense of realism Morgan exhibited throughout his military career are the results he claimed for this disastrous expedition and the assurance he gave his government that his command would be as strong as it had been when he "first entered the State."[29]

This, however, was to be the last of Morgan's much-touted raids. In

24. *Ibid.*, 28.
25. *Ibid.*, 47; Brown, *The Bold Cavaliers*, 262–64; Mason, *The Twelfth Ohio Cavalry*, 48.
26. *Official Records*, Vol. XXXIX, Pt. 1, p. 47.
27. *Ibid.*, 69. The total of Burbridge's losses was 34 killed, 158 wounded, and 206 missing. Unexplained is the reason why a single regiment, the 12th Ohio, should have lost 19 killed, 70 wounded, and 190 missing. *Ibid.*, 38, 43, 45, 48.
28. George C. Mosgrove, *Kentucky Cavaliers in Dixie: Reminiscences of a Confederate Cavalryman* (Jackson, Tenn., 1957), 149, 163–64.
29. *Ibid.*, 69. Colonel D. Howard Smith wrote: "That last raid into Kentucky was the death blow of the command. The men were so scattered and demoralized on the return that it was some time before General Morgan could get them together and effect a reorganization. . . . Notwithstanding his utmost efforts . . . [Morgan] found it impossible to restore the morale and efficiency of the command. Many of the men never returned, some went to other commands, and some to 'guerrillaing.'" Smith, *Services of D. Howard Smith*, 124.

the ensuing months enough recruits found him to rebuild the command to nearly 2,000 men, but the numbers meant nothing, for many of them lacked horses and arms, and there was little discipline. Spurred on by Morgan's own officers, the Confederate government was about to investigate the Mount Sterling and Lexington bank robberies. It may have been a mercy that he was caught on the rainy morning of September 4 at Greeneville, Tennessee, by General Alvan C. Gillem's cavalry, cornered in the garden of Mrs. Catherine Williams' house while trying to escape, and shot and killed by Private Andrew Campbell, Company G, 13th Tennessee.[30]

At the opposite end of Tennessee from Greeneville, and at nearly the same time that Morgan started out on his raid into Kentucky, Generals Washburn and Sturgis were concerting plans to redeem themselves for their failure to intercept Forrest after his Tennessee-Kentucky incursion. On May 5, Forrest reached Tupelo on his return from Tennessee. He reported to General S. D. Lee that he had a total of 9,220 men, only 5,416 of whom were armed.[31] He knew by May 20 that "the force of the enemy at Memphis [was] reported to be preparing for a raid." Nevertheless, he proposed to Lee that he be allowed to take 2,000 "picked men" and a battery of artillery, to try to cut the enemy's communication in middle Tennessee—the rail communications behind General Sherman, whose Atlanta Campaign had begun on the day Forrest reached Tupelo. His proposal was approved, and he left Tupelo on June 1 with the 2,000 "picked men," intending to pick up in Russellville, Alabama, the additional thousand men of Roddey's division that Lee gave him for the operation.[32] On the morning of June 3, however, he received a dispatch from Lee letting him know that "the enemy were moving in force from Memphis in the direction of Tupelo" and ordering his immediate return. Two days later, on the fifth, Forrest

30. *Official Records*, Vol. XXXIX, Pt. 1, pp. 489–90; Samuel W. Scott and Samuel P. Angel, *History of the Thirteenth Regiment, Tennessee Volunteer Cavalry, U.S.A.* (Philadelphia, 1903), 165–78; Holland, *Morgan and His Raiders*, 329–31, 337–44; Swiggett, *The Rebel Raider*, 259–64; Brown, *The Bold Cavaliers*, 267–71. Campbell was promoted to first lieutenant of Company E.

31. *Official Records*, Vol. XXXVIII, Pt. 4, p. 723. For the condition of Forrest's forces, see Henry, *"First with the Most" Forrest*, 278–80.

32. *Official Records*, Vol. XXXVIII, Pt. 4, pp. 729, 747, Vol. XXXIX, Pt. 1, pp. 221–22.

was back in Tupelo, and there he received word that the enemy force had reached Salem, fifty miles to the west.

The Federal force that brought Forrest back to Tupelo had been organized on General McPherson's orders, on the strength of information brought in by his scouts that Forrest was "preparing for some expedition," which was quite logically assumed to be intended "to operate on General Sherman's communications." The primary goal of the Federal countermove, to be commanded by Samuel Sturgis, was "to engage . . . [Forrest], and if possible to whip and disperse his forces"; secondarily, it was to destroy once again the Mobile & Ohio, which the Confederates had succeeded in placing "in complete running order" from Corinth down to Mobile. Sturgis was given for the expedition Grierson's cavalry division, numbering 3,300, made up of Waring's and Winslow's brigades; and infantry numbering 5,500, organized by Sturgis into an *ad hoc* division, to be commanded by Colonel William L. McMillen and consisting of the brigades of Colonels Alexander Wilkin, George B. Hoge, and Edward Bouton. The latter brigade was made up of two infantry regiments (55th and 59th United States) and a section of artillery, all Negro troops. Sturgis was also given 14 pieces of artillery and a train of 250 wagons loaded with ammunition and 18 (or by another account 20) days' rations for the men. To feed his nearly 5,000 horses and mules, Sturgis had to depend on what his men could find along the way, but, as Colonel McMillen wrote: "The line of march was through a country devastated by the war, and containing little or no forage, rendering it extremely difficult, and for the greater portion of the time impossible, to maintain the animals in a serviceable condition. The roads were narrow, leading through dense forests, and over streams rendered almost impassable by the heavy rains which fell daily."[33]

Sturgis appeared to have received command of the expedition somewhat by default. After his return to Memphis following his fruitless effort to intercept Forrest, Washburn ordered him to return to General Sherman, who sent him back to Washburn "under orders as equivalent to an order to give him the command to which his rank [as the senior brigadier general in Memphis] entitled him."[34] Washburn's

33. *Ibid.*, Vol. XXXIX, Pt. 1, pp. 85, 103, 100.
34. *Ibid.*, 86. Sherman wrote that "there was great danger, always in my mind, that Forrest would collect a heavy cavalry command in Mississippi, cross the Tennessee

cleverly worded report implies that he was bound by Sherman's orders and the army's hierarchical system to give Sturgis the command and hints that if he had had a free hand he would not have done so. It may be assumed that his language would have been different had the expedition been a success. It is important to note that Sturgis and the officers he was to command did not meet until June 2, the day *after* the troops left Memphis. Colonel Alexander Wilkin considered that "one great difficulty" of the expedition, and a contributing cause of its failure, was that "the command was composed of troops of different commands, unacquainted with and distrustful of each other and new to the general commanding."[35]

The expedition needed seven days—until June 8—to reach Ripley, eighty miles southeast of Memphis. There Sturgis held an informal council of war, attended by General Grierson and Colonels McMillen and Hoge. Grierson expressed the opinion that an advance beyond Ripley would "lead to disaster." Colonel McMillen remarked that he "would rather go on and meet the enemy, even if we should be whipped, than to return to Memphis without having met them," and made much of Sturgis' failure to meet Forrest on his previous expedition. Sturgis called attention "to the great delay we had undergone on account of the continuous rain and consequent bad condition of the roads; the exhausted condition of the animals; the great probability that the enemy would avail himself of the time thus afforded him to concentrate an overwhelming force against us . . . and the utter hopelessness of saving our train or artillery in case of defeat, on account of the narrowness and general bad condition of the roads and the impossibility of procuring supplies of forage for the animals." Nevertheless, but with "a sad foreboding of the consequences"—hardly a frame of mind promising of success—Sturgis decided to go forward.[36]

At 5:30 A.M. on June 10, the Union cavalry, with Waring's brigade in the lead and Winslow's brigade behind, started from their bivouacs

River, and break up our railroads below Nashville. In anticipation of this very danger, I had sent General Sturgis to Memphis to take command of all the cavalry in that quarter to go out toward Pontotoc, engage Forrest and defeat him." Sherman, *Memoirs*, II, 52.

35. *Official Records*, Vol. XXXIX, Pt. 1, p. 96. Sturgis said to the board appointed to investigate the disastrous expedition that he had led: "As I was an entire stranger to the troops and the organization, I thought they could be governed and handled better by dividing them into two divisions." *Ibid.*, 147, 149.

36. *Ibid.*, 199–200, 98, 99, 101, 207.

and marched southeast on the Ripley and Fulton road toward the Mobile & Ohio track at Guntown. At ten o'clock, about ten miles from their starting point, they came to an intersection called Brice's Crossroads, where the Baldwyn-Pontotoc road crossed the road they were on at a nearly exact ninety-degree angle. The intersection got its name from the Brice farmhouse, which stood a few yards from the crossing. The open fields of the Brice farm, about six acres in extent, were surrounded on all sides by dense forest, overgrown not only by trees but also by "blackjack and scrub oak so dense that in places the troops could with difficulty force their way through, and, being then in full leaf, it was possible to approach within a few yards without being seen."[37]

About five miles from its camps, McMillen's infantry and the trains were held up at the crossing of the Hatchie River: "The road through the bottom land of this stream was almost impassable, and we found it impossible to put it in good condition." As a result of this holdup, a gap of between five and six miles opened between the cavalry and the head of the infantry column. A second hazard still ahead of the infantry was the swampy bottoms of Tishomingo Creek (which has given its name to the battle in some accounts), about a mile and a half north of the crossroads and hence between the cavalry and the infantry. The road through the Tishomingo bottoms, on which the cavalry had already advanced, "took somewhat the character of a causeway, in length nearly three quarters of a mile"; it crossed the creek ("a sluggish stream") over a small wooden bridge.[38]

As soon as Waring reached Brice's Crossroads, he halted and, in keeping with good cavalry practice, sent scouting squadrons forward to the south in the direction of Guntown and to the east and to the west on the Baldwyn-Pontotoc road. While waiting for these squadrons to return, Grierson ordered Waring to turn left, on to the Baldwyn road, and dismount and deploy his men at the edge of the timber a half mile east of the crossroads in a line facing east, with his right-hand regiment just to the south of the Baldwyn road. Behind a fence along the same road and hence facing northeast, Waring posted a detachment of

37. Wyeth, *That Devil Forrest*, 353. "The opposing lines were at all points concealed from each other by the dense blackjack. . . . The underbrush was so thick that only occasional glimpses of the advancing enemy could be had." Scott, *Story of a Cavalry Regiment*, 240, 243.

38. *Official Records*, Vol. XXXIX, Pt. 1, pp. 103–104; *Battles and Leaders*, IV, 420n; Wyeth, *That Devil Forrest*, 353.

a hundred men with revolving rifles, as skirmishers. Winslow's brigade deployed to Waring's right, in the angle between the two roads, the two brigades forming a continuous arc, their left facing east and their right facing south.[39]

The first of Waring's scouting groups to report was Captain Robert M. Hanson's detachment of the 4th Missouri. He had been sent toward Baldwyn, the direction in which Colonel Waring thought the enemy ("Forrest and Lee, with their whole commands") would most likely be found. Hanson sent back word that he had encountered, and was skirmishing with, "quite a strong picket" of the enemy.[40] The reports of General Grierson, of Colonels Waring and Winslow, and of their regimental commanders make it evident that none of them had any clear idea at this point of just what enemy troops were behind the strong picket Captain Hanson had run into. Nor is there any suggestion that Grierson, who would have had to make the decision, had any inclination to drive ahead, which would have meant leaving the security of the Brice farm clearings to plunge into the dense woods to the east, and increasing the distance between himself and the infantry. Deploying in a defensive arc, as Grierson did, to wait for the infantry to arrive, might have been sound conservative tactics against any antagonist other than Forrest, but against him such timidity was fatal.

The postwar recollections of Forrest's principal subordinates, perhaps colored by hindsight, indicate that from at least June 8 on, he intended to meet and fight Sturgis at Brice's Crossroads, well west of the railroad, and also that he was fully and constantly informed of the size, composition, and progress of Sturgis' force.[41] On the morning of the tenth, Forrest had his men on the road from Boonville down to Brice's at four o'clock, an hour and a half before the Federal cavalry left their camps and three hours before the Federal infantry did so. The Confederates encountered by Waring's scouting detachment on the Baldwyn road were two companies of W. W. Faulkner's 12th Kentucky, which led the advance of Hylan B. Lyon's brigade of 800 men. Within a few minutes of the encounter, and while Lyon was deploying his men, Forrest joined him with his 85-man escort company and ordered an immediate

39. *Official Records*, Vol. XXXIX, Pt. 1, pp. 98–99, 132; *Battles and Leaders*, IV, 420, 420n.
40. *Official Records*, Vol. XXXIX, Pt. 1, p. 132.
41. *Ibid.*, 222; Wyeth, *That Devil Forrest*, 350.

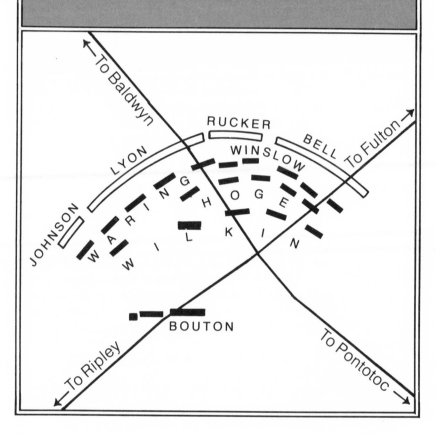

BATTLE OF BRICE'S CROSSROADS

attack, which, he explained to Lyon, was to be nothing more than a demonstration, but as noisy as possible, to keep the Federal cavalry pinned in place and prevented from going over to the attack themselves, before the arrival of additional units of Forrest's cavalry. To make the sham attack, Lyon disposed of 935 men, minus the horse holders, against Grierson's 3,200, similarly diminished.[42]

At about 11 A.M., Colonel Edmund W. Rucker joined Forrest; his 700-man brigade raised Forrest's numbers to 1,635, minus the casualties Lyon had sustained and the horse holders—enough, Forrest thought, for a real attack, not a demonstration this time, against Waring's line. This attack was repulsed, but as Lyon's and Rucker's men made their way back to their start line in the woods, Colonel William A. Johnson came up with his 500-man brigade of Alabamians, giving Forrest 2,135 men to pit against Grierson's 3,200.

Colonel Waring had barely completed the deployment of his brigade after sending out his scouting detachments when he was attacked by what he described as a "strong force" of the enemy, emerging from the woods to the east of the Brice farm; "a heavy engagement ensued, which resulted in their repulse." This "heavy engagement," lasting about an hour, was with the "demonstration" by Lyon's small brigade. Rucker having arrived, Forrest decided that the demonstration had accomplished its purpose, and ordered Lyon to withdraw into the shelter of the woods, a movement Colonel Waring may be excused for describing as a "repulse." But now, after a brief pause, came the Confederates' first real attack, made by Lyon and Rucker, with Forrest everywhere present as the directing force. This "desperate" attack, aimed at Waring's left, was followed by a third and equally "desperate" attack, directed against Waring's right and Winslow's left. Waring described these attacks as "exceedingly fierce, each consisting of a double line of skirmishers with an infantry line of battle, and a column of support behind, apparently numbering 4,000 men."[43] To mistake Forrest's dismounted cavalrymen for infantry was understandable, but to more than double their numbers was both a tribute to the ferocity of their attack and a black mark on the record of a colonel of cavalry of three years' experience.

42. Wyeth, *That Devil Forrest*, 353. Accompanying Lyon's brigade, but not a part of it, was Captain Henry Gartrell's 50-man company of Georgians.

43. Wyeth, *That Devil Forrest*, 353, 355, 356; *Official Records*, Vol. XXXIX, Pt. 1, pp. 132, 129; *Battles and Leaders*, IV, 420; J. P. Young, *The Seventh Tennessee Cavalry: A History* (Nashville, 1890), 89–90.

Neither Lyon's voluntary withdrawal, mistaken for a repulse and credited to the revolving rifles of the detachment Waring had posted on the flank, nor the repulse of the first of the Confederates' real attacks was followed by a counterattack that Grierson's men should have been capable of making. It must be repeated that a defensive remaining passive to this degree was not the way to "whip and disperse . . . [Forrest's] forces"; it in fact invited defeat.

As soon as Captain Hanson reported the presence of the enemy, Grierson sent the information back to Sturgis, who had remained with the infantry. Grierson added that he had found an advantageous position and would hold it. Sturgis started at once for the crossroads, but after riding a short distance, it occurred to him that "the enemy might be stronger than General Grierson had conceived," and he sent an aide back to Colonel McMillen with orders "to send forward the advance brigade of infantry . . . as rapidly as possible without distressing his men." Then came a second message from Grierson, "stating that the enemy was in considerable force, and that he had nearly all his command engaged." It may have been this message, the wording of which Grierson remembered as "I have an advantageous position and could hold it if the infantry was brought up promptly," or a third message to the same effect, that Sturgis read and had an aide take on to Colonel McMillen, with the request from himself that McMillen "lose no time in getting up." [44]

It is pointless to speculate on what Sturgis might have done, or what the course of the battle might have been, if he had reached the crossroads earlier than he did. By the time he arrived, at or shortly past noon, apparently during the pause between the Confederates' second and third attacks, Grierson's cavalry was already on the verge of being whipped. Sturgis found "considerable confusion about the cross-roads with the artillery and ambulances and led horses jammed in the road, and . . . [his] first attention was directed to clearing the road so that the infantry could get up." Grierson met Sturgis at the crossroads (whether it was before, during, or after the commanding general's road-clearing activities, does not appear) and urged him, so Sturgis reported, "to get the infantry up as quick as possible, as his men were

44. *Official Records*, Vol. XXXIX, Pt. 1, pp. 92, 129, 153, 208, Pt. 2, 97. It is impossible to be certain of the number of such messages Grierson sent. Only one, marked as sent at 10 A.M., appears in the *Official Records*.

worn out and must be nearly out of ammunition." Sturgis' response was to direct him "to organize all the idle men about the cross-roads, of which there were a great many, and skulkers, and put them into the fight where they were the most needed."[45] Sturgis claimed to have also received two or three messages from Colonel Winslow "in strong terms, almost demanding to be relieved," and one from Colonel Waring, asking also to be relieved.[46] Neither Grierson nor Waring mention these pleas for help, and neither does Colonel Winslow, who on the contrary states that he held his position "until twice ordered back by Brigadier-General Sturgis. . . . Though fiercely assailed by the enemy . . . I could have held our original position had not the retirement of Colonel Waring's command obliged me to fall back in order to keep up communication with the left."[47] What actually happened, as Lieutenant E. Hunn Hanson, 4th Missouri, recalled, was that when the third of Forrest's attacks came to within "fifty to seventy-five paces of the edge of the wood, along which Waring's brigade was, the center of that command slowly gave way. As a result, the entire brigade fell back." This uncovered Winslow's left and caused his brigade also to fall back.[48] Another version of the same incident has it that Rucker's brigade, spearheaded by the 7th Tennessee, C.S.A., broke through the center and right of Waring's line after a hand-to-hand fight.[49]

The tenth of June, 1864, was a typically hot, oppressively humid Mississippi summer day.[50] McMillen's infantry, in their woolen, dark-

45. *Ibid.*, Pt. 1, pp. 132, 153−54.

46. *Ibid.*, 92, 153, 154. In his formal report Sturgis was scathing about Winslow, who, he wrote, "was especially clamorous to be relieved, and permitted to carry his brigade to the rear." *Ibid*., 92.

47. *Ibid.*, 137.

48. *Battles and Leaders*, IV, 420−21. In a footnote, Hanson added, "There is a point in an engagement beyond which a struggle is seen to be hopeless. . . . that point had not been reached by the center, nor anything like it, and there was neither excuse nor justification for its retreat." *Ibid.*, 420*n*.

49. Young, *The Seventh Tennessee*, 90−94. Rucker's men attacked on foot, but he himself remained on horseback. "Several bullets passed through his clothing; his horse, five times wounded, fell at last from a mortal shot." Rucker was wounded in the abdomen but remained on the field until the end of the fight. Wyeth, *That Devil Forrest*, 357−58.

50. "A heavy rain had fallen on the 8th . . . and on the afternoon and evening of the 9th it came down in torrents and did not cease until after midnight; but about daybreak the clouds . . . vanished, and when the sun came up it ushered in one of those hot, humid and depressing days characteristic of this season of the year in this section of the Southern country." Wyeth, *That Devil Forrest*, 350.

blue, heat-absorbent uniforms, burdened with guns, ammunition, haversacks, blankets, and other gear, had upwards of five miles to cover to reach the cavalry. Colonel Hoge, whose brigade was in the lead, had his men alternate between a "very quick" and a "moderate" pace until he was within three-quarters of a mile of the crossroads, when he was ordered by McMillen "to move forward at a double-quick, which was . . . kept up until the head of the column arrived at the cross-roads."[51] The effect of the unaccustomed fast pace and the heat on the infantry was disastrous. Overcome by the heat, men were falling out at every step. At least forty of the 93rd Indiana Infantry fell out, and the rest reached their destination "very much exhausted." Lieutenant Colonel John F. King, 114th Illinois Infantry, passed "a great many men who had fallen out by the way on account of the heat" lying on the roadside, and lost a hundred men of his own—a quarter of his regiment—on the way. When his regiment was placed in the firing line, he heard several of his men say "that they were so much exhausted that they could not load."[52] One officer after another gave as the reason for the loss of the battle the state of exhaustion of his men when they reached the crossroads after their grueling march.[53]

Shortly after 1 P.M., the infantry arrived at the crossroads. Hoge's brigade was deployed mainly to the right of the Baldwyn road, at about the center of the Union arc, where the center and right of Waring's cavalry had been driven back. Wilkin's brigade, arriving a short time later, was divided, the 95th Ohio Infantry being posted on Hoge's left, the 114th Illinois Infantry and the 93rd Indiana Infantry on Hoge's right and extending as far as the Ripley-Fulton road. The two brigades of infantry thus formed an arc similar to, but to the rear of, the arc the cavalry had formed until Waring's brigade was pushed back. Colonel Edward Bouton's brigade, the rearmost unit of the infantry column that day, remained with the trains, which moved forward as rapidly as the poor road and the worn-out condition of its mules allowed. The head of the long line of wagons got as far as Tishomingo Creek and began to cross.[54]

51. *Official Records*, Vol. XXXIX, Pt. 1, p. 163.
52. *Ibid.*, 169, 173. Colonel Hoge estimated that "at least 20 per cent" of the men of his entire brigade had fallen out.
53. See, for example, *Ibid.*, 171, 175, 196, 205, 211.
54. *Ibid.*, 104. Sturgis had sent his sick and forty-one of his wagons back to Memphis from Ripley on June 8, but he still had more than two hundred wagons left.

The formal reports of Sturgis, Grierson, McMillen, and their commanders of brigades and regiments, by the very nature of such writings, give a misleading picture of what the situation must have been at and to the north of the crossroads on the early afternoon of June 10. Unintentionally, no doubt, they suggest an orderly advance and deployment of the infantry and an equally orderly retirement of the cavalry to their horses, behind the newly established infantry screen. We are shown the cavalry, having mounted, forming ranks by companies and regiments under their officers. There are, however, hints of confusion and disorder among the cavalrymen as they tried to reform behind the infantry. Colonel McMillen, who road ahead of his infantry, said that when he reached the crossroads, "the cavalry were falling back rapidly in disorder and the roads at Brice's house were filled with retreating cavalry, led horses, ambulances, wagons, and artillery, the whole presenting a scene of confusion and demoralization anything but cheering to troops just arriving. Great anxiety was manifested on the part of all for the quick arrival of the infantry, and I was frequently appealed to to know when the infantry would come up." Colonel McMillen's statement is borne out by Waring's admission that when he took up his new position after being driven back from the line he had occupied at the beginning of the action, he had "not more than 400 or 500 men in line"—no more than a third of his numbers when the action began.[55]

Tyree Bell's brigade, having covered twenty-five miles from Rienzi to the crossroads, and two batteries commanded by Captain John Morton (the latter having made an eighteen-mile march since daybreak "over roads so muddy that for much of the distance it was with great difficulty the horses could drag the pieces along") now arrived, adding 2,800 fighting men and twelve guns to Forrest's forces.[56] Positioning Bell on his left, Forrest now had his small army in a semicircle facing the Federal infantry. Rucker was on Bell's right, then came Lyon, and then Johnson on the extreme right. Both Johnson and Lyon were to the north of the Baldwyn road, facing the Ripley road. Forrest had no intention of allowing the Federal infantry time to catch their breath and become settled in their positions, and as soon as Bell had his brigade aligned where Forrest wanted them, his bugles blew the

55. *Ibid.*, 208, 191.
56. Wyeth, *That Devil Forrest*, 347.

charge, and his entire line, from end to end, swung forward.[57] But they had a fight on their hands; indeed, Hoge's men countercharged with the bayonet, and it required Forrest's and Bell's personal intervention to rally their men and resume their advance. "The battle was fierce, and the enemy obstinate," Forrest wrote.[58]

It was now nearly five o'clock. Bell and Rucker had checked Hoge's attack and were themselves attacking. Johnson, on the extreme right, was steadily forcing the left wing of Hoge's and Wilkin's lines back toward the Ripley road, their only feasible line of retreat to the trains and the support of the as-yet-unengaged brigade of Colonel Bouton. At this time, too, Colonel C. R. Barteau and his 2nd Kentucky, C.S.A., which Forrest had sent on a wide swing north to come in on Sturgis' rear, came to within charging distance of the Federal trains and Bouton's infantry at Tishomingo Creek and immediately attacked. Barteau had only 250 men, but he made noise enough for a brigade and caused someone (neither Sturgis nor Grierson mention in their reports having done so) to order the cavalry protecting Hoge's left flank to move back to Tishomingo Creek to help save the trains.[59]

The move of the cavalry to the rear exposed McMillen's left wing to the imminent danger of being encircled and denied access to their only line of retreat. With the left and center of his line already beginning to break to the rear "in considerable confusion" and the enemy about to cut the Ripley road behind him, McMillen had no choice but to give the order to retreat.[60] A sketchy rear guard of two regiments of infantry and 200 dismounted men of the 10th Missouri bought the time to allow most of McMillen's infantry to escape, but the only serious opposition to the enemy came from Colonel Bouton's two regiments, who, when their own ammunition gave out, maintained their position by using ammunition thrown away by their white brethren.

57. Colonel McMillen reported that he had not completed posting his infantry when "the enemy made a furious attack along the whole line and on each flank." *Official Records*, Vol. XXXIX, Pt. 1, p. 104.

58. *Ibid.*, 223. For Forrest's report, see *Ibid.*, 221–26. Hoge's counterattack was made by the 9th Minnesota and 93rd Indiana Regiments of Infantry. *Ibid.*, 105.

59. *Ibid.*, 121, 223.

60. *Ibid.*, 105. Sturgis' account differs from McMillen's. The disintegration, according to Sturgis, started with the giving way of the "cavalry" (not otherwise identified) he had sent to protect Hoge's right. "The scattered manner in which this cavalry came down," Sturgis said, "seemed to cause a kind of panic to the other cavalry and caused all to move to the rear." *Ibid.*, 155.

But except for these two regiments (Colonel McMillen wrote that they "fought with a gallantry which commended them to the favor of their comrades in arms") and Winslow's brigade, the army disintegrated.[61] In Sturgis' words: "Order soon gave way to confusion, and confusion to panic. . . . Everywhere the army now drifted toward the rear, and was soon altogether beyond control."[62]

The wagons of the train, now in an inextricable tangle, the guns and caissons of the artillery, and the ambulances were abandoned; rifles, ammunition, blankets were thrown away. The mob that had been Sturgis' army plodded on through the evening and the night, and all of the day and the night on the eleventh, until the men who were left reached Collierville on the morning of June 12, "worn and exhausted by the fatigues of fighting and marching for two days and two nights without rest and without eating," said Sturgis, and, he might have added, cast down by a humiliating defeat and having accomplished in forty hours a march that on the way south had taken them seven days. Missing from the ranks at Collierville were the 223 officers and men killed at Brice's Crossroads, the 394 wounded, and the 1,623 taken prisoner and missing in the battle and the retreat—nearly a quarter of the force with which Sturgis had started out.[63] The cavalry's share of the casualties was 34 killed, 105 wounded, and 194 captured and missing.[64]

Brice's Crossroads is Forrest's military masterpiece, the supreme illustration of the effect that personality and leadership qualities, added to tactical skill, can have on the conduct and outcome of a battle. It was a tribute to his tactics, as well as to the élan of his men, that

61. Bouton said to Colonel McMillen that he "thought if he could be furnished with ammunition . . . he could hold the enemy at bay. . . . I was delighted to meet with someone who expressed a determination to do something and gave the necessary orders to secure the . . . ammunition." As to Colonel Winslow, Sturgis wrote, how rightly or wrongly it is impossible to tell, "no power could now check or control the panic-stricken mass as it swept toward the rear, led off by Colonel Winslow, at the head of his brigade of cavalry, and who never halted until he had reached Stubbs', ten miles in rear." *Ibid.*, 94.

62. *Ibid.*, 93, 137, 145. See also Wyeth, *That Devil Forrest*, 366–68. Of the 926 men of Hoge's brigade who were able to escape to Collierville, 659 had lost or thrown away their guns. *Official Records*, Vol. XXXIX, Pt. 1, p. 120.

63. *Official Records*, Vol. XXXIX, Pt. 1, p. 94; Waring, *Whip and Spur*, 132–34. Forrest's provost marshal accounted for 1,618 prisoners. *Official Records*, Vol. XXXIX, Pt. 1, p. 227.

64. *Official Records*, Vol. XXXIX, Pt. 1, p. 95. Forrest reported his own losses as 96 killed and 396 wounded. *Ibid.*, 230–31.

the Federals credited him with a force of from 15,000 to as many as 20,000, instead of half the numbers they themselves had.[65] And after showing them how a battle should be fought, Forrest also showed them how a beaten enemy should be pursued. He kept up the pursuit on the evening of the tenth until it was too dark to see; he then allowed his men a brief time "to halt, feed, and rest," but resumed the pursuit at 1 A.M., himself and his escort company in the lead, and kept on the heels of the fleeing enemy as long as there were any of them left to be taken prisoner or any of their supplies to be gathered up.

One of the casualties of Brice's Crossroads was the Federal commander. The records make it abundantly clear, both directly and by implication, that he had no faith in the success of the expedition, that he had little control of the battle—he seems to have spent the major part of the day dashing from one point to another without any coherent purpose behind his movements—and no control at all of the retreat. It is quite obvious that the guidance the troops received came not from him but from Colonel McMillen and his subordinates. Faced with a situation he was unable to handle, Sturgis lost both his grip and his head. Sherman forwarded Sturgis' report of the battle to Washington with a charitable covering note ("misfortunes may befall us all, and these are rendered more likely in wooded countries, with narrow roads and deep mud"), and he was granted a "Board of Investigation" to "investigate and report the facts connected with the disaster to the late expedition," not, be it noted, to assess blame, to condemn, or to exonerate.[66] Within a day or two of his return to Memphis, Sturgis asked to be relieved of active duty. His request was granted. The Board of Investigation heard testimony from June 27 to July 30; Sturgis himself testified before it for three days. For more than a year, however, while the Civil War came to an end, Sturgis remained in limbo, "awaiting orders."[67]

As to the Union survivors of Brice's Crossroads, Colonel Waring's

65. Sherman wrote in a dispatch to Washburn: "It is all nonsense about Sturgis being attacked by 15,000 or 20,000. He was whipped by a force inferior to his own." *Ibid.*, Pt. 2, p. 124.

66. A number of witnesses testified that they and the troops in general lacked faith in Sturgis. There had been reports ("the slanderous charges with which the country is being flooded") that he was drunk at Brice's Crossroads. Nearly all the witnesses were questioned on that point by the board, but all denied that he had been. See also *Ibid.*, 124.

67. Cullum, *Biographical Register*, II, 160. Sturgis was appointed colonel of the 6th United States on August 24, 1865.

adjutant wrote in his brief sketch of the battle: "It is the fate of war that one or the other side should suffer defeat, but here there was more. The men were cowed, and there pressed upon them a sense of bitter humiliation, which rankles after nearly a quarter of a century has passed."[68]

In his report and in his testimony, Sturgis implied that his cavalry was responsible for the defeat at Brice's Crossroads, and a study of the surviving evidence makes it evident that for whatever reason, the Union cavalry failed to give a good account of itself on that occasion. It showed none of the élan, none of the remorseless drive, of the Confederate cavalry that won the battle for Forrest.

The day before Sturgis' defeat, two divisions of infantry of the XVI Army Corps, which Sherman had loaned to General Banks for the Red River Campaign, returned to Memphis in anticipation of joining General Canby in a campaign to capture Mobile. On June 14, however, Sherman learned of the disaster at Brice's Crossroads. He wrote to Secretary Stanton from Big Shanty, Georgia: "I will have the matter of Sturgis critically examined, and, if he be at fault, he shall have no mercy at my hands . . . but Forrest is the very devil, and I think he has got some of our troops under cower. I have two officers at Memphis who will fight all the time—A. J. Smith and [Joseph A.] Mower. . . . I will order them to make up a force and go out and follow Forrest to the death, if it cost 10,000 lives and breaks the Treasury. There never will be peace in Tennessee till Forrest is dead."[69]

A telegram went from Sherman to General Washburn the same day, canceling the expedition to Mobile and ordering that "Smith's command . . . go out and meet Forrest, and check him. . . . I don't see what Forrest can have except his cavalry, and the [Georgia] militia under [Samuel J.] Gholson. They should be met and defeated at any and all cost." Sherman's directions were reinforced two days later by General McPherson. Washburn was to "organize as large a force as possible . . . to pursue Forrest and punish him. This force should be large enough to deal with [him] handsomely, and will be composed of

68. *Battles and Leaders*, IV, 421n.
69. *Official Records*, Vol. XXXVIII, Pt. 4, p. 480.

infantry, cavalry and artillery, mainly of infantry, and should be got ready and started with all possible dispatch. Forrest should be followed until brought to bay somewhere and then whipped."[70] The reader will not fail to note the emphasis on the need for a large infantry component in the force to be organized.

Pursuant to these directions, Washburn assembled at LaGrange a force of about 14,000, made up of two divisions of infantry of the XVI Army Corps, commanded by General Mower and Colonel David Moore, respectively, Colonel Bouton's brigade of Negro infantry, a division of cavalry commanded by General Grierson, and twenty-four guns.[71] The expedition began its march southeast toward Ripley on July 5, the 7th Kansas marching ahead of the infantry, and Grierson's two brigades (Winslow's First, consisting of the 3rd and 4th Iowa and the 10th Missouri, and Colonel Datus E. Coon's Second, of the 9th Illinois, 2nd Iowa, and detachments of the 3rd and 7th Illinois) marching as a flank guard on parallel roads to the left (east) of the infantry, the direction from which a Confederate attack was most likely to come. Smith's advance was slow, cautious, and uneventful, with the weather, as usual, as the main source of hardship for the troops. On this occasion, it was not rain and mud, but heat and dust and the scarcity of water, that caused difficulties.[72]

Forrest learned from his scouts of Smith's march toward Ripley on the very day Smith left LaGrange. Five days later, after Smith had crossed the Tallahatchie at New Albany, Forrest knew that he was moving due south and began preparations to give him a typical Forrest reception nine miles south of Pontotoc, on a ridge lying beyond "a low swampy bottom through which . . . [ran] two creeks. This bottom was about a mile and a half in width, densely timbered, and . . . [he] rendered [it] almost impassable by felling trees across the road."[73] Smith occupied Pontotoc after driving McCulloch's brigade out of the town by means of a frontal attack by the 7th Kansas, supported by a brigade of infantry, and a simultaneous attack by Grierson on McCulloch's right

70. *Ibid.*, Vol. XXXIX, Pt. 2, pp. 115, 124.
71. The force was made up of 11,000 infantry, 3,200 cavalry, and 500 gunners. *Ibid.*, Pt. 1, p. 304; Wyeth, *That Devil Forrest*, 379.
72. For the role of the 7th Kansas, and of one of its troopers, later famous as Buffalo Bill Cody, on the march south, see Starr, *Jennison's Jayhawkers*, 305–307. See also Pierce, *History of the Second Iowa*, 97–100.
73. *Official Records*, Vol. XXXIX, Pt. 1, p. 250. For the capture of Pontotoc, see Pierce, *History of the Second Iowa*, 100–101.

flank. On the twelfth, Smith sent forward a "reconnoitering party" of the 9th Illinois, supported by the 52nd Indiana Infantry—it is to be noted that General Smith, like General McPherson, seemed to be of the opinion that cavalry needed a backup force of infantry to perform effectively even so elementary a cavalry function as a reconnaissance—and evidently received a detailed report on the formidable position Forrest had readied for his reception. He decided, wisely, not to fight Forrest on ground of the latter's choosing but to find and occupy a position favorable for the defensive and invite Forrest to attack him. Accordingly, on the morning of the thirteenth, he made a ninety-degree turn to his left and, with the cavalry division in the lead, marched off toward Tupelo and the Mobile & Ohio Railroad, eighteen miles to the east.

The 7th Kansas Jayhawkers, who had led the advance south of Smith's infantry, were again assigned the post of greatest danger on the march to Tupelo. They were to form the rear guard, to be supported when necessary by Colonel Bouton's brigade of infantry. Stephen D. Lee, who ranked Forrest by virtue of his lieutenant general's rank, as well as his position of commanding officer of the Department of Alabama, Mississippi, and East Louisiana, arrived on the evening of the twelfth. After what appears to have been a friendly debate, Lee urging Forrest to retain command of the operation inasmuch as the troops were his and accustomed to his style of leadership, and Forrest insisting that Lee, as "his superior in rank should assume and exercise the command," Forrest had his way.[74] Nevertheless, responsibility for the following day's events became the subject of acrimonious controversy in the postwar years. As soon as Smith's flank march was detected, Lee ordered Forrest to hound the rear of the Federal column with his escort company, Hinchie P. Mabry's brigade, and "Forrest's old regiment," while he himself, with the rest of Buford's and Chalmers' divisions, rode toward Tupelo on roads south of Smith's line of march, looking for an opportunity to attack the Federals in flank.

With Forrest himself directing the attacks against them, the 7th Kansas had their hands full. They were favored, however, by the terrain. Colonel Thomas P. Herrick was able to set one ambuscade after another "in the defiles and ravines of that hilly and heavily wooded country." The Jayhawkers had another factor in their favor. It was now

74. Henry, "First with the Most" Forrest, 318.

the summer of 1864; most of the enlisted men in the ranks were veterans with nearly three years of fighting experience, and more important, perhaps, most of the twenty-five officers (the 7th Kansas was a
ten-company regiment) had started as enlisted men and had earned
their commissions on merit. Nevertheless, despite the competence of
officers and men, from midmorning on, the Jayhawkers had to rely on
Bouton's infantry for help. It was by general agreement the hardest
day's fighting the regiment had ever had, and when they reached
Tupelo on the heels of the infantry, the men tumbled off their horses
and rolled up in their blankets to sleep, too tired to start their little fires
and cook supper.[75]

The battle of Tupelo (actually fought at the village of Harrisburg, a
mile away in 1864 but now a part of Tupelo), fought on the fourteenth,
was a series of attacks by Forrest's cavalry—the brigades of Lyon,
Mabry, McCulloch, Rucker, and Bell, a total of between 9,000 and
12,000 men—fighting dismounted, against Smith's infantry, lined up
on a ridge, with a wide-open field of fire and a clear view of the attackers coming toward them. Smith sustained casualties of 69 killed,
501 wounded, and 32 captured and missing. The 1,623 (or 1,618) captured and missing at Brice's Crossroads and the 602 at Tupelo is indicative of the essential difference between the two battles. Forrest reported his casualties as 210 killed and 1,116 wounded.[76]

Before the attacks on Smith's infantry began, a detachment of the
7th Kansas under Major Francis M. Malone "proceeded north from
Tupelo to Saltillo [about ten miles], thoroughly destroying the bridges
and watertanks on the line of the Mobile and Ohio Railroad."[77] Aside
from this, however, Tupelo was wholly an infantry-artillery battle.
Grierson's division was divided, one brigade being posted on each flank
of the infantry battle line, "picketing, demonstrating, and skirmishing,"

75. *Official Records*, Vol. XXXIX, Pt. 1, p. 319; Starr, *Jennison's Jayhawkers*,
308–309.

76. *Official Records*, Vol. XXXIX, Pt. 1, pp. 254–55, 324; *Battles and Leaders*, IV,
422n. The latter gives Forrest's casualties as 153 killed, 794 wounded, and 49 missing.
The commanding officer of every regiment of Bell's brigade was killed or wounded in
these attacks. For descriptions of the battle as a whole, see *Official Records*, Vol. XXXIX,
Pt. 1, pp. 251–52, 322–23; *Battles and Leaders*, IV, 421–22; Wyeth, *That Devil Forrest*, 383–96; Henry, *"First with the Most" Forrest*, 318–24; Pierce, *History of the Second Iowa*, 103–106; R. R. Hancock, *Hancock's Diary; or, A History of the Second
Tennessee Cavalry* (Nashville, 1887), 430. The figure of 9,000 as Forrest's strength is
Henry's (p. 319); the 12,000 figure is in *Battles and Leaders*, IV, 421.

77. *Official Records*, Vol. XXXIX, Pt. 1, p. 319; see also *Ibid.*, 305, 252.

but some of the men were at times dismounted to act as skirmishers in front of the infantry.[78]

The Tupelo battle did not by any means "whip" Forrest, but as General Washburn wrote in a somewhat self-congratulatory dispatch, the result of the expedition was "most satisfactory, and has thoroughly retrieved the disaster to . . . Sturgis. . . . [Forrest's] power has been very greatly impaired. . . . In addition to the great number of killed and wounded, the country has been filled with deserters and stragglers from the enemy endeavoring to get home." Notwithstanding this brave talk, however, the ending of the campaign was anticlimactic. On the morning after the battle, "it was found" that Smith's army had only one day's rations of hardtack left in the wagons, owing to the fact that much of it was already spoiled when it was drawn from the commissary warehouse in Memphis. This shortage of hardtack, coupled with the reduction of the artillery ammunition to what Smith considered an unsafe level by the previous day's battle, caused him to decide that he had done enough and that it was time to return to his base, which he accomplished in good order on July 21.[79]

The shortage of hardtack reported by General Smith was real enough. One of the troopers of the 7th Kansas recorded that on the march north, the cavalry were issued one hardtack per day; the foot-soldiers received two. The cavalry were doubtless assumed to be able to make up the difference, or more, by foraging. As to the horses, General Grierson reported after he reached LaGrange that "owing to the slow rate of march, the horses . . . [were] in fair condition." Colonel Winslow supplied more precise and more meaningful information. He reported that he had "marched a distance of 350 miles, a great part of the way being over very broken and barren country affording but little forage or water. With great difficulty the animals were supplied with about three-quarters rations of forage, consisting principally of wheat and oats in sheaf." Of the 1,325 horses with which he started the campaign, Winslow lost 19 killed, 32 wounded, and 40 abandoned, for a total of 91; by the standard of other campaigns, such losses were minute.[80]

Generals Smith and Washburn may have thought that the fight at

78. *Ibid.*, 304, 317.
79. *Ibid.*, 249, 252; see also Wyeth, *That Devil Forrest*, 400.
80. Starr, *Jennison's Jayhawkers*, 310; *Official Records*, Vol. XXXIX, Pt. 1, pp. 305, 307.

Tupelo had clipped Forrest's wings, but General Sherman did not think so. Indeed, he wired Washburn on July 20, "Order Smith to pursue and keep after Forrest all the time."[81] Thus urged on, Washburn asked the secretary of war for two batteries to replace guns that Sturgis had lost and told him, "General Smith whipped Forrest very badly in his late campaign, but I want to keep whipping him until his power is destroyed." It must be said that both Washburn and Smith proceeded with an energy that had not always been in evidence in Memphis previously, to assemble and equip forces for a new campaign. To make certain that lack of rations did not again force a premature retreat, the Memphis & Charleston was rebuilt as far east as Grand Junction, and the Mississippi Central thence south to Holly Springs, the latter to serve once again as a base of supplies.[82] As early as August 2, Washburn was able to send Sherman a flamboyant message to let him know that he had "sent forward a force that can whip the combined force of the enemy this side of Georgia and east of the Mississippi." Smith did in fact leave Memphis on July 29, with 10,000 of his own infantry, three Minnesota regiments of infantry of unknown size, 3,000 "colored troops from Memphis," and a 4,000-man "Cavalry Corps" commanded by Grierson and made up of the divisions of General Hatch and Colonel Kargé, the latter of whom took command of the division when Colonel Winslow became incapacitated.[83]

In the absence of a report by General Smith, it is impossible to tell what his plans were, but whatever they may have been, Forrest was not "whipped." Quite the contrary. Led by the cavalry, Smith's march south from Holly Springs was even more leisurely than his march to Pontotoc had been. The elements were at least partly to blame, for the August of 1864, unlike the normally dry Mississippi August, went down in local lore as "the wet August." It rained hard nearly every day, every stream and creek the command had to cross was out of its banks, and between rainstorms it was oppressively hot. Except at the crossings of the Tallahatchie and Hurricane Creek, the latter a short distance north of Oxford, Smith's cavalry had little opposition to face. Yet its progress, presumably because it was held down to the pace of the

---

81. *Official Records*, Vol. XXXIX, Pt. 2, p. 184. In an attack on the rear of Smith's column, as it was going into camp at Old Town Creek on the fifteenth, Forrest was painfully wounded on his right foot. Wyeth, *That Devil Forrest*, 402.

82. *Official Records*, Vol. XXXIX, Pt. 2, p. 204, 208.

83. *Ibid.*, 242, and Pt. 1, p. 371.

infantry, was exceedingly slow—it took three days, for example, to cover the thirty miles from Holly Springs to Oxford. Forrest, marching west from Okolona, reached Oxford on the evening of the tenth. His numbers had been reduced by his losses at Tupelo, detachments, and the straggling and desertion that were endemic in Confederate armies, to about 5,000, the brigades of Bell, Mabry, McCulloch, and James J. Neely.

On August 10, General Hatch had driven Chalmers' cavalry from the crossing of Hurricane Creek and through and beyond Oxford, but then he retreated to Abbeville, ten miles to the north. He then moved forward a second time, but on this occasion he was held up for three days at the Hurricane Creek crossing by stiff resistance that he was eventually able to overcome, although he was then ordered to return to the Tallahatchie. It is impossible to discern any coherent plan or purpose in these repeated advances and retreats of the Union cavalry. No doubt the resistance put up by Forrest in the week after his arrival at Oxford was a factor, but even if he had been able to place every one of his men in the firing line, he would have been outnumbered four to one and should not have been allowed to hold in check so long forces so much larger than his own. His ability to do it was made possible by what can only be viewed as a lack of enterprise on the part of his antagonist.

Enterprise, or daring, was a quality Forrest had in full measure, as he was about to demonstrate, and not for the first time. Late on the afternoon of August 18, he assembled his entire command, selected 2,000 of the best-mounted men, and started off on the most spectacular of his raids. He went from Oxford west to the crossing of the Tallahatchie at Panola, then north, first across flooded, sixty-foot-wide Hickala Creek (the "bridge" he had his men build in an hour to get them across was a masterpiece of ingenuity, skill, and hard work), and then to a crossing of the Coldwater River, also in flood, and finally at 3:15 A.M. on Sunday, August 21, to the center of Memphis, a journey of nearly a hundred miles in two and a half days.[84] This was not General Smith's style of marching, but it was Forrest's, and it had the effect he intended. General Chalmers, left behind at Oxford, had done a

84. For the Hickala Creek bridge, see Hancock, *Hancock's Diary*, 446. See also J. M. Hubbard, *Notes of a Private* (Memphis, 1909), 128; *Official Records*, Vol. XXXIX, Pt. 2, p. 282.

masterful job with his 3,000 to keep General Smith with his 20,000 blinded, busy, and immobile, and when word came south of Forrest's presence in Memphis, Smith began immediately to retreat.[85] He did so in such haste that he left undamaged the railroad bridge over the Tallahatchie at Panola and left undisturbed, for the Confederates to use after he was gone, a ninety-seven-mile telegraph line. About the only accomplishment of Smith's forces, but hardly one to boast about, was the burning of the courthouse and other public buildings at Oxford, set on fire, as the adjutant of the 7th Kansas explained, because on "the day this was done, Southern newspapers fell into our hands glorying over the burning of Chambersburg [Pennsylvania] . . . and Oxford was burned in retaliation."[86]

85. In an encounter with Chalmers on August 19, a torrential rain "soon rendered the Sharp's carbines, with which the Seventh Kansas were armed, unserviceable, when the Second Iowa, whose Spencer carbines were impervious to rain, were sent to relieve them. We now had it all our own way, for the rain had been as injurious to the rifles of the enemy as to the carbines of the Seventh Kansas, while our pieces emitted their deadly stream with as much certainty as if the day had been one of cloudless beauty." Pierce, *History of the Second Iowa*, 112–13.

86. Henry, *"First with the Most" Forrest*, 343, 341; Starr, *Jennison's Jayhawkers*, 314. Chambersburg, Pennsylvania, had been burned by Jubal Early's cavalry on July 30. For Smith's expedition as a whole and Forrest's Memphis Raid, see Henry, *"First with the Most" Forrest*, 328–42, and Wyeth, *That Devil Forrest*, 406–17.

XVIII

And Charge with All Thy Chivalry

THE EXPEDITIONS OF GENERALS STURGIS AND A. J. SMITH, described earlier, had a common goal: to cripple Nathan Bedford Forrest and make it impossible for him to interfere with the second (and in all essential respects, the more important) prong of Grant's design for beating the life out of the Confederacy, namely William Tecumseh Sherman's campaign to capture Atlanta. Discussions of the campaign, which was to coincide with the forward move of the Army of the Potomac against General Robert E. Lee's army, began in early March, upon Grant's appointment as general-in-chief of the Union armies. Active preparations for the campaign got under way on March 18, with the appointment of Sherman to succeed Grant in command of the Military Division of the Mississippi.

Toward the end of March, Sherman met in council with Generals McPherson, Thomas, and Schofield, commanding, respectively, the Armies of the Tennessee, Cumberland, and Ohio, which were to combine for the campaign with what had been two separate commands of infantry, the IV Army Corps of Gordon Granger (succeeded by Oliver O. Howard), and the newly created XX Army Corps, formed by the consolidation of the XI and XII Corps, which had been rushed west under Joseph Hooker at the time of the post-Chickamauga crisis. The three army commanders and Sherman "conversed freely and frankly on all matters of interest then in progress and impending"—not omitting the fate of high-ranking personalities. As Sherman explained in his reminiscences:

The great question of the campaign was one of supplies. Nashville, our chief depot, was itself partially in a hostile country, and even the routes of supply from Louisville to Nashville by rail, and by way of the Cumberland River, had to be guarded. Chattanooga (our starting point) was one hundred and thirty-six miles in front of Nashville, and every foot of the way, especially the many bridges, trestles, and culverts, had to be strongly guarded against the acts of a local hostile population and of the enemy's cavalry. Then, of course, as we advanced into Georgia, it was manifest that we should have to repair a railroad, use it, and guard it likewise.[1]

Thus was spelled out the first of the assignments of Sherman's cavalry: to protect his rail lifeline by means of defensive operations—to "guard" the railroads in the narrow sense of the word—and also by means of active preemptive operations against the enemy's cavalry—Forrest's and also that of other Confederate commanders—to keep them away from the railroad. The second and more traditional assignment of the cavalry was to accompany Sherman's infantry in their advance against the Army of Tennessee, commanded since December 27 by General Joseph E. Johnston.

The Confederates had wintered at Dalton, Georgia, and had been improved in "instruction, discipline and spirit" and increased in numbers, to just under 43,000 by General Johnston's account, or by another account to 53,000, by the end of April.[2] When General Johnston took over command of the army from Braxton Bragg, 6,000 of the infantry were without guns, about the same number lacked blankets, "and it was painful to see the number of bare feet in every regiment." It may be assumed that these shortages had been overcome for the most part by the end of April. Only about a third of Wheeler's cavalry were actually present with the Army of Tennessee. In January, Johnston had reported those under his eye as "not very efficient." The "want of harmony among the superior officers," he wrote, "causes its discipline to be imperfect."[3] Johnston added that he intended to improve the discipline of his cavalry, but the extent to which he succeeded in doing so may be open to doubt.

The Atlanta Campaign opened on May 5 with Sherman in command of a "grand aggregate" of 110,123 officers and men of all arms

---

1. Sherman, *Memoirs*, II, 8–9.
2. *Battles and Leaders*, IV, 261, 281n. Connelly, *Autumn of Glory*, 325, states that Johnston had 41,300 "effective infantrymen" on May 7.
3. Johnston, *Narrative of Military Operations*, 279, 273.

and 254 guns, divided among the three armies mentioned previously.[4] The Army of the Cumberland, by far the largest, in addition to its three corps of infantry, had divisional artillery, a separate artillery brigade, and some unattached troops, and totaled just over 64,000 men. It also had a Cavalry Corps commanded by General Washington L. Elliott numbering 9,826, rank and file, divided among the divisions of Edward M. McCook (now a brigadier general), Kenner Garrard, and Judson Kilpatrick. McCook's First Division contained the brigades of Colonel Joseph B. Dorr (8th Iowa, 2nd Michigan, 1st Tennessee, 4th Kentucky Mounted Infantry), Oscar H. LaGrange (2nd and 4th Indiana, 1st Wisconsin), and Louis D. Watkins (4th, 6th, and 7th Kentucky). Garrard's Second Division was made up of the brigades of Colonels Robert H. G. Minty (4th Michigan, 7th Pennsylvania, 4th United States), Eli Long (1st, 3rd, and 4th Ohio) and John T. Wilder (98th and 123rd Illinois, 17th and 72nd Indiana Regiments of Mounted Infantry). Kilpatrick's Third Division consisted of the brigades of Colonels Robert Klein (5th Iowa, four companies of the 3rd Indiana), Charles C. Smith (8th Indiana, 2nd Kentucky, 10th Ohio), and Eli H. Murray (3rd and 5th Kentucky, 92nd Illinois Mounted Infantry). Each of the three divisions had attached to it a battery of artillery.

Nearly all the cavalry that had been a part of General McPherson's Army of the Tennessee was left behind at Memphis; hence, with his three army corps of 23,702 infantry and artillery, he had only two regiments of cavalry (1st Alabama, 5th Ohio) plus several odd companies serving as escorts, the whole numbering 678 of all ranks. Since in the early stages of the campaign McPherson's infantry, on the right flank, served as the mobile body whose job it was to unhinge the Confederate position, Kilpatrick's division was attached to the Army of the Tennessee. The Army of the Ohio had Stoneman's cavalry of 2,891, rank and file, to go with its 9,971 footsoldiers and gunners. Stoneman had under him Colonel Israel Garrard's First Brigade (9th Michigan, 7th Ohio), Colonel James Biddle's Second Brigade (16th Illinois, 12th Kentucky, 5th and 6th Indiana), Colonel Horace Capron's Third Brigade (14th Illinois, 8th Michigan, McLaughlin's Squadron of Ohio Cavalry),

---

4. This and the figures that follow are as of April 30 and are taken from *Official Records*, Vol. XXXVIII, Pt. 1, p. 115. The strength figures in Sherman, *Memoirs*, II, 23–24, are considerably (and in the case of the cavalry, inexplicably) lower. The organization of the cavalry of the three armies is in *Official Records*, Vol. XXXVIII, Pt. 1, pp. 89–114.

and Colonel Alexander W. Holeman's "Independent Brigade" (1st and 11th Kentucky). On August 11, the command was reorganized as a division under Garrard (Stoneman and many of his men having been taken prisoner), consisting of two brigades, one designated "Mounted" and the other "Dismounted."[5]

The reader will note that Sherman's organization of his cavalry into brigades, divisions, and corps followed the pattern that by the spring of 1864 had become the accepted thing, in the West as well as in the East. It is also worth noting that nearly all the cavalry and mounted infantry regiments that made the Atlanta Campaign were units of veterans, commanded at all levels by officers who, for the most part, were themselves tried and tested veterans. What little information on the subject is available suggests that the condition of the mounted troops available to Sherman was generally good at the start of the campaign. Kenner Garrard's division, with 3,000 horses available on April 27, received 2,000 more that day, to raise its mounted strength to 5,000. Kilpatrick, normally a Pollyanna, reported his division "in good condition . . . ready and anxious for an order to strike the enemy."[6] The 7th Pennsylvania, after a "jubilant" reception when it reached home on veterans' furlough, returned to the army in early March with enough recruits to fill its ranks to the prescribed maximum plus a surplus of 600 men, and through the generosity of the Ordnance Department in Washington, it also had received "complete sets of horse equipments, Spencer carbines and sabers" to outfit the entire regiment. General Elliott, who inspected the Pennsylvanians just before the start of the campaign, found them with "every company full to the maximum, perfectly armed and equipped, and mounted upon horses of a uniform color," a showy luxury nearly unheard of so late in the war.[7] The 1st

---

5. It will be of interest to note the following tabulation (from *Official Records*, Vol. XXXVIII, Pt. 1, p. 117) of the strength of Sherman's cavalry from the start of the campaign to the capture of Atlanta:

April 30	12,455
May 31	12,908
June 30	12,039
July 31	10,517
August 31	9,398

6. *Ibid.*, Vol. XXXII, Pt. 3, pp. 511, 514, Vol. XXXVIII, Pt. 4, p. 97.

7. Sipes, *The Seventh Pennsylvania*, 95–96. The 9th Pennsylvania, which had its veterans' furlough a few weeks later, gained 621 recruits. Service in the cavalry was seemingly as attractive in the spring of 1864 as it had been three years before. Not sur-

Ohio, too, entered on the Atlanta Campaign, after its return from veterans' furlough, "better mounted, better armed and equipped, and better drilled, than ever before."[8]

As far as horses were concerned, appearances were misleading—even the splendors of the 7th Pennsylvania. The regiment had drawn 919 animals from the government corrals at Nashville. As was the case with newly purchased horses throughout the war, all the horses were untrained, and the majority were also too young for cavalry duty. Nearly half of these "green" horses were issued to the new recruits, some of whom "had never been on a horse" and many of whom had to learn the rudiments of caring for their animals.[9]

Colonel Watkins of McCook's division had an even grimmer experience with the government corrals at Nashville as a source of supply of horses for his brigade. "The great majority" of the 762 "convalescent" horses issued to him just before the start of the campaign were "nothing but skin and bones and the very best of them unfit for any kind of use"; his efforts to nurse the animals back to sound health were hampered by his inability to obtain "a full supply of forage" and by lack of grazing in the area. Despite his best efforts, "great numbers" of the 762 died, and "many were abandoned."[10]

Measured by the quality of the horses issued to the cavalry throughout the war and their suitability for hard service, the horses given to the 7th Pennsylvania were probably no better and no worse than the average. Indeed, the entire brigade of which the Pennsylvanians were a part had its "men and horses in good condition, good health, and also excellent spirits." At the start of the campaign, the 72nd Indiana Mounted Infantry of the Wilder brigade had "more men mounted, and they were mounted on better horses, than ever before," and officers were more particular about the way the men took care of their horses than ever before.[11]

As far as can be determined from the records, General Stoneman's Army of the Ohio cavalry was in a worse case than any of its fellows. In

---

prisingly, however, the veterans in the regiment formed "a closed club" that the recruits were unable to get into. Rowell, *Yankee Cavalrymen*, 175, 192.

8. Curry, *Four Years in the Saddle*, 164.

9. Alonzo Gray, *Cavalry Tactics as Illustrated by the War of the Rebellion* (Fort Leavenworth, Kans., 1910), 162.

10. *Official Records*, Vol. XXXVIII, Pt. 4, pp. 792–93; see also *Ibid.*, 797.

11. Vale, *Minty and the Cavalry*, 280; McGee, *History of the 72nd Indiana*, 291.

early April, Stoneman had taken over from Sturgis the task of re-mounting, reequipping, and reorganizing the cavalry of the Army of the Ohio, and he fell heir to all the delays and difficulties Sturgis had complained about. Still, he was able to report on April 18 that he ex-pected to have his entire force of 6,000 armed and equipped by May 1. Before that date, however, Schofield sent him orders to join the army with all the cavalry that was then ready and to let the rest follow "as soon as practicable." Stoneman replied the next day that he was starting out from Nicholasville with 2,000 men "fitted for the field"; of those he was leaving behind, 2,300 were mounted and equipped, but only partially armed. The rest, numbering about 1,700, "had nothing. . . . some [had] pistols without cases and carbines without slings," and neither horses nor pack mules were being received as fast as had been promised.[12]

Stoneman reached the army at Dalton with his initial lot of horse-men, increasing Schofield's cavalry to 3,190.[13] The story of the 1st Kentucky's march south, starting out 800 strong and arriving at Dalton with 2 officers and 71 men in the ranks, the rest, all of whom turned up eventually, having dropped out on the way to "visit the folks," has already been told.[14] Even aside from this, Stoneman's troubles con-tinued. He reported to Sherman shortly after the start of the cam-paign: "One great difficulty I have to contend against is the utter in-competency of subordinate officers. I have to post and put in every regiment myself and send out every party. I know that my movements appear tardy, but I can't help it; it is next to impossible to get up a trot even on the field. I called upon the regimental commanders night be-fore last for a report, giving the number of horses able to make a vig-orous night push, and the sum total out of the command was 1,238."[15] On the subject of horses, Stoneman wrote to General Schofield a few days later: "You must use your cavalry sparingly, and recollect that the horses, green and new, have averaged nearly twenty miles a day for the past twenty-three days, and that without hay or grass; and have on the average been under the saddle three-fifths of every day, or you will soon be without cavalry. . . . [I] consider it my duty to inform you

12. *Official Records*, Vol. XXXII, Pt. 3, pp. 269, 302, 361, 399, 500, 512.

13. *Ibid.*, Vol. XXXVIII, Pt. 2, p. 510, Pt. 4, p. 23.

14. See Vol. I, p. 171 of the present work. See also Tarrant, *Wild Riders of the First Kentucky*, 318–19.

15. *Official Records*, Vol. XXXVIII, Pt. 4, p. 268.

that our horses (I find from an inspection to-day) are pretty nearly played out." [16]

These reports of Stoneman's about the state of his horses were made when the campaign was barely under way. Efforts were made to spare the animals. Sherman himself thought it well to remind Kenner Garrard to make his men dismount and lead their horses when ascending or descending a mountain, and there is some evidence that the admonition filtered down to, and was actually observed, at the regimental level. "In no case," the historian of the 72nd Indiana Mounted Infantry reports, "were we to ride . . . [our horses] out of ranks; and if by chance a soldier should ride his horse faster than a walk he was promptly dismounted and compelled to lead his horse the balance of the day. . . . We were never allowed to ride up or down a hill." [17]

Despite such precautions, however, the loss of horses remained great, principally because of lack of forage. The historian of the 72nd Indiana Mounted Infantry noted on May 29: "Our horses had not had any grain for five days, and scores of them fell dead in the road that night. . . . [The foragers returned] with nothing but a few small bunches of green wheat in bloom which, in the exhausted state of our horses, was little better than nothing." By June 2, the regiment had lost a third of the horses with which it had begun the campaign less than a month before. Nor were such conditions confined to the Lightning Brigade. On May 19, Colonel Minty, acting on orders from General Garrard to move from Kingston, Georgia, to Gillem's Bridge across the Etowah River five miles away "at the gallop and hold the bridge at all hazards," reported that the five-mile gallop "rendered about 300 horses totally unserviceable." [18]

The horses of the 7th Pennsylvania were reported as starving

for want of feed. Five days without a mouthful of grain or hay. They peeled the bark from the trees. They ate dry leaves. They chewed the bridle reins and the picket lines. On the first of June . . . we distributed one quart of corn to each horse. . . . Our cavalry was ordered back to Etowah river for feed and rations. Over fifty horses dropped in the road from exhaustion, and were left to die, or by chance to be nursed by some poor family who were glad to own a horse that was so near dead that the soldiers did not want him. Some of

---

16. *Ibid.*, 287.
17. *Ibid.*, 29; McGee, *History of the 72nd Indiana*, 291, 294.
18. *Ibid.*, 305–306; *Official Records*, Vol. XXXVIII, Pt. 2, pp. 811–12.

these families, we know, did "right smart" ploughing with these broken-down chargers.[19]

After the capture of Atlanta, Major William H. Jennings, then in command of the 7th Pennsylvania, wrote, as has been mentioned, that the regiment began the campaign with 919 horses. On May 22, when the regiment received "the first forage the horses had for three days," during which time the animals had been under saddle for sixty of the seventy-two hours, company commanders reported 76 horses "as died of starvation and abandoned." The regimental veterinarian inspected the remaining animals that morning and "pronounced 43 more unserviceable and unfit to travel." The subsequent fate of the remaining miserable animals will be described later. It may be mentioned now, however, that in the entire campaign the regiment lost 401 horses, 230 "abandoned & died," and 171 "killed . . . [or] captured by the enemy."[20]

On June 2, General McCook wrote General Elliott that the horses of his division were "absolutely dying of starvation; five from one company dropped on picket this morning, totally exhausted for want of something to eat. The green wheat and leaves, the only food we can procure, neither strengthens nor nourishes them. I tell you their condition now so that you may not rely upon the division as serviceable, for it certainly is not."[21]

The reports concerning the state of the horses that have been cited could not have made their way up the chain of command to General Sherman, for he wrote on May 17 from Resaca to General Halleck: "It will take five days to repair the railroad bridge here. We are abundantly supplied, and our animals are improving on the grass and grain fields, which now afford good pasture."[22]

The Atlanta Campaign, in which Sherman, utilizing his nearly two-to-one numerical superiority, maneuvered the Army of Tennessee out of one well-chosen defensive position after another, from Dalton south to

19. Dornblaser, Sabre Strokes of the Pennsylvania Dragoons, 160–61; see also Sipes, The Seventh Pennsylvania, 118–19.

20. Letter of September 13, 1864, 7th Pennsylvania Volunteer Cavalry, Regimental and Company Order and Letter Books, Record Group 94, National Archives. The report also appears in Official Records, Vol. XXXVIII, Pt. 2, pp. 832–33.

21. Official Records, Vol. XXXVIII, Pt. 4, p. 387; see also Pt. 5, p. 67.

22. Ibid., Pt. 4, p. 219.

Kingston and then southeast across a succession of rivers and ridges to the outskirts of Atlanta, was almost wholly an infantry-artillery operation. Not until the preliminaries of the crossing of the Chattahoochee, within sight of Atlanta, was the Union cavalry given an independent role. In the first two months of the campaign, the cavalry, sometimes in brigade strength, less frequently in divisional strength, played a purely auxiliary role, leading the advance or protecting the flanks of the infantry, staging demonstrations to mislead the enemy, and scouting. At no time in the approach of the army to Atlanta was the united body of the cavalry, or even a major portion of it, turned loose against the enemy.[23] Even in the operation leading to the crossing of the Chattahoochee, Kenner Garrard and Stoneman were widely separated, Garrard several miles upstream and Stoneman several miles downstream of the main army. One at least of Sherman's cavalrymen, Edward McCook, was displeased by the limited scope of the warlike operations he was ordered to perform. He wrote General Elliott on June 23: "I am so tired of taking my share of this fight in little skirmishess [sic] and scouting parties that I would risk cheerfully the lives and wind of the few anatomical steeds I have left for the purpose of getting my proportion of the glory, if there is any for the cavalry, of this campaign. I recognize the certainty that whatever is done must be done quickly, if we do it mounted."[24]

General Sherman would doubtless have explained his lack of imagination in failing to make greater and more effective use of his cavalry by mentioning three inhibiting factors. He believed, first, that General Johnston's cavalry outnumbered his own (actually, the two mounted forces were nearly identical in numbers).[25] Of greater significance was

23. In turning down Frank P. Blair's request for two companies of cavalry to be assigned to his corps, Sherman wrote: "During our operations here . . . our cavalry must all be kept on the grand flanks and our communications. . . . I insist on all organized cavalry being massed on our flanks and rear." *Ibid.*, 541.

24. *Ibid.*, 575. On April 13, McCook sent to General Thomas "papers, memoranda, maps, etc.," including a map of Atlanta and vicinity, found on Captain F. R. R. Smith of Johnston's corps of engineers, whom McCook's scouts had captured. Wheeler, with 2,500 of his cavalry, was encamped twenty-six miles from McCook. Said McCook, in his sprightly manner, "If the general commanding sees proper to give me permission, I will give them so much work defending their own camp and outposts that they will have neither time nor opportunity to annoy me." Whatever McCook's shortcomings may have been, he did not seem to lack the "cavalry spirit." *Ibid.*, Pt. 3, pp. 341–42.

25. *Ibid.*, Pt. 4, pp. 219, 456; *Battles and Leaders*, IV, 281. By mid-May, Sherman's cavalry numbered 12,908; Johnston's, after he was joined by General W. H. Jackson's division, numbered 12,913.

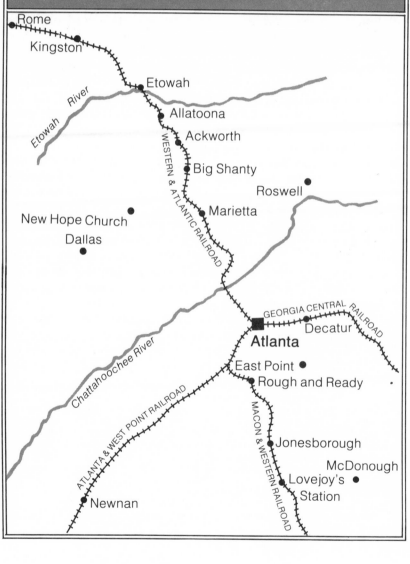

UNION CAVALRY OPERATIONS AROUND ATLANTA; SUMMER OF 1864

0   10
MILES

Rome

Kingston

Etowah River

Etowah

Allatoona

Ackworth

WESTERN & ATLANTIC RAILROAD

Big Shanty

Roswell

New Hope Church

Marietta

Dallas

Chattahoochee River

GEORGIA CENTRAL RAILROAD

Decatur

Atlanta

East Point

Rough and Ready

ATLANTA & WEST POINT RAILROAD

MACON & WESTERN RAILROAD

Jonesborough

McDonough

Lovejoy's Station

Newnan

the second factor, mentioned frequently in Federal cavalry reports, namely the terrain along the route of the campaign. In McCook's words, it was an area that could not have been "worse . . . to handle cavalry in," and two months later General Garrard reported, "The country being so unfavorable for cavalry, I was unable to reap the fruits of the victory gained by my dismounted men."[26] The third and probably decisive factor was Sherman's downright distrust of the reliability of his cavalry commanders. He knew he could count on McPherson, Thomas, and Schofield, and with reservations, even on Hooker, but his dispatches make it evident that he did not have an equal faith in Elliott, Stoneman, Garrard, or Kilpatrick.

Within ten days of the start of the campaign, Sherman sent orders from near Resaca to General Garrard: "If you can possibly cross Oostenaula make a strike for the [Western & Atlantic] railroad anywhere near Kingston. Do this in your own way, but do it thoroughly and well. . . . If it be impossible to cross the Oostenaula with even a raiding force, then threaten Rome, and the Coosa below Rome, that the enemy may not receive provisions, forage, or reenforcements from that direction. Make your own arrangements as to wagons and artillery; the less wheels you have, the better; but I leave it to you—only act with the utmost possible energy and celerity."[27]

From the standpoint of the commander of a division of cavalry, these were ideal orders. They gave him an independent operation, an alternate objective if the primary goal proved unattainable, and his freedom of action was not hedged about by elaborate restrictions. The following day, however, Sherman had to write to Garrard: "I regret exceedingly you did not avail yourself of the chance I gave you to cut the railroad. . . . Now [William T.] Martin's and Wheeler's divisions are covering the retreat of Johnston for Allatoona, and I want you to dash in and strike the retreating masses in flank and all round. Leave your artillery at the bridge, or better still, throw it into the Oostenaula and operate rapidly against the enemy. . . . Now, do not spare horseflesh, but strike boldly."[28] Two weeks later, Sherman sent Garrard orders to rush and seize Allatoona Pass, about halfway between Kingston and

26. *Official Records*, Vol. XXXVIII, Pt. 2, pp. 750, 808. In another connection McCook spoke of "a hilly, wooded country, utterly unfit for cavalry operations." *Ibid.*, 466.
27. *Ibid.*, Pt. 4, p. 187, Pt. 2, p. 803.
28. *Ibid.*, Pt. 4, pp. 197–98.

Marietta. "If you find the road occupied," he wrote, "attack the cavalry with cavalry and the infantry with dismounted men, and force your way into and through the pass. . . . Do not be deterred by appearances, but act boldly and promptly; the success of our movement depends on our having Allatoona Pass."[29] On this occasion, Garrard succeeded in fulfilling his mission, but to be told that he was not to be "deterred by appearances" should and must have rankled.

In mid-June, in a "not purely official" letter to Grant, Sherman wrote: "Our cavalry is dwindling away. We cannot get full forage and have to graze, so that the cavalry is always unable to attempt anything. Garrard is over-cautious, and I think Stoneman is lazy. . . . Each has had fine chances of cutting in but were easily checked by the appearance of the enemy."[30]

As the armies continued their slow movement southward, under a daily downpour from June 2 on, Sherman's orders to Garrard became increasingly sharp in tone. On June 10, in a dispatch from Big Shanty, after explaining that Johnston had "detached largely from his cavalry" to attack Sherman's railroad lifeline far to the rear, he prefaced his orders to Garrard with a wounding remark: "Surely if . . . [the enemy] cavalry can make such marches ours should do something." The orders were to circle around behind Johnston's army and "threaten, if not attack, the railroad between Marietta and the Chattahoochee."[31] After a week's delay, Garrard replied from the north bank of an obscure watercourse "not over twenty feet across" named Noonday Creek with suggestions for getting infantry across the creek out of sight of the enemy but saying nothing about his own plans to comply with Sherman's orders of June 10. This brought down on his head, as it should have, Sherman's wrath. Had Sherman been Sheridan, Garrard would have been relieved of his command and ordered to the rear, but among the traits of this most fascinatingly complex commanding officer was an

29. *Ibid.*, 367, and Pt. 2, p. 804.
30. *Ibid.*, Pt. 4, p. 507. Among cavalry commanders of lesser note, Colonel LaGrange was wounded and captured by the enemy on May 9, Kilpatrick was wounded on May 13 and did not rejoin his division until July 23, and on June 9 Colonel Wilder had to give up command of his brigade because of illness. His place was taken by Colonel Abram O. Miller. *Ibid.*, Pt. 2, pp. 751, 858, 848. A gunner of the 18th Indiana Battery, now a part of McCook's division, commented on Colonel LaGrange's wounding: "His loss will be very great to our Div. as he was the best officer we had in the div. by far." Rowell, *Yankee Artillerymen*, 196.
31. *Official Records*, Vol. XXXVIII, Pt. 4, p. 450.

amazing tolerance for the shortcomings of his subordinates, and all that happened to Garrard was that he received a severe rebuke: "The enemy has detached a great part of his cavalry back to our line of railroad where they are doing mischief. Now, if they can cross the Etowah, the Oostenaula, and Connesauga—large streams—it does seem that you can cross the little Noonday. I therefore order you to cross and advance against the enemy's cavalry. . . . Take no artillery or wagons with you, and leave all dismounted and ineffective men, but with the balance attack the enemy's cavalry and drive it back and interpose between the enemy and their detached infantry." [32] Poor Garrard pointed out the next day that he had tried five times in ten days to cross Noonday Creek, and that it was the enemy's cavalry, greatly outnumbering his, and not the creek, that prevented him from effecting a lodgement on the south bank. Having said this much, he came to the real point. "I regret exceedingly," he wrote,

that on several occasions the major-general commanding has seen fit to write as if he were dissatisfied with my activity and zeal. . . . The cavalry is a special arm of the service, and the commander of a division, situated on one of the flanks like mine, should possess the full confidence of the commanding general. Unless such is the case his sphere of usefulness is materially injured. . . . My service with the cavalry this campaign has been very unsatisfactory, for I have been made to feel more than once that it was not equal to the occasion. . . . Should the general commanding desire a change in command of this division, I will most cheerfully yield it and take command of a brigade of infantry. [33]

This polite but firm rejoinder caused Sherman to beat a graceful retreat and reestablish friendly relations with his unhappy subordinate. In the middle of a lengthy reply dealing with operational matters in his normal matter-of-fact tone, he wrote, "I assure you, spite of any little disappointment I may have expressed, I feel for you personally not only respect but affection, and wish for you unmeasured success and reputation, but I do wish to inspire all cavalry with my conviction that caution and prudence should be but a very small element in their characters." [34]

It is worthy of note that in these exchanges, Sherman dealt directly with Garrard, bypassing both General Thomas and General Elliott,

32. *Ibid.*, 542.
33. *Ibid.*, 555.
34. *Ibid.*, Pt. 5, p. 76.

to whose army and corps Garrard and his division belonged. Those who recall the famous Meade-Sheridan confrontation of May 8, 1864, over Meade's issuance of orders directly to Sheridan's divisional commanders, may wonder what might have happened on this occasion if Sheridan had been in Elliott's place.

This account of the Sherman-Garrard exchanges would not be complete without mention of the fact that on June 20, the day before General Garrard wrote his pained dispatch, Colonel Minty did in fact cross the creek but was then attacked "by Wheeler with six brigades, viz: Allen's, Iverson's, Hannon's, Williams', and Dibrell's. About 500 men of the Seventh Pennsylvania and Fourth Michigan . . . fought Williams', Hannon's, and Anderson's brigades for over two hours. The Seventh Pennsylvania and Fourth Michigan each made one saber charge, and two battalions of the Fourth Michigan repulsed three saber charges made by Anderson's brigade of regular cavalry." Minty was then reinforced by the Wilder brigade, but a charge of the six Confederate brigades, dismounted, drove him back across the creek with the loss of 65 killed, wounded, and missing.[35]

By the end of June, Sherman had succeeded in compelling Johnston to retreat to the Chattahoochee, seven miles northwest of Atlanta as it then was. There had been battles of some severity at Resaca, Adairsville, Cassville, Pickett's Mills and New Hope Church, Big Shanty, Brush Mountain, and on June 27, the major battle of the campaign at Kennesaw Mountain. But despite the apparent frequency of these engagements and despite the number of men killed, wounded, and missing (Sherman's totaled 9,299 in May and 7,530 in June), the campaign so far had been mainly one of maneuver, Sherman forcing Johnston to retreat step by step by threatening alternately, as the terrain suggested, his left flank and then his right.[36] The Confederate army, fighting on the defensive behind field fortifications, sustained considerably fewer casualties than Sherman's and also received substantial reinforcements (some, however, militia of questionable value) so that its numbers had increased by the end of June to about 65,000. Sherman, too, had been reinforced, by Frank P. Blair's XVII Army Corps, and on July 1 he had an "effective strength" of 106,070.[37] The mounted troops of the two armies were roughly equal, 13,318 Confederate to 12,039 Union. Earlier

35. *Ibid.*, Pt. 2, pp. 812, 820–21, 823, 849–50.
36. Sherman, *Memoirs*, II, 47–63.
37. *Battles and Leaders*, IV, 282, 289. On June 27, Colonel Eugene W. Crittenden's

in June, Sherman had wired Sooy Smith: "Continue to procure mounts for cavalry and send forward by regiments as they are ready. The enemy far outnumbers me in cavalry, and limits my operations, which, with more cavalry, I could make more rapid and decisive."[38] Given Sherman's poor opinion of his cavalry and of their commanders, it may be doubted that the accession of a few regiments of cavalry would have made an appreciable change in his operations.

His left threatened by a deep encircling movement, Johnston evacuated his Kennesaw Mountain position, and later the town of Marietta, and retreated to the previously prepared *"tête du pont"* on the north bank of the Chattahoochee. Up at the "earliest Dawn" on July 3, Sherman rode into Marietta, "just quitted by the rebel rear-guard, and was terribly angry at the cautious pursuit by Garrard's cavalry" and by the head of Thomas' infantry columns as well.[39] The position on the Chattahoochee to which Johnston retreated was too strong to be attacked frontally, and Sherman prepared to cross the river well upstream from it. He sent Stoneman, backed by McPherson, to Turner's Ferry and Sandtown, eight miles downstream, to cause Johnston to think that he intended to cross at one or another of these points. At the same time he sent Garrard and his division eighteen miles upstream to Roswell, and Schofield to an intermediate point "just below the mouth of Soap's Creek"; these were the two places where he actually intended to make the crossing. Stoneman, however, was expected to do more than merely demonstrate. Expecting that the crossing of the Chattahoochee by Garrard and Schofield would draw the bulk of Johnston's forces northward, leaving the forces guarding the river south of Atlanta "strung out," Sherman directed Stoneman to march east after crossing the river and attack, or at least demonstrate against, the Atlantic & West Point Railroad. He wrote Stoneman, "You may incur any risk sure of my approval, for whether you make a break of the road or merely cause a diversion, you will do good." Stoneman, however, decided not to raid the railroad, on the ground that "to attempt it would incur risks inadequate to the results." Clearly, Stoneman was not Sherman's kind of cavalryman.[40]

---

brigade of dismounted cavalry (12th Kentucky and 16th Illinois) joined General J. D. Cox's division of the XXIII Army Corps. *Official Records*, Vol. XXXVIII, Pt. 2, p. 683.

38. *Official Records*, Vol. XXXVIII, Pt. 4, p. 456.
39. Sherman, *Memoirs*, II, 66, 62, 65.
40. *Official Records*, Vol. XXXVIII, Pt. 5, pp. 99, 133, 145.

Garrard destroyed an "immense factory" at Roswell, then gained a foothold on the south bank of the Chattahoochee, making the "important ford" at that point available to the Union infantry.[41] Schofield at the same time crossed the river at Soap's Creek. His flank turned by these crossings, Johnston had no choice but to abandon his "*tête du pont*," which he did on the night of July 9. The entire Union army, after a pause of several days to accumulate supplies, crossed the river behind him, and the siege of Atlanta began. Under its new commander, John B. Hood, the Army of Tennessee sallied forth several times to try, never with success, to break up the investment of the city.

In the course of the war, Atlanta had become a sizable city and a major industrial center vital to the ability of the South to continue the war. The defense lines circling the city were too long to enable Sherman to surround the town completely; his armies were deployed in a five-mile semicircle, from below the Georgia Railroad running east to Augusta, then on a wide sweep north of the town, and continuing opposite the west face of the defenses as far as Proctor's Creek, a little less than a mile south of the Western & Atlantic track, Sherman's lifeline back to Chattanooga. Sherman's deployment left unblocked an arc about seven miles long, from Proctor's Creek on the northwest around to the southeastern end of the siege line. Through this gap ran the railroad from Atlanta south to West Point, where the tracks separated, the Macon & Western continuing south through Rough & Ready, Jonesborough, and Lovejoy's Station toward Macon, and the Atlanta & West Point southwest through Red Oak, Palmetto, and Newnan toward Montgomery, Alabama. Faced with the choice of making an all-out attack against a tough enemy manning elaborate fortifications, or using the threat of starvation to force Hood out into the open, Sherman chose the latter alternative and thereby opened the way for his cavalry to play a major role in the campaign, with the breaking of the two rail lines as their targets.[42]

Before crossing the Chattahoochee, Sherman had ordered General Lovell H. Rousseau, at Nashville, to collect from the numerous cavalry units scattered throughout middle Tennessee, "2,500 good cavalry,

41. *Ibid.*, Pt. 2, p. 804; Sherman, *Memoirs*, II, 68–69; Connelly, *Autumn of Glory*, 392–93.

42. Sherman, *Memoirs*, II, 72, 75. Hood was described by McPherson and Schofield, both of whom had been his classmates at West Point, as "bold even to rashness, and courageous in the extreme."

well armed, and a sufficient number of pack-mules loaded with ammunition, salt, sugar, and coffee, and some bread or flour," and proceed south to strike the Atlanta & West Point and Montgomery & West Point railroads somewhere between Tuskegee and Opelika. He was "to work night and day to destroy the roads "toward and including Opelika," then turn northeast and join the main army, "doing all the mischief possible" on the way.[43] Sherman reminded Rousseau that he was "to take no wagons" and spelled out for him in detail that when he reached the railroads, he was to "burn the ties in piles, heat the iron in the middle, and when red hot, let the men pull the ends so as to give a twist to the rails. If simply bent, the rails may be [re]used, but if they are twisted or wrenched, they cannot be used again."[44] Rousseau selected detachments of the 8th Indiana, 2nd Kentucky, 4th Tennessee, 9th Ohio, and 5th Iowa to make the raid. All these units except the Tennessee regiment lacked horses, and after a great deal of difficulty, Rousseau had to resort to the expedient of taking horses from other regiments to get his raiders mounted. Owing to "the difficulty in getting the pack train ready," Rousseau was a day late in starting. Four days later, on July 14, he ordered "a thorough inspection of the command" (a task that might perhaps have been performed earlier), with the result that 300 unfit horses and all the "ineffective men" were sent back, reducing the numbers of the column to under 2,300. On the evening of the seventeenth, the raiders reached the railroads. Rousseau gave his men a night's rest and then set them to work; in the next two days, they "completely destroyed" the track of the West Point & Montgomery "for several miles" and did the same for twelve miles in one direction and six miles in the other on the Atlanta & West Point Railroad. There is the customary conflict of opinion on the thoroughness of the destruction. General Rousseau, at any rate, reported on the basis of his "personal observation" that the "effectual manner" in which the work was done was "deserving of honorable mention."[45] General Sherman expressed the opinion that the raid "must have disturbed the

43. *Official Records*, Vol. XXXVIII, Pt. 2, p. 910.

44. The track of these two railroads was constructed in the same fashion as that of the Richmond & Danville, destroyed by Wilson in June, 1864: "The cross-ties were of pitch-pine, and into these were sunken stringers of the same kind of wood, and a light bar of iron spiked on the top" on which the wheels of the trains actually ran. *Ibid.*, 907. See also Vol. II, pp. 183–84 of the present work.

45. General Rousseau's report is in *Official Records*, Vol. XXXVIII, Pt. 2, pp. 904–909.

enemy somewhat; but, as usual, the cavalry did not work hard, and their destruction of the railroad was soon repaired."[46] Wherever the truth may lie, Rousseau and his men reached Marietta on July 22 with 400 captured mules.

The first of the raids on Hood's rail lines was assigned to Kenner Garrard. He was ordered on the night of July 20 to leave behind his wagons, led horses, and baggage and march his division to Covington, Georgia, on the Georgia Central Railroad thirty-five miles east of Atlanta. He was to destroy the railroad "effectually all the way," as well as the bridges across the Yellow River and the Ulcofauhachee east of Covington, and then make a wide circuit to the north to return to the army.[47] Garrard was back from the raid on July 24, and to make up for past sins, Sherman sent him an overwhelmingly cordial "welcome back" dispatch: "I am rejoiced to hear that you are back safe and successful. . . . I will give you time to rest and then we must make quick work with Atlanta. I await your report with impatience, and in the mean time tender you the assurance of my great consideration." Moreover, Sherman also distinguished him in his report of the campaign by stating that Garrard had "succeeded perfectly in his mission, and destroyed the bridge at Ulcofauhachee and Yellow Rivers, besides burning a train of cars, a large quantity of cotton (2,000 bales), and the depot of stores at Covington and Conyers Station, and bringing in 200 prisoners and some good horses."[48]

General Garrard's success caused Sherman to conclude that the Georgia Central had been sufficiently crippled for the moment at least to be "useless to the enemy," and he "addressed . . . [himself] to the task of reaching the Macon road, over which came the stores and ammunition that alone maintained the rebel army in Atlanta."[49] To break both the Macon and Montgomery branches of what Sherman consistently called "the Macon road," he sent out three cavalry raids: the first under Stoneman, July 27–August 6; the second, under General Edward McCook, July 27–31; and the third, under Judson Kilpatrick, August 18–22. The first two of these raids were actually two branches

46. Sherman, *Memoirs*, II, 69.

47. *Official Records*, Vol. XXXVIII, Pt. 5, pp. 209, 221, and Pt. 1, pp. 72–75.

48. *Ibid.*, Pt. 5, p. 245, Pt. 2, p. 804, Pt. 1, p. 75. Within a month, however, Sherman asked General Thomas to send out the Lightning Brigade to "break up another five miles of the road to make a sure thing of it." *Ibid.*, Pt. 5, p. 640.

49. *Ibid.*, Pt. 1, p. 75.

of a single overall plan and ended in disaster; the third was modestly successful.

Any cavalry operation to the south of Atlanta had a difficult terrain to negotiate. McCook noted that "the country is too broken and the woods too dense for mounted men to pass through, except on roads."[50] Since most of the roads were twisting, narrow lanes, which restricted any cavalry advance to a march in a strung-out column four (sometimes only two) abreast, the defense, whether infantry or dismounted cavalry, had a substantial advantage. Despite this handicap and the departure of time-expired troopers who had chosen not to veteranize, Sherman thought up an elaborate scheme for breaking up the "Macon road."

Stoneman was posted near Decatur, on the left rear of the Union army. His division was made up of three brigades—Colonel James Biddle had the First, consisting of about 700 mounted men of the 5th and 6th Indiana; Colonel Silas Adams commanded the Second, of 550 men of the 1st and 11th Kentucky; Colonel Horace Capron commanded the Third, of 800 men of the 14th Illinois, 8th Michigan, and part of the 1st Ohio Squadron.[51] Stoneman, called by Sherman "a cavalry officer of high repute," was to command, in addition to his own 2,050-man division, Kenner Garrard's division of about 4,000 troopers.[52] The function of the latter was to remain behind Stoneman and intercept any pursuit by the Confederate cavalry. Stoneman was to move out on July 27 "by the left around Atlanta [south] to McDonough" and was to reach the Macon road near Lovejoy's Station. "At the very moment almost of starting," Stoneman proposed an expansion of the plan. He requested permission, which Sherman granted, "after fulfilling his orders and breaking the road, to go on to Macon, 60-some miles to the south," to liberate the 1,500 Union officers held there as prisoners of war, and then go on to free the 23,000 prisoners penned up at Andersonville, "badly fed and harshly treated."[53]

The right-hand prong of the raid was to be Edward McCook's divi-

50. *Ibid.*, Pt. 5, p. 229.

51. *Ibid.*, Pt. 2, p. 915. With a section of 3-inch guns of the 24th Indiana Battery added, Stoneman's division numbered about 2,100.

52. Sherman, *Memoirs*, II, 87. In his official report, however, Sherman credited Stoneman and Garrard together with "an effective force of full 5,000 men." *Official Records*, Vol. XXXVIII, Pt. 1, p. 75.

53. *Official Records*, Vol. XXXVIII, Pt. 1, pp. 75–76; Tarrant, *Wild Riders of the First Kentucky*, 362. Sherman wrote that "there was something most captivating in the idea."

sion, with the 2,000-man division Rousseau had brought to the army (commanded by Colonel Thomas J. Harrison, 8th Indiana, Rousseau having been wounded on the raid) in support.[54] McCook's own command of 1,455, rank and file, which was to do the work, was made up of John T. Croxton's First Brigade (8th Iowa, 1st Tennessee, 4th Kentucky Mounted Infantry) and Colonel William H. Torrey's Second Brigade (1st Wisconsin, 2nd and 4th Indiana).[55] Sherman had Stoneman, Garrard, McCook, and Harrison meet him to receive a face-to-face explanation of the plan and of his wishes, "and they entertained not a doubt of perfect success."[56]

Stoneman's division left its camps, four miles north of Decatur, at 4 A.M. on July 27 and were met at sunrise by Garrard's division. Here, at the very start of the raid, Stoneman encountered one of the causes of his subsequent troubles; this was his inability to pin down the whereabouts, strength, and movements of the Confederate cavalry opposing him. Wheeler's Cavalry Corps was made up at this time of the divisions of William T. Martin (the brigades of William W. Allen and Alfred Iverson), John H. Kelly (the brigades of Robert H. Anderson, George G. Dibrell, and Moses W. Hannon), William Y. C. Humes (the brigades of Henry M. Ashby, Thomas Harrison, and John S. Williams), and lastly William H. Jackson (made up of the brigades of Frank C. Armstrong, Lawrence S. Ross, and Samuel W. Ferguson), a formidable-sounding force of forty-four regiments and eight smaller units.[57] The numerical strength of the corps is not in the records, but even if full allowance is made for the depleted (and constantly changing) strength of Confederate mounted units, Wheeler must have had about 7,000 men and perhaps more.[58] Whatever the exact strength of the Confederate cav-

54. *Official Records*, Vol. XXXVIII, Pt. 1, p. 75, Pt. 2, p. 762; Rowell, *Yankee Artillerymen*, 215.

55. *Official Records*, Vol. XXXVIII, Pt. 5, p. 257. Colonel Croxton gave the strength of his brigade as 940 officers and men, which would leave 515 as the strength of the Second Brigade. *Ibid.*, Pt. 2, p. 769.

56. *Ibid.*, Pt. 1, p. 75.

57. *Ibid.*, Pt. 3, pp. 665–66. The data are as of July 31. In the operation about to be described, William T. Martin's division was actually commanded by General Iverson.

58. Rowell, *Yankee Artillerymen*, 215, gives Wheeler's strength as 3,800, a suspiciously low figure for the number of regiments reported. For whatever the information may be worth, the historian of the 14th Illinois gives Wheeler's strength as 8,000 to 10,000, who had the further advantage that many of them were armed with long-range rifles, whereas Stoneman's men had short-range carbines and navy revolvers, "effective weapons in a cavalry charge, but inferior in fighting dismounted." Sanford, *History of the Fourteenth Illinois*, 191, 193.

alry may have been, Sherman wrote in his report on the campaign that his own four cavalry divisions should have been able to "whip all of Wheeler's cavalry and could otherwise accomplish . . . [their] task, and I think so still."[59] It may not be unfair to wonder what the outcome of the raid might have been if instead of sending three widely separated divisions on the raid, Sherman had joined all four of his divisions into a single corps, as James Wilson was to do for his Selma Campaign a few months later, and had sent them as a unit against the railroad and the Confederate cavalry protecting it.[60]

Having been taken prisoner on the raid, Stoneman failed to submit a detailed report of the operation.[61] Lieutenant Colonel Robert W. Smith, his assistant inspector general, wrote that a report that Wheeler's cavalry was waiting for him on ahead caused Stoneman to form a line of battle in preparation for a fight, but the report was erroneous, and Stoneman resumed his march after sending Garrard and his division to Flat Rock, eight miles southeast of Decatur.[62] There, according to Garrard's not entirely unbiased report, Stoneman "abandoned . . . [the Garrard division] to its fate." But, said Garrard, "after being surrounded by a superior force for over twelve hours, and contending against every disadvantage, in hopes of benefiting General Stoneman in his attempt to destroy the railroad, it extricated itself from its perilous situation."[63] Not mentioned by General Garrard is the fact that engaging the enemy at Flat Rock to keep them from pursuing Stoneman was precisely why Sherman had sent him on the raid. According to Colonel Minty, at daybreak on the twenty-eighth, Garrard at Flat Rock was "completely surrounded by three divisions (nine brigades) of rebel cavalry," but led by a charge of Colonel Abram O. Miller's brigade of

59. *Official Records*, Vol. XXXVIII, Pt. 1, p. 75.

60. A major "if" in any such supposition must be who among Sherman's cavalrymen had the ability to lead successfully a four-division body of perhaps 10,000 cavalry.

61. On August 6 he was allowed to send under flag of truce an explanation of his discomfiture, which he blamed in the main on the misbehavior of Colonel Adams' Kentucky regiments and secondarily on the misbehavior of Colonel Capron's brigade. *Official Records*, Vol. XXXVIII, Pt. 2, p. 914.

62. Flat Rock is also called "Flat Shoals" in some reports and "Flat Creek" in others.

63. *Official Records*, Vol. XXXVIII, Pt. 2, p. 804. General Garrard seemed to lack the milk of human kindness. He endorsed the report of Colonel Minty (who commanded his First Brigade), which mentioned him no less than six times, with the statement "Lest there be some misunderstanding . . . I would . . . state I was in command of the Second Cavalry Division during the past campaign." *Ibid.*, 811–15.

mounted infantry (the Lightning Brigade), the division "drove . . . [the] enemy in confusion" and escaped from the encirclement.[64]

After the false alarm at Decatur, Stoneman marched all day and most of the night of the twenty-eighth eastward along the line of the Georgia Central Railroad, past Stone Mountain, through Covington, and thence the next day south toward Monticello. Except for a stab by a 125-man detachment of the 14th Illinois to break the Georgia Central near Milledgeville, and another by a second detachment to break the same line "at or near Gordon," no serious effort was made to accomplish the principal objective of the raid. The two detachments, according to Colonel Smith, "reached the railroad with but little interruption, and each burnt some small bridges and culverts and tore up the road at these points for a distance of two or three miles." The two detachments also encountered and destroyed two or three (the accounts differ) trains of cars loaded with commissary and quartermaster stores, including "hogs and cattle for the Rebel army."[65] It is obvious, however, that Stoneman had decided on his own to reverse Sherman's priorities and to make the freeing of prisoners initially at Macon his primary objective. From Monticello he continued his march south through Clinton to within a mile of Macon.

Unable to force a crossing of the Ocmulgee River to get at Macon, Stoneman's first thought, as reported by Colonel Smith, was to try to make his escape through southern Georgia and Alabama to Pensacola, more than 300 miles away, but after marching in that direction for a

64. *Ibid.*, 813. Wheeler's report says nothing of the "encirclement" spoken of by Colonel Minty. He says, simply, that he had "driven the advance of Garrard's division across Flat Creek. He, finding himself so strongly opposed, retreated. . . . We pursued a few miles, capturing a few horses and arms, and . . . three wagons." *Ibid.*, Pt. 3, p. 953. See also Crofts, *Third Ohio Veteran Volunteer Cavalry*, 159, and Vale, *Minty and the Cavalry*, 327–28.

65. Colonel Capron stated in his report that he divided his brigade into detachments that destroyed 5 miles of track. *Official Records*, Vol. XXXVIII, Pt. 2, pp. 915–16, 926; Tarrant, *Wild Riders of the First Kentucky*, 361. Still another account has it that the 14th Illinois detachment, commanded by Major Francis M. Davidson, "struck the railroad seven miles east of Gordon, burned trestle work and bridge; destroyed everything at Gordon . . . 275 flat and box cars, mostly loaded with supplies and the best of refugee goods; 9 engines and 150 passenger and express cars. . . . Seven of the engines had steam on, which were destroyed by running them in a general smash and burning the whole thing. Destroyed the long bridge over the Oconee River, also over Buffalo Creek, and all between those points. Caught 4 trains between Gordon and Buffalo Creek; destroyed them entire." *Official Records*, Vol. XXXVIII, Pt. 2, pp. 920–21. See also Sherman, *Memoirs*, II, 98.

few miles, a scout's report of 1,000 to 1,500 Confederate cavalry ahead caused him to change his mind. Just what he intended to do at this point is unclear. His provost marshal, Major Haviland Tompkins, reported that he intended to break out northeastward, in the direction of Milledgeville, but General Iverson's brigade, which Wheeler had sent to Macon to oppose Stoneman while he himself dealt with Garrard and McCook, were in the way. It was now the morning of July 31; all of the raiders' "desperate efforts" to break free were driven back by Iverson's cavalry with the loss of "many valuable officers and men . . . [who] were nearly out of ammunition and fatigued almost beyond endurance." [66] By midafternoon, Iverson had Stoneman blocked in front and hemmed in on both flanks and in the rear. Bombarded heavily by Iverson's artillery and charged by his cavalry, Stoneman, apparently after some hesitation, decided to allow Adams and Capron with their brigades and most of the 6th Indiana—a total of between 1,200 and 1,300 men—to try to break out through a small crease in Iverson's lines, toward Eatonton, north of Milledgeville, while he himself, with his staff and about 200 of the 5th Indiana and a section of artillery, remained behind to hold off the enemy as long as possible before surrendering. [67]

One of the officers of the 1st Kentucky, Lieutenant Richard E. Huffman, Company E, wrote home three days after his return from the raid: "I have seen excitement in our regiment, but when our men, whose time was nearly out, learned that they were about to be made prisoners the excitement was uncontrollable. . . . Col. Adams . . . went to Gen. Stoneman and vehemently protested against surrendering his brigade; that it was unjust at the expiration of his own regiment's term of service to consign his men to captivity to waste their lives in the horrid prisons of the South." Given permission to try to break out, provided he took the responsibility if his brigade was "cut all to pieces and killed," Adams led the way, wrote Lieutenant Huffman. "Many from other regiments united with us and followed our leader. I know not how Col. Adams found the way; but he led us over hills and deep ditches— not the sign of a path being there and took us out between the Rebel pickets without firing a gun." [68] Capron took another route, had some fighting before he broke clear, and then allowed his men to "run . . .

66. *Official Records*, Vol. XXXVIII, Pt. 2, pp. 920, 916.
67. *Ibid.*, 914, 917.
68. Tarrant, *Wild Riders of the First Kentucky*, 365.

their horses to kill."[69] The two brigades met, joined forces, marched all night on July 31 and all day on August 1 and 2, north through Eatonton, Madison, and Watkinsville to near Athens, and then west toward Jefferson. On the second, Capron became separated from Adams, was attacked by "five hundred picked men under Col. [William C. P.] Breckinridge" sent ahead to intercept Capron and Adams and delay them as much as possible until the rest of Iverson's command could catch up with them. The Capron brigade was considerably cut up and scattered by Breckinridge's attack.[70] After another all-night march on August 2, Adams reached the Chattahoochee River and crossed it late on the evening of August 3 over "an old and difficult ford" twenty-five or thirty miles upstream from Marietta. The next morning, "stiff, sore and worn out," Adams and his 490 remaining men reached Marietta, "reporting, *as usual*, all the rest lost."[71] Three days later Capron and what was left of his brigade, in a "perfectly demoralized" state, also reached the Union lines.[72]

McCook's division, too, was on schedule in leaving its camps at Mason's Church, beyond the extreme right of the Union army. It crossed to the north bank of the Chattahoochee, then crossed back to the south bank on a pontoon bridge at Riverton, seven miles downstream from Campbellton, late on the afternoon of the twenty-eighth. Captain William Kossak, in charge of the pontoon train, reported that on the march to Campbellton, "the extreme heaviness of . . . [the] pontoon train and the miserable condition of the mules proved a serious drawback on the celerity and dispatch of . . . [the] cavalry movement" and that he lost on the way "18 mules, dropping dead in their harness."[73]

After the chest-pounding declaration that he "obeyed . . . [Sherman's orders] implicitly, and accomplished all that . . . [they] contemplated or directed," McCook listed the positive results of the raid: 2½ miles each of the Atlanta & West Point road near Palmetto and of the

69. For Capron's adventures, see *Official Records*, Vol. XXXVIII, Pt. 2, pp. 927–29.

70. Breckinridge was colonel of the 9th Kentucky, C.S.A.

71. Tarrant, *Wild Riders of the First Kentucky*, 368; Sherman, *Memoirs*, II, 97 (emphasis added); *Official Records*, Vol. XXXVIII, Pt. 2, p. 918.

72. Capron came into the Union lines with "not more than 100" men, but "small squads are coming in all the time," the report said. *Official Records*, Vol. XXXVIII, Pt. 2, p. 918.

73. *Ibid.*, Pt. 3, p. 69.

Macon & Western near Lovejoy's Station destroyed.[74] Before daylight on the twenty-ninth, between the two stations, Colonel Brownlow's regiment, in the advance, found and captured a Confederate train variously reported as of over 500 to as many as 1,160 wagons, some of which were loaded with officers' clothing, trunks, "and other valuables." The train guard was captured, the wagons destroyed, the best of the horses and mules taken for remounts, and the "poorest animals . . . [killed] with sabers, so as to avoid the noise of carbine reports."[75]

On his march to Lovejoy's Station, McCook had met no opposition. The only Confederate cavalry in the area was Jackson's division; why it did not, or could not, contest McCook's march does not appear in the records. McCook was intended to meet or "communicate with" Stoneman on July 28 at or near McDonough, thirteen miles due east of Lovejoy's Station, after destroying the railroad at the latter point. It does not appear that McCook made any strenuous effort to find Stoneman. On the strength of a report that "Wheeler's command" (which on the twenty-ninth could only have been one or both of General Jackson's brigades) was between him and McDonough, he decided to forget about Stoneman and head for the Chattahoochee and safety via the village of Newnan, thirteen miles downstream from Riverton. In the meantime Wheeler, in the north, received word that McCook (credited with a total force of 3,000) was advancing toward the railroads, and Hood ordered him "to move immediately to oppose this force with such troops as could be spared."[76] Leaving George C. Dibrell's brigade to hold Garrard in check, he sent orders to Robert H. Anderson to follow, and with Ashby's 500-man brigade he rode in all haste to Jonesborough, where a message from General Jackson was waiting for him. McCook,

---

74. *Ibid.*, Pt. 2, p. 762. In Colonel Brownlow's (1st Tennessee) opinion, the Macon & Western "was destroyed in such a manner as to render it unserviceable for about twelve or fifteen days." General Hood wrote simply that the destruction of 1½ miles of the road "was promptly repaired." *Battles and Leaders*, III, 314; *Official Records*, Vol. XXXVIII, Pt. 2, p. 774. Rowell says, without citing a source, that the line was shut down for three days. Rowell, *Yankee Artillerymen*, 226. General Stanley put it more bluntly, saying the raid did not amount "to one row of pins. . . . The damage to the enemy was nil." Stanley, *Personal Memoirs*, 179.

75. *Official Records*, Vol. XXXVIII, Pt. 2, pp. 762, 775, 783. McCook described the wagons as "including the headquarters trains of nearly . . . [Hood's] whole army, Hardee's entire transportation and the cavalry command supply trains." Also, McCook reported the number of mules killed as 800. *Ibid.*, 761. See also Rowell, *Yankee Artillerymen*, 217.

76. *Official Records*, Vol. XXXVIII, Pt. 3, p. 953.

Jackson wrote, had taken the road to Fayetteville, a road center eight miles southwest of Jonesborough and about twenty-two miles south of the Chattahoochee; he urged Wheeler "to follow and push them in rear" while he himself, with Harrison's and Ross's brigades, headed them off or attacked them in flank. An hour or two past midnight on the twenty-ninth, Wheeler caught up with the rear of McCook's column, and for the next forty-eight hours, the raiders were battered by unceasing attacks, day and night, front, rear, and flanks, by Jackson's two brigades, by Roddey's brigade of about 600 men (who had arrived at Newnan a short time before), by two brigades of infantry, by Ross's brigade of Texas cavalry, and by the 700 men Wheeler now had under his immediate command. Headed off from Newnan by Roddey and the infantry, broken up into regiments and detachments by attacks from the rear and flanks, confined to a "narrow, devious path, crossing innumerable ditches and bogs," and hemmed in by "an almost impenetrable forest," those of the troopers who had not been killed, wounded and left behind, or captured, did at long last reach the river, mostly in squads or singly—Colonel Brownlow with 28 men, Colonel Croxton with a single orderly—miles below Newnan and managed to cross, swimming their horses, in whatever canoes or boats they were able to find.[77] The largest group, the 8th Indiana, the 5th Iowa, parts of the 2nd Indiana and 4th Tennessee, and the gunners of Lieutenant Martin J. Miller's section of the 18th Indiana Battery (the guns and caissons were destroyed and abandoned), led by McCook himself, "cut a way through in the midst of a most terrible fire, and crossed the river at Philpot's Ferry, below Franklin."[78]

Writing on August 7, General McCook thought that his total loss, killed, wounded, and missing, did not exceed 500. General Wheeler claimed with considerable justice "the entire destruction" of McCook's

---

77. *Ibid.*, Pt. 2, pp. 771–74. Croxton reached the Union lines August 12. The numerous Union reports on the McCook raid will be found in *Ibid.*, 761–92, 802–803, 875–77. It is worthy of note that Lieutenant Granville C. West, 4th Kentucky Mounted Infantry, made mention in his report of "the utter worthlessness of the Ballard rifle, used by six companies of . . . [his] regiment. A great many became entirely useless during the action; some bursted from firing." *Ibid.*, 781. It may be noted also that the 8th Iowa had 24 officers and 292 men on the raid, "all that could be mounted and considerably less than one-third of the force of the regiment when it started on the [Atlanta] campaign less than 90 days before." Of the 316 men who started on the raid, only 20 returned. Ingersoll, *Iowa and the Rebellion*, 697–98.

78. *Official Records*, Vol. XXXVIII, Pt. 2, p. 763.

"entire command," which, he said, was "a picked body of cavalry, and its destruction destroyed the flower of General Sherman's vast cavalry organization."[79] General Sherman reported that "on the whole" the raid was not a success. It accomplished its objective of making a break in Hood's communications but did it on so limited a scale that the damage could be repaired in short order.[80] In his *Memoirs*, in which he could speak more freely, he wrote, "I now became satisfied that cavalry could not, or would not, make a sufficient lodgment on the railroad below Atlanta, and that nothing would suffice but for us to reach it with the main army." Just the same, he hastened to "recompose" his cavalry, an arm he considered essential, for both defense and offense. He posted Judson Kilpatrick and the Third Division on the army's right rear; Garrard and the Second Division were on the left, where Stoneman had been; McCook's division, reduced to 1,139 men, fewer than 500 of whom were mounted, were "held somewhat in reserve, about Marietta and the railroad."[81]

79. *Ibid.*, Pt. 3, p. 957. T. L. Connelly has called Wheeler's handling of his forces to oppose the raiders his "finest hour," but according to General McCook, Wheeler and his subordinates were "severely censure[d]" by Confederate newspapers "for not having, with their vastly superior force, entirely destroyed . . . [McCook's] whole command." Connelly, *Autumn of Glory*, 452; *Official Records*, Vol. XXXVIII, Pt. 2, p. 764.

80. *Official Records*, Vol. XXXVIII, Pt. 1, p. 77. Speaking of Wheeler's raid on his own railroad three weeks later, Sherman wrote, "cavalry has not the industry to damage railroads seriously." *Ibid.*, Pt. 5, p. 626.

81. Sherman, *Memoirs*, II, 98, 102; Rowell, *Yankee Artillerymen*, 226. The figure 1,139 was as of August 8. According to Sherman, however, McCook's "broken division" numbered 1,754 men and horses. Sherman, *Memoirs*, II, 98.

XIX

The Valley of the Shadow

UNWILLING TO INCUR THE CASUALTIES THAT A DIRECT AS-
sault on Hood's defenses around Atlanta would have entailed, and disenchanted with the cavalry's inability or unwillingness to destroy the
railroads feeding Atlanta so as to force Hood to move out of his trenches
into the open, Sherman concluded that "nothing would suffice but . . .
to reach . . . [the railroads] with the main army." To that end, he moved
the XIII and XIV Corps (a total of 30,000 infantry and artillery), plus
McCook's patched-up division of cavalry, to the extreme right of the
Union line, with orders on August 4 to "make a bold attack on the railroad, anywhere about West Point." There were delays caused first by
command problems (General John M. Palmer refused to serve under
Schofield, his junior, and resigned) and then by Sherman's decision to
try the effect of a softening-up bombardment of the city, intended
to "make the inside of Atlanta too hot to be endured."[1] It became obvious to him, however, that the "enemy would hold fast, even though
every house in the town should be battered down," and that he either
had to decoy Hood out of Atlanta for a fight in the open "or else, with
the whole army, raise the siege and attack his communications." He
chose the latter and on August 13 issued orders for his entire army,
less one corps, "to move bodily to some point on the Macon Railroad
below East Point."[2]

1. Sherman, *Memoirs*, II, 98–99, 101.
2. *Ibid.*, 102–103. "After the destruction of the Augusta road, the holding of Atlanta

Before these orders could be put into execution, Hood made a mistake that he was to repeat on a larger scale and with disastrous results later in the year. Having decided, with considerable justification, that Wheeler had effectively smashed Sherman's cavalry, he sent him off on August 10 with 4,500 men on a wide circuit around the Union rear to break up Sherman's railroad connection with Chattanooga and Nashville.[3] Wheeler marched around the Union left, burned the bridge over the Etowah (presumably the bridge located between Allatoona and Cartersville), "recaptured Dalton and Resaca; destroyed about 35 miles of railroad in the vicinity, and captured about 300 mules and 1000 horses."[4] To add insult to injury, Colonel Moses W. Hannon's brigade captured near Calhoun on the night of August 13 a herd of 1,020 beef cattle intended for Sherman's army.[5] Given the magnitude of Sherman's resources, the loss of the mules, horses, and beef cattle, and the destruction of some bridges and of a few miles of track, were no worse than temporary annoyances. Indeed, Sherman wrote in his report, "I could not have asked for anything better, for I had provided well against such a contingency, and this detachment left me superior to the enemy in cavalry."[6] He therefore suspended the flank march of his infantry toward the railroad and ordered Judson Kilpatrick, in command of "a well appointed force of about 5,000 cavalry," to make one more try by cavalry alone to interdict Hood's supply lines.

As soon as he learned of Wheeler's absence, Sherman ordered Kenner Garrard, on his left flank, and Kilpatrick, on his right, to make reconnaissances to their front. Garrard's excessively cautious execution of the order led to his supersession. Sherman's dispatch to General Thomas (who tried loyally to defend his unfortunate subordinate) indi-

---

. . . depended upon our ability to hold intact the road to Macon," Hood wrote later. *Battles and Leaders*, IV, 341. See also *Official Records*, Vol. XXXVIII, Pt. 5, 951.

3. *Battles and Leaders*, IV, 342. At the same time, Hood arranged for Forrest and General Dabney H. Maury's cavalry from Mobile to strike the line near the Tennessee River and in Tennessee. *Ibid.*, 342. See also Dyer, *"Fightin' Joe" Wheeler*, 187–88, and Horn, *Army of Tennessee*, 363.

4. *Battles and Leaders*, IV, 342; Sherman, *Memoirs*, II, 103. But "actually, Wheeler had done little damage to the railroad, and he certainly had burned no bridges and had destroyed no tunnel. Most of his efforts . . . were directed at less important objectives, such as capturing a few trains and mules, attacking outposts, and other minor operations." Connelly, *Autumn of Glory*, 457.

5. *Official Records*, Vol. XXXVIII, Pt. 5, p. 967, Pt. 1, p. 79.

6. *Ibid.*, Pt. 1, p. 79. The 4,500 (or by another account, 4,000) men Wheeler took with him amounted to "almost half of the army's cavalry." Connelly, *Autumn of Glory*, 457.

cates clearly enough what he expected, but failed to get, from his cavalry commanders: "I am willing to admit that General Garrard's excessive prudence saves his cavalry . . . but though saved, it is as useless as so many sticks. Saving himself, he sacrifices others operating in conjoint expeditions. I am so thoroughly convinced that if he can see a horseman in the distance . . . he will turn back, that I cannot again depend on his making an effort, though he knows a commander depends on him. If we cannot use that cavalry now, when can we?"[7]

Whatever the rights or wrongs of Sherman's strictures on Garrard may have been, Colonel Eli Long, 4th Ohio, "a hard-working and worthy cavalry officer" who was then commanding the Second Brigade of Garrard's division and who eventually took Garrard's place, was an inspired choice for divisional command.[8] On Sherman's recommendation, and with General Thomas' cordial concurrence, Long was promoted to brigadier general to give him the necessary rank and transferred, with his own and Colonel Minty's First Brigade, to the right, to take part in the operation against Hood's railroads.

Kilpatrick was Sherman's own choice to head the operation, on the strength of his conduct of the August 15 reconnaissance to his front that he had been ordered to make. As Sherman wrote General Thomas, Kilpatrick "has acted so as to show the enemy that he will fight. I do believe he, with his own and . . . Garrard's cavalry, could ride right around Atlanta and smash the Macon railroad all to pieces."[9] He had "displayed so much zeal and activity" in the operation that Sherman was "attracted to him at once" and was "so pleased with his spirit and confidence" that he decided then and there to give the cavalry one more chance to make a durable break in the railroad.

Shortly after midnight, August 17, Garrard's First and Second Brigades, a total of six regiments of cavalry, with two sections of the Chicago Board of Trade Battery—2,398 officers and men—left their camps near Peachtree Creek, northeast of Atlanta, to join Kilpatrick at Sandtown, west of the city.[10] Long's numbers were reduced on the

---

7. *Ibid.*, Pt. 5, p. 526.

8. *Ibid.*, 595. For additional dispatches on the Garrard-Long switch, see *Ibid.*, 509, 521, 524, 527, 569.

9. *Ibid.*, 525, 524.

10. Vale, *Minty and the Cavalry*, 337–38. In addition to his own division of cavalry, Kilpatrick also had two sections of the 10th Wisconsin Battery. Kilpatrick speaks of making the raid with 4,500; deducting Minty's and Long's 2,400 would leave 2,100 for the

march by about 100 because of "the giving out of horses." The two brigades were intended to devote the eighteenth to getting for themselves, and giving their horses, a good rest, but "the weather was very
hot, the flies and insects were swarming and the surroundings were
anything but inviting for a good day's rest." At five o'clock that day the
horses were fed and watered, and the troopers got their suppers. Toward sundown, the men drew sixty rounds of ammunition and saddled
their horses. Then Kilpatrick, never one to let an opportunity for or-
atory go unused, assembled the command in a hollow square, and
gave them of his best. They had been selected, he said, for a special
service and furnished with the best arms and equipment the government had. He had "all confidence" in their ability to accomplish their
mission and expected of all a hearty cooperation, willing obedience to
orders, and at all times prompt and energetic action.[11]

Having thus inspired his men, Kilpatrick marched out of his camps
on time, his own Third Division in the lead. Opposition, light at first,
was met within a few miles. Enemy barricades were encountered at
frequent intervals. It was a "bright, beautiful moonlight night," which
made the rail barricades easier to deal with. Nevertheless, they did
delay progress, and it was not until daylight on the nineteenth, near
Fairburn, that the Atlanta & West Point Railroad was reached.[12] Here
Minty's and Long's brigades were given the lead, and they drove the
enemy (Lawrence S. Ross's brigade of cavalry) out of a succession
of barricades as far as Flint River, within five miles of Jonesborough
and the Macon Railroad. For most of the advance so far—through
"country . . . thickly wooded and a very bad place for cavalry to operate"—the men had marched on foot. The bridge over Flint River had
been partially dismantled by the Confederates, who occupied "a strong
position" on the far bank, but they were driven off by Minty's artillery
and a dismounted charge of his troopers with their Spencers. The
bridge was hurriedly repaired, and both Minty's and Long's brigades

Third Division. *Official Records*, Vol. XXXVIII, Pt. 2, p. 560. Another source, however,
credits the Third Division with 2,400 men. Vale, *Minty and the Cavalry*, 347.

    11. *Official Records*, Vol. XXXVIII, Pt. 5, p. 839; Curry, *Four Years in the Saddle*,
172; Crofts, *Third Ohio Veteran Volunteer Cavalry*, 160. By another account, Kilpatrick
made no speech, but "an order was read" exhorting the command, "the last cavalry hope
of the army," to "start with the determination to 'do or die.'" Wulsin, *Story of the Fourth*,
53–54.

    12. Sipes, *The Seventh Pennsylvania*, 124.

crossed, driving the enemy, now joined by the brigades of Ferguson and Armstrong, toward Jonesborough.

The track of the Macon road ran down the main street of Jonesborough; both the track and the depot buildings were protected by a fort of cotton bales. Kilpatrick's artillery set fire to the "fort," the depot, and numerous other buildings. For five hours thereafter, the Third Division was engaged in tearing up the track, while Minty's brigade, to the north of the village, held off the Confederate troops coming down from Atlanta and Long's brigade did the same with those hurrying up from the south. Abut two miles of track were destroyed.[13] The historian of the 1st Ohio, of Long's brigade, recalled, "It was a wild night and a most graphic scene, the sky lit up with burning timbers, buildings and cotton bales, the continuous bang of carbines, the galloping of staff officers and orderlies up and down the streets . . . the terrified citizens, peering out of their windows, the constant marching of troops changing position, Kilpatrick's headquarters band discoursing national airs, with the shouts of the men—all made a weird scene never to be forgotten."[14]

Reports that the enemy troops to the south were infantry caused Kilpatrick to decide to withdraw from Jonesborough eastward toward McDonough and swing back to the railroad at or near Lovejoy's Station, there to continue tearing up track. He actually reached the railroad a mile above Lovejoy's Station at midmorning on the twentieth, but before he could begin breaking up the track, he discovered that the Confederates had him completely surrounded. There were three brigades of cavalry in his rear, a brigade of infantry to his front and left, and a division of infantry moving up on his right, and all the enemy troops not actually in the skirmish line were busy constructing barricades of fence rails and logs.[15] Kilpatrick and his 4,500 were hemmed in, in a space measuring not more than about three-quarters of a mile, by Confederate forces, horse and foot, that may have numbered as many as 12,000, including 1,000 Georgia militia.[16]

13. Curry, *Four Years in the Saddle*, 177, 178; Sipes, *The Seventh Pennsylvania*, 126; Vale, *Minty and the Cavalry*, 341.

14. Curry, *Four Years in the Saddle*, 178.

15. Sipes, *The Seventh Pennsylvania*, 128–29. For a somewhat different account of the encircling forces, see Curry, *Four Years in the Saddle*, 180.

16. Curry, *Four Years in the Saddle*, 180. While on the way to Lovejoy's Station, Minty's advance guard, the 7th Pennsylvania and the 4th United States, were ambushed

Now Kilpatrick made a decision that despite his weaknesses, entitles him to a high place as a cavalryman. He decided to try to break out. Moreover, instead of having his men try to escape by brigades and regiments wherever they could find a weak spot in the enemy position, he chose to assemble his entire command and risk the hazard of a mass charge, mounted, to get him through the Confederate lines. The breakout attempt was to be made in an eastward direction along the McDonough road, with his own division to the left of the road, and Minty, followed by Long, to the right, the mounted men, sabers drawn, in front in column of regiments and the dismounted men, ambulances filled with the wounded, ammunition wagons, pack mules, and the artillery following as closely behind the mounted men as possible. The charge had to be made through "an old, deserted plantation," over ground cut up by "ditches and washouts" and two or three lines of fences. Facing the Union horsemen were Confederate cavalry, dismounted, on the south of the road (the Union right) and infantry on the north. The Confederate infantry, so one of the Union regimental historians reports, were "formed in three lines, about fifty yards apart, in double rank; the first and second lines with fixed bayonets and the third line firing; in both the first and second lines the front rank knelt on one knee, resting the butt of the gun on the ground, the bayonet at a 'charge.'" Fortunately for Kilpatrick, Minty's charge struck the enemy cavalry, who "broke and fled in the wildest panic." The infantry stood firm but, with their flank exposed, were ridden down and sabered by Minty and Long, who changed direction to the left.[17]

Having broken through and gotten his command sorted out, Kilpatrick marched to McDonough in the midst of a torrential downpour, pursued by Confederate infantry. Long's brigade was rear guard.[18] The

by Confederate infantry, attacked in front and flank, and "forced back in utter defeat and badly cut to pieces." Casualties were heavy in both regiments. Vale, *Minty and the Cavalry*, 344; see also Wulsin, *The Story of the Fourth*, 57–58.

17. Vale, *Minty and the Cavalry*, 347, 348. A participant with the 4th Ohio in the charge wrote after the war, "Owing to the irregular nature of the ground . . . no regular alignment was possible, and it soon became a charge of squadrons, companies, squads and single riders." William E. Crane, "Bugle Blasts," MOLLUS, Commandery of Ohio, *Sketches of War History, 1861–1865*, (7 vols.; Cincinnati, 1888–1910), I, 247–48. See also William L. Curry, "Raid of the Union Cavalry, Commanded by General Judson Kilpatrick, Around the Confederate Army in Atlanta, August, 1864," MOLLUS, Commandery of Ohio, *Sketches of War History, 1861–1865*, VI, 252–74.

18. Long himself was wounded twice in the fighting and had to give up command of the brigade to Colonel Beroth B. Eggleston, 1st Ohio.

pursuit halted west of McDonough, and after a brief rest there, the retreat continued north to the crossing of the Georgia Railroad at Lathonia. To reach the railroad, the command had to cross the Cotton River at daylight on the twenty-first, the stream "swollen to an enormous height" by the rain. The bridge had been swept away, and the crossing had to be made by swimming the horses; one man of the Minty brigade, fifty of its horses, and nearly all its pack mules, carrying the men's cooking utensils and mess kits, were drowned.[19] Thereafter the return march was uneventful, and the next day the Minty and Long brigades were back in their camps after their five-day circuit around Atlanta. Casualties had been heavy: 451 officers and men lost, including 64 killed, an inordinately high price to pay for three miles of track Kilpatrick reported destroyed, which he estimated would take ten days to repair.[20] On August 23, within a day of his return to Peachtree Creek and just over three days following the destruction of track at Jonesborough, the besiegers saw "trains coming into Atlanta from the south." This, so far as Sherman was concerned, was conclusive. He said nothing (or nothing that has survived in the records) in criticism of Kilpatrick's performance, but it ended any idea of using cavalry to make a permanent break in the Macon road.[21]

Orders now went to Thomas, Schofield, and Howard to put into execution the plan, held in abeyance by news of Wheeler's raid, to march the entire Union army less the XX Corps, to the south and across the Macon road. The march began on the night of the twenty-fifth and continued until the twenty-eighth, when Generals Howard and Thomas reached the West Point railroad, which they broke up "thoroughly" from East Port on the north down to Fairburn on the south. A new note was added here to the usual burning of the ties and twisting of the rails: "many deep cuts . . . [were filled] with trees, brush, and earth, and comingled with them loaded shells, so arranged that they would explode on an attempt to haul out the bushes." On the thirty-

19. Curry, *Four Years in the Saddle*, 185.

20. Sherman, *Memoirs*, II, 104. The casualties of Minty's brigade were 17 killed, 31 wounded, and 18 missing; of Long's, 16 killed, 67 wounded, 17 missing; of Kilpatrick's division, 31 killed, 111 wounded, 143 missing. *Official Records*, Vol. XXXVIII, Pt. 2, pp. 827, 861.

21. Sherman, *Memoirs*, II, 104. In General Orders of August 31 to the Army of the Tennessee, General Howard wrote, "The gallant behavior of the cavalry division, under General Kilpatrick, in meeting the attack of the division of Cleburne is heartily appreciated . . . and will not remain unnoticed." *Official Records*, Vol. XXXVIII, Pt. 3, p. 49.

first, the entire army reached the stretch of the Macon road from Rough and Ready down to Jonesborough. Hood kept pace with the southward extension of Sherman's lines, but with his relatively limited numbers, he could not do so and at the same time maintain his hold on the Atlanta defenses. There was a fight at Jonesborough on September 1, and at daylight the next day, General Henry W. Slocum was able to enter Atlanta from the opposite direction, from the northwest. He met no opposition.

Atlanta had now been captured, and Sherman spent the next few days deciding what to do. The conclusion he came to was to turn his back on Hood's army below Lovejoy's Station and return with his own forces to Atlanta to "enjoy a short period of rest, and to think well over the next step required in the progress of events."[22] The reader will recall that as a warning to the French in Mexico and as a counter to their efforts to establish the Austrian Archduke Maximilian as emperor in that country, the authorities in Washington, and Secretary of State Seward in particular, began as early as the summer of 1863 to urge on General Banks the importance of "restoring the flag" in some point in Texas.[23] Galveston or Indianola were first proposed as possible targets, to be seized either by means of an overland campaign or a joint army-navy expedition. On second thought, General Halleck proposed "a combined military and naval movement up the Red River to Alexandria, Natchitoches, or Shreveport, and the military occupation of Northern Texas," along the lines of a plan General Banks had himself proposed some time before. General Halleck took the trouble to remind Banks of the advantages of the Red River plan and the disadvantages of the Galveston/Indianola alternative and in characteristic fashion concluded, "I write this simply as a suggestion and not as a military instruction."[24] Expressing initially a preference for a land campaign aimed at Galveston, Banks spoke of his shortage of cavalry, and in a later dispatch, wrote Halleck:

The want of cavalry is the greatest deficiency we suffer. It is indispensable in any movement in Texas that we should be strong in this arm. All the Texas

---

22. Sherman, *Memoirs*, II, 105, 110.
23. *Official Records*, Vol. XXVI, Pt. 1, p. 672. The dispatch is dated August 6, 1863.
24. *Ibid.*, 673.

troops are mounted men; their movements are rapid, and their concentration effective and powerful. We must meet them the same way, and I earnestly urge upon the Government the necessity of strengthening us in that arm. We also want horse equipments, carbines, and sabers for the negroes who will be enlisted in this service. Once in Texas, mules and horses will be abundant, but the equipments are indispensable.[25]

Halleck's reply gave Banks little encouragement. He was told that Grant, at Vicksburg, had been ordered to send on "all the reenforcements in his power; this, of course, includes cavalry." But, Halleck went on (his dispatch was sent six weeks after the draft riots in New York), "No reenforcements of any kind can be possibly sent to you from the Northeastern States at present . . . [or] for some time to come."[26]

In the event, Banks decided on an attack on the Sabine Pass, below Beaumont, Texas. The navy was expected to silence the fort at the mouth of the pass and lead the transports carrying General William B. Franklin, elements of the XIX Corps infantry, engineers, and artillery, and the 1st Texas, U.S.A., a force of about five thousand of all arms, up the Sabine River. Having landed, Franklin was to march north to Beaumont and "seize and hold" a position on the railroad connecting Beaumont and Houston. The expedition was, however, a complete fiasco.[27] Shallow water at the mouth of the Sabine limited the Navy to using four gunboats ("old boats of decayed frames and weak machinery, constantly out of repair"), and the fort guarding the Pass was far more heavily gunned than the naval authorities had anticipated.[28] The result was that when on the afternoon of September 8 the attempt was made to pass the bar, silence the Confederate guns, and land the troops, two of the ships were grounded and a third was "disabled by a chance shot." Franklin had to call off the operation and head back to his base.[29] A minor element in his decision to call off the operation was that a mere four days after his departure from New Orleans, his "stock of fresh water was nearly exhausted, and the animals were already on short allowances of water; the men were living on uncooked rations, and there was no fuel on shore for cooking."[30]

25. *Ibid.*, 690–91. In an earlier dispatch, Banks had written Halleck that Grierson desired to join any expedition to Texas. *Ibid.*, 683.

26. *Ibid.*, 699.

27. It is called an "unaccountable failure" in *Battles and Leaders*, IV, 598.

28. *Official Records*, Vol. XXVI, Pt. 1, p. 288.

29. Two of the gunboats, the *Clifton* and the *Sachem*, were disabled and captured by the Confederates. For reports of the expedition, see *Ibid.*, 286–99.

30. *Ibid.*, 297.

Having been foiled at the Sabine, Banks tried again two months later to "restore the flag" in Texas. This time, he himself led the expedition, made up of the Second Division, XIII Army Corps, an "attached" regiment of Maine infantry, a pioneer company, the 1st Texas, U.S.A., and the 1st Engineers and 16th Infantry, "Corps d'Afrique," *i.e.*, Negro troops. The objective was Brazos Island, at the mouth of the Rio Grande near Brownsville, and on November 2, Banks was able to notify his chief of staff in New Orleans, who in turn notified the president, that "The flag of the Union floats over Texas to-day at meridian precisely." What Banks had in mind after establishing a base at the mouth of the Rio Grande was to work his way northeastward and "occupy successively all the passes and inlets that connect the Gulf of Mexico with the land-locked lagoons or sounds of the Texas coast from the Rio Grande to the Sabine."[31] Banks had to spend time on an unavoidable involvement in more than normally volatile Mexican politics, but at the same time he strengthened his forces by enlisting recruits who came into his lines "in great numbers," bringing their own horses with them but requiring "horse equipments and cavalry arms," two thousand sets of which were sent on to him from New Orleans. To increase further the number of his mounted troops, Banks arranged to buy locally "about 600 horses (mustang)" but then discovered that to improve the condition of the animals, he had to have oats shipped to him from New Orleans.[32]

The immediate military (as distinguished from political) objective underlying these operations was to protect Louisiana against attack from Texas, where the armed strength of the trans-Mississippi Confederacy was concentrated. As Banks had written General Halleck in August, 1863, "The rebellion in Louisiana is kept alive only by Texas." The somewhat longer-range goal was to recapture western Louisiana and eastern Texas and thus restore to the Union what remained of the Confederacy west of the Mississippi, the population of which was already in the grip of what one author has termed "a weary mood of lawless apathy."[33] It was clearly seen by General Halleck, and perhaps less so by General Banks, that nibbling at the periphery of the region by

31. *Ibid.*, 396; *Battles and Leaders*, IV, 346.
32. *Official Records*, Vol. XXVI, Pt. 1, pp. 811, 843. In addition to buying mustangs in Texas, an officer was sent "into the interior of Mexico" to buy horses and mules, *Ibid.*, 413.
33. Kerby, *Kirby Smith's Confederacy*, 279.

landing troops at "all the passes and inlets" from the Gulf would not do the trick. The only effective way to reconquer the trans-Mississippi was an overland campaign, west via the Red River to Alexandria and Shreveport.

It was understood by everyone concerned that the contemplated operation, since it would depend heavily on the armed and logistical support of gunboats and transports steaming up Red River, would be impractical because of low water, particularly over the falls at Alexandria, until the spring runoff in March and April opened the river to navigation. Banks had a sizable force (its numbers not reported) at Brashear City—three divisions (seven brigades of thirty-four regiments and eight batteries) of the XIII Army Corps, commanded by Major General Cadwallader C. Washburn, and two divisions (four brigades of seventeen regiments and four batteries) of the XIX Army Corps, commanded by General Franklin, who was also in command of the entire force.[34] A peculiarity of the force was that all the regiments and batteries of the XIII Corps command came from the western states, mainly Illinois, Indiana, Iowa, and Ohio, whereas all those in the XIX Corps came from the eastern and New England states—New York, Maine, and Massachusetts. Included in General Franklin's forces were an "Artillery Reserve" of two batteries, three regiments of infantry and one battery "not brigaded," and General Albert L. Lee's Cavalry Division, made up of Colonel John G. Fonda's First Brigade (the 118th Illinois Mounted Infantry and six to nine companies of three regiments of Louisiana, Missouri, and New York cavalry), and Colonel John J. Mudd's Second Brigade (one to seven companies each from six regiments of Illinois and Indiana cavalry).

After the failure of the Sabine Pass enterprise, and before the successful Brazos Island operation, Banks made an attempt to reach Texas by marching Franklin's forces overland to Alexandria and Shreveport, through "Evangeline country," a land seamed with bayous and lakes left behind by the many changes in the course of the Mississippi over the ages. With Banks himself present, the campaign got under way on

34. *Official Records*, Vol. XXVI, Pt. 1, pp. 334–36. Richard Taylor estimated the XIX Corps numbers as about 10,000 and of the XIII Corps as "somewhat larger." *Ibid.*, 387. Franklin himself gave the numbers of the two XIII Corps divisions as "about 4,500" and "only about 1,100," respectively. *Ibid.*, 342, 343. Lee's cavalry numbered about 2,100. *Ibid.*, 343. Without citing a source, Kerby credits Franklin with a total strength of 20,000. Kerby, *Kirby Smith's Confederacy*, 242.

October 3. There were frequent skirmishes of no consequence with the Confederate forces led by General Richard Taylor, son of President Zachary Taylor and brother of Jefferson Davis' first wife, as the expedition moved north to Bayou Courtebleau, beyond Opelousas, where Franklin came to a halt, and then decided to retreat.[35] In the absence of a formal report by General Franklin, it is impossible to determine why he stopped the advance on October 25 and, after a pause of several days, chose to retreat to his base. Based on his experiences in this operation, General Franklin gave it as his opinion that

an infantry force is very hard to move on account of the scarcity of supplies, and, when moved, is of but little use. The enemy is nearly entirely mounted, and . . . the system of warfare . . . [is] merely that of annoyance. In no case will he risk a general battle, unless his forces are superior to ours and he certain of success. He has it in his power to hover on all sides of an infantry force, producing an annoyance the severity of which cannot be appreciated unless it be felt.

The only way of meeting this method of warfare is to keep a large force mounted. This force should be the main force of the army, and the infantry should be subordinate to it. . . .

All of the infantry should be mounted whose unexpired terms of service will justify the labor of teaching them to be cavalry, and about one-half should be mounted infantry, the remainder cavalry. . . . The question as to whether the animals belonging to the mounted force which I have indicated can be fed in the country is a grave one.[36]

Notwithstanding General Franklin's qualms, it may be assumed that an area that made it possible for General Taylor to subsist his "nearly entirely mounted" forces could have subsisted a Union mounted force as well. Where, however, in the universal shortage of horses, animals were to be found for mounting General Franklin's projected mounted infantry and cavalry was probably a more intractable problem. Banks's frequently (but politely) repeated pleas for more cavalry or, failing that, for horses to create his own cavalry were discussed in the latter part of

35. The "Record of Events of the Cavalry Division" states that on November 7 "the cavalry was strengthened by mounting infantry, and newly brigaded." *Official Records*, Vol. XXVI, Pt. 1, p. 378. One critic has written, not unfairly, that "once New Iberia was taken, Franklin seemed unable to decide how to proceed or what to do next. Instead of marching his column for a decisive thrust toward a stipulated objective, he dissipated his forces in scattered, piecemeal, leapfrog forays aimed, roughly, at the nearest roving detachments of Taylor's little army." Kerby, *Kirby Smith's Confederacy*, 243.

36. *Official Records*, Vol. XXVI, Pt. 1, pp. 390, 347–48.

Chapter XIII. In reply to one of Banks's applications, Halleck sent him on September 8 a firm "no."

I have already stated to you [Halleck wrote] that it would be impossible to send you any cavalry very soon from the north. The great losses in that arm in recent battles, and by the discharge of two-years' and nine months' men, and the great difficulty in procuring cavalry recruits, places this matter beyond question or discussion. Requisitions are received almost simultaneously with yours from nearly every other department for additional cavalry, some 20,000 or 30,000 being urgently asked for, it being alleged in many cases that operations cannot be continued without them. . . . I have not a single man to supply these demands. . . . As volunteering has virtually ceased, the only mode of supplying . . . [the new men needed due to expiration of terms of service] was by the draft, which, as yet, has been almost entirely unproductive.[37]

A minor factor, presumably beneath the notice of such highly placed officers as Halleck and Franklin, was noted by a real cavalryman, a trooper of the 2nd Illinois.

Our cavalry has shown such high efficiency that they considered that the only factor necessary to success was more cavalry. This they did not have, but it was easy to get. Cavalry was composed of men on horseback. Why not mount the infantry? If not enough, mount more infantry . . . and we were soon able to muster about nine regiments including ours and the 6th Missouri Cavalry. With this force we marched out to meet the enemy. . . . [Our] wings, composed of mounted infantry, soon began to fall back and to become displaced. They were good men but as little at home on horseback as a lands-man on a yardarm. They could not manage their horses and were greatly handicapped with their long guns. This gave them a grotesque appearance which would have been ludicrous had the situation been less grave.[38]

Despite his discouraging dispatch, Halleck found the means to help to increase Banks's mounted force. He arranged to have 8,000 sets of "horse equipments" sent to Banks and Grant, asked Grant to send Banks "all the cavalry he could possibly spare," and asked General Meigs, then on his way west, to give "his personal attention" to shipping Banks the largest possible number of horses from St. Louis.[39] Early in the new year, the 26th Massachusetts Infantry was converted to "cavalry," and at the end of January, better than his word, Halleck wrote Banks that three regiments of cavalry, one each from Maryland and Maine and a veteran unit from New York, were being shipped to him, with equipments but without horses, "as transportation for

37. *Ibid.*, 719–20.
38. Fletcher, *The History of Company A*, 122–23.
39. *Official Records*, Vol. XXVI, Pt. 1, p. 719.

horses by sea cannot now be procured."[40] General Meigs was to send horses for these regiments from St. Louis.

With his mind still on an invasion of Texas by a campaign up Red River, Banks communicated with Sherman, his neighbor to the north who was in the midst of planning for his Meridian Campaign. Writing on January 16, Sherman had written that the success of his Meridian operation, "and one similar on Shreveport as soon as Red River rises, would pretty well settle the main question in the southwest, and I would like nothing better than to unite with you in such a movement."[41] Banks had also been told by Halleck more than once that "the Red River is the shortest and best line of defense for Louisiana and Arkansas and as a base of operations against Texas. . . . If as soon as you have sufficient water in the Atchafalaya and Red Rivers you operate in that direction, Steele's army [in Arkansas] and such forces as Sherman can detach should be directed to the same object. The gunboats should also co-operate." In another dispatch Halleck mentioned a fact that, deservedly or not, was to make the Red River Campaign notorious. The campaign, Halleck wrote, "would open to us the cotton and stores in Northeastern Louisiana and Southern Arkansas."[42]

In a further exchange of dispatches and in a personal visit to New Orleans, Sherman expressed an eagerness to participate in a Red River Campaign. But, he said, it should not be undertaken until there were "twelve feet of water on the rapids at Alexandria," which limited the operation to the months from March to June, and he laid out a plan of campaign for Banks's benefit. He envisaged a fast-moving, three-pronged operation, General Steele to move directly on Shreveport from Little Rock with 10,000 infantry and 5,000 cavalry, Banks to move north from Opelousas by way of Alexandria with 10,000 men, and Sherman himself to move directly up Red River with "about ten thousand" men and a combined fleet of gunboats and transports. The three branches of the advance were to join at Shreveport "about a day appointed beforehand."[43] Grant, whose permission to take part Sherman

40. *Ibid.*, Vol. XXXIV, Pt. 2, pp. 75–76, 55, 171.

41. *Ibid.*, Vol. XXXII, Pt. 2, pp. 114–15. In the same dispatch, Sherman tried to excuse the seizure by his subordinates at Vicksburg and Natchez of "horses, stores, &c.," in transit to Banks from St. Louis.

42. *Ibid.*, Vol. XXXIV, Pt. 2, pp. 15, 56.

43. *Ibid.*, 266–67. (The same dispatch is in Sherman, *Memoirs*, I, 395.) Steele, however, was to protest energetically that he could contribute no more than 7,000 troops to the operation. *Official Records*, Vol. XXXIV, Pt. 2, p. 547. He actually contributed 11,499, as will appear below.

needed, disapproved of Sherman himself going, because there was "other important work for him to do." But he agreed to lend Banks for a limited time the 10,000 men Sherman had mentioned, notwithstanding that (as he later wrote) he had "opposed the movement strenuously, but acquiesced because it was the orders of my superior at the time"—*i.e.*, Halleck.[44]

Based on his proposal to Banks, and having obtained Grant's sanction, Sherman made up a two-division force of 10,000 infantry and artillery, taken in part from the XVI and in part from the XVII Corps. The two divisions were commanded by Generals Joseph A. Mower and Thomas Kilby Smith; the whole, not formally designated as a corps, was commanded by General Andrew J. Smith. On March 6, Sherman handed written orders to A. J. Smith. He was to embark his "strong, well-appointed" force, "little encumbered with wagons or wheeled vehicles, but well supplied with fuel, provisions, and ammunition," for a voyage up the Red River (which the historian of the navy's role in the campaign spoke of as "treacherous" and as a "crooked and turbid stream") to Alexandria, where he was to meet Banks about March 17, and then go on upriver to capture Shreveport.[45] Within thirty days after his arrival at Red River, Smith was to return to Vicksburg "with all dispatch" to join the Army of the Tennessee. It may be said now that General Smith's forces (having captured Fort De Russy, ten miles below Alexandria, on the way) and Admiral David D. Porter's gunboats reached Alexandria ahead of schedule and then had to wait several days for Banks. "These two divisions," Sherman wrote, "participated in the whole of General Banks's unfortunate Red River expedition, and were delayed so long up Red River, and subsequently on the Mississippi, that they did not share with their comrades the successes and glories of the Atlanta campaign. . . . indeed, they did not get back to Tennessee until December, nine months later, and barely in time to play a part in General Thomas' great victory at Nashville."[46]

Frederick Steele's negligible role in the campaign may be disposed

44. Grant, *Personal Memoirs*, II, 128, 139. His after-the-fact opposition may be contrasted with his statement in a March 16 dispatch to Banks: "I regard the success of your present move as of great importance in reducing the number of troops necessary for protecting the navigation of the Mississippi. . . . It is also important that Shreveport be taken as soon as possible." *Official Records*, Vol. XXXIV, Pt. 2, p. 610.
45. *Official Records*, Vol. XXXIV, Pt. 2, pp. 513–15; *Battles and Leaders*, IV, 362.
46. Sherman, *Memoirs*, II, 308.

of first. He had warned Grant and Sherman not to expect too much from him. "My cavalry," he wrote, "have not had a remount for a year. Many of them are dismounted and most of the horses on hand now are in poor condition. The same is the case with most of the batteries. . . . I shall . . . do the best I can." According to plan, his troops left Little Rock and Fort Smith on March 23; they numbered 11,499 effectives, 4,658 of them cavalry. They were organized into a division of infantry; a hybrid "Frontier Division," made up of regiments of white and Negro infantry and a three-regiment brigade of Kansas cavalry; General Eugene A. Carr's division of two brigades of cavalry; and lastly Colonel Powell Clayton's two-regiment Independent Cavalry Brigade.[47]

The 1st Iowa, one of the regiments of the cavalry division, waived its right to leave on veterans' furlough to go on the expedition. The 350 dismounted men of the regiment were organized as a "Dismounted Battalion" and marched along as infantry.[48]

Moving first southwest across the Prairie d'Ane and then east toward Camden, Steele's men were beset by supply difficulties—for three weeks they were on half rations—and had to make the exhausting physical effort of moving through swamps and on primitive roads. "Long stretches of the roads to Camden had to be corduroyed. Crossing Cypress Bayou meant simply wading through a swamp."[49] Steele wrote Sherman on April 22 from Camden: "We arrived here on the 15th . . . having been delayed about ten days by bad roads and the failure of the command from Fort Smith to join us according to agreement. We have been bushwhacked, attacked in front and rear and flank, and have driven [General Sterling] Price out of two defensive works."[50]

Opposing Steele's advance were Price's five brigades of cavalry. On April 18, a 198-wagon forage train Steele sent out was attacked and

47. *Official Records*, Vol. XXXIV, Pt. 2, p. 646, Pt. 1, pp. 657–59; *Battles and Leaders*, IV, 368.

48. Lothrop, *A History of the First Regiment*, 148; Ingersoll, *Iowa and the Rebellion*, 370–71. On April 17 a detachment of the mounted portion of the regiment captured a streamboat on the Ouachita River and brought it safely to Camden.

49. Ludwell H. Johnson, *Red River Campaign* (Baltimore, 1958), 179. See also Andrew W. McCormick, "Battles and Campaigns in Arkansas," MOLLUS, Commandery of Ohio, *Sketches of War History, 1861–1865*, VI, 2–4, for incidents of the march to Camden.

50. *Official Records*, Vol. XXXIV, Pt. 1, pp. 662–63. See also Castel, *General Sterling Price*, 173–74.

captured at Poison Springs by General Marmaduke. The train was escorted by 285 Kansas cavalry ("many of . . . whom had, in violation of orders, straggled from their commands"), 875 infantry, and four guns. The 1st Kansas Infantry, a Negro regiment, was part of the escort. Its Colonel James M. Williams reported, "Many wounded men . . . fell into the hands of the enemy, and I have the most positive assurances from eyewitnesses that they were murdered on the spot."[51]

On April 19, General E. Kirby Smith, in command of the Confederate Trans-Mississippi Department, took personal charge of the operations against Steele. Six days later, the cavalry brigades of James F. Fagan, William L. Cabell, and Jo Shelby (now a brigadier general) attacked at Marks' Mill a train of 240 wagons Steele was sending back to Little Rock for supplies. The train had an escort of 1,600 infantry, 400 cavalry, and five pieces of artillery, the whole under the command of Colonel Clayton. Attacked from two sides, the escort was overwhelmed "after a desperate fight of three hours, [and] the train, with all the artillery and the greater portion of the infantry and cavalry, was captured."[52] The loss of the train made it impossible for Steele to advance, or even to remain in Camden, and on the night of April 26 he set off on his return to Little Rock.[53] Under constant attack for several days, Steele made a stand on April 30 at the Jenkins' Ferry crossing of the Saline River. "The battle raged furiously nearly half a day, when the Confederate army was repulsed with heavy loss and withdrew from the field. . . . Price was so badly beaten that he made no effort to pursue north of the Saline River," and Steele made a leisurely march thence back to Little Rock.[54]

51. *Ibid.*, 744, 746, 754. Of the 438 officers and men the 1st Kansas Infantry had in the action, 117 were killed and 67 wounded, "some of them mortally." *Ibid.*, 746. Marmaduke had between 3,500 and 3,800 men in the action. *Ibid.*, 819; Castel, *General Sterling Price*, 177.

52. *Ibid.*, 665; O'Flaherty, *General Jo Shelby*, 210; McCormick, "Battles and Campaigns in Arkansas," 5–8. About 500 troopers of the 1st Iowa, released at last to go on veterans' furlough, "were a few miles in rear of the train when it was attacked. On hearing the firing, they pressed forward, but were met by a superior force, and fighting fell back." *Official Records*, Vol. XXXIV, Pt. 1, p. 668.

53. From dispatches found in the telegraph office in Camden, Steele learned that Banks had been "badly defeated" and "was in full retreat down Red River." McCormick, "Battles and Campaigns in Arkansas," 3.

54. *Battles and Leaders*, IV, 375. Castel, *General Sterling Price*, 181–83. Confederate losses at Jenkins' Ferry were 800 to 1,000 killed and wounded. Steele's casualties in the entire campaign were 2,750 killed, wounded, captured, and missing, plus 635 wagons and 2,500 mules. Johnson, *Red River Campaign*, 202–203.

The navy, composed of a "splendid squadron" of thirteen ironclads and seven shallow-draft gunboats ("tinclads") under command of Admiral Porter, escorting more than thirty transports carrying General A. J. Smith's troops and the army's supplies, occupied Alexandria on March 16, as has been mentioned. The third and principal prong of the enterprise, the XIII and XIX Corps infantry (15,392 rank and file present for duty, plus 1,535 "Corps d'Afrique"—four regiments of Negro infantry—and General Albert L. Lee's division of 4,635 troopers in seven regiments of cavalry and four of mounted infantry) left their base at Franklin, Louisiana, on Bayou Teche, for the 175-mile march via Opelousas and Bayou Boeuf to Alexandria on roads ruined by bad weather.[55] Lee and the cavalry reached Alexandria on March 19; the infantry and artillery arrived on March 25 and 26. It is stated that the week's delay in the arrival of the infantry had no effect on the campaign, because "the river, though slowly rising, was still so low that the gunboats had not been able to pass the difficult rapids that obstruct the navigation just above Alexandria.[56] Not until April 3 were thirteen of the gunboats and thirty of the transports able to get above the rapids.

The Confederate troops in the area, under General Richard Taylor, had evacuated Alexandria and moved west toward Shreveport, staying well out of reach of the advancing Federals. Banks's cavalry and infantry moved out from Alexandria on March 27 and, marching along the south bank of the river, reached Natchitoches and Grand Ecore, four marches short of Shreveport, on April 3. Here Banks made what proved to be a fatal decision. He could have continued to Shreveport on a road that ran along the south bank of the river and thus kept in contact with his ships, or he could have used the "inland" road that veered away from the river and led to Shreveport via Pleasant Hill and Mansfield. He chose the latter route. Banks's assistant medical director wrote after the war that the inland road "plunges into dense woods" after it leaves Grand Ecore, but it was reported to be the "regular, most trav-

---

55. *Battles and Leaders*, IV, 367.
56. *Battles and Leaders*, IV, 350. Seven of the gunboats and the "larger transports" drew too much water and had to remain below the rapids. The Mississippi Marine Brigade, which had gone upstream with the gunboats, left the expedition at Alexandria to return to Vicksburg. Many members of the brigade were "suffering from small-pox, which pervaded all the transports, and they were reported in condition of partial mutiny." *Official Records*, Vol. XXXIV, Pt. 1, p. 197. The brigade's campaign of pillage and destruction on its journey down Red River has been mentioned (see Ch. VIII, pp. 203–204 above).

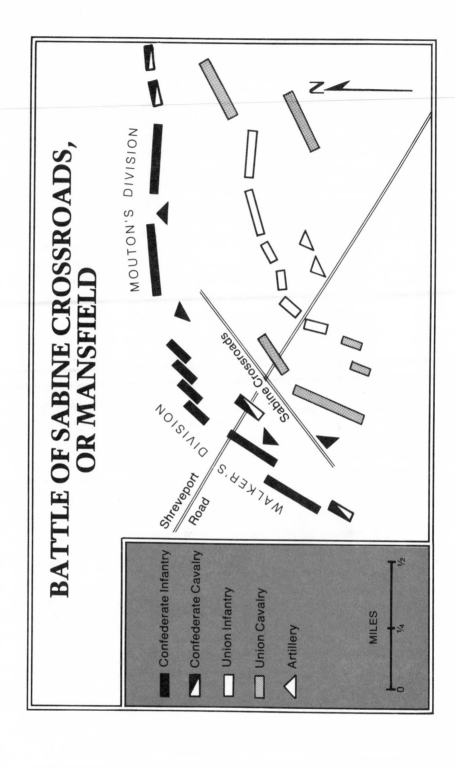

BATTLE OF SABINE CROSSROADS, OR MANSFIELD

MOUTON'S DIVISION

Sabine Crossroads

WALKER'S DIVISION

Shreveport Road

Confederate Infantry
Confederate Cavalry
Union Infantry
Union Cavalry
Artillery

MILES

0   ¼   ½

elled route," notwithstanding that, as he described it, it was "a narrow, sunken road through a pine forest, called in the rebel reports 'a howling wilderness,' a road more like a broad, deep, red-colored ditch than anything else, and one where it was impossible to turn a wagon around, except at intervals of several miles where might happen to be a clearing."[57] The result, dictated partly by the nature of the road and partly by deliberate choice, was that when the advance from Grand Ecore got under way, the Union army stretched out for a distance of more than a day's march from the head of the cavalry in front to the rear of General A. J. Smith's troops and the Corps d'Afrique at the far end of the line of march. General Lee's column of horsemen, itself strung out for a considerable distance by the narrow road, had behind it its train of more than 300 wagons and three batteries of artillery, covering a three-mile stretch of road. Behind the cavalry train came the XIII Corps infantry, followed by their train of 700 wagons. Then, after a gap of several miles, came the XIX Corps infantry and the rest of the army.[58] Thus was created the scenario (with which the reader is already familiar) for a disaster similar to Sturgis' defeat by Forrest at Brice's Crossroads three months later, but on a considerably larger scale.

Richard Taylor, short of cavalry until he was joined on April 4 and 5 by General Thomas Green's division of Texas mounted infantry, continued to retreat until he reached a road intersection named Sabine Crossroads, where there was a clearing bordered by dense woods to the north, an excellent position, he decided, on which to give battle. The clearing was 1,200 yards side to side and 800 yards north to south; a "deep ravine" ran through the middle of the clearing; the road to Shreveport, on which Lee was advancing, split the clearing into two

57. John Homans, "The Red River Expedition," *Papers of the Military History Society of Massachusetts*, VIII (1910), 77. Homans wrote: "On the river road we should have had plenty of drinking water, and should have been near the gunboats in case they had needed our assistance, and also they would have been a protection to ourselves in case of reverse and defeat. There were probably obvious reasons, such as swamps or impassable marshes and lowlands . . . that made our engineers choose the [inland] road." *Ibid.*, 77.
58. Aside from the fact that a day's march separated the head and tail of the Union column, it is impossible to be certain of the distances (and gaps) between the various units. See, for example, *Ibid.*, 77, 79. General Taylor's statement that "in the afternoon of the 7th I knew that the front and rear of . . . [Banks's] column were separated by a distance of twenty miles" is probably as accurate as any. Taylor, *Destruction and Reconstruction*, 162.

roughly equal halves from side to side.[59] On the morning of April 8, Taylor moved his forces into the woods at the northern edge of the clearing, three brigades of General John G. Walker's division of infantry to the west (right) of the Pleasant Hill–Mansfield road, and two brigades of General Alfred Mouton's infantry division to the east (left) of the road; Green's horsemen, dismounted, extended Mouton's line to the east. Including a regiment of mounted infantry posted well out on each flank and a third (X. B. Debray's) held in reserve, Taylor had 5,300 infantry, 3,000 mounted infantry, and 500 gunners on the field.[60] General Thomas J. Churchill's 4,400-man detachment of infantry from Sterling Price's army, marching down from Shreveport, did not join Taylor until the ninth, the day after the battle.

Lee's cavalry bivouacked on the night of the seventh at Carroll's Mill, twelve miles south of the crossroads. For the first time since the start of the campaign, they had encountered that afternoon something more than token opposition. Three regiments of Green's mounted troops opposed Lee's advance effectively enough to force him to dismount two of his brigades so that they could make their way through the woods; he deployed them in line to push the enemy out of the way. Green's delaying operation had another effect: it made Lee apprehensive and caused him on the evening of the seventh to ask General Franklin for infantry reinforcements. The message Lee sent General Franklin was to the effect that "the enemy were in considerable force, and I thought we were on them. . . . I wanted the infantry for the reason that it was necessary to dismount every cavalryman I put in the fight, and . . . their horses made a long, loose irregular train to lead and take about; and cavalrymen are not fit to fight on foot for a great length of time."[61] Franklin refused to send the reinforcements. It is said that he "had little confidence in the cavalry—[and was] afraid that his men would be left in the lurch in case . . . [the cavalry] were

59. Taylor, *Destruction and Reconstruction*, 160. *Battles and Leaders*, IV, 352, gives the depth of the clearing north to south as 900 yards.

60. Taylor, *Destruction and Reconstruction*, 162. Taylor writes that "dense forest prevented the employment of much artillery, and with the exception of [M. V.] McMahan's, which rendered excellent service, none was used in the action." *Ibid.*, 162. In contrast to Taylor's statement that he had 8,800 men present on April 8, he is credited with 11,000 in *Battles and Leaders*, IV, 352.

61. U.S. Congress, *Report of the Joint Committee on the Conduct of the War*, 38th Cong., 2nd Sess. (2 vols.; Washington, D.C., 1865), II, 59 (cited hereinafter as *Report of the Joint Committee*).

defeated."[62] Banks, however, overruled Franklin, who thereupon ordered Colonel Joseph W. Vance's brigade of the Fourth Division, XIII Army Corps, to be sent to Lee; later, on the morning of the eighth, Franklin also sent Colonel Frank Emerson's brigade of the same division to join Lee.

Lee was also conscious of the potential danger of having his train strung out in single file for a distance, he wrote, of "two or three miles" immediately behind him. He had asked Franklin "very often" to be allowed to join his trains to those of the infantry, in rear of the XIX Corps; Franklin turned down the request each time Lee made it, "saying that it was the cavalry's business to look after its own train."[63] One reason (perhaps the main one) Lee had for wanting to be relieved of his train was that guarding it took "from one-third to one-half of . . . [his] force." The real vice of the arrangement, however, and probably the main contributing factor of the eventual Federal disaster, was that it created too great a gap between the cavalry and the head of the infantry column, thereby increasing greatly the time the infantry needed to come to Lee's assistance, should the cavalry get into trouble, as they did.

Having received the infantry reinforcements he had asked for, and ordered to go on to Mansfield, Lee moved off at sunrise on the eighth and at once met powerful opposition. He deployed a regiment of infantry in line of battle on each side of the road, preceded by dismounted cavalry skirmishers, and moved forward "very slowly, about half a mile an hour." It was noon when Lee reached the ridge overlooking the "large open field" (which he described as "perhaps a mile in extent in each direction") beyond which Taylor had posted his troops. Banks was with Lee, in the advance; told by Lee that the Confederates were present in force, he ordered Lee to deploy and sent orders back "to hurry forward" the infantry, whose march that morning had been "impeded" by "very heavy rains . . . [which] made the single road . . . almost impassable."[64]

Facing the Confederates at the crossroads, Lee deployed the 3rd Massachusetts and the 31st Massachusetts Mounted Infantry of Colo-

62. Johnson, *Red River Campaign*, 126; *Report of the Joint Committee*, II, 29.

63. *Report of the Joint Committee*, II, 59; Homans, "Red River Expedition," 78; Johnson, *Red River Campaign*, 125.

64. *Report of the Joint Committee*, II, 60; Johnson, *Red River Campaign*, 128; *Battles and Leaders* IV, 353; *Official Records*, Vol. XXXIV, Pt. 1, p. 181.

nel Nathan A. M. "Gold Lace" Dudley's brigade on his left flank, a third regiment of the brigade, the 2nd New Hampshire, on the right, and its fourth regiment, the 2nd Illinois, in reserve, a half mile to the rear. To Dudley's right, he placed the two brigades of infantry that General Franklin had sent him. Next to the right came Colonel T. J. Lucas' First Brigade of cavalry, dismounted, and on the outer flank, as has been mentioned, the 2nd New Hampshire.[65]

It is worthy of notice, as a portent of what would shortly happen, that the Emerson brigade of infantry had been sent to Lee in response to a plea from Colonel William J. Landram (who was actually in command of the Vance brigade). "My men," Colonel Landram wrote, "have skirmished and marched through the bushes and thickets for 8 or 9 miles. . . . They have no water, and are literally worn out. Can you have them relieved soon? General Lee insists on pushing ahead." General Thomas E. G. Ransom, to whose division both brigades of infantry belonged, noted in his report that the second brigade he sent had "much difficulty in passing the cavalry train, which obstructed the road."[66]

The only activity in the early hours of the afternoon at the crossroads was a desultory fire by the skirmishers of both sides. At 4 o'clock, "the enemy showing no disposition to advance," Taylor ordered his entire force to attack.[67] Advancing in two lines and sustaining heavy casualties—General Alfred Mouton himself (succeeded in command of the division by General Camille Armand Jules Marie, Prince de Polignac) and four colonels were killed, and more than a third of Mouton's division were killed or wounded—the Confederates nonetheless maintained the momentum of their attack and in a short time had also turned Lee's left flank. Charged by Walker's division, the 23rd Wisconsin Infantry of the Vance brigade and the Massachusetts regiments of cavalry and mounted infantry on Lee's left gave way in less than twenty minutes.[68] Thereupon Lee's entire line collapsed, and now the

65. *Official Records*, Vol. XXXIV, Pt. 1, pp. 451, 456–57. The Third Cavalry Brigade remained in the rear to guard the train, the head of which was 1¼ miles in rear of the position occupied by Lee. *Ibid.*, 457. In his testimony before the joint committee, Lee stated that the head of the train was a half mile behind his line. *Report of the Joint Committee*, II, 61. The 31st Massachusetts Mounted Infantry was also known as the 6th Massachusetts Cavalry. Ormand F. Nims's battery of horse artillery and two sections of the 6th Missouri Howitzer Battery were interspersed with the regiments of infantry and cavalry.

66. *Official Records*, Vol. XXXIV, Pt. 1, p. 265.

67. Taylor, *Destruction and Reconstruction*, 163.

68. *Report of the Joint Committee*, II, 61; *Official Records*, Vol. XXXIV, Pt. 1, p. 458.

presence of the cavalry trains immediately behind the front and filling the narrow road turned defeat into rout, and rout into disaster. The train made an orderly retreat impossible, notwithstanding General Lee's later claim that "the cavalry (mounted) formed repeatedly lines behind our retreating forces and stayed the advance of the rebels." It negated any effort—which might have been fruitless in any case—to organize a solid line behind which the fugitives could rally.[69] Lastly, the blockage of the road hampered the advance of the infantry that General Franklin hurried forward in response to Banks's orders. General Robert A. Cameron's division needed two hours to cover five miles, and by the time it got within reach of where Lee's line had been, it was too late. Lee's own men and the two brigades of infantrymen had "crumbled everywhere and were falling back" in disorder. Lee had sent orders to the rear when the battle began "to get that train back as fast as they could. . . . But there were conflicting orders, and a great deal of confusion about it." When the beaten troopers and infantrymen got back to the train, they found total chaos: "a hundred or more of these wagons stopped there; some of them were not turned round; the most of them were turned around; but a great many of them were in ruts, against trees, the mules shot, etc., and we lost some artillery there by reason of it."[70]

It is of interest to note the judgment of surgeon John Homans, an intelligent and disinterested observer, to account for the Sabine Crossroads disaster. "Why we lost the battle of Sabine Cross Roads," Homans wrote, "is plain enough. The country was not one to manoeuver in. Our cavalry had no business in front. They had to ride along a sunken road

---

The twenty minutes is General Lee's estimate. General Banks reported that the troops held out for an hour before they broke. *Official Records*, Vol. XXXIV, Pt. 1, p. 182.

69. *Official Records*, Vol. XXXIV, Pt. 1, p. 452. General Banks said in his report: "Upon the retreat of the advanced guard the enemy instantaneously enveloped the train . . . and it was impossible to withdraw the artillery in consequence of the preoccupation of the ground by the wagons; and the encumbered roads impeded the movements of troops and caused many prisoners to fall into the hands of the enemy. The disasters of the day are to be attributed to the fatally incautious advance of the large cavalry train and the surplus artillery rather than to the strength of the enemy, his unexpected resistance, or the deficient valor of our troops." *Ibid.*, 182.

70. *Report of the Joint Committee*, II, 61; *Official Records*, Vol. XXXIV, Pt. 1, p. 458. Lee stated his loss here as 156 wagons (mostly loaded with forage) and about 800 mules. *Report of the Joint Committee*, II, 62. Taylor claimed as "the fruits of victory" 2,500 prisoners, 20 guns, several stands of colors, many thousands of small arms, and 250 wagons. Taylor, *Destruction and Reconstruction*, 164.

in a pine forest, dismount, drive the enemy, come back for their horses, mount again, and soon fight again as foot soldiers. They were practically infantry, with inferior arms, and bothered by their horses. . . . Cavalry was out of place; they could not be used. Then again, our army was strung out over thirty miles of road, no two detachments being in supporting distance of each other."[71] Admiral Porter, no admirer of Banks, put it more simply in a letter to General Sherman. After remarking that "the army has been shamefully beaten by the rebels," he called the campaign "an affair the management of which would be discreditable to a boy nine years of age." He blamed the actual defeat on Lee and the cavalry, who, he said, had allowed themselves to be led into a trap, and when attacked by Taylor's 15,000 infantry, they "broke and fell back on the wagons, the wagons stampeded and blocked up the road . . . [and] such a scene ensued as was never seen before except at Bull Run."[72]

The retreat of the beaten troops did not come to a halt until they found refuge behind General William H. Emory's division of the XIX Corps, drawn up in line of battle facing an open field, three miles south of Sabine Crossroads. Notwithstanding "a tremendous rush made on the line by the mass of fugitives," followed by an attack by Taylor's forces, Emory was able to hold his ground. Banks then held a council of war to decide whether to remain where he was to await the arrival next morning of A. J. Smith's two divisions or to retreat fifteen miles to Pleasant Hill, where Smith had halted for the night, and join him there. The decision was to retreat. As General Banks explained, "The want of water, the weakness of the position we held, and the uncertainty of General Smith being able to reach the position we occupied at day-break, led to the adoption of the second course."[73] The march to the rear began at midnight, and at 8:30 A.M. on the ninth, the army was reunited at Pleasant Hill. Banks then ordered Lee to detach a force of 1,000 of his cavalrymen (Lee chose 500 men each from his First and Fifth Brigades) to remain with General Franklin "to act as scouts and skirmishers." With the rest of his division and "whatever was left of the detachment of the 13th corps, and some negro troops that were there . . . [Lee was to] take the trains and the majority of the

71. Homans, "Red River Expedition," 82.
72. *Official Records*, Vol. XXXIV, Pt. 3, pp. 153, 170.
73. *Ibid.*, Pt. 1, pp. 392, 257, 183, 201; *Report of the Joint Committee*, II, 62.

artillery of the army [six or eight batteries] to Grand Ecore."[74] Lee departed just as the "desperate and sanguinary" battle of Pleasant Hill was beginning, a battle in which, as General Banks reported, "the defeat of the enemy was complete," a statement, so General Taylor wrote, in which the proportion of fiction was greatly in excess of the proportion of fact. The accuracy of Banks's claim is, however, borne out by General E. Kirby Smith, who reported that "Taylor's troops were repulsed and thrown into confusion."[75]

Whatever the truth of these conflicting claims may have been, another council of war held by Banks that evening determined, on the "urgent recommendation of all the general officers," to retreat the next day to Grand Ecore and form a junction with the fleet. From Grand Ecore to Alexandria, where the retreat halted because low water over the rapids made it impossible for the navy to go on, "the Army of the Gulf left behind it a smoldering wasteland." Lee did not remain in Alexandria to witness the memorable feat of Lieutenant Colonel (later Major General) Joseph Bailey, 4th Wisconsin Infantry, who designed a series of dams that the army proceeded to build, to raise the depth of the water over the rapids and enable the gunboats and transports to reach deep water below.[76]

Admiral Porter was not alone in assigning to Lee and the cavalry a large share of the responsibility for Sabine Crossroads. On April 18, Lee was relieved of his cavalry command; he was ordered to "proceed forthwith to assume charge of the cavalry depot in New Orleans for the purpose of reorganizing the cavalry of the department." Demoted with Lee was Colonel Dudley, relieved of his command of the Fourth Brigade of the Cavalry Division and sent to New Orleans to assist Lee in "reorganizing the cavalry of the department." Lee's place in active command of the Gulf cavalry was taken by General Richard Arnold, translated to that job from his post of chief of artillery of the department, first to command the cavalry left with the army at Grand Ecore and then to assume the duties of chief of cavalry, Department of the Gulf. Banks explained that he relieved Lee of his command—an act he "afterwards regretted"—"because the general officers expressed . . .

74. *Official Records*, Vol. XXXIV, Pt. 1, p. 459; *Report of the Joint Committee*, II, 62.
75. *Official Records*, Vol. XXXIV, Pt. 1, p. 202; Taylor, *Destruction and Reconstruction*, 175; see also Homans, "Red River Expedition," 81–82.
76. Johnson, *Red River Campaign*, 223; *Official Records*, Vol. XXXIV, Pt. 1, pp. 401–405; *Report of the Joint Committee*, 40–42; *Battles and Leaders*, IV, 358–60.

so positively their want of confidence in the organization and condition of the cavalry, and advised so earnestly a change." Banks himself professed to have "no complaint to make of General Lee's general conduct. He was active, willing, and brave."[77] But the testimonial, however flattering it might have been, did not save Lee from being demoted.

General Arnold was still in Alexandria and had had the cavalry command for a scant three weeks when he felt "obliged to state that the condition of my cavalry is such that for any immediate operations requiring energetic action it is utterly unfit. The men are able to endure much more, although fatigued, but I believe one-half of my horses would be completely broken down if compelled to move tonight or tomorrow on a scout. Since I have had this command every portion of it has been severely worked, and it is now in so crippled a condition that, for the benefit of the service, I am compelled to make this statement." On May 9, in preparation for the departure of the army from Alexandria, Arnold was ordered to detail five hundred of his men, under "officers of responsibility and character," to "protect the town . . . taking every precaution possible to [prevent] any conflagration or other act which would give notice to the enemy of the movements of the army." It is reported that despite these precautions, as the army marched out, "apparently scores of fires were set simultaneously. Looting was widespread." Some of the cavalrymen "did what they could to help the people in fighting the fire . . . but the fires had been set in so many places and the wind spread them so quickly that nothing could be done. By noon most of the town had been leveled. . . . Cavalry and mounted infantry were specifically mentioned by witnesses as spreading the fire."[78]

As the army marched east from Alexandria, "the country," the historian of the 3rd Massachusetts wrote, "was in flames. Burning buildings could be seen as far as the eye could reach. Somebody had applied the torch to everything. . . . Great clouds of smoke rolled up against the northern sky. The crackling of the flames, the falling timbers, the burning embers mingled with the roar of guns and the report of rifles, made up a picture that was impressive in the extreme."[79]

77. *Official Records*, Vol. XXXIV, Pt. 3, pp. 211, 294; Johnson, *Red River Campaign*, 220.
78. *Official Records*, Vol. XXXIV, Pt. 3, pp. 497, 521, Pt. 1, p. 212; Johnson, *Red River Campaign*, 269, 271.
79. Ewer, *The Third Massachusetts Cavalry*, 169. The regiment had lost 73 killed, wounded, and missing, and 137 horses, at Sabine Crossroads.

After fights at Mansura, Moreauville, and Bayou De Glaize, Banks's army crossed the Atchafalaya on May 19, and the luckless Red River Campaign, in which the Union losses were 454 killed, 2,191 wounded, and 2,600 captured and missing, was over.[80] As Lieutenant Colonel Richard B. Irwin, Banks's assistant adjutant general has written in the best brief account of the campaign:

On both sides this unhappy campaign . . . raised a great and bitter crop of quarrels. Taylor was relieved by Kirby Smith, as the result of an angry correspondence; Banks was overslaughed [by General Edward R. S. Canby], and Franklin quitted the department in disgust; [Charles P.] Stone was replaced by [William] Dwight as chief-of-staff, and Lee as chief of cavalry by Arnold; A. J. Smith departed more in anger than in sorrow; while between the admiral and the general commanding, recriminations were exchanged in language well up to the limits of "parliamentary privilege."[81]

Colonel Irwin denies that the campaign was a colossal cotton speculation, but his denial does not carry complete conviction. He is correct, however, in his further comment that after the Red River Campaign, "no important operation was undertaken by either side in Louisiana."[82]

There was one modest exception to Colonel Irwin's dictum, an operation typical of the winding-down phase of a long war. The chief of cavalry of the Department of the Gulf in the autumn of 1864, with 7,514 mounted troops in his domain, was Colonel John P. Sherburne; restored to favor, and in command in the field of the Cavalry Division, was General Lee.[83] Above both, as chief of cavalry of General Canby's Military Division of West Mississippi, was General John W. Davidson. In mid-November, Davidson proposed to send (or to lead) Lee's division, reinforced by one or two regiments of cavalry, on a raid to destroy once again the oft-destroyed and oft-rebuilt Mobile & Ohio Railroad, this time between Meridian and Mobile, and instead of hazarding a return to base, to "drop down to Biloxi or some available Gulf port near by." The project was approved, and when Lee returned "badly used up" and in a state of "utter prostration" from a successful raid (in which he captured 200 prisoners and 600 to 800 head of horses and

80. These figures are given as "approximate" in *Battles and Leaders*, IV, 367.
81. *Ibid.*, 361.
82. *Ibid.*, 362.
83. *Official Records*, Vol. XLI, Pt. 2, p. 494, 591, 598. General Arnold reverted to his post as chief of artillery. On December 28, Joseph Bailey, infantryman, engineer, and builder of the dam at Alexandria, with no experience whatever with or in command of mounted troops, succeeded Lee in command of the cavalry division.

mules, and "destroyed immense stores"), Davidson took direct command of the raid. He marched out from Baton Rouge on November 27 with 2,000 rank and file of Lee's division plus 1,200 of E. J. David's brigade, after issuing strict orders forbidding "in the most positive manner" "all plundering and straggling."[84]

The utility of Mobile to the Confederacy had largely disappeared on August 5, when Admiral Farragut fought this way past the forts at the entrance to Mobile Bay, and while the city at the head of the bay remained in Confederate hands, the Davidson raid had little in the way of military value to recommend it. It went forward nonetheless. The route chosen by General Davidson led "through a barren, sparsely settled country . . . covered with scrub and pitch pine and interspersed with swamps. The streams were swollen and almost impassable and the roads were so bad that the expedition was compelled to abandon a number of its wagons. . . . Forage was scarce and the men were soon reduced to quarter rations." The 1st Texas, U.S.A., composed largely of Comanche Indians, did its best to save the command from starvation. Detailed as foragers, the Texans "kept the command well supplied with fresh beef; these Indians all carried lassoes made of horsehair and could catch any animal that came within reach of the rope." The Texans' efforts were, however, inadequate, and until the raiders reached the Gulf at Pascagoula Bay, they lived mostly on sweet potatoes, which caused them to insist that the purpose of what they called "Davidson's sweet potato raid" was "to clear the country of that vegetable." The men had been given to understand that the object of the raid was to assist General Thomas in his efforts to deal with Hood's invasion of central Tennessee and to aid Sherman's campaign in Georgia. Its effectiveness in both respects may be gauged by the fact that "there were not more than a dozen shots fired upon the whole trip."[85]

84. *Ibid.*, Pt. 4, pp. 559–60, 653, 638, 685–89.

85. Fletcher, *The History of Company A*, 155–56; Smith, *"Scott's 900," Eleventh New York*, 188–92. The units that made the raid were the 1st Texas, 1st Louisiana, 2nd New York Veteran, 11th and 14th New York, 2nd and 12th Illinois, 4th Wisconsin, 6th Missouri, 118th Illinois Mounted Infantry, two batteries of horse artillery, and a Pioneer Corps with a pontoon train. Smith, *"Scott 900," Eleventh New York*, 188. General Davidson's report on the raid will be found in *Official Records*, Vol. XLV, Pt. 1, pp. 787–89.

XX

Once More unto
the Breach

SOMETIME BEFORE STEELE STARTED ON WHAT CAME TO
be known as the Camden Campaign, General Price proposed to E. Kirby
Smith an invasion of Missouri. "If you," he wrote, ". . . will either go in
person or send me into Missouri with a competent force, such as you
might easily spare, we would not only be able to sustain ourselves
there, but attract to our army thousands and tens of thousands of recruits."[1] The Camden and Red River campaigns then supervened and
provided occupation for the outnumbered Confederate troops in the
Trans-Mississippi. After the battle of Jenkins' Ferry, Kirby Smith directed Price "to accumulate supplies and gather intelligence about the
enemy in preparation for a northern campaign." Smith actually intended Richard Taylor to command the campaign; he wrote President
Davis that while Price's "name and popularity would be a strong element of success in an advance on Missouri," he was incapable of "organizing, disciplining . . . [or] operating an army."[2] But after a Taylor–
Kirby Smith quarrel and General Simon Bolivar Buckner's refusal to
head the expedition, command of it went to Price by default.

Not until August 4, in a meeting at Shreveport, was a firm decision

1. Castel, *General Sterling Price*, 172. In a later dispatch, Price spoke of attracting
not less than thirty thousand recruits. *Ibid.*, 200.
2. *Ibid.*, 196. Kirby Smith later added that militarily speaking, Price was "good for
nothing." *Ibid.*, 202.

reached to mount an invasion of Missouri. Kirby Smith was ordered to transfer all his infantry east of the Mississippi to create a diversion in favor of the Confederate forces in Georgia and Alabama; hence the invasion of Missouri was to be an all-cavalry affair.[3] Its military objectives were to seize St. Louis, "its supplies and military stores," and to "enlist recruits, collect arms, and gather supplies"; should Price be forced to retreat from Missouri, he was to do so via "Kansas and the Indian Territory, sweeping that country of its mules, horses, cattle, and military supplies." To these military aims, Price added a political objective: to hold elections for governor and a legislature and, with the aid of the secret Order of American Knights, to join Missouri to the Confederacy.[4]

Delayed by the late arrival of "needed ordnance stores," Price set off for Missouri from Princeton, Arkansas, on August 30 at the head of two divisions—Fagan's, and Marmaduke's less Shelby's brigade—in which his cavalry was then organized. From Princeton to Dardanelle, where Price crossed the Arkansas River, was a march of 165 miles; from Dardanelle to St. Louis was another 191 miles; from St. Louis to the Kansas border via Jefferson City added 325 miles more to the distance Price had to cover on his outward march. To make the march and to fight the Federal forces he would encounter in Missouri, Price started out with between 9,000 and 12,000 men (he himself claimed 12,000; his inspector general gave the smaller figure), at least 2,000 and perhaps as many as 4,000 of whom were unarmed. The feckless way in which the entire operation was conducted makes it impossible to say how many recruits joined Price in Missouri, and if, or to what extent, their numbers made up for the "thousands" he brought north from Arkansas who simply walked away, taking their weapons with them, when they came within reach of their homes in Missouri.[5]

Facing Price in Missouri was General Rosecrans. For good reasons

3. *Ibid.*, 200–201; Kerby, *Kirby Smith's Confederacy*, 385.

4. Castel, *General Sterling Price*, 202, 193–94; Kerby, *Kirby Smith's Confederacy*, 336; Lamers, *The Edge of Glory*, 420–21, 426; see also *Official Records*, Vol. XLI, Pt. 1, p. 307. In General Sherman's opinion, "the movements of Price and Shelby . . . were mere diversions. They cannot hope to enter Missouri except as raiders." Sherman, *Memoirs*, II, 115.

5. J. H. Parks, *General Edmund Kirby Smith, C.S.A.* (Baton Rouge, 1954), 449; Kerby, *Kirby Smith's Confederacy*, 340. A considerable portion of Price's troops have been described as "at best partisans and at worst marauding bandits." Kerby, *Kirby Smith's Confederacy*, 340.

or bad (Grant's personal dislike of Rosecrans cannot be discounted as a factor) Missouri had been stripped of troops. Thirty-two Federal regiments of infantry had been removed from the state between May and early August, leaving Rosecrans a force, scattered among more than fifty garrisons, of 14,000 national troops and 2,600 Missouri militia, some of the latter of uncertain loyalty, as demonstrated by the "Paw Paw Rebellion" in northern Missouri.[6] Rosecrans' somewhat hyperactive intelligence service brought him word "from early in the spring" that "it was known through[out] the lodges of the O[rder] of A[merican] K[nights] and other rebel sources that Price intended a great invasion of . . . [Missouri] in which he expected the co-operation of that order and of rebels generally, and by which he hoped to obtain important military and political results." After entertaining each other with caustic remarks at Rosecrans' expense, Grant and Halleck decided to play it safe and, in the light of the mounting rumors of an impending invasion of the state, gave him permission to enlist and arm for such period as in his opinion "the exigency may require" as many volunteers as he thought were needed. Pursuant to this authorization, Rosecrans issued a call for nine regiments of infantry to serve for twelve months; three additional regiments were to be raised if enough volunteers came forward. He asked Washington for 5,000 sets of cavalry arms and horse equipments; they were ordered to be forwarded to him "immediately."[7]

By October 1, five regiments of twelve-month infantry had been mustered, and Rosecrans' forces had increased to 17,500 Federal troops and 15,000 Missouri militia.[8] A part of the increase was the result of Rosecrans' efforts to help his own cause (if not his standing with the

6. Kerby, *Kirby Smith's Confederacy*, 336; *Official Records*, Vol. XLI, Pt. 3, p. 773. Typical of Grant's attitude was his October 11 dispatch to Stanton in which he urged that "a proper regard for the present and future interests of the service demands the removal of Rosecrans." On this date Price's troops were plundering the pro-Confederate population of Boonville, Missouri.

7. *Official Records*, Vol. XLI, Pt. 1, p. 307, Pt. 2, pp. 322, 358, 504.

8. *Ibid.*, Pt. 1, p. 307; Kerby, *Kirby Smith's Confederacy*, 337. For the defense of St. Louis, Rosecrans obtained the services of six regiments of hundred-day infantry from Illinois. *Official Records*, Vol. XLI, Pt. 1, p. 318. Of the Missouri State Militia Cavalry, only between half and two-thirds were mounted. *Official Records*, Vol. XLI, Pt. 2, p. 656. Their arms, if one may generalize from a report on the 1st Missouri State Militia Cavalry, were scandalously inadequate. Their arms were reported to be "very poor and of every possible kind and pattern, nearly worthless; sixteen different patterns of breech-loading, nine of muzzle-loading, some double barreled guns, and some men have nothing but revolvers." *Official Records*, Vol. XLI, Pt. 3, p. 417.

War Department) by in effect kidnapping two regiments of cavalry, the 1st Iowa and 1st Missouri, that were on their return from veterans' furlough to General Steele's army in Arkansas.[9] General A. J. Smith's corps of about 9,000, on its way up the Mississippi to join Sherman after the Red River Campaign, was intercepted at Cairo and diverted to St. Louis.[10]

Included in Rosecrans' accession of strength were the 7th Kansas. Jennison's Jayhawkers had just recently returned from veterans' furlough to Tennessee. They received orders on the night of September 6 to return to Memphis in preparation for departure "without delay" for Missouri. "Without delay" in this instance meant departure from Memphis six and eight days later, as shipping became available and as Rosecrans and General C. C. Washburn conducted a debate by telegraph (which Rosecrans eventually won) to decide whether the Jayhawkers should (Rosecrans) or should not (Washburn) be allowed to take their horses with them to Missouri.[11]

In addition to the Jayhawkers, detachments numbering about 1,900, rank and file, of Colonel Edward F. Winslow's cavalry division were also ordered to Missouri. They crossed the Mississippi to join General Steele's forces in Arkansas, greatly to Colonel Winslow's displeasure. "The command will suffer in many points almost beyond recovery. . . . I can hardly hope to keep my animals in good condition for any length of time when the country has been desolated by the enemy and the growing corn almost gone," he complained. But after crossing the river and marching a hundred miles toward Little Rock, they were redirected to Missouri. On the march to Cape Girardeau, where they were to take ship for St. Louis, "notwithstanding every possible effort," Winslow was unable to "get . . . [his] horses shod, and because of this many were abandoned."[12]

9. *Official Records*, Vol. XLI, Pt. 2, pp. 175–76.

10. The corps actually arrived in two installments; 4,500 men of what had been Kirby Smith's division came first; Joseph A. Mower's division of about the same strength reached Cape Girardeau on October 5 ("out of supplies, his teams worn down, part of his cavalry [Winslow's] dismounted, and many horses unshod"). Transports brought the division to St. Louis October 8 and 9 and then carried them up the Missouri to join A. J. Smith. *Ibid.*, Pt. 1, p. 311. For reasons not indicated, Mower himself was not with the division; he joined Sherman in Georgia. *Ibid.*, Vol. XXXIX, Pt. 2, p. 366.

11. *Ibid.*, Vol. XLI, Pt. 2, p. 550, Pt. 3, pp. 141, 164, 174, 189.

12. *Ibid.*, Pt. 1, pp. 327–29, Pt. 3, pp. 46, 187. After arriving in St. Louis, Winslow "turned in all unserviceable animals" and received 500 fresh horses, and "much needed" clothing was issued to the men. *Ibid.*, Pt. 1, pp. 327–28.

On September 16, at Pocahontas, Arkansas, General Shelby, who had been off on a highly successful foray north of the Arkansas River, joined Price. General Joseph West had had a fruitless chase after Shelby with 2,000 cavalry, a regiment of infantry, and two sections of the 5th Ohio Battery. On his return to Little Rock, he reported, "The miserable condition of the cavalry and artillery horses satisfied me that the enemy could and had marched three miles to my two. Abandoned the idea of a successful pursuit. . . . Upon this expedition, as upon a previous one made earlier in the month, the miserable plight of animals that had at any time for months back only been partially foraged, and sometimes left entirely without any, rendered any rapid movement an impossibility." [13]

The return of Shelby with a large number of recruits caused Price to regroup his cavalry into three divisions, Fagan's Arkansans, Marmaduke's Missourians, and Shelby's, made up of units from both states. To make provision for the thousands of anticipated Missouri recruits, all three divisions consisted in part of what in today's terminology would be called "cadres"—skeleton regiments and brigades. So organized, Price crossed into Missouri on the nineteenth, with his forces "in fine health and spirits"; marching in three widely separated columns, he reached Fredericktown, seventy-seven miles north of the state line and on the direct road to St. Louis, on the evening of the twenty-fourth. There his scouts brought him word that 5,000 of A. J. Smith's infantry had arrived in St. Louis to reinforce the garrison. Deciding, wisely, not to risk an encounter with so large a body of veteran infantry, Price veered off westward in the direction of Jefferson City and on the twenty-sixth reached Pilot Knob, at the end of the Iron Mountain Railroad, eighty-six miles southwest of St. Louis. [14]

A telegram of September 3 from General Washburn in Memphis "sounded the tocsin," bringing Rosecrans word that there was "a big raid on foot for Missouri, under Price, Marmaduke, and Shelby, all mounted." Rosecrans made what preparation he could, including locating General Pleasonton in Philadelphia and recalling him from leave with the message "There will be a heavy invasion. You will command the cavalry." But he was hampered by uncertainty about Price's

13. *Ibid.*, 327–28.
14. Kerby, *Kirby Smith's Confederacy*, 388–89, 342; *Official Records*, Vol. XLI, Pt. 1, pp. 627–28, 307, Pt. 3, p. 46.

likely route. Price had a choice of three: one northeast via Pocahontas (the route he actually took), a more central route via Rolla to Jefferson City, and the one farthest to the west, which led north through Springfield and Sedalia.[15] Pending definite word of Price's route, Rosecrans concentrated his troops in three places, Springfield, Rolla, and Sedalia. Then on the twenty-fourth came word that Shelby was approaching Pilot Knob, and Rosecrans ordered General Thomas Ewing, Jr., to assemble his forces there. On Monday, September 26, Ewing, with 489 "raw troops" and 562 "old troops," all Missourians except five companies of the 14th Iowa Infantry, occupied Fort Davidson at Pilot Knob. The fort was a strong hexagonal work, mounting seven 32- and 24-pounder guns, but overlooked on three sides by an encircling range of hills, all within musket range.[16] Price could have battered the fort into submission by dragging his artillery up to the hilltops surrounding it, as his chief engineer suggested, but on the strength of assurances by Fagan and Marmaduke that they could take the fort by assault in twenty minutes or less, Price opted for a direct attack by his cavalry, dismounted.[17] The attack, poorly coordinated, was repulsed with ease. At little cost to themselves, Ewing's scratch force inflicted a humiliating defeat, damaging to morale, on the two Confederate divisions, which sustained an estimated (and probably greatly underestimated) 450 casualties, killed and wounded.[18] A Price biographer has stated that "the fighting edge of Fagan's division was badly blunted for the remainder of the campaign. Marmaduke's division was exposed as unreliable in battle, and the morale of the . . . [army] as a whole (except for Shelby's command) seriously impaired. As soon as the fighting ended, large numbers of deserters began wending their way back to Arkansas or headed for homes in Missouri."[19]

Despite his victory, Ewing realized that he could not hold the fort against a sensibly planned attack. He decided to evacuate Fort Davidson during the night; not even the blowing up of his powder magazine

15. *Official Records*, Vol. XLI, Pt. 3, pp. 302, 378, 405, Pt. 1, p. 307.

16. Ewing's "old troops" included seven companies of Missouri State Militia Cavalry. *Ibid.*, 446.

17. *Ibid.*, 448; Castel, *General Sterling Price*, 213–16.

18. In Albert Castel's opinion, Price's casualties may have been as high as 1,500. Castel, *General Sterling Price*, 218, 218n. Shelby's division was not involved in the attack. Price had sent them to circle Pilot Knob and break up the railroad north of it.

19. *Ibid.*, 218–19.

in an explosion "which shook the hills" could rouse the Confederates to what was happening. Ewing and his men got away: his infantry, outdistancing the pursuing cavalry of Marmaduke and Shelby, reached Rolla, seventy miles away, in safety.[20]

Price's march, slow by cavalry standards up to Pilot Knob, became even slower thereafter. Averaging only ten miles a day, he reached Jefferson City late on the afternoon of October 7. The city was held by the united forces of Generals John McNeil, John B. Sanborn, Clinton B. Fisk, and Egbert B. Brown, 4,100 cavalry and 2,600 infantry, "mostly the new and partially organized twelve months' men, with a few citizens and militia, manning a defensive line, which with industry and good judgment had been prepared by the entire laboring force, civil and military." After viewing the "five forts and long lines of connecting rifle pits, all heavily manned and protected by palisades and chevaux-de-frise," Price decided not to attack the place, and set off toward the Kansas border, accompanied by his immense train, swollen to five hundred wagons (which the soldiers believed were loaded with "the private loot of staff officers and camp-followers," as doubtless some of them were), and by "a rabble of deadheads, stragglers and stolen negroes on stolen horses."[21]

Pleasonton arrived at Jefferson City on the eighth, "under orders to assume command." He organized all the available cavalry—increased to about 6,600 when Colonel Winslow arrived—in a "Provisional Division" of four brigades under General Sanborn and sent them "as a corps of observation after the enemy, to harass and delay him as much as possible until other troops [*i.e.*, A. J. Smith's infantry] could be brought forward."[22] For reasons not explained in his report, Pleasonton did not take personal command of this cavalry force, as he might have been expected to do, until the nineteenth, by which time, after repeated skirmishes with the retreating enemy, Sanborn had reached the village of Dunksburg, seventy miles west of Jefferson City.

At the same time that Pleasonton's cavalry dogged Price's footsteps, and A. J. Smith's corps (which had now been joined by General Jo-

20. *Official Records*, Vol. XLI, Pt. 1, pp. 448–51; Castel, *General Sterling Price*, 216–18.

21. Kerby, *Kirby Smith's Confederacy*, 343; *Official Records*, Vol. XLI, Pt. 1, p. 311; Castel, *General Sterling Price*, 224, 223.

22. *Official Records*, Vol. XLI, Pt. 1, p. 340.

seph A. Mower's division) was closing up as fast as the men's legs and logistics allowed, Rosecrans kept General Samuel R. Curtis, commanding the Department of Kansas, informed of Price's progress, as the invading army moved westward through Boonville, Marshall, and Waverly.[23] Curtis had returned a month earlier to his headquarters at Fort Leavenworth from the western edge, several hundred miles west of the Missouri border, of his vast department. He was followed east by General James G. Blunt's First Division, Army of the Border, which reached Olathe, Kansas, on October 10. In addition to Colonel Charles R. Jennison's 15th Kansas, a battalion of the 3rd Wisconsin, detachments of the 14th Kansas and of the 6th Regiment, Kansas State Militia (Mounted), which joined him a few days later, Blunt had the 11th Kansas, detachments of the 5th and 16th Kansas, and portions of the 5th and 10th Regiments of Kansas State Militia (Mounted).[24] Other than these troops under Blunt, Curtis had only a battalion of hundred-day men whose brief term of enlistment had nearly expired, and the 2nd Colorado at Kansas City, a grand total of about 4,000 men. He notified Governor Thomas Carney of Kansas that he would "again have to ask the militia of Southern Kansas to aid in checking rebel approaches." Because of the forthcoming elections, and a campaign embellished by the vicious bitterness customary in Kansas politics, between the governor's own faction and that of U.S. Senator James H. Lane, Carney had to be cajoled into calling out the militia and later into allowing them to serve a few miles beyond the Kansas border.[25] Successful in both respects, Curtis brought Blunt north and sent him forward to Lexington, Missouri, where he was attacked on the nineteenth and driven back toward Independence, his retreat covered "in a gallant manner" by Colonel Thomas Moonlight's 11th Kansas.[26]

It is said that after beating Blunt back to Independence and be-

23. On October 13 Price sent two brigades on a raid across the Missouri to Glasgow (which was captured with its 550-man garrison on the fourteenth), and on October 15 a raid by a third brigade forced the surrender of the militia holding Sedalia. Price claimed in his report that "800 or 900" prisoners were taken at Glasgow. *Ibid.*, 632–33; Castel, *General Sterling Price*, 227.

24. *Official Records*, Vol. XLI, Pt. 1, p. 572.

25. *Ibid.*, 464–65, 467–69, 471. Curtis described the Kansas militia as "little better than rabble." Castel, *General Sterling Price*, 346. Wearing their everyday clothes, they were told to wear sprigs of sumac, scarlet in October, in their hats for identification.

26. *Official Records*, Vol. XLI, Pt. 1, pp. 312, 573–74. Blunt's command present at Lexington numbered about 2,000.

yond, Price could have turned south and made (or tried to make) his escape back to Arkansas. For "reasons that remain incomprehensible," he chose instead to continue to march northeast through Independence and Kansas City to the Kansas border. But as he must have realized, he was already in serious trouble. Pleasonton's cavalry was right behind him; Curtis was in a position to stop, or at least delay, his westward progress; and the infantry of A. J. Smith's corps, "racing forward at a killing pace," was reaching a position from which they could either block his escape southwest or attack him in flank if he continued on his westward course.[27]

On the twentieth, Blunt took up a "strong natural" defensive position on the west bank of the Little Blue, a northward-flowing tributary of the Missouri, nine miles east of Independence, where he intended to keep Price in check until Rosecrans' forces could come up behind him. He sent to General Curtis for reinforcements but was told that "in consequence of the action of the Governor of Kansas and other of the State authorities he [Curtis] was unable to move the State militia farther into Missouri."[28] Curtis ordered him to leave an outpost on the Little Blue and retreat with the rest of his troops to the camp of the Kansas militia on the Big Blue, just west of Independence, where defensive works had been constructed. Blunt reached the Big Blue position late in the evening, after an all-day fight, first with Marmaduke's division and then with both Marmaduke's and Shelby's divisions.

McNeil's brigade (17th Illinois, 13th Missouri, 5th Missouri State Militia Cavalry, and detachments of the 7th Kansas, 2nd Missouri, and the 3rd and 9th Regiments of Missouri State Militia Cavalry) led Pleasonton's advance on October 20 and 21 through Lexington (where they found no forage for their animals) and across the Little Blue on a hastily constructed crude bridge.[29] McNeil's cavalrymen, fighting on foot against W. F. Slemons' brigade of Fagan's division, which made up Price's rear guard, pressed forward in a series of skirmishes to the eastern edge of Independence. Directed to drive Slemons out of the town, McNeil had his troopers mount and, with the 13th Missouri in the lead, supported by the 7th Kansas and the 17th Illinois, had them

27. Kerby, *Kirby Smith's Confederacy*, 346–47.
28. *Official Records*, Vol. XLI, Pt. 1, pp. 574, 476–78; Castel, *General Sterling Price*, 229–30.
29. *Official Records*, Vol. XLI, Pt. 1, p. 371.

"charge through the town, and on the enemy's rear, saber in hand." The charge resulted in the capture of two of Fagan's guns "and the killing and wounding and capturing [of] a large number of his men."[30]

With Slemons driven out of Independence, Pleasonton decided to keep up the pressure all through the night. Replacing McNeil's brigade in the lead with Winslow's, he had them dismount; led by the 4th Iowa (armed with Spencers) and "thrown forward in a number of successful charges," they drove Fagan's entire division "some six miles to the Big Blue" by daylight.[31]

By the evening of October 22, the noose had tightened considerably around the hapless Price's neck. Blocked by the Missouri River on the north, his army was wedged in a narrow space between Curtis, on the Big Blue, and Pleasonton, now west of Independence. Rosecrans, made aware of the situation by Curtis' and Pleasonton's dispatches and "supposing the enemy could not cross the Big Blue in the face of Curtis," wired Pleasonton his opinion that Price would turn south and suggested that Pleasonton should leave McNeil's brigade behind to harass Price's rear and with his other three brigades should move south about eighteen miles toward Lone Jack, join General Smith's infantry, and force Price to fight them to open a way south.[32] This was strategically sound advice, but Pleasonton chose to ignore it. Deciding that he needed the help of infantry to force his way across the Little Blue fords southwest of Independence, he compromised; he sent only McNeil's brigade to Little Santa Fe (on the Missouri-Kansas border, about ten miles due south of Westport, as it then was) but kept the rest of his cavalry in the north and asked Rosecrans to order Smith to join him in Independence. Rosecrans professed to do so reluctantly, but he did issue the orders Pleasonton requested and thereby deprived Smith of any useful role in the campaign.[33]

Price spent the night of the twenty-first in Independence, ten miles east of Kansas City in 1864. After his retreat from the Little Blue that

30. Ibid., 371. "I am confident," General John McNeil (a St. Louis hatter and politician in civil life) wrote, "that this day's work of the Second Brigade did much to convince the enemy of the fighting qualities of our men and to inspire a wholesome respect for their prowess." Ibid., 371–72.

31. Ibid., 336–37.

32. Ibid., 312.

33. Kerby, Kirby Smith's Confederacy, 349; Official Records, Vol. XLI, Pt. 1, pp. 313, 337. Pleasonton's report does not mention Rosecrans' suggestion. He speaks of his orders to McNeil but not of the orders to A. J. Smith.

day, Blunt was deployed in the hurriedly prepared defenses—abatis, rifle pits, and "other field works"—above the west bank of the Big Blue, as the right of Curtis' line; the Kansas militia held the left, or northern, end of the line.[34] In Blunt's command was Jennison's small brigade-by-courtesy, formally organized a week earlier, consisting of the 15th Kansas, a detachment of the 3rd Wisconsin, and five small mountain howitzers manned by cavalrymen. In the fight on the Little Blue on the twenty-first, "the first general one in which . . . [the brigade] had been engaged . . . [it] gave evidence," in Colonel Jennison's opinion, "of great proficiency in drill, unhesitating obedience, and . . . a courage and determination worthy of any veteran corps."[35] Early on the morning of October 22, Blunt sent Jennison to Byram's Ford, four miles upstream, to prevent an enemy crossing at that point and sent Colonel Moonlight with his Second Brigade to occupy Hinkle's Ford, midway between his own position and Bryam's Ford.[36]

Having learned on the evening or night of the twenty-first that Blunt's forces on the Big Blue ("a position strong by nature and strengthened by fortifications, upon which all their art had been exhausted") had been joined by Curtis and had thereby increased in numbers to "between 6,000 and 8,000 men," Price decided to change direction the next day.[37] He sent Colonel Sidney D. Jackman's brigade of Shelby's division to demonstrate in the direction of Kansas City, and with the rest of his forces, Shelby in the van and Marmaduke bringing up the rear, he veered off southwest on the "Santa Fe road, which had been obstructed by felling trees."[38] To continue on this route, he had to cross the Big Blue at Byram's Ford. Jennison's brigade had been joined there by a detachment of Kansas militia, who made themselves useful by felling trees to obstruct the ford. Shelby's van reached Byram's at 11 A.M., with the assignment of effecting a crossing and clearing the Federal forces holding the ford out of the way so that Price's immense

34. General Curtis described the terrain between the Little and Big Blue as "rough and thickly timbered and the streams bordered by precipitate banks, which render it generally impassable for cavalry and artillery." *Official Records*, Vol. XLI, Pt. 1, p. 479.

35. *Ibid.*, 581, 583.

36. *Ibid.*, 575. Colonel Moonlight calls the ford "Simmons" in his report. *Ibid.*, 593.

37. *Ibid.*, 634. Counting the Kansas militia Curtis had a total of 15,000 troops deployed in a "more or less continuous 15–16 mile line from the Missouri River in the north to near Hickman Mills in the south." He believed that Price had an army of 30,000. *Ibid.*, 479.

38. *Ibid.*, 634.

trains could cross the river and go on to Little Santa Fe on their way south.

There are two principal versions of what happened at Byram's Ford on October 22. Price's version has it that Shelby, less Jackman's brigade, met "some opposition . . . which was soon overcome," and after crossing the river himself, Shelby "engaged the enemy to cover the crossing and the passage of the train." Jennison's version was to the effect that the Confederates were repulsed each time they tried to cross, that his brigade "held the enemy effectually in check, notwithstanding his great superiority in numbers, until about 3 P.M.," when, having succeeded in crossing the river both above and below the ford, the enemy threatened both his flanks and made it necessary for him to order his troops to retire westward, toward Westport.[39] It may or may not be significant that Shelby, whose reports seldom err on the side of modesty, makes no mention whatever of forcing a crossing of the Big Blue but does speak of a hard fight until dark "within sight of the domes and spires of Westport."[40] That there was a fighting of some severity here is borne out by the fact that before it was over, Shelby had to ask for help to hold his own. The Federals opposing him were Jennison's brigade, reinforced by the equally small brigade of Colonel Moonlight, which was made up of the 11th Kansas, two companies each of the 5th and 16th Kansas, and four mountain howitzers manned, like Jennison's, by cavalrymen. Pressed back initially nearly to Westport and the Kansas state line, but retreating in good order, Jennison and Moonlight "got stubborn" (in Shelby's words), counterattacked, and forced Shelby to retreat in his turn.[41]

Under the cover of Shelby's fight with the Federal cavalry, Price's trains got across the Big Blue and moved on toward Little Santa Fe. More important, however, was the fact that by forcing a crossing of the river, Shelby had turned the flank of Curtis' position and opened the way to the escape of Price's entire army south if Price chose, and if he was allowed by the Federals, to take advantage of it.

Separated from Curtis, Blunt, and their troops by Price's army and the rough, wooded terrain, Pleasonton's cavalry nevertheless made a

39. *Ibid.*, 634, 585, 575.
40. *Ibid.*, 658, 584–85, 575. For still another version, see Castel, *General Sterling Price*, 231.
41. *Official Records*, Vol. XLI, Pt. 1, pp. 591, 584–85, 592–93. Colonel Moonlight called this fight "a very pretty one." *Ibid.*, 593.

major contribution on the evening of the twenty-second to the ultimate Union victory. After driving William Cabell's brigade of Fagan's division out of Independence, Pleasonton decided to "push them all night" ("The enemy seemed to be in haste," he wrote in his report) and ordered Winslow's brigade to dismount and drive the enemy.[42] With the 3rd Iowa in the lead, the brigade did so, with a series of charges that drove Fagan's Arkansans six miles to the Big Blue and ultimately into a state of panic. A part of Marmaduke's division, hurried to the rear to rescue Fagan (the rest of the division was in the fight near Westport, helping Shelby), was caught up in the panic.[43] General John B. Clark, Jr., who succeeded to the command of Marmaduke's division a few days later, testified to the effectiveness of the attacks delivered by Winslow's men. "Notwithstanding the almost impenetrable darkness of the night," Clark wrote, "they rushed upon us with a reckless fierceness that I have never seen equaled."[44] When exhaustion at length brought an end to Winslow's attacks, Fagan had been driven westward on to Shelby's position south of Westport. Marmaduke, in the Confederate rear, was able to come to a halt at Byram's Ford, where he occupied (and later improved) the defenses Jennison had held in the morning.

Winslow's men were understandably "very much worn down" by their all-night, six-mile running fight, dismounted, with Fagan's and Marmaduke's forces. Hence, Pleasonton ordered General Egbert B. Brown to move his First Brigade (1st, 4th, and 7th Regiments of Missouri State Militia Cavalry) to the front and to "attack the enemy at daylight." The sun rose, but there was no sign of the attack Brown had been ordered to make, and Pleasonton rode forward to investigate. He "found Brown's brigade . . . so disordered as to be in no condition for fighting" and saw no indication that Brown had made any preparations to carry out the order. Pleasonton immediately placed Brown in arrest and directed Colonel John F. Philips, 7th Missouri State Militia Cavalry, to take command of the brigade. For good measure, Pleason-

42. *Ibid.*, 336.
43. *Ibid.*, 635, 641. There is considerable confusion in the records about the exact status of Marmaduke's command; it is called sometimes a brigade and sometimes a division.
44. *Ibid.*, 683, 328–29. On the morning of October 23, Colonel Winslow was wounded (a rifle bullet in the leg—his second wound of the war) and had to turn over command of his brigade to Lieutenant Colonel Frederick W. Benteen, 10th Missouri.

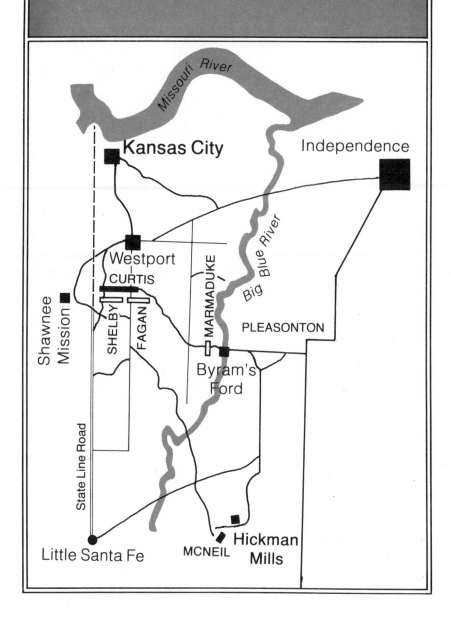

BATTLE OF WESTPORT

Missouri River

Kansas City

Independence

Westport

CURTIS

Big Blue River

MARMADUKE

SHELBY

FAGAN

PLEASONTON

Shawnee Mission

Byram's Ford

State Line Road

Little Santa Fe

MCNEIL

Hickman Mills

ton also placed in arrest Colonel James McFerran, 1st Missouri State Militia Cavalry, "whose regiment was straggling all over the country, and he was neglecting to prevent it." Needless to say, General Brown denied Pleasonton's charges and protested his supersession with considerable heat.[45]

General Brown's real or supposed failure to follow orders was not Pleasonton's only problem with balky or incompetent subordinates on that twenty-third of October. There may have been legitimate excuses for Brown's failure to take the place of Winslow's worn-out men at daybreak. There were none for John McNeil's failure to be at Little Santa Fe "by daylight," as he had been ordered. It is true that his brigade had been marching or fighting for nineteen hours without a break when he received Pleasonton's orders, and to get to Little Santa Fe by daylight would have required a long, wearing march in the darkness for desperately tired men on tired and hungry horses. Nevertheless, it could have been done. But McNeil got only as far as Byram's Ford, miles short of his destination, by 4 A.M., and stopped there to feed his horses. He was still there at daylight and then moved off "cautiously." The effect of his inertia will be seen shortly; it may be said in the meantime that Pleasonton was amply justified in remarking in his report, "I trust that this conduct on the part of General McNeil will meet the marked disapprobation of the major-general commanding [Rosecrans] as it has mine."[46]

The result of the fighting on the day and night of the twenty-second was to align Price's forces facing north in the dense woods bordering both banks of Brush Creek (an eastward-flowing tributary of the Big Blue, some two miles south of Westport) and in the open prairie to the south of the creek.[47] Shelby held the left of the line, Fagan the center, and beyond a considerable gap, on the right was Marmaduke. On the Union side, Curtis had his troops in motion at 3 A.M. Leaving a small garrison of militia in Kansas City, he moved forward with Blunt's forces, reinforced by large numbers of Kansas militia. As his report fails to make entirely clear, he crossed Brush Creek and deployed on the prairie south of it. Here he was attacked by Shelby and two brigades

---

45. *Ibid.*, 337, 346–50, 360.
46. *Ibid.*, 372, 337.
47. General Curtis wrote that Brush Creek was "skirted by a dense forest some two miles wide." *Ibid.*, 485.

of Fagan's division, and driven back into and beyond the woods on the north bank of Brush Creek.[48] But Confederate success against Curtis and Blunt at Brush Creek was coupled with disaster to the east, at Byram's Ford. Here Marmaduke's division was charged repeatedly at Pleasonton's cavalry—Winslow's and Philips' brigades, with Sanborn's brigade in support—and was at length driven back and routed, pursued at the gallop by Pleasonton's troopers, who collected prisoners by dozens.[49]

With Marmaduke driven out of the way, Pleasonton was in a position to attack Fagan in flank and rear as soon as he could collect his men, some of whom were engaged in shooting or hanging those of their prisoners who were wearing Union army overcoats. In the meantime, Curtis had brought forward the major portion of the Kansas militia and reoccupied the woods along the north bank of Brush Creek. Jennison's and Colonel James H. Ford's brigades had already crossed the belt of woods and were skirmishing with Fagan's division on the edge of the prairie, when Curtis, who had been shown a way across the woods and across the creek "by an old man, a Missouri patriot of seventy-five years," came up and ordered Jennison and Ford to charge the enemy. Supported by their artillery, the 15th Kansas, portions of the 2nd Colorado and the 3rd Wisconsin, and Blunt's bodyguard charged and dislodged the enemy and drove them south at the same time that Pleasonton's cavalrymen, harrying Marmaduke's broken division before them, emerged from the woods to the southeast of Curtis' battle line. With Fagan on his right driven back, Shelby and his division became isolated; Blunt's cavalry and masses of Kansas militia, "swarming out of the forest," had a clear path to attack his right flank and rear.[50] Jackman's brigade, which had been sent at a gallop to help Fagan, had been engulfed in Fagan's collapse, and Shelby had no option but to try to cut his way through the Kansans and the masses of Pleasonton's victorious cavalry to reach what was left of Price's defeated and retreating army. To reach Price, Shelby's men had to "run for it" through the "debris marking the wake of a beaten army, 'dead horses, saddles, blankets, broken guns, and dead rebels.' A thousand dead and wounded Confederates lay sprawled on the prairie below Westport, at

48. Ibid., 575–76.
49. Ibid., 341, 635; see also Castel, General Sterling Price, 234.
50. Official Records, Vol. XLI, Pt. 1, p. 486.

least another five hundred dead had been abandoned on the fields between Lexington and the Big Blue, and two thousand prisoners remained behind in the custody of the Federals."[51]

In midafternoon of a day, which, Shelby wrote, had "dawned upon . . . [the Confederates] clear, cold, and full of promise" and ended in disaster, the victorious Union commanders and some of their subordinates met in a farmhouse near Indian Creek, to discuss their next move.[52] Governor Carney and General George W. Deitzler (the latter in command of the Kansas militia), both of whom were present, urged that their men be discharged, and Curtis agreed. Pleasonton, whose horses (as well as Blunt's) General Curtis reported to be "in fine condition," asked to have his command released to return to Missouri on the ground that those of his troops who had come from Arkansas (presumably Winslow's brigade) had to have rest and that the Missouri regiments should be allowed to get home by election day. Having made the soldierly decision that it was his duty to mount a "vigorous pursuit" of a "much demoralized enemy . . . if provisions . . . [could] be brought forward fast enough," Curtis persuaded him to remain and join in the pursuit.[53]

After a greatly needed rest on the night of the twenty-third, the pursuit got under way the next morning, with Blunt in the lead and Pleasonton right behind him. The pursuit, which eventually ended at the Arkansas River, nearly three hundred miles south of Westport, might not have been necessary had General Smith's infantry not been ordered north on the evening of the twenty-second. Without that order, they could have been squarely athwart Price's line of retreat. Pleasonton's request for Smith's help in the north, made in the heat of battle, was at least excusable. Not so was John McNeil's failure to intercept Price's trains. After his predawn halt to feed his horses, he resumed his march toward Little Santa Fe, with his regiments strung out on the road, the 7th Kansas in the lead. At about 1 P.M., the Jayhawkers, commanded by Major Francis M. Malone, rode up the east side of a north-south ridge at Hickman Mills, and "there, on the road running south a little to the west of the base of the ridge on which they stood, was

51. Kerby, *Kirby Smith's Confederacy*, 349; Castel, *General Sterling Price*, 235.

52. *Official Records*, Vol. XLI, Pt. 1, pp. 658, 491.

53. *Ibid.*, 491–92. Most of the Kansas militia were discharged that day; the remainder were discharged at Fort Scott two days later.

Price's . . . wagon train, guarded by a meager escort."[54] There were regimental commanders in the Union cavalry, R. H. G. Minty and Peter Stagg, to mention only two, who, seeing before them the answer to a cavalryman's dream, would without hesitation have ordered a saber charge on the train, but Major Malone saw his duty otherwise. He sent an orderly to the rear to locate the general and report that the enemy had been found. By the time McNeil reached the scene, an hour had passed; he ordered a charge, but it was too late. The Jayhawkers had been spotted and the Confederates deployed dismounted men (many of them unarmed recruits but they made an imposing show at a distance) and artillery in position to rake the Jayhawkers in flank had they charged the train; to add a crowning touch to a tale of incompetence, McNeil had halted the rest of the brigade a mile short of the ridge, too far back to be able to support the 7th Kansas. McNeil canceled his order to charge, and the train escaped unscathed.[55] Pleasonton reported with some chagrin that "General McNeil . . . instead of vigorously attacking the enemy's wagon train, which was directly in front of him with but little escort . . . contented himself with some skirmishing and cannonading, and the train escaped." Furthermore, he pointed out, "The rebel General Marmaduke stated after he was captured that had McNeil attacked at this time they would have lost their whole train," a view Pleasonton found clearly in accordance with the facts.[56]

Charting the course of Price's retreat from October 24 until the ragged, starving remnants of his army reached and crossed the Arkansas on November 7 and General Curtis halted the pursuit, would add little of value to the tale of cavalry operations in the West. Curtis, with a total of 7,000 cavalry, part his own and part Pleasonton's, following a trail "marked by broken wagons and caissons, discarded rifles and blankets, bits of harness and debris, and by sick, wounded, and exhausted Confederates lying by the wayside waiting to be captured," caught up with Price at the Marais des Cygnes River after dark on the twenty-fourth, but did not deliver a full-scale attack until noon the next day, twelve miles farther south, at the crossing of Mine Creek.[57] With

54. Starr, *Jennison's Jayhawkers*, 338.
55. *Ibid.*, 338; see also 338*n*.
56. *Official Records*, Vol. XLI, Pt. 1, p. 337.
57. Castel, *General Sterling Price*, 238. For the fight at the Marais des Cygnes, see *Official Records*, Vol. XLI, Pt. 1, pp. 493–95.

the ford across the creek—"a deep, high-banked stream"—blocked by Price's wagons, the brigades of Colonels Philips and Benteen, in the van of the pursuit, came face to face with what was left of Fagan's and Marmaduke's divisions, which Price had left as rear guard north of the stream while he himself started off with Shelby's division to try to capture weakly held Fort Scott, with its stores of supplies. Seeing the Federal cavalry advancing, Fagan and Marmaduke chose an unusual scheme of deployment. Armed as their men were with infantry rifles, they would normally have dismounted them to withstand the Federal attack they could see coming. This time, however, they ordered their men to remain mounted, and deployed them in three lines on the open prairie. Colonel Benteen, surveying the Confederates' deployment from a distance of six hundred yards, saw an opportunity for an attack that he was not deterred from exploiting by the fact, also clearly visible, that his and Philips' 2,500 troopers were outnumbered two to one by Marmaduke and Fagan. But by this time, as Forrest would have said, the Federals had the "skeer" on Price's army. Benteen had his buglers blow the charge and rode for the center of Marmaduke's line. A few moments later Philips' brigade also charged, riding for the left flank of Fagan's division. After a single discharge of their infantry rifles (which could not be reloaded on horseback) failed to halt the oncoming Federals, both divisions broke and fled in all directions. The Federals, using their sabers, revolvers, and carbines, killed and wounded 300 of Fagan's and Marmaduke's men and captured 900 (including General William L. Cabell and Marmaduke himself, who was taken prisoner by Trooper James Dunleavy, 3rd Iowa), as well as all eight guns of the Confederates' artillery.[58]

Except for a fight at Newtonia, Missouri, on October 28 that General Blunt blundered into and from which he escaped only with the help of General Sanborn's brigade, there were only skirmishes as Price's disintegrating army continued to trudge southward. Fatigue affecting both sides, coupled in the case of Price's remnants with starva-

58. *Official Records*, Vol. XLI, Pt. 1, pp. 495–502. General Curtis calls this the "Battle of the Osage" in his report. See also Lumir F. Buresh, *October 25th and the Battle of Mine Creek* (Kansas City, 1977), 86–137; Castel, *General Sterling Price*, 240–45. In his report on the Mine Creek fight, Colonel Philips wrote, "A number of prisoners taken in this fight were dressed in our uniform, and in obedience to existing orders from department headquarters, and the usages of war, they were executed instanter." *Official Records*, Vol. XLI, Pt. 1, p. 352.

tion and disease, became more and more a factor. On one occasion, McNeil's and Benteen's brigades found the enemy formed in line of battle and tried to charge, but "the utmost exertions of officers and men could not move the horses to a trot or gallop."[59] During the night following the Mine Creek disaster, Price ordered all "superfluous" wagons—which amounted to a third of those still able to move—destroyed, and day by day thereafter more of the wagons were either broken up, burned, or abandoned. Even wagons loaded with small-arms ammunition were set on fire and left behind. The desperate Confederates made a futile effort to at least slow down the pursuit "by the fire and smoke created by their burning of the hay and grain and grass along their route." Toward the end, even the weather turned against the unfortunate raiders: it became "bitterly cold, with rain, sleet, and finally snow falling."[60]

Price's plight, bad as it was, would have been worse had it not been for Pleasonton's and later Rosecrans' strange conduct. Late in the evening following the Mine Creek fight, despite General Curtis' protests, Pleasonton decided to take himself and all his cavalry except, for some strange reason, Benteen's and McNeil's brigades, out of the pursuit.[61] "The exhausted condition of my men and horses," he wrote, "having marched near 100 miles in two days and a night, and fighting the last thirty miles, required that I should proceed to the vicinity of Fort Scott for forage and subsistence."[62] Fort Scott was six miles (he had been told two and a half miles) to the west of his line of march, and the forage and subsistence could have been brought to him from the fort. In-

59. *Official Records*, Vol. XLI, Pt. 1, p. 373. "Sanborn's brigade had marched 102 miles in 36 hours when it intervened in the fight at Newtonia, and the Jayhawkers' horses had not been fed for forty-two hours when the regiment arrived there at midnight after the battle." Starr, *Jennison's Jayhawkers*, 349.

60. *Official Records*, Vol. XLI, Pt. 1, p. 502; Castel, *General Sterling Price*, 246.

61. *Official Records*, Vol. XLI, Pt. 1, p. 502.

62. *Ibid.*, 341. Because of a misunderstanding of orders, Blunt, seeing Pleasonton's men turning off on the road to Fort Scott, followed suit and took himself out of the chase also. Then, to complete the cycle of mischances, the wagons loaded with rations and forage that had left the fort pursuant to General Curtis' orders to meet the cavalry on the main north-south road, met Pleasonton on his way to the fort and thereupon turned around and went back to the fort also. (In February, 1865, Pleasonton was in Philadelphia, "under medical treatment," when both John Pope and General Dodge asked for him to join them. On April 17, he was announced as "Chief of Cavalry and Artillery" under Pope, who had command of the recently created Military Division of the Missouri. *Ibid.*, Vol. XLVIII, Pt. 1, pp. 746–47, 761, Pt. 2, pp. 111, 159.)

deed, General Curtis had sent orders to the fort to that effect, and a train of wagons carrying forage and rations started east from the fort when Pleasonton turned west to march to the fort. General Curtis' dispatch to General Halleck, intended for the eyes of the general-in-chief, tells a sad tale of frustration.

The militia caviled about going beyond State lines; and General Rosecrans' commanders, except one or two, ever since we formed a junction, expressed a conviction that they had done enough. . . . I used argument, expostulation, and orders, and held the troops together till we fought at Charlot, opposite Fort Scott. Here General Pleasonton, without consulting me, flanked off most of his force, and insisted that farther pursuit was needless. . . . I . . . informed . . . [him] that I assumed and must exercise the prerogatives of my rank and direct him to resume the pursuit. To this he yielded and ordered his brigades to join me.[63]

But time had been lost, and then, for better or worse, Pleasonton himself decided to leave the operation. He informed Curtis on October 27 that "from the effects of a severe fall and exhaustion from . . . [his] late arduous services," he was unable to move. He enclosed a certificate of his medical director's to that effect and requested permission to return to St. Louis, where he could "obtain proper care and attention."[64] In the "Roll of Honor" ("to be transmitted to posterity") General Curtis appended to his report of the campaign, he listed Pleasonton's name second, following James G. Blunt's.[65]

No sooner did General Curtis settle matters with the balky Pleasonton than Rosecrans, keeping up with the pursuit after a fashion, a hundred miles to the rear, decided that enough had been done for the honor of the Department of the Missouri. He sent orders to the brigades of cavalry in Pleasonton's command, all of which except Winslow's belonged to his department, to abandon the pursuit. Given the hardships of the campaign, it is understandable that the brigade commanders were happy to comply and left at once for the rear.[66] With only a thousand

63. *Ibid.*, Vol. XLI, Pt. 4, p. 330. All but Winslow's brigade of Pleasonton's cavalry belonged to Rosecrans' Department of the Missouri and hence were not subject to the orders of General Curtis, who commanded the Department of Kansas.

64. *Ibid.*, 286.

65. *Ibid.*, Pt. 1, p. 519. General McNeil's name was fourth on the list, ahead of the names of the far more deserving Sanborn, Ford, Moonlight, and Benteen.

66. See, for example, Colonel Philips' dispatch of October 27 to General Curtis: "My command is exhausted . . . and the horses so jaded and sore that I can scarcely travel. . . . My command have now been in the saddle thirty-one days, and have not had

effective men of Blunt's division at his disposal, Curtis nevertheless wanted to continue the chase. At Neosho, Missouri, during the night of the twenty-ninth, he received Grant's orders, via Halleck, that Price was to be pursued to the Arkansas River.[67] He dispatched at once couriers to McNeil and Sanborn, ordering them to rejoin him, but it was too late.[68] The condition of the men and horses of a typical regiment, the 4th Iowa, that had participated in the pursuit, was described thus:

> In a campaign so long and active army clothing would go to pieces. Many of the men had not enough left to keep them warm. On the ice and frozen ground their cheap army boots gave out, and a large number of them were not only dismounted but barefoot. Many were hatless, all were ragged and shivering. All the remaining horses were greatly jaded, many permanently injured, and none were able to move with any speed. At the end of the march there were not one hundred horses in the whole brigade able to carry their owners. . . . In the bitter weather, without shelter, without sufficient food, that shabby and weary column dragged itself painfully along.[69]

The orders to return were received by McNeil and Sanborn, but difficulties of one kind or another—General McNeil called them "the belly impediment"—prevented, or were cheerfully allowed to prevent, these brigades from taking further part in the chase. Perhaps it was just as well that they did not try to do more, for on November 6, three of General McNeil's six regiments, the 7th Kansas, 2nd Missouri, and 5th Missouri State Militia Cavalry, mustered an aggregate of a mere 587 men.[70]

General Price's report of his Missouri-Kansas raid must have provided grimly entertaining reading for those of his command who were fortunate enough to survive the expedition. The results of the raid, he wrote, were "of the most gratifying character." He made grandiose claims of the Federal troops, guns, small arms, and supplies he captured and the railroad track, depots, and bridges, and "Missouri property" in general, he destroyed.[71] Not listed among the items destroyed

---

in all this time a change of clothing. If you can possibly relieve us without damage to the glorious work of your pursuit of Price we will be grateful." *Ibid.*, Pt. 4, p. 279.

67. *Ibid.*, 330, 287, and Pt. 1, pp. 330–31.

68. The whereabouts of Benteen's and Philips' brigades at this moment are unclear. See, however, Castel, *General Sterling Price*, 248n.

69. Scott, *Story of a Cavalry Regiment*, 346–47. Scott's regiment belonged to Winslow's brigade.

70. *Official Records*, Vol. XLI, Pt. 1, pp. 395–96, Pt. 4, p. 459.

71. *Ibid.*, Pt. 1, p. 640.

was his own army. Its state after it crossed the Arkansas was described thus by Shelby's biographer: "After crossing the Arkansas the worst stage of misery came upon the army, and the sufferings were intense. Horses died by thousands; the few wagons were abandoned . . . the sick had no medicines and the healthy no food; the army had no organization and the subordinate officers no hope. Bitter freezing weather added terrors to the route and weakness to the emaciated, staggering column. Smallpox came at last, as the natural consequence, and hundreds fell out by the wayside to perish without help and to be devoured by coyotes without a burial."[72] This was the Civil War as experienced by those who fought it; the scent of magnolias in the moonlight came years after the war had been lost.

Price had no choice but to furlough those of his men who had not already furloughed themselves; he himself, with remnants of his force, went on to Texas. A court of inquiry, appointed by General Kirby Smith, to look into Price's management of the raid, assembled on April 21, 1865, and met a number of times, but before it could complete its work and render a report, the war came to an end and the court disbanded.[73]

The reader will be spared a recital of yet another chapter of the excessively familiar tale of atrocities committed by both sides, by Price's men while their route lay on the Kansas side of the Kansas-Missouri border, as far south as the Marmiton River, and by the Federal troops, Blunt's command in particular, farther south, in Missouri and in Arkansas and on their return march from the Arkansas River as well. It may be noted, for what little it was worth, that Colonel Jennison, who either tolerated or actively encouraged the atrocities committed by the 15th Kansas, was court-martialed as the direct result of the complaints of several of his own officers and, having been found guilty on a number of the charges on which he was tried, was dishonorably discharged from the service.[74]

The Price court of inquiry and the Jennison court-martial wrote an epilogue with little intrinsic significance to the long war in Missouri

72. Edwards, *Shelby and His Men*, quoted in Castel, *General Sterling Price*, 248.
73. *Official Records*, Vol. XLI, Pt. 1, pp. 701–29; Castel, *General Sterling Price*, 269. It may be noted as an oddity that as a step in rebuilding his division, Shelby organized Alonzo W. Slayback's battalion of Missourians, whom he equipped with "lances, tipped with steel and decorated with gay flags made by fair hands." This was one of General John Magruder's ideas. Edwards, *Shelby and His Men*, 496.
74. Starr, *Jennison's Jayhawkers*, 358, 365–69.

and Kansas. Except for the operations, long past the end of the war, of guerrillas, gangs, or individuals professing still to be laboring for the Confederacy, the Civil War west of the Mississippi came effectively to an end when Price crossed the Arkansas River on November 7, 1864.

XXI

Swifter than Eagles, Stronger than Lions

AT THE MOMENT WHEN GENERAL SLOCUM MARCHED HIS XX Corps into Atlanta and received from the mayor the surrender of the undefended city, Hood and Sherman and their armies stood facing each other at and near Lovejoy's Station, where the Federal infantry had at length succeeded in making a permanent break in the rail lines serving Atlanta. Battle losses and desertions in the long campaign, 50,000 in the aggregate, reduced Hood's numbers to 23,000 infantry and 39,000 of all arms.[1] Sherman's casualties totalled 32,000; he lost thousands by expiration of their terms of service and had to detach thousands more to garrison sensitive points on the railroad back to Chattanooga. Nevertheless, he had as of September 1 just under 82,000 of all arms, including 9,394 cavalry.[2] Despite his two-to-one numerical superiority, Sherman decided to leave Hood to his own devices, to give

1. Connelly, *Autumn of Glory*, 467. Another tally of Confederate losses, exclusive of those of the cavalry and also of desertions, gives a figure of 34,979. Sherman, *Memoirs*, II, 132.

2. Sherman, *Memoirs*, II, 133, 135. Illustrative of the losses in the campaign, Colonel Minty's brigade, which had marched 925 miles, been in thirty-one fights, in skirmishes without number, and put in fourteen days of serving as infantry in the trenches before Atlanta, started the campaign with 2,515 oficers and men, 2,279 good horses, and 2,001 carbines. At the end of the campaign the brigade had 736 officers and men, 811 horses (which it had to turn over to Kilpatrick's division), and 1,001 carbines. Vale, *Minty and the Cavalry*, 376.

his men (and himself) a period of rest while he puzzled over his next move, and on September 8 he and his troops were back in Atlanta.[3]

Materially as well as spiritually, the loss of Atlanta was a body blow to the Confederacy. Its most urgent problem now was to decide on a strategy for Hood's depleted, ragged army, short of supplies, of ammunition, and of morale.[4] President Davis himself traveled west to confer with Hood, review and encourage his troops, make speeches, smooth out or eliminate personality conflicts in the higher ranks of the army, and do his best to restore morale both in the army and in the sorely beset civilian population.

The strategy for the coming months that evolved after much debate, and was modified considerably as time went on, was distinctly a second-choice affair. Unable to mount a direct attack on an enemy much too wary and powerful, Hood would force Sherman to take the offensive by using all of his own army, not his cavalry alone, to break up the latter's rail connection with Chattanooga and beyond. The break was to be made as far north of Atlanta as possible, to draw Sherman out of his position in central Georgia.[5] A few weeks later, Hood superimposed on this plan a far more ambitious project: to "cross the Tennessee River . . . at Guntersville, destroy Sherman's rail communications in the Stevenson-Bridgeport area, rout any defensive forces in Tennessee, capture Nashville, and invade Kentucky. Then . . . continue into northeastern Kentucky, threaten Cincinnati, and await Sherman. If . . . [he] did not come . . . either . . . send detachments to aid [R. E.] Lee or . . . march directly through the Cumberlands . . . and threaten Grant's rear."[6] After Grant's success at Vicksburg, made possible by his decision to cut loose from his base, the Confederate authorities might have considered the possibility that Sherman would be less concerned to protect his rail lifeline to the rear than the military textbooks said he should have been. It was taken for granted that Sherman would not dare to ignore a full-fledged attack on his communications and, in a textbook counter to such an attack, would retreat from Atlanta toward or into Tennessee.[7]

3. Sherman, *Memoirs*, II, 110.

4. For the material effect on the Confederacy of the loss of Atlanta, see Connelly, *Autumn of Glory*, 467–68.

5. *Ibid.*, 476–77.

6. *Ibid.*, 483. For earlier versions of the plan, see *Ibid.*, 477, 478; see also Hood, *Advance and Retreat*, 266–68.

7. An all-out attack on "Sherman's communications" by all the cavalry in Missis-

Wheeler and his cavalry had been operating for some time on Sherman's railroad. In a report characterized as "grossly misleading" and as failing to reveal that his "corps was practically destroyed," Wheeler claimed to have broken up fifty miles of track and "several key bridges" on the stretch between Chattanooga and Nashville.[8] After meeting Wheeler on September 20, Forrest wrote General Richard Taylor:

His command is in a demoralized condition. He claims to have about 2,000 men with him; his adjutant-general says, however, that he will not be able to raise and carry back with him exceeding 1,000, and in all probability not over 500. One of his brigades left him and he does not know whether they are captured or have returned, or are still in Middle Tennessee. He sent General Martin back in arrest, and his whole command is demoralized to such an extent that he expresses himself as disheartened, and that, having lost influence with the troops, and being unable to secure the aid and co-operation of his officers, he believes it to the interest of the service that he should be relieved from command.[9]

Despite the difficulties he described to Forrest, Wheeler was preparing for another expedition against Sherman's railroad. Moreover, Forrest, on the basis of his own proposal to President Davis, was now ordered by Richard Taylor, the new commander of the Department of Alabama, Mississippi, and East Louisiana, "to proceed at once into Tennessee . . . for the purpose of breaking the lines of communication of General Sherman."[10]

Unaware, probably, of the state of Wheeler's command, Sherman telegraphed General Halleck, "I can whip . . . [Hood's] infantry, but his cavalry is to be feared." Based on his experience with his own cavalry, Sherman explained that he had "little fear of the enemy's cavalry damaging our roads seriously, for they rarely made a break which could not be repaired in a few days," but he concluded with an opinion he was to abandon later—that "it was absolutely necessary to keep . . .

sippi and Tennessee had been suggested by General R. E. Lee as early as July 12. Henry, *"First with the Most" Forrest*, 347.

8. Hood, *Advance and Retreat*, 198–99; Connelly, *Autumn of Glory*, 477.

9. *Official Records*, Vol. XXXIX, Pt. 2, p. 859.

10. *Ibid.*, Vol. LII, Pt. 2, p. 732. Taylor's justification for sending Forrest into Tennessee was his assessment of the "campaign in Georgia [as] of paramount importance." Forrest had wired President Davis, "If permitted to do so with 4,000 picked men and six pieces of artillery of my present command, I believe I can proceed to Middle and West Tennessee, destroy enemy's communication or cripple it, and add 2,000 men to my command." *Ibid.*, 731.

Hood's infantry off our main route of communication and supply." [11]

Hood started to put his plan into execution on September 19 by leaving Lovejoy's Station. Eight days later, with forces numbering between 33,000 and 40,000, he crossed the Chattahoochee. Leaving behind the XX Corps to hold Atlanta, Sherman took off after Hood with five corps "very much reduced in strength by detachments and discharges" but numbering still about 60,000 infantry and artillery plus Kilpatrick's and Kenner Garrard's small divisions of cavalry. [12] As Sherman noted, the "cavalry could do little against . . . [Hood's] infantry in the rough and wooded country . . . which masked . . . [his] movements." [13]

The ensuing campaign, in which the main armies never came in sight of each other, nevertheless had its dramatic moments, highlighted by General John M. Corse's defense of Allatoona (his message to Sherman—"I am short a cheekbone and an ear, but am able to whip all hell yet"—belongs in any work that deals with America's military past). An interesting sidelight on the campaign, illustrating the degree of expertise the Union army's technique for repairing breaks in the railroad had reached, is given by General Sherman: "The rebels had struck our railroad a heavy blow, burning every tie, bending the rails for eight miles . . . so that the estimate for repairs called for thirty-five thousand new ties, and six miles of iron. Ten thousand men were distributed along the break to replace the ties, and to prepare the roadbed, while the regular repair-party . . . came down from Chattanooga with iron, spikes, etc., and in about seven days the road was all right again." [14]

Notwithstanding such feats of restoration, Sherman came gradually to the conclusion that changed the face of the Civil War, and perhaps of war in general. He wired Grant from Allatoona on October 9: "It will be a physical impossibility to protect the roads now that Hood, Forrest, and Wheeler, and the whole batch of devils, are turned loose without home or habitation. . . . I propose we break up the railroad from

11. Sherman, *Memoirs*, II, 144, 146.

12. In addition to Kilpatrick's and Garrard's divisions, which took part in the chase after Hood, Sherman also had the division of Edward McCook and the Fourth Cavalry Division then commanded by Colonel George Spalding. *Official Records*, Vol. XXXIX, Pt. 1, pp. 724–25.

13. Sherman, *Memoirs*, II, 152.

14. *Ibid.*, 151. It was at this time that the Confederate remark originated crediting Sherman with carrying along a duplicate tunnel to replace the one near Dalton that Wheeler had supposedly blown up.

Chattanooga, and strike out with wagons for Milledgeville, Millen, and Savannah. . . . By attempting to hold the [rail]roads we will lose 1,000 men monthly, and will gain no result. I can make the march, and make Georgia howl."[15] In numerous messages on subsequent days to Grant, Sherman elaborated and refined the idea, to persuade a reluctant general-in-chief to allow him to deviate from a cardinal rule of military science by seeking a geographic goal rather than the destruction of the enemy army.[16] Sherman convinced himself, and then at least half-convinced Grant, that Hood "had no intention to meet me in open battle, and the lightness and celerity of his army convinced me that I could not possibly catch him in a stern-chase." A more weighty argument Sherman advanced was that by making the march from Atlanta to Savannah ("smashing things to the sea") he would retain the initiative: "Instead of being on the defensive . . . [he would] be on the offensive," and instead of having to guess what Hood was planning to do, Hood would have to try to guess *his* plans.[17]

Quite early in the course of the Sherman-Hood military ballet, Forrest, with "a heavy force," captured Athens, Alabama, on September 24.[18] Anticipating more attacks on his railroad, which eventually came to pass, Sherman sent a division of infantry back to Chattanooga and another to Rome, Georgia; a few days later, "to meet the danger in Tennessee," he sent General Thomas back to Chattanooga with another division of infantry.[19] The exchanges between Sherman and Grant on the one hand and Grant and Halleck on the other, which led

15. *Official Records*, Vol. XXXIX, Pt. 3, p. 162.

16. At one point Grant proposed, but did not order, that as a "first step" Sherman "drive Forrest out of Middle Tennessee." *Ibid.*, Pt. 2, p. 478; Sherman, *Memoirs*, II, 141.

17. Sherman, *Memoirs*, II, 157, 154.

18. For Forrest's raid (September 21–October 8), made with a force of 4,500 (thought by the Federals to be 8,000), see Henry, *"First with the Most" Forrest*, 352–65; *Official Records*, Vol. XXXIX, Pt. 1, p. 506; Wyeth, *That Devil Forrest*, 422–51. Aside from the usual toll of prisoners and supplies captured (the latter enabled Forrest to distribute to his men "as much sugar and coffee as they needed" and "boots, shoes, hats, blankets, overcoats, oil-cloths and almost everything necessary for their comfort"), he also destroyed a long stretch of the Nashville & Decatur Railroad but inflicted only minor damage (repaired in a day) on the far more important Nashville & Chattanooga Railroad. Henry, *"First with the Most" Forrest*, 357–58.

19. Sherman, *Memoirs*, II, 144. General Rousseau, sent with a division of infantry to try to intercept Forrest, reported to General Sherman from Tullahoma: "Forrest is here to stay unless driven back and routed by a superior cavalry force. Infantry can cause him to change camp but cannot drive him out of the State. . . . Cavalry is wanted. I have here about 3,000, not enough to fight him without support." *Official Records*, Vol. XXXIX, Pt. 1, p. 506.

eventually to Grant's somewhat grudging approval of the March to the Sea, dealt more and more with the disturbing possibility that Hood would not follow Sherman eastward but would take advantage of his departure to invade Tennessee. Would General Thomas in that event have the forces needed to "hold the line of the Tennessee"? Intent on making his march—"a movement . . . not purely military or strategic, but it will illustrate the vulnerability of the South"—Sherman assured Washington that Thomas would have the necessary force, but he protested too much. Years after the war, he still felt the need to justify his decision to leave it to Thomas to deal with Hood, by presenting a less-than-convincing tabulation of the forces Thomas would have to do the job. These would include "eight or ten thousand new troops and as many more civil employes of the Quartermaster's Department," divisions at Chattanooga and Murfreesboro, and another at Decatur and Huntsville, Alabama. To these Sherman added, by his own reckoning, 15,000 men of the IV Corps and 12,000 of the XXIII Corps, and lastly, the 8,000 to 10,000 men of A. J. Smith's corps, who were marching from Missouri to join Thomas.[20] Had Sherman's figures been correct, Thomas would have had between 65,000 and 70,000 troops, although nearly 20,000 of them were of questionable quality and the timely arrival of Smith's command was doubtful.[21] But Sherman overstated the strength of the IV and XXIII Corps by 6,000, and in crediting Thomas with "eight or ten thousand new troops," he saw fit to ignore the fact that as fast as he was receiving these "new troops," Thomas was losing veterans because of the expiration of their terms of service.[22]

The Union cavalry, which was to play a decisive role in the campaign, its command structure, organization, and logistics, requires separate discussion. It is to be noted in the meantime that on October 26, at Gaylesville, Sherman decided that he had pursued Hood far enough. He turned about and headed back to Atlanta, leaving Hood to be dealt with by General Thomas. After sending back the "immense amount" of surplus stores from Atlanta and all his wounded, sick,

20. *Official Records*, Vol. XXXIX, Pt. 3, p. 358; Sherman, *Memoirs*, II, 162–63.
21. General Smith's troops arrived in Nashville in installments from November 30 to December 2, at the same time that Hood reached the city.
22. In early November, as Sherman was about to leave Atlanta, Thomas had an effective force, by his own reckoning, of 12,000 in the IV Corps, 10,000 in the XXIII Corps, and 7,700 cavalry under Hatch, Croxton, and Capron, for a total of 29,700, plus garrisons guarding the railroad at Murfreesboro, Stevenson, Bridgeport, *etc. Battles and Leaders*, IV, 473; see also McKinney, *Education in Violence*, 377, 381.

lame, and halt soldiers, Sherman cut his telegraphic link to the North on November 12, and having broken up the railroad north of Atlanta and "so damage[d] the country [behind him] as to make it untenable to the enemy," he began the great March to the Sea. [23]

Readers of the first volume of this history will recall that on September 30, General James Harrison Wilson turned over command—which he had exercised without any particular distinction—of the Third Division, Cavalry Corps of the Army of the Potomac, to George Custer and traveled West to become chief of cavalry, under General Sherman, of the Military Division of the Mississippi. Sherman had been quick to accede to Grant's suggestion that he should have "an officer in command of cavalry, whose judgment and dash could both be relied on." "I do want very much a good cavalry officer to command," he wired Grant. "My present cavalry needs infantry guards and pickets, and it is hard to get them within ten miles of the front. If you think [Romeyn B.] Ayres will do, I would like him. . . . I would prefer [David McM.] Gregg or Wilson; still, any body with proper rank will be better than [Kenner] Garrard. Kilpatrick is well enough for small scouts, but I do want a man of sense and courage to manage my cavalry, and I will take any one that you have tried." [24]

Sherman's dissatisfaction with his cavalry commanders, and by extension with his cavalry in general, is exemplified in a dispatch he sent a few days later to the officer who was then his chief of cavalry, General Washington L. Elliott.

I reiterate my order for all the cavalry to act boldly against Hood to-morrow, leaving all trains and artillery with the infantry. Of course I don't want them to attack infantry in position, but to strike detachments. . . . At all events keep . . . [Garrard] out and hang close upon the enemy. We must not let Hood send off all his cavalry and hold ours at bay by mere squads. It does look as though our cavalry was afraid to meet an inferior force. Let them wipe out this impression. The fact that a single regiment [of infantry] went out to-day where a division of cavalry would not venture elicited universal comment. . . . I was asked by a hundred where our cavalry was, and why it did not reconnoiter instead of men on foot. [25]

23. Sherman, *Memoirs*, II, 169, 171.
24. *Official Records*, Vol. XXXIX, Pt. 2, pp. 438, 442. Sometime before, Sherman had tried to get General Mower for the post.
25. Sherman had written General Halleck, "[Forrest's] cavalry will travel a hundred miles in less time than ours will ten." *Ibid.*, Pt. 3, pp. 107–108, 110, 126–27, Pt. 2, p. 517.

The selection of Wilson ("he is the best man for the position") to send to Sherman was ultimately made by General Sheridan, whom Grant had instructed to send A. T. A. Torbert, Sheridan's chief of cavalry, or Wilson. Sherman, Grant had written, was "absolutely without a man who can command cavalry."[26]

Except for six months in command of a cavalry division in the field and three months in command of the Cavalry Bureau in Washington, Wilson brought no cavalry experience to his new post, in which he was to command seventy-two regiments of cavalry and mounted infantry, nominally about 50,000 men "present and absent." What he brought west instead were "certain conclusions, not only from the study of military history, but from observation in the field, as to the proper functions of cavalry and the necessity of handling it in masses against the enemy's front, flanks, and communications."[27] He would now have the opportunity to put these conclusions into practice, for Sherman, eager to be off on his march to Savannah, directed him after a brief conversation to draft the orders establishing the "Cavalry Corps, Military Division of the Mississippi," with himself in command and with the authority "to make such dispositions and arrangements as . . . [he] might think best for getting the largest possible force into the field and inflicting the greatest possible amount of damage upon the enemy."[28] It is to be noted that Wilson's command was to extend over the cavalry of the entire military division and hence would absorb and supersede the commands of the cavalry forces of the Departments of the Cumberland, Tennessee, and Ohio. The new arrangements, and Wilson's status, were spelled out in General Orders issued on October 24.[29]

Mentioned in neither Sherman's nor Wilson's dispatches was the fact that the military division already had a chief of cavalry, to wit, Gen-

26. *Ibid.*, Vol. XLIII, Pt. 2, pp. 170, 218, 249. Wilson's own comment on his appointment, characteristic of his brashness, was, "While Grant authorized Sheridan to send either Torbert or myself . . . both Sheridan and I felt that the great task was really intended for me, and as Torbert did not care to leave the Army of the Potomac, the detail fell to my lot." Wilson, *Under the Old Flag*, I, 566.

27. Wilson, *Under the Old Flag*, II, 5, 7.

28. *Ibid.*, 12. Sherman's rather casual attitude toward spelling out Wilson's status and duties may have been due to the fact that, as he himself said, he "had not so much faith in cavalry as . . . [Grant] had." It may be noted that Washington never approved formally the establishment of the cavalry corps, which therefore had only a de facto existence, based on Sherman's authority. *Official Records*, Vol. XLV, Pt. 1, p. 554; Wilson, *Under the Old Flag*, II, 61–62; Sherman, *Memoirs*, II, 160.

29. *Official Records*, Vol. XXXIX, Pt. 3, p. 414.

eral Richard W. Johnson, headquartered in Nashville. His fall from grace was eased by appointment to command a division of infantry in the XV Corps and, a few days later, to command of a division in the new Cavalry Corps. Nor was Johnson's head the only one to roll under the new dispensation. Kenner Garrard, whom Wilson had succeeded earlier in the year in command of the Cavalry Bureau, was removed from the command of the Second Division of Cavalry, to spare him the embarrassment of serving under a man greatly his junior in Regular Army rank as well as in cavalry experience; he, too, was given an infantry command. Elliott, Stoneman, and Grierson, chiefs of cavalry in their respective armies, were all Wilson's seniors, and he "thought it best for all concerned that they should be disposed of as Garrard had been," and with Sherman's consent, all three were relieved "from further service with the cavalry." [30]

Wilson's most urgent task was to make ready Kilpatrick's division for the March to the Sea by getting it fully mounted and armed (which he was able to do only by taking horses and arms from Garrard's and McCook's divisions) and supplied with ammunition, clothing, wagons, and whatever else it needed. His next job was to prepare for the field the rest of the cavalry of the military division, wherever found, "and help Thomas as best as . . . [he] could to defeat and destroy Hood." [31] Sherman was of the opinion that there were enough cavalrymen in the military division to make up two or three small divisions besides Kilpatrick's. Wilson, on the other hand, thought that there were enough of them, "if they could be got hold of, to make six, certainly, and perhaps seven, large divisions." [32] Wilson's problem was to find and collect these men, get them mounted, armed, equipped, and officered, and formed into a cavalry army ready to be hurled "into the bowels of the South in masses that the enemy cannot drive back as it did Sooy Smith and Sturgis." [33]

30. *Ibid.*, 415, 613, 705; Wilson, *Under the Old Flag,* II, 19–20. In Wilson's opinion and evidently in Sherman's also, Garrard and Elliott were better suited to command infantry than cavalry. *Official Records,* Vol. XXXIX, Pt. 3, p. 443.

31. *Official Records,* Vol. XXXIX, Pt. 3, p. 13.

32. *Ibid.*, 13. It was in the dispatch to Wilson directing him to make up three divisions, "each of 2,500, for the hardest fighting of the war," that Sherman used the memorable phrase "I am going into the very bowels of the Confederacy, and propose to leave a trail that will be recognized fifty years hence." *Official Records,* Vol. XXXIX, Pt. 3, p. 358. For the state of the cavalry when Wilson took command, see General R. W. Johnson's and his own reports in *Ibid.*, 439–44.

33. *Official Records,* Vol. XXXIX, Pt. 3, p. 443. Wilson asked for Emory Upton,

The most immediate challenge presented to Wilson and Thomas was, however, Hood's presence at Tuscumbia and what was obviously to be his next move, an invasion of Tennessee. Starting from his crossing of the Tennessee River at Tuscumbia, Hood's most feasible route north was over the turnpike that ran from Pulaski through Columbia, Spring Hill, and Franklin to Nashville. In anticipation of Hood's probable use of that route, General Thomas sent the 23,000 infantry of the XXIII and IV Corps, under Schofield, to Pulaski with orders to delay Hood's northward advance as long as possible.

Guarding the crossings of the Tennessee and disputing Hood's progress as well as their scanty numbers permitted, were the cavalry of Edward Hatch's "efficient division," joined later by the "fairly good" brigades of John T. Croxton, Horace Capron, and Thomas J. Harrison, a total of about 4,300, rank and file, opposing the Confederate 5,000, who were thought by the Union command to be 8,000 or as many as 12,000.[34] After Hood had actually reached Nashville, Thomas was given permission to seize horses wherever Wilson's men could find them and was able by that means to increase the number of his mounted troops to 12,000.[35] In the meantime, however, as Schofield retreated north from Pulaski, Wilson, as new to his officers and men as they were to him, had the unenviable task of trying to block with detachments of his small force crossings over distances of as much as twenty-five miles, first of the Duck River above and below Columbia, then of the Harpeth River above and below Franklin.

Forrest had joined Hood on November 15 and was given command of all the cavalry of the Army of Tennessee.[36] With the advantage of the

---

Ranald Mackenzie, George Custer, Alexander C. M. Pennington, Jr., and Marcus A. Reno to command his divisions and brigades. Upton was the only one on the list he actually got.

34. *Ibid.*, Vol. XLV, Pt. 1, pp. 70, 752; Wilson, *Under the Old Flag*, II, 32, 33–34; Henry, *"First with the Most" Forrest*, 384.

35. *Official Records*, Vol. XLV, Pt. 2, pp. 16, 18, 35.

36. *Ibid.*, Pt. 1, p. 1211. Before joining Hood, Forrest had performed one of the most spectacular feats of his career. Having escaped, after his September 16–October 6 raid, the trap General Thomas had organized to catch him, he was ready at once for another expedition to cut Sherman's line of communications. This time his goal was the huge Federal depot at Johnsonville, Tennessee. Supplies for Sherman's army were shipped up the Tennessee River to Johnsonville, to be warehoused and forwarded thence via Nashville and Chattanooga to Atlanta. He started on the raid on October 16. He left Johnsonville on November 4 after destroying four Union gunboats, eleven steamboats,

initiative, Forrest could choose the river crossing or crossings that best suited the tactical situation or Hood's wishes and concentrate his command accordingly. The first such operation occurred on November 28, with Schofield occupying the north bank of Duck River at Columbia. Hood put into execution a well-conceived plan, ultimately a failure, to get two corps of his infantry and Forrest across the turnpike in Schofield's rear at Spring Hill, a road center twelve miles north of Columbia, while most of a third corps of infantry and most of the army's artillery remained on the south bank and staged a noisy demonstration to prevent discovery of the threat to Schofield's rear. Forrest crossed the river upstream from Columbia and, after laying a pontoon bridge for the infantry to use, drove Wilson northeastward—that is, away from the turnpike from Columbia to Franklin.[37] At 1 A.M. on November 29, Wilson notified Schofield that Forrest had crossed the river and urged him to get back to Franklin as quickly as possible and "to get to Spring Hill by 10 A.M."[38]

Hood had his infantry in motion before daylight on the twenty-ninth to cross the river at Davis' Ford on the pontoon bridge Forrest had laid the previous day. Alarmed by Wilson's 1 A.M. dispatch, Schofield started General David Stanley, with George D. Wagner's division of his IV Corps and the army's train of eight hundred wagons, north on the turnpike. By marching Wagner's men on the double, Stanley got them to Spring Hill before Forrest arrived there, and deployed them in an arc to the east of the village so as to block the latter's access to the turnpike. Wagner's riflemen and gunners beat off a series of attacks by For-

---

fifteen barges, and most of the stores stacked up on the landing and in the warehouses. General Sherman wrote after the war that this exploit of Forrest's was "a feat of arms which, I confess, excited my admiration." Henry, *"First with the Most" Forrest*, 369–78; Wyeth, *That Devil Forrest*, 455–66; Sherman, *Memoirs*, II, 164.

37. After driving off Wilson to the northeast, Forrest turned west toward Spring Hill, leaving General Lawrence S. Ross's Texas brigade to keep Wilson moving. Wilson, *Under the Old Flag*, II, 45–47.

38. *Official Records*, Vol. XLV, Pt. 1, p. 1143 (Wilson also kept General Thomas informed; see *Ibid.*, 1145, 1146); Wilson, *Under the Old Flag*, II, 40–42; Henry, *"First with the Most" Forrest*, 388. For a splendid account and analysis of Wilson's performance on November 28–29, see Thomas R. Hay, "The Cavalry at Spring Hill," *Tennessee Historical Magazine*, VIII (1924), 7–23. In Hay's opinion, "The cavalry had performed most creditably throughout the retreat to Franklin and it is hardly too much to say that Wilson's work saved Schofield from being cut off and defeated." *Ibid.*, 21. See also Thomas R. Hay, *Hood's Tennessee Campaign* (New York, 1929), 105–109.

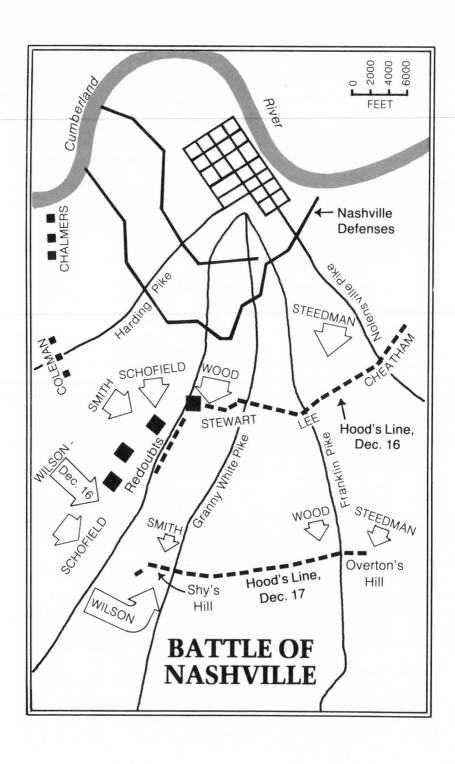

BATTLE OF NASHVILLE

rest's cavalry and kept open the turnpike for the all-night march of the rest of Schofield's infantry to Franklin and safety. Assigning responsibility for the Confederates' failure to trap Schofield at Spring Hill became in the postwar years second only to Longstreet's supposed failure at Gettysburg on July 2 as an inexhaustible subject for acrimonious dispute.[39]

Having escaped destruction at Spring Hill, Schofield posted his troops on November 30 below the left bank of the Harpeth at Franklin to give his train time to get across the river. He was now eighteen miles from Nashville. Early in the afternoon, Forrest's cavalry and Hood's infantry came up and saw, beyond a rolling terrain of cleared fields some two miles wide, Schofield's infantry and artillery in intrenchments that ran in a semicircle from the river above the town to the river below. It was clear to Forrest, to the Confederate generals, and to Hood himself that Schofield's position could be flanked by crossing the river upstream from Franklin, and that is what Forrest actually proposed: "Give me one strong division with my cavalry," he said to Hood, "and within two hours' time I can flank the Federals from their works."[40] For reasons impossible to fathom, Hood turned down Forrest's offer and ordered a frontal assault on Schofield's position that in its murderous stupidity is exceeded only by Grant's order of the frontal assault at Cold Harbor. In a fight lasting no more than two hours, the Confederates lost 1,750 officers and men killed, 3,800 wounded, and 702 taken prisoner, for an appalling total of 6,200.[41] Especially ominous for the future was the loss of high-ranking officers. In addition to divisional commanders Patrick Cleburn killed and John C. Brown wounded, 4 brigade commanders were killed, 5 were wounded (one mortally), and 4 were missing; of regimental commanders, 14 were killed, 26 were wounded, and 8 were missing or taken prisoner. In the fight at Nashville two weeks later, two of Hood's divisions, thirteen of his brigades, and no fewer than fifty-one of his regiments had new commanding

39. Henry, *"First with the Most" Forrest*, 389–96; Hood, *Advance and Retreat*, 282–91; Horn, *Army of Tennessee*, 384–93.

40. Henry, *"First with the Most" Forrest*, 397; Wyeth, *That Devil Forrest*, 480. Aware of this possibility, Schofield sent a brigade of infantry to guard the turnpike north of the river. *Official Records*, Vol. XLV, Pt. 1, p. 343.

41. Connelly, *Autumn of Glory*, 536. The Federal loss was 2,326. For an excellent description of the battle, see Horn, *Army of Tennessee*, 395–403. One of the Federal casualties was General David Stanley, wounded severely in the neck. *Official Records*, Vol. XLV, Pt. 1, p. 343; Wilson, *Under the Old Flag*, II, 54.

officers, with all that implied in terms of loss of cohesion, responsiveness, and morale.[42]

After turning down Forrest's proposal to flank Schofield out of his position, Hood permitted or ordered him to send one of his divisions—he chose William H. Jackson's—to cross the river above the town, swing to the west, and attack Schofield's trains moving toward Nashville. Jackson crossed the river at Hughes' Ford, three miles above Franklin, but he was met head on by Hatch's division and attacked in flank by Croxton, and by nightfall was forced to recross the river. Hatch and Croxton earned Wilson's praise for the manner in which they conducted this minor operation.[43]

On the night following the slaughter at Franklin, Schofield retreated to Nashville. His report suggests that he was less than happy with the performance of his cavalry in the campaign. His remark that "My experience on the 29th had shown how utterly inferior in force my cavalry was to that of the enemy, and that even my immediate flank and rear were insecure, while my communication with Nashville was entirely without protection" indicates a lack of confidence in his cavalry that may have been his own or merely inherited from Sherman. He is also credited with saying, "Wilson is entirely unable to cope with" Forrest.[44] On the other hand, he wrote either more accurately or more charitably in his reminiscences: "During . . . the operations between Pulaski and Nashville . . . the cavalry was never seen by me. They were far out in front or on the flank, doing all the 'seeing' for me, giving me information of vital importance in respect to the enemy's movements. . . . I believe no cavalry ever performed that important service more efficiently. At no time during that short campaign did

42. Henry, *"First with the Most" Forrest*, 399–400.

43. *Official Records*, Vol. XLV, Pt. 1, p. 550. Wilson was in error in stating that Buford, too, had crossed the river with Jackson. Buford's men, dismounted, were on the right flank of Hood's attack on the Federal infantry at Franklin. Wyeth states that "Wilson was unable notwithstanding his superior force . . . to drive the Confederates south of the river until dark, when Forrest . . . withdrew his troops to the south side of the Harpeth." Wyeth, *That Devil Forrest*, 482. Schofield said to Wilson on the evening after the battle, "If you had not succeeded [in beating back Forrest] our victory here would have been in vain, for with Forrest upon our flanks and rear it would have been impossible for us to have withdrawn our trains, artillery and troops from this position." Hay, *Hood's Tennessee Campaign*, 129.

44. *Official Records*, Vol. XLV, Pt. 1, p. 343; Wilson, *Under the Old Flag*, II, 54; Stanley F. Horn, *The Decisive Battle of Nashville*. (Baton Rouge, 1956), 18.

I suffer any inconvenience from lack of information that cavalry could possibly give."[45]

A possible indication that the cavalry had done its share of the work in the retreat from Pulaski to Nashville is that its numbers shrank from about 4,300 to 3,000. Horace Capron's brigade, for which accurate figures are available, had started the campaign with 1,500, rank and file, but on November 30 reported 411 "for duty," only 267 of whom had serviceable horses and 81 of whom were without guns.[46] On its arrival in the Nashville defenses on December 1, the cavalry, in Colonel Croxton's words, describing the state of his own brigade, was "shattered by long and severe service . . . need[ed] rest, and must have it."[47] The men also needed footwear and clothing, nearly all the surviving horses needed reshoeing, and after weeks of marching and standing in mud, many of them were incapacitated by "scratches."[48] The main problem, however, was that hardy perennial of cavalry afflictions, a shortage of horses throughout the command. The brigades and regiments of Wilson's forces, as they reached Nashville, were ordered into camps at Edgefield, across the Cumberland, and they and Wilson "went to work at once . . . to repair the damages of the campaign, to rest and build up both men and horses, to reequip and remount the dismounted troopers, and finally to bring forward every cavalry organization as soon as it could be got ready to take the field."[49]

An example of what the process of remounting meant is the state of the Sixth Division, now commanded by General Richard W. Johnson. Johnson took their horses from those troopers of the 8th Michigan and 14th Illinois who had them, to fully mount the 750 men of the 16th

45. Schofield, *Forty-Six Years*, 227. This passage has been quoted in Vol. I, p. 10, note 16 of the present work.

46. *Official Records*, Vol. XLV, Pt. 2, p. 17, Pt. 1, pp. 550, 1181. General Johnson, to whose division Capron's brigade was assigned, reported it as "800 mounted men, poorly armed and equipped, and . . . considerably demoralized by an unsuccessful campaign of some duration against an enemy superior to them in numbers, mount, and equipment." *Ibid.*, Pt. 1, p. 597.

47. Quoted in Horn, *Decisive Battle of Nashville*, 46.

48. *Official Records*, Vol. XLV, Pt. 1, p. 911. An inspection of the horses of the 2nd Iowa (of Hatch's division) on November 25 showed that out of "over 400 . . . less than sixty were serviceable, the balance being rendered unfit for service by greese [sic] heel." However, the regiment "picked up" in two days in the Columbia area horses "in sufficient numbers to give . . . [it] the best remount . . . [they] had had since . . . [they] veteranized." Pierce, *History of the Second Iowa*, 133, 136–37.

49. Wilson, *Under the Old Flag*, II, 57.

Illinois and 7th Ohio, which made up his First Brigade. In his Second Brigade, only the 5th Iowa, an exceptionally large regiment of 590 men, was fully mounted; the other two regiments of the brigade, the 5th and 6th Indiana, were dismounted.[50] This juggling of horses was the order of the day throughout the corps, based on a circular of Wilson's directing division commanders to "take instant measures to mount regiments complete by dismounting partially dismounted regiments."[51] It was at this time also that the Nashville area and the southern and western counties of Kentucky as far north as Louisville (where General Long seized 1,130 animals) were combed for horses to be seized for the cavalry, pursuant to authority granted by Washington, which enabled Wilson to increase the number of his mounted troops to about 10,000.

Other shortages could not be cured by heavy-handed seizures from the civilian population. Wilson's special inspector, Major W. P. Chambliss, reported from Louisville on November 16 that "articles of equipment" ordered in September had not yet arrived, and neither had blankets ordered from New York on October 27, which should have been in Louisville by November 1. When the Ordnance Bureau overcame what General Johnson called its "proverbial inefficiency" and shipped the arms and equipment the cavalry needed, then the "transportation department" fell down on the job. As a result, General McCook reported from Louisville on November 27 that Colonel Oscar H. LaGrange's brigade of his division was about to leave for Nashville without carbines, and went on to explain: "There are no carbines here, and I much prefer having my command go into the field without them to taking such inferior arms as they have had heretofore. . . . We have never been thoroughly armed, and I would like to put the division into a fight once with arms in which the men have confidence." A week later, it was General Eli Long's turn. He inquired of Wilson from Louisville whether he should arm the Second Division "with muskets or any-

50. *Official Records*, Vol. XLV, Pt. 1, p. 1026, Pt. 2, p. 151. The 5th Iowa had acquired about 300 of its horses ("very poorly shod") by seizure in the Hopkinsville, Kentucky, area. *Ibid.*, Pt. 2, p. 137.

51. *Ibid.*, 135. General Wilson wrote in his article "The Union Cavalry in the Hood Campaign" that in seven days from his arrival in Edgefield the numbers of his mounted troops had increased to 12,000, besides which he had about 3,000 dismounted men organized as infantry. *Battles and Leaders*, IV, 467. The returns for December 10 show 11,591 cavalry "Present for Duty—Equipped" at Nashville and Edgefield. *Official Records*, Vol. XLV, Pt. 1, p. 55.

thing I can get" and was told in reply that if the proper arms were not available when his division was fully mounted, he should accept whatever firearms he could get.[52]

General Grierson's Fourth Division presented a problem of a different character, and it was the general himself. He had been ordered on October 26 to collect his own division and Colonel Benteen's (formerly Winslow's) brigade (on its way east after its participation in the pursuit of Price to the Arkansas River) and hurry them to Nashville. Nearly a month later, Wilson asked Grierson, in harsher tones than brigadier generals were accustomed to reading, why he had failed to comply with these "clear and unmistakeable" orders and why he himself, instead of being in St. Louis to arrange for the shipment of these troops to Nashville, was in Chicago. "There being no record at army headquarters of a leave of absence to you," Wilson wrote, "you will report without delay by what authority you are absent from Saint Louis or Memphis." Grierson's lame replies of November 23 and 30—by which time he had made no move to comply with orders already more than a month old—make it obvious that he had no intention whatever of giving up his quasi-independent status in Memphis to become a mere cog in a corps commanded by a man ten years his junior who, moreover, was clearly lacking in the respect that the commander of Grierson's Raid had the right to expect. Without actually denying that he had been in Chicago, he claimed that he had been sent to Missouri and Illinois "on military business connected with . . . [his] command" and had gone to Springfield, Illinois, "to confer with the Adjutant-General with regard to filling up the Sixth, Seventh, and Ninth Illinois Cavalry Regiments." Lieutenant Henry E. Noyes, whom Wilson sent to Memphis to hurry forward Grierson's and Benteen's commands, reported having learned that "Grierson was at his home in Jacksonville, Ill. He had been absent several weeks." So far as one can judge from the records, Wilson's order of December 13 relieving Grierson of the command of the division was fully justified. Grierson's replacement was one of the outstandingly fine officers of the Union army, General Emory Upton, who was ordered to "proceed to Louisville, Saint Louis, and Memphis for the purpose of collecting the men, horses and transportation of his division and bringing it to Nashville."[53]

52. *Official Records*, Vol. XLV, Pt. 1, pp. 598, 908, 1092–93, Pt. 2, pp. 47, 75.
53. *Ibid.*, Vol. XXXIX, Pt. 3, p. 459, and Vol. XLV, Pt. 1, pp. 954–55, 1003, 1179, Pt.

While Wilson and his officers were struggling to add the 6,000 or 7,000 mounted, armed (after a fashion), and equipped horsemen to the effective strength of the Cavalry Corps to raise its numbers to the 10,000 General Thomas thought he needed to cope with the 12,000 cavalry Forrest was thought to have, and to protect his flanks as he attacked Hood, Thomas himself became the victim in one of the most shameful episodes in American military history, the inexcusable harassment he was subjected to by Grant. Even Wilson, an admirer of Grant's, had to confess that the latter's behavior to Thomas in the first two weeks of December was "perhaps the least creditable incident in . . . [Grant's] whole military career."[54] Urged on initially by the president and Secretary Stanton, paying no attention to Thomas' pleas for time to collect and organize his forces and to build up his cavalry to a level he considered prudent, he was urged, badgered, and at the last ordered (from a distance of five hundred miles!) to attack Hood, lest Hood flank Nashville, cross the Cumberland, invade Kentucky, and reach the Ohio, which, in midwinter weather and after his losses at Franklin, Hood had as much chance of doing as invading the moon.[55] Against his better judgment Thomas was about to obey the orders to attack, despite the fact that neither his infantry nor his cavalry were ready, when a sudden storm and drop in temperature to 10° F coated the entire area with a sheet of ice and made movement on the hilly terrain totally impossible.[56] General Jacob D. Cox, who was in Nashville in command of a division of the XXIII Corps, wrote: "The slopes in front of the lines were a glare of ice so that movement away from the roads and broken paths could be made only with the greatest difficulty and at a snail's pace. Men and horses were seen falling whenever they attempted to move across country. A man slipping on the hillside had no choice but to sit down and slide to the bottom, and groups of men in

---

2, pp. 9, 61, 17. Colonel Winslow, recovered from his wound and back in command of his brigade, wrote from Memphis on December 15: "I do not know by what authority we are kept . . . [in Memphis] but do know that my whole command is suffering very much by this long-continued separation. . . . had my efforts here been properly seconded by . . . Grierson . . . we should now be in Nashville." *Ibid.*, Vol. XLV, Pt. 2, p. 204.

54. Wilson, *Under the Old Flag*, II, 84.

55. For the exchanges between Grant and Thomas (and those between Thomas and Halleck) see *Official Records*, Vol. XLV, Pt. 2, pp. 15–17, 55, 70, 96, 97, 114–16, 143, 155, 171. For John Schofield's actual or possible role in these events, see Horn, *Decisive Battle of Nashville*, 53–57.

56. By another account, the temperature dropped to 10° F below zero. Pierce, *History of the Second Iowa*, 140.

the forts and lines found constant entertainment in watching these mishaps. . . . manoeuvers were out of the question for nearly a week."[57]

All this time the drumbeat of Grant's exhortations and orders to attack continued. Orders were at length drawn up, but fortunately not sent, relieving Thomas of command and replacing him with Schofield, under whom (his inferior in rank) he was ordered to serve. Acting in what can only be interpreted as a frenzy of fear for his own position, Grant next sent General John Logan to relieve Thomas if he had failed to attack Hood in the meantime, and finally, started west himself; he got as far as Washington, where he was met by news of Thomas' great victory of December 15. Grant's motivation in all this is clear enough. Against his own better judgment, he had allowed Sherman to march off toward the sea on the strength of the latter's assurances, which he did not bother to question, that he was leaving Thomas with adequate forces to deal with Hood's veterans. Should Hood now avoid Thomas and invade Kentucky, it would be discovered that a large part of the forces given to Thomas were civilians, rejects of Sherman's own army, untrained recruits, Negro infantry without battle experience, and one body of veteran infantry who might not arrive (and very nearly did not arrive) in Nashville in time.[58] The most charitable view of Grant's conduct, and a cautious surmise of its source, was General Wilson's: "Here, if at any time during the war, Grant lost his head and failed to act with his usual sound sense. It is, of course, impossible to say with certainty . . . how far Grant's judgment may have been disturbed by his fear that Thomas would fail to hold Hood, and that this would condemn both himself and Sherman for stripping Thomas and leaving him with widely dispersed forces to contend against Hood's compact veteran army."[59]

57. Jacob D. Cox, *Military Reminiscences of the Civil War* (2 vols.; New York, 1900), II, 352–53 (previously quoted in Vol. I, p. 12, note 22 of the present work). General Wilson wrote that "the glare of snow and ice" made it "impossible to move cavalry not especially rough-shod for the occasion. In fact, neither infantry nor cavalry could have made any progress whatever over a battlefield so undulating and broken and so covered with ice and frozen snow." Wilson, *Under the Old Flag*, II, 99–100. See also Grant, *Personal Memoirs*, II, 379–83, for an outstanding example of special pleading, obfuscation, and outright distortion of the record.

58. Wilson called Sherman's march "his holiday excursion," which, given the quantity and quality of the opposition he met with between Atlanta and Savannah, it certainly was. Wilson, *Under the Old Flag*, II, 105.

59. *Ibid.*, 65–66; see also Donn Piatt and H. V. Boynton, *General George H. Thomas* (Cincinnati, 1893), 574–77.

General Thomas' plan for attacking Hood had been elaborated and discussed with his subordinates before the ice storm made an attack impossible. Hood had added to his follies in the meantime by sending Forrest with Buford's and Jackson's divisions of his cavalry plus two brigades of infantry, a total of 6,000 men, to attack Murfreesboro, held by a Federal garrison of 8,000. The purpose was "to ascertain if it was possible to take the place"; the only results of the operation were to demonstrate the unreliability of some of Hood's infantry and, more important, to keep 6,000 men and Forrest away from Nashville when their, and especially his, presence might have made a major difference in the events of December 15–16.[60]

When Hood arrived before the Nashville defenses, his engineers laid out a line for his troops to occupy. The line was about five miles long and fronted, at a distance of about two miles, the southeastern face of the Nashville defenses. Starting at the Nashville & Chattanooga Railroad on the east, the line crossed the Nolensville, Franklin, and Granny White pikes, which radiated like the fingers of a hand southeastward and southward from Nashville, and it ended at the Hillsboro Pike on the west, where it was "refused" and its southward extension protected by five large redoubts and also by a stone wall, behind which infantry could shelter, running for a distance of about a mile and a quarter along the eastern edge of the pike. Cheatham's infantry held the eastern (right) end of Hood's line; Stephen D. Lee's corps held the center; and A. P. Stewart's the left, including the redoubts and the stone wall along Hillsboro Pike. Chalmers' cavalry division (the brigades of Edmund W. Rucker and Jacob B. Biffle) patrolled and held loosely a line about four miles long from the Hillsboro Pike northwestward to the Cumberland River.

There is a considerable variance in the number of troops on the eve of the battle credited to Hood by various sources. He himself gives the figure of 23,053, exclusive of the infantry and cavalry absent at

60. *Official Records*, Vol. XLV, Pt. 1, p. 654. Hood does not explain in *Advance and Retreat* why he sent Forrest to Murfreesboro. See, however, Henry, *"First with the Most" Forrest*, 402–405, which calls it "a pointless and fruitless division of forces." Hood also sent 800 "undisciplined and but poorly organized" cavalry under General Hylan B. Lyon to break up the Louisville & Nashville Railroad. Wilson sent McCook's division in pursuit, but Lyon (500 of whose men deserted on news of Hood's defeat at Nashville) escaped to Alabama. The principal accomplishment of his raid was the burning of eight courthouses in Kentucky. *Official Records*, Vol. XLV, Pt. 1, pp. 45, 561, 791–806; Wilson, *Under the Old Flag*, II, 143–45.

Murfreesboro; other accounts give him as many as 38,000 and as few as 15,000, with a figure of 26,877 between the two extremes. Given the number of his men taken prisoner in and after the battle and the number of those who deserted, the 15,000 figure seems far too low. Perhaps the figure of 23,000 he himself has given is reasonably close to the mark. In any event, albeit with the advantage of fighting on the defensive and having possession of commanding ground, Hood was about to face an attack by an army nearly twice the size of his—43,260 (including 6,600 cavalry) actually engaged.[61]

A thaw on December 14 melted the ice and made movement on the hills and fields south of Nashville possible. Thomas' plan of attack for the next day, confirmed in a meeting with his subordinates in the evening, called for General James B. Steedman's Provisional Division of about 5,000, newly arrived from Chattanooga, to make a "heavy demonstration" straight ahead against Cheatham, on Hood's right. It is to be noted that Steedman's command was "made up of fragments of 200 ill-provided regiments. A large proportion were unfit for duty. Thirty-five per cent of them were scarcely convalescent. Fifty per cent were recruits. . . . There were no ambulances or wagons. Some of these troops were not armed until the evening of the fourteenth."[62] A. J. Smith's command, supported by the IV Corps on its left, was to deliver the principal attack, aimed at Stewart's corps on the Confederate left.[63] The cavalry was to attack on Smith's right, "turn and envelop the enemy's left flank, and, if possible, strike him in the rear."[64] Wilson was to have three full divisions (Hatch's Fifth, Richard Johnson's Sixth, and Joseph F. Knipe's Seventh) plus Croxton's brigade of the First Division in the attack. One brigade each of the Sixth and Seventh Divisions was mounted, and the other dismounted; Hatch's division and Croxton's brigade were mounted. To avoid misunderstandings and mistakes, Wilson

61. Hood, *Advance and Retreat*, 298 (the figure is as of December 10); *Battles and Leaders*, IV, 474 (according to which another 12,000 men were absent at Murfreesboro); McKinney, *Education in Violence*, 406; Connelly, *Autumn of Glory*, 508. The Federal numbers in *Battles and Leaders*, IV, 473, use the figures of Colonel Henry Stone of General Thomas' staff.

62. McKinney, *Education in Violence*, 404.

63. General Schofield claims that he persuaded General Thomas to move the XXIII Corps and have it, rather than Smith's command, make the principal attack. There is no mention of this change in General Thomas' report. Horn, *Decisive Battle of Nashville*, 64–65; see also *Official Records*, Vol. XLV, Pt. 1, pp. 344–45.

64. *Official Records*, Vol. XLV, Pt. 1, pp. 37–38; Wilson, *Under the Old Flag*, II, 107.

assembled his division and brigade commanders, showed them "the ground over which they were to advance," went over with them verbally the plan of attack, gave each of them his instructions in writing, and then assigned one of his staff officers to each of the three divisions "to see that everyone was in his place and did his part in conformity with the general plan of operations." The corps was to make the attack with "something over" 9,000 mounted and 3,000 dismounted men.[65]

Reveille in the Union camps was blown at 4 A.M., and by daylight the troops were ready to move.[66] A dense fog, however, made it impossible for them to move until midmorning. As soon as the fog lifted, the attacks went in. The main cavalry contribution that day was made by the brigades of Colonels Datus E. Coon and Robert R. Stewart of Hatch's division, and in particular the regiments of Colonel Coon's brigade (6th, 7th, and 9th Illinois, 2nd Iowa, and 12th Tennessee).[67] Advancing dismounted to the right of Smith's infantry, under orders to "touch to the left and guide right," they captured first Redoubt No. 5, then, hardly pausing for breath, Redoubt No. 4, each with four guns and the latter with 250 prisoners.[68]

The capture of the redoubts, and Schofield's advance into the space between his own left and Smith's right, made it possible for Wilson to order Hatch's men to mount and ride forward to the Hillsboro Pike, to the south of and behind the Confederate infantry manning the stone wall. But Knipe and his brigade, crossing the Hillsboro Pike to Hatch's right, got to the Granny White Pike, even farther to Hood's rear; and to Knipe's right, Croxton's brigade and Johnson's division, meeting light opposition, were also able to advance as far as the Hillsboro Pike. The cavalry, in Wilson's summation, "had driven back the enemy's entire

65. Wilson, *Under the Old Flag*, II, 107–109, 188. The reader will note the large discrepancy in the strength of the cavalry (6,600 vs. 12,000) between Colonel Stone's and General Wilson's figures. There is no explanation in the records of the difference.

66. Hood's spies had brought him word on the evening of the fourteenth that his left was to be attacked the next morning. Connelly, *Autumn of Glory*, 509.

67. In the initial attack, the 12th Tennessee captured Chalmers' headquarters and baggage, 14 wagons and 43 prisoners. The Tennessee regiment was commanded by Colonel George Spalding of Michigan. This success, Wilson wrote, "fully vindicated my action in putting a Northern field officer in charge of a Tennessee regiment"—an action for which Vice President elect Andrew Johnson never forgave him. Wilson, *Under the Old Flag*, II, 110.

68. In Wilson's report, Coon is credited with the capture of four guns and 65 prisoners in Redoubt No. 5, and six guns and 175 prisoners in Redoubt No. 4. *Official Records*, Vol. XLV, Pt. 1, p. 551.

left wing an average of over four miles, and had placed itself in a position from which it was enabled to renew the attack on the enemy's left and rear the next day with deadly effect." General Wilson's claim, although basically correct, failed to give adequate credit to General Smith's footsoldiers, attacking abreast of his troopers, but he was wholly correct in his further statement that "for the first time on any American battlefield all the available mounted force, a full army corps in strength, were massed on the flank of an advancing army, making a turning movement of the first importance against an enemy occupying a strongly fortified position. For the first time in our country the horsemen on foot had charged side by side with the infantry, carrying the enemy's entrenchments, taking his field guns, and capturing the detachments told off for their support."[69] Wilson would demonstrate in another four months that his cavalry could accomplish all this and more, entirely on its own and without the support of infantry.

A comment by a regimental historian is to be taken into account in considering the course of attacks by dismounted cavalry, especially when such attacks required marches over a considerable distance, as did the charge of Coon's brigade on the morning of December 15 to capture Redoubt No. 4. After the capture of Redoubt No. 5, the historian writes, "the boys unused to marching on foot, had now charged for near a mile, and were so completely exhausted as to be wholly unable to move faster than a slow walk. . . . now some one too much fatigued to go farther, would sink down behind a tree, and there discharge his seven loads and reload his carbine, and then slowly drag himself up the fearful hights [sic]."[70]

In one of the minor military miracles of the Civil War, Hood's army retained its cohesion despite the drubbing it had taken on this day and also despite the threat to its left flank and rear.[71] The survivors of the day's fighting came to rest about two miles to the rear of their original lines and a short distance north of the Brentwood Hills. Their new line, facing mainly north, was about three and a half miles long and was fortified after a fashion in the dark by men exhausted by a day of

69. Wilson, *Under the Old Flag*, II, 112–13.

70. Pierce, *History of the Second Iowa*, 144.

71. Hood's losses this day were remarkably small. Fighting mainly behind defenses, his loss in killed and wounded was minimal, but 1,200 of his men were taken prisoner. He also lost sixteen guns. *Official Records*, Vol. XLV, Pt. 1, p. 39.

fighting and marching. The right of the line was anchored on Peach Orchard (or Overton's) Hill, and the left, in a salient extending northwestward like the prow of a ship, on a promontory that acquired that day the name of Shy's Hill. Bate's infantry, returned from Murfreesboro, had joined Hood the previous evening, too late to take part in the day's fighting; they were posted on and to the right of Shy's Hill, behind breastworks they worked all night to construct. On their left and facing west was Cheatham's corps, moved there after dark from the right; Stewart's corps, which had borne the brunt of the fighting on the fifteenth, lay in the center; and Lee's corps on Peach Orchard Hill, on the right.

The Federal troops, shuffled into place in the dark after the fighting ended on the fifteenth, faced the new Confederate line with Steedman's division and the IV Corps on the Union left facing Lee, Smith in the center, Schofield in a curved line facing Cheatham from the north and west, and Wilson's cavalry, with its right on the Granny White Pike, positioned well to the south end of Cheatham's line. Thomas' orders for the sixteenth to Steedman and the corps commanders were simple: advance straight ahead at daylight; if the enemy was still in place, attack; if he had decamped during the night, pursue. Then, however, Thomas had a strategically splendid afterthought: the main effort was to be made by Schofield and Wilson on his right, both directing their attacks in an east-northeast direction, so as to try to cut off Hood from the Franklin Pike, his main escape route south. By midmorning, Wilson had General John H. Hammond's brigade of Knipe's division and all of Hatch's division in a line a mile and a half long, pressing Cheatham diagonally from southwest to northeast, toward the rear of Shy's Hill. Hammond's and Hatch's advance carried them into the Brentwood Hills, "densely covered with underbrush and broken by fences which made the wooded country entirely impracticable for mounted men"; hence, the cavalry advanced on foot.[72] Croxton's brigade, in support of Hammond and Hatch, followed on their heels, and Johnson's division, making a wider swing to the south, forced its way across the Hillsboro Pike.

Now came a strange incident. Schofield was to attack in echelon with the cavalry. The horsemen had launched their attack and had

---

72. McKinney, *Education in Violence*, 411–12; Wilson, *Under the Old Flag*, II, 114.

reached the rear of Shy's Hill. Now was the moment for Schofield to make his attack. It was already past three o'clock on a rainy, cloudy, midwinter day and getting dark. Whatever his reasons may have been—they are not to be found in the records—Schofield failed to move.[73] Even stranger is the fact that General Thomas, who was with Schofield at the time, failed to order him to do so until after Wilson had ridden to find the commanding general and "urged . . . [him] with ill-concealed impatience, to order the infantry forward without further delay." General John McArthur, who had been sent with his division of Smith's corps to reinforce Schofield, decided not to wait longer for the XXIII Corps to move, or indeed for orders for his own division to attack, and moved out on his own initiative to capture Shy's Hill. Bombarded by the Union artillery from three directions, under attack by McArthur from the north, by Schofield (whose attack, when he finally launched it, was a halfhearted affair, as demonstrated by his 163 total casualties compared with A. J. Smith's 744 and the cavalry's 616) from the west, and by Wilson's cavalrymen from the south, Shy's Hill was captured.[74] At nearly the same time, the Peace Orchard Hill position also fell, captured by an attack by Steedman's and Wood's infantry. With the anchors at both ends of his position gone, Hood's entire line collapsed, and with the exception of Lee's corps, which retained its cohesion, there was a panic-stricken rush to the rear by those of the Confederate infantry and gunners who managed to outdistance the onrushing Federals.

Hatch, Knipe, and Hammond captured this day fifteen more pieces of artillery and several hundred prisoners, but they had gotten a considerable distance in advance of their horse holders. By the time they found their horses, mounted, and rode off in pursuit of the fleeing infantry, it had begun raining heavily, the rain was turning into sleet, and it had gotten pitch dark. Wilson's orders to his men were to ride south on the Granny White Pike to its junction with the Franklin Pike, where he hoped to intercept the fleeing Confederates. Chalmers, who had been moved to the rear sometime before for just that purpose, was

73. Schofield wrote in his report that his order to General Cox to capture Shy's Hill "was not executed with the promptness or energy which . . . [he] had expected." *Official Records*, Vol. XLV, Pt. 1, p. 346. But see Van Horne, *George H. Thomas*, 331–32. Allowance must, however, be made for Van Horne's pro-Thomas bias.

74. Wilson, *Under the Old Flag*, II, 116; *Battles and Leaders*, IV, 463–64; *Official Records*, Vol. XLV, Pt. 1, p. 47.

able to find a good location to set up a barricade of logs, fence rails, and brush across the Granny White Pike, and from behind it, he brought the advance of the Union cavalry to a halt.[75] Colonel Spalding captured Colonel E. W. Rucker in a saber duel, and even members of Wilson's staff and their orderlies, caught up in the excitement, thrust themselves into the melee at the barricade. "It was a scene of pandemonium," Wilson wrote, "in which flashing carbines, whistling bullets, bursting shells, and the imprecations of struggling men filled the air."[76] Not until midnight did mutual exhaustion bring the fighting to a halt, but Chalmers had held up Wilson long enough to allow the infantry, ambulances, and train to get well ahead of the Federal pursuit. General Lee's infantry performed a similar service on the Franklin Pike, seven miles north of Franklin, against the none-too-vigorous pursuit of the IV Corps infantry.

Meeting and recognizing Wilson in the rain and the dark, General Thomas, an officer in the Second Dragoons in the "Old Army," shouted to him, "Dang it to hell, Wilson, didn't I tell you we could lick 'em?"[77]

The pursuit of Hood's beaten, ragged, starving, demoralized army, many, perhaps thousands, of the men trudging barefoot through the slush and freezing mud, is a tale of horrors that fortunately does not require retelling here. The able commander of Forrest's artillery, Captain John W. Morton, Jr., recorded that "the sufferings of the soldiers on both sides were indescribable. The coating of ice on the roads gave way to mud, and the continued rainfall froze on the guns and pistols, making it agony for the numb fingers to fire them." Nevertheless, one of the pursued Confederates was of the opinion that the pursuing Federal cavalry "was very poorly handled. In fact, the conduct of the officers, had they been Confederates, would have been regarded as criminal." On the other hand, a better-qualified judge, General Lee, thought that the pursuit was remorseless. On the morning of the seventeenth, he wrote, the Federals "commenced a most vigorous pursuit . . . [their] cavalry charging at every opportunity and in the most daring manner. It was apparent that they were determined to make the retreat a rout if possible."[78] Initially, Wilson's entire corps was engaged

75. Wilson, *Under the Old Flag*, II, 121. General Johnson's division was to march south on the Hillsboro Pike and cut across to the Franklin Pike south of the Harpeth River.

76. *Ibid.*, 124.

77. *Ibid.*, 126.

78. J. W. Morton, *The Artillery of Nathan Bedford Forrest's Cavalry* (Nashville,

in the pursuit, but on December 20 he sent Johnson's and Knipe's commands back to Nashville, and went on with those of Hatch, Croxton, and Hammond.[79]

Forrest, recalled from Murfreesboro, rejoined Hood south of Franklin on the afternoon of the eighteenth and was given command of the rear guard, consisting of 3,000 of his own men and 1,850 infantry ("fully 400 of whom were without shoes"), the remnants of eight brigades.[80] He managed somehow to keep the pursuit in check day after day, stopping to fight wherever the terrain gave him a reasonable chance to do so and earning thereby General Thomas' generous praise. "With the exception of the rearguard," Thomas wrote, Hood's army "had become a disheartened and disorganized rabble of half-armed and barefooted men. . . . The rearguard, however, was undaunted and firm, and did its work bravely to the last."[81] Forrest himself reported to General Taylor: "The Army of Tennessee was badly defeated and is badly demoralized, and to save it during the retreat . . . I was compelled almost to sacrifice my command. Aside from the killed, wounded, and captured . . . many were sent to the rear with barefooted, lame, and unserviceable horses, who have taken advantage of all the confusion and disorder attending the hasty retreat of a beaten army, and are now scattered through the country or have gone to their homes."[82]

The long agony of the retreat came to an end on December 28, when General Edward C. Walthall and his detachment of 200 men crossed the Tennessee River at Bainbridge (the main body had crossed on the two previous days) and took up their pontoon bridge behind them. A few days later, Colonel William J. Palmer, with his 15th Pennsylvania and a detachment of 300 men taken from the 2nd Tennessee

---

1909), 287; James Dinkins, *Personal Recollections and Experiences in the Confederate Army* (Cincinnati, 1897), 250; *Official Records*, Vol. XLV, Pt. 1, p. 689.

79. Wilson, *Under the Old Flag*, II, 137. For the logistics of the pursuit in which the cavalry is said to have had "over 6,000 horses disabled, and many of them had to be abandoned or destroyed," see McKinney, *Education in Violence*, 416; Piatt and Boynton, *General George H. Thomas*, 591. For Wilson's tactical handling of the pursuit, see Wilson, *Under the Old Flag*, II, 129–30. It may be noted that on December 21, Captain J. W. Harper, 9th Illinois, was directed to return to Nashville "with the enlisted men of his regiment whose terms of service have expired, for the purpose of having them mustered out of the service of the U.S." *Official Records*, Vol. XLV, Pt. 2, p. 303.

80. Henry, *"First with the Most" Forrest*, 412.

81. Quoted in *Ibid.*, 417. For an example of these rear-guard affrays, see Pierce, *History of the Second Iowa*, 148–53.

82. *Official Records*, Vol. XLV, Pt. 2, p. 756.

and the 10th, 12th, and 13th Indiana, stumbled upon the pontoon train near Russellville, Alabama. The train, lightly guarded ("we met no resistance," Colonel Palmer reported), "extended for five miles, and consisted of 78 pontoon-boats and about 200 wagons, with all the necessary accoutrements and material, engineering instruments, &c.; all the mules and oxen, except what the pontoniers and teamsters were able to cut loose and ride off, were standing hitched to the wagons." Colonel Palmer burned the entire train "in the most thorough manner."[83]

General P. G. T. Beauregard, nominally Hood's superior, hurried from Charleston and Savannah to visit Hood's army at Tupelo, Mississippi, on January 15. What he found was, in his words, "in the strict sense of the word a disorganized mob, [and] it was no longer an army."[84] On January 13, Hood had telegraphed Secretary of War James A. Seddon to ask to be relieved of the command of the Army of Tennessee. The request was granted at once, and General Richard Taylor was directed to take his place. Hood turned over to his successor about 15,000 men, "fewer than half . . . [of whom] were still equipped or considered effective. . . . Some thirteen thousand small arms were missing, and wagon transportation had been annihilated."[85] Mainly at Nashville, and then in the retreat, Hood lost fifty-four guns, nearly all he had, and while his losses in killed and wounded were relatively small—due no doubt to the fact that both at Nashville and on the retreat, his men fought behind defenses of some sort—his loss in men taken prisoner was large: 4,462, including 4 generals. In addition, thousands of his men deserted, some to the Federals, and probably many more who simply went home.[86]

On the Federal side, the loss in the two days of fighting at Nashville was 387 killed, 2,562 wounded, and 112 missing; the cavalry's share of the casualties was 36 killed, 270 wounded, and 23 missing. In the entire campaign, however—in the move from Pulaski north to Nashville,

83. *Ibid.*, Pt. 1, p. 643. General Thomas added in his report that on the following day, Colonel Palmer caught another train of 110 wagons near Aberdeen, Mississippi; he burned the wagons and "sabered or shot" the 500 mules hitched to them. *Ibid.*, 45.

84. Horn, *Army of Tennessee*, 422. The January 15 date is given by Horn; Connelly, *Autumn of Glory*, 513, gives January 14.

85. Connelly, *Autumn of Glory*, 513.

86. Horn, *Army of Tennessee*, 417–18. In the period September 7, 1864, to January 20, 1865, the Department of the Cumberland captured 11,857 prisoners and received 1,314 deserters. *Official Records*, Vol. XLV, Pt. 1, p. 47.

the battle, and the pursuit south to Bainbridge—the cavalry lost 122 officers and men killed, 521 wounded, and 259 missing.[87] What the Union gained in exchange for these losses was the virtual destruction of the Army of Tennessee, the only force of any size and military effectiveness the Confederacy had left in the huge area bounded by the Ohio River, the Gulf, and the eastern seaboard, and the Indian lands west of the Mississippi, as the fourth year of the Civil War approached its close.

It is impossible to close this account of the Nashville Campaign without quoting what General Thomas had to say about Wilson and his men in the recommendations for promotion he sent General Halleck without waiting for the end of the pursuit. Thomas recommended first of all Wilson's promotion from brevet rank of major general

to the full rank of major-general of volunteers, for the excellent management of his corps during the present campaign, in which it has peculiarly distinguished itself, attempting such things as are not expected of cavalry, such as assaulting the enemy in intrenched positions, and always with success, capturing his works, with many guns and prisoners. His corps has also been conspicuous for its energy in the pursuit of the retreating rebel army, which has cost the rebel commander many men, several pieces of artillery, and tended much to the demoralization of his army.[88]

87. *Official Records*, Vol. XLV, Pt. 1, p. 105; Wilson, *Under the Old Flag*, II, 146.
88. *Official Records*, Vol. XLV, Pt. 2, p. 343. General Thomas also recommended that Hatch be promoted from brigadier general to major general.

XXII

All Thy Banners Wave

WHILE MAJOR EVENTS INVOLVING THE UNION CAVALRY were taking place on the Kansas-Missouri border and at Nashville, commanders in the West remained aware of the opportunity to reach the heart of the Confederacy through the back door of the gaps and passes in the Alleghenies. Readers will recall that General George Stoneman was taken prisoner when his mishandled raid to Macon was intercepted and broken up by Confederate cavalry. He was exchanged after a brief captivity and returned to Knoxville, where John Schofield, still in command of the Department of the Ohio, appointed him his second-in-command, greatly to Secretary Stanton's disgust. "If you approve of his doing so," he wrote Grant, "I am content, although I think him one of the most worthless officers in the service, and who has failed in everything intrusted to him." Grant replied the next day: "I am not in favor of using officers who have signally failed when intrusted with commands in important places . . . [but] as a general rule, when an officer is intrusted with the command of a department, he ought to be allowed to use the material given him in his own way. I would simply suggest the transmission of this dispatch to General Schofield, and leave it discretionary with him to employ General Stoneman, or relieve him from duty, as he deems best."[1] The result of

1. *Official Records*, Vol. XLV, Pt. 2, p. 54.

these exchanges was that Stoneman kept the post to which Schofield had appointed him and was thus enabled to go forward with a project he had offered for Schofield's consideration on November 26, namely, to cross the mountains with a force of from five thousand to ten thousand, destroy the saltworks—a resource essential to the Confederacy in an age before refrigeration—at Saltville, and then go on to invade North Carolina and perhaps South Carolina as well.[2]

The importance of Saltville to the Confederacy had been recognized in the North from the beginning of the war, and as recently as September, 1864, General Stephen G. Burbridge, commanding in Kentucky, proposed moving with his "available mounted forces" against the saltworks there. Schofield and General Halleck approved; the only reservation came from General Sherman, in characteristic language: "I doubt the necessity of . . . sending far into Virginia to destroy the salt-works. . . . we must destroy their armies." Burbridge had two veteran regiments of cavalry, the 12th Ohio and the 11th Michigan, and a number of twelve-month mounted infantry regiments of Kentuckians to take on his expedition. He started out on September 20 and crossed Laurel Mountain in a violent equinoctial storm. As a member of the 12th Ohio described it, this

was one of the darkest passages in the whole experience of the regiment. The path, at best, was a wretched one—steep, uneven and dangerous. On one side rose the mountain, rugged and precipitous; on the other yawned an abyss whose depth could only be guessed from the roar of the torrent that poured along the bottom of the gulch. . . . The night was so dark that men and horses walked against cliffs and trees, and it was only by the greatest care and the most marvelous good fortune that the casualties were so few. The men mostly dismounted, and, leading their horses through the fathomless mud, at length reached the valley beyond.[3]

Joined by two regiments—the 11th Kentucky and the 5th United States Colored (the latter dismounted)—from General Alvan C. Gillem's east Tennessee forces, Burbridge now had 4,200, rank and file. On the march to Saltville, "the colored soldiers, as well as their white officers, were made the subject of much ridicule and many insulting remarks

2. *Ibid.*, Pt. 1, pp. 1073–74. General Gillem wrote that the destruction of the saltworks "would be a ruinous blow to the Confederacy." *Ibid.*, Vol. XXXIX, Pt. 2, p. 398. The saltworks were a series of wells from which brine was pumped into large pans, or "kettles," in which the brine was evaporated, leaving the solid salt.

3. *Ibid.*, Vol. XXXIX, Pt. 2, pp. 360, 447; Mason, *The Twelfth Ohio Cavalry*, 27.

by white troops, and in some instances petty outrages, such as the pulling off of caps of colored soldiers . . . were practiced by the white soldiers."[4]

At the start of the discussions that led up to the sanctioning of the expedition, General Gillem wrote that he was "confident that there . . . [were] not 200 men at the salt-works" and that the Confederates could not collect a defensive force of more than 2,500 from southwest Virginia and east Tennessee. Burbridge, however, was to credit the defense he encountered with 6,000 to 10,000 men—a great exaggeration—and counted the number of his own troops actually engaged as 2,500. He found the Confederate troops deployed halfway up the side of a high mountain "behind rifle pits made of logs and stones to the height of three feet."[5] Attacking on October 2, Burbridge failed to carry the rifle pits, and with his ammunition expended, he withdrew, abandoning his wounded. His casualties were 350 (of the 400 of the 5th United States Colored in the attack, 114 men and 4 officers were killed or wounded); he had nothing to show for his losses but the destruction of "some of the outer salt-works."[6]

A Confederate cavalryman, George D. Mosgrove, 4th Kentucky, C.S.A., told the story of what happened early the next morning.

As usual, a dense fog enveloped mountain and valley. . . . Presently I heard a shot, then another and another until the firing swelled to the volume of that of a skirmish line. . . . the Tennesseeans were killing negroes. . . . I cautiously rode forward and came upon a squad of Tennesseeans, mad and excited to the highest degree. They were shooting every wounded negro they could find. Hearing firing on other parts of the field, I knew that the same awful work was going on all about me. . . . Very many of the negroes standing about in groups were only slightly wounded, but they soon went down before the unerring pistols and rifles of the enraged Tennesseeans. . . . About this time General Breckinridge, General Duke and other officers appeared on the scene. General Breckinridge, with blazing eyes and thunderous tones, ordered that the massacre should be stopped. He rode away—and the shooting went on.[7]

4. *Official Records*, Vol. XXXIX, Pt. 1, pp. 555–57.

5. *Ibid.*, Pt. 2, p. 361, Pt. 1, pp. 552, 557.

6. *Ibid.*, 552–53, 557; see also Mason, *The Twelfth Ohio Cavalry*, 66.

7. Mosgrove, *Kentucky Cavaliers in Dixie*, 206–207; see also Mason, *The Twelfth Ohio Cavalry*, 70. Surgeon William H. Gardner, 30th Kentucky Infantry, who was left behind to care for the Union wounded, reported that on the morning following the battle, "several armed men" entered the field hospital, took out 5 wounded Negro enlisted men of the 5th United States Colored, and shot them. Four days later, armed men wearing Confederate uniforms entered the hospital and killed 2 more of the Negro wounded and a wounded lieutenant of the 13th Kentucky. *Official Records*, Vol. XXXIX, Pt. 1, p. 554.

The raid or invasion General Stoneman proposed was to be a more ambitious operation than Burbridge's had been. Burbridge was to participate with 4,000 cavalry and mounted infantry—"every available man he could mount . . . and in order to enable him to mount as many men as possible," Stoneman reported, "I authorized him to impress horses wherever he could find them." Burbridge was to cross the mountains at Cumberland Gap and then be joined by a 1,500-man contingent (made up in part of two regiments of Ohio heavy artillery, serving as infantry) under General Gillem. These were troops Stoneman had been able to collect at Knoxville after the "personal animosities" that had resulted from a stinging defeat (the "Bull's Gap Stampede") the east Tennessee troops had sustained a month earlier "were somewhat abated; criminations and recriminations by commanders . . . which had extended to the commands themselves, were in great measure silenced." On December 11, Gillem met Burbridge. Two days later, he attacked and dispersed a "brigade" of about 800 men Basil Duke had assembled from the wreckage of John Hunt Morgan's command. Gillem took 84 prisoners, including Morgan's brother Richard, captured Duke's wagon train, and scattered the remnants of the brigade to the four winds. Five days later, reinforced by the 11th Michigan and 11th Kentucky, lent to him by Burbridge, Gillem "attacked, routed and pursued" to Wytheville the forces of General John C. Vaughn, capturing all his artillery and trains and 198 of his men.[8] On December 17, Stoneman detached Colonel Harvey M. Buckley's brigade of Burbridge's command and sent them to destroy "everything that was destructible" in the lead mines seventeen miles from Wytheville, which Federal reports claimed Buckley succeeded in doing. As is common in such situations, one Confederate report had "the injury to the lead mines . . . very slight," and another claimed that the damage done could be repaired in eight days.[9]

On December 20 the united forces of Burbridge and Gillem reached Saltville, after a fight with Breckinridge near Marion, and devoted the following day to the destruction of the saltworks, which, Stoneman claimed, was "total . . . as far as [was] in the power of man to accomplish." In his detailed report he wrote that all of the day and the night of the twenty-first were devoted "to the destruction and demolition of

8. *Official Records*, Vol. XLV, Pt. 1, pp. 809, 819–20, 811, 816, 818.
9. Stoneman claimed "the total destruction, as far as in the power of man to accomplish, of the lead works." *Ibid.*, 808, 826, 830.

the buildings, kettles, masonry, machinery, pumps, wells, stores, material, and supplies of all kinds. . . . The wells . . . were, by the use of bombshells, railroad iron, spikes, nails, &c., put into such condition as to render it impossible to use them until they were cleared out."[10]

The objective of the expedition having been accomplished, Stoneman sent Burbridge back to Kentucky and Gillem and his men to Knoxville. Both commands had before them "a long and arduous march through rivers swollen by the recent and almost continuous rains, along roads which had become nearly impassable, and over mountains slippery with ice and covered with snow."[11] To supplement the conventional language of Stoneman's report, it will be salutary to read the story of a night and a day (December 22–23) of the return march to Kentucky, as described by a trooper of the 12th Ohio.

A furious gale froze the heavy rain as it fell, and the road was soon covered with a thick, slippery coating of ice. Horses could no longer walk with certainty, and after a dozen falls, most of the men dismounted and led their animals. . . . Stiffened as their clothing was by the frozen rain, many of the men found walking almost impossible, and the frequent falls that ensued disabled many a soldier. . . . The terrors of the march [on the twenty-third] eclipsed all the previous sufferings of the expedition. The storm continued, and the poor horses, worn out with a month of terrible exertion, were fast yielding to famine and exhaustion. They fell by dozens in the miry, slippery road, and could not be induced to rise. They were unsaddled and left to perish, their riders marching thenceforward on foot. . . . To add to the suffering of the troops . . . [their] worthless shoes and boots began to fail. Long before the crest of the mountain was reached many men were walking over the frozen road with their feet wrapped only in shreds of cloth torn from their saddle blankets and overcoats. . . . Scores of men had their hands and feet frozen, many of these cases being so severe as to finally result in amputation of one or both feet. . . . Of the forty-four hundred animals which carried Burbridge's men into Tennessee a month before, only eight hundred lived to recross the Cumberlands.[12]

There was to be one more raid across the mountains led by General Stoneman. In the light of Grant's later derogatory comment on the operation, it should be remembered that the initial suggestion for it was his, in a dispatch of January 31, 1865, to General Thomas. "An expedition from East Tennessee under General Stoneman," Grant wrote,

10. *Ibid.*, 808, 813–14. In addition to the destruction of the saltworks and wells, the raiders also burned down the town of Saltville, where the operators of the saltworks lived.
11. *Ibid.*, 813.
12. Mason, *The Twelfth Ohio Cavalry*, 91–93.

might penetrate South Carolina well down toward Columbia, destroying the railroad and military resources of the country. . . . Of the practicability of doing this General Stoneman will have to be the judge. . . . Sherman's movements will attract the attention of all the force the enemy can collect, thus facilitating the execution of this. Three thousand cavalry would be sufficient force to take. . . . To save time I will send copy of this to General Stoneman, so that he can begin his preparations without loss of time. . . . As this expedition goes to destroy and not to fight battles . . . it should go as light as possible.[13]

The "preparations" Stoneman had to make entailed the usual search for more cavalry, more horses, and more firearms. To make up the 3,000 cavalry Grant had mentioned, Stoneman needed 1,007 more cavalry (he asked for 2,000), 2,000 horses, and 600 Spencers.[14] Major W. P. Chambliss, Wilson's inspector of cavalry, reported on February 14 from Louisville that he could "perhaps" equip Stoneman in ten or fifteen days, but to collect the horses Stoneman needed and to assemble the widely scattered regiments to be taken on the raid took not ten or fifteen days but six weeks. In the meantime Grant wired General Thomas repeatedly to ask if Stoneman had started and to urge that he start as soon as possible.[15] Finally, perhaps in desperation (it should be said in Grant's behalf that at the same time that he was receiving a stream of excuses for Stoneman's failure to get started, he was receiving similar excuses for Wilson's delay in starting on his expedition to Selma), he wired Thomas on March 19: "If Stoneman has not got off on his expedition, start him at once with whatever force you can give him. . . . He will not meet with opposition now that he cannot overcome with 1,500 men."[16]

On March 20, Stoneman did get away at last. He left Knoxville with a cavalry division of which General Gillem had immediate command; under Gillem were the brigades of Colonel William J. Palmer (12th Ohio, 10th Michigan, 15th Pennsylvania), General Simeon B. Brown (11th and 12th Kentucky, 11th Michigan) and Colonel John K. Miller (8th, 9th, and 13th Tennessee).[17] With the exception of a scratch

13. *Official Records*, Vol. XLIX, Pt. 1, p. 616.

14. *Ibid.*, 662, 679, 680, 700, 703, 709.

15. *Ibid.*, 725, 773, 916. On February 27, Grant directed a change in Stoneman's itinerary. "Stoneman being so late in making his start," he wrote, "and Sherman having passed out of . . . South Carolina, I think now his course had better be changed. . . . It will be better . . . to keep Stoneman between our garrisons in East Tennessee and the enemy. Direct him to repeat his raid of last fall, destroying the railroad as far toward Lynchburg as possible." *Ibid.*, 777.

16. *Ibid.*, Pt. 2, p. 28.

force—its artillery commanded by Colonel John C. Pemberton, formerly a lieutenant general and in command of the Vicksburg defenses—at Salisbury, North Carolina, which the raiders brushed aside on April 12, they met no opposition worth mentioning as they rode on a seemingly aimless course along the east face of the Blue Ridge in Virginia and then across the northwest corner of North Carolina as far as Hendersonville.[18]

With only token opposition to face, the raiders were free to concentrate on their primary goal of wrecking railroads. The East Tennessee & Virginia Railroad, running southwest from its connection at Lynchburg with the Petersburg & Lynchburg, received the raiders' particular attention; having undisturbed possession of ninety miles of the road from Wytheville to Salem, they destroyed all of its bridges, as well as the "iron and cross-ties" for twenty miles east of New River. Indeed, the historian of the 10th Michigan noted that for "125 miles substantially every bridge and trestle of any importance had been destroyed."[19] Then, marching northeast, the raiders struck the North Carolina Railroad, a southward continuation of the Richmond & Danville, and destroyed its track and bridges for a distance of fifteen miles north of Salisbury.[20]

Worthy of notice is Stoneman's realization that a wagon train and

17. *Ibid.*, Pt. 1, p. 325. A postwar account gives a somewhat different list of the units making up Brown's and Miller's brigades and also gives the strength of the division as 6,000, "all veterans, well mounted, and in perfect condition." Frank H. Mason, "General Stoneman's Last Campaign," MOLLUS, Commandery of Ohio, *Sketches of War History, 1861–1865*, III, 23.

18. The raiders took 1,364 prisoners at Salisbury and captured fourteen (or eighteen) of Pemberton's guns. The twenty-four hours following the capture of the town were devoted to putting to the torch the "immense depots and magazines" in the place and destroying large quantities of weapons, ammunition, cotton, rations, medical stores, clothing (including 250,000 blankets imported from England), and miscellaneous stores. "But the part of the work . . . in which Stoneman's troopers took most delight was the burning of the infamous prison pens in which so many thousand brave men had been starved and frozen to death." *Official Records*, Vol. XLIX, Pt. 1, pp. 334, 336; Mason, *The Twelfth Ohio Cavalry*, 101–102; Mason, "Stoneman's Last Campaign," 26–29.

19. *Official Records*, Vol. XLIX, Pt. 1, p. 322; Luther S. Trowbridge, *A Brief History of the Tenth Michigan Cavalry* (Detroit, 1905), 39–40. "About twenty miles east of Christiansburg the railroad crosses the Roanoke river six times in as many miles and the 10th Michigan destroyed six beautiful bridges." Luther S. Trowbridge, "The Stoneman Raid of 1865," MOLLUS, Commandery of Michigan, *War Papers No. 7* (Detroit, 1888), 8–9.

20. *Official Records*, Vol. XLIX, Pt. 1, p. 324; see also Mason, "Stoneman's Last Campaign," 26.

an excess of artillery were not compatible with the mandatory rapid pace of a cavalry raid. Hence he took along a single four-gun battery instead of the more usual three six-gun batteries, one for each of his three brigades. Then, on March 23, five days' rations, one day's supply of corn for the horses, and four horseshoes and nails were issued to all troopers, after which "the command moved, cutting loose from all in-cumbrances in the way of trains. One wagon, ten ambulances, and four guns, with their caissons, were the only carriages that accom-panied the expedition."[21] After the five days' rations and one day's corn were consumed, the men and their horses lived well for fifty-eight days on what they foraged in a countryside not previously ravaged by the march of armies.

On April 17, Stoneman left the raiders to return to Knoxville. The records do not indicate why he did so. General Gillem took over the com-mand and spent the next few days trying to reach Asheville by a roundabout route via Hendersonville, but in midafternoon on the twenty-third he received notice under a flag of truce of the Sherman-Johnston armistice, and for the raiders the war was over.[22]

In transmitting Stoneman's report on the raid to the War Depart-ment and to Grant, General Thomas took pains to "specially . . . [invite] their attention to the importance of the work performed by General Stoneman, who in spirit fully executed the orders given him before starting on the expedition." Grant, on the other hand (and unfortu-nately for Stoneman, it was Grant's opinion that mattered) found fault with Thomas for failing "to get Stoneman off in time"; then, comment-ing on the three expeditions that he had "tried so hard to get off," Wilson's to Selma, Canby's to Mobile, and Stoneman's to the Carolinas, he wrote: "They were all eminently successful, but without any good result. Indeed, much valuable property was destroyed and many lives lost at a time when we would have liked to spare them."[23]

The story of James Harrison Wilson's invasion of Alabama, first to Selma, thence east to Montgomery, and then on to Columbus and

21. *Official Records*, Vol. XLIX, Pt. 1, p. 330; Trowbridge, "The Stoneman Raid," 33.

22. *Official Records*, Vol. XLIX, Pt. 1, pp. 384, 344–46. Stoneman had not received notice of the Sherman-Johnston truce when he left the command.

23. *Ibid.*, 323; Grant, *Personal Memoirs*, II, 413–14, 518. Grant had evidently for-gotten that his initial orders to Thomas spelled out the goal of the Stoneman raid as not to fight but to destroy the "railroad and military resources of the country."

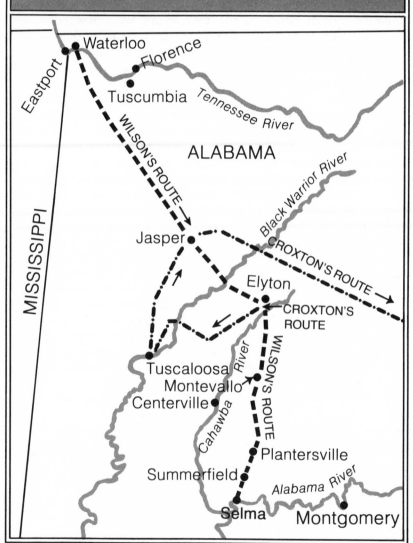

SELMA CAMPAIGN

MILES

0 10 20 30 40 50

Eastport

Waterloo

Florence

Tuscumbia

Tennessee River

WILSON'S ROUTE

ALABAMA

MISSISSIPPI

Black Warrior River

Jasper

CROXTON'S ROUTE

Elyton

CROXTON'S ROUTE

Tuscaloosa

Cahawba River

WILSON'S ROUTE

Montevallo

Centerville

Plantersville

Alabama River

Summerfield

Selma

Montgomery

Macon, Georgia, where he received his first trustworthy notice that Generals Lee and Johnston had surrendered and that for him, too, and for his cavalry corps, the war had ended, has been told in the opening chapter of Volume I of the present work.[24] It was given pride of place in this history of the Union cavalry because of the author's conviction (as it was General Wilson's) that this campaign, its planning, organization, tactics, and operations, from the departure of the corps from the Tennessee River on March 22 to the capture of Selma eleven days later, are a model of their kind and show the officers and men of the Union cavalry in the Civil War at the height of their powers and effectiveness. They show, too, the Union cavalry in the West reaching, as did their colleagues in the East under Sheridan at nearly the same moment, the culmination of a grim, costly four-year apprenticeship, in the course of which they had to learn a trade for which there were practically no native precedents, and what precedents were imported from abroad were largely misleading.

A month after the war ended, Wilson wrote "unofficially" to General Sherman: "I have now 13,500 men for duty . . . thoroughly armed, well mounted and equipped. I believe . . . that they cannot be excelled. I regard this corps to-day as the model for modern cavalry in organization, equipment, armament, and discipline, and hazard nothing in saying that it embodies more of the virtues of the three arms, without any sacrifice of those of cavalry, than any similar number of men in the world."[25] And he closed by recommending for promotion his commanders of divisions and brigades, "the best cavalry officers I ever saw," Generals Upton, Long, Croxton, McCook, Alexander, and Winslow, and Colonels Minty, Miller, and LaGrange.[26]

24. Detachments of the corps (the 1st Wisconsin and 4th Michigan) participated in the pursuit and eventual capture of Jefferson Davis. Wilson tried hard to keep the corps in being and offered it ("the best cavalry in the world") for service in Texas and presumably in Mexico. His offer was not accepted, and the corps was formally dissolved on June 26, 1865. *Official Records*, Vol. XLIX, Pt. 1, pp. 515–45, Pt. 2, pp. 903, 1035. For Wilson's farewell order, see *Ibid.*, Pt. 2, p. 1059. In mid-May, Wilson's men captured Confederate Vice-President Alexander Stephens and Captain Henry Wirz, commandant of the Andersonville prison camp. *Ibid.*, Pt. 2, pp. 734, 800; see also E. N. Gilpin, "The Last Campaign; A Cavalryman's Journal," *Journal of the United States Cavalry Association*, XVIII (1908), 668. Official word of the Sherman-Johnston truce reached Wilson on April 21.

25. *Official Records*, Vol. XLIX, Pt. 2, p. 663. Wilson had written in his report on the Selma Campaign, "The great fault in our cavalry system had previously been overwork in detachments, and the absence of instruction, organization, and uniformity of equipment." *Ibid.*, Pt. 1, p. 355.

26. Wilson was careful to exclude McCook from his list of the best cavalry officers;

There are points not mentioned in the account of the Selma Campaign in Volume I that, with the perspective of four years of cavalry operations, East and West, it will be useful for the reader to note. Wilson's corps had been practically dismounted at the end of the pursuit of Hood in December, 1864, but most of the wastage was replaced, notwithstanding that the government was now having to pay $144 to $185 for horses suitable for the cavalry, an increase of 20 percent or more over the 1861 prices, and Wilson was thus able to start the Selma Campaign with 12,000 of his 13,500 men mounted.[27]

The situation was less favorable with respect to armament. Wilson expected to receive, but failed to get, 3,000 Spencer carbines per month, and as late as February 26, reported that "Croxton's and Hatch's veterans . . . [were] armed with every species of arm from Springfield rifles to Hall's carbines."[28] He was able to approximate a uniformity of armament in his command by accepting Colonel Datus E. Coon's voluntary offer to turn over to Croxton's men the Spencers of his own brigade.[29] Despite Colonel Coon's unselfish offer, however, "a few hundred" of Wilson's men had weapons other than the Spencer carbine when they left on the campaign. Those who hold to the conviction that the Confederacy was overwhelmed by the limitless industrial might of the North may wish to consider the plaint of General Hatch, written not in the summer of 1861 but in March, 1865, that only the 2nd Iowa and the 6th Illinois of Colonel Coon's brigade of his division had received Spencers and that the 3rd and 7th Illinois and the 12th Missouri of the same brigade had for eight months past carried guns that had previously been condemned. General Hatch pointed out that all these regiments had been promised that they would be rearmed with

---

nevertheless, he recommended him for promotion to major general of volunteers by brevet. *Ibid.*, Pt. 2, p. 663.

27. *Ibid.*, Vol. XLV, Pt. 2, pp. 489, 517, 522, 575. But to get up to the 12,000 figure, Wilson had to take the horses of Hatch's division. *Ibid.*, Vol. XLIX, Pt. 1, pp. 355–56; Weigley, *Quartermaster General of the Union Army*, 257. The wages cavalrymen received increased also, privates from $13 to $16 a month, corporals from $14 to $18, sergeants from $17 to $20, and orderly sergeants from $20 to $24. Scott, *Story of a Cavalry Regiment*, 386.

28. *Official Records*, Vol. XLIX, Pt. 1, pp. 596–97, 773. In January, the corps received no Spencers at all. *Ibid.*, p. 744. The Burnside Arms Company was now also manufacturing Spencer carbines under license from the Spencer company. The 3,000 carbines per month Wilson was to receive were to come from the Burnside company.

29. *Ibid.*, 808, 909, and Pt. 2, p. 19. The basis of Colonel Coon's offer was the fact that Croxton's brigade was to go on the Selma Campaign; his own brigade was not.

Spencers as an inducement to reenlist as veterans in early 1864. He added that he had no arms of any kind for the recruits he was receiving daily and that he had sent one of his officers to Nashville a few days before "for muskets, despairing of obtaining a cavalry arm."[30]

A minor but nevertheless striking aspect of the Selma Campaign was General John Croxton's "Naval Expedition"—the march of his brigade from Tuscaloosa, Alabama, to join the Cavalry Corps at Macon, Georgia, nearly a month later.[31] It will be of interest to those who recall the reports in 1861 and 1862 of the mountains of baggage that individual cavalrymen and regiments of cavalry thought essential to fighting a war, that Croxton's men carried nothing but their haversacks and weapons and that the brigade made its march of more than six hundred miles without wagons, ambulances, or artillery.[32]

Lastly, having participated on the Union side in the attack of Eli Long's division on the Selma defenses on the late afternoon of April 2, the reader will wish to see the attack from the Confederate side. Franklin A. Montgomery, 1st Mississippi, C.S.A., a part of Frank C. Armstrong's 1,400-man brigade, was in the section of the defenses facing northwest. "The romance of war was gone," Montgomery wrote, "only a sense of duty sustaining the cause." Long's division, hidden from the view of the defenders manning the Selma parapets by a low ridge, was in the process of deploying into line. "An occasional shell was fired at the ridge which hid the enemy from us," Montgomery remembered. "They presently brought up a gun and returned our fire, and we all supposed this would be about the extent of the fight that day, for none of us thought the enemy would assault the works, exposed as they would be in an open field for some hundreds of yards. . . . While we were all looking—the sun was almost down—a long, dark line of men appeared on the brow of the ridge; they moved slowly forward for a while, and then broke into a cheer and charged."[33] Montgomery's regiment fought its last battle of the war that April afternoon; "almost to a man" they were killed, wounded, or captured.[34]

30. *Ibid.*, Pt. 2, p. 39. The 2nd Iowa and 6th Illinois Spencers were those turned over to Croxton's brigade.

31. See Vol. I, pp. 33–34, footnote 74 of the present work.

32. Homer Mead, *The Eighth Iowa Cavalry in the Civil War* (Carthage, Iowa, 1925), 17.

33. F. A. Montgomery, *Reminiscences of a Mississippian in Peace and War* (Cincinnati, 1901), 241. See also *Official Records*, Vol. XLIX, Pt. 1, pp. 359–61, 438–39, 473.

34. Montgomery, *Reminiscences of a Mississippian*, 245. "The last to leave their

Mention has been made of the fact that General Long, whose practice it was to lead his men in battle, charged the Selma defenses with
his division and fell with a severe scalp wound. In a striking display of
vitality and fortitude, he remained with the division while it made the
march to Macon, and did not leave for the rear until April 23, when
the campaign and the war were over. His farewell order to his command, so characteristic of a sentimental age, is a fitting note on which
to bring these comments on the Selma Campaign to a close.

According to the advice of the surgeon, I leave you for a time; how long I am
unable to say. I do not feel like separating myself from you, possibly forever,
without in a few parting words expressing my entire and heartfelt gratification
at your gallant and soldierly conduct since I have had the honor and good fortune to command you. . . . Having naturally no love for war, and if it should be
my fortune, as I hope it may be, never again to hear the fire of a gun in battle, I
shall consider it is honor enough to last me the remainder of my life to have
had the honor to command you . . . [at Selma]. Whether or not all or any portion of us may meet again, I shall watch your career with interest, and my
prayers shall be for your welfare and happiness.[35]

---

position were the 1st Mississippi Cavalry. . . . They stoutly stood until the enemy were
completely in their rear, so that the Colonel, the Lieutenant-Colonel and most of the
intrepid officers and men were captured." Deupree, "The Noxubee Squadron," 128–29.

35. *Official Records*, Vol. XLIX, Pt. 2, pp. 444–45.

XXIII

Now the Battle Day
Is Past

GENERAL SHERMAN MARCHED AWAY INTO THE VOID ON
November 12 with what it would not be an exaggeration to describe as
the finest mainly veteran army of its size in American military history:
55,000 infantry and artillery and 5,000 cavalry.[1] The infantry, divided
symmetrically into two "wings," the right, under General O. O. Howard,
made up of the XV and XVII Army Corps, and the left, under General
Henry W. Slocum, of the XIV and XX Army Corps. As has been mentioned, the cavalry, technically the Third Division of Wilson's Cavalry
Corps, was commanded by Judson Kilpatrick and was under the immediate direction of General Sherman.[2] The division was divided into
two brigades, the First under Colonel Eli H. Murray (8th Indiana, 2nd,
3rd, and 5th Kentucky, 9th Pennsylvania) and the Second under Colonel Smith D. Atkins (3rd Indiana, 9th Michigan, 5th, 9th, and 10th
Ohio, 92nd Illinois Mounted Infantry, and the McLaughlin Squadron
from Ohio).[3] Not brigaded, and not a part of the division, were the

1. The figures are as of November 10. Sherman, *Memoirs*, II, 172. Kilpatrick stated
in his report that he had 2,800 in his First Brigade and 2,700 in the Second, for a total of
5,500. *Official Records*, Vol. XLIV, 362.
2. Sherman, *Memoirs*, II, 172.
3. *Official Records*, Vol. XLIV, 25. Colonel Atkins noted in his report that his brigade
was organized as such just before the march began; hence, "the regimental organizations were unaccustomed to act together, and officers and men were strangers."
Ibid., 393.

1st Alabama and the 9th Illinois Mounted Infantry. For his artillery, Kilpatrick had Captain Yates V. Beebe's 10th Wisconsin Battery.[4]

General Sherman wrote and believed that his entire army was made up of "able bodied, experienced soldiers, well armed, well equipped, and provided, as far as human foresight could, with all the essentials of life, strength, and vigorous action." Each of the four corps had its own train of 800 wagons and 150 ambulances, each wagon drawn by six mules, and each ambulance by two horses. A part of each corps train were pontoons sufficient to cross a stream nine hundred feet wide.[5] The wagons were loaded with ammunition, twenty days' supply of hardtack, forty days' supply of sugar and coffee, and a double allowance of salt to last forty days. Behind the marching columns of men came herds of beef cattle, a forty days' supply of fresh beef on the hoof. The army was instructed to forage "liberally" (and did so) in order to maintain the supplies of hardtack and beef at a constant level as a reserve.[6]

The left wing marched out of Atlanta east to Covington and then turned southeast toward Milledgeville. There, in seven days, it was to make junction with the right wing. The latter, with the cavalry on its right flank, was to make a "strong feint" toward Macon, breaking up railroads on its way. Driving out of its path detachments of Wheeler's cavalry and Georgia militia, the cavalry division met the enemy in some force on November 22 at Griswold Station, or Griswoldville, on the Central Georgia Railroad near Macon. Kilpatrick's pickets and skirmishers were driven in by an attack of Wheeler's entire corps reinforced by three brigades of infantry, but a counterattack by the 9th Pennsylvania and 5th Kentucky ("the saber being principally used") first checked and then drove back the Confederates.[7] Milledgeville was occupied without incident. Orders for the next stage of the march directed Kilpatrick and the right wing to cross the Ogeechee River and

---

4. *Ibid.*, 25. Just before the campaign began, 440 enlisted men and 9 officers of the 5th Ohio whose terms of enlistment had expired, were ordered home for muster-out. Twelve officers whose terms of enlistment had also expired were, however, ordered by General Howard to remain in the army. *Ibid.*, 398.

5. Sherman, *Memoirs*, II, 172, 176. Each corps train occupied five miles of road.

6. *Official Records*, Vol. XLIV, 8.

7. *Ibid.*, 363, 407. A few days earlier, the 3rd Kentucky of the First Brigade had made "a most brilliant and successful saber charge," and in another action the same day, the 10th Ohio of the Second Brigade "made a gallant saber charge against the enemy posted behind rail barricades." *Ibid.*, 369, 389.

then proceed via Waynesboro and the line of the Augusta & Savannah Railroad to Millen, where Union prisoners of war were thought to be held.

At Waynesboro on November 27, after experiencing the previous day a succession of attacks by Wheeler on his flanks and rear, Kilpatrick was attacked again during the night. He then learned that the prisoners of war had been removed from Millen, and he thought it best to retreat for support to the position of General Absalom B. Baird's division of the XIV Corps. He was still under attack by Wheeler, and it was therefore necessary to manage the retreat by having his two brigades leapfrog each other to the rear. The circumstances are anything but clear, but after retreating for some time and apparently outdistancing the pursuit, Kilpatrick decided that Wheeler needed "a severe repulse." Accordingly, he "took up a strong position and constructed a long line of barricades, with . . . [his] flanks thrown well to the rear. These dispositions were scarce completed ere the enemy came in sight, and in a few minutes made one of the most desperate cavalry charges . . . ever witnessed, but he was most handsomely repulsed." General Wheeler's version of the course of the Federals' retreat is quite different from Kilpatrick's. Calling it a "chase," Wheeler wrote that on their retreat, the Federals set fire to "all corn cribs, cotton gins, and [a] large number of barns and houses" along their route, as well as the town of Waynesboro. Wheeler claimed that he had succeeded in driving back the Federals, "capturing a number of prisoners, arms and horses, and killing a great many who refused to surrender, and who were shot in the pursuit which ensued. The rout was complete, and General Kilpatrick was himself very nearly captured." And as to the "desperate charge" that Kilpatrick claimed had been "most handsomely repulsed," in Wheeler's version it "routed Kilpatrick's entire force, capturing, killing, and wounding nearly 200, and completely stampeding the whole force."[8]

There is another witness, perhaps not entirely objective in his reporting, to the performance of Kilpatrick's cavalry on this march. This was Major James A. Connolly of the XIV Corps. Kilpatrick himself, the major thought, was "the most vain, conceited, egotistical little popinjay I ever saw." As to his men, Connolly wrote, they were "a positive

8. *Ibid.*, 364, 408.

nuisance; they won't fight, and whenever they are around they are always in the way of those who will fight." And the next day: "Confound the cavalry. They're good for nothing but to run down horses and steal chickens. I'd rather have one good regiment of infantry than the whole of Kilpatrick's cavalry."[9] Unquestionably, the good major was guilty of a considerable degree of bias, but his views, slanted though they may have been, have a special meaning. They may only be the traditional disparagement of one branch of the service by another, but they may also indicate the survival of the "who ever saw a dead cavalryman?" attitude, so prevalent at the beginning of the war, into its waning months, by which time the cavalry had furnished its fair share of the dead.

On December 3, after several days of maneuvers that took the cavalry southwest to Louisville, Kilpatrick was ordered by General Sherman "to engage Wheeler wherever we met him." Kilpatrick ordered all "surplus animals and all non-combatants [sent] to the wagon train" and announced that "in the morning the command would move to engage, defeat, and rout the rebel cavalry encamped at Waynesborough."[10] He found the enemy dismounted and "strongly posted behind long lines of barricades, with their flanks well secured." An initial attack by the Second Brigade failed to budge the enemy. Thereupon Kilpatrick had the 92nd Illinois Mounted Infantry, dismounted, attack the barricade with their Spencers; the 10th Ohio and 9th Michigan, mounted, in columns of four by battalions charged the barricades on the right and the 9th Ohio, deployed similarly, charged on the left. "All being ready, the charge was sounded, the whole line moved forward . . . and never halted for one moment until the barricades were gained and the enemy routed."

After beating off several countercharges that Wheeler ordered to save his dismounted men, Kilpatrick reached the town of Waynesboro, where he found Wheeler occupying another line of barricades, with "his flanks so far extended that it was useless to attempt to turn them." He therefore decided to attack the center of Wheeler's position with the 8th Indiana, dismounted, in the lead as skirmishers, followed by the 3rd Kentucky, mounted, in columns of four by battalions in the center, the 9th Pennsylvania, similarly deployed, on the left, and the 5th

9. Connolly, *Army of the Cumberland*, 348, 333, 335, 331, 345.
10. *Official Records*, Vol. XLIV, 364.

and 2nd Kentucky on the right. "The advance was sounded, and in less than twenty minutes the enemy was driven from the position, the town gained, and Wheeler's force completely routed. The Fifth Ohio, Fifth Kentucky, and a portion of the Ninth Pennsylvania followed in close pursuit . . . [for] a distance of eight miles. . . . upward of 200 [of Wheeler's wounded] left in our hands were wounded by the saber alone." [11]

In Wheeler's account it is not recognizable as the same engagement, but the accuracy of Kilpatrick's version is supported by the diary entry of a trooper of the 9th Pennsylvania, who noted that the charge of his own and of the other regiments of cavalry "drove . . . [Wheeler] Back in great Disorder," and by the report of James Moore, assistant surgeon of the Pennsylvania regiment, who spent the night following the fight caring for the wounded of both sides and was apparently the source of Kilpatrick's statement that 200 of the enemy prisoners had been wounded with the saber. [12] And *mirabile dictu*, even the persnickety Major Connolly had to admit, albeit he did so with a qualification, that "Kilpatrick's men have behaved very handsomely today. They did *all* the fighting, and whipped Wheeler soundly, killing, wounding, and capturing about 300 of his men, and losing only about 50 themselves. But then Kilpatrick's men had the moral support of two of our brigades that were formed in line right behind them and kept moving forward as they moved, so that our cavalry all the time knew that there was no chance of their being whipped." [13]

On the day before this fight, General Sherman, pausing for a day at Millen, learned that General Wade Hampton, who had been appointed a short time before to the command of the Cavalry Corps of the Army of Northern Virginia, had been relieved of that command and ordered to Augusta, Georgia, "to organize a large cavalry force to resist . . .

11. For the fight at Waynesboro, see *Ibid.*, 365, 634–35, 409–10. Kilpatrick claimed that Wheeler had 6,000 men in four divisions, plus two "independent brigades." Wheeler said that Kilpatrick's numbers were "at least double" his own and that Kilpatrick was reinforced besides by "one or more divisions of infantry." *Ibid.*, 365, 410. Kilpatrick himself acknowledged that General Baird "tendered" him a brigade of infantry to support his attack. *Ibid.*, 634.

12. Rowell, *Yankee Cavalrymen*, 214.

13. Connolly, *Army of the Cumberland*, 345. "A cavalry fight," Connolly wrote, "is just about as much fun as a fox hunt; but of course in the midst of all the fun, somebody is getting hurt. . . . But it is by no means the serious work that infantry fighting is." *Ibid.*, 345.

[Sherman's] progress."[14] Nevertheless, the last few days' march to Savannah proceeded without incident. The infantry columns met no opposition whatever, and the cavalry, marching first in rear of the XX Corps and then of the XVII Corps, had only a skirmish on December 7 with Samuel W. Ferguson's cavalry to report, before the army came up to the Savannah defenses on December 8, 9, and 10. Kilpatrick's only problem at the moment seemed to be a loss of horses, and the number brought back by his foragers either fell considerably short of replacing his losses or was improperly distributed. The 9th Pennsylvania, for example, reported after its arrival in Savannah that in the course of the march from Atlanta it had captured 288 horses but "abandoned" 441, leaving 153 men dismounted.[15] The wastage throughout the division had been sufficiently serious to cause Sherman to issue an order on December 6 directing each of his four corps commanders "to collect from his command 100 horses, the best adapted to cavalry uses . . . and dispatch them . . . to the cavalry command of General Kilpatrick," and at the same time he had his aide-de-camp write Kilpatrick, "You may always rely upon the general for cavalry horses, as, in order to keep you well mounted, he will dismount every person connected with the infantry not necessary for its efficient service, and take team horses, even if the wagons and contents have to be burned."[16]

This reflection of Sherman's newfound confidence in his cavalry was apparently more than just a polite commonplace. The general himself wrote in his report of the campaign that "General Kilpatrick, who commanded the cavalry of this army, has handled it with spirit and dash

14. Sherman, *Memoirs*, II, 193. The orders sending General Hampton to the Carolinas were not issued until January 19. Douglas Southall Freeman, *Lee's Lieutenants: A Study in Command* (3 vols.; New York, 1942–44), III, 639.

15. *Official Records*, Vol. XLIV, 389. The Pennsylvanians also captured 152 mules and lost 13. A contrast with this experience is found in the account of a trooper of the 92nd Illinois Mounted Infantry, who wrote: "The cavalry marched [from Milledgeville] early on November 25 . . . and they captured hundreds of horses. . . . The captured animals were a great incumbrance, and after each trooper had secured a good mount, over five hundred horses were killed by the second brigade." Smith D. Atkins, "With Sherman's Cavalry," MOLLUS, Commandery of Illinois, *Military Essays and Recollections* (5 vols.; Chicago, 1891–94), II, 389–90. See also Sherman to Grant: "It looks to me, in riding along our columns, as though every officer has three or four led horses, and each regiment seems to be followed by at least fifty negroes and foot-sore soldiers, riding on horses and mules." Sherman, *Memoirs*, II, 208.

16. *Official Records*, Vol. XLIV, 638, 649. In asking Sherman for "some few hundred" horses, Kilpatrick pointed out that when ordered, as he then was, to protect the rear of the infantry instead of its front or flank, it was impossible for his men "to find a single horse or mule." *Ibid.*, 635.

to my entire satisfaction, and kept a superior force of the enemy's cavalry from even approaching our infantry columns or wagon trains." [17] Sherman's words of praise may be contrasted with Major Connolly's somewhat sour disparagement of the cavalry, quoted previously.

The chief claim of the March to the Sea in Civil War folklore, North and South, lies in the exploits of Sherman's foragers, or "bummers." As the army marched southeast on a number of more or less parallel roads, it stripped in a band sixty miles wide a rich countryside of its livestock, poultry, cornmeal, the contents of its smokehouses and barns, "and every thing else that could be used as food or forage." One report of many, from the pen of the historian of the McLaughlin Squadron, relates that "the army left Atlanta with twenty days' rations . . . in wagons, but the wagon covers had not been unfastened—not a hardtack or a pound of sowbelly had been issued. The cavalry had the usual advantage in the matter of supplies. Covering so much ground untrodden by the feet of the infantry, the rollicking troopers had their pick from the field, orchard, garden, smokehouse and barnyard. . . . The boys enjoyed a protracted picnic. . . . the army was in the highest possible physical condition. Sickness was almost unknown . . . and everybody waxed fat and saucy." [18]

From General Sherman's vantage point, "as a rule" his men destroyed nothing, but they did keep the wagons full and the mules and horses well fed. Major Connolly, however, seeing the situation from a less exalted level, recorded that "columns of smoke by day, and 'pillars of fire' by night, for miles and miles on our right and left indicate to us daily and nightly the route and location of the other columns of our army. Every 'Gin House' we pass is burned; every stack of fodder we can't carry along is burned; every barn filled with grain is destroyed; in fact everything that can be of any use to the rebels is either carried off by our foragers or set on fire and burned." [19]

17. *Ibid.*, 14.
18. Sherman, *Memoirs*, II, 181–82; *Official Records*, Vol. XLIV, 13; Hinman, *Story of the Sherman Brigade*, 904. Jacob Bartmess, 8th Indiana, wrote his wife from Savannah: "We always had plenty of meet [sic] and ham, and honey and butter when we could get it, and sweet potatoes without end and chickens much the same. It have [sic] been the time in the service for me. We burned cotton enough to nearly buy the state of Indiana." Jacob W. Bartmess, "Civil War Letters," *Indiana Magazine of History*, LII (1956), 177.
19. Connolly, *Army of the Cumberland*, 314. Those fortunate enough to escape a visit by Kilpatrick's cavalry had good reason to fear a visit by Wheeler's horsemen, whose "alleged depredations and straggling propensities and reported brutal interference with

After describing with considerable glee the foraging exploits of his bummers, General Sherman thought it well to add, "No doubt, many acts of pillage, robbery, and violence, were committed by these parties of foragers . . . for I have since heard of jewelry taken from women, and the plunder of articles that never reached the commissary; but these acts were exceptional and incidental."[20] However "exceptional and incidental" such acts of robbery may have been, they were not thereby made more bearable for those on whom they were inflicted. For a more revealing account of what foraging visits by Kilpatrick's cavalry were actually like, one must read the letters and journals of the widow Mary Jones and her pregnant daughter, Mary Jones Mallard, of Montevideo Plantation, south of Savannah.[21]

Colonel Thomas Jordan, whose 9th Pennsylvania was sent to forage in the area in which the Jones plantation was located, and may well have been the regiment that stripped it of everything edible, wrote his wife: "We have not been supplied either with forage or rations, and often both horses and men have been in a state of starvation which can only be relieved by long trips to the country where we live upon the people. 'Tis teaching them a very salutary lesson & one that the people will not soon forget. We find them living in plenty, with fine horses, carriages, &c., and leave them too poor to know where their next meal will come from."[22]

Savannah, on the south bank of the river of that name, had a garrison of about 10,000 troops under General William Hardee manning a series of forts blocking access to the town from the sea via the Savannah

private property have been common by-words in every country where it has been their misfortune to pass. Public rumor condemns them everywhere," as Colonel Alfred Roman reported to General Beauregard. Dyer, *"Fightin' Joe" Wheeler*, 212–14.

20. General Sherman may not have been aware of a fact noted by Major Connolly: "Our soldiers and even some officers have been plundering the [Georgia] State library today, and carrying off law and miscellaneous works in armfuls." Connolly, *Army of the Cumberland*, 318.

21. Robert Manson Myers (ed.), *The Children of Pride* (3 vols.; New York, 1972), II, 1222–33, 1237–40, 1251, 1256, III, 1284–85. See also William D. Hamilton, *Recollections of a Cavalryman of the Civil War After Fifty Years* (Columbus, Ohio, 1915), 168–69.

22. Letter of January 7, 1865, in *Jordan Letters*. In an earlier letter, Jordan described the silver plate, specie, *etc.*, "found" by his men, doubtless with the aid of escaped slaves who had helped their erstwhile masters bury it in the swamps and woods. "Silver cups," the colonel wrote, "are as common in the command tied to the saddle straps of the men for drinking purposes, as tin ones used to be." Letter of December 18, 1864, in *Ibid*.

River on the north and Ossabaw Sound and the Great Ogeechee River on the south. The Union fleet, loaded with supplies for Sherman, was understood to be waiting for him in Ossabaw Sound.[23] Sherman's army approached Savannah from the southwest, across a land of salt marshes and rice paddies, seamed with innumerable streams, large and small. Blocking communication between the army and the fleet in Ossabaw Sound was Fort McAllister, with twenty-three large-caliber guns, located on the south bank of the Great Ogeechee River twelve miles south of the town, and manned by about 200 infantry and gunners. Sherman had sent his cavalry south of the Great Ogeechee to try to open communications with the fleet. Kilpatrick, his ambition pitched to a higher key by his successes on his march to Savannah against Joseph Wheeler, his West Point classmate, offered to capture the fort by using his "old infantry regiments, with Spencer rifles," to force the defenders to keep their heads down below the level of the fort's parapets while they worked their way to within a short distance of the earthworks and then "deliberately [?] storm[ed] the works."[24] Sherman, however, preferred to have the fort stormed by General William B. Hazen's division of the XV Corps, who duly accomplished the job on the afternoon of December 13, and communication with the fleet was opened.[25] On December 21, Hardee evacuated Savannah, and the March to the Sea, which had cost the cavalry 38 officers and men killed, 159 wounded, and 168 missing, was officially at an end.[26]

The latter part of December and all of January until the twenty-eighth was for the cavalry a period of comparative rest. Camped near King's Bridge on the Ogeechee to guard the depot of supplies established there, the cavalry picketed a line across the neck of land between that river and the Savannah and spent some days breaking up the three railroads serving Savannah. The work was light and made it possible for Kilpatrick to permit brigade commanders to "detail one

23. The only supplies he actually needed, Sherman wrote Grant, were clothing, sugar, coffee, and some hardtack. Sherman, *Memoirs*, II, 202. The army's greatest need was the mail, which happily arrived on December 16. *Ibid.*, 204.

24. *Official Records*, Vol. XLIV, 10, 690, 698.

25. *Ibid.*, 110–11, 366; Sherman, *Memoirs*, II, 199. The storming party met stiff opposition and lost 24 officers and men killed and 110 wounded. Some of the killed were blown "to atoms" by a "line of torpedoes" planted just outside the works, "many of which were exploded by the tread of the troops." *Ibid.*, 110–11.

26. *Ibid.*, 366. General Sherman, however, gives the casualties of the cavalry as 93 killed, 127 wounded, and none missing. The casualties of the infantry and artillery totaled 65 killed, 301 wounded, and 278 missing. Sherman, *Memoirs*, II, 221.

battalion each day . . . with their officers, to proceed (mounted) to . . . Savannah to see the city and enjoy themselves generally." "It is to be hoped," Kilpatrick added, "that these officers and men while in the city will so conduct themselves as to reflect no discredit upon the command."[27]

There was a grand review of the army in Savannah on January 12, with General Sherman and Secretary of War Stanton taking the salute, and a few days later, preparations began for the next stage of the campaign.[28] In place of Grant's initial idea to have Sherman's army brought by sea to be added to the forces facing Richmond and Petersburg, Sherman proposed, and Grant eventually accepted, the scheme of a campaign by Sherman's army north through the Carolinas via Columbia (bypassing Charleston, "a mere desolated wreck . . . hardly worth the time it would take to starve it out," Sherman wrote) and Wilmington to Raleigh. When his army reached Raleigh, Sherman wrote Grant, "The game is . . . up with Lee," and he added, "I attach more importance to these deep incursions into the enemy's country, because this war differs from European wars in this particular: we are not only fighting hostile armies, but a hostile people, and must make old and young, rich and poor, feel the hard hand of war." Even aside from military considerations, Sherman was eager to get moving. He "was quite impatient to get off . . . for a city life had become dull and tame, and we were all anxious to get into the pine-woods again, free from the importunities of rebel women asking for protection, and of the civilians from the North who were coming to Savannah for cotton and all sorts of profit."[29]

General Beauregard had arrived from the West to assume direction of the forces that were to try to block Sherman's progress north, and General Hampton arrived to beef up and take command of the cavalry. But what Sherman had mainly to contend against was neither Beauregard nor Hampton, nor any of their troops, but the elements. "The heavy winter rains," as Sherman called them, began in early January. Every stream, major and minor, flowing eastward from the Appalachian chain toward the sea, was out of its banks, and Sherman had to cross them all.

27. Sherman, *Memoirs*, II, 215; *Official Records*, Vol. XLIV, 785.
28. The secretary brought to Savannah the commission by brevet of major general of volunteers for Kilpatrick and commissions by brevet of brigadier general of volunteers for Colonels Murray and Atkins. Letter of January 15, 1865, in *Jordan Letters*.
29. Sherman, *Memoirs*, II, 225, 227, 252.

Other than the accession of recruits and the departure of time-expired men and officers, the campaign through the Carolinas was made by the same forces that had made the March to the Sea. John Schofield's XXIII Corps joined Sherman at Goldsboro, North Carolina, on March 21, but by then the campaign was nearly over. The cavalry, numbering 5,068 for duty, was described by Kilpatrick as "indifferently mounted [and] badly armed." It was now organized into three brigades: the First, commanded by Colonel (later General) Jordan, consisted of a battalion of the 3rd Indiana, the 8th Indiana, 2d and 3rd Kentucky, and 9th Pennsylvania; the Second, commanded by General Smith D. Atkins, included the 92nd Illinois Mounted Infantry, 9th Michigan, 9th and 10th Ohio, and McLaughlin's (Ohio) Squadron; and the Third, commanded in succession by Colonels George E. Spencer and Michael Kerwin and General Thomas T. Heath, was made up of the 1st Alabama, 5th Kentucky, 5th Ohio, and 13th Pennsylvania. As the campaign progressed, Kilpatrick also organized a Provisional Fourth Brigade, commanded by Lieutenant Colonel William B. Way and composed of three "regiments," to each of which were assigned the dismounted men of the brigade bearing the corresponding number. The artillery, increased from one battery to two, was made up of the 10th Wisconsin and 23rd New York Batteries.[30]

Concerning his men's weapons, Kilpatrick reported from his King's Bridge camp on January 3 that "no arms of any kind . . . [were] to be had at . . . [Savannah], as . . . [he] expected there would be. The Joslyn carbine, with which the Ninth Pennsylvania is armed, and the majority of my Sharps carbines are utterly worthless." He begged for 300 Spencer carbines to be sent to him as soon as possible and added, with perhaps a touch of exaggeration, "My troops are worse armed at present than Wheeler's irregular cavalry."[31] Colonel W. D. Hamilton of the 9th Ohio concluded his report of the campaign with this statement: "During the latter part of the campaign my command was rendered to a considerable extent ineffective on account of the lack of ammunition

30. *Official Records*, Vol. XLVII, Pt. 1, pp. 857, 55. General Sherman, however, reported the strength of the cavalry as 4,438 on February 1, as 4,401 on March 1, and as 4,781 on April 1. Sherman, *Memoirs*, II, 269. In addition to the cavalry in Kilpatrick's division, the 29th Missouri Mounted Infantry was in the XV Corps, and the 9th Illinois Mounted Infantry was in the XVII Corps. *Official Records*, Vol. XLVII, Pt. 1, pp. 48, 50.

31. *Official Records*, Vol. XLIV, 361. From Fayetteville, North Carolina, Colonel Jordan wrote his wife, "Before leaving here we expect to be all armed with Spencer Rifles 7 Shooters, and can walk over the Jonnies [*sic*] with ease." Letter of March 12, 1865, in *Jordan Letters*.

for our carbines (Smith) a large portion of it having been rendered worthless by the rains . . . I regard the weapon for that reason, and for its liability to get out of repair, as one which should not be used in the service."[32]

Bearing out Kilpatrick's discouraging appraisal of the state of his division was the report of Lieutenant Colonel Fielder A. Jones on the condition of his 8th Indiana at the start of the new campaign. "My command," he wrote, "left Savannah, Ga., in very poor condition; our animals had been nearly starved at Savannah and only by the most untiring efforts were our horses kept in anything like serviceable condition. Added to these embarrassments was the fact that seventeen of the old and tried officers of the command were mustered out and their places filled by men who, although they proved themselves deserving soldiers had not yet shown their capacity for command."[33]

Some of Kilpatrick's regiments acquired recruits in considerable numbers to replace men who had not "veteranized" and had now gone home for muster-out. Data of a sort are available on only three regiments. The 9th Pennsylvania, which had acquired "a lot of new recrutes [sic]" in September, acquired eighty more in Savannah. These were all one-year men, some new to the army; others had already served one term of enlistment and were induced to reenlist by the federal, state, and local bounties. It is reported that more than half of the men of the 9th Pennsylvania who made the campaign from Savannah to Raleigh were these one-year men.[34] In the absence of comment in the history of the regiment, it may be assumed that these recruits were better physical specimens than those received by the 4th Iowa earlier in the year; many of those six hundred recruits had been "physically or mentally, quite unfit for the service." Indeed, some of those "bounty men" were "proofs of shameful frauds upon the government," and the surgeon of the regiment declared that the "surgeons who passed these men and boys ought to be shot."[35]

General Sherman's plan for the initial stage of the march north was

---

32. *Official Records*, Vol. XLVII, Pt. 1, p. 890.

33. *Ibid.*, 870.

34. Rowell, *Yankee Cavalrymen*, 192, 200. The 11th New York, stationed in Baton Rouge at the time, received in September, 1864, "a large number of recruits, who had enlisted for one year. . . . Many of these men had served for two years or longer in the Army of the Potomac." Smith, "Scott's 900," *Eleventh New York*, 173.

35. Scott, *Story of a Cavalry Regiment*, 223–25.

to threaten, or to seem to threaten, Charleston by massing his right wing at Pocotaligo, South Carolina, and to use his cavalry and left wing, assembled at Sister's Ferry, on the Savannah River forty miles upstream from the town, to threaten a movement on Augusta, Georgia. The cavalry got a foretaste at Sister's Ferry of the conditions they (and of course the infantry and artillery) were to encounter for much of the way north; the Savannah River had been turned by the rains into a sheet of water three miles broad.[36] The 58th Indiana Infantry, serving as engineers and pontoniers with the left wing, placed their nine hundred feet of pontoons in midstream, built a thousand feet of trestle work at each end of the bridge, and corduroyed the road beyond the outer ends of the trestles. To get wagons and the artillery across, the cavalry had to dismount, and they and the infantry pushed and pulled in water up to their armpits.[37] On the right-wing front, to which the 1st Missouri Engineers had been assigned, twenty-two bridges, scattered over a mile of swamp and averaging about twenty-five feet in length, had to be built or rebuilt on the night of February 4, and "the whole road through the swamp was corduroyed."[38]

What fighting there was, was done for the most part under similar conditions; at Barnwell, to force a crossing of the Salkehatchie River, the 92nd Illinois Mounted Infantry and the 9th Ohio attacked dismounted "through the swamp, men wading in the water up to their armpits."[39] On February 25, the First Brigade of cavalry reached Lancaster, South Carolina, "having marched for two days through mud and water knee-deep to . . . [its] horses, and on the night of March 8, Colonel Jordan had to dismount his brigade, then acting as rear guard of the cavalry division, "to draw the artillery and wagons through the swamp [of Drowning Creek] more than a half a mile wide."[40] The historian of McLaughlin's Squadron wrote:

The campaign from Savannah to Raleigh . . . proved to be one of almost incredible hardship, privation, and fatigue. For a long distance the . . . route was

36. *Official Records*, Vol. XLVII, Pt. 1, p. 17.
37. The army had 68 guns, 2,500 wagons, and 600 ambulances. Sherman, *Memoirs*, II, 269.
38. *Official Records*, Vol. XLVII, Pt. 1, pp. 169–70.
39. *Ibid.*, 858. Downstream from Barnwell, where the XVII Corps was to cross, the stream had swollen to the width of a mile. Sherman, *Memoirs*, II, 256.
40. *Official Records*, Vol. XLVII, Pt. 1, pp. 866–67. These conditions were of course the same for the infantry. See the report of General John M. Corse, *Ibid.*, 337–38.

through the swampy lowlands of South Carolina. The season was much more than usually wet. . . . For weeks men and horses floundered through literal oceans of mud. . . . All the streams were torrents. . . . The whole country was a vast quagmire. All the roads had to be corduroyed for the passage of the artillery and wagons. No vehicle could move without a detail of men to push and lift and pry and yell. . . . For weeks the clothing of the soldiers was saturated with water and splotched with mud.[41]

Fortunately for Sherman's waterlogged soldiers, horse and foot, enemy opposition to their march was generally negligible. What infantry General Hardee had was "utterly unable to meet . . . [Sherman's] veteran columns in the open field." The Confederate cavalry could offer little more than token opposition to the Federal advance; Wheeler's division, "reduced to the size of a brigade by . . . hard and persistent fighting ever since the beginning of the Atlanta campaign," could do little more than hover along the flanks of the Federal advance and engage in skirmishes with Kilpatrick's flank and rear guards.[42] The only cavalry engagement worthy of the name before General Hampton took a hand in the proceedings at the head of Matthew C. Butler's and his own newly raised cavalry, occurred at Aiken, South Carolina, on February 11. General Atkins, on a reconnaissance to the village with his entire brigade, was "most furiously attacked by Wheeler's entire command" and was driven back on the rest of the cavalry division, engaged in breaking up the South Carolina Railroad at Johnson's Station. Here the attack was checked, with the loss to the Confederates, as Kilpatrick claimed, of 31 killed, 160 wounded, and 60 taken prisoner.[43]

His successes in these minor operations raised Kilpatrick's normal state of euphoria another notch or two and produced a series of boast-

41. Hinman, *Story of the Sherman Brigade*, 908–909.

42. Sherman, *Memoirs*, II, 271. According to the historian of McLaughlin's Squadron, "Wheeler's division had lost much of its vim and vigor." Hinman, *Story of the Sherman Brigade*, 910.

43. *Official Records*, Vol. XLVII, Pt. 1, pp. 858–59, 866, 879, 882. The 92nd Illinois Mounted Infantry, leading the brigade, was trapped in Aiken, but Lieutenant Colonel Matthew Van Buskirk, in command, "left a skirmish line to hold the enemy in front, and, facing to the rear, charged through the enemy and regained the brigade. . . . The Ninety-second was completely enveloped by overwhelming numbers, and came up to . . . [the brigade] line of battle so mixed up with the enemy that . . . [the brigade] did not dare to fire; each was claiming the other['s] prisoners and pulling one another off their horses, neither being armed with sabers." The 92nd Illinois Mounted Infantry casualties were 5 killed, 11 wounded, 7 missing. Colonel Van Buskirk "killed two of the enemy himself and knocked a third off his horse with his empty pistol." *Ibid.*, Pt. 2, pp. 879, 882.

ful dispatches to General Sherman. He announced on February 7 that "at any moment you desire I can drive Wheeler into the Edisto, and . . . save any bridge you may name." Nine days later he let it be known that "I don't fear Wheeler and Hampton combined, even without supports." And after another two weeks, in a patronizing tone that went well with his recently acquired second star: "My officers are fast learning to be good cavalrymen. All little expeditions sent out have been characterized by that enterprise and dash so requisite to success." Perhaps Kilpatrick's high spirits were induced or furthered by the presence in his entourage of a "tall, handsome, well-dressed woman," a trophy of war acquired in Savannah, no doubt.[44]

General Kilpatrick received his well-earned comeuppance on March 10. In contact with Hardee's infantry, he was marching toward Fayetteville, North Carolina, "over the most horrible roads, swamps, and swollen streams," when he learned that General Hampton, with his cavalry, was coming up behind him. In a tactically misguided scheme to intercept Hampton, Kilpatrick placed his three brigades on three widely separated roads where they were out of touch with one another. He remained himself with the smallest of the three, the Third Brigade, joined on this occasion by the 400 dismounted men of Colonel Way's "Fourth Brigade." But General Hampton was too experienced a hand to be snared by so obvious a scholar's gambit. He reconnoitered the positions of Kilpatrick's brigades, determined that the Third and Fourth (with whom Kilpatrick established his headquarters for the night) were the most vulnerable, and, just as the Federal buglers were blowing reveille on the morning of March 10, came charging into their camps with the divisions of Butler, William W. Allen, and William Y. C. Humes.[45] Colonel Way's camp, the brigade and division headquarters and train, the house in which Kilpatrick and the "tall, handsome, well-dressed woman" were spending the night, and the major portion of the Third Brigade camp were overrun, the divisional artillery captured, and the men not shot down or taken prisoner chased into a swamp "a few hundred yards in rear." Kilpatrick, wearing nothing but his night-

44. Ibid., Pt. 2, pp. 338, 450, 651; Rowell, Yankee Cavalrymen, 229.
45. Official Records, Vol. XLVII, Pt. 1, p. 884. Johnston credited Hampton with 4,000 "effectives" (half the number Sherman thought he had)—3,000 in Wheeler's division and 1,000 in Butler's. Johnston, Narrative of Military Operations, 377; Sherman, Memoirs, II, 299.

shirt, had come running out of his quarters at the sound of battle and, barely avoiding capture, ran to join his men in the swamp. The Confederate cavalrymen, as their brethren had done at Cedar Creek a few months earlier, scattered to plunder the abandoned Federal tents and wagons. While they did so, Kilpatrick and the other officers got a counterattack organized, recaptured their artillery and turned it on the intruders, and eventually drove them out of their camps. By the time General John G. Mitchell's brigade of infantry, marching cross-country to the sound of the guns, arrived on the scene, the enemy was gone, and the infantrymen, as Kilpatrick was careful to point out, did not have to fire a single shot.[46]

Colonel Spencer lost in this engagement 18 killed, 70 wounded, and 170 (an amazingly high number) missing; Colonel Way failed to submit a complete report of his casualties. The Confederates left behind, when they retreated, 103 dead, "a large number" of wounded, and "about" 30 prisoners, by Colonel Spencer's count.[47]

On March 16, at Averasboro, on the road between Fayetteville and Goldsboro, Kilpatrick's cavalry had its last fight of the campaign.[48] With the exceptions noted, their encounters with the enemy had been skirmishes: "A crash of horses, a flashing of sword blades, five or ten minutes of blind confusion, and then those who have not been knocked out of their saddles by their neighbors' knees, and have not cut off their own horses' heads instead of their enemies', find themselves, they know not how, either running away or being run away from." As Jacob Bartmess of the 8th Indiana wrote his wife, Amanda, from Fayetteville: "We have had but little fighting on this trip. The rebel cavalry have been watching us very close, we have marched side by side with them nearly all the time, but they have not seamed [sic] anxious to fight, neither have we. . . . Our march over the country has been like a blighting pestilence, for we have taken or turned upsidedown every thing before us." Indeed, few of the villages and towns through which

46. Descriptions of what was called the battle of Monroe's Cross-Roads are in *Official Records*, Vol. XLVII, Pt. 1, pp. 861–62, 894–95, 904–905, Pt. 2, p. 786.

47. *Ibid.*, Pt. 1, p. 894. Surgeon Moore of the 9th Pennsylvania (which was not in the fight) reported that "there were 600 Rebels wounded and captured and . . . the houses all along the Confederate line of march to Fayetteville were filled with wounded." Rowell, *Yankee Cavalrymen*, 233. Hampton and Wheeler claimed having taken 500 prisoners. Johnston, *Narrative of Military Operations*, 381.

48. The name is spelled as in the text in the *Official Records* but as "Averysboro" in the *Atlas* volumes and in Sherman's *Memoirs*.

the Federal cavalry marched escaped burning; Barnwell, South Carolina, on February 6 and Lexington, South Carolina, ten days later, are examples.[49] And foraging having been thought a necessity, its inseparable byproduct, robbery, went on also, committed not only by the cavalry, but also by infantry foragers who acquired horses and mules to ride. General Frank P. Blair, Jr., wrote on March 7: "Every house we pass is pillaged. . . . There is no cure except the entire cessation of foraging. The system is vicious and its results utterly deplorable."[50]

It may not be unfair to assume that the atrocities committed against Union soldiers in the Carolinas were in retaliation for the kind of foraging General Blair condemned. And these atrocities were bad enough. Eighteen of Kilpatrick's men, apparently a foraging party, were killed after they had surrendered, and the bodies marked with a warning that all foragers would be similarly dealt with. Private Charles Wright, 9th Ohio, found 21 infantrymen in a ravine, near a main road, "with their throats cut and stripped of their clothing," and a trooper of the 92nd Illinois Mounted Infantry "was found hung to the limb of a tree near the roadside." Lieutenant David H. Kimmel, 9th Pennsylvania, reported the losses of his regiment over the entire course of the campaign as 10 killed, 26 wounded, and 32 missing, and added, "The great loss, independent of . . . [22 killed and wounded at Averasboro] was occasioned by foraging, where . . . [the men] would rashly contend with superior numbers of the enemy."[51]

On February 22, General Joseph E. Johnston was given the unenviable assignment to "concentrate all available forces . . . [in the Carolinas] and drive back Sherman." General Johnston had first of all to assemble his widely scattered forces and then try to prevent the junction of Schofield's corps, marching up from New Berne, and Sherman's army. On March 15, after crossing the Cape Fear River at and below Fayetteville, Sherman resumed his march north toward Raleigh. Kilpatrick's division had the lead on the left and was followed by four

49. Hinman, *Story of the Sherman Brigade*, 911; letter of March 14, 1865, in Jacob W. Bartmess, "Civil War Letters," *Indiana Magazine of History*, LII (1956), 181; Rowell, *Yankee Cavalrymen*, 225, 227.

50. *Official Records*, Vol. XLVII, Pt. 2, p. 717. Kilpatrick complained to General Sherman that on February 23, five of his men, "detached to forage for . . . [the] wounded," were arrested by the XX Corps provost marshal, tied to a tree with "inscriptions on their breasts 'House Breakers,'" and kept there while the XX Corps marched by. *Ibid.*, 554.

51. *Ibid.*, 544, 554, 876.

divisions of infantry. The following day Kilpatrick, reinforced in the meantime by a brigade of infantry, found Hardee's forces of about 20,000 "with artillery, infantry, and cavalry in an intrenched position . . . in the narrow, swampy neck between Cape Fear and South Rivers, in hopes to hold . . . [Sherman] to save time for the concentration of Johnston's armies at some point in the rear." Riding with the infantry, Sherman ordered an immediate attack, with General William T. Ward's division of the XX Corps deployed in front, marching over ground "so soft that horses would sink everywhere, and even men could hardly make their way over the . . . pine barren."[52] Hardee's first line, held by a brigade of heavy artillerymen serving as infantry, was driven back to the second line, stronger than the first. This position was attacked by Ward's division on the left, with General Nathaniel J. Jackson's division on its right. Colonel Fielder A. Jackson's 8th Indiana attacked on the right of Jackson's infantry, and eventually the rest of the First Brigade of cavalry joined in the attack, in support of the Indiana regiment. The main burden of the battle on the Union side fell on the cavalrymen (Colonel Jordan was brevetted brigadier general for his skilful handling of his regiments in this engagement), with alternate advances and retreats by the two sides.[53] The day's fighting ended with Hardee still in possession of his line; having accomplished his purpose of delaying Sherman's advance toward Goldsboro, he retreated during the night.

Three days after the fight at Averasboro, Kilpatrick's division skirmished with the Confederate cavalry pickets at Bentonville, and was "ready and willing to participate in the battle . . . but the opportunity did not offer." After the battle, the cavalry was ordered to Mount Olive, on the Wilmington & Weldon Railroad, and in the midst of a countryside "full of forage" went into camp to recover from the stresses and strains of "the long and arduous campaign" they had undergone. On April 7, Sherman wrote in orders to Kilpatrick to move his division to Raleigh and "act against the flanks of the enemy . . . boldly and even rashly now, for this is the time to strike quick and strong."[54]

52. Johnston, *Narrative of Military Operations*, 371; *Official Records*, Vol. XLVII, Pt. 1, p. 24.

53. The Second Brigade joined in the fight as the First Brigade began to run low on ammunition.

54. *Official Records*, Vol. XLVII, Pt. 1, p. 862, and Pt. 3, pp. 11, 29, 123; see also *Ibid.*, Pt. 3, pp. 132, 172.

Kilpatrick reported on the morning of the thirteenth that he was "heavily engaged with Wheeler's and Hampton's combined forces" but said in a later dispatch the same day that "the [enemy's] cavalry is totally demoralized. We have taken barricade after barricade of the strongest character and with but little loss. . . . I have been scattering Wheeler's cavalry all day, driving it off upon the side roads."[55] Wheeler's men may well have been "demoralized," but they were still capable of inflicting punishment and casualties, including the killing of two troopers of the 9th Pennsylvania. Two days later, however, a flag of truce appeared at Kilpatrick's outposts at Durham's Station with a dispatch for Sherman from General Johnston, asking for "a temporary suspension of active operations," and the fighting days of Kilpatrick's cavalry were effectively ended. Perhaps as a compliment, in the dispatch asking for "a good company" of cavalry to escort him to the meeting with Johnston, Sherman invited Kilpatrick to accompany him to the meeting. Kilpatrick in turn did the handsome thing; he had the commanding general's escort made up of four men from each company of his regiments. The whole was commanded by Major John M. Porter, 9th Pennsylvania.[56]

In early May, after the furor over the terms of the armistice Sherman had negotiated with Johnston had settled, the XIV, XV, XVII, and XX Corps of Sherman's army marched through Virginia to Washington. On May 23, the Army of the Potomac, led by its Cavalry Corps, was reviewed by the new president, the cabinet, and all the notables and populace of Washington plus as many people from out of town as could crowd into the city. Among those in the reviewing stand was General Sherman, who viewed the appearance and bearing of an army quite different from those of the men he had led through Georgia and the Carolinas.

On the next day, the twenty-fourth, as beautiful as the day that had graced the review of the eastern army, and before crowds as large and as enthusiastic as those of the previous day, Sherman led his men down Pennsylvania Avenue and past the dignitaries in the reviewing stands. Behind him and his staff marched the XV Corps, then, in order, the XVII, XX, and XIV, constituting in the judgment of their com-

55. Ibid., Pt. 3, pp. 107, 198; see also Ibid., Pt. 3, p. 214.
56. Johnston, Narrative of Military Operations, 400; Official Records, Vol. XLVII, Pt. 3, p. 235; Rowell, Yankee Cavalrymen, 246, 253.

mander "the most magnificent army in existence."[57] In the marching column were the army's footsoldiers and gunners, pioneers and contrabands, and even the "bummers," suitably bedizened. Every branch of the service but one, that had the right to be present, was there. The one conspicuous exception was the western cavalry. A part of it had been left behind in western Tennessee, a part at Gravelly Springs, some in the Department of the Gulf, some in Kansas, a sizable body with General Wilson in Macon, Kilpatrick's and Gillem's divisions in North Carolina.

The cavalry of the western armies had overcome great obstacles to find its place in the sun, to achieve the capability to make a worthy contribution to the winning of the war in the West. In recognition of that achievement, it would have been appropriate to have a representative body, perhaps Eli Long's Second Division of Wilson's corps, which had stormed the Selma fortifications, or General John T. Wilder's Lightning Brigade, or even Kilpatrick's division, which had made the march from Atlanta to Savannah and thence north to Raleigh, present in the line of march, but May 24, 1865, was not their day.

57. Margaret Leech, *Reveille in Washington, 1860–1865* (New York, 1941), 416–17.

Epilogue

IN STUDYING THE OPERATIONS AND DEVELOPMENT OF the Union cavalry in the West, one must try to answer two basic questions. First, did the western cavalry differ in any important respect from their brethren in the East, and if so, in what ways? Second, did the Union cavalry in the West evolve in the course of the war in ways similar to, or different from, the evolution of cavalry in the East? Did the western cavalry become better, more skilful *cavalry*, or did it evolve into something quite different, namely, an effective mounted infantry?

To answer the first question is not difficult. There were indeed differences between the eastern and western horsemen of the Union army, but they were differences of degree, not differences in kind. The casual disregard of "spit and polish" in the western armies, horse and foot, in contrast with the paper collar niceties favored in the East, is one of the staples of Civil War literature. Personal grooming, and the grooming of horses and equipment, never among the strengths of the eastern cavalry, was even less so in the West. And this was so with most of the courtesies and graces of life in the army and, unfortunately, in the far more important area of discipline as well.

There was little enough discipline in the European sense in the eastern armies; west of the Alleghenies there was even less. Except for regiments raised in large cities like Cincinnati and St. Louis and made up mainly of German immigrants, the western soldiers' attitude toward authority, as represented by officers ("shoulder straps") or by textbooks on the military art, was a mixture of amused tolerance, disdain, and outright hostility. Men who had (or whose parents or grandparents had) settled what was then the West—the states of Ohio, Indiana, Michigan, Illinois, Wisconsin, Iowa, and Kansas—a few short decades before, were individualists and egalitarians. They had little patience for the formalities West Point–trained officers, and even many volunteer officers, were fond of. It is quite significant that the western armies did not produce a McClellan. There was fondness and even admiration for "Uncle Billy" Sherman and "Old Tom" Thomas, but a capacity for hero worship was not in the equipment of the western volunteer. Many thousands of enlisted men who lost their lives in the Civil War would have lived had there been less contempt in the army for what the men spoke of as "red tape foolishness."

The ability of troopers to function effectively as cavalry depended to a great extent on having "serviceable" horses to ride. Despite this, an unwillingness to take proper care of the horses supplied by the government was well-nigh universal. Grooming their horses and doing what they could to protect them from the elements were neglected equally by the city boys in the East and farm boys in the West, and cavalry officers everywhere were equally remiss in keeping their men up to the mark in this vital respect. Lastly, the outstanding sin of the cavalry, straggling on the march and its concomitants, robbery, pillage, and arson, were or seemed to be more prevalent in the West than in the East, with the scales weighted against the West by regiments from Kentucky, Tennessee, and Kansas.

As to the second of our questions, the accepted military wisdom has it that European cavalry tradition, culminating in the Napoleonic wars, was never fully naturalized in the United States; hence the cavalry of the Civil War, both Blue and Gray, developed spontaneously, as a substitute, a native cavalry doctrine, namely that of the mounted infantry. Cavalry in the European tradition, when not engaged in battle, had two primary functions: reconnaissance, to locate and shadow the enemy army, and screening, to prevent the enemy cavalry from locating and shadowing its own army. In battle—and by devotees this was held to be the cavalry's main reason for being—its essential function was the massed charge with the saber on bodies of enemy infantry and cavalry. There was also another cavalry tradition, of more re-

cent vintage, also imported from Europe. This was represented in the
United States Army until August, 1861, by two regiments of dragoons,
armed with short muskets ("musketoons"), sabers, and "horse pistols,"
who were intended to be equally adept at skirmishing and fighting on
foot as infantry and on horseback as cavalry. In addition, as a wholly
native response to the needs of warfare against the Plains Indians,
there was the Regiment of Mounted Riflemen, armed with rifles and
trained to fight on foot, and using their horses merely as a means of
transportation.

The records make it evident that the men who enlisted in the volunteer cavalry regiments after Fort Sumter, as well as their officers,
expected to serve as cavalry in the traditional European sense, and
nearly every regimental history tells of the hours they spent learning
and practicing the saber drill. From early 1862 on, however, by which
time the hostile armies began to find their bearings, the Union cavalry
developed more and more in the direction of the dragoon concept. Although in the absence of direct evidence it cannot be said with complete certainty, this process of evolution seems to have been more
widespread and to have moved faster in the West than in the East.

There are a number of reasons to account for the evolutionary process taking this direction. There is no proof whatever that it came about
as a conscious, considered response to the greater accuracy, range, and
killing power of the infantry rifle. The reasons—and there were several—appear to have been less direct. The principal reason, in all probability, was that the horses issued to the cavalry were totally untrained
(thousands of them were not even broken to the saddle) and that many
cavalry enlistees—apparently the great majority—had never learned
to ride before they joined the cavalry. An attempted mass saber charge
on untrained horses and with riders in momentary danger of parting
company with their mounts would have been a travesty. In European
armies, by contrast, horses were trained by expert horsemen for as
much as two years before being issued to the cavalry, and cavalry conscripts were trained in horsemanship for as long as two years before
they were allowed to take their places in the ranks.

The second factor was the lack of uniformity of armament. The
cavalry enlisted in 1861 were armed with whatever weapons, good,
bad, or indifferent, a desperate Ordnance Bureau was able to find for
them. More often than not, there was no uniformity of weapons even

within a single regiment. It is to be noted in this context that the quality of arms issued to the cavalry varied, intentionally or otherwise, with the distance of a given regiment from Washington: the greater the distance, the worse the weapons. Third, while there were cavalry manuals for officers to study, there was no one with the authority to ensure strict adherence to the "letter of the law" as prescribed by the tactical pages of the manual. It may be noted also that while lieutenants and captains of the Regular Army were permitted to become colonels or lieutenant colonels of the new volunteer regiments of cavalry and contributed their expertise to them, there were not enough such officers to ensure uniformity of practice throughout the mounted service.

Next, the "massed charge" of the textbooks made sense only if executed by much larger bodies of cavalry than the few dozen men of a squadron or battalion or the three hundred or four hundred a regiment had after a few months of campaigning. These were the units of cavalry that commonly conducted operations. With the exception of John Pope in the West, not until well on in the war did army commanders learn the wisdom of employing their cavalry (or the portion that at any given moment had "serviceable" mounts) in divisional or even brigade strength. As late in 1864, General Sherman, who had under him in the Atlanta Campaign three divisions in an officially designated "Cavalry Corps" plus an oddly organized four brigades of cavalry of the Army of the Ohio, never used them as a unit but only as individual divisions on or beyond the wings of his army. Not until Sheridan did so in the Shenandoah Valley in the East, and James Wilson in his Selma Campaign in the closing weeks of the war in the West, was the cavalry employed in sufficient numbers (and, it must be added, with adequate weapons) to be able to demonstrate its capabilities when massed.

Another factor militating against the employment of traditional cavalry tactics was peculiar to the western armies. The clamor of successive army commanders for more mounted troops was commonly met by authorizing them to mount regiments of infantry in whatever numbers horses could be found for them. The government furnished the horses and equipment and occasionally, but not often, cavalry arms. The officers of these regiments of instant cavalry, from colonel down to the lieutenants, however worthy they may have been as infantrymen, had no cavalry experience, and since such conversions were frequently made in midcampaign or when a campaign was about to get under way, there was never any time or opportunity for cavalry training worthy of the name.

The last of the factors making the employment of traditional cavalry tactics impossible was the terrain. In the 1860s much of the area in which the armies operated was still a heavily wooded wilderness, even in the relatively well-settled East. The armies had to move, and even fight, on narrow paths, in thick woods and heavy underbrush, and on farm or plantation clearings in the forest. Readers will recall the kinds of terrain in the Wilderness, at Chickamauga, at Brice's Crossroads, and at Sabine Crossroads, on which cavalry tactics in the European sense would have been manifestly impossible.

Notwithstanding these obstacles, the Union cavalry never lost completely its tenuous hold on European tradition. There were numerous regiments in the Union armies, especially in the West, that were called "cavalry," but had been organized as, or converted to, mounted infantry and did all their campaigning as such, using their horses only for transportation, although it was not uncommon even for such regiments to arm their two flank companies with saber and pistol or carbine and call them their "cavalry companies." Some of these regiments achieved careers of distinction and were proud to be known as mounted infantry and not cavalry. General John T. Wilder's Lightning Brigade of four such regiments, and the 92nd Illinois Mounted Infantry, are conspicuous examples. It is to be understood, however, that such regiments were far from being representative of the Union cavalry as a whole. It must be emphasized that despite the fact that for the reasons discussed, the Union cavalry did much of its fighting on foot, it never ceased to be *cavalry* properly speaking, capable, and proud of it, of charging the enemy with the saber, mounted. The same regiments that advanced on foot, with their carbines blazing, to attack and breach the Selma fortifications on April 2, 1865, had charged with the saber, mounted, and driven back Confederate infantry and dismounted cavalry deployed behind field fortifications at Montevallo on March 30 and at Ebenezer Church on April 1.

Colonel G. F. R. Henderson, the British military historian, demonstrated many years ago the falsity of "the common belief that the American horsemen were merely mounted infantry. The truth is," he wrote, "that the Americans struck the true balance between shock and dismounted tactics. They were prepared for both, as the ground and the situation demanded; and . . . they used fire and *l'arme blanche* in the closest and most effective combination, against both cavalry and infantry." And Colonel Henderson concluded that "it may be . . . unhesitatingly declared that the horseman of the American war is the model of the efficient cavalryman."

Appendix: The Mutiny of the 15th Pennsylvania

GIVEN THE SHAKY STATE OF DISCIPLINE IN THE UNION army generally and the absence of the habit of command among many of the volunteer officers, it is not surprising that there were occasional flareups of mutinous conduct in one regiment or another, in reaction to real or fancied mistreatment or in protest against the deprivation of rights or privileges the men thought themselves entitled to. One such incident occurred in the 14th Illinois on October 30, 1864. After being promised that they would be rearmed with sabers, revolvers, and Spencer carbines, the men learned that there were no cavalry arms to be had. Then, the regimental historian explains: "The emergency of the service demanding that we should at once take the field, and as no other weapons were available, Springfield muskets were issued . . . a weapon with which . . . [we] had no experience, and a more unsuitable weapon could not be [found]. . . . This had a most damaging effect. . . . [The] men had been much encouraged to expect that they would be properly armed, and they actually refused to receive the muskets. Many broke them around the trees and an open mutiny was the result, taxing the officers heavily to quell." [1]

This flurry of insubordination was put down without serious trouble or untoward consequences. That was not true of all such incidents, the most serious of which involving the cavalry occurred in the 15th Penn-

1. Sanford, *History of the Fourteenth Illinois*, 227.

sylvania. The regiment was also known as the "Anderson Cavalry," inasmuch as its single-company nucleus had been organized, mainly in Philadelphia, to serve as a body guard for General Robert Anderson, from whom it was inherited by General Don Carlos Buell. The circumstances of the mutiny, and even references to its having taken place, are absent from the monumental, 784-page regimental history.[2] It is, however, documented at considerable length in the *Official Records*.[3]

The circumstances leading up to the mutiny are set forth in the report of Assistant Inspector General Major N. H. Davis, who was sent from Washington by Secretary Stanton, clearly under political pressure, to investigate and report on the event. The major's lengthy report agrees to a remarkable degree with one prepared by the highly articulate and literate committee of spokesmen for the regiment, for submission to a committee of Philadelphians, chaired by a clergyman, "deputed to inquire into the condition of the Anderson Cavalry," and with another the regimental spokesmen prepared for submission to Major Davis.

In the fall of 1861, Captain (later Brigadier General) William J. Palmer had organized a troop of "select and intelligent young men, as a body guard to General Anderson." After being inherited by General Buell, they "rendered valuable and efficient service as guards, escorts, scouts, &c.," so much so that the general asked for, and obtained in July, 1862, permission "to have raised three more companies of like class of men, all to be officered from the old troop on his selection and united with it as a battalion." A recruiting party headed by Captain Palmer returned to Philadelphia to enlist the additional men and met with "unprecedented" success. Its "fancy recruiting office . . . was daily crowded by respectable young men, anxious applicants for membership in the Anderson Troop, none being considered eligible to membership save those who could produce unexceptionable written recommendations, attesting good moral character, general intelligence, and stern integrity." Notwithstanding such high standards, in no time at all the recruiters had not just the three hundred men needed to make up the battalion, but nearly a thousand, enough to make up a regiment. There is considerable doubt as to whether, and if so from

2. Kirk, *History of the Fifteenth Pennsylvania*.
3. *Official Records*, Vol. XX, Pt. 2, pp. 345–80.

whom, Captain Palmer ever received permission to go so far beyond his original authority.

A camp for the recruits was established on the outskirts of Carlisle, Pennsylvania, adjacent to the United States Cavalry barracks. Dismounted drill began at once, under the tutelage of "the old regular sergeants of the barracks." A major source of the subsequent difficulties was the failure to "perfect the organization." Of the forty-one field and line officers the regiment should have had, only twelve were appointed, and the men were not given the opportunity to elect the rest, still the normal practice in 1862. Considering the normal attitude of volunteers toward their officers, appointed or elected, it is startling to find that a major complaint of the mutineers was that they had not been properly officered, the few appointed being "mostly young, rash, incompetent, and inexperienced," in the opinion of their men. Whether it was due to the lack of a sufficient number of officers or the incompetence of those they did have, "preparations were retarded, discipline lax, and camp or garrison duties more or less neglected." The emphasis on this ground of complaint, and on a second, namely that Palmer proceeded to recruit a full regiment without obtaining the consent of the men who had enlisted when only a battalion was to be raised, suggests that the legal profession was well represented among the recruits of "good moral character," *etc.*, in the regiment.

The Confederate army now intervened to bring the difficulties of the infant regiment to a temporary halt. In response to Governor Andrew Curtin's call, on the occasion of the Antietam Campaign, for fifty thousand militia to defend the border of Pennsylvania from invasion by General Lee's forces, the Andersons were hastily armed (by their account, "partially equipped, in many instances, with wholly worthless arms") and sent to act as scouts in the Cumberland Valley. In these operations, which culminated in the battle of Antietam, Captain Palmer was taken prisoner.

The enlistment of recruits beyond the number needed for a battalion caused "many of those previously enlisted . . . to be alarmed . . . fearing they had been deceived by the enlisting officers, and were not to perform the service they were enlisted to do." Then, shortly after their return to Carlisle, they learned that General Buell had been removed from command of the Department of the Ohio. On the assurance that General Rosecrans, Buell's successor, would accept the regiment to "do special service as an independent organization," they decided with some misgivings to forgo "any decisive action to attain . . . [their] just rights"; they agreed to obey orders to entrain for Louisville, where, they understood, they were to be met by the rest of their regimental quota of officers. Louisville proved to be a disappointment: they were met by only one officer. This, they decided, was "a miserable farce and a base deception." When, in addition, they learned on "excellent authority" that Rosecrans did not want them as an escort and intended instead to have them brigaded with other regiments of cavalry, they drew up petitions to Governor Curtin and the War Department, signed by nearly every member of the organization, requesting an honorable discharge "on the ground of false enlistment." At this time or perhaps a short time later, they received "the legal opinion of eminent lawyers in Philadelphia that they . . . [could not] be held in the service."

The regiment was issued horses in Louisville and was then ordered to march south to Nashville. When these orders were announced, "a very large percentage of the troop stacked their arms in front of their tents, refusing to march any farther." But on receiving "the positive and most solemn assurance that all . . . [their] grievances would be redressed" in Nashville, they agreed to march. While still on the road to Nashville, they were told that they were to report to General David Stanley, Rosecrans' chief of cavalry, for assignment.

Indicative of the atmosphere in the regiment is the language in which their spokesmen expressed their belief that "having been inveigled by our officers from Carlisle to Nashville, we deemed it our duty to make a stand . . . [at Nashville] until fully satisfied of not being further deceived." A committee on which all companies of the regiment were represented waited on Lieutenant Colonel William Spencer on Christmas Day to learn what was to become of them. Colonel Spencer was unable to supply answers, whereupon the committee, after consulting their constituents, returned to warn him that if the regiment received marching orders "before being satisfied in the particulars, they would stack arms and refuse to obey."

On the morning of December 26, Rosecrans started from Nashville on the operation that was to culminate in the battle of Stones River. The Andersons were ordered to march with the rest of the army. All the officers (one of whom was killed and another mortally wounded at

Stones River) and about two hundred of the men obeyed.[4] The rest refused to move "on the ground of insufficiency of officers and incomplete organization." On December 28, Rosecrans met one of the mutineers' demands by appointing twenty-three "acting" officers to serve until they or others could be regularly commissioned.[5] The next day, he tested the effect of severity; after declaring that he would not "submit to their whims," he threatened to disgrace the regiment "as well as make them otherwise bitterly regret their folly."

On December 31, the military authorities in Nashville decided to force a showdown. Ordered to march with other troops to escort supplies to the army at Stones River, all but "a very few" of the Andersons refused. The mutineers were thereupon ordered to turn in their arms and equipment; 309 of them were confined in the Nashville workhouse, and 101 in the yard of the county jail. The latter group were given their tents after "a few days."

The mutineers' statement to Major Davis accounts for the large discrepancy between the 400-odd men incarcerated and the total strength of the regiment with the explanation that "some are quietly sleeping the sleep that knows no waking . . . others are sick and wounded, and [have] found temporary refuge in humane institutions; but the vast majority are missing; why they are missing, and where they are, the veil that obscures the future can only disclose."

The conditions under which the prisoners were held do not seem to have been unduly severe. The policing of the large room in the workhouse where they were, and of the yard of the county jail, was less than adequate, but as Major Davis reported, "Far greater privileges and liberties were extended to these prisoners than is customary in the military service for offenses of a much less criminal character. For some time (days) they were allowed to go about town and board at hotels and private boarding-houses. Their friends were allowed to visit and take them such articles as they pleased. If sick, they were allowed to be removed to hospitals or private houses. Medical officers visited

---

4. These officers and men took part in the battle of Stones River, but seventy-three of the men, including eight noncommissioned officers, joined the mutineers on their return to Nashville.

5. Rosecrans' action was later revoked. Officers were appointed, and commissioned by Governor Curtin, on the basis of Colonel Palmer's much more effective plan of reorganization.

the prison. They were as well supplied with rations and fuel as the other troops at the post; had their clothing, blankets, &c."

On January 20, acting on orders from Rosecrans, General R. B. Mitchell, commanding at Nashville, offered to release from confinement all who "would go to duty." All the men in the jail yard accepted and were released, but only about 40 in the workhouse did so, leaving 208 still in confinement there.

In the meantime the Philadelphia committee representing the mutineers' friends and relatives informed Secretary Stanton that the men were "confined in loathsome prisons," and they asked that the regiment be disbanded and the men given honorable discharges. In support of their request, they listed the same grievances the men had previously set forth, laying special emphasis on the contention that "deception was used in enlisting them by making false representations as to the duties they were to perform, and the position in which they were to be placed." Induced to do so by this petition, Stanton sent off a curt telegram to General Mitchell. He repeated the petitioners' claim that the men in confinement were "treated in a cruel and improper manner" and that Mitchell had "uttered threats against them, and expressed a desire and determination to have some of them shot." He directed the general to treat the prisoners "in a humane manner, cause them to be imprisoned in a proper place, and properly supplied and cared for."

After receiving a second, even blunter telegram on the same subject from the secretary two days later, Mitchell, not to be browbeaten by any civilian, however highly placed, replied, "I have said to them that mutiny in the face of the enemy was punishable by death, and unless they reconsidered their action some of them would be made examples of." To show that he was well aware of the source of the secretary's concern for the mutineers' welfare, Mitchell added, "I have refused to allow them to board at first-class hotels, and have also refused admittance to persons from the city of Philadelphia, who have been publicly encouraging them in their course, and promising to sustain them at home and at the capital." The latter part of the general's statement is supported by Major Davis, who reported to Washington that "one or more of the committee recently here from Philadelphia have induced the last act of mutiny and disobedience," and by Provost Marshal Colonel John A. Martin, who reported that the men's refusal of the offer General Mitchell made to them on January 20 "was induced by the influence of certain visitors from Pennsylvania, who told them to hold out a little longer and the regiment would be disbanded."

On January 17, a court-martial, ordered by Rosecrans, had assembled to try the mutineers, eighteen of whom, presumably the ringleaders, were found guilty and sent to the Tennessee penitentiary to await promulgation of their sentences. But now the sun began to break through the clouds. Captain (who had in the meantime become Colonel) Palmer, whose presence with the regiment might well have prevented the mutiny, had escaped from captivity, hurried west, and was authorized by Rosecrans on February 8 to reorganize the regiment, nominate the line officers to be commissioned, and report what horses and gear the regiment needed to be ready to take the field.

Palmer wrote Rosecrans' chief of staff after his arrival in Nashville that the condition of the regiment "was just about as bad as it was possible to be. Even the men who went to the front had since become demoralized with the prospect of disbandment, and the unfortunate encouragement given to the mutineers by various committees from Philadelphia, and sympathizing meetings in that city, at which the doctrine of military despotism was preached." Palmer's subsequent conduct as commander of the regiment, and then of a brigade, shows him to have been a man of considerable ability and sound sense. He went to Nashville with a complex but effective scheme for reorganizing the troubled regiment and appointing a full slate of officers for it. He caused to be revoked an idiotic War Department order granting discharges from the service to six of the mutineers (precisely what they and their friends wanted) and had the eighteen in the penitentiary released, their sentences suspended "dependent on the good conduct of the regiment." There was thus a tacit amnesty; all past sins were forgiven.

When Colonel Palmer rejoined the regiment, it had only 15 horses left, about 250 sabers and carbines, a few tents, and no wagons. To get it reorganized and reequipped, he wrote, was "rather worse than beginning afresh," but at least the mutiny had ended, leaving, so far as can be determined, no permanent scars. Officers were appointed and duly commissioned, the men were resupplied with horses, weapons, and equipment, and the 15th Pennsylvania was ready to embark on what was to be a career of considerable distinction in the war in the West.

Addenda to Bibliography

Adams, Henry C. "Battle of Prairie Grove." MOLLUS, Commandery of Indiana, *War Papers*, 451–64. Indianapolis, 1908.

Ambrose, Stephen E. *Halleck: Lincoln's Chief of Staff*. Baton Rouge: Louisiana State University Press, 1962.

Bacon, David L., ed. *Wartime Letters of Gen. Thomas J. Jordan to His Wife Jane, 1861–1865*. Privately Printed, 1978.

Beatty, John. *Memoirs of a Volunteer, 1861–1863*. Edited by Harvey S. Ford. New York: W. W. Norton, 1946.

Bearss, Edwin C. "Cavalry Operations in the Battle of Stones River." *Tennessee Historical Quarterly*, XIX (1960), 25–53, 110–44.

Buresch, Lumir F. *October 25th and the Battle of Mine Creek*. Kansas City: Lowell Press, 1977.

Cimprich, John, and Robert C. Mainfort, Jr., eds. "Fort Pillow Revisited: New Evidence About an Old Controversy." *Civil War History*, XXVIII (1982), 293–306.

Connelly, Thomas L. *Army of the Heartland: The Army of Tennessee, 1861–1862*. Baton Rouge: Louisiana State University Press, 1967.

———. *Autumn of Glory: The Army of Tennessee, 1862–1865*. Baton Rouge: Louisiana State University Press, 1971.

Cotterill, Robert S. "The Louisville and Nashville Railroad, 1861–1865." *American Historical Review*, XXIX (1924), 700–715.

Dinges, Bruce J. "The Making of a Cavalryman: Benjamin H. Grierson and the Civil War Along the Mississippi, 1861–1865." Ph.D. dissertation, Rice University, 1978.

Greene, Francis Vinton. *Campaigns of the Civil War, VIII: The Mississippi*. New York: Charles Scribner's Sons, 1882.

Hay, Thomas R. *Hood's Tennessee Campaign.* New York: W. Neale, 1929.

[Hinton, Richard J.] *Rebel Invasion of Missouri and Kansas and the Campaigns of the Army of the Border Against General Sterling Price.* Chicago: Church & Goodman, 1865.

Homans, John. "The Red River Expedition." *Papers of the Military History Society of Massachusetts*, VIII (1910), 67–97.

Hubbell, John T., ed. *Battles Lost and Won.* Westport, Conn.: Greenwood Press, 1975.

Kennedy, Jos. C. G. *Preliminary Report on the Eighth Census, 1860.* 37th Congress, 2nd Session, House of Representatives, Executive Documents No. 116. Washington, D.C., 1862.

Kerby, Robert L. *Kirby Smith's Confederacy: The Trans-Mississippi South, 1863–1865.* New York: Columbia University Press, 1972.

Longstreet, James. *From Manassas to Appomattox: Memoirs of the Civil War in America.* Philadelphia: Lippincott, 1896.

McCormick, Andrew W. "Battles and Campaigns in Arkansas." MOLLUS, Commandery of Ohio, *Sketches of War History, 1861–1865*, VI, 2–13. 7 vols. Cincinnati: Robert Clark, 1888–1910.

McDonough, James Lee. *Stones River: Bloody Winter in Tennessee.* Knoxville: University of Tennessee Press, 1980.

McDowell, Robert Emmett. *City of Conflict: Louisville in the Civil War.* Louisville: Louisville Civil War Round Table, 1962.

McWhiney, Grady. *Braxton Bragg and Confederate Defeat.* New York: Columbia University Press, 1969.

McWhiney, Grady, and Perry D. Jamieson. *Attack and Die: Civil War Military Tactics and the Southern Heritage.* University, Ala.: University of Alabama Press, 1982.

Miers, Earl Schenk. *The Web of Victory: Grant at Vicksburg.* New York: Alfred A. Knopf, 1955.

Miller, Francis T., ed. *The Photographic History of the Civil War: The Cavalry.* New York: Review of Reviews, 1912.

Monaghan, Jay. *Civil War on the Western Border, 1854–1865.* Boston: Little, Brown, 1955.

Myers, Robert Manson, ed., *The Children of Pride.* 3 vols. New York: Yale University Press, 1972.

Nye, Wilbur S. "Cavalry Operations Around Atlanta." *Civil War Times Illustrated*, III (1964), 46–50.

Rowell, John W. *Yankee Artillerymen: Through the Civil War with Eli Lilly's Indiana Battery.* Knoxville: University of Tennessee Press, 1975.

Sanborn, John B. "The Campaign in Missouri in September and October, 1864." MOLLUS, Commandery of Minnesota, *Glimpses of the Nation's Struggle*, 3rd Series, 135–204. New York, 1893.

Sanger, Donald B., and Thomas R. Hay. *James Longstreet.* Baton Rouge: Louisiana State University Press, 1952.

Scott, William F. "The Last Fight for Missouri." MOLLUS, Commandery of New York, *Addresses Delivered Before the Commandery*, 3rd Series, 292–328. New York, 1907.

Starr, Stephen Z. "Colonel George St. Leger Grenfell: His Pre–Civil War Career." *Journal of Southern History*, XXX (1964), 278–97.

———. "The Second Michigan Volunteer Cavalry: Another View." *Michigan History*, LX (1976), 161–82.

———. "The Third Ohio Volunteer Cavalry: A View from the Inside." *Ohio History*, LXXXV (1976), 306–18.

Sunderland, Glenn W. *Lightning at Hoover's Gap: Wilder's Brigade in the Civil War*. New York: T. Yosseloff, 1969.

U.S. Congress, *Report of the Joint Committee on the Conduct of the War*. 38th Congress, 2nd Session. 2 vols. Washington, D.C., 1865.

Weigley, Russell F. *The American Way of War: A History of United States Military Strategy and Policy*. New York: Macmillan, 1973.

Index